DEFENDING BATTERED WOMEN ON TRIAL

Law and Society Series
W. Wesley Pue, General Editor

The Law and Society Series explores law as a socially embedded phenomenon. It is premised on the understanding that the conventional division of law from society creates false dichotomies in thinking, scholarship, educational practice, and social life. Books in the series treat law and society as mutually constitutive and seek to bridge scholarship emerging from interdisciplinary engagement of law with disciplines such as politics, social theory, history, political economy, and gender studies.

A list of titles in the series appears at the end of the book.

DEFENDING BATTERED WOMEN ON TRIAL

LESSONS FROM THE TRANSCRIPTS

Elizabeth A Sheehy

21 20 19 18 17 16 15 14   5 4 3 2 1

Printed in Canada on FSC-certified ancient-forest-free paper (100% post-consumer recycled) that is processed chlorine- and acid-free.

Library and Archives Canada Cataloguing in Publication

Sheehy, Elizabeth A., author
   Defending battered women on trial: lessons from the transcripts / Elizabeth A. Sheehy.
(Law and society series)

Includes bibliographical references and index.
Issued in print and electronic formats.
ISBN 978-0-7748-2651-8 (bound). – ISBN 978-0-7748-2652-5 (pbk.). –
ISBN 978-0-7748-2653-2 (pdf). – ISBN 978-0-7748-2654-9 (epub)

   1. Abused women – Legal status, laws, etc. – Canada – Cases. 2. Assault and battery – Canada – Cases. 3. Self-defense (Law) – Canada – Cases. 4. Defense (Criminal procedure) – Canada – Cases. 5. Trials (Assault and battery) – Canada. 6. Trial transcripts – Canada. I. Title. II. Series: Law and society series (Vancouver, B.C.)

KE8925.5.S54 2013	345.71'025553	C2013-906378-1
KF9322.S54 2013		C2013-906379-X

Canada

UBC Press gratefully acknowledges the financial support for our publishing program of the Government of Canada (through the Canada Book Fund), the Canada Council for the Arts, and the British Columbia Arts Council.

This book has been published with the help of a grant from the Canadian Federation for the Humanities and Social Sciences, through the Awards to Scholarly Publications Program, using funds provided by the Social Sciences and Humanities Research Council of Canada.

UBC Press
The University of British Columbia
2029 West Mall
Vancouver, BC V6T 1Z2
www.ubcpress.ca

Contents

Acknowledgments

This book was inspired by the ground-breaking work of Judith Herman, Elizabeth Schneider, and Evan Stark, whose insights and analysis have shaped my thinking, and by Kim Pate and Lee Lakeman, whose advocacy with and for battered women provide leadership for us all.

I am deeply grateful to many people who read, edited, and commented on the draft chapters of this book: Randy Schmidt of UBC Press, my structural editor Kevin Burns of Seven Stories, my partner Dean Beeby, and my dear friend Elizabeth Pickett, who each read every word with care, several times, and rallied me when I faltered; my friends and colleagues Constance Backhouse, Susan Boyd, Kim Brooks, Emma Cunliffe, Nora Currie, cj fleury, Holly Johnson, Darlene Johnstone, Kim Pate, Rakhi Ruparelia, Louisa Russell, and Julia Tolmie, who provided valuable feedback and encouragement on individual chapters; my research assistants and former students Leighann Burns, Martha Butler, Mary Anne Carter, Charlene Davidson, Julie Desmarais, Shushanna Harris, Christel Higgs, Amy Jackson, Maya Krishnaratne, Lindsay McIntosh, Kerry McVey, Jeewon Min, Samar Musallam, Frederico Pasquarelli, Martin Tooke, Johnna Van Parys, and Stacey Wells, who helped me find the women and document their stories. Thank you all. Forgive me if I have left anyone out. Of course, any errors are mine.

Funding from the Social Sciences and Humanities Research Council, Standard Research Grant, and the Law Foundation of Ontario is gratefully acknowledged, as is the support I have received from the University of Ottawa Faculty of Law, Common Law Section. I also want to thank the women of the Women's Writing Retreats at the University of Ottawa; these retreats are funded in part by the Centre for Academic Leadership. I am so fortunate to be surrounded by such brilliant and sustaining colleagues! And thank you, cj fleury, for gracing the book cover with your gorgeous sculpture.

DEFENDING BATTERED WOMEN ON TRIAL

Introduction

In the Beginning: Angelique Lyn Lavallee

In September 1986 in Winnipeg, Manitoba, Angelique Lyn Lavallee killed her common law partner Kevin "Rooster" Rust in a situation not recognized by Canadian law as allowing self-defence. Rather than killing in an ongoing physical confrontation, she fired a gun as he turned and walked from the room after assaulting her and swearing that he would "get" her later. Lavallee's counsel, Greg Brodsky, made legal history by asking the Supreme Court of Canada to affirm the admissibility of expert evidence on "Battered Woman Syndrome" to reinterpret self-defence in light of the experience of battered women like Lavallee.[1]

Brodsky's argument was a bold one, for the criminal justice system – its procedures, assumptions, and rules – was never designed for women, especially those who kill their husbands or partners. In fact, the law historically authorized husbands to exercise violent authority over their wives and made it very difficult for women to escape from brutal husbands. The phrase "rule of thumb" is inherited from the notion that men were entitled to beat their wives with sticks as long as they were no thicker than a man's thumb.[2] The precedent-setting decision of *Hawley v Ham*, delivered in Kingston, Ontario, in 1826, set out the common law position in Canada. According to Chief Justice William Campbell, a man had "a right to chastise his wife moderately." To warrant leaving her husband, "the chastisement must be such as to put her life in jeopardy."[3] Campbell's ruling endorsed as permissible the behaviour of a husband who flourished a riding whip over his wife's head, with threats of flogging.[4]

Wife killing, through an excess of "chastisement," was often not condemned as murder but as "chance medley" – accidental homicide or what we today would call manslaughter. Husband killing, however, was worse than murder: it was treachery, a form of treason. The offence of petit treason – the killing of one's lord and master – garnered a special punishment of public burning at the stake until it was abolished in 1790.[5]

Criminal prosecution of wife beating was possible at least by the 1830s,[6] due to reforms to property, family, and criminal law and to public campaigns aimed at "redefining abusive spousal behaviour as criminal."[7] These reforms, spearheaded by early feminists and the temperance movement, began to untie the knots of patriarchal power by allowing abused women to keep their own property when fleeing violent husbands,[8] apply for maintenance,[9] retain custody of their children,[10] and press criminal charges.[11] There were isolated prosecutions for wife assault throughout history,[12] but it was not until the 1960s that large-scale and persistent second wave feminist demands returned to focus on this issue.[13] In the 1980s, the Canadian legal system began to respond with policies aimed at prosecuting wife battering more rigorously.[14] Yet the ideas and privileges protected by the law's established approval of wife beating survived beyond legal change on the surface.[15] And, when women like Lavallee kill their male partners, police and prosecutors bring the full force of the law to bear against the woman, sometimes acknowledging the deceased's past violence but characterizing it as legally irrelevant to her right to use lethal self-defence.[16]

Before the Beginning: Jane Hurshman

Canadian jurors given liberal access to the woman's story – frequently constrained by the rules governing the admissibility of evidence in criminal trials – are often quite fair with battered women, arguably displaying the "common sense" for which the jury system is praised. The trial of Jane Hurshman,[17] who killed her common law husband, Billy Stafford, in 1982 in Bangs Falls, Nova Scotia, provides a powerful example.

Hurshman experienced "captivity" in her life with Stafford, a descriptor drawn from Dr Judith Lewis Herman's book *Trauma and Recovery*.[18] Dr Herman demonstrates that the psychological trauma of war and its aftermath of Post-Traumatic Stress Disorder (PTSD) are mirrored in the lives of women entrapped in domestic relationships with abusive men. "Traumatic events," she writes, "are extraordinary, not because they occur rarely, but rather because they overwhelm the ordinary human adaptations to life ... They confront human beings with the extremities of helplessness and terror, and evoke the responses of catastrophe."[19] These events can include being subjected to or exposed to violence, where "action is of no avail." Traumatic experience overwhelms and disorganizes the psyche, producing "profound and lasting changes in physiological arousal, emotion, cognition and memory."[20] The symptoms of PTSD – hyperarousal, when the body and mind go into high alert; intrusion, when the event is relived repeatedly through dreams and flashbacks; and constriction, when the mind escapes through altered states of consciousness or disassociation – persist long after the traumatic event.

Dr Herman explains that, while singular traumatic events can occur anytime and can arise from natural disasters, the experience of repeated trauma occurs only in captivity, such as that experienced by prisoners of war, members of cults, persons in institutions, and women in "domestic captivity." She says that "[t]he worst fear of any traumatized person is that the moment of horror will recur, and this fear is realized in victims of chronic abuse."[21] She describes the mechanics whereby men can accomplish and maintain the captivity of women and children who, to the external world, appear "free" to attend school, work, and live their lives.

Abusive men achieve domination by subjecting women to repeated psychological trauma, through threats to kill or wound them or those whom they love; surveillance of and control over women's movements, bodies, and bodily functions; sexual violence and degradation; sleep deprivation; interrogation; enforcement of petty rules; and destruction of their attachments to family photographs, loved ones, and cherished values. Batterers can use minor violence or resort to violence infrequently to reinforce their control by keeping women in a state of dread or to secure their compliance. But simple compliance is often not enough, according to Dr Herman. An abusive man requires gratitude, admiration, and love: "His ultimate goal is the creation of a willing victim."[22]

Batterers deploy additional methods when women attempt to separate: promises to change, apologies, and declarations of love; efforts to further isolate women from familial and social supports; and escalating threats to kill them should they leave. These men seek total surrender, which they achieve by forcing women to violate their own boundaries and moral codes, participate in their own humiliation, or sacrifice others – children, family, friends. Thus "broken," a woman is at risk of losing the will to live.

Release from captivity required that Hurshman kill Stafford. No one else was going to save her. Her story is told in a best-selling work of non-fiction by Brian Vallée, *Life with Billy*.[23] The CBC's current affairs program, *The Fifth Estate*, interviewed Hurshman after her initial acquittal and documented her struggle with the effects of trauma.[24] The recording technician stopped because he thought that something was wrong with his equipment: as Hurshman relayed Stafford's brutal attacks, the lapel microphone picked up the sound not only of her voice but also of her relived terror, betrayed by the sound of her wildly pounding heart.[25]

From 1977, when Stafford first attacked Hurshman, through to 1982, when she killed him, he kept up a relentless campaign of material deprivation, control, intimidation, extreme violence, and degradation against Hurshman; Allen, her son from her first marriage; and Darren, the child whom she conceived with Stafford. Her co-workers described Hurshman as constantly bruised and black-eyed. Stafford fired bullets in her direction, knocked her unconscious, sexually degraded her in horrifying ways, and assaulted and punished her children with deliberate cruelty. He was notorious as a violent bully who boasted having killed a man by throwing him overboard at sea. He so terrified other sailors that all refused to testify with respect to this death. He had raged at authorities and openly defied police and court orders.

It is perhaps not surprising that Hurshman had never once reported any of his hundreds of assaults against her and her boys.[26] She knew that his two prior wives had fled the province to escape. Should she try to leave, Stafford threatened, he would not be a "three time loser": he would kill her family members one by one until she returned. She contemplated killing Stafford in bed, once putting a loaded gun to his head while he slept, but she worried about Darren seeing the aftermath. She considered suicide but could not bring herself to leave Darren alone with his father. She thought about killing Darren and then herself but could not kill her son. Hurshman even tried unsuccessfully to hire a man to kill Stafford.[27]

One night in March 1982, Stafford announced that he would set fire to a trailer next door with neighbour Margaret Joudrey and her husband inside and "deal with" Allen, vowing that he would clean them all up at the same time. Hurshman killed Stafford with his shotgun after he passed out drunk in his truck outside their home. She drove the truck away with his body in it and left it to be found on a country road.

She was brought in for questioning by the police the next day. Within twelve hours, she confessed. The police seemed sympathetic, but Staff Sergeant Peter Williamson recorded her confession and left out all the abuse that she recounted. Yet he said to another officer, within her hearing, that "[s]he deserves a medal. She probably saved a couple of our officers' lives. He always had loaded guns. I'm sure we would have gone out there one day and he would have shot one of us."[28] Two weeks before the killing, her lawyer learned, Hurshman had attended the station to beg the police to cancel a summons against Stafford for shooting deer out of season. They ignored her bruises and black eyes.

The provincial Attorney General's (AG) office insisted on pursuing first-degree murder charges against Hurshman, repudiating her lawyer's offer of a guilty plea to manslaughter. Because she had shot Stafford while he was unconscious, the AG believed that her actions displayed "planning and deliberation" deserving of the most serious sentence available for murder: life imprisonment without parole eligibility for twenty-five years.[29] As the prosecutor, Blaine Allaby, told the jury at her trial, "[w]e may sympathize with Jane [Hurshman] in her situation, but the law is the law."[30]

Defence lawyer Alan Ferrier painted a picture for the jury of Stafford's brutality. One woman testified that Stafford tried to run her down while she crossed a street with her baby in a stroller. When she reported him to the police, a bullet was fired through the window of her home. Another woman was threatened by Stafford after she complained to the police that he had shot her dog. A man was punched, chased, and shot at by Stafford; another man committed perjury in a deer-jacking charge against Stafford because he was so terrified of retaliation; another man ran barefoot from the Stafford house in the snow with his wife and son after Stafford suddenly became a raging madman and hit him for no reason. Stafford's two ex-wives described how they fled Nova Scotia with their children and went into hiding. Three doctors also testified for the defence: one of them was a forensic and child psychiatrist who evaluated Darren as an abused child and who gave evidence on "battered women" and "the syndrome."[31]

Ferrier asked the jury to consider self-defence and defence of others, which would result in acquittal if successful, but his main focus was on persuading them to return a manslaughter verdict on the basis that either Hurshman was provoked or she had no intent to kill.[32] The presiding judge, Mr Justice D Burchell, meticulously reviewed the testimony of the forty-six witnesses who testified over nineteen days. He spent seven and a half hours charging the jury. After eighteen hours of deliberation, with two nights in sequestration, the jury returned an acquittal for Hurshman. The courtroom exploded with the jubilation of spectators.[33]

Public reaction to Hurshman's acquittal was positive – but not that of the legal profession. Ferrier was shocked by the acquittal, for he thought that a manslaughter conviction was the appropriate verdict.[34] Dalhousie University law professor Wayne McKay criticized the result, saying that Hurshman's circumstances and lack of options should not have been considered with respect to her guilt or innocence. Instead, he said, these were matters for sentencing: "[I]n its quest for justice in the individual case, a jury should not be permitted to distort principles."[35]

The AG's office filed its appeal within three weeks. Hurshman was told by the RCMP officer who served the appeal notice that "I'm really sorry to have to give this to you. I can't see what they hope to gain. Every officer across the country has followed this case, and it should have ended when they acquitted you."[36]

The Nova Scotia Court of Appeal agreed with the Crown appeal and ordered a new trial.[37] The judge should not have allowed the jury to consider either self-defence or defence of others because no one faced "imminent harm" while Stafford slept. Furthermore, all evidence of Stanford's rampant violence should have been ruled inadmissible because it was not relevant to a viable defence. Hurshman offered to plead guilty to manslaughter to avoid a second trial. This time the Crown accepted readily.

At the sentencing hearing, Allaby asked Mr Justice Merlin Nunn to impose a jail sentence as a deterrent to others. Justice Nunn commented that Hurshman had endured a hard life but warned that "[w]ives don't have the right to take the lives of their husbands."[38] He sentenced her to six months of imprisonment, denouncing her for playing "judge, jury and executioner."[39]

An editorial in the *Liverpool Advance* by Jock Inglis expressed the community's outrage at the AG's conduct:

> The Crown got its pound of flesh through the incarceration of Ms. Stafford, but at what cost to our judicial system? ... There are those of us who felt that the jury was the pillar of our judicial system, that once we were found to be innocent by a group of our fellow citizens we were free to go about our business. We know now that this is not so. We also wonder how, in the future, the Crown can expect we citizens to do our duty as jurors, to sit hour after hour, day after day, studying the testimony and finally to be told, once our verdict has been rendered, that no, our opinion was not really wanted after all, only that of the lawyers. What did the Crown really accomplish through this exercise? Did they prove to the citizens of Queen's County, beyond a reasonable doubt that Ms. Stafford committed a crime against our society? Did they show society that she deserved to be punished? Will the sentence stop others from protecting themselves from physical or emotional violence perpetrated by their mates? Did our society derive meaningful benefit from the second trial? We think not.[40]

Hurshman became a public figure in Nova Scotia, where she spoke out against wife battering and supported other women's efforts to escape from violent men. Nova Scotia's AG Henry How insisted on speaking with

Hurshman at a hotel just before she was to address a women's conference in Lunenburg, Nova Scotia, in February 1985. According to Vallée, "he apologized for granting appeal in her case, but said he had no choice."[41] How explained that she did not kill in response to "sudden provocation," since Stafford was asleep, and the law did not recognize "slow burn" or cumulative provocation; he also said that self-defence covered only an immediate confrontation. Then, How said, "[n]ow Jane – off the record – I want to say, that cocksucker should have been shot a long time ago."[42]

How was later appointed the Chief Judge of Nova Scotia's Provincial Court, where he served until his retirement in 1988. Hurshman did not fare so well. She died in February 1992, likely by her own hand.[43] Although she escaped from Stafford, she never recovered from his effort to break her body and spirit, and her terrible legal ordeal took its toll.

Hurshman was condemned by prosecutors and judges for not choosing the appropriate route to deal with Stafford's reign of terror. But no one specified what that route was. She was credited with "choice" and therefore responsibility for how she secured her and her children's safety, while AG How, arguably one of the most powerful men in the province, claimed that he had no choice and therefore bore no responsibility for the legal injustice committed against her. The state justified its response by reference to "the law" and its principles, when a jury of her peers understood all too clearly that "the law" had nothing to offer Hurshman.

A New Paradigm for Self-Defence?

Lavallee changed the law of self-defence in 1990, thereby resolving the unfairness that had confronted battered women on trial for murder. Or did it? True enough, expert evidence on Battered Woman Syndrome, a subset of PTSD, was ruled admissible to support self-defence. *Lavallee* also put to rest the common law "imminence" requirement deployed against Hurshman: women do not need to wait for the "uplifted knife" to act in self-defence.[44]

Legal researchers looking for *Lavallee*'s impact were disappointed. Early assessments in 1994 and 1995 detected only two cases in which prosecutors declined to prosecute women when evidence of serious violence by the deceased against their female partners emerged.[45] Beyond these prosecutorial stays, few women were known to have been acquitted based on *Lavallee*.[46]

In 1995, Judge Lynn Ratushny, as she then was, was appointed by the federal government to conduct an *en bloc* review of the homicide convictions of women who alleged that they had killed male partners in self-defence, on the basis that they arguably had not received the benefit of the

Lavallee ruling. This review was the product of initial research and lobbying by the Canadian Association of Elizabeth Fry Societies.[47] The Terms of Reference asked Judge Ratushny to review the applications for review of eligible women to ascertain whether their cases warranted a recommendation to the government for granting the royal prerogative of mercy and to identify appropriate law reforms stemming from the review.

Judge Ratushny's *Self-Defence Review* (*SDR*) received ninety-eight applications from women convicted before and after *Lavallee*. Judge Ratushny developed legal standards for review of the women's cases, and, after compiling and analyzing the applications in light of those standards, she rejected all but fourteen women's claims. She interviewed those fourteen women, but in the end she made recommendations for seven;[48] the federal government granted some relief to only five of the women; and no woman was released from prison as a result of the *SDR*.[49] Judge Ratushny also made a number of law reform recommendations that have languished without federal response in the fifteen ensuing years. I discuss these recommendations in the chapters that follow where relevant.

The results of the *SDR* were extremely disappointing to the women and their advocates, but they should not be read as confirmation that the justice system works fairly for battered women on trial. I have explained elsewhere how the legal standards for review, the burden of proof that falls on those who challenge their convictions, the unfairness of some of the legal requirements for self-defence for battered women, the lack of a systemic analysis of male violence against women, the restricted availability of counsel for the women, and Judge Ratushny's experience of resistance and interference by government officials[50] together blunted access to justice for the women involved.[51] Battered women advised by counsel to plead guilty rather than go to trial, those who went to trial but did not raise self-defence, and those whose lawyers raised self-defence but nonetheless made strategic decisions about the evidence and the arguments were out of luck for a remedy unless there was new evidence or evidence whose significance was unappreciated at the time. In the absence of clear incompetence, counsel's strategic decisions, especially in light of the complex law of self-defence, the rarity of its interpretation in cases of battered women, and the high stakes presented by a murder conviction, could not be reviewed by the *SDR*, potentially leaving deserving women without a remedy.

The *SDR* recognized, consistent with the work of feminist scholars,[52] that one salient effect of *Lavallee* was to facilitate plea bargains for manslaughter and compassionate sentences for battered women, in circumstances in which they might have achieved acquittal based on self-defence had they gone to trial. Inherent in such plea bargains is the notion that the crime was committed while the woman was in a provoked or intoxicated state, in which she did not have the intent to kill required for murder because her mind was affected by Battered Woman Syndrome. In some of these cases, judges have mitigated women's manslaughter sentences in light of the battering that the women endured, imposing suspended sentences, conditional imprisonment (house arrest), and sentences of less than two years of imprisonment.

Thus, instead of the legal system recognizing that the woman's act was justified by the complete defence of self-defence, her act is "excused" by the prosecutor's acceptance of a manslaughter verdict based on compassionate considerations. This looks like mercy, not justice, according to Rebecca Bradfield: "The classification of the sentence as 'merciful' ... renders the battered woman's case as exceptional and outside the legitimate mitigatory framework. The use of the concept of mercy perpetuates the judicial system's willingness to express sympathy and compassion for these women, while not recognising the legitimacy of their actions."[53]

Are these results just? Are Canadian women receiving equal access to a fair trial when they kill violent male partners? To adopt the definition proposed by Holly Maguigan,[54] do women have access to a trial in which they can put to the jury the full contexts of their acts and receive the benefit of judicial instruction that relates the contexts in which they killed to the law? Would our legal system respond today to a woman in Hurshman's situation as it did in the 1980s?

Searching for Justice

Using trial records of women's homicide trials that were previously not transcribed, a clearer picture emerges of how the Canadian justice system deals with these difficult cases. I searched electronic legal and news databases[55] to identify 141 cases in which women were charged with killing their male partners from 1990 to 2005; I then secured transcripts when they were available and within my research budget.

Of course, not all 141 women killed in circumstances that raised the issue of self-defence: some were found unfit to stand trial or not criminally responsible on the basis of mental disorder; others alleged an alternative defence or mitigating circumstance. I excluded from further study those women who, from the available information, made no claim to have experienced abuse. I also excluded a number of women who may have fit my criteria, but the available information was incomplete. The remaining ninety-one women's cases are shown in the Appendix of this book. For these women, self-defence was at least arguable. All experienced prior abuse, the majority being described in news accounts and judgments as having been "battered." These results (65 percent) are generally consistent with earlier work by Statistics Canada, which reported that 68 percent of husband killings involved a history of domestic violence.[56]

Seventy-two of the ninety-one women whose cases are recorded in the Appendix were killed in the course of an ongoing altercation that involved some form of physical conflict or threat. Nine of the remaining nineteen were women who killed sleeping male partners, and two women conspired to kill with the aid of others. However, this group also included women who killed upon discovering that the deceased had sexually assaulted them or their children, women who killed in anticipation of physical conflict, and women who killed during a lull in a physical confrontation. These results, which suggest that only 20 percent of the ninety-two women did not kill during physical conflict, parallel those found by US author Maguigan in her study.[57]

In cases in which there was some evidence of prior abuse, I attempted to gather basic information about the relationship, the circumstances surrounding the homicide, the charges laid, the arguments advanced, the legal resolution of the charges, and the sentence, if the woman was convicted. Charges were declined, dropped, or stayed by the prosecutor, or the accused was discharged by the judge after a preliminary inquiry, in seven of these cases. Guilty pleas to manslaughter (and two to conspiracy to commit murder) were entered by forty-nine women (54 percent of total, or 58 percent of those against whom the prosecution proceeded); one other woman pled guilty to second-degree murder after multiple trials. Of the thirty-four women who went on to trial, two were convicted of first-degree murder, one of second-degree murder, and nine of manslaughter, totalling twelve convictions (13 percent of total, or 14 percent of those against whom the Crown proceeded). The remaining twenty-two women were acquitted of all charges (24 percent of total, or 26 percent of those against whom the prosecution proceeded), including one woman acquitted by the court of appeal and another acquitted after a new trial. In the end, out of ninety-one women, sixty-two were convicted of some form of homicide (68 percent of total): fifty-six of manslaughter; two of conspiracy to commit murder; two of second-degree murder; and two of first-degree murder. Another twenty-nine women (32 percent of total) were either spared a trial or were acquitted.

More recent work tracking battered women's homicide cases from 2000 to 2010 shows similar patterns: thirty-six women were charged; twenty pled guilty, nineteen to manslaughter and one to murder (56 percent); one charge was stayed; and, among the fifteen who went to trial, eleven were acquitted (30.5 percent).[58]

From my research base, I ordered thirty-six transcripts[59] of preliminary inquiries, trials, and sentencing hearings. I chose to analyze eleven of these women's cases, selected to show the range of issues that arises in battered women's trials, the different outcomes, and the strategies and arguments advanced by their lawyers. I also chose these cases taking into consideration the length of the transcript, the availability of additional secondary materials such as reported decisions in the matter and newspaper coverage, and, in the case of Aboriginal women, the prevalence of their cases among my sample.

This study presented methodological challenges, to be sure. These databases allowed me to retrieve a number of sentencing reasons where women pled guilty or were found guilty of manslaughter[60] and appeal decisions on jury instructions or sentence. Jury acquittals and convictions are not reported in legal databases unless they raise a legal issue, such as parole eligibility, or are appealed; guilty pleas, where the reasons for sentence are brief, are rarely reported in legal databases. Newspaper databases revealed many more cases, probably because husband killing remains relatively infrequent and therefore more "newsworthy," but the details provided are often sketchy. In some cases, further media reports on the progress of the case could not be found. Thus, neither search method yields a complete picture of women who kill male partners in Canada. Statistics Canada reports that approximately 273 women killed male partners in my study period,[61] so my research has captured approximately half of the known cases.

Although my research base does not perfectly match the statistics, it allows a snapshot of the results of battered women's homicide charges post-*Lavallee*, revealing charging patterns, the predominant outcome of guilty pleas to manslaughter, and a surprising number of acquittals based on self-defence. This study also provides a context within which to make sense of the eleven cases that I analyze in depth, using a case study approach. For each case, I explain legal aspects for the general reader; situate it within my larger study of ninety-one cases; and show its relationship to the broader social and legal contexts in which it occurred to highlight the systemic forces that shaped the homicides and the legal resolution of the charges. The case study approach to criminal trial transcripts does not lend itself to definitive conclusions about guilt or innocence or the "right" or "wrong" trial strategy, but it nonetheless offers valuable insights into the barriers and challenges facing battered women on trial.

Defining My Terms

For the purposes of this book, I use the term "battering" to describe the systemic use of threats and acts of violence, whether minor or serious, by male partners to get their way – to enforce their authority, to isolate, intimidate, and silence their female partners, and to control them.[62] Also called "intimate terrorism" in the literature, battering is overwhelmingly committed by men against women, is motivated by the desire to dominate and achieve control over another, and tends to escalate over time.[63] Battering draws on structural inequalities experienced by women – women's unequal access to social, political, and economic resources. Societies more rigidly stratified by gender have higher rates of battering.[64]

Battering is used to enforce women's traditional roles – to force women to serve their male partners by cooking and cleaning, bearing and raising children, and being sexually available; to restrict or supervise what women wear, whether they pursue educational or employment opportunities, and whom they associate with;[65] and to reflect men "at twice their natural size."[66] Melanie Randall sums up battering as "simultaneously express[ing] and reproduc[ing] sexual inequality on both individual and societal levels; it is both a cause and effect of sex inequality."[67]

Battering is distinguished from "situational couple violence," which denotes common couple violence in which women as well as men might on occasion use violence outside a larger pattern of control or coercion in order to get their way in a particular situation.[68] Relationships are described as battering ones when there is evidence of threatening behaviour, sexual or physical abuse by the man, coupled with his effort to control and dominate the woman. In such cases, the implication is clear to both partners: if he needs to use more serious violence to achieve his goal, he will. Lisa A Goodman and Deborah Epstein elaborate: "Even nonviolent control tactics take on a violent meaning through their implicit connection with potential physical harm."[69]

The term "battered women" is used throughout this book, even though it implicitly suggests a category of women whose experiences are universal and who are somehow set apart from "other" women.[70] In the context of criminal trials, in which nuance is abandoned by Crown and defence lawyers who present competing narratives about women on trial as either violent, manipulative frauds or wholly innocent, deserving wives and mothers, claiming the experience of battering carries particular risks. Women who fail in any way to meet the preconceptions of battered women can have their credibility destroyed and their chances of acquittal undercut. For example, in one case in my study of ninety-one women, the prosecutor argued at sentencing that the woman was "often drunk, profane, verbally abusive, physically aggressive, prone to lying and exaggeration, that she was not in fact the submissive, passive, vulnerable woman who lived in the state of learned helplessness."[71] Some Canadian judges have attempted to disrupt this binary, insisting that, although a woman might use violence or coarse language or in other ways present as less than perfect, this does not mean that she has not experienced battering.[72] Yet Crown attorneys and defence lawyers continue this battle for the hearts and minds of jurors by presenting contrasting and stark portraits of the woman's (and the deceased man's) goodness or evil.

To further complicate matters, many women, US author Martha R Mahoney explains, avoid calling themselves "battered." She identifies "the gap between my self-perceived competence and strength and my own image of battered women, the inevitable attendant loss of my own denial of painful experience, and the certainty that the listener cannot hear such a claim without filtering it through a variety of derogatory stereotypes."[73] Even women convicted of killing their batterers might reject the label because they have grown up with male violence as a constant, internalized it as their fault, thought that the violence they experienced was not severe enough, or believed that if they fought back they could not be a battered woman.[74] Thus, the practices of batterers and the consequences for women whose lives have been affected by them remain relatively invisible in our society and legal system[75] and continue to be distorted by misconceptions.

A Word about Transcripts

Trial transcripts in Canada are very difficult for researchers to obtain. The preparation and release of transcripts are subject to different rules in each province. They also require lengthy waits and are extremely expensive to acquire, if the tapes have indeed been preserved. For example, until recently, Nova Scotia destroyed tapes and transcripts after two years.[76] Although new practices using digital records will allow much longer retention in the future, on average jurisdictions retain tape recordings for between five and ten years. In some jurisdictions, the tapes follow the court reporter, requiring the researcher to locate the court reporter, who then has to find her tapes.

Even then, the court reporter might not have the time – or the researcher the money – to type the record, at an average cost of $3.50 per page.

Worse are jurisdictions such as British Columbia and the Yukon, which have privatized the enterprise, enabling court reporter services to charge fifteen dollars per page to produce the transcript and high fees even for photocopies of trial records that have already been transcribed, and claim copyright in public records. British Columbia has further revised its policy as of February 2011 to require a court order before transcripts of criminal proceedings can be released to a member of the public.[77] These barriers to transcript-based research mean that the Canadian public loses knowledge and history as a consequence.

Finally, if one gets the transcript, one can be surprised by the variability of what it includes or omits. Some transcripts exclude all oral argument by lawyers on points of law before the judge when the jury is absent; many exclude matters such as jury selection; and critical matters such as the final jury addresses are sometimes excluded, for no apparent reason. Video or audio recordings entered into evidence are rarely transcribed, so the researcher is acutely aware that she is not reading the whole story. Even when supplemented by in-court observation, a transcript provides a partial glimpse into what happened, as lawyers, witnesses, and judges deploy the rules of evidence to shape the evidence presented in the courtroom.[78]

The Chapters

The chapters in this book are driven by the narrative of each transcript and are presented in an accessible form for the general reader.

Chapter 1 explores Angelique Lyn Lavallee's trial, made possible only because Greg Brodsky retained a copy of her transcript in his files and generously shared it. This chapter contextualizes Brodsky's advocacy in the *Lavallee* case by reference to the work of feminist activists and lawyers who prepared the groundwork and advanced the arguments in US courts on behalf of battered women who kill. Here I explain the theory of Battered Woman Syndrome, using Lenore Walker's work,[79] and review the critiques and problems associated with invoking this theory. The *Lavallee* case is lauded around the world as the most progressive decision among Western nations for battered women who kill: this chapter explains the role played by Justice Bertha Wilson in the decision and why the judgment held so much promise for battered women. It situates this case within the feminist movement's efforts to put wife battering on the public agenda and the backlash against so-called violent women engendered by feminist demands for formal equality whereby women would be treated the same as men.

Chapter 2 steps back from women's murder trials to examine the other side of the coin: what of those battered women who do not kill? This chapter explores what we know about wife battering, police intervention, women's options for escape, and the risks of intimate femicide, for this is the dangerous sea in which most women who kill male partners must swim. I use Bonnie Mooney's civil lawsuit against the AG of British Columbia and the police for failing to protect her and her loved ones against the violent rage of her ex-partner to illustrate how the "social entrapment" of battered women narrows their options for escape from abusive men. James Ptacek argues that women are not only held captive by abusive men: "Individual women are assaulted by individual men, but the ability of so many men to repeatedly assault, terrorize, and control so many women draws on institutional collusion and gender inequality."[80] What exactly do we offer by way of safe passage for women seeking to escape from batterers?

Chapter 3 exposes a major barrier to women's access to a fair trial on the merits: the mandatory life sentence for murder. I tell Kim Kondejewski's story in this chapter to show how the mandatory life sentence makes the line between guilt and innocence arbitrary when a battered woman is charged with homicide, particularly first-degree murder. Although I use her transcript to tell "the facts," I also draw on the work of Emma Cunliffe[81] and Austin Sarat[82] to explore the limitations of trial transcripts. The Kondejewski case illustrates some of the risks of using Battered Woman Syndrome evidence and raises the question of whether self-defence is available for planned and deliberate murder and for defence of one's children. Finally, I invite the reader to consider the psychological price paid by battered women who undergo murder trials.

Chapter 4 explores what happens to Aboriginal women who kill, whose experiences might not easily be captured by Battered Woman Syndrome. Both Gladys Heavenfire and Doreen Sorenson killed non-Aboriginal male partners who were able to draw on systemic racism to further dominate them. Their domestic captivity was enabled by colonial practices of the state that heightened their vulnerability to male violence. This chapter argues that Aboriginal women's dilemmas must be understood within the context that these women are dramatically more likely to be the victims of intimate femicide than other women. Not surprisingly then, they appear disproportionately in my study, comprising 41 percent of my ninety-one files. I use the work of Sherene H Razack[83] in this chapter to explore how the role of racism can be rendered invisible in Aboriginal women's homicide trials, at the risk of further shoring up racist stereotypes and white privilege. The Heavenfire and Sorenson transcripts raise delicate questions about how a defence lawyer can expose unconscious racism that might affect how the credibility of witness testimony, especially that of the client, is evaluated by the jury.

Chapter 5 uses a major study by Anne McGillivray and Brenda Comaskey[84] to show the role of colonization in Aboriginal women's experience of male violence. This chapter identifies the common features of Aboriginal women's homicides, focusing on those women who kill Aboriginal male partners. Aboriginal women almost invariably kill during an altercation and not when their partner is asleep or passed out, yet they are more likely than others to plead guilty and forgo their right to argue self-defence. The chapter examines the trials of two women who did not plead guilty: Donelda Ann Kay and Denise Robin Rain. Their cases illustrate the serious barriers to acquittal for Aboriginal women who are invariably portrayed as aggressors, not "real" battered women. In light of the escalation of the federal incarceration of Aboriginal women by 151 percent between 1997 and 2007,[85] making them the fastest-growing prison population in Canada, this chapter seeks to understand why so many Aboriginal women are convicted of killing violent male partners. These transcripts reveal strategies that might be used to challenge stereotypes about Aboriginal women and to position their actions within a self-defence paradigm. The chapter then turns to the well-known case of Jamie Tanis Gladue, whose guilty plea led to a sentencing decision that made legal history in 1999.[86] I ask whether she should have gone on to trial rather than pleading guilty in light of the exculpatory evidence available through her preliminary inquiry and sentencing hearing.

Chapter 6 asks whether self-defence is or should be available to those relatively rare women who kill their batterers in non-confrontational situations, such as when the man is asleep. Lilian Getkate's murder trial raises the question of whether Battered Woman Syndrome is appropriate when little evidence corroborates the woman's claim of abuse and when the woman does not match the stereotypes associated with battered women. An alternative defence theory might be "Coercive Control,"[87] which shifts the focus away from a man's discrete acts of violence and toward his pattern of psychological domination and pervasive threat "to secure privileges that involve the use of time, control over material resources, access to sex, and personal service."[88] This chapter also considers whether overzealous Crown prosecutors of battered women violate their ethical obligation to act in the public interest to ensure that justice is done,[89] given that the same prosecutors must assure battered women that their accounts of battering will be believed and prosecuted according to the law. Is there an inherent ethical and moral conflict posed for Crown prosecutors in these cases?

Chapter 7 shows how, in order to survive battering, women use alcohol and drugs; they suppress their fear and anxiety; and they dissociate from reality. Some have experienced traumatic brain injuries from being hit on the head, strangled, and thrown into walls and down stairs. The transcripts of Margaret Ann Malott and Rita Graveline demonstrate these additional hurdles for battered women on trial, whereby their partial or wholly absent memory can compromise their ability to argue self-defence. I discuss here other defences advanced in these trials – intoxication, provocation, and automatism – and their limitations for battered women who kill. The chapter uses the work of Evan Stark and Anne Flitcraft[90] to examine the role of the medical profession in women's social entrapment by treating women for depression and prescribing anti-depressants and anti-anxiety medications. It also discusses psychological abuse by batterers as a form of torture that risks the destruction of the psychological self. Does or should the law of self-defence recognize psychological self-defence? Does our law of self-defence fairly capture women's survival dilemmas?

The Conclusion identifies changes that could be put in place to secure for battered women on trial for homicide their equal right to a fair trial on the merits: what can we do to alleviate the pressure to plead guilty and avoid a trial? I highlight successful defence strategies, especially relating to the choice of alternatives to Battered Woman Syndrome and of experts to testify to the theory. I also suggest changes to prosecutorial policies and practices, to the sentencing of murder, to legal aid, and to the law of self-defence that arise from my study of the transcripts.

In the Conclusion, I also outline the new law of self-defence, which passed in June 2012,[91] after I completed this book. The new provision replaces sections 34-37 of the *Criminal Code* and applies to all offences that a person might commit in self-defence, including non-violent offences.[92] This new defence addresses many of the uncertainties that I identify through my analysis. Still, my study remains relevant for lawyers, activists, and researchers because the new law uses the same principles as the old did[93] and because lawyers and judges will continue to draw from prior practice and precedent in its interpretation. I end by discussing the legal, economic, and social changes needed to secure for women in Canadian society their due: safety and freedom.

Elizabeth M Schneider names the work of the battered women's movement in the United States as "feminist lawmaking" that "seeks to transform social meaning."[94] She describes a dialectical process between the social movement and legal change whereby theory and practice talk back to each other: "[T]heory emerges from practice and practice then informs and reshapes theory."[95] In Canada, this dialectical process of revision has been stunted by the fact that neither the battered women's movement nor feminist litigators have been involved in crafting battered women's defence strategies. I hope that this book can contribute to dialogue and revision among feminist activists, legal researchers, and lawyers who defend battered women on trial.

Dealing with a Dilemma

Criminal trials, especially murder trials, are matters of public record. All of the cases described in this book are documented in newspapers, legal reports, and transcripts. Press bans are ordered by judges to protect the identities of women and others who are sexually assaulted – unless they themselves are charged criminally. This means that, though battered women charged with killing their abusers have almost always been raped, and this information emerges from their trials, they are not granted the same anonymity granted to other women. Some legal reporter services mask the identities of women sentenced for spousal manslaughter by substituting initials for names in their reports, but the women's names are readily available in other reporters that do not employ the same practice and in newspaper accounts of the women's prosecutions.

I am acutely aware that the women whose trials I describe will experience suffering by having their cases once more discussed and debated. Each woman has already lost so many years to captivity and then to criminal justice adjudication. None should be asked to suffer further. I considered trying to mask their names somehow, but documenting my sources while concealing their names would have created intractable problems for presenting a credible record of these events. And anyone who wishes to discover their names can easily do so from any partially altered sources that I might have devised. I wish that I could do justice to these women's lives and struggles without subjecting them to renewed public scrutiny, but I could not find a way to do so that would have both protected them and furthered our knowledge of battered women on trial. I have endeavoured to treat each woman's story with integrity and respect.

1

Angelique Lyn Lavallee

"You're my old lady and you do as you're told."[1]

The headline of the *Winnipeg Free Press* story on the city's seventeenth homicide of 1986 foreshadowed the essential conflict in a soon-to-be-famous murder prosecution. The headline, "Murder Charge Raises Concern about Violent Women,"[2] reflected Staff Inspector George Pike's view that "[n]ot only are women becoming involved in more crimes in general, but the crimes are becoming more serious and more violent."[3] The same story quoted Carole Bhakar, executive director of the Elizabeth Fry Society, who gave a different explanation: "[V]ictims of abuse are lashing out at their abusers more often."[4]

Twenty-two-year-old Angelique Lyn Lavallee was not named in this first of many news stories about her case, but it posed the central questions that her jurors would later face. Was she part of an alleged trend[5] whereby young women are becoming more violent? Or was she the real victim?

The Case for the Prosecution

Lavallee would not be the easiest client to defend on charges of second-degree murder. Her statement to the police upon her arrest was "long and rambling," posing "discrepancies and conflicts" with her own and other evidence.[6] According to Lavallee, either she accidentally shot her common law partner, Kevin "Rooster" Rust, intending to shoot above him, or she fired the gun deliberately in self-defence.

Her counsel would worry about whether it would be wise for her to test-ify. Lavallee would be vulnerable in cross-examination because she had lied to medical personnel and others about the source of her many injuries while living with Rust. She was also traumatized and grief stricken. She told her psychiatrist that she still loved the deceased and was deeply remorseful. It had emerged at the preliminary inquiry that a Crown witness had seen her point a loaded rifle at Rust on two prior occasions and heard her threaten to kill him if he touched her again.[7]

Lavallee was arraigned in Winnipeg on 8 April 1987, where she entered a plea of not guilty. Her counsel, Greg Brodsky, an experienced Winnipeg de-fence lawyer, was pitted against Crown Attorney Bruce Miller, who was later appointed to the Provincial Court and became its Associate Chief Judge in 1995. It was not the last time that Brodsky and Miller would oppose each other in a highly contested murder trial.[8]

Jury selection took place the morning of 14 September 1987, and the trial commenced that afternoon before one female and eleven male jurors. Miller's opening statement described the relationship between Lavallee and Rust as "stormy," involving "continuous arguments" and on occasion "vio-lent physical altercations between the two."[9] On the night of the homicide, Miller told the jury, the two held a raucous party. By 1 a.m., it had reached such a crescendo of music, yelling, and screaming that two neighbours called 9-1-1. Rust was so intoxicated that he vomited in the basement and passed out. While he was inside, Lavallee evicted his sister Wendy and her friends. Summoned to the altercation, Rust briefly came outside to inter-vene. His sister departed, he returned to the house, and Lavallee, according to Miller, stomped around angrily on the second floor.

When the remaining guests heard a shot ring out from the second floor, Rust went up alone to speak to Lavallee. Six minutes after the first shot, the guests heard a second shot. They saw Lavallee run from the house, and an-other guest, awakened from the living room couch, ran upstairs to find Rust dead. His head was a bloody mess; human tissue was splattered in the up-stairs hall. Miller's forensics expert would testify that Rust was shot in the back of his head from a distance of approximately six feet.

In Canadian criminal courts, unlike those depicted in television dramas, defence lawyers are not permitted, absent rare circumstances, to provide their opening address until the Crown's case is complete.[10] Lawyers such as Brodsky must use cross-examination of Crown witnesses to outline the de-fence in order to begin to presuade the jury. Brodsky made sure that the jury never forgot he was there.

Miller presented fifteen witnesses for the prosecution, starting with the police and a pathologist. Constable Gerald Roberts took the jury through the layout of the property, as shown by police photos, including the two separate bedrooms in which the couple slept. Three guns were found in the closet of a storage room upstairs, and the rifle used to kill Rust was found in the "woman's bedroom." Roberts introduced a piece of window screen with a bullet hole to show that the first shot had been fired through Lavallee's bedroom window. Shell casings were matched to the rifle, as were her fingerprints to the ammunition box.[11]

On cross-examination, Roberts admitted that he could not ascertain whether Lavallee's fingerprints were recent, whether anyone else had handled the ammunition, or who had loaded the gun. The reliability of the police search of the townhouse was put into question when Roberts denied having seen the "caved in portion, a half-moon shape," at the bottom of Lavallee's closet door. This mark, Brodsky suggested, showed that the door had been kicked in. Roberts also missed a three-inch by three-inch hole in the wall behind the closet, which Brodsky claimed had been caused by punching.[12]

Miller's next witness was Dr Peter Markesteyn, introduced as a medical practitioner. Brodsky interjected and demonstrated to the jurors his fair-mindedness by extolling the witness's expert credentials: "More than that, My Lord, he is a forensic pathologist and well able to conduct autopsies and to do those matters that the office of a Chief Medical Examiner requires."[13]

The cause of death was a single gunshot wound to the brain, the shot having been fired from behind the deceased's head. Dr Markesteyn described bruising on the deceased's shin: "[W]henever I see a wound on a shin from an investigative point of view, I always say was there a woman involved ... Because women so commonly when in an altercation will kick the shin of a person, whereas a man very seldom will do that."[14]

In cross-examination, Dr Markesteyn acknowledged that the bruising found on the knuckles of the deceased was consistent with having hit someone. Was the bruising shown in photographs of Lavallee consistent with the bruises on the deceased's hand? "Medically that would be entirely possible, yes."[15]

Brodsky took a risk and asked Dr Markesteyn a pointed question: "Can you tell the jury in connection with ... the injuries you saw in the photographs of the accused ... what ... Battered Wife Syndrome refers to?"[16] The Crown's witness then launched into a lengthy exposé that alerted the jury to the defence strategy and educated them about battering relationships. Dr Markesteyn said that it is usually women who find themselves experiencing physical, emotional, and sexual abuse and that, without intervention, the situation usually gets worse. The woman often tries to hide her injuries, "usually by giving explanations of trivial injuries like I only knocked myself slightly and I bruised all over,"[17] and might return to the batterer for many reasons, including economic and emotional dependency. Although he disclaimed expertise, he was invited by Brodsky to admit, modestly, that he had delivered public lectures on Battered Woman Syndrome.

On re-examination of his witness, Miller attempted to regain the upper hand by having the doctor confirm that Battered Woman Syndrome is not a psychiatric term. Instead, his witness claimed, "it is an entity, not only recognized by psychology, psychiatry, but also by emergency physicians who see them as people who come back with bruises all the time."[18] When Miller tried to get Dr Markesteyn to agree that the photos of Lavallee did not show "tremendous bruising," Brodsky dropped his accommodating approach and rose to object. He slipped in the defence theory: "[I]f my learned friend's point is that there wasn't serious and severe bruising on this lady, I am taking exception to my learned friend pursuing it, for the simple and very obvious reason that my learned friend must be seriously facetious in his questioning in that the deceased died before the attack could conclude." Associate Chief Justice of the Queen's Bench Richard Scott[19] responded dryly: "Well, that's your case, Mr Brodsky. We haven't heard anything about that yet."[20]

Brodsky had introduced to the jury a taboo subject – wife battering. Only four years before, in 1982, MP Margaret Mitchell was greeted by guffaws and shouts of laughter from male MPs[21] when she spoke to the first parliamentary report on wife battering.[22] The battered women's movement, composed of women who had experienced male violence, shelter and crisis centre workers, and feminist advocates, had developed a sophisticated analysis of wife battering and had succeeded in bringing the issue into the public sphere. As early as 1972 in Canada, women began to set up networks of safe houses to shelter women and children who fled from abusive men and to form support groups in which women shared their experiences and came to understand how rape, sexual harassment, and wife battering had shaped their lives.[23] The battered women's movement insisted that wife battering was not a "private" issue but one deserving a public response.[24] This movement criticized the role of the state – police, judiciary, legislators – in perpetuating battering and demanded arrest and charging policies, taking the onus off women to lay charges themselves and placing it instead on police and prosecutors.

In the four years of Lavallee's relationship with Rust, 1982-86, the battered women's movement in Canada succeeded in instigating sweeping changes in public policy.[25] Women's advocates persuaded the Solicitor General of Canada in 1982 to direct the RCMP to lay charges in cases of wife battering where grounds existed. He wrote to police chiefs urging them to adopt strong charging policies for wife assault; provincial attorneys general followed suit in 1982 and on.[26] In 1983, for the first time, Ottawa designated government funding for shelters and transition houses, to be developed through cooperative funding with provincial governments.[27] The increase in criminal charging of batterers led to greater media interest, which in turn heightened public attention to the challenges confronting battered women.[28]

Brodsky had also alerted the jury to Battered Woman Syndrome, another outcome of the advocacy work of the battered women's movement. Elizabeth M Schneider describes the two-pronged strategic litigation engaged in by feminist lawyers, researchers, and activists in the 1970s and 1980s in the US to challenge the masculine bias of the law of self-defence. When battered women required legal defence for killing violent men, they found themselves disadvantaged by the law of self-defence, premised on norms that represented men's, not women's, lives and experiences. Women on trial were also disadvantaged by the social reality that wife battering was a hidden crime, subject to widespread public denial and minimization, as the eruption in our House of Commons in 1982 illustrated.

The battered women's movement criticized the law's focus on the immediate circumstances in which the homicide took place and its exclusion of the batterer's prior violence against other female partners as inadmissible.[29] Even the woman's prior experience of violence at the hands of the deceased could be characterized as legally irrelevant.[30] Similarly, the requirement that the defender deploy "equal force" could disentitle a woman who used a gun to defend herself against a larger and stronger man. Finally, assessment of the woman's culpability that did not require jurors to step into her shoes and gauge "reasonableness" based on her past experiences also disadvantaged women.[31]

In a landmark appeal, Schneider and her co-counsel Nancy Stearns, on behalf of the Center for Constitutional Rights, persuaded the Washington Supreme Court in 1977 in *State v Wanrow*[32] that these self-defence standards denied women their "equal right to trial." Instead, legal standards must include women's experiences. In another series of appellate cases, the first being *State v Kelly*[33] decided in 1984, feminist litigators persuaded the courts to admit expert testimony on Battered Woman Syndrome to inform the jury about the realities of wife battering and dispel the negative stereotypes about battered women so that jurors could step into the shoes of those women.

These developments in US law were of great interest to the battered women's movement in Canada. The risks and benefits of reliance on Battered Woman Syndrome evidence in women's homicide trials were debated within Canadian circles as early as 1987.[34] In fact, Brodsky had already used Battered Woman Syndrome evidence in another trial a year before he represented Lavallee. Victoria Savoyard, a Métis woman, was acquitted of manslaughter by her Kenora, Ontario, jury in May 1986,[35] and other women's sentences had been mitigated by such evidence.[36]

Obviously, Brodsky had not missed the precedents secured by the battered women's movement south of the border. It seemed, however, that Miller might have.

Miller then called to the witness stand Lavallee's two neighbours. Dennis Dyer testified that the noise emanating from the party prompted him to call the police at 1 a.m. They had not yet responded when Dyer heard what he thought was a gunshot at 1:59 a.m. Six minutes later he heard another shot and this time, convinced that it was gunfire, looked outside and heard what "sounded like a child crying." He heard a woman say "[f]uck, he punched me in the face. He punched me in the face."[37] Dyer saw a female come out from the townhouse, fall to her knees, raise her arms in the air, and wail in "anguish ... she's very sorrowful and very upset."[38]

Theodore (Ted) Hladky, the second neighbour, had more to say. He also called the police first at 1 a.m. to complain about the raging party next door. About twenty minutes later, "everything went berserk ... It was the wildest thing I have ever heard."[39] Hladky went downstairs armed with a "companion" – a broom because he could not find a baseball bat – and told his wife to call the police a second time. He heard Lavallee say "I didn't say anything to your sister. I didn't do anything."[40] Rust's tone was "argumentative." Hladky returned to bed, only to be startled five to ten minutes later by gunfire. He leapt up: "I instructed my wife to phone the Police Department one more time and ... not to be nice this time."[41]

Outside, Hladky heard yelling and screaming from the neighbour's house, the sounds of people running up and down stairs – "it sounded like an army arguing."[42] When he heard the second shot, five to ten minutes

after the first, he ordered his family inside. He grabbed the telephone re-
ceiver to tell the police "to get their butts down here now." People in the
townhouse next door began to empty out. Lavallee caught Hladky's attention because she was hysterical and repeating "I shot him in the head. I
killed him. I killed him. You guys are my witnesses."[43]

Brodsky asked in cross-examination whether Hladky had heard a mere
argument between the first and second shots. Hladky's sense of foreboding
was palpable:

> There's no question there was a fight ... I remember recalling, I wished the
> police would just hurry up and get here because ... the whole evening was
> just turning sour from about 1:00 o'clock on. And I had a feeling at that
> point in time to be honest with you that something was going to happen
> and that's what really kept me there because the violence, there was vio-
> lence inside the house.[44]

As Brodsky pressed, Hladky said that he could not say who was being beaten,
but "there was definitely a fight in there and the screams that I heard were
not male screams. They were female screams ... These were not screams of
joy, Mr Brodsky. They were screams of pain and I think fear ... I would have
to draw the conclusion that she was scared."[45]

The Crown then called Wendy Rust, Rust's sister. Of Lavallee, she said,
"not friends, really."[46] Lavallee had demanded that she leave because she
was drinking "their" beer. When Wendy challenged Lavallee, "she took a
swing at me."[47]

Wendy's friend, Angela St Laurent, described Lavallee as a rough woman:
"She looked at me and she said to me, 'What the fuck are you staring at?' So
I went to answer her and then she says, 'Get the fuck out of my yard.' Just
like that."[48] After reporting the conversation to Wendy, St Laurent gathered
her beers from the fridge and left. Lavallee's tone was "threatening."[49] Under
cross-examination, St Laurent told Brodsky that Rust had grabbed Lavallee
to stop her from attacking Wendy.[50]

David Keith Wright, Rust's friend, had witnessed quarrels between Rust
and Lavallee but had never seen violence. He had seen Lavallee with stitches
on her lip but claimed that she had told him something about a horse. At the
party, he had lain down on a couch on the main floor to sleep. A shot and
female screaming had woken him abruptly. Wright had run upstairs, found
Rust prone on the floor at the top of the stairs, and yelled for an ambulance
to be called.

Brodsky's cross-examination focused on Wright's state of intoxication: Wright must have been very inebriated to have slept through the wild party and the first gunshot. Brodsky circled around to the injury that Wright saw on Lavallee's face two weeks before the homicide:

> Q: And you asked her how she got this fat lip and she mentioned something about a horse?
>
> A: Yes.
>
> Q: You didn't pursue it?
>
> A: No
>
> Q: In fact, you never even asked her if she had been on a horse? You never even asked her if she had been on a horse that day, the day she got the fat lip?
>
> A: No.[51]

Herb Kaglik testified that he, Norm Kolish, and Joanne Wright had tried to dissuade Rust from going up to check on Lavallee after the first shot. Rust had gone to the second floor alone. They had returned to the basement but could hear "pushing, shoving, like fighting."[52] At the second shot, they had run from the basement to the living room as Lavallee raced down from the second floor and flew out the door.

Brodsky lit into Kaglik: why had he not rushed upstairs at the first gunshot to check whether Lavallee had killed herself? "You could hear the crying right away," explained Kaglik. Brodsky persisted: "Wouldn't you want to go up and see what condition she was in?" Rather than running upstairs after the second shot, Kaglik and the others had gone outside. Brodsky asked: "Did you call an ambulance, the police, any assistance?" "No."[53]

Brodsky attacked Kaglik's inability to recollect key events, including where Rust was when the first shot was fired.[54] Kaglik conceded that "I got troubles with the time, you know."[55] He admitted that the sounds he had heard upstairs between the first and second shots could have been Rust "beating the tar out of Lyn."[56] Brodsky asked why none of them had run upstairs to intervene: "Is it because it was nobody's business how Lyn and Rooster lived their lives?" Kaglik replied: "Well, yes. Yes."[57] He claimed that he never saw physical violence between the two but admitted that, whenever altercations began, he left the premises.[58] "So you don't know how any of that ended up?" "Never, never asked."[59] Kaglik was forced to concede that it was possible Rust was upstairs with Lavallee when the first shot was fired.[60]

Norm Kolish, another of Rust's friends, acknowledged that Rust and Lavallee fought a lot. He described it as mutual: "[S]he fought with him and he fought with her."[61] He told Miller that he had never seen the fighting escalate beyond a verbal screaming match.[62]

After the party, Kolish, Kaglik, Joanne, and Rust took the music system to the basement and sat around talking while Lavallee went upstairs, "banging things around" and saying "[f] this and stuff like that."[63] They heard a shot fired from upstairs, and all ran up to the main floor. Rust went up to "calm Lyn down," after failing to persuade the other three to go up.[64] While Rust was upstairs, Kolish said, they could still hear Lavallee "smashing things around."[65] He heard Rust say "[c]ome on, Lyn, put the gun down."[66] Then, he said, "Rooster had come back down the stairs and just said that, you know, she's really, she is going crazy, she is upset, da, da, da and then he proceeded to go up there and try and calm her down again."[67]

Kolish and the others returned to the basement. They could hear the ensuing fight – loud banging and other noises – and then a second shot. Lavallee's screaming followed immediately. "It was just screaming, hysterical screaming."[68] As they ran upstairs and Lavallee ran down from the second floor, "she was crying and screaming and saying 'Rooster was beating me so I shot him.'"[69]

Brodsky's cross-examination of Kolish established that he had consumed fifteen beers and numerous shots of vodka and had been "feeling pretty good."[70] At the preliminary inquiry, he had said that Rust was chasing Lavallee around the backyard;[71] she had used Kolish as a shield by hiding behind him. Rust had challenged him: "What are you doing? Sticking up for the old lady?"[72] Kolish also admitted having described Rust's mood as "mean"[73] and "Lyn [as] afraid of him"[74] at the preliminary inquiry. Brodsky reminded Kolish that at the preliminary inquiry he had testified that Lavallee said "[l]eave me alone" a minute or two before the first gunshot – a point critical for the defence – even though he was now claiming that Rust did not go up until after the first shot.[75]

Brodsky read in Kolish's evidence from the preliminary inquiry that Rust might have said that he was going upstairs to "straighten her out" rather than "settle her down."[76] Both Miller and the judge were skeptical about the significance of the phrasing. But Brodsky ingeniously asked Kolish to explain what "straightening someone out means." Kolish replied: "Well, when someone gets out of hand, you know ... generally causing trouble, it is time to straighten the guy out." "By doing what?" "Well. Throwing him out, getting rid of him or whatever, what have you, whatever needs to be done."[77]

Joanne Wright, the wife of Keith Wright, had a "good" relationship with Lavallee.[78] Rust and Lavallee argued in front of her, but she never saw physical violence or injuries. Yet Rust was "strict" with Lavallee: "If we decided to go out, she would tell me that he said no and so I didn't think it was fair."[79] Joanne relayed a conversation that she had had with Lavallee the night of the party. Miller asked if it was "woman talk," then tried to correct the patronizing tone: "And I don't mean that to be a slur. I mean, men talk as well."[80] Joanne continued: "[S]he was telling me apparently one time she had an abortion and Rooster made her go to a social of some kind and she said she was still bleeding and she didn't want to go."[81]

Joanne's evidence provided insight into why Lavallee did not like Rust's sister. Despite having lived together for four years, "when she goes on the bus Wendy doesn't talk to her ... or say hi to her or anything."[82] Joanne described the tension in the backyard with Lavallee "calling down" Wendy and deciding to "throw her out ... because she didn't acknowledge her on the bus."[83]

Joanne returned to the house with the others not long after Wendy left. Five minutes later they heard a shot: "Norm yelled, 'Lyn's committed suicide.'"[84] Then, she testified, Rust ran straight up to the second level. From the main floor, they heard thumping and yelling and screaming. Then Rust descended. He wanted Joanne to go up and calm Lavallee down. She refused: "I didn't know what was going on with those guys and I didn't want to get involved."[85]

Just as Joanne returned to the basement, she heard a "pop" and ran back upstairs. "Lyn was running around the living room ... [s]creaming, crying, whimpering," and saying "[y]ou know how he treated me. You got to help me."[86] Joanne offered to go with her to the police station, but "Lyn said that there was no need for me to go with her, that she did it herself, she can handle it herself."[87]

In cross-examination, Joanne acknowledged that she had never asked Lavallee why she did not leave Rust.[88] Brodsky asked: "Did she tell you also that she didn't want the abortion in the first place and that was Rooster's idea?" and "that she wasn't happy at all about the whole state of affairs, anything to do with the abortion?"[89] Joanne did not remember this, but Brodsky had inserted another aspect of Rust's control over Lavallee.

Brodsky clarified Lavallee's state of mind before the homicide: "She never said, 'I'm going to shoot him, kill him, stab him, beat him, bash him, throw him down the stairs, get somebody else to do any of those things?'"[90] Joanne agreed that Lavallee had cleaned Rust after he vomited, not been yelling at him, and "seemed friendly enough."[91]

Rust's best friend, Robert Ezako, testified next. He had seen maybe three or four of Rust and Lavallee's many arguments turn physical.[92] When they did, he left: "I don't like to be around stuff like that."[93] Lavallee was "gettin' mouthy, gettin' smart and snotty all the time." Rust would warn her: "You know, if you keep it up you're gonna get it."[94] The slapping, hitting, punching, and scratching was "mutual." Rust had once shown Ezako a deep scratch on his chest, allegedly caused by Lavallee. Ezako had seen Lavallee with a black eye: Lavallee and Rust said that she had fallen down the stairs.[95]

Ezako's evidence painted a most damaging portrait of Lavallee. Once Ezako and Rust were moving a couch into the house and Rust called for Lavallee to come and hold the door for them. She was "mouthing off" to Rust and then picked up a baseball bat, swung it, and hit him on the arm. Rust took the bat and told her that she was going to "get it." Lavallee went upstairs and returned with a rifle:[96] "She stood halfway up the stairs and ... said 'If you ever touch me again [...] I'm gonna kill you.'"[97]

Another time Ezako visited their home Lyn became upset when he saw some framed photos on the wall. Rust said to her: "You wait. You're gonna get it."[98] Lavallee went upstairs and returned holding a .22 rifle. She was "very upset and hysterical and like freakin' out" and said "'[i]f you ever – if you ever try that or hit me again,' or something, 'you'll be sorry.'"[99] Ezako stayed away after that until the night of the party: "[G]uns kill people and I just had no part of him after that."[100] Ironically, it was Ezako who had sold a .22 rifle to Lavallee and a .303 to Rust – the weapon that caused his death.[101]

Ezako acknowledged that Lavallee had told him Rust beat her: "As I told Kevin, on occasions of fighting and beatings, I said it was none of my business."[102] He explained: "I've got problems of my own."[103] Miller asked Ezako if Lavallee had ever left Rust: "There was two or three occasions where she had moved out and moved right back in. Within a few days to a week later, she'd be back in there ... I told Rooster, 'Like, you know, what are you takin' her back for?'"[104]

Brodsky's cross-examination of Ezako produced a starkly different portrait of the frequency and seriousness of Rust's violence. Lavallee was sleeping when they came to the door with the couch, and Rust repeatedly screamed "[f]ucking Bitch, get on down here."[105] She came down the stairs "mouthing off." Brodsky then asked Ezako pointedly: "He had, to your knowledge, beaten her up pretty good a few times?"[106] Ezako agreed. He saw physical violence almost every time he visited the couple: "A good beating, many slaps and punches and throwing around." He specified: "Throwing into walls and, you know, over the couch and across the room." How often? "Every day pretty well."[107]

Brodsky asked Ezako about the times when the beatings would go on for several days. Ezako denied that this had occurred, only to be confronted with his evidence at the preliminary inquiry, where he had said just that. Brodsky pressed on: "And if he wanted to beat her up every day, two, three days in a row straight ... [?]" Answer: "It's his business, not mine."[108] Rust slapped and backhanded Lavallee almost daily, not just in their home but in other homes as well.[109] Ezako did not intervene even when Lavallee was "screaming like a pig being butchered." He instead told Rust to "'do it in your own privacy. I don't like to see that.'"[110]

Brodsky also established that the threats issued by Rust were to be taken seriously: "He would say to her, 'You're going to get it' ... [W]hen he said that, he meant it?" Miller must have cringed at Ezako's answer: "Obviously, otherwise he wouldn't have said it." Brodsky continued, "you fully expected that she was going to get it later?" Answer: "Yeah. Lickin', slap, punch, whatever. If that's the way he handles things, that's the way he handles them."[111] Ezako agreed that the two times Lavallee threatened Rust with a gun he had first warned her "[y]ou're going to get it."[112]

After the second gun incident, "that was the end ... 'cause guns scare me." Brodsky challenged Ezako: "Well, what about husbands beating up on wives like he was beating up on her; didn't that scare you too?"[113] Ezako agreed: "Yeah, that scared me, but, like I said, I'm not gettin' involved."[114] The police arrived at the premises three or four times to Ezako's knowledge, but all they did was give a warning and leave.[115]

Lavallee was afraid of Rust, "but ... she was very aggressive and she never backed down. She always fought right back."[116] Pressed, Ezako conceded that "quite often" Lavallee got the worst of it. Brodsky reminded him about the incident in the truck when he was driving with Lavallee seated between him and Rust. As Lavallee dozed off, her head on Rust's shoulder, her hand fell to Ezako's leg: "[Rust] slapped her in the face and it scared her. It scared me ... [H]e grabbed her and they were shakin' and yelling ..."[117] He said that Rust "thought she was making a sexual advance on me because her hand was on my lap."[118] Wisely, perhaps, Miller declined re-examination.

The prosecution then called police witnesses to fill in details of the homicide. Kenneth Derendorf testified that the fatal shot to Rust's head was fired from two metres away by a rifle not subject to discharging accidentally.[119] In cross-examination, the defence tried to establish whether the rifle was pointed up, down, or straight ahead when fired. Derendorf acknowledged that it was possible Lavallee fired the weapon from a seated or prone position.[120]

Before his last witnesses took the stand, Miller explained that he would be introducing evidence that normally would first be tested for admissibility with the jury excluded. Brodsky elaborated: "[W]e wish the jury to hear all of the evidence that my learned friend has to offer."[121] He waived the *voir dire* – a hearing in the absence of the jury, here to determine the admissibility of statements made by Lavallee to persons in authority – and he accepted that any statements made by her to police were made voluntarily, without threat or promise of reward.

Winnipeg constable John Popplestone relayed Lavallee's statements made in the police car en route to the station. Her first words were "I didn't mean to do it."[122] Her statements were punctuated by crying, her head in her hands: "He kept beating me all the time. I just couldn't take it anymore ... He said if I didn't kill him first he would kill me. I hope he lives. I really love him." And then "I didn't mean to do it. I'm too young to go to jail and he told me he was gonna kill me when everyone left."[123]

At the station, Lavallee was read her rights, and the only person whom she wanted to call was her mother.[124] Lavallee was, after all, only twenty-two years old. As she waited for her parents, she kept talking: "He kept egging me on, telling me to shoot him."[125] "He hit me twice ... He's done it before. Check the records. Three weeks ago he hit me so hard my tooth went through my lip. Before that he broke my ribs and he broke my nose."[126]

Lavallee was asked only two questions by the police: what weapon had she used, and whose gun was it? Moments later a knock on the door and some news: Rust had died, and she would be charged with murder. It took her parents, who arrived soon after, to calm her wild sobbing. Only then did Lavallee ask for a lawyer.[127]

Waiting for counsel, Lavallee, in shock and full of frenetic energy, asked question after question. Would she be able to go to the funeral? Would the incident be on television? How would the other female inmates in jail treat her? What about the money Rust owed her? He had promised her his motorcycle in his will – would she still get it? Who was going to look after her cat? Was the house locked up?

Brodsky asked Popplestone to repeat all of Lavallee's statements, ensuring that the jury absorbed every one. Referring to her remark "[c]heck the records," he asked whether the police had checked either police or hospital records.[128] They had not. Brodsky's concluding questions were rhetorical devices aimed at countering the aggressive, "unwomanly" image of Lavallee that the Crown witnesses had painted: "At any time that you were with that young lady did she ever make you nervous because of any aggressive attitude on her part?" "Did she ever act in any way that wasn't completely cooperative with you?" "Did she always do what she was told when she was told?" "Aside from crying a lot, did she make your job difficult in any way?" The answer, over and over, was "[n]o."[129]

Constable Robert McQuat testified that, when he and Sergeant Sundell met Lavallee at the station, she told them "[a]ll I know is I was scared. I was fucking scared. It's not the first time."[130] Then, on the advice of her lawyer, Miss Maltz, she provided a written statement. But first, more questions came from Lavallee. She wanted to know where Rust had died: "It really means a lot if I knew where he died." "Does his mom know he died?" "Where was he shot, in the head? All I remember is I saw his head flying off."[131] "Is my house all locked up?"[132] "I want to know who said I didn't love him. I heard some chick say that upstairs."[133]

Lavallee's written statement explained that, at the party hosted at their home, she became embroiled in an argument with Rust about his sister. He pushed her; she ran upstairs and hid in a bedroom closet. He came up after her.

> He wanted me to come out but I didn't want to come out because I was so scared. He grabbed me by the arm right there (points to inside of right forearm) there's a bruise on my face also where he slapped me. He didn't slap me right then first he yelled at me then he pushed me and I pushed him back and he hit me twice on the right side of my head. I was scared. All I thought about was all the other times he used to beat me, I was scared, I was shaking as usual. The rest is a blank all I remember is he gave me the gun and a shot was fired through my screen. This is all so fast. And then the guns were in another room and he loaded it the second shot and gave it to me. And I was going to shoot myself. I pointed it to myself, I was so upset. OK and then he went and I was sitting on the bed and he started going like this with his finger (indicated shaking pointer finger at her) and said something like "You're my old lady and you do as you're told" or something like that. He said, "wait till everybody leaves, you'll get it then" and he said something to the effect of "either you kill me or I'll get you" that's what it was. He kind of smiled and then turned around. I shot him but I aimed out. I thought I

aimed above him and a piece of his head went that way. There was blood and he kept calling my name.[134]

McQuat confronted Lavallee with the essential contradiction between the other witnesses and her statement. She claimed that Rust had come upstairs, loaded the gun, and given it to her before she fired the first shot out the window. In contrast, the others said that Rust had been downstairs with them when she fired the first shot. Her response was consistent: "I remember him upstairs."[135] McQuat also reviewed the bruising and scrapes on Lavallee's face, midriff, right hand, and forearm. Under cross-examination, McQuat said that Lavallee had broken down and wept three times. She had said that she was "scared, really scared," no fewer than six times.[136]

Brodsky's Defence of Lavallee

Brodsky's opening jury address was delayed by a Crown objection. The jury excused, Miller argued that, if Lavallee did not testify, then Brodsky would be introducing medical and psychiatric evidence without an evidentiary foundation:

> [U]nless we hear from the actual so-called batteree, then I don't see as there's a connection between any of these visits to the hospital and the deceased, and I don't believe, with respect, that any explanation that may or may not have been given to an emergency surgeon at a hospital by this person is admissible without having first heard that from her ... We haven't heard any indication of feelings of worthlessness or helplessness. My learned friend is putting the cart before the horse.[137]

Justice Scott refused to constrain Brodsky's conduct of his case: "If the experts deal with a hypothesis, and there's no evidence to substantiate the hypothesis, ... then the opinion is worthless and I will tell [the jury] that."[138]

Brodsky's opening remarks were terse. Brodsky reminded the jury that they had already heard that Rust had assaulted Lavallee:

> I propose to call a number of doctors, not to go through each and every injury that Lyn suffered, not to call each medical record from each traumatic beating that she sustained in every hospital in Winnipeg, but just to go through a representative sample of traumatic incidents so that you'll understand and be able to put in context what Lyn was saying when she told

the police he used to beat her before, put her tooth through her lip, broke her ribs.[139]

He named the misconceptions surrounding wife battering, explicitly asking jurors to set aside such beliefs if they held them:

[Y]ou may wonder to yourself, "Why would she keep going back ... where she was going to continue to be beaten time and time again?" ... Why couldn't she leave? It's for that reason, to help you understand her mind at the time, that I propose to call Dr Dirks ... and a psychiatrist to explain the mind of a lady or spouse that lives in such an environment. Because we shouldn't get into believing the myths, that is: She wants it. She likes it. She can control it. It's her fault. She precipitated it. You have to put that out of your mind, pay attention to the reality. The reality, I hope, will come from the witness box, after which you can use your own good common sense to arrive at an appropriate verdict.[140]

Finally, Brodsky told the jurors to focus on self-defence: "Whether in fact Lavallee was defending herself at the time of the first shot, second shot, what was she defending herself from, did she have any place to run away to ... in the end, when you decide whether she's guilty or not guilty ... that's what you are going to have to decide."[141]

Brodsky's first witness was Dr Henry Dirks, Director of Emergency at Concordia Hospital. His records indicated that Lavallee had received emergency treatment at Concordia eight times in the period 1983-86 for various physical injuries: chest pains, a fractured foot (allegedly caused by dropping a cement block on her foot), chest pain from being kicked in the chest, a black eye, nasal pain and fractures to her hand (allegedly caused by falling off a horse), overconsumption of pain pills, a cut to the finger joint that required sutures, and a cut to the upper lip (allegedly caused by falling into the corner of a couch) that went "through to the inside of the mouth in a gaping fashion" and also required sutures.[142] Brodsky clarified: "She never told you that Kevin Rust hit her in the face." Dr Dirks explained that Lavallee gave no such information, not surprisingly, since Rust was with her at the hospital for the last incident.

Brodsky asked: "Can you tell us about the reliance you place on the history women give of how they received the traumatic injury that you see in hospitals?" Miller was on his feet to object, complaining that this topic of battered women was not within the doctor's expertise. As Brodsky started to explain the work of emergency room physicians, Dr Dirks lept in to defend his expertise:

> As the director of emergency I'm also a physician in the community. Battered-wife abuse and battered women is now part of the protocol ... because we have now been instructed by the attorney general to be – become aware and report incidents ... [D]uring one Friday night and separated by one week ... I had two incidents of battered women who were wives of Winnipeg policemen.
>
> So actually we have become, with time, ... experts in this ... [I]t's become one of the things that we've got to watch for like we have to watch for venereal disease, trauma and everything else.[143]

Justice Scott allowed Dr Dirks to continue. Brodsky asked Dr Dirks to explain the term "battered women." Women go to emergency departments with multiple and traumatic injuries, and if "the patient returns continually with bruises ... there's a call for help, but not directly."[144] Several courses of action might be pursued – the police might be notified, the patient might be referred back to her family doctor, in the hope that that doctor is better able to intervene, or the woman might discharge herself, with or without her batterer present.

On cross-examination, Miller first tried to establish these as Lavallee's only hospital visits, regardless of Brodsky's claim to be merely providing a "representative sample": "Despite my friend's gracious desire to move ahead with this and not go through each and every month of the year, am I fair in saying ... that there were no visits in 1984 documented ...?"[145] Dr Dirks qualified his response. There was none recorded "in my hospital."

Miller three times tried to get Dr Dirks to admit that one emergency visit a year is normal. Dr Dirks navigated around this question: "[Y]ou'll find very often that a person visits your hospital in July, is at Seven Oaks in August, is at the Misericordia in September, is at the St. Boniface in October."[146] When Miller persisted, Dr Dirks insisted that "you'll find many people who have – go from hospital to hospital with injury."[147] Miller again claimed that annual emergency visits are normal. And again Dr Dirks disagreed: "Well, with injuries it is ... Most people get once [sic] injury in five years." Referring to someone with a heart condition, Miller suggested that "it's not unusual for a person like that to come in consistently, is it?" Dr Dirks answered: "But [for] a young person it is unusual."[148]

Miller suggested that Lavallee's "blunt trauma" injuries could have had an innocuous source. Here he secured a slight concession from Dr Dirks. Yes, it was possible that Lavallee was injured while handling a concrete block, but "it's unusual," he cautioned.

Miller proposed that Dr Dirks's staff erred in allowing Lavallee to leave the hospital with her father when she was brought in after having been kicked in the chest, because her injuries could have been caused by a battering parent. This suggestion the doctor dismissed out of hand. Lavallee was then eighteen and living away from home – conditions highly unlikely to produce a "battered child."

When questioned about the injuries that Lavallee received from allegedly falling off a horse, Dr Dirks said that normally such falls cause fractures to the wrist, dislocated shoulders, and fractures to the lower limbs. Lavallee's injuries, therefore, "were inconsistent with falling from a horse."[149] As the Crown pressed, now hinting that it was unethical to allow Lavallee to leave the hospital with Rust without having her stomach pumped to rid her of the pain killers that she had swallowed, Brodsky objected: "My learned friend is making an editorial comment that is completely uncalled for." The judge agreed: "Mr Miller, stick to the facts of the case please."[150]

Miller made a last ditch attempt to gain some concession from this witness. He tried to establish that Lavallee's injuries were probably not caused by wife battering because Lyn usually presented singular injuries to emergency doctors. His question: "[I]f we heard of a continual fight over minutes, punching, slapping, scratching, you would expect to see more than a single bruise?" The answer: "If you have continuous fighting."[151] Miller finally abandoned this witness.

In redirect, Brodsky asked when the Attorney General's office issued a new directive regarding the prosecution of wife assault. Dr Dirks's answer was that it was post-1983.[152]

Dr Edward Kesselman was the second witness. As an emergency physician from the St Boniface General Hospital, he testified that Lavallee had been treated at his facility on 1 December 1983 for a bruise over her eye, a bruise over her nose, a bleeding nose, scratches on her neck, and front teeth that were painful to the touch.

The defence's third witness was Dr Fred Shane. With the jury out of the room, Miller informed the judge that he wished to challenge the expert qualifications of this witness. Dr Shane, a psychiatrist, would be called to testify to her state of mind when Lavallee fired the fatal shot, not "as an expert just on spousal abuse."[153] Ordinary witnesses are not permitted to offer their opinions to jurors but are confined to testifying about what they saw, heard, or felt. Experts can provide opinions, but the lawyer who wishes to present their evidence must first demonstrate that the "subject matter of the inquiry [is] such that ordinary people are unlikely to form a correct judgment about it, unless assisted by persons with special knowledge."[154] The lawyer must also demonstrate that the proposed witness is an "expert" in the subject area, to the satisfaction of the presiding judge. Brodsky was perplexed by Miller's insistence that Dr Shane's expertise needed to be proven: "I don't object. I don't know – it's as a matter of courtesy I have no objection, although I don't know how my learned friend could have him ruled not an expert. He's an expert in psychiatry. That's why I'm calling him. He dealt with Angelique Lyn Lavallee."[155]

The normal process in such a *voir dire* is for the lawyer who wishes to call the witness to adduce the witness's "expert" qualifications through direct examination. Confidence in his witness led Brodsky to spurn this opportunity, stating "that would be a total waste of time." Miller thus proceeded directly to cross-examine Dr Shane on his qualifications.

In a matter of minutes, the judge cut off Miller's cross-examination. Dr Shane's lengthy curriculum vitae showed that his expertise regarding spousal abuse and Battered Woman Syndrome was undeniable.[156] Brodsky offered to provide Miller with six or seven articles written by Dr Lenore Walker, the author whose work Dr Shane relied on in his clinical practice. Miller responded, sarcastically, "[f]or a moment I thought this was Dr Walker here, but obviously that's not the case."[157]

Dr Shane's expert opinion was based on five visits with Lavallee, an interview with her mother, and a review of hospital, police, and court records. Dr Shane described her homicidal act as "a reflection of her fear, her catastrophic fear that she had to defend herself." It was, he said, one of loss of self-control, of self-defence, and of accumulated "violent feelings."[158] He explained how victims of traumatic violence can become bonded to their aggressors and experience barriers to extricating themselves, including "learned helplessness."[159]

Rust begged Lavallee to lie to doctors and others about her injuries and threatened to tell her parents that she had had an abortion and was a "baby killer."[160] Explaining why she had returned to Rust, Dr Shane said that "she came back because of her own disturbed personality and her own sense of, I think, helplessness and vulnerability and her victim mentality ... [S]he came back in a magnetic sort of way."[161]

The tensions in the relationship were escalating – the couple had separate bedrooms by the time of the homicide – and "she was hit and beaten in varying degrees almost every day of their relationship."[162] Dr Shane described Lavallee's prior threats to Rust as self-defensive threats, not homicidal fantasies or evidence of premeditation. On the night of 31 August 1986, "[h]e had, apparently, pulled her out [of the closet] and had grabbed her arm and bruised her, had given her a gun, a rifle, according to her, said that, you know, that something was going to happen, that he was going to get her, and she became very frightened. She lost total control and she shot him."[163]

Miller cross-examined Dr Shane with impatience and incredulity. The interruptions of Dr Shane caused the judge to reprimand Miller: "Let him finish his answer."[164] Questioning Dr Shane's evidence that Lavallee had been assaulted on every part of her body, Miller asked: "And yet she was obviously, you would agree with me, able to function? She worked. She went to work she told you every day?" She covered up with sunglasses and clothing, said Dr Shane. Miller responded: "Did she say she wore a veil to work?"[165]

Miller suggested that Dr Shane's conclusion that Lavallee had been battered was fragile because it was based solely on what she had told Dr Shane privately, not subject to cross-examination or independent verification.[166] On this point, Dr Shane fought back: the medical records from the hospitals provided ample corroboration of her account.

Miller then asked: "You indicated that if some of her information, if not all of it, were erroneous you'd have to reassess your opinion; correct?" "That's true," Dr Shane responded. "I believe you indicated to us that she advised you that at no time had she ever thought of killing Mr Rust; correct?" Miller continued: "I take it then you would be most surprised if you heard of a situation ... when she levelled a loaded rifle at the man and threatened to kill him if he ever touched her again?" Dr Shane explained that this "was a reflection of her fear – that she – that she had to defend herself ... an impulsive, spontaneous act."[167]

If Rust's assaults were daily and escalating, Miller asked, why did not Lavallee pull the trigger when she had pointed the gun on other occasions?[168] Rust's words – "[y]ou're going to get it" – had been used before. As Miller put it, "there have been ... countless other occasions when, if your theory holds true, her life would have been on the line?"[169] Dr Shane explained that "you maintain a certain level of control ... and I think the factors, all the background and the drinking and perhaps the marijuana and the ensuing several months that their relationship had been deteriorating, it all built to where the proverbial, you know, straw that broke the camel's back."[170]

Miller pressed on: "What, Doctor, in your opinion is the significance, if any, of the fact that it would appear as though Mr Rust was on his way out of her room at the time he was fatally shot?" Dr Shane answered: "Well, I can speculate. I mean that's – " Miller cut in: "Well, you've been doing a very good job." Dr Shane attempted a polite response: "Well, that's a matter of opinion. We'll have to agree to disagree on that issue."[171] He said that Lavallee felt threatened by Rust even while he was leaving the room.

Returning to the issue of premeditation, Miller asked: "One of the things that was building up in her mind was the fact that, 'The only way to extricate myself from this situation is to kill him.' Is that a possibility, Doctor?" Dr Shane agreed.[172] Miller then proposed that Lavallee's thinking was as follows: "I'm drawn to him as if he were a magnet, so I can't extricate myself from the situation, but I have to survive and I put those two together and then I shoot him in the head."[173]

Dr Shane rejected this theory: "[P]eople who have lived in these sort of circumstances ... often do not think of actually consciously or fantasizing violent reactions until they get driven to the point because they're so sapped of energy to react or to extricate themselves that they can't – and then it erupts – " Miller snapped: "Well, she was sapped of enough energy to fire the rifle?"[174]

Miller then suggested that Dr Shane's reliance on the hospital records as corroboration of Rust's violence was misplaced because Lavallee's injuries were consistent with her contemporaneous accounts. Dr Shane was incredulous: "[C]onsistent doesn't mean that's what happened."[175] He continued: "You know, I think she hoodwinked the doctors. She didn't fall off any horses."[176] Miller clarified that only once did she claim that she fell off a horse.

He was surely hoping to end his cross-examination with his next question: "The bottom line is that you were accepting everything that she was saying to you?" But Dr Shane answered "[n]o." Miller pounded away on the point for the next ten minutes. Dr Shane explained that Lavallee told him the truth because she knew that hospital records could be checked, and in fact her story was borne out by the records.

Miller needed to score some points from this long wrangle. Dr Shane had to agree that "people do lie," but he would not agree with the follow-up: "[Y]ou've heard the expression a con man or a con woman, a con person, somebody who, you know, is really smooth ...?" "But she wasn't conning me." "Not in your opinion." Dr Shane leapt back in: "I think we'll have to agree to disagree why she attended the hospital ... and the jury will make the decision."[177]

Brodsky had no questions in redirect. In what was surely a risky move, he closed his case at this point, keeping Lavallee off the witness stand. He would have to hope that the jurors would not think that his client had something to hide. His entire case for self-defence therefore rested on her unsworn statement to the police, his cross-examination of the Crown witnesses, and his three medical witnesses.

Turning to Judge and Jury

Before closing arguments began, Miller argued, in the absence of the jury, that Dr Shane's testimony should be excluded from their consideration. Dr Shane had inappropriately testified to the "ultimate issue," whether Lavallee had killed in self-defence, thereby crossing the permissible boundary of a witness's testimony. Miller also objected that he had testified regarding Lavallee's sincerity based on her interviews with him. Miller was objecting to "oath helping," which refers to historical forms of trial whereby accused persons could secure acquittal by having their "helpers" come to court and swear that their testimony was truthful. Worse, Lavallee herself had not testified, making Dr Shane's "oath helping" more significant.

Brodsky disagreed: expert witnesses are permitted to testify to the accused's state of mind, as in a trial in which insanity is the defence. Furthermore, Dr Shane had not simply asserted Lavallee's credibility but had provided the basis for his opinion.

Justice Scott quickly disposed of the Crown's motion, advising Miller that his concerns "could be met through an appropriate charge to the jury."[178]

It was now time for Brodsky to give his closing address to the jury. Under Canadian law, the defence lawyer who calls no evidence is permitted to address the jury last. Since Brodsky called evidence, he was required to close before the Crown[179] and to anticipate what Miller would say.

Brodsky's two-hour address impressed on the jury the primacy of their role: "You are the judges of the guilt or innocence of Lyn Lavallee."[180] This job is entrusted to ordinary people from all walks of life "because we trust their common sense." Brodsky repeated: "Lyn trusts you."[181]

He briefly alluded to the law's history of sex discrimination when women were the property of their husbands. Men, he pointed out, were expected to stand their ground in a fight; they did not have to run away. Today "[w]omen, the same as men, don't have to leave the matrimonial home if somebody continues to beat them up."[182]

Recognizing that jurors might nonetheless find it difficult to understand why Lavallee did not leave, Brodsky suggested that, if they were assaulted repeatedly, they too would be focused on preventing the next assault.[183] Moreover, "[y]ou lose the ability to think of yourself as an important person, especially if the people around you seem to think it's okay." Ezako did not tell Rust not to assault Lavallee, only not to "do that when I'm around."[184] Even Ezako said that Rust's violence scared him – "if it scared him, what do you think it did to Lyn?"[185]

Brodsky reviewed Lavallee's motive. This was not a planned killing: Lavallee was dragged out of the closet, and Rust said that, if she did not kill him first, he would kill her. She told police that Rust had hit her before – they should "check the records." "Who called that evidence?" he asked rhetorically.[186]

Brodsky predicted that Miller would cast her act as deliberate retaliation. Recall, Brodsky said, that Lavallee told police "I hope he lives ... I really love him. I didn't mean to do it."[187] He reminded jurors subtly that she was almost a child: "[Y]ou remember she didn't want to see the lawyer because who she wanted to talk to was her mom when she was told she could see the lawyer."[188] "She wanted to call her mom, this killer."[189] Lavallee had cleaned and comforted Rust earlier in the evening and asked police about going to his funeral – "this person that the Crown is going to say deliberately killed."[190]

Brodsky told the jury that the exact number of times Rust beat Lavallee was less important than the fact that she was "totally under the control of ... [and] subservient to ... one person ... See whether or not she didn't adhere to every single wish of Kevin."[191] Brodsky read back Lavallee's police statements, punctuating them with his commentary: "[S]o you see, she's doing what she's told ... Did she say, 'Just a minute. I'm busy right now'? No."[192]

Count the number of times that Lavallee described herself as "scared" in her statements, Brodsky advised.[193] "You don't have enough fingers and toes to count up all the times she says that, which leads me to suggest to you that [that] was the predominant thing in her mind at the time ... she was confronting this fellow."[194] Referring to her words "I was shaking like usual," he asked: "Have you ever been that scared? Have you ever been that scared? She was."[195]

Lavallee's statements were corroborated by the physical evidence: the damage done to the bedroom and closet, the trajectories of the bullets, the bruises and cuts on her body, and the hospital records. The Crown's own witness, Dr Markesteyn, had explained "battered women's syndrome," how women fail to disclose the true causes of their injuries, and why "ladies ... don't leave abusive relationships, why they end up hiding in closets as opposed to going ... away."[196] Even Ezako, Rust's best friend, did not believe Lavallee's explanations of her injuries: "But Mr Miller's going to ask you to believe it and you're not his best friend ..."[197]

No one, Brodsky told the jury, was going to help Lavallee that night: "You could tell the attitude of the people that were in the house because when they thought, as they testified, that she'd committed suicide did they call an ambulance? No. Police? No. A doctor? No. Anybody? No. They just went downstairs and had another beer."[198]

Brodsky peppered his address with rhetorical questions. Repeating the words that Rust screamed at Lavallee to get her downstairs to help him and Ezako with the couch (fucking bitch), Brodsky asked: "Is that what your husband calls you? When you're getting your wife down in the middle of the night is that how you salute her?"[199] Referring to Ezako's description of how Rust beat her – "throwing into the wall and, you know[,] over the couch and across the room," Brodsky asked the jury: "Is that how you train your wife?"[200] He personalized "learned helplessness" by asking this question: "And what do you think would happen to your wife if [she were assaulted] every day for two or three years or every week for two or three years?"[201]

As for the inconsistencies between Lavallee's story and those of other witnesses, Brodsky acknowledged that Lavallee might have been mistaken about whether Rust was upstairs when she fired the first shot. But, said Brodsky, "it's not the actual facts that are important, because she's on trial. It's what she thought was happening."[202] And, of course, "if you're that hysterical, ... you're just getting impressions and blurs."[203] He predicted that Miller would tell them that Rust had said before "she was going to get it," without lethal consequences. The question, he said, was not what they made of those words but what Lavallee understood them to mean.

Brodsky urged the jury to remember that Miller's witnesses were all inebriated that night and made mistakes in their evidence. Jurors should rely more heavily on the neighbours' independent and sober recollections.

Finally, Brodsky reviewed Dr Shane's testimony on Lavallee's state of mind:

> The issue is not whether Lyn made the same choice on this day ... as you would have made ... [but] whether she thought she had to do what she did. That's the issue. And if you have a reasonable doubt on ... that, you're

bound, as I explained earlier and as his lordship will tell you later, you're bound to give the benefit of that doubt to Lyn Lavallee.[204]

Miller's address to the jury was shorter by almost an hour. First, Miller focused on the technicalities of the law of homicide and self-defence. His emphasis on dry legal doctrine must have contrasted sharply with Brodsky's impassioned plea. Miller reviewed the *Criminal Code* provisions in detail and tried, line by line, to convey to the jury how his evidence showed an intentional killing and ruled out self-defence.

Lavallee was the aggressor: "We're not, I suggest to you, dealing with a meek and mild young lady who was cowering in the corner during the course of that evening. No, we're dealing with a lady who was foul-mouthed, who was aggressive, who was feisty."[205] "Lyn wanted to fight," he told the jury. "She wanted to fight that evening. There's nobody else ... as aggressive ... as she was."[206]

Miller pointed out testimonial inconsistencies, including whether Rust gave Lavallee the gun, whether he was present when she fired the first shot, and whether the guests planned to stay the night, making his threat to get her when everyone had gone implausible. Miller pointed out that the bruising claimed by Brodsky was not visible in the police photographs.[207]

Miller also minimized the number and seriousness of Lavallee's injuries and suggested that they were consistent with the explanations that Lavallee provided to hospital personnel. He urged jurors to attach no weight to Dr Shane's opinion, which relied on statements by Lavallee and her mother untested by cross-examination.[208] Dr Shane was mistaken that Lavallee never contemplated killing Rust. She had twice pointed a loaded weapon at him and threatened to kill him, and this showed that "she ... seize[d] the opportunity to shoot him in the back of the head."[209]

Miller proclaimed that "the myth is, in this particular case, that Miss Lavallee was a battered woman."[210] Her statements about Rust's violence and his threat that night were concocted and self-serving. No member of Lavallee's family took the stand – "I submit to you that's because they had nothing enlightening to add."[211]

Finally, Lavallee's fingerprints were on the ammunition box.[212] This suggested that Lavallee loaded the weapon herself. While Hladky heard screaming and thumping upstairs between the first and second shots, those inside the house said that Rust was downstairs for some of that time while Lavallee was alone upstairs, carrying on.

Miller wrapped up his murder case by reminding the jury of their oath: "I ask but one thing from you, and that is a true verdict in accordance with the oath or affirmation that you took one week ago today, a verdict based upon all of the evidence, a verdict free of sympathy or prejudice, a verdict, I suggest to you, of guilty of murder."[213]

Justice Scott reviewed the testimony of the witnesses and the positions of counsel. He told jurors that they were to determine what, if any, weight to give to Dr Shane's evidence where it was unsupported by other evidence: "If the premises upon which the evidence is substantially based [have] not been proven in evidence, it is up to you to conclude that it is not safe to attach a great deal of weight to the opinion."[214] Brodsky was wrong to hint that Lavallee had visited the hospital beyond those visits introduced into evidence: "It is not evidence and must be completely disregarded by you."[215] Justice Scott instructed the jury on self-defence and provocation and left them with three possible verdicts: guilty of second-degree murder, guilty of manslaughter, or not guilty.

After the jury retired to deliberate, Brodsky was on his feet objecting to the judge's failure to instruct the jury on the defence of "accident." The judge had also neglected to review the evidence of Hladky, one of the few witnesses who knew neither the accused nor the deceased and who had been sober that night. Justice Scott was not prepared to raise "accident" with the jury but reminded them that Hladky had heard Lavallee screaming from the second floor of the house, in pain and fear, between the first and second shots.[216]

The jury returned five hours later to ask the judge to explain again the legal requirements for manslaughter and for self-defence.[217] Brodsky jumped up again, this time asking the judge to tell the jury that Lavallee had no obligation to retreat from her house before defending herself. Justice Scott reacted strongly: "Mr Brodsky, why are you pulling these things out of the woodwork at this juncture?"[218] He refused this request because Miller had not suggested that Lavallee should have retreated before shooting Rust.

A couple of hours later, in response to more jury questions, the judge clarified what kind of "unlawful assault" triggers the right to use self-defensive violence. Again Brodsky objected because the judge had failed to provide examples of the deceased's behaviour that might amount to an "unlawful assault" but had provided the example of firing the gun – Lavallee's act. Justice Scott conceded: "Well, Mr Brodsky, I think you're wearing me down. I guess the moral of the story is persistence pays off."[219] The jury was brought back in and told that "activities of the deceased about which you heard, such as chasing Lyn Lavallee around the yard, the blows, the yelling, the screaming, the threats that went on upstairs, if you find that those things took place, could also constitute an assault by the deceased to the accused so as to trigger one of the criteria under s. 34 [self-defence.]"[220]

Forty-five minutes later the jury returned with a verdict – only ten hours after they began deliberating. The foreman announced that Lavallee was not guilty of murder and not guilty of manslaughter. Justice Scott reminded the jurors that their deliberations were secret and not to be disclosed on pain of criminal penalty. Unlike in the United States, where jurors can discuss – even sell – accounts of their deliberations, in Canada the *Criminal Code*[221] criminalizes disclosure to afford jurors the security of knowing that their questions, comments, and positions will be immune from public scrutiny. No one outside the jury room therefore knows with certainty what moved the jury to acquit Lavallee.

She emitted a "sheepish grin" on hearing the verdict, then collapsed sobbing in the arms of her mother. As she left the courtroom, she said that "[i]t hasn't sunk in just yet. I really don't know what to think."[222] Days later Lavallee spoke about her ongoing grieving for Rust and her feelings of guilt over killing the man whom she had known since she was six years old and moved in with at the age of eighteen.[223] She continued to place flowers on his grave and contemplated leaving the province: "Some people have changed their opinion of me. It makes me wonder if some of them are beating someone they know."[224]

Brodsky hoped that the acquittal would raise public awareness about wife battering: "I think it will encourage more shelters and encourage more hospitals to set up protocols that will explain to doctors and emergency physicians what to look for."[225] Women's groups hoped that the acquittal signalled a changed societal understanding of wife abuse. Toni Nelson, for the Manitoba Committee on Wife Abuse, criticized the narrowness of the law of self-defence: "The woman was frightened 24 hours a day. She wasn't reacting only to that day. She was reacting to the many times he had done this to her."[226]

The Appeal Process

Not everyone was happy with Lavallee's acquittal. Rust's sister, Wendy, wept openly. His uncle angrily denounced the acquittal as "a crock."[227] The prosecution filed its appeal soon after and encountered success at the Manitoba Court of Appeal. Two of three justices on the panel overturned the acquittal because the trial judge had failed to warn the jury about the dangers of relying on the unsworn statement of Lavallee to the police that contained her version of the events. The judge had also failed to adequately caution the jury on the frailties of Dr Shane's testimony since Lavallee did not testify, leaving much of his opinion based on second-hand information.

Luckily, for Lavallee, one justice of the three-justice appeal panel disagreed on the legal question of whether the judge had erred in instructing the jury. This dissenting opinion by Justice Charles Huband guaranteed her right to appeal to the Supreme Court of Canada.[228] Lavallee's unsworn statement had been introduced by the Crown, and its own expert, Dr Markesteyn, had testified to "abused-wife syndrome." Furthermore, the judge had indeed directed the jury to consider whether Dr Shane's opinion was supported by corroborative evidence and pointed out several such gaps. Justice Huband concluded with a vote of confidence for the jury system: "This accused was acquitted by a jury of her peers on the basis of self-defence, which might strike some as being somewhat fanciful. We should not, however, search out semantic excuses to order a new trial, at high public cost, in the belief that the jury should have been more sceptical and arrived at a different verdict."[229]

Brodsky wasted no time in appealing to the Supreme Court of Canada. He argued the appeal himself on 31 October 1989. He and George Dangerfield, for the Manitoba Attorney General's office, "painted vastly different pictures"[230] of Lavallee. Dangerfield described her as "a combative woman, a woman who was antagonistic, who for her size was quite strong, who fought back on every occasion." He "ridiculed the term battered wife syndrome," saying "how can Shane imply in his evidence ... that this woman was the cowering creature who resorted to murder?"[231] In contrast, Brodsky argued that "there was plenty of evidence at the trial chronicling a regular pattern between Rust and Lavallee of verbal jousting, threats ('if you keep it up you're going to get it'), and finally, physical violence." Dr Shane's testimony was critical: "The jury has to be told why when you were taken to hospital because of those beatings, you tell them you fell off a horse, you do not say he did it. This is a special syndrome."[232]

The "Difference" that Justice Bertha Wilson Made

The Supreme Court reserved judgment, and while it deliberated Canada's first woman justice appointed to the Supreme Court, Her Honour Bertha Wilson, delivered an explosive lecture on the enterprise of judging. On 9 February 1990, three months after the oral argument in *Lavallee*, Justice Wilson gave the Barbara Betcherman Memorial Lecture[233] at Osgoode Hall

Law School at York University in Toronto, entitled "Will Women Judges Really Make a Difference?"[234] Her speech addressed the relevance of gender to the task of judging and contemplated the nature of judicial independence and impartiality.

Breaking with the judicial tradition of public silence on matters deemed "political," Justice Wilson told the room of 350 lawyers, law students, and members of the public that some areas of law display a "distinctly male perspective," producing legal principles that are "not fundamentally sound." Moreover, she said, "[s]ome aspects of the criminal law in particular cry out for change; they are based on presuppositions about the nature of women and women's sexuality that, in this day and age, are nothing short of ludicrous."[235] According to Toronto lawyer Brian Bucknall, "[a]t the end of the speech the room erupted into a standing, cheering ovation. I have never seen an argument of such breadth and subtlety communicated with such direct and simple force."[236]

Even as her Betcherman lecture provoked complaints about her "feminism" to the Canadian Judicial Council,[237] it prompted Justice Wilson to put her words into action as she contemplated her judgment in *Lavallee*. To her biographer, Ellen Anderson, she said:

> It was when I was writing [that speech] and thinking about it that I realized that there were quite a number of aspects of the law that needed to be rethought from a gender perspective and ... that was a chance to begin doing it by looking at the defence of self-defence and how it was essentially male oriented. And I thought to myself, now here was a chance to give some leadership to what I have said in my speech.[238]

The force of Justice Wilson's argument persuaded all of the male justices of the Supreme Court to her view of the case. Chief Justice Brian Dickson, for example, is reported to have held a contrary first impression of the case. His biographers comment that "*Lavallee* demonstrates Dickson's growing attachment to Wilson's equality views and his receptivity to her feminist perspective, which re-examined traditional legal doctrines in light of their effect on women."[239] Anderson reports Justice Wilson's surprise and her resolution:

> I have always seen that case as the biggest mystery of all my judgments because how it ended up was as a unanimous judgment when they all thought I was mad to think there was anything that could even be said in

her favour ... [I]t did show me ... that if you have done your homework and you could present a case in a plausible and forceful way, then male judges would move.[240]

When Justice Wilson delivered her ruling in *R v Lavallee*,[241] overturning the Manitoba Court of Appeal and reinstating Lavallee's acquittal on 3 May 1990, it made front-page news in papers across the country: "Battered Wife Acquittal Upheld";[242] "Beaten Wife Had Reason to Kill Man, Court Rules";[243] "Top Court Backs Battered Wife in Killing";[244] "Battered Wife Case Hailed as Landmark for the Abused";[245] "Court Upholds Battered Wife's Acquittal in Husband's Murder."[246]

The *Lavallee* decision was a monumental one for criminal law, both in Canada and in other common law countries.[247] The only woman on the Supreme Court had managed to unify it and produce a decision telling Canadians that women are entitled to use self-defensive violence – pre-emptive violence even – when protecting themselves against battering husbands. Battered women, declared Justice Wilson, need not wait for "the uplifted knife" before protecting themselves. It would be condemning women like Jane Hurshman and Lyn Lavallee to "murder by instalment," she cautioned, if they are required to wait until a lethal attack is in full swing before using justifiable force.[248]

There is no strict requirement of imminence for self-defence in the *Criminal Code*, Justice Wilson wrote, and none should be read in. Section 34 simply requires the accused to have faced an "unlawful assault" that was threatened but not necessarily in progress or imminent. The person must have actually and reasonably perceived herself to be in danger of death or grievous bodily harm. And she must have actually and reasonably believed that she could not, other than by killing, have preserved herself from death or grievous bodily harm.

Furthermore, Justice Wilson wrote, the law of self-defence must be interpreted in light of the realities faced by battered women. They cannot be judged by the usual "ordinary man" standard of criminal law: "If it strains credulity to imagine what the 'ordinary man' would do in the position of a battered spouse, it is probably because men do not typically find themselves in that situation."[249] Reasonableness here must be informed by the woman's experience of her batterer's patterns of violence, the size and strength differences between the woman and her partner, men's and women's different socialization as it affects the use of violence, a woman's experience of "traumatic bonding" or "learned helplessness" in response to battering, and the real limitations on her ability to escape safely.

For the first time in Canadian law, a court examined the roots of the law of self-defence and exposed its underpinnings as premised on the male accused and the masculine experience. Historically, self-defence was developed by England's judges to allow juries to acquit men who were either suddenly attacked by other men, who killed to save themselves, or who, engaged in fighting, attempted to quit the conflict but were forced to defend their lives with deadly force in an assumed physical conflict between equals, in circumstances in which men found themselves, such as duelling. It presumed that the men were strangers to each other, such that retreat would have ensured safety or the end of the conflict.

Justice Wilson described law's historical role in shoring up wife battering by permitting men to "discipline" their wives. She set out the myths about women in violent relationships that persist long after the law had reversed its earlier stance and begun to condemn wife battering as criminal assault. These myths include the idea that such women "like" violence and that, if it really were that bad, a battered woman would have left the relationship. Justice Wilson refuted these myths in her judgment, noting, for example, the many reasons why women might not be able to leave a violent man, including their fear of retaliation.

Justice Wilson rejected the Crown's argument that jurors have no need to hear expert testimony because they are "thoroughly knowledgeable about 'human nature'" and "are, so to speak, their own experts on human behavior."[250] She instead ruled that expert evidence is admissible in order to disabuse the jurors of prevalent myths and stereotypes about wife battering and abused women and to assist the defence in fleshing out self-defence. Jurors are therefore entitled to hear evidence about a woman's experience of violence at the hands of her partner and expert evidence about the consequences of this violence – Battered Woman Syndrome. "[I]t is not," Justice Wilson reasoned, "for the jury to pass judgment on the fact that a battered woman stayed in the relationship. Still less is it entitled to conclude that she forfeited her right to self-defence for having done so."[251]

A First for Battered Women?

Justice Wilson's judgment shut the door on Lavallee's legal peril and opened a window for battered women who kill their abusers. Women's groups praised the ruling for taking wife assault seriously and attempting to incorporate women's realities into legal doctrine.[252] The *Toronto Star* editorialized: "By itself the verdict won't end wife abuse. But it puts the law on the side of innocent victims who've long been treated as if they were criminals."[253] The Montreal *Gazette*, the *Calgary Herald*, the *Edmonton Journal*, and the *Ottawa Citizen* followed suit with positive editorials.[254] Certainly, some columnists and editors disagreed,[255] but the lively public debate that continued for months in the nation's newspapers showed that no one thought *Lavallee* insignificant.

News reports described Lavallee's acquittal as a "first" for battered women, as did Brodsky.[256] Was it really? Battered women had been acquitted as early as 1965, when a Toronto jury acquitted Maggie MacDonald of killing her husband, Angus "Soup" Campbell, while she was in a dissociated state.[257] Battered Woman Syndrome evidence was also introduced in the trial of Jane Hurshman, who was acquitted in 1982.[258]

Lavallee, however, was the first time that an appellate court affirmed that Battered Woman Syndrome evidence was admissible as expert testimony. Although *Lavallee* dealt only with this form of expertise, offered by a psychiatrist, its principles provided a precedent to argue for the admissibility of other forms of knowledge about the experiences of battered women[259] and for a broader cast of witnesses to be qualified as experts, including psychologists, social workers, and counsellors. *Lavallee* was possibly the first time that a battered woman was acquitted without testifying, the expert testimony having filled the gaps in the self-defence claim. It was also the first appellate decision in Canada to uphold a battered woman's jury acquittal, providing a precedent where none existed before.

Moreover, Justice Wilson's decision in *Lavallee* reached far beyond the bare legal argument in Brodsky's factum supporting the admissibility of Battered Woman Syndrome evidence based on the general law of evidence.[260] Interestingly, her judgment was not directly influenced by feminist legal intervention in the case. Although the impetus for new US self-defence rulings came from feminist litigators who represented battered women on appeal or intervened in their cases through *amicus curiae* briefs,[261] in Canada the Women's Legal Education and Action Fund (LEAF) had just been founded in 1985, after the section 15 equality guarantee in the *Canadian Charter of Rights and Freedoms*[262] was declared in force. LEAF's mandate included intervening in cases that implicate the constitutional right to equality in order to shape the legal interpretation of this important right to women's benefit. But in those early days, LEAF was focused on using its scant resources for cases in which the newly proclaimed section

15 was directly at issue. In *Lavallee*, the issue had been narrowly framed without reference to section 15 of the *Charter*,[263] leaving Justice Wilson to develop this larger legal context.

Brodsky had supplied in his factum, without elaboration, an article written by his son Daniel Brodsky. The article reviewed US case law and articles on the admissibility of Battered Woman Syndrome evidence and its function in self-defence cases and urged Canadian courts to follow suit.[264] Justice Wilson, known as a superb legal researcher before she was appointed to the bench, clearly had read Daniel's article and sources with care. Her decision probed the issues more deeply, citing to the publications of US feminist scholars.[265] Her decision was indeed "a first" for being premised on women's entitlement to equality before the law[266] and for her contextual approach incorporating legal history, social science evidence, and psychological knowledge aimed at giving women equal benefit of the criminal law.[267]

Battered Woman Syndrome and Self-Defence

Justice Wilson's judgment carefully explained what Battered Woman Syndrome is and articulated its relevance to the law of self-defence. Relying on the work of Dr Lenore Walker, who has undertaken studies of women's experience of wife battering and published numerous volumes on her results,[268] Justice Wilson's judgment introduced the terms "battered woman," "cycle of violence," and "learned helplessness" to Canadian lawyers.

According to Dr Walker, the cycle of violence in battering relationships has three stages: tension-building, acute battering, and loving contrition. During the tension-building stage, the man begins verbal, psychological, and perhaps physical assault against his partner. He expresses demands, hostility, and dissatisfaction; she responds by placating and avoiding him, sometimes precipitating his inevitable violence. In the second stage, the acute battering incident, the man "unleashes a barrage of physical and verbal aggression that can leave the woman severely shaken and injured."[269] Finally, in the loving contrition stage, the man apologizes, expresses love, and attempts to win back his partner's trust.

According to Dr Walker, a "battered woman" is one who has gone through this cycle of violence more than once. Dr Walker documents the psychological results of battering, which can include the development of what she calls a "syndrome" by which the woman "bonds traumatically" with her abuser, loses self-esteem, and becomes focused on survival as her efforts to stop the violence or free herself are thwarted by the man. She experiences paralysis and "learned helplessness" in terms of resolving her safety, such that she is either too humiliated or afraid to report the violence, attempt to leave, or ask for help. In the end, a battered woman might kill when she perceives that the threat to her life has ceased to be survivable.

Justice Wilson held that Battered Woman Syndrome evidence can be used in support of self-defence. First, it can be used to show how and why a woman actually and reasonably perceived an "unlawful assault" when those less familiar with her batterer might not have registered the signs. Second, it can also be used to show why her belief that she was threatened with death or grievous bodily harm was reasonable, as required by the *Criminal Code*. Third, this evidence can be used by jurors to assess whether the woman's belief that nothing less than deadly force was required to preserve herself was both honest and reasonable.[270]

Moreover, Justice Wilson emphasized that, since traditional self-defence doctrine does not require that men retreat from their own homes before legitimately killing an intruder, women could not fairly be held to a higher standard: "A man's home may be his castle but it is also the woman's home, even if it seems to her more like a prison in the circumstances."[271] Having reviewed the jury charge, Justice Wilson held that Justice Scott had accurately conveyed how jurors were to weigh Dr Shane's evidence where corroborative evidence was unavailable for all of the underlying facts on which his opinion depended.

An Advance for Battered Women?

Lawyers used the *Lavallee* precedent successfully within months after the Supreme Court released its decision.[272] Many more lawyers used *Lavallee* to negotiate their clients out of murder charges and into guilty pleas to manslaughter where evidence of Battered Woman Syndrome was available to mitigate the sentence.[273] *Lavallee* was also used to argue on behalf of men who killed in violent prison milieus that they should not be disqualified from self-defence because they did not wait for the "uplifted knife."[274] *Lavallee* also supported acquittals for battered women, where lawyers argued that the women's acts did not display "criminal intent"[275] or relied on the defences of necessity[276] and duress.[277]

Most legal academics recognized the *Lavallee* decision as a positive shift in Canadian self-defence law that addressed a gap for women. But one male academic called Battered Woman Syndrome evidence "a pious fraud," "junk science," and an "abuse excuse" that relies on the "inherent idiocy" of the notion that a woman experiencing "learned helplessness" can suddenly "rear up" and fire a bullet at her partner's head.[278] Yet even this author acknowledged the important role that Battered Woman Syndrome played in tearing "us from our rigid patterns of thinking."[279]

Feminist commentators were more nuanced in their criticism of *Lavallee*. Many expressed concern that reliance on "syndrome" evidence would prove detrimental to the legal defence of battered women.[280] Battered Woman Syndrome evidence can pathologize the woman, suggesting that she has a mental problem as opposed to a normal response to trauma. As Jennie Abell pointed out, Brodsky's comments to the media only reinforced this worry. Brodsky said that "[t]he ordinary person would say 'what kind of self-defence is that?' ... But the Supreme Court of Canada said because of the battered woman syndrome that's what was her perception ... She's not the average type of person. Otherwise she would not have found herself in this situation."[281] Implicit in his comment is the notion that Lavallee's experience was "abnormal."

By conveying women's experience of Battered Woman Syndrome as somehow abnormal, this strategy can undercut rather than support self-defence. This is because self-defence requires that the accused has reasonably assessed both her danger and the lack of alternatives. If her perceptions are clouded by the syndrome and are unreasonable, then a jury might well conclude that she was not justified in killing in self-defence.[282] Some authors have argued that syndrome evidence points to an "excuse" defence, whereby the accused is not acquitted but the gravity of her offence is mitigated by her inability, due to the syndrome, to conform to our expectations of reasonable persons. In such cases, the evidence can support a conviction of manslaughter on the basis that the woman had no intent to kill.[283]

Another difficulty with syndrome evidence is that it can take the focus off the dangerousness of the batterer's conduct and train it on whether the battered woman suffered from the "syndrome."[284] Lawyers and jurors might be less concerned about whether she was battered than about the impact of the man's battering on her.[285] Did she experience "learned helplessness"? Does evidence of the woman's help-seeking behaviour suggest that she did not experience "learned helplessness"? The defence can become mired in a battle of the experts, whereby the prosecution's expert contests the diagnosis made by the defence's expert.

Battered Woman Syndrome can also imply that "a single effect or set of effects characterizes the responses of all battered women,"[286] which in turn can suggest that some women are not "real" battered women.[287] The danger that individual women might be unfairly denied the benefits of this expert evidence is perhaps most apparent when the woman is portrayed as an equal partner or initiator in the violence or when racial stereotypes suggest that they are not "helpless" but themselves violent.[288] Battered Woman Syndrome might do little for Aboriginal and racialized women whose lives, experiences of battering, and avenues of escape and aid might be structured by colonization and racism.[289]

Finally, feminists have pointed out that Battered Woman Syndrome evidence presents a misleading picture of wife battering as an unfortunate but individualized experience. Rather than drawing the link between women's inequality and their vulnerability to male violence and illuminating how batterers draw on men's social power to control women, syndrome evidence focuses on diagnosing an individual woman's mental condition. Such evidence can mask the impacts of systemic inequalities, including racism, that abet batterers in entrapping women. It encourages pity for women's "tragic lives"[290] instead of resolve to change the social, political, economic, and legal structures that shape women's choices. If conceptualized in this individualizing way, it can also provide grist for backlash, allowing men to claim that women too are "batterers."

Reformulations of Syndrome Evidence

Dr Walker addresses some of these criticisms in the third edition of her book *The Battered Woman Syndrome*. She reports on her latest research – the first scientific study of the phenomenon using testable hypotheses.[291] The Battered Woman Syndrome is that cluster of symptoms that occurs after a woman has been physically, sexually, and/or psychologically abused to force her compliance with her partner's demands. Dr Walker does not use the phrase "Battered Spouse Syndrome" because there is no empirical evidence or theorization to support the claim that men experience the same impacts if they are assaulted by female partners.[292]

Dr Walker describes six criteria for the syndrome:

1 Intrusive recollections of the trauma event(s).
2 Hyperarousal and high levels of anxiety.
3 Avoidance behaviour and emotional numbing usually expressed as depression, dissociation, minimization, repression and denial.
4 Disrupted personal relationships from batterer's power and control measures.
5 Body image distortion and/or somatic or physical complaints.
6 Sexual intimacy issues.[293]

The first three criteria are common to PTSD, recognized by the American Psychiatric Association as a psychiatric condition. The rest are specific to those whose trauma is repeated and originates in their intimate relationships. The additional threshold criteria to diagnose PTSD require that the person has experienced a traumatic event that made her fear death or bodily harm, causing after-effects extending beyond four weeks, and that affects her life in a significant aspect, such as employment, education, or relationships.[294] Battered Woman Syndrome is widely recognized as a subset of PTSD,[295] even though it is not specifically listed in the fourth edition of the *Diagnostic and Statistical Manual of Mental Disorders*.[296]

Dr Walker argues that the critical reaction to her phrase "learned helplessness" has missed the underlying theory. It is not that battered women are or become helpless but that they have "lost the ability to predict that what [they] do will make a particular outcome occur."[297] When women's help-seeking strategies fail, or when women are too terrified to attempt escape, they develop complex skills to survive and cope with the abuse. Dr Walker concludes that, "until they are able to regain the belief that they can safely escape, breaking the learned helplessness, they will not be able to leave the relationship psychologically."[298] "They reach for a gun," she explains, "because they cannot be certain that any lesser action will really protect themselves from being killed by the batterer."[299]

Several insights from this latest research are highly relevant to battered women on trial for homicide. For example, Dr Walker reports that 92 percent of the women believed that the batterer could or would kill them.[300] Two-thirds of the women reported that battering became more frequent over the course of the relationship, and 73 percent said that the man's psychological abuse became more severe.[301] Her research also shows that "the impact from the most recent event would include the totality of the battering experience."[302]

But Battered Woman Syndrome testimony in women's homicide trials is not limited to diagnosing the woman as having the syndrome. Experts who testify on battered women's behalf often use the syndrome as the basis for much more wide-ranging evidence about the prevalence and potential lethality of wife battering, the dynamics of abusive relationships,[303] and the limited availability of resources and strategies for women to end the battering or escape from the batterer. And, as Elizabeth M Schneider notes, the battered women's movement never envisioned Battered Woman Syndrome evidence being heard in isolation; indeed, "it should be integrated with overall defense strategy, tied to the particular facts of the case, and focused on the particular defense problems in the case."[304]

Others argue for alternatives to Battered Woman Syndrome evidence. For example, some propose that reliance on the work of Dr Judith Lewis Herman would avoid the stigma associated with being diagnosed as having a "syndrome."[305] As discussed in the Introduction, Dr Herman adapts PTSD to fit the aftermath of prolonged terror and repeat trauma. Changes to the personality ensue that render the woman "vulnerable to repeated harm, both self-inflicted and at the hands of others."[306] Dr Herman provides a new diagnosis now recognized as Complex PTSD, which might be more compelling for judges and juries due to the analogy drawn between survivors of combat and battering.

Evan Stark proposes another model to assist jurors in seeing potential lethality beyond those battering relationships characterized by extreme physical violence: Coercive Control.[307] This theory attempts to capture the wide range of strategies apart from physical assault that men use to restrict women's freedom and cause them to fear for their lives. It holds the promise of accounting for and valorizing women's efforts to fight back and seize control of their lives without portraying them as helpless or mentally ill. I will elaborate on this model in Chapter 6.

Finally, an alternative form of evidence – social context evidence – that neither diagnoses nor pathologizes battered women's resort to homicide has been advanced by others. One major US study reports that expert evidence regarding "battering and its effects" has been admitted in criminal trials in all US states and the District of Columbia.[308] This strategy is grounded firmly in social science evidence and feminist analysis of the realities of women's lives.[309] Evidence regarding women's vulnerability to intimate femicide, particularly when separating, as well as evidence about the limited availability of shelters, police protection, and economic independence for women who flee violent men would be key aspects of this defence strategy.

Women's groups, academics, and lawyers all had high hopes for the potential impact of the *Lavallee* decision. Before turning to my study results and the trials that have followed on the heels of this case, I first examine in more depth the question that Justice Bertha Wilson so poignantly asked in her judgment: "Why doesn't she leave?"[310]

2

Bonnie Mooney

"I could feel him coming out my pores."[1]

Bonnie Mooney used these words repeatedly in a civil trial in British Columbia's Supreme Court in February 2001 to describe her intense fear of her former common law partner, Roland Kruska. Mooney sued the federal and provincial Attorneys General responsible for policing, as well as Constable Craig Andrichuk, for negligence in the incompetent investigation of her report that Kruska had threatened her on 11 March 1996 in Prince George, British Columbia. Andrichuk did not act on her report and instead advised her to retain a lawyer and to "stay in public places."[2] Seven weeks later, on 29 April 1996, Kruska broke into Mooney's rural home, shot and killed her friend Hazel White, maimed Mooney's twelve-year-old daughter Michelle by almost blasting off her arm, terrorized her six-year-old daughter Kristy, set the house on fire, and then turned the gun on himself, ending his own life.

With Kruska dead, criminal prosecution was foreclosed. Instead, Mooney filed civilian complaints against police officers and supervisors. Such complaints are normally investigated by police themselves – often by the same units – and have a low rate of success.[3] With one exception, all of her complaints were dismissed. Mooney also pursued disciplinary complaints against a prosecutor and defence counsel earlier involved in other charges against Kruska; these the Law Society of BC dismissed after investigation. Mooney filed claims with the BC Criminal Injuries Compensation Board and here met with success: Michelle was awarded the maximum of $25,000 for her injuries and disablement;[4] Mooney received $4,500 for physical and psychological injuries incurred while escaping from the house; and Kristy received $1,500.[5]

Mooney then engaged lawyer Henry Wood, QC, to argue her civil claim that police negligence had facilitated Kruska's murderous acts. Mooney hoped that success would change police responses to battered women. A civil suit differs from a criminal prosecution in that its purpose is primarily compensatory as opposed to punitive, but it can prompt institutional change. A civil trial is pursued by an individual, not the state as represented by a Crown attorney; it carries a less onerous burden of proof – "on a balance of probabilities," not "beyond a reasonable doubt." Parties to civil actions have mutual obligations to disclose evidence in their possession through a process called "discovery," whereas generally in criminal trials disclosure obligations rest solely on the prosecutor.[6]

Wood argued that Andrichuk, the police, and the Attorney General of British Columbia had a legal obligation to use care in responding to her urgent request for help when Mooney reported Kruska's threatening behaviour. Sending Mooney away without seeking particulars from her or other witnesses fell below the standard of professionalism that the officer was obliged to fulfill, especially in light of the province's *Violence against Women in Relationships Policy*.[7] This claim was supported by Andrichuk's reprimand from senior officers for failing to investigate Mooney's report. Wood argued that the police failure to arrest and detain Kruska had played a causal role in his homicidal violence, emboldening him through their inaction and leaving him free to attack. Kruska's actions had caused physical, psychological, and economic harm to Mooney and her daughters, for which the police should pay monetary compensation.

George Carruthers defended the lawsuit on behalf of the police and the Attorney General. In his opening address, he said that to impose a legal duty on the police would hinder the execution of their duties. Even if a duty had been owed, he continued, Andrichuk had performed a competent investigation and consulted with a senior officer. Police inaction should not be seen as having "caused" the violence of an unpredictable third party. Furthermore, Mooney and her children suffered pre-existing psychological injuries before March 1996.

Carruthers proposed that Mooney had contributed to her suffering by her own actions. Even though "contributory negligence" is only a partial defence in a negligence claim, shifting the blame to Mooney had the potential to demoralize her and to cleanse the negative police image generated by this litigation. Carruthers criticized her for staying in the relationship with Kruska, not fully cooperating with the police on earlier charges against him, and failing to ask for help from family and shelters. His defence thus mirrored popular beliefs about battered women: they do not help themselves; they are irrational; they cannot be helped; and, ultimately, they deserve what they get.

His secondary strategy characterized Kruska as a psychopath,[8] too irrational and wildly unpredictable[9] to be stopped by the police. This is an oft-told tale about men who rape, batter, and murder women: they are monsters, almost subhuman. They are so unlike "normal" men that their actions can be neither understood nor prevented.

These two tropes – one about battered women and the other about battering men – seem unrelated at first glance. In fact, though, they work together to insulate the police, lawyers, and judges from legal responsibility for failing to protect women and to encourage us all, collectively, to look away. After all, there is nothing to be done. Or is there?

Why Didn't She Leave?

Carruthers repeatedly asked Mooney why she did not leave Kruska[10] even though she *had* left him more than five months prior to his final attack. A woman who had sought police intervention, who had left her abuser, and whose ex-partner, in his last desperate attempt to control her, had killed her best friend and attempted to kill Mooney and her daughters was being admonished for "failing to leave."

Speaking for the Supreme Court of Canada in *Lavallee*, Justice Bertha Wilson offered several answers to the question of "why doesn't she leave?" She credited "learned helplessness" and "Battered Woman Syndrome" as explaining a woman's psychological responses to her thwarted efforts to escape or to stop her partner's violence. She also referred to "traumatic bonding," whereby a victim can become emotionally dependent on and worshipful of her captor.[11] Yet there was no evidence to suggest that Mooney was "traumatically bonded" to Kruska.

When Carruthers pressed Mooney in cross-examination to explain why she did not leave after Kruska's first three assaults, she said "Mr Carruthers, um, what you need to understand here is, I was paralyzed with fear from this man. I couldn't even think straight, 'cause alls I thought about was safety, what he was up to, trying to keep him happy ... [T]hat's all I could think about."[12]

Angela Browne elaborates: "Women progress from being horrified by each successive incident to being thankful they survived the last one. Survival becomes the criterion ... They [are] involved in a constant process of assimilation and readjustment."[13] According to Norma Cashen, battered women exhibit

> hyper-vigilant behaviour, monitoring his behaviour to know all the time what he is up to. They become experts of his cues, very externally motivated ... They monitor their own behaviour to see what they can do to maintain control over the situation ... [Their] survival has been so focused on maintaining peace, their energy is so channelled, they lose their ability to have perspective.[14]

Mooney's separation precipitated a tsunami of violence by Kruska, which Mooney had imagined, dreaded, and ultimately faced unaided. Ann Jones argues that the question why a woman does not leave "is not a real question but rather a judgment." It transforms an "immense social problem into a personal transaction" and implies that "help is available to worthy victims."[15] So powerful is this question that it is asked even when women like Mooney *have* left.[16]

One might ask instead how Mooney found the courage to leave in the face of such danger and terror. Beyond bravely facing the real risks of deadly violence, women face the complex process of separation, requiring emotional detachment, ability to overcome psychological denial, safety planning, practical preparations, action, and maintenance of separation.[17] Justice Wilson noted in *Lavallee* that "environmental factors may also impair the woman's ability to leave – lack of job skills, the presence of children to care for, fear of retaliation by the man, etc. may each have a role to play in some cases."[18] Which, if any, of these factors affected Mooney's decisions?

Women's "Lack of Job Skills"
Justice Wilson's reference in *Lavallee* to women's "lack of job skills" pointed to women's economic inequality and the larger question of whether a battered woman can support herself and her children if she leaves her abuser.[19] Mooney, before and during her marriage to the father of her three children,

worked outside the home in low-pay employment as a nurse's aide in a retirement residence, a clerk in K-Mart, a hairdresser, and a manual labourer,
loading freight trains.[20] She stopped working at the dissolution of her marriage because she was "a nervous wreck." Mooney believed that her husband was a good father and provider and was devastated when criminal
proceedings were commenced against him. She separated from him, but her
son went to live with his father when he was acquitted of the charges.

Mooney's economic marginality is reflected in national data. Women in
Canada on average earn 64.5 percent of what men earn;[21] remain occupa-
tionally segregated in the low-paying and insecure employment sectors;[22]
are economically disadvantaged by divorce compared with men, especially
if they take on the role of unpaid homemaker and caregiver;[23] and are "the
poorest of the poor."[24] Women's poverty is increased by structural inequalities such as racism, the long-term effects of colonization, and disability
discrimination, putting Aboriginal women, "visible minority" women, and
women with disabilities at the very bottom.[25] Aboriginal women who leave
their homes on reserve lands are at risk of losing their right to return, ex-
acerbating their economic vulnerability.[26]

Mooney relied on child support and welfare for a brief interval. In this,
she was lucky. Many women on social welfare, having left abusive men, experience further abuse at the hands of the welfare system. Rather than allowing women to flee and make new lives for themselves and their children,
social welfare systems can force women back into unsafe situations.[27] If welfare rates are so low that women cannot afford telephones, warm winter
clothing, and safe housing for their children, or if they must perform work-
fare without reliable and secure daycare, then their only option might be to
return to abusers.[28]

Women on welfare are required to contact their former partners to request child support, a practice that individualizes and privatizes the costs of
raising children.[29] Worse, as one woman explains, "[i]t's crazy to have women
track men down (for support), you're running from him, for God's sake."[30]
Abusive men use "snitch lines" to falsely report that their ex-partners have
a "spouse in the house"; they secure access to women's current addresses
when welfare forces women to process child support applications, endangering them and their children.[31]

Social welfare did not, however, press Mooney back into the marriage.
Instead, she met Kruska. And in this she was not so lucky. At that time,
she had just separated and soon received her share of the proceeds of the

matrimonial home. She used this money to buy a rural home in Clucultz Lake, British Columbia, for herself and her daughters, without a mortgage. She later secured employment at a mill in the nearby town of Vanderhoof.[32]

Mooney thus managed financially and was not economically dependent on Kruska, unlike many battered women. Women's economic vulnerability is increased when they end up attached to violent or controlling men.[33] Economic abuse is a key strategy that abusers use to control their partners, as Nina Tarr explains: "Financial independence, regardless of class, income, or economic status, is a challenge to the batterer's need to control, so he will try to undermine the woman's ability to work."[34] An abusive man may prevent his partner from working outside the home because he is jealous of her contact with others, he might insist that she provide full-time domestic labour, and he might not want her to have her own money. A batterer might stunt her career by preventing her pursuit of higher education, job training, and advancement, thus undercutting her financial independence. She might lose her job because he causes her to miss work, monitors her constantly at work, or drops in or waits outside, creating fear and anxiety among other employees.[35] Women disabled by their partners' abuse, whether physically or psychologically, are hindered in their ability to maintain employment.

Abusive men also seek control over women's economic resources and live off their female partners' money, especially when they are debt ridden or unemployed like Kruska.[36] Mooney supported him and put his name on the Clucultz Lake title even though he contributed not a penny. She explained: "I wanted to make Roland happy. At this time, I ... already ... was beginning to be scared of him[,] and ... I would do anything to make Roland happy and so he wouldn't be on edge."[37] His sole contributions were physical improvements he made to the property, with materials purchased by Mooney.

Women need not necessarily leave their homes to escape batterers. Unless they live on reserve lands, they can apply under provincial family laws for "exclusive possession" of the home if they were married or live in a province such as British Columbia, which grants this right to common law partners,[38] and if they can satisfy a court that their spouse has been violent.[39] Mooney did not need to get an order to get Kruska out – he went to live with his mother. Yet he used his claim on the title to force Mooney to negotiate with him, thereby maintaining power over her. When she gave him legal papers to sign after they reached an agreement to sell the house so that she could pay him $15,000 to release his claim, he incinerated the papers.[40] Mooney testified that she would have given up the house "if I would have thought that that was what it was going to take to get Roland out of my life, he could have had the whole house, but I knew that wasn't what it was going to take."[41]

Economic insecurity was not what kept Mooney tied to Kruska.

"The Presence of Children to Care For"

Under cross-examination, Mooney repeatedly said that Kruska was good to her kids; she never feared for their safety: "[T]he only one he was after was me."[42] In hindsight, of course, she was dead wrong. He would do anything to get at her – even hurt her daughters.

Justice Wilson described "the presence of children" as another factor preventing women's escape from violent partners. Women's bonds with their children and their concern to protect them make flight from abusers difficult. Some mothers' concern is not to deprive their children of their fathers,[43] which might postpone exit from a marriage. But when a man is bent on controlling his partner, he might use the children, harming them physically, sexually, or psychologically, to control their mother.[44] Abusers know that it works: battered women will often do anything to protect their children, including staying with their abusers.

Women who leave abusers have a tough road ahead to ensure their children's safety. Exposing the man's violence and the mother's inability to protect her children can result in removal of the children by child welfare authorities.[45] Women who run and leave their children behind face temporary, if not permanent, loss of custody as well as social approbation and the guilt attached to leaving their children exposed. Those who flee with their children are forced to stay in the same jurisdiction, within reach of the perpetrators, at least until an agreement or court order grants them custody and permits a move.

Abusers are not likely to agree to women's sole custody of the children.[46] Litigation might be inevitable unless women accede to pressures from their partners, lawyers, and mediators to accept joint custody.[47] With some exceptions,[48] the majority of joint custody court claims are made by fathers and resisted by mothers.[49] Yet many of these fathers show no willingness to cooperate with the mothers or any ability to put their children's interests first.[50] The emphasis on "equal" parenting, regardless of the quality of that parenting before or after separation, combined with the legal system's tendency to see abuse as discrete incidents of violence as opposed to a pattern of intimidation and control,[51] supports a norm of joint custody commonly ordered by judges.[52] Many judges pay attention to mothers' allegations of abuse and exercise caution in custody decisions,[53] but there is no guarantee that joint custody will be denied.[54] Some judges disconnect wife battering from its impacts on children's psychological well-being,[55] concluding that the man can still be a good father.[56] Others discount battered mothers' anxieties that former partners might harm their children.[57]

A woman who secures sole custody can remain in jeopardy from her abuser. Judges can order shared legal decision making (also called guardianship) with the father, subjecting her to his continuing efforts to control her, thwarting her aspirations for autonomy, and jeopardizing her safety.[58] And, when women do manage to secure both custody and guardianship, they must be prepared for the fact that fathers are rarely denied access rights to their children. Judges in Canada promote "maximum contact" between children and their fathers, even when fathers have been violent to mothers and sometimes when they have been violent to their children.[59] Judges might allow access where there is evidence that the father uses child contact to continue his abuse of his ex and regardless of the severity of the abuse.[60] Visits with children provide opportunities for batterers to gain access to their former partners[61] and put the children at risk of "revenge killing" by estranged fathers.[62]

Women with sole custody whose former partners have access rights cannot relocate without securing the fathers' agreement or seeking court permission. This too can be a difficult hurdle in the context of the court's preoccupation with fathers' access.[63] Women who can prove the abuse and their need to create distance have an easier time of it,[64] but if they cannot corroborate their accounts of violence they might be forced to stay close to an abuser or surrender custody by moving.[65]

"Tangential spouse abuse" was one form of control that Kruska did not exert, according to Mooney. Fear of losing or being unable to protect her children was not a conscious barrier for her to leave him.

"Fear of Retaliation by the Man"
The third factor cited by Justice Wilson to explain why battered women stay with their abusers is their reasonable fear that they will be murdered if they pull away from them. Mooney begged the Prince George police for help in March 1996 because she was persuaded that Kruska would kill her. She met him in 1991, and after only six weeks of romantic involvement she became fearful of him: "His eyes ... when he got mad ... I would feel death come over me."[66] Her first experience of fear was triggered by his intense jealousy: "He would always ask me questions whenever I went to town. He

was jealous if I had a girlfriend; he was jealous if I had male friends; he was jealous of the neighbours."[67]

Kruska was "broad-shouldered, [with] big arms." According to the police, he had a "[t]hick neck. He looked like a very muscular, very strong man."[68] Mooney's daughter Michelle described his frightening demeanour:

> [W]hen you looked at him when he was angry, you could just see the hatred in his eyes, the anger and it just – it was scary. When you looked at him, you knew he was – there was something wrong with him and just the looks he gave, you knew he was ... he was capable of doing something.[69]

Kruska's first assaults on Mooney were not murderous. Kruska became angry when she suggested hiring painters after he complained about painting her home. He threw an entire gallon of paint in her face and stomped off.[70] On another occasion, he found bear spray in her purse and calmly and deliberately sprayed her face with the burning substance.[71] A third assault was more ominous. Michelle described Kruska choking her mother before Mooney escaped and ran into the girls' room, where they attempted to barricade the door. Kruska crashed in, threw her mother to the floor, and began kicking her in the stomach and hips.[72] When Michelle tried to intervene, Kruska put his face inches from hers and growled "[s]hut up, bitch."[73]

Kruska perpetrated an even more frightening attack on 4 November 1995. His friend Glenn Miller was visiting that day, and Michelle was present. When Miller slumped in his chair, passed out from consuming too much alcohol, Kruska suddenly accused Mooney of having telephoned Miller.[74] He became enraged, and Mooney leapt up and fled to a bedroom, with him in chase, wielding a cane. Michelle heard her mother's screams from the room. There Kruska choked Mooney into unconsciousness, leaving handprints on her throat and bursting the blood vessels in her eyes. When she came to, he was smashing the cane on her hip, opening the skin on her left buttock. She staggered out the door, trying to run, but he brought the cane down again, this time on the back of her head. He wrested the car keys from her as she fled to the neighbours to call 9-1-1.[75] Mooney had almost died; she was acutely aware of her endangerment.

Every woman involved with a violent or controlling man faces the prospect that he will continue or escalate the violence if she leaves. Men's deliberate use of threat and violence to prevent a woman from leaving is part of the power struggle of battering. The dangerous and intentional pattern of escalation by men in response to women's decision to leave is what Martha Mahoney names "separation assault."[76] Separated women experience violence from their former partners at nine times the rate of married women, and separated Aboriginal women are another four and a half times more likely to experience this violence than non-Aboriginal separated women.[77] Studies in Canada, the United States, and Australia indicate that recent separation or the threat of separation greatly elevates the risk of more serious, including lethal, retaliation.[78] The risk of intimate femicide – the murder of a female intimate partner – is also heightened ninefold post-separation.[79]

Risk factors and additional consequences of intimate femicide are detailed in studies undertaken in Ontario. In 1989, the Women We Honour Action Committee set out to document intimate femicide, a task never before undertaken in Canada.[80] While men in Canadian society are twice as likely to be victims of homicide as women, both women's and men's greatest risk of violent death resides in men.[81] Intimate femicide is a gendered crime: women are more likely to be killed by their male partners and former partners (61-76 percent) than by others, and women are four[82] to five[83] times more likely to die at the hands of their partners than are men. Although husband killing is usually motivated by self-defence,[84] intimate femicide usually stems from men's jealousy and a need to control;[85] they kill post-separation and in response to perceived or actual infidelity; and they plan murder-suicide.[86]

Two studies by the Women We Honour Action Committee (covering 1974-90 and 1991-94) identified patterns and risk factors for intimate femicide using police files, hospital files, and coroners' records of women who had been murdered. This research confirms that intimate femicide is a crime of power, control, and domination. The batterer's instrumental use of force and threat secures the compliance of his partner to his domination. Her efforts to expose his violence or separate are deeply threatening. Intimate femicide is the ultimate exercise of control: "If I can't have her, no one will."

Kruska's final acts were predictable based on this research. Mooney understood her risk of dying intuitively and viscerally. That Kruska had strangled her was an important predictor of lethal violence. Strangulation raises the risk of intimate femicide at least sevenfold.[87] The Abuse Assessment Screen used by health practitioners in the United States has been revised to include non-lethal strangulation,[88] and some twenty-nine US states have drafted new criminal laws to facilitate its prosecution.[89] In Ontario, the Domestic Violence Death Review Committee, which studied 253 intimate homicide deaths between 2002 and 2008,[90] identified strangulation and other factors that would have placed Mooney in the highest risk category, including the history of domestic violence, actual or pending separation, and obsessive behaviour.[91]

Kruska had threatened suicide were he to be sent to jail. Mooney testified that this threat had frightened her because she suspected that he would kill her first.[92] In fact, 31 percent of perpetrators of intimate femicide also commit suicide.[93] "Threats to commit suicide" and "escalation of violence" share fifth place as risk factors for intimate femicide.[94] Mooney had every reason to be deathly afraid.

The Women We Honour Action Committee further found that men who kill their intimate partners also kill their children, family members, and friends in some cases.[95] In other words, seeking help from family members, as suggested by Carruthers,[96] can render those loved ones vulnerable to homicidal violence. Many women understand that this advice endangers others.

Tragically, Mooney discovered the risks of accepting help from loved ones too late. Could she have escaped by "going underground"?

"Going Underground"

Mooney did not choose to "go underground." Battered women might contemplate leaving their jurisdictions, travelling as far away as they can from their abusers, assuming new identities, and creating new lives, but this option is dangerous and fraught with legal risk. First, if women take their children, they increase their chances of being located because so many clues are inevitably provided by children.[97] Mothers will be prosecuted for kidnapping if caught and will likely lose both custody and access, unless they can establish that fleeing was "necessary" to protect their children.[98]

Even if women do not have children or leave without them, disentangling from one's friends, family, contacts, and assets is almost impossible. There are many ways for a batterer obsessed with finding a woman to succeed. Women can be betrayed by the simplest of details and by well-meaning people. Battered women in witness protection programs have been exposed to grave danger by the errors of others.[99] If her batterer finds her, the woman has none of the safeguards to dissuade him from killing her, such as police intervention or watchful neighbours, precisely because she has been living under an assumed identity.

Beyond the danger and illegality of going underground with children with new identities, this strategy brings endless complications for securing employment, social welfare, or even housing. Lawyers might be ill equipped to provide legal assistance for a plan to go underground, and their ethical obligations can be compromised if they provide "how to" advice.[100]

Finally, going underground means an isolated and lonely life that few can sustain. Women must be perpetually vigilant, trust no one, and maintain secrecy in all relationships and those of their children. Most battered women do not choose this route.

Women's Shelters

Mooney stayed at a women's shelter with her daughters for one night after the assault in which Kruska smashed her head against the floor and began kicking her.[101] He "was on the loose somewhere," she testified, while she was at the shelter.[102]

Women of the battered women's shelter movement, which emerged in Canada in 1972,[103] have saved countless women's and children's lives as well as the lives of many men.[104] Shelters have "safe houses," with unlisted addresses and telephone numbers. They use safety protocols to ensure, to the best of their abilities, that their residents are safe.[105] Still, shelters cannot imprison women: they must work, take their children to school, and live their lives.

Shelters have nurtured local and national anti-violence movements; produced a sophisticated feminist analysis of male violence against women; provided counselling and advocacy for battered women; delivered public education around male violence; and instigated reform efforts aimed at changing police practices as well as welfare, immigration, and social housing laws and policies.

Shelters were originally run by women and for women, without state assistance, until feminists insisted that the government shelter women from predictable violence.[106] Emergency and transitional shelters provide temporary space[107] for women and their children, and second-stage shelters provide longer-term respite[108] and a stepping stone to new lives. All forms of "shelter" are needed if women are to escape from male violence, including subsidized housing.[109]

Shelters across the country are bursting, however. In Ottawa alone in 2007, 5,150 women were turned away by the seven shelters that serve the area because they had no beds left.[110] A "snapshot" study in British Columbia reported that 550 women, youths, and children were turned away on a single day in 2009.[111] Smaller cities and rural communities experience similar capacity issues.[112] Women wait in hotels for weeks,[113] stay with friends, or turn to homeless shelters or even the street when they cannot get to women's shelters. Thousands are stuck in violent homes; we will never know how many women's and children's lives have been lost because shelters were full.[114]

Second-stage shelters lag even further behind women's demands. Only 20 percent of shelters are second stage. Some jurisdictions, such as the Northwest Territories and Nunavut, where the need is greatest, have none,[115] reflecting the scarce resources and weak commitments to women's shelters in smaller communities. Rural women might have no shelters within reach of their homes.[116]

Shelters might serve Aboriginal women, but not all are equipped to meet Aboriginal women's unique needs,[117] and fewer still are on reserve lands.[118] The first Aboriginal-run shelters in Ontario opened their doors as early as 1978, offering services based on values and practices that address the devastation that colonization has caused to Aboriginal cultural, familial, and spiritual bonds.[119] Immigrant and refugee women similarly have unique experiences of male violence, racism, and immigrant status that are met by only six in ten shelters.[120] Women with disabilities face up to three times the risk of intimate violence, but they too face barriers from the physical structures and services offered by shelters.[121]

Finally, the continuing dismantling of the welfare state in Canada, with corresponding cuts to legal aid, social assistance, child care, and services for persons with disabilities, and the systematic defunding of women's advocacy groups, have further weakened the safety net that shelters provide.[122] Changes to the law governing charitable status by the federal government have put pressure on women's shelters and rape crisis centres to curtail their advocacy and reinvent themselves as professional service providers. The limits and cuts have helped to depoliticize some women's shelters, with corresponding losses to battered women, whose lives and futures depend on women's equality aspirations, not on the professional delivery of "victim" services.[123]

Corporal Curle counselled Mooney to call for officer escort to Omineca Safe House, a shelter across the street from the police station in Vanderhoof,[124] when she was released from hospital on 5 November after Kruska strangled her. Mooney did not follow up, believing that the police would immediately arrest and hold Kruska. Only later, during her civil trial, did Mooney turn to her local shelter for support and advice and to the Vancouver Rape Relief and Women's Shelter (VRRWS). VRRWS initiated a national letter campaign by shelters protesting to the Attorneys General Federal and British Columbia, demanding that they stop fighting Mooney in court.

The Police and the Justice System

Mooney invoked the police and the justice system on four occasions. At every turn, she was misinformed and confused about what would happen and why. She was given neither protection nor information to enable good decision making.

In reporting the abuse, Mooney joined a small minority of women who contact the police in the wake of male violence.[125] Although the police, lawyers, judges, and laypersons might think that police intervention is an obvious and effective strategy, it is seldom employed by women who experience intimate violence. At least seven and up to nine of ten assaulted women do not report the assaults to the police.[126] Over two-thirds of women have been assaulted more than once before they contact the police, and more than a quarter have been assaulted at least ten times before they first call the police.[127] Almost two-thirds of those who get to a shelter do not report the violence to the police.[128]

Women fear retaliation by the abuser, his family, and his friends,[129] and they worry that the police will see the assault as too minor.[130] Mooney might have perceived the paint can and bear spray assaults as likely to be dismissed by the police or explained away by Kruska. When the police express disbelief, contempt, or indifference, women become discouraged.[131] Women who report to the police and then try to withdraw the charges can be charged with public mischief.[132] Humiliated by their partners' acts, women can internalize the message that they deserve the abuse.[133] Racialized women, particularly African Canadian women, do not trust the police and might fear the consequences for their partners should they report them.[134] Other women fear the economic implications for their families of their partners' arrests or know that they will be deported if their partners withdraw sponsorship.[135]

Some women have experienced "equality with a vengeance."[136] The police can interpret "mandatory" arrest policies as requiring them to arrest women when their male partners claim to have been assaulted, even when it was the woman who called the police.[137] Statistics Canada reports that men and women say that they have experienced spousal assault at roughly the same rates but that the nature of those assaults and their impact are vastly different: women are much more likely to experience repeat assaults; be at the receiving end of serious violence, including sexual assault, strangulation, and being threatened with a gun or knife; experience more devastating physical injuries and emotional suffering; and ultimately be killed.[138] Women's acts of resistance and self-defence – including minor acts such as pushing a man away, throwing a plastic water bottle, or biting a partner who is pinning her down – can become the basis for assault charges. Being charged as an "abuser" seems to be a particular risk for African Canadian and Aboriginal women,[139] who can be viewed through racial stereotypes as assertive and violent. If charged, women become vulnerable to losing not only their jobs but also their children.[140] Women who are charged often swear that they will never again call the police,[141] which further empowers the batterer and immunizes him from repercussions.

Statistics Canada reports that, though abused women are likely to be assaulted multiple times, they tend to call the police only once.[142] This pattern might reflect women's negative experiences with the police. Women's reporting rates have steadily decreased in the past five years,[143] as has the rate at which their reports result in charges.[144]

Women such as Mooney calculate when to call the police, knowing that this is a direct challenge to their partners' control. Abusers whose control is threatened raise the ante with more serious threats, violence, and humiliation to re-establish domination. If the police or the criminal justice systems respond negatively or weakly, then the woman's endangerment escalates.[145]

"Left Me to Die"

Mooney's first effort to access the criminal justice system resulted in charges against her first husband, but he was acquitted at trial. Explaining her initial hesitation to contact the police regarding Kruska's violence, Mooney testified that she did "not want to put [her family] through the court system again."[146]

Her second effort to secure legal protection came in November 1995 after Kruska almost killed her by strangulation. When Curle drove her to the hospital, she disclosed Kruska's three prior assaults. Curle took Mooney to the emergency department at St John Hospital in Vanderhoof, then returned to the station to check Kruska's criminal record. The printout revealed that Kruska had been convicted of manslaughter,[147] forcible confinement, and two sexual assaults.[148]

Curle returned to the hospital to interview Mooney in her room, where she was heavily sedated and suffering from the effects of strangulation. Strangulation causes no visible injuries in half of battered women studied, and another 35 percent have injuries difficult to photograph, which in turn means that the police may lay minor charges. One study reports that, "unless the victim had significant visible injuries or complained of continuous pain requiring medical attention, the police were inclined to handle the incident as minor – almost as if the victim had been slapped, rather than having been strangled."[149]

Curle testified that he did not see bruises on Mooney's neck but noted the burst blood vessels in her eyes, her hoarse voice, and her obvious pain. He assumed that Mooney had been administered pain relief.[150] She was in poor shape to give a statement and to be her own advocate. And she needed one.

Curle recorded her account, but Mooney became beset by worry that Kruska was watching. She was convinced that he knew everything she did and said. She refused to sign her statement for fear of retaliation.[151] Her instincts were dead-on. That day Kruska prowled the hospital corridors looking for her room.

Mooney testified that, if she was too frightened to sign the statement, then obviously she was too frightened to testify against Kruska. She communicated her terror to Curle, who said that the police had more than enough evidence without her testimony. She knew that her injuries were recorded by Dr Willis at the hospital and observed by the police and that Michelle had seen Kruska chase her into the bedroom and heard her screams. When challenged by Carruthers to locate Curle's assurance in the written statement, Mooney protested: "[H]e was the one doing the writing, not me."[152]

Curle recorded Mooney's decision in contradictory terms: "MOONEY was reluctant to sign the statement as she greatly fears reprisals from KRUSKA. MOONEY is prepared to follow through with court action for this assault."[153] Curle believed that, once she had a chance to think things over, Mooney would cooperate,[154] but he denied telling Mooney that she need not testify.[155]

Mooney thought that Curle would arrest Kruska for his attempt on her life. In fact, Curle had no plan to request a warrant until Monday.[156] Nor was any sort of security or warning placed by the police or hospital officials in her room or on her file, a failing that put her at grave risk.[157]

All of these missteps left Kruska free to act. A nurse informed Mooney that Glenn Miller had arrived to see her; instead, Kruska sauntered into her room. He blurted out an apology, then slipped from the room. Mooney testified that in spite of her injuries she scrambled out of bed and ran down the hall to inform a nurse: "That wasn't Glenn Miller, that was Roland Kruska, the guy that they're looking for. There's a warrant out for his arrest."[158] But Kruska had accomplished his goal: he had reminded Mooney that he was everywhere and unstoppable. He would never let her go.

Throughout the civil trial, the lawyer for the police attempted to blame Mooney for failing to protect herself. In cross-examination, Carruthers demanded to know what she had done when Kruska appeared in her hospital room. Had she called the police? Had she instructed the nurse to do so?[159] Mooney stood up for herself: "I shouldn't have to tell the nurse to phone the police." "And in my state of mind – I mean, I was – they had me severely sedated, um, I was badly beaten, and was frightened."[160]

Mooney was discharged the afternoon of 5 November and went home to Clucultz Lake, mistakenly believing that the police had arrested Kruska. There was no vehicle in her driveway. Her heart almost stopped when she found Kruska in her house, armed with a gun.[161] He swore that he would kill himself rather than be sent back to jail. He demanded that she concoct a story blaming herself for his assault, and he promised that he would sign the house over to her and leave her alone if she kept him out of jail. Mooney agreed: "I was scared to death of him. I ... thought, you know, maybe he's going to kill me too."[162]

While Kruska was there, Corporal Michael Pisio pulled into the driveway. Kruska ran outside to hide while Mooney spoke with the officer. Pisio asked whether she had seen Kruska. She told him that Kruska had been there earlier, apologized, and left. She explained in her testimony: "Roland was outside in the bushes with a gun and – Mr. Pisio came alone, there was no other officers with him."[163] In spite of possibly having spared the officer's life by staying silent, Mooney testified, "I remember feeling so inadequate and you know, I – God, I remember feeling that I just wanted to drop to my knees, but again, I – I was so scared."[164] After Pisio left, Mooney's friend Karen Neal dropped by, but Mooney stopped her at the door and shh'd her by holding her finger to her lips to let her know that Kruska was there.[165] Asked in cross-examination why she did not ask Neal to call police, Mooney replied: "I knew she was going to get the police."[166]

Kruska had slipped through the fingers of the police several times in less than twenty-four hours. His power over Mooney grew correspondingly. That afternoon she called the police to report that she had forgotten that she had started the altercation by assaulting Kruska with a poker. Kruska stayed overnight. The next morning he hovered while she, under his direction, called lawyers, trying to find one to help her tell a new story to the court about his attack. Kruska's lawyer, Steven Peleshok, accepted. He told her that she "needed to stick with that story or Roland was going to be facing four to five years."[167] "So," Mooney testified, "in the eyes of Roland, I was feeling helpless."[168]

Peleshok arranged to meet Mooney and Kruska at the courthouse on the morning of 6 November to discuss her evidence. Peleshok sent Mooney to ask Crown prosecutor James Swales if he would drop the charges. When Swales opened his door and Mooney identified herself, he asked her if that was Kruska standing behind her. When she replied yes, he slammed the door and summoned the police to handcuff Kruska on the spot.[169] He was arrested and charged with assault with a weapon and assault causing bodily harm.

Kruska's acts and intent were homicidal, but their seriousness was not reflected in the charges, suggestive of an intimacy "discount" that seems to apply to men who batter their female partners.[170] More appropriate charges would have been attempted murder or aggravated assault because his acts had endangered Mooney's life.[171] These more serious charges carry much higher maximum sentences of life and fourteen years imprisonment. They would have been supported by medical evidence showing that, beyond the risk of immediate death, women who have been strangled can experience respiratory difficulties, cerebrovascular accidents within weeks of strangulation, brain damage, paralysis, and memory loss.[172]

Once Kruska was dispatched to a holding cell, Swales heard Mooney out. According to her evidence, he responded that "there's no goddamn way I believe this story, Bonnie. Look at you ... [Y]ou're totally black and blue underneath the eyes; you've got broken blood vessels; you have handprints on your neck."[173] Swales told her that he could prosecute her for contempt of court.[174] Mooney testified that she began to cry and replied, "if you get me for contempt of court and I go to jail, at least I'm safe."[175] She told him that she was terrified of Kruska. Swales reassured her that they could convict him without her evidence.

Swales denied telling Mooney that she did not need to testify. He informed her that it was Crown policy to attempt to prosecute wife assault regardless of the wishes of the victim. But on cross-examination, Swales acknowledged that his words were intended to convey that the decision to proceed with charges was his, not hers; he could force her to testify by issuing a subpoena but was unlikely to do so; and he would proceed to prosecute Kruska.[176]

Furthermore, Swales acknowledged, had Mooney testified, Kruska's sentence would have been "somewhere probably more than six months, perhaps up to about two years, maybe a bit over two years."[177] This was far below the sentence of three to five years that Carruthers claimed in his opening address would have been imposed had Mooney not recanted[178] and the four to five years that Peleshok told her were inevitable if she did not "stick with the story."[179] No wonder Mooney was confused.

Swales conceded that he could not recall making any effort to ascertain whether Mooney had recanted because of her fear of her abuser,[180] the predominant reason why battered women withdraw from prosecution.[181] Lacking this crucial information, he might have viewed her as uncooperative and not a "true victim."[182] He could not recall her injuries but admitted that severe injuries would have been material to the potential success of a prosecution without her testimony.[183]

With the changed story and the claim that Mooney was not fearful, Swales's case for detaining Kruska in custody pending trial was compromised even though batterers are at high risk to reoffend while on release.[184] At the bail hearing the same morning, Peleshok conveyed Mooney's new story to the presiding justice. Kruska was released from custody but ordered to stay at least one-quarter mile from her home and avoid contact with her. According to Swales, having "lost" the advantage of detaining Kruska in custody pending trial,[185] he discussed with Peleshok the possibility of accepting a guilty plea to a lesser charge. He believed that without Mooney the case was weak.[186] Sometime between Kruska's release on 6 November and his next court appearance, Swales accepted a plea bargain.

Kruska's sentencing hearing was held two weeks later. The night before the hearing Miller called Mooney to tell her that Kruska was going to jail for only twenty-one days, boasting that Kruska "could do this standing on his head."[187] She did not believe the story – "that never came from Swales, that came from him and Peleshok, so I thought it was just a bunch of baloney."[188]

Just before the hearing, Swales spoke briefly with Mooney: she did not want a "no contact" order added to Kruska's sentence for her protection. As she said later at the civil trial, "I was trying to do everything in my power to get Roland off the hook because Peleshok told me this is what I needed to do. Kruska told me this is what I needed to do, and I just felt overwhelmed."[189] She believed that Kruska had been charged with attempted murder and was going to jail for a long time. She thought that Swales was referring to non-contact after Kruska came out of jail, four to five years down the line.[190] Minutes before the hearing, according to Swales, he "misinformed her about the sentence because I thought it was going to be a bit higher" – "I told her either 40 or 45 days."[191]

Kruska pled guilty to a reduced charge of assault, based on an agreed statement of facts that Mooney had started the altercation by hitting him with a poker. She did not testify. The original charges were dismissed by the plea agreement. To Mooney's shock, Kruska was sentenced to a mere twenty-one days of imprisonment – a lengthy sentence by some standards.[192] The judge's reasons referred to Mooney's statements that Kruska's assault was "unusual" and attributable to his consumption of alcohol and that Kruska was a good husband and father. The judge told Kruska that "I may be placing too much emphasis upon your rehabilitation and not enough emphasis upon protection of the public and protection of Ms Mooney, but I'm relying a great deal upon what Ms Mooney has told me." To her, he said that "Certainly Ms Mooney ought to feel confident enough in the judicial court system that if Mr Kruska was to raise one hand or make one threat against Ms Mooney, she should not hesitate to complain to the authorities."[193] Unfortunately, this was an empty promise.

Mooney was devastated and confused, believing that there was enough evidence to put Kruska away for years. In the civil trial, Carruthers expressed disbelief at this. After all, she had provided a concocted story to the court: how could she have been surprised at the outcome?[194] Mooney maintained that she understood that Swales would pursue conviction and a serious sentence: "I don't believe any of them believed about the poker ... including the police."[195]

Mooney's third attempt to secure protection from the police came four months later. Kruska was released from his short sentence for assault at the beginning of December 1995. He did not fulfill his promise to sign over the house and leave Mooney alone. He instead began a protracted property negotiation aimed at maintaining contact and keeping her in anxiety and dread. He rejected every proposal, including sale of the property so that she could pay out his claim. He stalked her and phoned her constantly.[196] Mooney installed a "jail door" (bars) on her back door and telephoned Kruska to assess his mood and alleviate her fears, knowing that he was eighty kilometres away (an hour by car) from her rural property.[197]

On 11 March 1996, Kruska called to ask Mooney to meet him in Prince George to discuss the house arrangements. He proposed a McDonalds. When he arrived, he said that he wanted to talk elsewhere and asked her to meet him at Fort George Park. She agreed, knowing that it too was a populated area. Once there Mooney pulled her vehicle next to his in the parking lot, left her driver's door open, and cautiously sat on the passenger seat in Kruska's truck, leaving his passenger door open. Within seconds, Kruska became highly agitated. She knew that his violence was imminent because he was "shuffling those big arms of his."[198] They had not even begun discussion before his rage erupted.[199]

Mooney leapt from his vehicle to her own and tried to drive out of the parking lot. As she tried to back up and drive away, Kruska pulled his truck over to block hers, threatening to ram her vehicle.[200] "I was looking through my rearview mirror and I could see Mr Kruska was going like this at me and, you know, baring his teeth and –" Henry Wood interjected to confirm "going like this" meant that Kruska was clenching his fist. She continued: "Oh, when he would do that, he looked just like a wolf, he was so scary looking."[201]

Mooney drove around his truck and escaped from the parking lot, but Kruska gave chase. She drove through stop signs and red lights and almost hit pedestrians as he tailed her pickup at high speeds: "[H]e was going to start ramming my truck because he was right on top of – like, the truck wasn't actually on top, but right – well, bumper to bumper."[202] She circled a friend's apartment building, honking, and then stopped to ask a woman named Cindy to run upstairs and get her friend Chris. Kruska finally drove off. When Chris descended, she persuaded Mooney to go to the police.

She went to the Prince George RCMP detachment, where Rebecca Jones, a civilian member, was on intake. Shaking and crying, Mooney relayed the events. In testimony, Jones said that Mooney was "very, very frightened."[203] She stood out in Jones's mind as one of the two most upset women who had reported domestic violence in her eighteen months doing intake.[204]

Jones paged the on-duty officer and completed a form tersely summarizing the complaint while they waited for the officer's return. Mooney provided the names of two witnesses – Chris and Cindy. "What really struck me is her hands were shaking so violently," testified Jones, "and I remember looking at her jewellery and her nails, and her hands were just shaking so violently, that really impressed me. And she was crying and her voice was shaking."[205] Mooney's demeanour did not change while waiting for the officer.

Constable Craig Andrichuk arrived between 11:30 and 11:35 a.m. and took Mooney into an interview room to take her statement. She testified that Andrichuk removed his black leather gloves and wrote on a clipboard as she spoke.[206] She told him: "Roland had just got done chasing me at high speed through Prince George and I had to go through stop signs and red lights, and he was waving his fist at me, and I felt he was going to kill me."[207] Carruthers demanded that Mooney explain why these details were neither in the police report nor in her statement. She testified that she assumed that they would be in Andrichuk's report.[208]

Andrichuk left and conferred with Staff Sergeant John Lloyd. He returned and said "that he was sorry, but there was nothing that they could do for me and that I needed to stay in public places and I had lots of reason to be scared, he was a scary, scary man. And I told him that I lived out at Clucultz Lake and how was I supposed to stay in the public? Take a park bench down at the mall?"[209]

At that time, the RCMP operational manual had adopted the Attorney General of British Columbia's 1993 *Violence against Women in Relationships Policy*,[210] regarded as among the strongest policies in the country. It mandated thorough investigation of all allegations, obtaining statements from victims and witnesses, and arresting if there are grounds to believe that an offence has been committed, particularly when there is a history of violence by the offender. It emphasized women's fear as a strong indicator of the level of danger.

Although these "mandatory" policies have drawn the ire of judges and the police alike for their purported interference in the realm of prosecutorial discretion,[211] they have never been truly mandatory or enforceable as law. They are intended to guide the discretion of the police and prosecutors in their daily work. Many police do not actually follow these policies, as women[212] and police themselves[213] report. And as Mooney discovered.

Andrichuk indicated that he would not assist Mooney in pursuing a criminal peace bond application under section 810 of the *Criminal Code* and advised her to hire a lawyer. He was indirectly counselling her to file for a civil "restraining order" in the family courts, consistent with the preference of some police forces.[214] Breaches of both peace bonds and restraining orders can be prosecuted as offences,[215] but the police are more reluctant to charge breaches of restraining orders. By recommending that women invoke restraining orders from the family courts, which the police are less likely to enforce, they effectively treat wife assault as a "private," "non-criminal" matter.[216]

Mooney despaired: "When I left the police station I felt like there was no hope. I felt that I needed to go out and actually purchase a gun ... I just figured I – I guess I'm going to have to take the law into my own hands now. Nobody wants to help me."[217] If the police could do nothing, then a lawyer would be useless.[218]

Carruthers pressed Mooney to admit that Andrichuk told her that the criteria for a peace bond had not been met; it would take up to ninety days to secure one in any event; and she should hire her own lawyer to get a restraining order because that would be faster. Mooney was certain:

No, he never suggested that at all. He – as far as I was concerned, he – he never – I mean, he knows all the ropes – the – what way you have to do ... I didn't know anything. I'd never been in trouble with the law before or even been involved with the law. He never tried to show me any proceedings on what I should be doing and, Mrs Mooney, we can't help you, but here, listen, this is what we can do to get you some proper help. He never did any of that ... [H]e basically left me to die, is what he did.[219]

Seven weeks later, on 29 April 1996, Kruska called Mooney "yelling and screaming," calling her "all sorts of names." He was furious because she was allowing Hazel White to build a cabin on the back of the Clucultz Lake property: "[T]here was people there helping me build this ... little cabin ... and he was angry with the people who were there. He didn't like anybody around me."[220] This autonomous act, much like disclosing his violence to others and calling the police, challenged his control and threatened his access to her.

Hours later, in the middle of the night, Mooney heard a noise. She crept downstairs, and her worst nightmare materialized. Kruska was at the front door, not the "jail door," holding a gun. He motioned to her to open the door. She began screaming to wake White, who yelled, "Bonnie, go. He's here for you and you only."[221] Mooney stood there, paralyzed with fear. "I thought I was moving but I wasn't going anywhere."[222] White gave her a shove, and she ran to the bathroom. Mooney kicked out the window, then jumped out.

As she fell, she heard the glass door inside break when Kruska used the butt of the gun to smash his way in. Mooney landed below, hitting her head on a rock, and, as she tried to stand, she found herself covered in blood and unable to use one of her legs properly. She thought that she had been shot. She could hear White begging for her life inside. Somehow Mooney summoned the strength to run, dragging her injured leg.

Arriving at her neighbours' home, Mooney fell to her knees. "I couldn't believe I had actually made it."[223] She called 9-1-1 while cowering under a kitchen table: "[I]t was like a fish bowl in there," with the lights on at night. "I didn't know whether he was going to come and shoot me."[224] While on the phone, she suddenly saw flames shooting from the roof of her home. She began screaming at the operator that her kids and her friend were inside a burning building. As she hung up, she heard "[m]ommy, mommy." Her daughter Michelle was on the front steps of the neighbours' house, dripping with blood, her arm "hanging by a thread." Mooney called 9-1-1 again to get instructions on how to stem the bleeding and keep Michelle alive until the ambulance arrived.

Michelle had managed to push her little sister Kristy out the bathroom window first, saving her before Kruska could get at her. Kristy ran in the opposite direction and huddled in a neighbour's dog house with his "mean dogs." The owner heard a huge commotion from his dogs and discovered a frightened child hiding in the dog house. When the paramedics, fire-fighters, and police arrived, they found the bodies of White and Kruska inside. Mooney's uninsured house – Kruska would never agree to insurance[225] – was severely damaged but not destroyed. The community later created a benefit fund for Mooney and her girls to repair the house.[226]

The human damage, however, was irreparable. As Mooney testified, "the weight that I carry on my shoulders from the death of my friend and my daughter being shot has been tremendous. I will carry that weight to my grave."[227]

Andrichuk contradicted most of Mooney's evidence about their inter-action on 11 March. He denied that Mooney disclosed anything resembling an assault or threat by Kruska:

[I]t was a very casual conversation. She had mentioned that she had some problems back, I believe, in November of '95 ... I was of the opinion that it was just to make us aware that he was in the area and that if she needed help, to give us – you know, that we would be aware that he was around. Her concern level was relatively low.[228]

He denied that he took notes while she spoke and claimed that she had com-pleted her written statement before he arrived at the detachment. He denied that Mooney was fearful. She was, he said, calm and relaxed.[229] He denied being made aware that she lived on a rural property out at Clucultz Lake.[230]

However, even in direct examination, Andrichuk gave the impression that he was attempting to cover his own tracks. Jones's written summary stated that Kruska had tried to ram Mooney's truck. Andrichuk had crossed out "ram" and changed it to "stop" because Kruska had not actually hit Mooney's vehicle.[231] In an internal report on his interaction with Mooney, Andrichuk stated that Kruska had "followed" her, not "chased" her, as indi-cated by Jones and Mooney.[232] Yet Andrichuk contradicted himself by writ-ing in his report, in response to an internal investigation, that Mooney had felt threatened.[233] He admitted that he had not explained the difference between a peace bond and a restraining order.[234]

Andrichuk added a time to the document showing that Mooney's statement was made at 11:50 a.m., even though he denied having been present then. Yet he testified that *after* his interview with Mooney to review her statement he left the room to perform a criminal records search. That search was tagged at 11:40 a.m., meaning that her statement had to have been made earlier. The criminal records search revealed not only Kruska's lengthy record of violent offences but also that Kruska was on probation for his earlier attack on Mooney.[235]

Andrichuk admitted under cross-examination having spent less than five minutes speaking with Mooney before he left to view Kruska's record and consult his superior.[236] Andrichuk did not pursue any information from the two witnesses listed on the report, nor did he attempt to contact Kruska.[237] According to a report by Superintendent Hall, he failed to pay attention to Mooney's distressed state, which should have "set off alarm bells."[238] He took not a single note on his interaction with Mooney. He acknowledged that treating the incident as a civil matter and referring her to a lawyer saved him a huge amount of paperwork.[239] Wood also established that Mooney's rural address was on the form that Andrichuk signed, undercutting his claimed ignorance about where Mooney lived.

Andrichuk acknowledged that his superiors had ruled that he had failed to competently investigate her report, in violation of policy. Staff Sergeant Frederick found on 3 September 1996 that Andrichuk had failed to conduct an adequate investigation. This finding was upheld by Superintendent Hall:

> Although you did consult with your supervisor, Staff Sergeant Lloyd, as a result of a lack of a proper interview statement, I believe that you were not able to properly provide a clear picture of the circumstances involving Ms. Mooney and Mr. Kruska. This gave rise to Staff Sergeant Lloyd recommending that the matter be better dealt with via the *Family Relations Act*.[240]

The senior officers in the internal review believed the description of Mooney's terrified demeanour over Andrichuk's more benign depiction. They also pointed out the inherent contradiction in his statements: "Ms. Mooney also relates that you advised her to be very cautious and to stay in public places considering Kruska's criminal history. This contradicts your statement that you did not feel Ms. Mooney was in danger."[241]

The practices of police such as Andrichuk are shaped by the belief that women who report wife abuse are reluctant witnesses unlikely to testify against their batterers.[242] The police blame these women for wasting police resources and are often oblivious to the confusion and the terrible bind in which women find themselves when an abuser demands that they recant. Women who recant are constructed as "typically ungrateful when 'rescued,' fostering an unhealthy ambivalence, even hostility[,] towards battered women's calls for assistance."[243]

Defending his failure to probe Mooney's statement, Andrichuk indicated that he "didn't want to jeopardize the investigation by leading a witness." Frederick countered in his report that "Andrichuk is very confused if he's afraid to ask victims or witnesses questions for fear of leading them. This certainly is the case when dealing with very young victims of abuse and certain other individuals; however, I'm not quite sure how an investigator can gather the information he requires if he is afraid to ask questions of the victim/witness."[244] Andrichuk used an approach reserved for young, impressionable, and otherwise unreliable witnesses, suggestive of an underlying attitude toward women like Mooney. He made her responsible, without telling her, for identifying and recording any significant details:

> In speaking to her about what she had written, I felt that's all I had to work with. And again, I didn't want to solicit more. I didn't want her to bring out more than was necessary. I felt if she came in on the incident and it was serious to her, every detail would have been put down on that form that was important to her.[245]

Andrichuk had another concern about asking Mooney for more information: "[B]y pushing it one way or another I felt it would be unfair to the other party as well."[246] He confirmed that it was Kruska whom he wanted to treat fairly. Wood asked: "At the time you were trying so hard to be fair to the other party, as you phrased it – you knew that Mr Kruska had assaulted this woman and been sentenced for it and was on probation for it about four months earlier; right?" "And you knew that he had the conviction for manslaughter and a violent history; right?" Andrichuk answered: "Yes."[247]

His concern about being "fair" to someone "red-flagged" in the RCMP database as extremely dangerous might seem unusual until one considers the "domestic" context, in which prejudice can affect decision making. His explanations suggest a belief that women lie about or exaggerate violence and threat by their male partners and presume that they are equally likely to be the aggressor.

Statistics Canada studies show that men report violence inflicted against them by their female partners, but the nature, severity, intent, and effects of this violence are simply not comparable to those of the violence that men inflict on their female partners.[248] When Mooney tried to free herself as Kruska strangled her, she yanked his hair and kicked him, attempting to knee him in the testicles. Does this mean that she was "violent" and should have been sanctioned?[249]

Andrichuk said that, even had he understood the facts as relayed by Mooney, he might not have pursued criminal charges. He speculated that Kruska "may have just been trying to apologize." Wood was dumbfounded: "You mean he may have been trying to catch up with her so he could say he was sorry?" "He may have."[250]

Mooney turned to the justice system for the fourth and final time in 2001 to ask for compensation from British Columbia and the police for negligence in failing to protect her and her daughters. Justice Collver of the BC Supreme Court accepted that Andrichuk and the RCMP detachment owed Mooney a legal obligation to use due care in investigating her allegations, ignoring the "Bonnie was the author of her own misfortune" theme advanced by the defence. Justice Collver also found that the police had patently failed to meet their own standard of professionalism in investigations: "I conclude that the investigation that Superintendent Hall criticized as being incomplete failed because it was never properly commenced."[251] He held that Andrichuk had failed to appreciate that "his principal duty was to assess Bonnie Mooney's subjective feelings of fear."[252] Justice Collver also based this finding of negligence on Andrichuk's failure to question Mooney, to follow up with witnesses, and to allow a justice to decide whether a peace bond was warranted rather than pre-empt that process.[253]

The defence did succeed, however, with its characterization of Kruska as "unpredictable," disconnecting police inaction from his final homicidal acts. Justice Collver declared that Mooney "could not explain" why her plan to build a cabin for White at the back of the property enraged Kruska,[254] in spite of her testimony about his intense jealousy of anyone who was around her and the threat to his control that her act signalled. Justice Collver ruled that "even after the unusual meeting at Fort George Park on March 11th [there was] no indication that Kruska was bent on harm,"[255] a conclusion at odds with his own finding that Andrichuk had failed to appreciate the significance of Mooney's fear and Kruska's actions. The "absence of any communication between Ms Mooney and Kruska in the ensuing seven weeks suggests that the brief encounter on March 11th was of little if any significance with respect to what happened on April 29th."[256] Justice Collver concluded that Andrichuk's "inaction did not materially increase the risk of harm to the extent that he must bear responsibility for Kruska's acts."[257] Justice Collver assessed the monetary damages incurred by Mooney and her children should his ruling on liability be overturned on appeal.[258]

Wood appealed to the British Columbia Court of Appeal, arguing that the judge had failed to properly apply the law on "causal effects." A stringent test for causal connection – clear proof that had the police acted Kruska would not have committed these acts – would be impossible to prove, leaving women with a right to a proper investigation of threats to their lives but no remedy if this obligation is unfulfilled.[259] Carruthers cross-appealed, arguing on public policy grounds that the police should not bear legal obligations to citizens; the police decision here was a mere error in judgment rather than negligence; and damages should have been reduced in light of Mooney's alleged "contributory negligence."

The VRRWS intervened to support Mooney's appeal in a rare but significant strategy for a women's shelter. It secured Court Challenges funding and *pro bono* assistance from a feminist legal team to ask the court to consider how Mooney's section 15 *Charter* right to equality and women's systemic experience of male violence and police neglect ought to shape the legal test for causal connection. Gail Dickson,[260] on behalf of VRRWS, urged the court to find that the *Violence against Women in Relationships Policy* itself made the causal link between police inaction and Kruska's violence. The policy was put in place to increase police intervention on the understanding, based on police experience, that strong and consistent law enforcement responses deter further violence by batterers. To find no causal link would encourage the police to ignore their own policies and further weaken the protections available to battered women. Dickson also argued that the defendants' invocation of "contributory negligence" against Mooney was rife with discriminatory stereotypes that blame women for men's violence.

The BC Court of Appeal dismissed the appeal and the cross-appeal in a 2-1 decision. The two judges who decided against Mooney's appeal, Justice John Hall and Justice Kenneth Smith, wrote separate decisions. They agreed that Kruska's acts were too remote from the police failure of duty to hold the police accountable.

Justice Hall was unsympathetic. He described Mooney as having "complained about a great many people."[261] He credited Andrichuk with having performed an "investigation," in contrast to the trial judge, who said that an investigation had not been commenced. Justice Hall also recast what the judge had called a reprimand as something much more innocuous: "[A] superintendent at the Prince George detachment advised Constable Andrichuk that his investigation on 11 March could have been more thorough."[262]

Justice Hall took up the theme that Kruska was "nuts," quoting from Mooney's evidence. He referred, for the first time in the legal record, to the fact that Kruska was under a deportation order that had never been implemented due in part to his disabilities arising from a car accident when he was a child: "It seems fair to describe him as having a mental difficulty and a 'short fuse.'"[263] Justice Hall ruled that the trial decision on causality was factual, deserving of deference. Police intervention or non-intervention was irrelevant to Kruska's actions, which Justice Hall detached from Mooney and from what is known about intimate femicide: "Absent deportation from Canada or permanent incarceration, it appears he posed a continuing risk to do harm to persons with whom he had contact."[264] Justice Smith concurred: "[I]t is difficult to imagine a sanction with realistic potential to forestall further violence by Mr Kruska."[265]

Justice Ian Donald was persuaded by the arguments of Wood and the VRRWS and would have allowed the appeal. He focused on the need for an effective remedy for a significant policy breach. He quoted from the judge who had sentenced Kruska to a mere twenty-one days of jail for strangling Mooney: "The ... passages bear a direct relationship to the public policy considerations supporting liability in this case. An experienced trial judge predicted further violence and gave Bonnie Mooney an assurance that the authorities would respond to any complaint if she were threatened again."[266]

Justice Donald rejected the claim that criminal intervention demonstrably would have made no difference. He relied on the Attorney General's own policy: "Increased public awareness, ... coupled with a rigorous arrest and charge policy, have been shown to reduce violence committed against women by their partners."[267] Recognizing that causal connection cannot be definitively proven either way, he argued that causation "requires flexibility ... so that compensation for a wrong will be provided where fairness and justice require."[268] Justice Donald reasoned that "the right to police protection in these circumstances is so strong and the need for teeth in the domestic violence policy so great that the causal linkage must be found sufficient to ground liability."[269] He concluded that, "by not dealing with Kruska's intimidation and threatening behaviour, the police failed to reduce the risk of more violence,"[270] which thus increased Mooney's endangerment.[271]

Justice Donald's dissenting judgment rejected the argument by Carruthers that Mooney had contributed to her own loss by failing to leave, by not taking steps to protect herself, and by telephoning Kruska: "[T]he police left Bonnie Mooney to her own devices. She kept in contact with Kruska for the comfort of knowing where he was and to resolve the property issue."[272]

At the same time, even Justice Donald accepted the defence characterization of Kruska as "erratic, irrational." And, after setting out the reasons why battered women cannot easily extricate themselves from abusive men,[273] he subtly attributed fault and irrationality to Mooney:

> The relationship between Bonnie Mooney and Kruska fits the classic profile of the battered woman syndrome. She felt powerless under his control; her decisions, often unwise, were prompted by fear and low self-esteem. Some internal dark force draws her to abusive partners. Modern law enforcement now recognizes that some victims of abuse cannot act rationally in their own best interests.[274]

But what would Justice Donald have had Mooney do rationally and in her own best interest? Could anyone have guaranteed, had she chosen a given option, that she and her loved ones would have survived?

Mooney's lawyer attempted to appeal further to the Supreme Court of Canada, but leave was refused.[275] Apart from seeking vindication in the international arena,[276] Mooney was left with no further legal recourse.

She was not the first woman in Canada to be denied police protection from a violent man; nor will she be the last. Sherri Lee Guy attempted to secure police aid in Ottawa in 1995 before her common law partner shot and killed her.[277] Brenda Moreside in Alberta made desperate 9-1-1 calls in 2005 when her ex tried to break into her home. The police refused to attend, even though Stanley Willier had a record for serious violent offences, including manslaughter, "because he was breaking into his own home."[278] Moreside was found murdered in her home in High Prairie. Lucie Gélinas reported in 2001 to Laval police, days before she was murdered and her three friends injured, that her ex-boyfriend Jocelyn Hotte, an RCMP officer, was stalking and threatening to kill her. Her complaint was "unfounded," and no report was even filed by the officers whom she contacted.[279] In

Calgary in 2003, Blagia Feteke repeatedly contacted the police in fear to report that her former husband was threatening to kill her and her three-year-old son. Her complaints were characterized as a chronic nuisance, and no action was taken. Mother and son were both murdered by the husband, who then killed himself.[280] Sheila Amero,[281] Gayle Hull,[282] and Wyann Ruso[283] survived deadly attacks by their former partners and initiated civil suits against the police for failing to respond appropriately to their calls for help in the face of grave danger.

Police, prosecutorial,[284] and judicial failures,[285] together with the other social, legal, and economic barriers surveyed in this chapter, prolong women's entrapment by raising the "costs" of leaving and driving the women back to their abusers.[286] Mooney left Kruska, but her decisions were criticized by the police, lawyers, and judges, making his reign of terror seem inconsequential. Ann Jones argues that the question "why didn't she leave?" avoids confronting "the failure of the police and courts to protect this woman; they could think instead that [she] might simply have walked away."[287]

Where does the *Mooney* decision leave battered women? If policies for arrest and prosecution of batterers are not enforceable in civil law, and if courts tell women that violent men are so unpredictable that the policies will not work anyway, what are women to do to save their lives?[288] Had Mooney acted pre-emptively and lain in wait to kill Kruska once the police told her that they could not help her, would she have been charged with first-degree murder? Would self-defence have been available to her? The murder trial of Kimberley Kondejewski, profiled in the next chapter, offers some answers.

3

Kimberley Kondejewski

"Kim was a profound victim of the Battered Woman Syndrome."[1]

On 15 May 1997, Kimberley Kondejewski waited in her darkened bedroom cradling a shotgun. When her husband, military sergeant and battle school instructor John Kondejewski, angrily burst into the room after a night out with his girlfriend, she shot him three times and then turned the gun on herself. The following spring at her murder trial in Brandon, Manitoba, her lawyer seized on Battered Woman Syndrome to advance self-defence.

Kim was hospitalized with her injuries while the police investigated and mulled over the charges.[2] *The Brandon Sun* reported "an unfounded complaint that one of the parents had assaulted one of the children."[3] A neighbour said that "yelling could be heard constantly from the home."[4] The newspaper also reported that the police had removed more than fifty weapons from the home[5] and that the military had confiscated unauthorized weapons-related items belonging to the army. The presence of potentially explosive artillery bomb casings, gunpowder, and primers required the services of the Emergency Disposal Unit.[6] The police continued to investigate Kim's motive.[7]

Five days after the homicide, and while still in Brandon General Hospital, Kim was charged with first-degree murder.[8] To secure a first-degree murder conviction, her prosecutor would have to prove that the murder was both planned (a calculated scheme or design)[9] and deliberate (considered, not impulsive).[10] Although those who kill intimate partners are less likely to be charged with first-degree murder than those who kill others,[11] Kim was among seventeen battered women charged with first-degree murder whose cases implicated self-defence.[12] Only two of them would be convicted of this most serious offence.

The Case against Kim

Kim's murder trial commenced 13 May 1998. Her family from Ontario and her friends filled the front row of the courtroom. In the prisoner's box, Kim clutched the rosary beads that she would finger throughout the trial.

Prosecutor Garry Rainnie's opening address sketched the evidence that Rainnie would call. Jennifer, the fourteen-year-old daughter of Kim and John, asked her father for the bedroom key when he returned home at 11 p.m. on 15 May 1997 because the door was locked and her mother failed to answer. On opening the door and seeing her mother with the gun, Jennifer let loose a small scream and turned to tell her father. Seconds later Jennifer saw her father fall backward from the bedroom doorway, blood spurting, while her mother stood holding the gun. Jennifer raced to call 9-1-1. She heard two more shots while she was on the telephone with emergency personnel. Three police officers attended the scene and found John lying in a pool of blood on the floor. Kim was conscious but wounded in the bedroom. The officers collected a suicide note from the bed.

Rainnie told the jury that Karla Sweeting would testify that she had accepted John's proposal of marriage four days prior to his death. Rainnie presented no motive for the murder, nor was he obliged to by law. It is enough if the Crown can prove intent to kill to secure a murder conviction. However, his reliance on Sweeting's evidence might suggest that Kim had killed her husband out of jealousy. Rainnie knew that the jury would need to make sense of why an ordinary woman like Kim would shoot and kill her husband, especially with both of her children in the house.

The Crown's first witness was Jennifer. Within minutes of taking the stand, she needed to take the first of several breaks, her eyes welling with tears.[13] Richard Wolson for the defence used the break to ask Justice Rodney H Mykle to inform jurors that he was not permitted to deliver his opening address immediately after that of the prosecutor: "[T]hey may feel, well, why isn't the defence saying something[?]"[14] After the break, Jennifer's grandmother sat beside Jennifer as a support person, as contemplated by the *Criminal Code*.[15] Jennifer testified that her mother said she might not be home that evening, uncharacteristically, and to take her house keys when she went out. When Jennifer found her parents' bedroom door locked on her return, she suspected that her mother was home after all. Rainnie asked

Jennifer to label stick figures on a sketch "mother" and "father" and to describe the blood and tissue emanating from her father's body as he fell.

Jennifer pinpointed the location of her father's guns throughout the house – in the laundry room, in her brother's bedroom, under her parents' bed, and in the family room.[16] She acknowledged that Sweeting was her father's girlfriend and that her mother "suspected." Jennifer "had to babysit for Karla's kids"[17] but did not know that Karla and her father were engaged to be married or if her mother was aware of their plans.

Wolson's cross-examination of Jennifer was anything but hostile. Delicately, Wolson led her through all the evidence that Rainnie had declined to elicit. This was painful for Jennifer, because Wolson probed her father's abuse of her mother, herself, and her brother with a cadence that repeatedly reinforced her father's cruelty:

Q: And for as long as you can remember your father would verbally abuse your mother.

A: Yes.

Q: He yelled at her all the time, didn't he.

A: Yes.

Q: What are the kinds of things he said to her when he yelled at her?

A: He called her a bitch and said that she was worthless, fat, and lazy.

Q: A bitch and worthless, fat, and lazy. How many jobs did your mother work at?

A: Two.

Q: What time did she start work?

A: Seven-thirty.

Q: Seven-thirty in the morning?

A: Yeah.

Q: And what time did she finish work?

A: Ten-thirty.

Q: She worked more than twelve hours a day.

A: Yes.

Q: And she took care of the house as well.

A: Yes.

Q: She cooked when she was home?

A: Yeah.

Q: And your father called her a lazy bitch?

A: Yeah.

Q: And he said these things to her, putting her down and calling her names for as long as you can remember. Isn't that right?

A: Yes.

Q: And her reaction to all of this was that she would cry a lot, wouldn't she.

A: Yes.

Q: She didn't fight back too often, did she.

A: No.

Q: And if she fought back it would just get worse. Isn't that so.

A: Yeah.

Q: He was always putting her down, wasn't he.

A: Yeah.

Q: And embarrassing and humiliating her.

A: Yes.

Q: Your father totally dominated and controlled your mother, didn't he.

A: Yeah.

Q: How would you describe him? What word would you use to describe your father?

A: A tyrant.[18]

The lack of interrogatory punctuation as well as the use of "didn't he" and "isn't that so" suggest that Wolson's questions to Jennifer were statements needing only her affirmation. Wolson was a master of rhetoric. Although the prosecutor had not yet unleashed a powerful narrative account to condemn Kim – just the bare fact that she had killed her husband – Wolson wasted no time introducing another story. Of course, leading questions are the prerogative of the cross-examiner, but this was a skilled monologue presented as a dialogue. This style of rhetoric risks the appearance of a manipulated performance,[19] but Jennifer's youth and her distress likely made the need for direction obvious to the jury. Wolson's interchange with the Crown's first and most important witness, delivered within seconds of commencing his cross-examination, might have begun to shift the jury's sympathies.

Wolson continued, through Jennifer, to expose the "private" life of the deceased and the pain that he had caused to his family. Using the same pattern and pace, Wolson asked Jennifer to agree that she had frequently seen bruises on her mother, her mother often wore turtlenecks in summer, her father had put his fist through a door in their home, and she had heard her father yell "I'll kill you!" on the phone before driving to her mother's place of work. This threat had prompted Jennifer to call and warn her mother.

A written transcript has a muting effect on the lived reality of a criminal trial, but Jennifer's anxiety was palpable as the cross-examination continued. Emma Cunliffe says that a transcript is "merely a similitude of the spoken proceedings it represents."[20] Although trial transcripts are seen as exact renditions of the event, transcription is unable to record all oral communication, such as sighing, gasping, or weeping. Choices are made about punctuation, spelling, even words themselves by the transcriber when the witness's enunciation or meaning is unclear; judges are given opportunities to correct transcripts. Although transcripts cannot effectively convey nonverbal cues such as facial expression, tone of voice, manner of dress, and indicia of social class and "race," this transcript does record some of the emotion of the witnesses and even of counsel.

Austin Sarat suggests that transcripts must be read also for their silences, for what "cannot-be-said."[21] Wolson caused Jennifer to panic when he noted that she was seeing counsellors to deal with her relationship with her father. The weight of what "cannot-be-said" increased her suffering in the stand. Wolson asked her if she was okay, then said "[t]ake a deep breath, and tell the judge if you need a break, and if you do, by all means."[22] Jennifer had learned not to talk back to her father and to do what he told her to do. He had grabbed her arm and slapped her face; he had called her a bitch; and, proposed Wolson, "there were other times where your dad has done things to you that you told me that you don't want to talk about?"[23] Thus, what is presented as evidence and recorded on a transcript is not the whole or the only truth. As Cunliffe comments, "[t]he stories told in the legal forum are not necessarily the same stories that the speaker would tell at a different time, in a different place, to a different audience."[24]

Later in cross-examination Wolson reminded Jennifer that she was angry "at everybody" when she first provided a statement to the police: "[Y]ou weren't telling everything in terms of the whole situation in the family. You didn't want to talk about it, did you."[25] He also stated: "You're [sic] come here today and you've talked to the members of the jury about your family life, and I know it hasn't been easy but I'm accepting that what you've told them is all true."[26] Jennifer answered yes to both questions.

Here Wolson attempted, indirectly, to explain why her evidence at trial had shifted from her first statements to the police, when she had little good to say about her mother. Children who have been injured by fathers who also abuse their mothers have conflicting feelings about both parents. They might feel angry toward their fathers but still love and idealize them.[27] They also often feel abandoned and therefore angry with their mothers for failing to protect them,[28] even when there was little or nothing their mothers could do. When their mother then kills their father, children might be sad and angry yet relieved. What a confusing mess of feelings for Jennifer, especially when forced to testify against her mother.

Her father's treatment of Chris, her twelve-year-old brother, Jennifer agreed, was "even worse." Chris, the jurors learned, had been hit so hard by his father that he had marks on his body and had been removed by Child and Family Services for six weeks a few years earlier. Chris, Jennifer, and their mother had been forced to lie about his injuries; her mother and brother had fled to a women's shelter, leaving Jennifer alone with her father. Here again Jennifer struggled to continue.[29]

Wolson developed a portrait of Jennifer's father: "Would it be fair to say your mother virtually had nothing and your father had all kinds of toys?" The jury learned that her father had owned two boats, a pool table, a truck, all sorts of new clothes, and a massive weapons collection. Showing photograph after photograph, Wolson repeatedly asked Jennifer to identify shotguns, rifles, handguns, machetes, bayonets, ammunition clips, boxes of ammunition, bows and arrows, another forty-seven or forty-eight rifles, expensive reloading machines, all belonging to "[m]y dad."[30] Sweeting was not her father's first girlfriend. Far from it. Jennifer recalled at least four earlier girlfriends.[31]

Wolson used cross-examination to get the "why didn't she leave?" question out in the open, before it could begin to trouble the jurors as they listened to the terrible life that Kim had faced:

Q: And you asked your mother on a number of different occasions throughout the years why she continued to live there and not leave, and what was her response?
A: She was there for us.
Q: She was there for you. To protect you.[32]

Wolson thus used a question that is usually a hostile one to shine a light on Kim's love for her children and her ability to put them first. He reminded Jennifer that her mother had stood up for her and Chris against their father, even though he would then go after her.[33] Jennifer's mother was not in the least unhappy about her father's extramarital relationships. When John was out with his girlfriends, Kim told Jennifer, "at least there's peace at home, and I can be with my two children."[34] Any "jealous wife" motive that Rainnie might float was deflated.

Wolson also drew from Jennifer a very different interpretation of the night's events than that presented by Rainnie. Before the shooting, she overheard her father yelling angrily at her mother, telling her to kill herself, she should have done it before, and that she was to make it look like an accident so that he could collect insurance money. "And you heard him say that if he had the money he could live better and take care of the kids better." "Yes."[35] Jennifer confronted her mother, but her father became "very, very angry." Dinner at the family table on 15 May was eerily quiet. It was followed by her father screaming at her mother in their bedroom. Her father stomped out soon after, gun in hand. Jennifer's story was backed by her and her mother's discovery of two insurance policies after John's death. Both policies on Kim's and John's lives had been taken out by John on 1 April 1997. The defence entered the documents as exhibits.[36]

By the time that he finished with this first Crown witness, Wolson had managed to put before the jury all the elements of self-defence. But the rhetorical device that surely stuck with the jurors came at great personal cost to Jennifer and her mother:

Q: You had a dog, a cocker spaniel?

A: Yes.

Q: Your father was quite attached to that dog, wasn't he. He liked that dog.

A: Yes.

Q: He treated that dog particularly well, didn't he.

A: Yeah.

Q: As a matter of fact, if the dog had an accident or did something that your father was unhappy about, he would just accept it from the dog, wouldn't he.

A: Yes.

Q: But if your mother ever did anything that he was unhappy with, the [sic] didn't accept that, did he.

A: No.

Q: Who was treated better in that house, the dog or your mother?

A: The dog.

Q: By your father.

A: Yes.[37]

The Crown's attempt to re-examine Jennifer failed miserably. By this time, Jennifer had found her voice. When Rainnie suggested that her mother had assumed the traditional parenting role, leaving discipline to her father,

Jennifer balked: "She didn't have a choice."[38] When asked to agree that her brother got into trouble requiring fatherly discipline, she again balked: "Not that bad."[39]

Rainnie asked whether Jennifer's father took her mother with him to gun shows on the weekends. Wolson objected: this was not a proper question for re-examination since he had not raised it in cross-examination. Rainnie submitted that "essentially the defence's position is that Ms Kondejewski was isolated from the public by essentially being a prisoner in her own home. I think this is going to go to the defence being raised by my learned friend."[40] The defence had staked out no such position. In fact, Wolson's questions to Jennifer had revealed that Kim worked outside the home in two different jobs. However, it was clear that Wolson was building a case for self-defence and would be relying on Battered Woman Syndrome.

The problem is that Battered Woman Syndrome evidence lends itself to generalizations that can undercut a self-defence claim, allowing lawyers to fall into oversimplifying distortions and stereotypes.[41] Here Rainnie hoped to show that, because Kim was not isolated and imprisoned in her home, she was not a "real" battered woman. As discussed in Chapter 1, Dr Lenore Walker, the originator of the theory, does not claim that a woman must literally be "imprisoned."

Over Wolson's objections, Justice Mykle directed Jennifer to answer. Her mother did not accompany her father to gun fairs, did not belong to any organizations or clubs, and was never away from her children in the evenings unless she was working.[42] Rainnie struck out.

Rainnie then asked Jennifer to expand on her evidence that her father had yelled at her mother for failing to kill herself. Her father, she explained, had been referring to the weekend before, when her mother had gone to Winnipeg. The children had been told that she needed "to get away," but Jennifer had learned the truth from overhearing her father screaming:

A: She went to Winnipeg the weekend, that weekend, and he told her how to do it.
Q: How to do?
A: Kill herself, get in a car accident.[43]

Rainnie closed with this witness and moved on to the technical proof of his case against Kim, and here he was on far more solid ground. He called Sergeant Rodney Koscielny, who described the scene and the evidence: the gun, shell casings, and the note that Kim had left on the bed.

Wolson asked him if the police had engaged in "good police work" by questioning neighbours about violence at the address. Koscielny explained that this had been done by other police officers, but Rainnie spoke up to say that these officers would not be called as witnesses by the Crown. He offered that Wolson was free to call them as his witnesses.[44]

Members of the jury might not have appreciated that a defence lawyer would be taking a huge risk in calling an investigating officer as a witness, but they might have begun to wonder about the objectivity of the Crown. Why were the witnesses and the evidence so selectively presented by one charged with securing justice?

Wolson had the officer read the words that Kim had written:

Jen and Chris, Please forgive me for what I've done. Just know in your hearts I had no choice. I couldn't let him destroy this family any further. In years to come try to understand what I put up with. I love you both dearly and I'm sorry it came to this. You'll be better off without either one of us because we are both too screwed up to help you. I love you dearly. Mum.[45]

Rainnie then called Constable Marc Kowal, who described the location of John's body and Kim's condition. He testified that "firearms [were] scattered throughout the house."[46] Wolson's cross-examination painted a terrifying picture of John's weapons collection. Kowal saw guns, bayonets, "boxes upon boxes of ammunition, ... military paraphernalia," and reloading machines in the home. Although Kowal could not specifically recall the bows and arrows, clips of ammunition, handguns, rockets, and grenades, Wolson called the jury's attention to the photos of these items removed from the house. In his eight years on the force, Kowal had never seen such an extensive weapons cache.[47]

Dr Michael Petrinak, Medical Examiner for Manitoba, was Rainnie's next witness. Three shells had been fired into the body. Wolson's cross-examination revealed that John was well muscled and that the injuries to his left arm and hand were consistent with an attempt to grab the barrel of the shotgun.[48]

Rainnie's final police witness, Sergeant Robert James, had photographed much of the evidence found in the house. Only through Wolson's cross-examination did it emerge that the military had come to the house after the shooting and seized certain articles. James had neither seen nor photographed them, but Wolson used his denials to enter into evidence a litany of weapons.[49] He asked Sergeant James, rhetorically, "[d]o you know why you'd need rockets in Brandon, in a house?"[50] Wolson summed up: "[O]ver a hundred kinds of dangerous weapons ... not including bows and arrows and knives and machetes and bayonets."[51]

Lest the jury think this the mere inventory of a weapons collector, Wolson asked: "Gun collectors can't have rockets in their homes, can they?" On receiving James's negative answer, he continued "or grenades?" or "contraband that bomb disposal units have to get rid of?" He was referring to a find by another officer: "Gunpowder in furnace room on floor, steel wool exposed, gas, paint. Powder keg ready to blow."[52] Wolson mused out loud: none of the officers called by the Crown was a firearms expert; the officer who had removed and catalogued the extensive weapons collection was missing from the Crown witness list. Again jurors might have wondered whether the Crown was presenting the whole picture.

Wolson used James to plant one more seed. Referring to a photograph of the bedroom closet whose top shelf held videotapes, he asked: "Pornography?" "I have no idea." "So if I suggest to you that they are pornographic movies you can't say one way or the other. You didn't look?" "No, sir."[53] The jury was left waiting for the other shoe to drop.

Rainnie's last witness was Sweeting, John's "fiancée." She was a single mother of two children who was completing her BSc in psychology and planned to continue with her master's degree and PhD. She had been involved romantically with John for three years: he had told her that he and his wife had been separated for some time. By the spring of 1997, they were seeing each other every night after supper and most days for lunch. On Mother's Day 1997, four days before his death, John proposed marriage. Sweeting spent the evening of 15 May with him at a gun club, and then they went out for coffee before he dropped her off at home. He seemed quite distracted that night.[54]

John had never been violent or threatened Sweeting. Of her relationship, she said "I thought we were close."[55] She had spent many evenings – at least a dozen – at "John's" house watching movies, often for three hours or more. Although his children were always there, she had never seen Kim at the house. Nor had she expected to. She had, however, spoken to her on the telephone several times and left messages for John with Kim. Kim had never once asked her who she was or questioned her relationship with John.

Wolson handled her cross-examination with compassion. "This man," he began, "you know today ... was living two separate lives." John had never separated from his wife: "he played you for a fool." Sweeting responded: "Yes, that's how I feel."[56] John had massively deceived her, her background in psychology notwithstanding.

Wolson again embarked on a series of questions that affirmed Sweeting's innocence and John's brutality.

Q: Did he tell you that he smacked his wife, hit her?
A: No.
Q: Kicked her?
A: No.
Q: Punched her?
A: No.
Q: No. Abused her, demeaned her?
A: No.
Q: Put her down?
A: No.
Q: Called her a lazy fat bitch. Did he tell you that?
A: No, he didn't.
Q: No. Treated her like a dog. Did he tell you that?
A: No.
Q: No. You wouldn't have been very impressed with a man like that at all, would you.
A: No, I wouldn't have been.[57]

Wolson asked whether Sweeting knew that John had punched his son in the face? Choked him? Yelled in his face and called him useless? Hit his daughter? "You didn't know this man at all, did you?" "I guess not."[58] Sweeting was unaware that Kim lived in the house because, as Wolson suggested, "there didn't seem to be much clothing belonging to her."[59] She answered: "There didn't seem to be any there." Only once did she see a pair of shoes belonging to Kim, which had "genuinely upset" John: he had raged that Kim was prohibited from entering "his" house without his permission.[60]

Had John told Sweeting that Kim worked two jobs, sometimes fifteen or sixteen hours a day? "No." Kim had always been polite to Sweeting on the phone, but John's response on hearing that Kim had taken her phone messages had been to tell Sweeting that "she [Kim] wasn't supposed to be in the house": John would change the locks to keep her out.[61] Sweeting and John had watched movies in his home – not pornographic ones. But, she said, "[h]e had told me that he had an extensive collection."[62]

Wolson returned to the night of the homicide. For some reason, Sweeting had told police, John wanted her to go with him to his gun club; he was distracted and distant.

> Q: Did he tell you that he had told his wife that she should kill herself that night?
> A: No.
> Q: And that he was to be with you because that was going to be an alibi for him?
> A: I was not aware of it.
> Q: You wouldn't have been with a monster like that, would you?
> A: No.[63]

Wolson's final questions for Sweeting made for a dramatic conclusion. Wolson returned to Mother's Day, when John had proposed co-habitation and marriage to Sweeting. He suggested that Mother's Day is usually spent with one's wife and children. He continued: "In order to get married his wife would have to be out of the picture, right?" "Right," Sweeting replied.[64] With that, he thanked the witness.

Rainnie then closed the case for the prosecution, having presented the physical evidence, Jennifer's account, and Sweeting's observations of John that night. At the same time, these witnesses had been deployed by Wolson to generate a solid evidentiary basis for self-defence.

In the absence of the jury, Wolson argued two motions for the defence. First, he asked the judge to dismiss the charge of first-degree murder, leaving second-degree murder as the sole charge. He argued that the Crown had failed to provide any evidence of planning and deliberation supporting a first-degree murder charge. The grammar of the note, he said, showed that it was written after Kim shot John. Even if Jennifer's observation of Kim holding a gun moments before the homicide could be evidence of deliberation, there was nothing to suggest that she had planned a murder.

Rainnie countered that the note used the past tense only because it was intended to be read by the children after Kim had carried out her intentions. Furthermore, he said, a plan need not be elaborate to ground first-degree murder. Rainnie was right on the law: the standard for committal to send someone on to trial on a given charge is low[65] – too low, according to many defence lawyers. The judge agreed with Rainnie in a two-sentence ruling: he found that there was "some evidence" to support first-degree murder and declined to withdraw it from the jury.[66] Twenty-five years without parole were still on the line for Kim.

Christopher: The Witness No One Wanted

The defence's second motion, argued by co-counsel Darwyn Ross, asked the trial judge to call Kim's son Chris as a witness. Ross argued that Chris's story was part of the "narrative," especially since several Crown witnesses had already referred to Chris in their testimony. He had been called by the Crown at Kim's preliminary inquiry, showing that he had essential evidence to give. It would be unfair to force the defence to call him themselves, particularly since the defence would then not be able to lead the evidence of this young witness.

Rainnie opposed this motion on a narrow interpretation of the "narrative": since Chris was in the basement the night of the homicide, "[a]nd that's really why we're here,"[67] he had nothing essential to offer. Justice Mykle rejected this attempt to separate the homicidal moment from the larger context in which Kim acted. He decided to call Chris himself and allow both sides to cross-examine him.

Wolson was the first to question this boy, who, unlike Jennifer, needed no help in delivering his story to the jury. From him, they learned that his father's many possessions, beyond those already described by Jennifer, included a satellite television and a special chair. These were not family possessions: John had allowed no one to even touch any of these expensive purchases.[68]

Chris had experienced violence at the hand of his father; his mother's efforts to protect him had only increased his father's violence.[69] His father slapped and punched him in the face, woke him up in the middle of the night to force him to complete chores such as vacuuming, and burned his hand with a match to teach him not to play with matches.[70]

The incident that brought the intervention of Child and Family Services occurred when his mother was at work and his father slapped him repeatedly in the face until Chris finally yelled back at him. His father threw him down a flight of stairs and strangled him, leaving hand prints on his neck. His father then retrieved a shotgun and a box of shells and began walking back upstairs, where Chris had retreated. In terror, Chris jumped out the second-floor window.[71] He disclosed this assault to his teacher, who in turn contacted authorities. His father later explained his innocent intent: he was just getting his gun and ammunition to show Jennifer the weapon for her hunter safety training course.

Chris had witnessed many assaults by his father on his mother. He had seen him slap her in the face, choke her, punch her, kick her, throw an iron at her, and point a gun at her head and pull the trigger.[72] Chris had asked his mother why she did not leave, and she had told him that she stayed for him and his sister. His father had told her that if she left "he would hunt her down."[73] He heard his father threaten to kill his mother on many occasions and heard him order her to kill herself and make it look like an accident so that he could collect the insurance money.

More details about John's plan emerged from Chris's evidence: Kim was to rent a car in Winnipeg and drive it into a semi-trailer. Chris heard his father say "[i]f you fuck this up I'll kill you."[74] On 15 May, Chris came home after school to find his father yelling and his mother crying. After a quiet dinner, his father left for the evening. When Chris left to go out, his mother seemed very sad. She told him that she might not be there when he got home.[75]

Rainnie's cross-examination of Chris tried to minimize and rationalize John's abuse. Referring to Chris's evidence that his father yelled at his mother over the telephone while she was at work, Rainnie asked, "when you say 'yelling,' was he really yelling or was he arguing with her in a loud voice?" Answer: "Like he was screaming at her."[76] Rainnie suggested that his father had Chris's best interests at heart when he "disciplined" his son, but Chris disagreed: "[H]e would get mad ... because [the school] called him ... He didn't care unless it affected him."[77] Rainnie asked Chris whether he told his mother about all the violence. Chris did not, for "she might have talked to my dad about it and they'd just start another fight."[78]

The Defence Witnesses

Through cross-examination, Wolson had already developed a strong narrative of Kim as a hard worker and an exemplary mother. This contrasted with John's portrayal of her as fat, worthless, stupid, lazy, a loser, and a bitch.

Wolson first called Sharon Struth, Kim's co-worker at Assiniboine Community College Food Services. She described Kim as "a very caring, sincere, very good person."[79] On a daily basis, she drove Kim to work for her 6 a.m. shift; Kim would then wait until 7:30 a.m. for her own shift to start. At 2:30 p.m., Struth would drive Kim to her second job at McDonald's, where she worked until approximately 10 or 10:30 p.m. Struth testified that Kim was often crying when she picked her up at 5:40 a.m. She had seen many bruises and marks on her and had observed her limping.[80] When Struth asked about her injuries and distress, Kim admitted that her husband had hit her.

John frequently called Kim's place of work. He treated Struth like "his slave" and was obnoxious to her on the telephone and even worse in person when he showed up at the workplace.[81] Kim was a happy, confident person when John was not around, but her personality changed completely in his presence – "very … quiet, you know, very down."[82] She lived for her children, according to Struth. When she asked Kim why she did not leave, Kim told her that he would not let her take the kids and would kill her.[83]

Rainnie asked Struth why Kim had not sought medical treatment. "If John found out that she was, then it would be another beating."[84] Rainnie tried to ascertain Kim's role in the arguments and whether Kim ever hit John back. Struth answered: "If you knew John you wouldn't hit him back."[85] Rainnie then turned to John's army career, suggesting that it affected how John dealt with his family: "A little too much army?" Struth replied: "Oh! I couldn't have raised mine that way." He tried to normalize her shocked reaction by saying "[a]ll right. Too strict, obviously, you would say." "Oh!" was all she could manage.[86]

Rainnie asked Struth whether she was aware that John held something over Kim that stopped her from leaving the marriage. "Did he say that he might, for example, send something to her family or to friends that might be very embarrassing to her, that she could never stand for him to disclose? For example, pictures of her?" Struth acknowledged that John held something over Kim; he had told her that she would "never, ever get the kids."[87] Rainnie persisted, asking for other explanations of why Kim did not leave, as if only "embarrassment" kept her in John's power. Struth insisted that Kim would never leave the kids behind with John, who would have tracked her down and killed her if she left.

Rainnie asked Struth whether she was aware of "other problems that Chris may have had in terms of behaviour," hoping perhaps to undercut his damaging testimony. Struth asked Rainnie whether he was referring to "the beatings and that," but Rainnie said no, he was more interested in Chris's behavioural problems. Struth acknowledged that the Kondejewskis had "lots of problems with Chris."[88]

Wolson used his re-examination to clarify her remark regarding "the beatings." Struth explained: "John beat Christopher all the time … [E]very time Kimberley tried to protect Christopher then she got another beating."[89]

Wolson then called Amber Page, the nineteen-year-old next-door neighbour, to the stand. She had also worked with Kim when she held a job at

Walmart. Page described Kim as a very nice woman: "Whenever I could talk to her she was always very pleasant."[90] John forbade her from speaking to Kim.

Wolson asked Page to describe John. She could not contain her anger and contempt: "He was an asshole." Justice Mykle sternly rebuked her: "Witness, I appreciate your editorial comment, but there are other ways of conveying the same meaning without using what we would call vulgarity." Page rephrased: "He was an extremely mean man."[91] Wolson directed her that she should, however, use vulgar language if she were quoting John.

Page heard her neighbour screaming at his family every time he was home. She tried to block the sound out by closing the windows and blasting the volume on the television, but she could still hear his tirades. She witnessed John assault Jennifer, who was then ten or eleven years old, on their deck by wresting a broom away from her and whacking her hard across the back twice with it, yelling "[y]ou fucking idiot. What the fuck do you think you're doing?"[92] Page relayed another incident in Walmart when John began screaming profanities at his wife and pushed her. Security intervened, and he was asked to leave the premises.[93] She also testified that, when she was turning seventeen, she knocked on the door of the Kondejewski home, and as she spoke to Kim in the doorway John began screaming at Kim: "Get your fucking ass up here right now." He stormed downstairs, where Page asked him whether it was okay if she had a party that might cause some noise. He replied: "I don't fucking care. Just get the fuck out of here."[94] Page told the jury that she was afraid of John,[95] as were his children.[96] Rainnie declined cross-examination.

Kim Takes the Stand

Wolson anticipated Kim's anxiety and asked her to speak loudly and slowly. As she told her story, her "voice rose to choking sobs and fell to nearly indecipherable whispers."[97] She was from a military family, she testified, and she began dating John when she was fourteen years old after they met in the Air Cadets. Three years later she married him, under pressure from John, who claimed that he was about to be transferred to Germany: if they did not marry on the spot, he would not see her for five years. He never was transferred.

John adhered rigidly to sex role expectations, and "he was very jealous, very possessive. I wasn't allowed to work because no wife of his was going to work." "Things were to be his way. A man was in charge of the home. I was responsible for cooking and cleaning and he was responsible for bringing home a pay cheque."[98] It was her job to polish his military boots and to have sex on demand:

> He wanted it all the time ... [B]efore the kids were born he'd come home on his coffee breaks and expect to get it. He would come home at lunch and expect to get it, and if I ever turned him down then he would tell me it was a wife's responsibility and that it was his right to have it whenever he wanted it.[99]

These are typical demands of abusers,[100] and these are the material rewards of their behaviour.

It eventually became her job to support the family financially as John commandeered her paid labour as well as her unpaid labour: "It didn't matter what time I got home from work – he'd be home from around four o'clock. If I got home at ten o'clock I'd still be expected to cook a full meal and clean the house before I went to bed."[101] Kim lived like a pauper: John would haggle with her over whether she needed a new ten-dollar pair of shoes – she had only one pair, and she wore them to both of her jobs, holes and all.[102]

Kim made one attempt to leave before they had children. She could no longer bear his constant yelling: "He was phoning me at work and starting fights. He was coming down to work and yelling at me if something wasn't right ... Nothing was ever right, nothing was good enough."[103] The night she left he loaded a gun, and she thought he was going to shoot her. Instead, he locked himself in the apartment bathroom and fired a shot through the ceiling. Fortunately, the neighbour upstairs was not hurt, but John was convicted of firing a gun and lost his licence; his weapons were removed for five years. He pressed Kim to return, bringing her flowers and promises to change (even to share the housework), and enlisted his mother as his advocate. Kim succumbed. After she gave birth to Jennifer a short while later, she was truly trapped.

The delivery was so difficult that Kim later asked John to get a vasectomy. He refused – that was her problem. She tried to arrange her surgery but by then was already pregnant again. John's abuse escalated soon after Chris was born. John harangued Kim to return to work as soon as her unemployment benefits ran out while still expecting her to assume full responsibility for both babies. He complained about her weight, her low income, that she was not "satisfying him enough sexually,"[104] and that she "wasn't worth her rations."[105] He monitored her, demanding to know where she was, whom she was with, and when she would be home. He slapped, punched, and kicked her.[106]

Kim cried a lot, struggled with depression, and even tried to end her life several times. These suicide attempts made her even more vulnerable to John's power. When she broached the possibility of separating, John told her that she would never get the children because of her instability.[107] She was too afraid to seek legal advice. One of his stock phrases was that "what happened in the house stayed in the house and if it were to go outside the home that I would pay for it."[108] Kim began to internalize the abuse: "I was beginning to believe everything he was saying, that I wasn't worth anything, that I couldn't do anything right, that I was fat and everything he said about me." At this point, the transcript records her voice breaking.[109] Wolson responded: "I'm sorry."

Kim detailed the increasing violence: John pushed her down stairs, choked her, threw things at her, and raped her. He punched her in the stomach, kicked her thighs, and threw her into walls. She was working around the clock at two, sometimes three, jobs, but these were the times when she felt good about herself.[110]

Her children were everything to her, so John attacked her mothering skills. Kim sobbed: "He constantly told me that I wasn't there for the kids and that I wasn't a good mother."[111] While she was working evenings and weekends, John did not stay with the children but was out fishing, hunting, and dating. These relationships were her fault, John said, "because I wasn't doing enough for him sexually and I was too fat and I was too ugly to be seen with him in public, and he couldn't take me anywhere so he had to have somebody."[112]

Yet John undermined her efforts to lose weight. After Kim lost twenty-five pounds and was close to her weight when she was seventeen, he flatly pronounced: "You're still fat."[113] When she joined a gym, he forced her to quit, telling her that it took away from "family time" and that she "had no right."[114] On one occasion, Kim confided John's abuse to his mother, who responded: "Just protect the children."[115]

John told Kim that if she left "he would hunt me down like an animal and I wouldn't see it coming, and he didn't care who he took out with me."[116] By this point in his military career, he was in intelligence, so she had good reason to fear his ability to track and kill her. She did not contact the police – "I was afraid that they couldn't do enough and if he was arrested and got out on bail that he would kill me" – echoing the experience of many battered women.[117] Moreover, John did target practice with police friends at his shooting club and told her that "they were his buddies and they wouldn't believe me."[118] He had friends among the Brandon police, the RCMP, and the military.[119] Kim did not seek medical attention in spite of severe injuries to her throat, legs, and arms "because I would have to tell them how it happened, and then I would have to pay for it in the end."[120]

With Kim working outside the home and expressing her desire to separate, John had to find new ways to enforce her captivity. As Dr Judith Herman explains,[121] by making women violate their moral core, abusers seek to break their will to ensure compliance. John forced Kim to pose for explicit videotapes that he claimed he needed while he was away on secondment in Quebec so that he would not have to get a girlfriend.[122] He used violence to make her redo the shots when she failed to smile and act like she was enjoying it.[123] He later used these tapes to threaten her with exposure to her family and employees at work should she try to escape.[124]

John became obsessed with the idea that they would have sex with another couple. Kim said that at first he begged her to do it to show that she loved him, and then, when she refused to cooperate, he resorted to threats, then to rape. After three failed efforts, John finally forced Kim to participate. He swore that it would be the first and last time because "he would get what he wanted out of it." Even then he was angry because she had not waited until he was in the room to watch her have sex with another man.[125] He wanted her to describe the details so that he could enjoy what was for her a rape. By this point in her evidence, Kim was crying so hard that she could no longer speak. The court recessed.

After the break, Wolson directed Kim to the financial difficulties that had led John to insist that she kill herself. He had insisted they buy a house that they could not afford, forcing them to take a second mortgage. He had maxed out his credit card buying clothes and pursuing his pastimes, and he had two personal loans. She was already working two full-time jobs. Still he chided her for not doing enough for the family – she was "the family fuck-up."[126] Creditors were calling their home and John's work. Kim wanted to sell the house, but he refused – "he wasn't taking a step down."[127]

Kim testified that John first broached his suicide plan for her at Christmas in 1996. He thought that a drastic solution to their financial bind was needed. She should kill herself and make it look like an accident so that he could use the insurance proceeds to pay off the debts. He would give her a decent burial, he promised, and she would give her kids a better life because she was not a good mother anyway. He would be a better father to them if he were debt free as he would not be so stressed out and would stop abusing them.[128] Kim told him that he was crazy, that there were other solutions, but he would not let it go. He began waking her in the middle of the night to harangue her about his plan.

By February 1997, John had convinced Kim that their dilemma was her fault and that they would all be better off without her. Suicide is a mortal sin to Roman Catholics like Kim. His insistence that she end her own life struck yet another blow to her moral core and her very personhood. His first plan was that she would rent a car in Winnipeg and drive head on into a tractor trailer on the highway. She did rent a car and drove to Winnipeg but could not follow through and hurt another driver.[129] When Kim returned home, John was furious and went on a violent rampage, throwing her over furniture and punching and kicking her. She promised to try again, and he continued to wake her up at night to enforce his relentless campaign. Kim embarked on a repeat journey in early May, but again she sat in her hotel room crying and praying. John was seething: "I had wasted his money again ... I fucked up everything I touched."[130]

John told Kim that time was running out, she testified. She had to do it by 15 May, when all the bills would be coming in. This time he decided that she would electrocute herself by plunging his electric razor into a sink of water. She did as he demanded, but nothing happened. John raged in a violent fit. He then instructed her to drop the radio into her bath. Kim prepared for her death, crying and praying, but again nothing happened. John was beside himself but would not give up. He frayed the electric cord of the radio so that she could make things right by killing herself. This time she did not obey because she had become ill and could not get out of bed.

Now Kim had really done it. The next day was 15 May, and John ran through everything that she had to do to make sure that it appeared an accident. She must do it when he was at work so that he would have an alibi. Kim did as he demanded, but again nothing happened: she sat shaking and crying in the tub with the live radio in the water beside her. She panicked when he called and she answered the phone. John came roaring home from work, "flying through the door ... 'You fucking bitch, how could you do this to us?'"[131] After assaulting Kim, he demanded that she come up with a plan for her "accidental" death. If she got it wrong, then he would hunt down every member of her family.

During the next few hours, he repeatedly demanded to know what her plan was. Kim tried to make dinner and keep her children calm throughout, but she just could not think. Her only idea was to "fall" into the river and drown because she could not swim, but John told her that would look like suicide and there would be no insurance payout for him. Finally, it was time. He left to go to the gun club so that he would have an alibi: "His parting words were if I was alive when he got home he would kill the kids and then me because he'd have nothing left to lose."[132]

Kim was devastated. John had never before threatened to kill Jennifer and Christopher. And he told her that it was a promise, not a threat. Like other battered women who kill, she identified a change in his patterns that signalled to her that something had shifted and her endangerment had reached an acute level.[133]

Kim sat in her darkened bedroom holding a gun to feel safe and trying to think. She cried and prayed, hoping for a miracle. Time passed. The next thing she knew the door flew open, and John was screaming at her, charging toward her. She closed her eyes and pulled the trigger. He fell, and as she approached he tried to grab the gun. As they struggled, it fired again, hitting their dog, which loped off whimpering. Then, she said, the gun "went off" again. Kim testified that it was a pump action gun – she had been taught to pump it automatically after discharging a shell.

"Why did you do it?" asked Wolson. "I didn't want him hurting the kids. The kids didn't deserve it." The transcriber notes that "THIS WHOLE SECTION HAS BEEN DIFFICULT AS THE WITNESS WAS CHOKED WITH WEEPING ... LONG PAUSE FOR HER TO REGAIN CONTROL."[134] Kim could not recall when in the sequence of events she wrote the note to her children, but it was before she fired the gun at her abdomen.

Rainnie tread carefully in cross-examination of Kim, possibly to avoid appearing to victimize her further in front of the jury. Nevertheless, his questions required her to elaborate on painful details. Her voice kept dropping to a whisper according to reporters.[135] She was reminded repeatedly to speak up.

Rainnie started off with what he euphemistically called "wife swapping," asking Kim to provide details. Without challenging his use of this benign phrase to capture her experience of facilitated rape, Kim said that she and Jennifer found John's correspondence when they were packing up the house after it was sold. They discovered, to Kim's shock, that until his death John had been trading photographs of Kim with other men. Rainnie quickly abandoned this topic.

He then asked whether Kim and John explored financial counselling or bankruptcy. Her answer only strengthened the defence. John rejected financial counselling because he claimed that he would be kicked out of the military if he declared bankruptcy. Rainnie asked Kim to explain how she and

Chris ended up in a women's shelter after Chris was removed by Child and Family Services. Chris ran away from Child and Family Services and threatened to commit suicide if he was not allowed to stay with his mother, so a night at a shelter was the compromise. Rainnie asked Kim if her family helped with their debt, and she explained that John had assaulted her to get her to lie to her family to obtain their aid. Why, Rainnie asked, did she not seek confidential legal advice or counselling? She was afraid that John would find out: he had once found a shelter telephone number in her pocket, for which he beat her.

When Rainnie asked her when she quit "trying" to make their marriage work, Kim clarified: "As in I wasn't going to try to lose weight any more because nothing was ever good enough, and I wasn't going to participate in his – other activities."[136] Even had Kim persisted in the self-abnegation required to make her abusive marriage "work," John would not have been happy until she took the final step by committing suicide.

The only tough questions came later in cross-examination. Kim admitted to Rainnie that John was not carrying a weapon when he entered her bedroom that night.[137] Rainnie asserted that Kim was involved in another relationship. He was forced to apologize and admit that he had bad information when she told him that was incorrect.[138] Rainnie then accused her of believing that John deserved to die. She answered quietly: "No one deserves to die."[139]

His last question to her was about her purchase of lottery tickets. Hoping perhaps to secure an admission of planning and deliberation, he asked: "Did you ever dream o[r] fantasize what it would be like without him, not to have him around?" "No," she answered, "just ... where we talked about ... the kids and I leaving and he could have everything."[140]

Wolson did not re-examine his witness. No serious damage had been done.

The Expert and the Syndrome

Wolson then called Dr Fred Shane to the stand – the same psychiatrist who had testified for Lavallee in her 1987 murder trial in Winnipeg. In some ways, calling an expert witness at this point was both unnecessary and risky. It was unnecessary because Kim's evidence provided a solid evidentiary foundation for self-defence, and John's abuse was corroborated by many other witnesses, including his demand that Kim commit suicide.

Introducing Dr Shane's evidence was risky because the psychiatrist could undercut self-defence inadvertently. First, he had been excluded from the courtroom during the trial and so was unaware of what had been said by other witnesses, most importantly Kim. There was a real possibility that he could contradict her account of the homicide. With the exception of the accused person, who has a legal right to be present for the whole trial, witnesses are excluded from the courtroom until they have given their testimony. This practice is based on the premise that witnesses might consciously or unconsciously shade their evidence in response to what they have heard and so must not have their evidence "tainted."

Wolson, like many defence lawyers in these cases, had requested that his expert be allowed to sit in and hear the testimony of others, particularly that of Kim. This exception is to enable the witness to testify with a wider knowledge base about the evidence. Crown attorneys often do not object to this request,[141] but Rainnie did.

Second, Dr Shane's testimony could muddy the waters for the defence. By framing Kim's actions in terms of the "syndrome," Dr Shane would be attaching a psychiatric label that could damage her credibility. Furthermore, self-defence requires "reasonableness" of both the woman's belief that she was in grave danger and her belief that she had no recourse other than to kill. By casting Kim as suffering from a syndrome, Dr Shane could imply that she was mentally ill and thus largely *un*reasonable.[142] And if the woman deviates from the generalizations used to describe Battered Woman Syndrome, she can be vulnerable to conviction.[143]

Third, reliance on Battered Woman Syndrome evidence is also potentially damaging for women on trial on a personal level. Recovery from battering and captivity demands not only mourning violence and loss but also recognizing one's courage and survival skills as part of reclaiming the self and resisting future abuse.[144]

In fact, Kim sought to avoid John's worst moments by telephoning before arriving home, gauging his moods, and delaying her return to the house. She intervened to shield her children in any way available and to divert her husband's wrath away from them and toward herself. She turned herself inside out trying to appease John. She tried to leave the relationship on one occasion. She reported to the police when he fired a gun through the bathroom ceiling. She disclosed his violence to family members and colleagues and told him repeatedly that she wanted to leave.

Such acts seem to fly in the face of "learned helplessness," the main diagnostic criterion for Battered Woman Syndrome. Thus, defence lawyers like Wolson do not emphasize these strategies of resistance to juries.[145] Even if acquittal is ultimately secured, the courage and resourcefulness of the woman

– qualities that she will need for her recovery – are downplayed or sub-merged. As Evan Stark recounts,

> Battered women often complain that they do not recognize themselves in their representation as pathetic victims of another's will in the courtroom. What they mean is that the portrait of their victimization fails to capture the feverish and moment-to-moment calculation by which they have at-tempted to retain their integrity while keeping themselves safe. A woman who had mounted a traditional battered woman's defense told me that she felt like her ex-partner was talking during a closing argument in which her lawyer stressed her abuse-induced incapacities.[146]

The Crown did not contest Dr Shane's expertise, but Wolson nonethe-less ensured that the jury knew that Dr Shane had treated hundreds of battered women and qualified as an expert witness in courts in six prov-inces. He had met with Kim on three occasions, interviewed both of her children, and visited their family home, which he described as conveying "a sense of despair, a family that had been ravished ... [I]t was like attending a graveyard."[147]

Dr Shane retold Kim's story in its essential features, carefully matching her to the profile of Battered Woman Syndrome. He used the word "clas-sical" nine times[148] to describe how the relationship and Kim fit the syn-drome. He told the jury that she was "highly authentic."[149] Her belief that John would hunt her down and kill her if she left or contacted the police was honest. John's use of brainwashing to get Kim to take her own life was, Dr Shane said, "a form of murder."[150]

The major theme in his evidence was that John's threat to kill the chil-dren was the turning point for Kim.[151] Over and over Dr Shane stated that her children were her life – "they were sacred to her, they were precious."[152] Her act, he said, was not intentional: "This was a mother's instinct to pro-tect her children."[153] Dr Shane assessed John at "very high risk" for killing his children.[154] Just before Wolson closed his examination-in-chief, he asked: "Do you have any doubt at all that what she did, she did to defend her chil-dren?" "I have no doubt," Dr Shane replied.[155]

In spite of this strong testimony, some of the risks of Battered Woman Syndrome evidence materialized. Dr Shane declared that Kim was "a clas-sical victim of the Battered Woman's Syndrome,"[156] repeating[157] that she was a victim "of the syndrome." Although the jury could not have missed that

John was the agent of Kim's suffering, this unfortunate word choice allowed his responsibility to be obscured, even if momentarily.

Dr Shane also located the barriers to escape in Kim's mind rather than her objective reality. He drew on an analogy used to explain "learned helplessness," derived from experiments in which caged dogs are repeatedly shocked when they attempt to escape from the cage. Then, when the cage is opened, the dogs no longer try to escape, even in the absence of further shocks.[158] Dr Shane explained that Kim had become "trapped psychologically."[159] In cross-examination, he said:

> She was trapped. It's very disorganizing, frightening, and there's a fence, a psychological steel wire fence around it. You don't see it but it's in her mind, and she's traumatized and she's a victim. She's a prisoner of war. She sees no hope. This is in her head, and that's the issue when you look at battered women with this sort of history who have fallen into this trap of helplessness and the hopelessness. It looks like they can escape, but if you're standing there, if you draw an analogy and you're a prisoner of war and you see people out there with guns you know that if you try to escape it's useless.[160]

Dr Shane contradicted Kim's evidence in several material respects. He said that Kim recalled Jennifer entering the bedroom when she was sitting in the dark holding the gun, a fact that she did not remember when testifying. Dr Shane acknowledged that Kim had not mentioned the note that she had written until their last session. More worryingly, his description of the three shots fired by Kim into her husband's body conveyed a more deliberate series of acts than those relayed by Kim. Finally, Dr Shane could not dispute the possibility that Kim wrote the note before her husband came home[161] – a key element in Rainnie's first-degree murder theory.

Fortunately for Kim, Dr Shane was an experienced witness who avoided some of the other traps that Rainnie attempted to set. Dr Shane insisted that when the note was written was irrelevant: this was not a premeditated act. Rather, Kim was reacting to "the lethality of the moment."[162] Rainnie proposed that Kim realized the only path to survival was to kill John. Even then Dr Shane resisted: "I don't think she formulated it that way. I think at that point – you know, you're an animal trapped in the jungle ... There's an instinctive survival."[163]

Rainnie questioned whether it was consistent with her fear for the safety of her children that Kim did nothing to get them out of the house before

John returned. Again Dr Shane defended Kim, describing John as a stalker from whom she saw no escape. Rainnie closed his cross-examination, having at least unearthed some inconsistencies in the evidence.

Wolson leapt back in to briefly re-examine so that Dr Shane could explain that he could only guess at the exact sequence of events after Kim shot her husband. He did not know how many minutes passed between when Kim fired the last shot at John and when she turned the gun on herself. Wolson closed his case.

Then, in the absence of the jury, Wolson argued to Justice Mykle that he should, in fairness, be permitted to give his closing address after Rainnie's, as an exception to what he called a "bad rule." Predictably, his motion was rejected, but Wolson still wanted his effort noted on the legal record, "in the event that matters change in the future, and I'm sure they will somewhere down the line."[164] What he did achieve, however, was the judge's agreement that, if Rainnie's summation were to raise matters not addressed by Wolson, he would get the last word after all.

Addressing the Jury

Wolson's summation to the jury was a masterpiece of rhetoric and a passionate defence of his client. Kim's father, seated with family members, wept during the summation.[165] Wolson repeated John's "haunting" threat on the night of the homicide and reminded the jury at least eleven times that Kim's sole motive was to protect her children: "[W]hat she did, she did to defend her children. She didn't care about herself. She did it to protect her children."[166] He told them that they could not, on the evidence presented, come to a conclusion of guilt beyond a reasonable doubt.

Wolson listed all the important aspects of Kim's defence on which Rainnie had not cross-examined or offered contrary evidence, leaving her defence intact. Rainnie had failed to challenge the evidence that John had abused his wife and children; he had failed to challenge Dr Shane's expertise or the "cold, hard fact" that Kim suffered from Battered Woman Syndrome; and he had not challenged that she had killed John in self-defence and had not planned the homicide.

Wolson shifted from a matter-of-fact rendition of the failures of the Crown case to an angry condemnation. In doing so, he took the jurors into his confidence:

And Mr Rainnie – and I couldn't believe it when he did this – he cross-examined Christopher, trying to say to him, Your father just wanted you to do well, and he was just trying to discipline him. Discipline you? Burning his hand with a match when he was six or seven years old? Punching him in the face? Choking him? There are teachers on this jury, there are parents on this jury. You love your children, you nurture them, you provide stability for them. You don't carry on like this beast, throwing him down flights of stairs, choking him, kicking him, throwing things at him, taking part of a cupboard and hurling it at him.[167]

Wolson confessed his strategic shift to the jurors on how to handle John's "fiancée." "[A]s I came out to Brandon and was preparing the case, I thought, I'm going to rip into Karla Sweeting in cross-examination, how could she be out with a man that was married. And then I realized – and I didn't do that by the way – and I realized that she too was a victim."[168]

Wolson cast the jurors as Kim's protector: "Fight for Kim. No one has in so many years."[169] "She throws herself upon you for protection."[170] At one point in his address, Wolson seemed to choke up: "Sorry if I get emotional. I've never seen anything like this. This abuse is – it's beyond words."[171]

Wolson told jurors: "There aren't enough adjectives to describe this man, this despicable human being that he was. And raping her, raping her. And forcing her to have all kinds of disgusting sexual acts on camera, and beating her if she didn't. To engage in sexual relations with another man so he could watch – just despicable. It's unthinkable brutality. It's unthinkable!"[172]

In his one-hour address, Wolson used every negative adjective that he could conjure up to dehumanize the deceased, calling him a lunatic, sadistic, a horrible human being, a sickening human being, a tyrant, a monster, disgusting, a beast, a predator, selfish, a poor excuse for a man, a murderer, an executioner, and a horrible, horrible beast. He told the jury that Kim's Mother's Day gift from her husband was "[e]lectrocution. She was on Death Row, Ladies and Gentlemen ... He was her executioner and it was going to be by way of electrocution."[173]

His last words to the jury were that Kim had already spent seventeen years imprisoned. Wolson asked them to give Kim her freedom back so that she could get her life with her children back together. He delivered a final impassioned plea: "I ask, Ladies and Gentlemen, that you find her not guilty. She begs you for that chance, that verdict, not guilty. The evidence cries out, Ladies and Gentlemen, not guilty."[174]

Rainnie took the floor for his summation and told jurors that, though the deceased had not apparently been a good husband or good father, the case was not about condoning or defending his behaviour – it was "about the killing of a human being."[175] The first shot hit John squarely in the chest: the evidence suggested that Kim must have been close to John when she fired that shot, especially since she said that she closed her eyes when she squeezed the trigger. The third shot was fired at close range, belying her claim that she did not intend to kill him. Rainnie reminded the jurors that Kim denied recalling Jennifer entering the bedroom before the homicide and failed to tell Dr Shane about her suicide note. The evidence suggested that Kim wrote the note before John returned home, while she was calm. Her use of the past tense reflected that she expected her children to read the note after her death.

John did not burst through the door – it was already open – and he was not armed when he entered the room. There was no corroborating evidence that Kim was in imminent danger when she fired that gun. The jury should not allow Wolson's "emotional summation"[176] to hamper a "full, fair and dispassionate consideration of the evidence," which, Rainnie said, proved the Crown's case.[177]

Leaving no stone unturned, Wolson took the opportunity to respond to Rainnie's summation. He told jurors that Rainnie's interpretation of the note required them to guess when Kim had written it: a guess cannot support proof beyond a reasonable doubt. He told them that the physical evidence of a spent shell near the bed supported her testimony that she had fired the first shot from there. That the door was off its hinge supported her evidence that John had "burst" angrily into the room. Finally, Rainnie had failed to cross-examine Kim on the question of whether she had thought she faced imminent danger, disentitling him to challenge that point now.

The jury was excused at noon that day, leaving the lawyers and judge to discuss how Justice Mykle would charge the jury. Again Wolson moved to have the first-degree murder charge withdrawn from the jury because there was inadequate evidence to support planning and deliberation. He wanted manslaughter offered to the jury as an alternative, and he asked the judge to consider not only section 34(2), self-defence, but also section 37, defence of others (in light of the threat to the children), and section 27, use of force to prevent the commission of a crime, any one of which would support acquittal. By 9 a.m. the next morning, just before the jury was brought in, Wolson had changed his mind. He asked the judge to put only section 34(2), self-defence, before the jury because he thought that the other defences would confuse them.

Wolson's decision to request Justice Mykle not to ask the jury to consider whether Kim killed to protect her children pursuant to sections 27 and 37 of

the *Criminal Code* illustrates a difficulty in the law of self-defence. These
sections use different formulations than section 34, the main self-defence
provision. For example, section 37 justifies an accused who acts to protect
herself or someone under her protection if she "uses no more force than is
necessary to prevent the assault or the repetition of it." Section 37 cannot
justify the wilful infliction of hurt that is excessive, "having regard to the
nature of the assault that the force used was intended to prevent." Use of
the word "necessary" and reference to "excessive force" can make this a nar-
rower defence than section 34 because the standard might be assessed on a
strictly objective basis (as opposed to what Kim reasonably believed was
necessary) and might be read as requiring retreat from the danger before
resort to fatal violence. On the other hand, one author argues that section
37 should be read using the same mixed subjective-objective test as section
34.[178] Furthermore, Wolson would have had a strong case in arguing that a
battered mother relying on section 37 should be given the full benefit of
the interpretive principles of the *Lavallee* decision. But since no court had
broached these interpretive questions, Wolson understandably shied away
from these alternative defences.

This legal uncertainty put him in an awkward situation. Wolson had
pressed his case on the basis that Kim was acting not to save her own life
but to protect her children. He was now asking the jury to focus on whether
Kim killed to preserve her own life.

Justice Mykle charged the jury on second-degree murder and manslaughter only, telling them that he had withdrawn first-degree murder from their
consideration. The justice who had presided over Kim's preliminary inquiry
had decided that there was some evidence of planning and deliberation sufficient to commit Kim to trial on first-degree murder, and Justice Mykle
had also found at the close of the Crown case that there was sufficient evidence such that a properly instructed jury could find Kim guilty of first-
degree murder beyond a reasonable doubt. After hearing the defence case,
he must have decided that it would be "unsafe" to allow the jury to deliberate on first-degree murder.

Justice Mykle went further. Based on the uncontradicted evidence of
Kim and Dr Shane, it would be difficult to conclude that she had the specific
intent for second-degree murder.[179] He charged the jury on self-defence,
noting that the evidence that Kim was a battered spouse was also unchal-
lenged. Jurors should consider her experience of violence at the hands
of the deceased in deciding whether she had a reasonable apprehension of
death or grievous bodily harm. In fact, Justice Mykle said, "he had tried to

kill her before, murder by remote control, by demanding repeatedly that she kill herself."[180] Even though John did not have a gun in his hand, he possessed numerous firearms with which to carry out his threat. As for the aspect of self-defence that the accused reasonably believed that she could not otherwise preserve herself, the judge referred to Dr Shane's evidence as well as John's friendships with the police and his threat to hunt her down if she left.

Defence of others – her children – was the second and only other defence that the judge left with the jury. For this defence to be met, Kim had to have used force to prevent John's assault and no more force than was "necessary." But, Justice Mykle said, a person in an emergency situation in which her children are under threat of death "cannot be expected to weigh precisely the exact measure of force that is necessary."[181] In fact, he said, "on reflection you may have little difficulty in coming to the conclusion that she used no more force than necessary to defend her children."[182]

With that rather generous instruction, the judge sent the jury off to deliberate at 10:01 a.m. Wolson put on record several concerns about the charge: he wanted the judge to more clearly tell the jury that they need not work out whether Kim's act was murder or manslaughter if they had a reasonable doubt that Kim acted in self-defence; he wanted the judge to repeat that the intent required for murder is the specific intent to kill; and he asked the judge to clarify that Kim's unlawful act of pointing a firearm, an element of manslaughter, would not be unlawful if Kim acted in self-defence. Justice Mykle declined to recharge the jury.

Over an hour later – at 11:20 a.m. – the jury returned. One of the jurors nodded to Kim's family and friends in the front row, as if to reassure them.[183] The six-woman, six-man jury delivered its verdict: not guilty. There was an audible gasp from Kim's supporters, and many began to cry.[184] Wolson shook the hand of each juror as they filed out, while Kim "gently shook her head no when asked to comment."[185]

She left the courthouse weeping, surrounded by friends and family. Wolson and Kim's father, as well as some of her friends, spoke to the media. Wolson said that he had not seen a more compelling case than this: "In my view this was not a case of murder and it never was. I'm just so happy that the jury saw things in an honest way and a true way."[186] Kim's father, Bernie Lynn, said: "It's an awful life she's gone through."[187]

Crown Attorney Rainnie accepted defeat and announced immediately that the Crown would not appeal: "Twelve people heard all the evidence and have drawn what can only be regarded as a reasonable conclusion."[188]

The Power of First-Degree Murder Charges

Kim's trial illustrates the power of the discretion vested in Crown attorneys to shape criminal justice outcomes by effectively determining both charge and sentence. Prosecutors can either accept guilty pleas to manslaughter, in which their sentence recommendations to the judge are highly influential, or pursue murder convictions that carry a mandatory life sentence. Both second- and first-degree murder carry an automatic life sentence. The difference lies in eligibility to apply for parole. For second-degree murder, the judge sets the period of ineligibility between ten and twenty-five years, on the advice of the jury; for first-degree murder, parole ineligibility is set at twenty-five years.[189]

When so few women – two of the seventeen charged with first-degree murder in my study – are convicted of first-degree murder, why do prosecutors pursue this charge against battered women? According to a 2003 Department of Justice study, there are many reasons: "Police and prosecutors may 'charge up' to demonstrate that they are not being too lenient, to allow room for possible plea negotiations, or to allow for the possibility of evidence that may be uncovered during the investigation that supports a more serious offence."[190] In fact, plea bargains were leveraged from eight of the seventeen women in my study charged with first-degree murder and from thirty-one of those forty-nine women charged with second-degree murder.

Like many women prosecuted for husband killing, Kim was the subject of a first-degree murder charge at least partly because she did not deny her responsibility, giving the prosecution an easy *prima facie* murder case.[191] Furthermore, the evidence of her daughter and the suicide note must have emboldened the Crown to pursue planned and deliberate murder. Rainnie might have pursued a first-degree murder charge to appear "tough" on husband killing.

Alternatively, he might have been convinced that self-defence could not excuse what he saw as a planned execution, in accordance with some US jurisprudence.[192] Self-defence's requirements – that an accused reasonably believes that she is being assaulted, faces grievous bodily harm or death, and cannot otherwise preserve herself – might be difficult to reconcile with planning to kill another person. Furthermore, the aggravating element of "planning and deliberation"[193] and the moral repugnancy of contract killing can be said to preclude access to self-defence, a defence that "justifies" rather than "excuses" murder.[194] Justifications convey the message that the actions of the accused person were rightful (and we have no right, therefore, to condemn them), while excuses suggest that, though the person's acts were wrongful, we will extend mercy to "excuse" what we regard as forgivable human frailty, such as acting under provocation.

No Canadian court has ruled on whether self-defence is available for planned and deliberate or contract murder, though a recent decision of the Nova Scotia Court of Appeal suggests that self-defence is unavailable for a battered woman who attempted to contract her abuser's death on just this reasoning.[195] An alternative argument is that Battered Woman Syndrome prevented the woman from being able to plan and deliberate, making her guilty instead of second-degree murder.[196] Still, this approach assumes the woman's culpability for murder and simply reduces its degree by treating the woman's experience of battering as an "excuse" based on her limited capacity.

Nevertheless, *Lavallee* can be used to argue that self-defence is available as a complete defence even for first-degree murder. *Lavallee* rejected any requirement that the anticipated assault be "imminent" before women act in self-defence, opening the door to pre-emptive killing. Furthermore, women's experience of battering as a pattern of ongoing threat and oppression helps to characterize a batterer's violence as omnipresent as opposed to a singular and isolated event.[197] When every day brings the risk of serious or lethal violence from a dedicated adversary prepared to escalate his violence should the woman attempt separation, she faces continuous "unlawful assault" that justifies defensive action whenever feasible. Some US courts have permitted women to advance evidence of Battered Woman Syndrome in cases involving contract murders,[198] and one judge of the Supreme Court of South Africa would have acquitted a battered woman in these circumstances.[199]

Dr Lenore Walker reports that, although three-quarters of battered women in her study feared that their batterers could or would murder them, even then they underestimated their risk: "We wondered if the women knew how close to death they actually were."[200] At the same time, the psychological effects of these traumatic experiences of intimate violence increase "geometrically rather than additively," such that "the most recent event would include the totality of the battering experience up until that event, rather than simply measuring the impact from that single event."[201]

Regarding the claim that planned murder is morally repugnant, how can women who are trapped by a terrifyingly violent male partner ensure that they save their own lives without "planning"? Battered women are assaulted by men using their hands, fists, and feet.[202] Although husbands who kill their wives are more likely overall to be convicted of murder than wives who kill their husbands,[203] those men who kill by beating their partners to death are rarely convicted of first-degree murder. In fact, they might not be convicted of second-degree murder either: the prosecutor might not be able to prove intent to kill when death has been perpetrated without using a weapon.[204] Even men who strangle their female partners to death might be convicted of manslaughter rather than murder.[205]

The vast majority of women cannot defend themselves against violent men without weapons. Is there a moral difference between spontaneous self-defence, when a woman happens upon a weapon at just the right moment to fend off a potentially murderous attack, and planned self-defence, when the woman tries to guarantee her own survival by preparation? With no other option that would demonstrably save her life, seeking aid from a third party might well be a woman's last resort. Jane Hurshman tried and failed to hire a hit man to kill Billy Stafford. In the end, she committed the homicide herself, but does that change the fact that in either scenario she was acting in self-defence?

Bonnie Mooney's only escape from her nightmare would have been to kill Roland Kruska. Instead, Hazel White was slaughtered by Kruska, and Mooney and her children suffered incalculable injuries. But, unlike Kim, Bonnie could not have waited for a final confrontation and then defended herself because his consistent method of attack was to take her by surprise. To kill Kruska would have required her either to hire a hit man or to devise a plan to lie in wait and take him unaware. Had she pursued either route, she surely would have faced a first-degree murder charge, with a more challenging self-defence argument and arguably more credibility issues than Kim faced. Do the differences in how and when women kill abusive partners, dictated by women's physical capacities, socialization, and individual experience of entrapment, warrant harsher punishment?

Undergoing Trial by Ordeal

In medieval times, guilt and innocence were a matter of determining God's will by subjecting the accused to life-threatening ordeals.[206] Kim's jury spent seven days in court and needed only an hour to deliberate before they acquitted Kim. We will never know whether the decision was based on her need to defend herself or her children or both. Whatever its basis, the acquittal was swift and supported by largely uncontested evidence, casting considerable doubt on the wisdom of the prosecution.

What were the Crown's ethical obligations in such a situation? Defence lawyers must vigorously pursue every avenue of defence available within the law and seek acquittal for their clients. Crown attorneys' ethical obligation is not the mirror image. It is not to seek conviction but to "ensure that justice is served by presenting all available legal proof of the facts to the court."[207] Crown prosecutors are instructed to proceed with prosecution only when there is "a reasonable likelihood of conviction" in light of the evidence, including available defences, and the prosecution is in the "public interest." If there is no reasonable prospect of conviction, then there is no "public interest" to consider in deciding whether to continue.[208]

Kim's prosecutor had in hand voluminous testimony from the preliminary inquiry of John's violence against Kim and both of her children that supported defence of others and self-defence. Rainnie also had John's conviction for a firearms offence, the Child and Family Services investigation of his abuse of Chris, and knowledge of the weapons cache removed from the home. Either the charge screening test was improperly applied by the Crown office or Kim's case shows that it is set too low. For example, Judge Ratushny in the *Self-Defence Review* argued that prosecutorial guidelines ought to adopt the more stringent test requiring a "substantial likelihood of conviction" used by British Columbia.[209]

Even if there truly had been a "reasonable prospect of conviction," how was it in the interests of justice to proceed with Kim's prosecution full tilt? Crown attorneys can and do take into account the suffering of witnesses in deciding whether and how to proceed.[210] Furthermore, Rainnie did not present to the jury all of the available evidence – much of it gathered by the police – forcing Wolson to call the neighbours interviewed by the police and to speculate about the other missing evidence.

The Crown's office could have decided to stay the charges against Kim and to explain that decision in open court by referencing the overwhelming evidence of the deceased's actual and threatened violence if public backlash was anticipated. Instead, Kim was forced to undergo what can only be described as legalized torture, a "trial by ordeal." Her trial exacted personal costs over and above the years of suffering and humiliation that she had already endured in her seventeen-year marriage to the deceased.

The insistence on a trial for Kim in spite of all the exculpatory evidence available is suggestive of a commitment to "equality" with a vengeance. Women who kill their abusers will themselves be prosecuted to the full extent of the law, mirroring the way in which zero tolerance policies requiring the arrest of batterers have also been turned against women. Kim's trial suggests that justice is not free: wives who kill violent husbands must pay at least the price of public exposure and spectacle if they are to regain their freedom. They must forgo the anonymity accorded to other women who are raped or assaulted by male partners that is afforded by the publication ban.[211]

Battered women on trial for murder must somehow speak the unspeakable, break the silence enforced by the batterers, and articulate the pain that they inflicted.[212] Elaine J Lawless, relying on the work of Elaine Scarry on the experience of pain,[213] writes that,

> As long as women and children are kept in this mode (constant state of fear and anxiety), there is no discourse available to them to talk about what is happening. Scarry says: "Pain is characterized by its 'unsharability'; it dismantles the victim's capacity for language and therefore the capacity to represent that pain to others." A woman who is being beaten becomes immobile, which, of course, is the intent of the abuser. As long as she cannot speak the pain to others, she remains imprisoned in her own body of pain, and he is safe from her reprisals and the eyes of the world.[214]

To testify about one's experience of battering in one's own murder trial requires re-experiencing and sharing that pain, explains Lawless: "We must remember at all times that this act of speaking is an entirely new and different experience for the women who have just emerged from lives of violence. The very act of speaking the pain to others, and admitting it out loud to herself, is uncharted territory."[215]

Battered women must take a terrifying leap of faith and trust that those who judge them will be able to bear witness to that pain without engaging the strategies commonly used in social discourse to deny, hide, and minimize men's violence.[216] Even while forced in testimony to describe their suffering, battered women anguish about exposing their loved ones and children to the details of what they went through. Worse still, they might be put in the untenable position of instructing their lawyers to cross-examine their children or call them as witnesses on their behalf.

Pleading Guilty

Kim's prosecution thus sheds light on some of the reasons why so many battered women plead guilty rather than go on to trial. Murder charges, especially first-degree murder, put enormous pressure on battered women to enter a guilty plea to manslaughter and secure agreement from the Crown on a range of sentences rather than take their chances in a trial.

The Canadian Association of Elizabeth Fry Societies (CAEFS), which advocates on behalf of incarcerated women in Canada, believes that battered women who have valid self-defence claims still end up behind bars by virtue of guilty pleas, in spite of Justice Wilson's ruling in *Lavallee*. In 1995, Kim Pate, the executive director of CAEFS, persuaded Justice Minister Allan Rock[217] to launch a review to identify and remedy the convictions of those women where the legal impact of wife battering had not been recognized either by lawyers or by judges as relevant to a claim of self-defence.[218] For only the second time in Canadian history,[219] a judge was asked to review the convictions of a group rather than that of an individual. Although the *Self-Defence Review* recommended only seven of the ninety-eight women who applied for a remedy,[220] Judge Ratushny identified a major systemic problem, concluding that battered women are driven by "irresistible forces" to forgo apparently valid self-defence claims and instead enter pleas of guilty to manslaughter.[221]

The mandatory life sentence for murder is the major culprit,[222] Judge Ratushny argued, which of course confronts all persons accused of murder. But its crushing prospect is heightened for women like Kim whose self-esteem has been deliberately attacked, who have children to care for, who cannot put the abuse behind them but must relive it publicly in open court, often in front of the deceased's family and friends, and who experience genuine remorse: "[E]ven though she feels she had to act to defend herself, she has difficulty justifying taking another person's life even to herself."[223] Judge Ratushny also pointed to the complexity of the law of self-defence,[224] the very few reported cases in which women have successfully raised self-defence, and the fact that wife battering is often committed without witnesses and is usually undocumented. This means that self-defence might rest on the woman's credibility before a jury.[225]

Lawyers retained by battered women accused of killing male partners face both these legal uncertainties and the vulnerabilities of their clients. Women charged with crimes constitute a tiny proportion of most criminal lawyers' daily practice. Defence lawyers are commonly retained to defend men accused of violence against women, whether sexual assault or assault against their intimate partners. As a result, their worldviews and understandings of battered women's lives and choices might be subtly shaped and limited by virtue of that perspective. Defence lawyers might not "see" the violence or threat posed by the behaviours described by battered women, or they might not appreciate the ways in which women's options are circumscribed by economic, social, and legal inequalities.

Furthermore, without claiming that men and women are naturally or inherently different, sex role socialization has implications for how women present as clients. This can in turn affect how lawyers assess the culpability of women who kill their husbands and the available defences. For example, juror studies have revealed that women and men judge battered women differently, with women jurors more likely to rate the battered woman as "justified, mentally stable, reasonable, credible, and having fewer options available to her than were the men."[226] Battered women are particularly likely to blame themselves for their partners' abuse, and criminal lawyers are accustomed to hearing women recant[227] and take responsibility for striking first or "provoking" the violence.[228] The challenge for defence lawyers confronted by women clients who have killed is to see the battered woman's story as somehow extraordinary. In the United States, for example, battered women appeal their convictions based on the "ineffective assistance of counsel." These appeals succeed when lawyers advise women to enter guilty pleas without investigating the evidence pointing to self-defence, calling the women to testify, or introducing expert testimony in support of self-defence.[229]

A real difficulty arises even for highly competent lawyers like Wolson who appreciate a client's self-defence claim and understand the need for her testimony to be supported by expert evidence. Because a lawyer cannot anticipate the judge's rulings on the evidence or instructions to the jury, and cannot be certain how witnesses' credibility will be assessed by jurors, conviction remains a serious risk. The defence lawyer is bound to present all possible outcomes to the client. Given the choice between pleading guilty to manslaughter, knowing that the sentence will be considerably less than life imprisonment, and undergoing a murder trial, at which she must expose the abuse and undergo cross-examination, at which her friends and family – possibly even her children – can be called as witnesses against her, and at which she risks a murder conviction, often a battered woman will forgo her right to a trial.

When a guilty plea is negotiated in such cases, the deceased's abuse will be characterized as mitigating the woman's crime. A psychologist's report that the woman experienced Battered Woman Syndrome might be put before the sentencing judge, and the facts agreed to by the Crown and defence will often include but minimize the surrounding facts that suggest self-defence. Lawyers must tread carefully in such situations: although they want the sentencing judge to appreciate the mitigating facts, if they suggest that the woman acted in self-defence, the judge will be obligated to reject the guilty plea. This is known as an "equivocal plea," when the person is ac-knowledging guilt while maintaining innocence at the same time. Some authorities take the position that Crown prosecutors can only accept un-equivocal guilty pleas,[230] but it is a practical reality that "equivocal" guilty pleas are negotiated daily, and some result in wrongful convictions.[231]

According to Judge Ratushny, it is not unprofessional for defence lawyers to agree to a guilty plea when the client is not prepared, for good reason, to accept the risks of a trial for murder. This practice of pleading guilty in these circumstances is understood as "making the best of a bad situation."[232] Judge Ratushny was sufficiently concerned about the unfairness occasioned to bat-tered women that she recommended that Crown attorneys downgrade mur-der charges to manslaughter when battered women offer "equivocal" pleas when there is evidence of self-defence and the Crown would be willing to accept a guilty plea to manslaughter. If manslaughter is instead the charge, then the woman could accept responsibility for her act by pleading guilty to it, but she could alternatively proceed to trial on that charge and put her self-defence claim before a jury. By removing the spectre of a life sentence, battered women's guilty pleas would more closely approximate a truly vol-untary choice and the truth of what happened.

In fact, unknown to Kim's jury, in the months before her trial, Kim had instructed Wolson to persuade the prosecutor to accept a guilty plea to manslaughter and her offer to serve five years in a penitentiary.[233] Had the prosecutor negotiated, Kim would have relinquished her right to argue self-defence in exchange for five years of her life and the stain of a homicide conviction. A woman with this much evidence of self-defence, with no cred-ibility problems such as a criminal record, a substance abuse problem, or past violence against the deceased, is still vulnerable to the pressure to plead guilty. She might be represented by an accomplished lawyer who believes strongly in her innocence yet beg her prosecutor to take her guilty plea. Where, then, might we find the reliability and justness of other battered women's guilty pleas? The next chapter addresses those women who are most vulnerable to entering guilty pleas – Aboriginal women.

4

Gladys Heavenfire and Doreen Sorenson

"[W]e were dispossessed of our inherited rights, lands, identities, and families."[1]

On 26 August 1990 in Shepard, Alberta, a hamlet ten kilometres southeast of Calgary, Gladys Heavenfire, an Aboriginal woman, killed her white male partner, Derrick John Falardeau. She was charged with second-degree murder three months after the Supreme Court of Canada released its *Lavallee* decision. "You really don't expect this to happen in the country," said Councillor Jean Isley. "It's scary – it belongs in the city, not the country."[2] Although an odd comment, given that domestic violence and homicide know no boundaries,[3] it arguably signified this as a "racial" crime – one belonging to the inner city, where, as Sherene H Razack explains, "all that is not respectable is contained."[4]

CM "Mac" Jones, a lawyer and an Anglican priest who ministered to the inmates in Drumheller Institution,[5] prosecuted Heavenfire. Of the possible conflict of interest between prosecuting and then preaching to prisoners, Jones said: "I've got no difficulty with sending them there and still feeling sorry for them."[6] In 1990, when approximately 5 percent of Alberta's population was of Aboriginal descent, one in four of Drumheller's inmate population was Aboriginal.[7]

Heavenfire was one of thirty-seven identifiable Aboriginal women among my ninety-one files, reflecting 41 percent of the women charged with killing their male partners. Yet my research might well undercount the Aboriginal women charged since government reports conclude that Aboriginal women are eight times more likely to commit spousal homicide than non-Aboriginal women.[8] In many of my files, it is simply not possible to assert that any given woman is *not* Aboriginal. For example, the woman whose case is known around the world as an early and ground-breaking decision, Angelique Lyn Lavallee, is widely supposed to have been an Aboriginal woman,[9] but the legal record sheds no light on her origins. Many other women in my files are quite possibly Aboriginal based on their names and circumstances.

In 1999, the Supreme Court of Canada decided that judges who sentence Aboriginal offenders must consider their Aboriginal backgrounds.[10] However, Aboriginal women's origins are not necessarily identified in pre-1999 cases, those in which women were acquitted or convicted of murder (which has a mandatory life sentence), or those in which the women's origins are not evident in news accounts. Furthermore, hatred of and discrimination against Aboriginal peoples in Canada can lead some Aboriginal women to deny their heritage. The legacy of residential school and child welfare policies that resulted in the widespread removal of Aboriginal children from their families and communities also means that some Aboriginal people are unaware of their origins. Furthermore, the Canadian criminal justice system has a history of erasing "race" from its official accounts.[11]

In this and the following chapter, I explore a number of Aboriginal women's homicide trials: there is a danger that one Aboriginal woman's case might be seen as exceptional and, without the benefit of the larger context of Aboriginal women's experiences of violence and their involvement in homicides, inexplicable. This chapter looks at the homicide trials of Aboriginal women who killed white male partners, while Chapter 5 examines those who killed Aboriginal male partners. Both groups of women are affected by the racist legacy of colonization, past and present, but Aboriginal women who live with white male abusers experience different forms of dominance and, when they kill white men, face a credibility contest framed by discrimination. Both chapters show what differentiates Aboriginal women's homicides from those committed by other women in Canada and demonstrate the striking parallels among Aboriginal women's lives that bring these women to kill their abusers.

Sharon McIvor and Teressa Nahanee argue that the experiences of Aboriginal women must be analyzed in light of colonialism and racism:

> This cycle of terror makes studying Aboriginal violence a unique and distinct undertaking. General studies of sexual or physical violence cannot account for the Aboriginal experience in Canada. Any researcher purporting to do so ignores the specific socio-cultural and historical contexts

in which violence is manifested in our communities. Mainstream feminist or systems approaches cannot begin to fathom the absolute brutalization of Aboriginal peoples without considering imperialism, racism, colonialism, and the particular consequences of growing up "Native."[12]

Standing at the intersection of the ravages of colonization and the subjugation of women, Aboriginal women's life histories are more likely to reflect a long trajectory of deprivation and abuse originating in state policies and practices, setting Aboriginal women up for further degradation and endangerment, usually but not always at the hands of men, state indifference to that abuse, and, simultaneously, criminal intervention when they have resisted abuse through violence. Can Aboriginal women benefit from the *Lavallee* interpretation of self-defence and Battered Woman Syndrome?

Gladys Heavenfire

> "If there was a battered spouse in that relationship, it was
> Rick Falardeau."[13]

Alain Hepner secured Heavenfire's release on bail pending her trial,[14] a huge benefit to any accused preparing for trial. For battered women, this freedom is critical: it allows them time to seek counselling for the abuse that they have experienced; to come to terms with grief, self-recrimination, and any addiction; and to assist in the preparation of their defence. Heavenfire secured bail because she did not present a flight risk or a substantial likelihood of committing violent acts while awaiting trial.

Hepner represented Heavenfire before a five-man, seven-woman jury trial[15] over six days, commencing 17 June 1991 in Calgary in the Court of Queen's Bench. The trial was presided over by Madam Justice Elizabeth A McFadyen.[16] Hepner made an early attempt to "destigmatize" his client in the eyes of the jury. He asked that Heavenfire be allowed to sit at the counsel table with him because she had been out on bail prior to the trial, presented no escape risk, and would find the trial anxiety producing. No objection was voiced by the Crown, yet the judge refused the application, saying that the jury would have more difficulty seeing Heavenfire if she were seated at the table instead of in the prisoner's box.[17]

The Crown theory was that Heavenfire was the aggressor who instigated the conflicts in their "stormy" relationship "when they both and especially the accused was drinking. Under the influence of liquor, she became extremely jealous, physically and verbally violent."[18] Heavenfire was thus framed by the prosecution within the discriminatory stereotype of Aboriginal women as intoxicated aggressors – a stereotype[19] that would make self-defence a challenging argument.

On the day of the homicide, Heavenfire found Falardeau at a bar in the late afternoon where he was drinking with friends from work. She accused him loudly of infidelity with a waitress at the bar, shoved him against a wall twice, and threatened "I will fuckin' kill you." The bar's owner saw Heavenfire punch Falardeau in the stomach several times on the dance floor. The owner's wife also observed this interaction and was surprised by the force that Heavenfire used since Falardeau was quite a large man – over six feet tall and more than 180 pounds – while Heavenfire was tiny – five feet two inches.

Falardeau and Heavenfire were asked to leave the bar. Out at his truck, according to witness Kathy Kennedy, Heavenfire continued the conflict by slapping Falardeau while Kennedy held onto his arm to prevent him from retaliating when he flexed his fist. When Kennedy let go, Falardeau punched Heavenfire repeatedly in the face while she curled up under the dashboard. Falardeau asked Kennedy to take Heavenfire home in her car, but after Heavenfire went back to the truck to get her shoes the couple drove home together.

An hour later Heavenfire called 9-1-1, sobbing that she had shot Falardeau in the head. He was dead, she managed to choke out to the operator, and she loved him. The deceased was described as "an elderly gentleman"[20] by the paramedic on the scene, though he was only forty years old at the time of his death. Testimony at trial revealed that he was both a serious drinker and a drug user, which might have explained his appearance.

Eleven of Falardeau's friends testified for the prosecution. All described Falardeau as an easygoing, passive man and Heavenfire as possessive, jealous, and verbally and physically abusive when drinking. William Stanko had seen Heavenfire use one of Falardeau's guns to shoot at targets and had once seen her load and fire the weapon. In cross-examination, it became clear that Stanko visited Falardeau daily and saw him order Heavenfire around and her obey. Another friend of the deceased, John Thompson, had seen Heavenfire load and fire Falardeau's gun. Both men described the deceased as a gentle, soft-hearted man who would never hurt anyone. Brian Boake, another friend, testified that he had seen Falardeau "battered up" and his face "scratched all the way down real deep from his forehead all the way down."[21]

Many of these witnesses admitted under cross-examination having either seen Falardeau punch Heavenfire in the face or seen her with black eyes, a swollen face, or an injured nose. Marlene Conlin, the deceased's cousin, claimed that she knew of Falardeau having been violent on two occasions only, yet when asked whether she spoke to him about his violence against Heavenfire she replied: "Yes, I did many times."[22] Hepner's cross-examination revealed these witnesses as unwilling to become involved or to condemn the violence: Edmund Crabtree admitted that he had never asked Heavenfire about her black eyes;[23] Conlin answered in the negative when Hepner asked whether she had urged Falardeau to seek counselling.[24]

Jones introduced police testimony that they had received no reports of violence against Heavenfire by Falardeau, but medical personnel testified that at the time of her arrest Heavenfire had two black eyes, a hematoma on her skull behind her ear, abrasions on her hand and finger, and bruising and scratches on her body. Police testified that Heavenfire's name was in their computer five times – once when Heavenfire was the victim of a hit and run – leaving jurors to speculate whether the other four occasions involved crimes by her.[25] The risk that jurors would draw a negative inference from this evidence was acute. Aboriginal women in Canada and particularly those in the Prairies are charged, convicted, and incarcerated at rates vastly exceeding their representation in the population.[26]

Hepner's opening address told the jury that his case rested on Battered Woman Syndrome. They would hear that on the night of the homicide Falardeau ordered Heavenfire to shoot him; in response, she picked up the gun, and it discharged accidentally. Hepner would call witnesses who had seen her many injuries, a witness from the bar, and a doctor who would explain how Battered Woman Syndrome applied to Heavenfire.

Heavenfire was called first. Her life story mirrored that of many Aboriginal women, whose family histories and experiences of intimate partner violence are the long-term outcomes of colonization and colonial practices. Anne McGillivray and Brenda Comaskey write that, "[w]hile there may be disagreement on whether First Nations experienced or countenanced intimate violence in partner relationships, there is wide agreement that contact with Europeans exacerbated it."[27] Trade, missionary work, and "the devaluation of culture and femaleness in the intensified cultural conversion projects, policies, and laws of the nineteenth century" all destabilized the roles of Aboriginal women in their nations, where they had often participated as equals.[28]

Canada adopted laws that criminalized Aboriginal spiritual practices, confined Aboriginal people to reserve lands, and destroyed their traditional leadership. Aboriginal women's status was undermined by the *Indian Act* of 1857, which allowed Aboriginal men, but not women, to give up their "Indian" status and reserve lands in order to become Canadians and exercise the right to vote. The *Indian Act* of 1869 stripped Aboriginal women and their children, but not men, of their "Indian" status and ousted them from reserve lands if they married non-status partners. It abolished all hereditary leadership and offices, which had been occupied by women and men alike, and replaced traditional structures with band councils, which only men were eligible to vote for and join.[29]

Together these laws furthered the colonial project of claiming land while simultaneously undermining Aboriginal women's authority and creating their subordination to men. The imposition of male authority disrupted nations, communities, families, and relationships, leading to marital discord and male violence. McGillivray and Comaskey comment: "Widespread acceptance of subordination to men, dependence on men and male systems, and physical, psychological, and social isolation contribute to intimate violence."[30]

The Aboriginal woman was conjured by white settler society as either "Indian princess" or "sq**w drudge,"[31] a profane, racial slur that sexualized Aboriginal women and dehumanized them by reducing them to their sexual organs.[32] They were characterized as "accustomed to being bought and sold by their own elders and to being mistreated by their own men,"[33] freeing white men from moral responsibility for abuse and violence. By the late nineteenth century, Aboriginal women were also represented as "bad mothers," justifying the removal of their children into residential schools and, later, foster care and adoptive families.

The residential school policies, at their height in the 1930s, attacked Aboriginal women's roles as mothers, tearing apart families and communities. These policies destroyed Aboriginal children's links with their heritage of language, identity, culture, and spirituality, and streamed the children into gendered, low-wage occupations. They subjected the children to physical, psychological, and sexual abuse, creating generations of children who grew up without parenting and experienced violence and shame as a way of life. By the time the last of the residential schools closed in 1996, at least 150,000 Aboriginal children had been taken from their families and placed in 130 such schools. Many Aboriginal communities across the country have yet to recover from the devastation caused to the subsequent generations – the children of the residential school survivors. Justice Murray Sinclair argues that Aboriginal people absorbed the message of inferiority conveyed by colonial practices and policies, resulting in what he calls "collective social depression."[34]

Heavenfire's mother was of the residential school generation. She was unable to parent or protect her daughter: Heavenfire experienced maternal neglect and abuse at the hands of her alcoholic mother, who one time beat her and left her unconscious on railway tracks.[35] She was five years old and survived only because her brother scooped her away from the tracks as a train bore down on her. Heavenfire also survived violence at the hands of her brothers and sexual assault from a young age, facilitated by her mother. Her family doctor "came ... in laughing and said so you finally did it, eh,"[36] reinforcing her powerlessness and teaching her that seeking assistance from authority figures is risky. Heavenfire had been in at least one violent relationship before moving in with Falardeau. None of this violence had been reported to the police or social workers.[37]

The legacy of her childhood could be seen in Falardeau's ability to dominate her. Heavenfire had four daughters when she met the deceased and gave up custody of each one because "[h]e didn't want any children around."[38] Her Aboriginal heritage enhanced his positioning in terms of his power. When Hepner asked whether Falardeau said anything about her being "Native," she replied:

> [W]hen I had been drinking ... he would say you act just like a fucking Indian, and I'd say, well, I am an Indian ... [T]here were times that I sat there and he and his friends were talking, and he would bring up Natives, Indians live off the taxpayers, we support the whole Native Colonies and all this stuff, and he said they're all a bunch of lazy bums, and he would go on. And I'd tell him: Rick, I'm an Indian, too, and then he'd say: Yeah, but you are different. And I never really asked him what did he mean by I was different.[39]

Hepner asked if her family ever visited the home that she shared with Falardeau in addition to the steady stream of his friends. She testified: "No, they didn't. I – there was a friend that we had that we worked with when we were at the gravel pit. He used to come out fairly often and visit us, but gradually, Rick told me he didn't want me inviting him out there anymore because he acted like a goddamn Indian when he was drunk."[40]

Through Heavenfire's testimony, as well as the cross-examination of several of the Crown's witnesses, the basis for her "jealousy," pointed out by so many Crown witnesses, was revealed. Richard Stanko testified that Heavenfire was jealous of Falardeau's friends because Falardeau spent more time with them than with her. She was offended by his display in their kitchen of a calendar depicting naked women. Teresa Olsen described a violent confrontation between the accused and the deceased that started when Falardeau asked Olsen point blank "do you want to fuck?" in front of Heavenfire and others in the car.[41] On another occasion, Heavenfire came home to find a woman asleep in their bedroom;[42] another woman repeatedly telephoned Falardeau in the middle of the night.[43]

The account that Heavenfire gave of the night that she killed Falardeau corresponded with the Crown witnesses' testimony. She was surprised to find him in the bar since he had told her he would not be wasting his money there anymore. She was upset because when she arrived he was dancing with the waitress – the woman who called Falardeau at night– and then he went out with her to the parking lot. Heavenfire admitted pushing him against the jukebox in anger and pushing his legs off a table so that she could pass by, causing him to fall off his chair. She testified to a memory loss until she was outside the bar and found Falardeau in his truck, where he accused her of breaking a window and then backhanded her. She responded by yelling and screaming, and then she began hitting him back. When he backhanded her again, her head hit the truck, and she slid down to the floor, where he continued hitting her as she tried to protect her head.

Heavenfire recalled calming down and driving home with Falardeau but had no memory after they pulled into the driveway until she found herself sitting in the dining room. From there, Falardeau dragged her to the bedroom, threw her on the bed, rummaged in the closet, and then turned around to point a gun at her head. He put the clip in the gun, threw it at her, and started yelling: "Shoot me, you fucking bitch. Shoot me, you stupid slut. Shoot me, or ... " She described herself as separating from her body – pulling away and watching herself – when she obeyed him. She raised the gun, and "it went off."[44] Heavenfire had another memory loss between the moment that the gun fired and when she came to and found Falardeau lying on the floor beside the bed.

Heavenfire acknowledged that she knew how to put bullets into the clip but claimed that she had never loaded the clip into the gun herself: Falardeau had always loaded it for her. She also testified that she thought the clip was empty, because three weeks earlier Falardeau told her that they were out of bullets. When Hepner asked whether she recalled what she told the 9-1-1 operator when she called that night, she replied that she could not remember. The 9-1-1 operator tape-recorded her words as she wept that the deceased had been beating her, that he would not stop hitting her in the face, and that her face hurt. Her statements to the police on the scene and to hospital personnel repeated these themes: "He was hurting me." "I was trying to protect myself." "He kicked me in the back." "[H]e gave me the gun and he said 'You son of a bitch shoot me, or I'll kill you,' and so I shot him."[45]

In cross-examination, Jones attacked her accounts of violence as completely uncorroborated. He asked Heavenfire to explain why she did not leave Falardeau when he was first violent with her. When she answered that she loved him, he asked why she did not contact the police. She did not want to jail him, she replied. Jones established that she had sought medical attention on two occasions and had dropped charges the only time that she had called the police.[46] When he asked why she returned to Falardeau rather than ask her family or friends for financial help and a place to live, she answered that she did not want to involve her family.[47] Jones suggested that her words "I pulled the trigger" and "I shot him" to the 9-1-1 operator, the ambulance attendant, and the police spoke to deliberate actions rather than an accident. Heavenfire could only answer "I wasn't thinking very clearly then."[48]

Other defence witnesses offered compelling corroboration of the aftermath of Falardeau's violence. Linda Newton, a counsellor at a vocational college where Heavenfire had commenced her upgrading, saw bruising on her face on at least five occasions. Heavenfire's explanations were telling: "I was beaten up by some women in the Co-op parking lot ... [A] woman had beat her up in a bathroom at a New Year's Eve party ... One was that she had been sleep walking, and this time she was really bruised, and I remember thinking there is no way you could walk that hard into furniture or a wall, because the whole side of her face was black."[49] On another occasion, Heavenfire told Newton that she had been fixing a car and something had fallen on her, bruising her arm, and yet another time she had to take time off work to see a doctor about her ruptured ear drum.[50] As the frequency of her injuries increased, her attendance dropped markedly along with her ability to concentrate in classes.

Jones tried to undercut Newton's conclusion that Heavenfire was being beaten by her partner. Newton acknowledged that she accepted the first explanation offered by Heavenfire for her injuries. Jones reviewed each subsequent explanation, suggesting that "that was a logical explanation, wasn't it?" and "again those things do happen, don't they?" On the third occasion, when Heavenfire claimed to have been beaten up by a woman at a party, Newton resisted: "Well, they don't normally happen that often, I don't think." Jones leapt on this response: "Miss Newton, read the paper. Those kind of things happen with great frequency here in the City of Calgary, don't they?"[51] He gave up this pursuit when Newton stood her ground. She insisted that it is just not "normal for people to come in to school that often looking beat up."[52]

Joy Cooney, a student from the college, also testified that Heavenfire started out attending daily and then began coming to school with injuries that increased in frequency and severity and for which her explanations were implausible: "[S]he gave explanations, such as sleeping on the couch and she rolled off and hit her face on the coffee table for black eyes."[53] When she was absent, "she usually came back with bruising on her face."[54] Only while temporarily separated from Falardeau did Heavenfire confide his violence to Cooney. He came to the school once to pull Heavenfire out of class: "[W]hen I walked by him the hairs on the back of my neck stood up for some reason, just something about him didn't sit right with me."[55] As her injuries and absences increased, Heavenfire withdrew from their friendship.

Her brother's wife, Sophie Rowan, testified to Heavenfire's increasing distance from her family. Even when Heavenfire visited, she spent her time on the telephone to Falardeau, promising him that she would be right back. She would stay for only ten or fifteen minutes, where previously she had visited for hours at a time, sometimes spending the night.[56] Under cross-examination, Rowan stated that she had seen Heavenfire bruised and battered at least five times. When asked why she did not report this to the police, she retorted: "Because it wasn't my place to do it. I know what it is to be abused."[57]

Heavenfire's sister, Alvina Heavenfire, described bruising and injuries that caused Gladys to limp as well as additional improbable explanations: "A few times, she said a curtain rod fell on her."[58] Heavenfire became nervous and jumpy, and "when she does visit she is always on the phone or, you know, hurrying off home to cook supper or something she says."[59] Alvina spoke about meeting her sister at a celebration on the reserve and, once up close, realizing that she was wearing heavy makeup to cover two black eyes.[60]

Heavenfire's brother, Thomas Heavenfire, saw her injuries and heard her explanations: "[S]he said that they were out camping for the weekend and then she ran into the camper door. On another occasion she said she was taking laundry down the stairs, and that's when she fell down the stairs, but those bruises they will not happen because of falling."[61] His concern was heightened by the frequency of her injuries: "She had bruises on her cheeks, on her forehead, and black eyes, had this every time I saw her."[62]

Thomas was also troubled by Falardeau's racism:

> I was sitting at Gladys' place, and then he came in, Rick, and then just glanced over at me, and I guess they were supposed to go somewhere, and then he asked Gladys, "are you ready?" And Gladys said, "Well, I'm getting ready," and then Rick, Rick, well, Mr. Falardeau said, "Oh, well, then it's these damn Indian sq**ws," he said, "they always like that." And I looked at Rick, and I said, "What? What? Rick, can you repeat it again?" And then he looked at me, and then I guess he realized who I was, and then he said, "Nothing, nothing at all," and "I didn't mean your sister," he said, and that was the last of it.[63]

Under cross-examination, Thomas acknowledged that he had been a tribal police officer but had not reported his sister's victimization because he was no longer an officer at the time. Furthermore, he had neither the evidence nor his sister's admission of Falardeau's battering.

The penultimate defence witness was David Peebles, a musician who had been performing with the band that night in the bar where the deadly confrontation between Heavenfire and Falardeau began. He saw the fight between the couple erupt "at least six times."[64]

> [E]very once in a while there would be a skirmish break out at the table, and she would lunge across the table and try to throw punches at him. All he did was back up and avoid the confrontation ... [H]e appeared to be like taunting her into violence, and he seemed to get a laugh out of the fact that she would go after him.[65]

This was a telling observation from an independent witness. Batterers are known to deliberately provoke their female partners into initiating violence and then mock their weakness.[66]

Peebles saw Falardeau disengage from dancing with the accused and then lean up against the wall, "as if he was not interested in dancing anymore," and dance with another woman.[67] Then he saw them talking in the pool room – she with her back to the wall and he facing her, leaning above her with his hands on the wall. Peebles then saw Falardeau slap Heavenfire across the face with an open palm and walk out of the bar, saying "all right then you are a fucking sq**w."[68]

The last defence witness, Dr William Alan Weston, had been permitted to hear all of the witnesses, including the testimony of Heavenfire. He testified that she suffered from Battered Woman Syndrome.[69] He focused on five childhood factors: (1) witnessing or experiencing battering; (2) sexual abuse or exploitation; (3) critical periods when the child experiences non-contingent control, such as through a parent's alcoholism or frequent moves; (4) exposure to stereotyped and rigid sexual roles; and (5) health problems and chronic illness. Then he outlined seven adulthood factors in women who experience Battered Woman Syndrome: (1) experience of the cycle of violence; (2) frequent and increasingly severe violence; (3) sexual abuse; (4) jealousy and efforts to isolate the woman; (5) threats to hurt or kill; (6) violence against others, such as children, family members, or animals; and (7) alcohol or drug abuse by either partner.

Weston told the jury that the vast majority of domestic homicides are of women.[70] Heavenfire's experience of depersonalization and the threat made by the deceased – kill or be killed – are typical: "[T]he fear of being killed is a reality to them."[71]

In response, Jones suggested that Heavenfire did not display all of the risk factors that correlate to Battered Woman Syndrome. Specifically, after asking the witness to explain forms of non-contingent control and getting the answer that it includes loss of one's parents, alcoholism in the parent, frequent moves, and stigmatization, Jones proposed that "there was no evidence that she felt stigmatized by her racial background."[72] Dr Weston conceded that no specific evidence on this issue had been introduced, missing, for the moment, the evidence of Falardeau's racist abuse. Jones also tried to get Dr Weston to agree that there was no evidence to support all seven factors associated with adulthood, including evidence of the man's violence against others, children, animals, or objects. Dr Weston noted Falardeau's strong interest in guns, but Jones replied: "You would get into an awful argument with the National Rifle Association, Doctor, I think." Dr Weston responded: "I might but I still think that there is a relationship between violence and the use of guns."[73]

Jones reminded Dr Weston that women with the syndrome typically attempt to appease and placate their batterers by using "anger reduction techniques." He highlighted three incidents in which Heavenfire "was certainly not trying to placate Mr. Falardeau."[74] She went out in public; she did not conceal her injuries, unlike the "real" battered woman.[75] Heavenfire had separated from the deceased for almost six months, showing that she was able to leave her partner,[76] again in contrast to the "typical" battered woman. Jones asked Dr Weston to agree that it is not necessarily the wife who is most likely to die in a domestic homicide but the "battered person," a proposition that Dr Weston accepted after some resistance.[77]

When Jones proposed that Heavenfire displayed a great deal of anger on the night that she killed Falardeau, Dr Weston refused to budge. He maintained that her testimony demonstrated not her anger but Falardeau's. When pressed to agree that when a "battered person reaches the point that he or she must kill or be killed"[78] the act can be characterized as "deliberate," Dr Weston insisted that the correct description would be "inevitable" – not deliberate.

In re-examination, Dr Weston testified that Heavenfire had been psychologically tortured by her partner's verbal abuse, which included name calling such as "Indian sq**w" and "fucking bitch."[79] Moreover, by hitting Falardeau when taunted to do so, Heavenfire was placating him.[80]

This completed the case for the defence. The jury excluded, Justice McFadyen expressed concerns about putting self-defence to the jury, noting that the accused had only once described the threat by the deceased – "shoot me, or I will kill you" – and had not testified that she was afraid of Falardeau, one of the elements of self-defence. But Hepner did not give up. He argued that the 9-1-1 tapes and Heavenfire's statements to the police and medical personnel were more telling of her state of mind, given Dr Weston's testimony about her state of depersonalization or detachment.[81]

Justice McFadyen also raised the possibility of provocation on the basis that Falardeau had allegedly thrown the gun at the accused and threatened her.[82] Hepner went out on a limb and rejected provocation as a stand-alone defence. Provocation would have allowed the jury to find Heavenfire not guilty of murder but guilty of manslaughter, a compromise verdict giving the judge a wide range of sentencing options, with life imprisonment as the maximum, not minimum, sentence. Hepner did not want the jury distracted by a middle ground of provocation and the characterization of Heavenfire as having acted out of anger rather than fear. Instead, he wanted the jury put to a stark choice: guilty of murder, or innocent of all charges.

In his closing address, Hepner placed before the jury two defence arguments. First, Heavenfire had accidentally killed the deceased; she had testified that she did not know the gun was loaded. Second, he recalled for the jury all of the statements made by Heavenfire on the night of the homicide that strongly supported self-defence as well as her "black and blue" physical condition. She was a truthful witness who did not attempt to elaborate on those statements recorded by 9-1-1 and the police but testified honestly about what little she could recall. Hepner reminded jurors of the police interrogation of his client; they had tried but failed to get her to acknowledge that she was angry about being used "as a punching bag for quite some time" and must have been mad when she picked up the gun.[83]

In contrast, Jones submitted that Battered Woman Syndrome did not apply to the accused, and he urged the jury to reject self-defence. Heavenfire was never in danger from the deceased; in fact, Falardeau was the battered spouse, according to Jones.[84] Heavenfire had threatened to kill Falardeau in the bar and had made contradictory statements to 9-1-1, doctors, and the police. Her black eyes and bruised condition came, Jones said, from her own knees hitting her face while she crouched on the floor of the truck to evade the blows from Falardeau, blows unleashed only after great provocation and assault by Heavenfire. She escalated conflict with him, unlike a battered woman, and could have left him as she had on two prior occasions. Finally, Jones said, self-defence and accident were fundamentally inconsistent explanations: "[T]his accused cannot maintain that she thought the gun was unloaded and then say, 'I had to kill to defend myself.'"[85]

Justice McFadyen summarized the evidence of both sides for the jury, describing the relationship as "abusive," "stormy," and "punctuated from time to time with some mental provocation on the part of Falardeau knowing that his common-law spouse was somewhat jealous of him."[86] She instructed that, if jurors accepted or had a doubt that the gun had gone off accidentally while the accused was picking it up, they should acquit. If they found instead that Heavenfire had deliberately pulled the trigger, if they had a doubt about whether she had intended to kill, then they should convict her of manslaughter. If she had intended to pull the trigger or to kill Falardeau, then they were to consider self-defence.

Justice McFadyen emphasized that a battered woman cannot justify homicide simply because she has been battered or suffers from the psychological effects of battering.[87] The chief difficulty of self-defence was that Heavenfire did not testify that she actually feared death or serious bodily harm from the deceased that night or believed that she could not otherwise preserve herself. However, Justice McFadyen told jurors, they might infer her fear from her injuries and her statements to the police that he was beating her that night or from her statement to the 9-1-1 operator that he told her to shoot him or he would kill her. They could, if they accepted the basis for his opinion, rely on Dr Weston's testimony that Heavenfire believed that she had to "kill or be killed."[88] Even if she feared for her life and saw no way out, they must also consider whether her beliefs were reasonable: "[D]id she have reason to believe that the extreme force of firing the gun was necessary to preserve herself from the attack?"[89]

The jury began deliberating on 24 June and reached a verdict in only three and a half hours. At 5:30 p.m., the jury rendered a verdict of not guilty, making Heavenfire the first Aboriginal woman to be acquitted after the *Lavallee* ruling of 1990.[90] She absorbed the verdict in silence, "shaking like a leaf"[91] and bursting into sobs only as she and Hepner walked out into the pouring rain.[92] Hepner told the media that she "feels sick about the whole thing."[93] He cautioned that "her acquittal doesn't give battered women in Alberta 'carte blanche' to kill their spouses, but in cases where a spouse is left with no choice but to kill to survive, the law will protect them."[94]

Falardeau's cousins decried the verdict. Marlene Conlin called it "unbelievable." Another cousin chimed in: "If you want to shoot and kill someone, all you have to do is get them to slap you a couple of times and then it's OK."[95] Falardeau's father told the media that his son "certainly was no wife beater," but compounding the tragedy, it was John Falardeau who had given his son the gun with which he had been killed.[96]

The Ravages of Colonization

The Heavenfire trial transcript allows us to look at how colonization continues to be manifested in violence, exclusion, and deprivation, resulting in two solitudes. Throughout, non-Aboriginal witnesses described Heavenfire in ways unrecognizable to her, her family, and her community. In fact, had one disinterested witness, Peebles, not testified near the end of the trial, the jury would have had to choose between two diametrically opposed versions of who thirty-three-year-old Heavenfire was and why she had killed Falardeau.

The prosecution's account of Falardeau as the "battered spouse" misrepresents battering as a course of conduct equally available to a young woman to dominate her older male partner. Its preposterousness is magnified when its "racelessness" is challenged.[97] Falardeau was valorized by the Crown witnesses as a physically large but essentially passive (white) man driven to violence by the aggression and jealousy of his younger and much smaller but surprisingly powerful (Aboriginal) female partner. Razack's comment that "perceptions of white vulnerability frequently exist in [a] manner disproportionate to actual documented incidences of crime"[98] captures the irony here. While Falardeau enacted his masculine and racial superiority through violence, control, and abuse,[99] his actions were por-trayed by witnesses as caused by Heavenfire.

Falardeau's racist language and verbal abuse were absent from the white witnesses' evidence, as were his banishment of Heavenfire's children and his exclusion of her Aboriginal friends and family from their home. Heavenfire was isolated and disempowered not only by his battering but also by her positioning as an Aboriginal woman living with a white man in a white rural community, among his friends. Her efforts to maintain contact with her family and to pursue her education were thwarted by his escalating vio-lence. Even those Crown witnesses who admitted having seen her injuries could not "see" her vulnerability.

Canadian law, according to Mary Eberts, has constructed Aboriginal women as "prey" by stripping them of citizenship in their own nations and withholding it from them in the new nation, along with the rights that go with "belonging," such as access to property and economic opportunities: "[W]hat is essential to grasp is that ... the Canadian state transformed Aboriginal women into civil and legal non-entities, officially devoid of value as citizens, community members and parents."[100]

The modern manifestations of Aboriginal women's status as prey are frightening: Aboriginal women are eight times more likely to be killed by male partners than non-Aboriginal women.[101] The Ontario Native Women's Association reports that, while one in ten Ontario women has experienced assault from a male partner, eight in ten Aboriginal women in Ontario have been so assaulted.[102] They are more likely to experience severe violence and correspondingly more debilitating effects.[103]

In fact, Heavenfire's story in many ways exemplifies the title of McGillivray and Comaskey's book *Black Eyes All of the Time.*[104] Here they provide a com-posite or aggregate picture of the twenty-six Aboriginal women whom they interviewed who had experienced intimate partner violence:

> She is a thirty-three-year-old woman of Indian status born and raised on a prairie reserve. Of her two or more children under the age of eighteen, at least one is in the care of others. She has not completed high school, and her annual income is under $10,000. She has been a victim of intimate violence since early childhood. She grew up witnessing the abuse of other children and women, including her own mother. She has herself lived with two abusive partners, becoming involved with the first while she was in her mid-teens. She experienced intimate violence about three years ago. Although she has a peace bond or restraining order against her abuser, and

charges laid against him have been settled, she is currently being stalked and harassed or still fears that he may come back into her life ...As a child, she experienced physical, sexual, and emotional abuse at the hands of family members and neighbours. She was physically and emotionally abused by her mother and sexually abused by a male relative. For a long time, she did not recognize that what was being done to her was wrong; she thought no one would believe her or help her, or that there was nothing unusual about her situation that would merit help. She tried to protect herself in various ways. If social services were available, she did not know about them. In adolescence and adulthood, she was humiliated by her partner and frequently and severely assaulted.[105]

Aboriginal women's lives and deaths remain relatively invisible to the larger society,[106] increasing their endangerment. Warren Goulding describes the investigation and trial of John Crawford, who killed at least four Aboriginal women before he was stopped. Indifference was the official and unofficial stance regarding these women's murders, from police who failed to halt an assault on one woman through to media that failed to cover the story.[107] Amnesty International's more recent *Stolen Sisters*[108] report provides many examples of neglect and disinterest on the part of the police when Aboriginal women are threatened, go missing, or are found murdered. Robert William Pickton was able to continue the massacre of forty-nine women, many if not most Aboriginal women, precisely because the police refused to investigate reports of missing women.[109]

Aboriginal women also have a highly problematic relationship with the police. According to Statistics Canada research, Aboriginal women are at least as likely as non-Aboriginal women to seek police intervention.[110] The authors of *Black Eyes All of the Time* report that all of the women whom they interviewed had contacted the police themselves at some point, out of fear for their own safety and their children's. Some called frequently and became discouraged by the police response: "[O]h it's her again," and "I should charge you for harassing, phoning here all the time."[111] The women described lengthy waits for assistance[112] as well as insulting police responses.[113] Many deplored the utter failure of child welfare and hospital personnel to react to the endangerment of their children.[114] McGillivray and Comaskey provide shocking examples of what women did to get police aid: a baby passed through an office window to call for help; rocks thrown at the window of another police station on reserve.[115] One report concluded that "[e]nforcement of the provincial 'zero tolerance' policy is all but non-existent on Manitoba reserves."[116]

Worse, Aboriginal women fear that their calls to the police will result in more violence, that the police will take their children away, or that the police will charge them instead. One woman responded to police advice with this question: "You're telling me to go back there when you know for a fact that I am in danger?" She was charged while attempting to lay charges against the abuser, held in a cell, and refused her epilepsy medication because she was believed to be drunk. In consequence, she suffered a grand mal seizure.[117] Four women in the McGillivray and Comaskey study were charged under the "zero tolerance" policy, though these charges were eventually dropped. Still, police decisions to lay charges against abused Aboriginal women can escalate into volatile situations that result in multiple charges against the woman,[118] with potentially deadly effects when women are afraid to ask for help: "I'm kind of scared to phone them anymore. I'm scared to get thrown in jail again."[119]

Beyond neglect and counter-charging as risks for Aboriginal women who seek help from the state is the possibility of assault and rape by the police themselves. Turning to the state for aid can be life threatening for some women, as documented in both reported cases and studies.[120]

Had Heavenfire pursued police intervention, she would have risked being charged and convicted, particularly in light of the many witnesses who claimed that she was the violent one. As an Aboriginal woman with a white partner, her chances of being disbelieved or criminalized by the police might have been elevated, particularly because, like other Aboriginal women, she fought back and at times might have been the first to strike when egged on by Falardeau.

US studies report that African American women are more likely to fight back physically than other women.[121] Although there are no similar studies in Canada of battered women who fight back, two of the conditions that seem to explain why African American women are more likely to fight back – their decreased access to outside resources to escape or stop the violence and their sense of themselves as strong and resilient survivors[122] – might predict that Aboriginal women are also more likely to defend themselves with physical force. The Canadian Association of Elizabeth Fry Societies writes that "the state has effectively trained many Aboriginal women to believe they are on their own in circumstances where they face violence. Women are then faced with the prospect of no hope and likely death or the need to fight."[123]

If a prosecutor can successfully label the woman on trial as a fighter or a danger, then her claim to have suffered from Battered Woman Syndrome and to have acted in self-defence becomes more precarious. One study of Canadian sentencing decisions involving women who killed abusive male partners suggests that women who fought back are judged more harshly, at least when they are sentenced for homicide. Elisabeth C Wells found that women seen by judges as violent or aggressive "were construed as active participants in the assaults that took place in the relationship" and were "presented as capable and assertive, the very antithesis to the battered woman as described by the [Battered Woman Syndrome] literature."[124] In turn, these women were "significantly more likely to receive a sentence of imprisonment compared to those not depicted as participants in mutually violent relationships."[125]

Racial stereotypes and prejudice can also play a role in whether the woman is seen as threatening or violent. To illustrate, one African American woman on trial for killing her batterer said that "I was told to act like a little white girl ... to look sad, to try to cry, to never look the jury in the eye. It didn't really work for me because the judge took one look at me and said, 'You look pretty mean; I bet you could really hurt a man.'"[126]

In another US trial involving a Native American woman charged with murdering her batterer, the prosecutor cross-examined her to show that "she liked to fight" and fought with her brothers and sisters. Her jury rejected self-defence and convicted her of murder.[127]

The Heavenfire case demanded exceptional defence work given the unanimous and damning portrait painted by the Crown witnesses. Fortunately, Hepner was able to recognize and indirectly expose the racism that framed both Falardeau's dominance and the witnesses' testimony, without inflaming the judge or jury. Lawyers,[128] judges,[129] and legislators[130] who dare to name racism can unleash a furious backlash, which a defence lawyer would want to avoid for the sake of the client. Hepner worked with Heavenfire's family and friends to show the jury her humanity and the reality of Falardeau's violence. He persisted with Battered Woman Syndrome evidence, in spite of the difficult fit, by using an expert who could reinterpret her experience as an Aboriginal woman.

Her acquittal gave Heavenfire a chance to escape from the additional years of violence to which she would have been condemned by a prison sentence. She turned her life around, reunited with her children,[131] kept a dry home,[132] completed her university preparation courses, enrolled in university to seek her degree in accounting, and served as treasurer for the

Hobbema First Nation. She spoke publicly about being entrapped in a battering relationship and urged medical professionals to find ways to reach battered women like her:

> Heavenfire says most of the medical professionals she dealt with "came across like they're not used to dealing with abuse." The most common response from physicians at the hospitals or clinics where she sought help was direct confrontation. "They'd say, 'He's doing this to you, isn't he?'" Heavenfire recalls. "But you're already defensive – I felt they were going to blame me if I said yes. Usually if they said something to me it didn't come across like they were trying to help – came across as criticism."[133]

In the same interview, Dr Weston said that a characteristic feature of Battered Woman Syndrome is the inability to disclose abuse.[134] Heavenfire no longer looks away: "Now if I see a woman with bruises on her face I get quite upset, and I don't stay out of it ... I'll say I know, I've used that excuse too."[135]

Doreen Sorenson

> "I know about 50 Ukrainian people living with Native girls and they're all jealous."[136]

Doreen Sorenson was charged with having murdered Danny Lund, her non-Aboriginal partner, in downtown Saskatoon on Sunday, 21 September 2003. Lund, like Falardeau, was a serious drinker – an alcoholic, according to Crown witnesses.[137] He frequently missed work due to his drinking.[138] When he did not show up for work at 3 a.m. Monday morning, a co-worker came looking for him. He saw Lund's body through the front door glass but assumed that he had just passed out and left.[139] Another friend, Eldon Baptiste, tried the door later in the morning, found it open, and entered the hallway where Lund's body lay. Lund had been stabbed in the back and chest and had died from the wound to his heart.

Sorenson was arrested on 4 February 2004, four and a half months after Lund's death. Donald Yonkman for the police later explained that they did not arrest her immediately because first there was the funeral, and then she underwent a major surgery. After that, the police became busy with other files. It cannot be ascertained whether Sorenson was released or detained pending her trial, but the case for detention would have been a difficult one for the Crown to make given the casual approach taken by the police regarding her arrest.

The entire prosecution rested on Sorenson's statements to her friend, Tansu Oktay, and to the police. There was no forensic evidence linking her to the homicide. It was not the police who brought Sorenson in for questioning but her daughter, Tracey Fiddler, who suspected that her mother had been involved in Lund's death and insisted that she "make things right" by speaking to the police several days after the homicide, on 25 September. Because she was not arrested at that time, Sorenson was neither asked about nor searched for injuries, though one officer noticed that she had a Band-Aid on one of her fingers.[140]

Sorenson's trial took place in late March 2006, in the Court of Queen's Bench, Saskatoon, presided over by Madam Justice Allisen R Rothery. Eight years earlier the Supreme Court of Canada had acknowledged that widespread prejudice against Aboriginal persons suggested a reasonable possibility that potential jurors hold unconscious or conscious bias that could deprive an Aboriginal accused of the presumption of innocence.[141] However, from Sorenson's transcript,[142] it appears that her lawyer did not invoke her right to challenge the jurors "for cause."

Because Sorenson's prosecution also contained what the Supreme Court called "an interracial element," her lawyer, Daryl Labach, was entitled to ask each potential juror whether the fact that Sorenson was Aboriginal and the victim white might cause him or her to favour the Crown over the accused. Most people answer in the negative – not surprisingly given the unconscious nature of most prejudice – but some admit their biases.[143] Furthermore, the discomfort that others display when answering this question can lead defence lawyers to exclude the juror from the panel.[144] It is difficult to know why counsel apparently did not seize this opportunity to pursue a fair trial for Sorenson.

In his opening address, Crown Attorney Perry Polishchuk told the ten women and two men jurors[145] that he would be calling twenty-eight witnesses – half of them police, the other half civilians – to prove his second-degree murder case against Sorenson. Police described the scene where Lund's body was found and their unsuccessful efforts to locate the knife. Confident that this was a simple murder case, they did not test any of the blood found on the deceased's clothes or the blood discovered throughout the home – on the couch in the living room, in the bathroom sink, or on the door handle in the hallway where the body was found.[146] Police testified that Lund had been convicted of common assault against Doreen and had received a conditional discharge.[147] The pathologist, Dr Dana Diudea, testified to three stab wounds, several other minor cuts or puncture wounds and abrasions, and slash wounds on his hands, one of which was "consistent with a defence wound."[148]

Polishchuk's main witness was Oktay, interviewed by the police on 24 September. He testified that Sorenson showed up at his home in the early hours of the morning on Monday to tell him that she had stabbed Lund and thrown the knife in the river.[149] She asked him to help her clean up the blood and was very teary and remorseful.[150] In response to the question whether Sorenson told him why she had done this, Oktay said that he had seen her "with a black eye or punched in the chin" – there was "an overall accumulation of a lot of ... physical violence between those individuals."[151]

On cross-examination, Oktay acknowledged that he had told the investigating officers that Lund had called Sorenson "an Indian slut or used some sort of racist comment."[152] He had seen her with physical injuries "all the time":[153] "black eye, punctured ear one day, bruises on shoulders in the summer ... [M]ost of the time she was physically battered ... [A] broken nose, half of her hair is missing in the back."[154]

Lund was extremely jealous, becoming furious when Oktay bought Sorenson a beer.[155] Oktay offered: "I know about 50 Ukrainian people who are living with Native girls and they're all jealous." Labach did not take too kindly to this generalization, asking the witness if all Ukranians were jealous, informing Oktay that he too was Ukrainian – "I'm interested."[156]

The Crown also called Fred Kanwischer, whose apartment Sorenson had visited after she was at Oktay's home. To Kanwischer, she had said nothing about the homicide, so he had little to offer. In a risky move, Labach asked the witness if he had observed any injuries on Sorenson that night. Kanwischer replied in the negative. Labach then asked "did you see her naked?" to qualify the denial. He did the same with police officer Lawrence Schulte.

Polishchuk called both of Sorenson's adult daughters to testify against their mother since she had made self-incriminating statements to each. They were allowed to provide what is called hearsay evidence: evidence based on what someone else has said rather than the witness's direct observation. This evidence is presumptively inadmissible for its truth because the person with direct knowledge is not on the witness stand and cannot be cross-examined on the evidence. Since Sorenson's statements to her daughters were characterized as "admissions against interest," they were able to provide these statements as evidence. The assumption is that, when people confess their crimes to others, these statements are more likely to be true.

However, every time Labach cross-examined Sorenson's daughters about what they knew about Lund's brutality toward their mother, Polishchuk objected to their evidence unless they had witnessed his assaults. This highlights one of the real difficulties for battered women on trial: scrupulous enforcement of the rule against hearsay can keep from the jury critical evidence of the nature and extent of the deceased's violence against the accused woman. She might be forced to take the witness stand to get this evidence in. Even if she testifies, she might not have full recall of all the assaults, making hearsay evidence by others critical to her defence. And of course the testimony of other witnesses regarding her disclosures can shore up her credibility and her claimed efforts to seek assistance. In the end, the jury heard some but not all of the statements that Sorenson had made to her daughters.

Tracey Fiddler described herself as "one of Jehovah's Witnesses." Her mother, she testified, was a very gentle, loving person who was never violent, even when drinking. Her mother's first husband, Sam Sorenson, a white man, had been very mean, very violent; Darryl Spence, with whom Sorenson had a subsequent relationship, was a violent alcoholic, according to Fiddler. Both daughters testified that her drinking started only when she left her marriage and increased when she began living with Lund.

Fiddler had hauled her mother down to the station on Thursday, 25 September, telling Police Constable Scott Joslin that her mother was there "to confess."[157] Even though at that point Fiddler was uncertain whether her mother was responsible, she earnestly believed that, "if she did it, she should confess,"[158] without considering whether her mother needed legal advice.

Fiddler had spoken on the telephone with her mother on Sunday evening and had hung up, upset that Lund was bad-mouthing her husband in the background. Like Oktay, Fiddler described Lund as extremely jealous. In fact, he had convinced himself that there was something sexual between Fiddler's husband and her mother. So obsessed was Lund with this belief that he would not allow Sorenson to talk to her daughter's husband. Fiddler was aware that Lund was violent to her mother when he was drinking. She had seen him in a rage, throwing furniture off their balcony. She had also seen photographs of her mother's head where her scalp was red and raw from her hair having been torn out. Fiddler described bruising on her mother's legs a "few days" after the homicide, "like she was defending herself or something."[159]

Sherry Sorenson, Sorenson's daughter from her first marriage, in direct examination by the Crown, retold the account of the homicide relayed by her mother to Sherry and her brother Terry. Because Sherry was recounting a narrative wherein her mother admitted the killing, the Crown did not stop her. She said that Lund usually let her mom leave when they were arguing, but this time he blocked one door and then the other when she tried to escape.[160] Sorenson told her that she grabbed a knife and stabbed Lund in the back. When she realized that she had seriously harmed him, she tried to wake him up, started crying, and then panicked. She wrapped the knife up and left the house to throw it in the river.

On cross-examination, Sherry testified to having witnessed terrible violence perpetrated against her mother by her father, Sam,[161] and by Spence, who had broken her mother's arm.[162] Len Stewart, another of her mother's partners, had also been "physical" with her mother.[163] Lund was a great person when he was not drinking, but Sherry had seen many injuries on her mother while she was with Lund: "[A] black eye, broken finger and there was cuts to her head from having her head smashed in a door, her whole face was full of blood from the blood pouring from all the cuts on her head."[164] She photographed her mother's injuries, but her mother begged her not to go to the police and refused to seek medical attention. Sherry was also aware that Lund had kicked her mother in the crotch and buttocks.[165] He was racist toward her mother for "being Native, sq**ws he mentioned."[166]

Sherry was the Crown's last witness, leaving Labach to open his case to the jury. In his address, he pointed out that none of the Crown's witnesses was present when Sorenson stabbed Lund, but she had both confessed to the homicide and voluntarily attended the police station. He told the jury that he would not summarize her defence for them but would allow them to draw it from her testimony: "Why it happened is the single most important issue i[n] this case ... So for 12 honourable people who are entitled to know why it happened, my first witness is ... Doreen Sorenson."[167]

Sorenson was a fifty-one-year-old residential school survivor. She recalled seeing her own mother being carried home in a bloodied blanket when she was five years old. Her mother was abused by her father, but "she didn't do anything, she just stood there and – while he beat her."[168] Her father was frequently jailed for his violence.

A soft-spoken woman whose voice in the courtroom required a microphone, Sorenson readily acknowledged her criminal record for impaired driving and breach of bail for drinking while awaiting trial.[169] She lived on the Sturgeon Lake Reserve until she was eight, when she was sent to residential school for six or seven years. Sorenson was beaten on her behind and hands by the nuns and principal, forced to wear her urine-soaked blankets, and hit on the head if she spoke Cree. She left school after grade five and gave birth to Tracey when she was fourteen or fifteen years old. Her father took out his rifle and asked her if he should shoot the baby now or later when she took Tracey to show her parents.[170] A teen mother with an abusive family, Sorenson really was on her own. She married Sam two years later, desperate for family and stability. She stayed with him for twenty-one violent years.

Sam was jealous and abusive not only to Sorenson but to the children as well, punching them in the stomach and head even when they were toddlers. When Tracey was fifteen, he beat her very badly. He used racist epithets to humiliate Sorenson, calling her a "wagon-burner,"[171] and treated her like an object.[172] She was too terrified to seek police aid,[173] and although she left him she was afraid to refuse when he tracked her down and ordered her to return home.[174] One of those times he drove her to a remote area, pulled a hunting knife across her throat, and told her that, if he could not have her, nobody would. She begged for her life and swore that she loved him and would never leave him.[175] She later managed to leave him, only to end up with an equally violent and jealous man, Darryl Spence, who checked her undergarments for evidence of infidelity and cut the clothes off her body if she looked too good.[176] She described her next partner, Len Stewart, as a "psycho." He broke her wrist, punched her in the eye, and monitored her movements in the home.

Her relationship with Lund followed the same pattern. He was extremely jealous and became violent when drinking. He isolated her from her friends and called her "an Indian slut and just f'ing Indian."[177] Sorenson testified: "I didn't like it, but my husband used to call me that too, so I just – just – more or less just got used to it, I guess."[178] The abuse started about a year into their relationship and escalated when Lund began kicking her in the legs and hips, dragging her by the hair, and pounding her face into furniture and doors. Kicking her in the crotch was his pattern, one time kicking her so hard that he bruised her entire pelvis.[179] Sorenson had many health problems, including depression and uterine cysts that caused pain and bleeding and necessitated a hysterectomy days after Lund's death.

Sorenson tried to get help once from a stranger on the street, without success,[180] and another time was driven to the hospital by the police, who subsequently charged Lund with assault causing bodily harm. She agreed to have the charge downgraded to simple assault so that he could plead guilty, secure a discharge, and not lose his job.[181] She became financially dependent on him after she quit her job because he would bother her at work with his jealous obsessions, asking her whom she was sitting with and demanding that she phone him every time she went for a break.[182]

Sorenson had no bank account and no money of her own. Lund gave her the occasional twenty-dollar bill, and she bought her clothes from second-hand clothing stores.[183] Apart from his sexual jealousy, Lund was a good person, Sorenson said, when he was not drinking. So she was loathe to charge him for his attacks on her when he sobered up. She began running away every time he drank because she knew what was coming.[184] Lund had also raped her. Yet she returned because he was good to her on his good days and because she blamed herself for being abused, as her mother had done.[185]

On the night of the homicide, Sorenson testified, she and Lund were both drinking, and she was "loaded." She described the telephone call to her daughter Tracey, when Lund began loudly criticizing Tracey and her husband, and Tracey hung up the phone. Lund then pulled the phone off the wall and put it in the bedroom, telling Sorenson that it was his phone, he paid for it, and she could not use it. As he ranted on about her daughter's family, Sorenson told him that she was leaving. In response, Lund tried to kick her in the crotch, missed, and got her in the leg. She tried to leave the house, but he blocked her exit and locked the door. He came after her and tried to get a hold on her, but she ran to the kitchen and grabbed a knife, warning him to stay away from her. She began swinging the knife to keep him at bay as he cursed her, calling her a "stupid f'ing Indian slut."[186]

The struggle moved to the living room, and Sorenson caught Lund in the shoulder with the knife as she tried to defend herself: "And he got even madder yet and we struggled at the back there and then that's when I – for fear that he was going to hurt me bad when – and if he got the knife and so I just – it happened so fast, I – he fell, he fell on the floor. And the knife ..." At this point, she was crying so hard that her testimony became inaudible. She struggled to compose herself and continued: "on the top of his chest, I didn't know what to do ... "[187] "I didn't think he was going to die from it."[188] Her last words in direct examination were that she was devastated by his death. Lund was a good person when he was not drinking, she repeated.[189]

Polishchuk's cross-examination focused on two main themes. First, Polishchuk repeatedly asked Sorenson to explain why she did not invoke other options such as calling the police when Lund was violent. She insisted that she was too afraid of him to involve the police, but the prosecutor reminded her that she had contacted the police when Stewart had broken her wrist and when her son Terry had assaulted her. Polishchuk dwelt on the fact that Sorenson had left Lund on prior occasions, sometimes for days, but had always returned to him. She held her own when Polishchuk suggested that the violence was mutual. She might have slapped Lund once, she admitted, but she had never pulled a knife on him.

Polishchuk's second theme was to challenge Sorenson's characterization of Lund's death as accidental. Polishchuk went over and over the sequence of events, to the point where the defence objected that he was trying to confuse Sorenson.[190] She was unable to explain, one by one, each of the injuries on the deceased's body. Repeatedly, she responded that "it just happened so fast." With regard to the stab wound to the deceased's heart, she said that "I blocked a lot of the stuff out." Polishchuk challenged whether she was swinging the knife wildly: "[I]f you're swinging the knife as opposed to thrusting it how do we get 4-5 cm into Danny's body?" Sorenson broke down again, weeping. Still, she insisted that she was not the aggressor but was terrified and just trying to defend herself.

When Dory Cook, the next witness, took the stand, the defence case took a downward turn. Cook was neither a psychiatrist nor a psychologist but a social worker who had counselled Sorenson since her arrest. Cook was to testify that the violence in Sorenson's past had resulted in Battered Woman Syndrome.

The defence attempted to have Cook recognized as an expert, in the absence of the jury. Labach argued that *Lavallee* did not limit what type of expertise was required for expert qualification in this regard. Cook received her Bachelor of Indian Social Work from the Saskatchewan Indian Federated College in 1998, taught courses on the subject, completed assessments for social services, worked with "hundreds and hundreds" of battered women, and counselled Aboriginal women dealing with violence. She clearly had important knowledge to offer about Aboriginal women's experience of male violence and the challenges they face in escaping from their batterers.

Unfortunately, her self-described qualification for diagnosing Battered Woman Syndrome was that she herself was a battered woman from the age of thirteen on, in at least five battering relationships.[191] In a lengthy monologue, Cook recounted terrifying experiences of being choked, having her clothing ripped off, being sexually assaulted, and being called vile names.

Her evidence in chief fell well short of qualifying her as an expert on Battered Woman Syndrome. More than that, her personal story allowed her objectivity to be questioned, although she had not been in a battering relationship since 1991.

Polishchuk had an easy time destroying Cook's credentials. In light of her earlier testimony that 85 percent of her clients were battered women, he asked how many of her clients experienced Battered Woman Syndrome? Cook answered 80 percent, but when he sought to clarify she asked him whether "the woman has to be in two – more than two relationships to be classified as a battered woman; is that correct?" Polishchuk corrected Cook on this point,[192] then asked her to explain the difference between being a battered woman and being diagnosed with Battered Woman Syndrome. Her answer seemed to focus on the fact that someone with Battered Woman Syndrome would kill her abusive partner. This response prompted Polishchuk to ask if 80 percent of her clients had killed, which further confused Cook:

> With the – the definition of a battered woman is one who is repeatedly subjected to ... continual physical and psychological behaviours by a man in order to coerce her into doing something he wants her to do, without any regard to her rights. So given that definition of battered woman, then I have counseled 80 percent of women who have [been] battered. I have also counseled 85% of women who had been – who have been – okay wait a minute, I'm getting confused myself. Okay. So say 85 percent of – would have battered women – no, 80 percent pardon me, would have battered women's syndrome and 80 – and 85 percent would be battered women then. So 5 percent would be battered women.[193]

Polishchuk reframed his question, advising Cook that being a battered woman was the threshold, but to have the syndrome one must also meet the diagnostic symptoms. Cook testified that, although her one psychology course did not qualify her to diagnose PTSD, she relied on her clinical experience to determine that virtually all of her clients who had been battered experienced PTSD. She preferred to call it an assessment rather than a diagnosis. When Polishchuk then asked her if she was qualified to diagnose Battered Woman Syndrome, a subset of PTSD, she said that she was. He then confronted her: "Didn't you just tell me that you don't believe you're entitled to diagnose certain things because you're not a doctor?"[194] She answered: "No, I – no, I believe I am entitled to – to classify a woman if she has – if she has battered – been battered in a relationship because I'm dealing with her reality." Polishchuk prodded further, asking Cook to provide the symptoms for PTSD. She answered:

> Very jumpy, coming in regressed in a – in a – acting like a – terrified child perhaps or a terrified person that was – that was – you know, doesn't – doesn't know how to breathe properly. Headaches, all kinds of body symptoms, back aches, neck aches, migraines, panic – oh, especially panic and anxiety attacks ... Insomnia, mind racing, massive guilt, toxic shame and embarrassment, rage.[195]

Polishchuk asked if a certain number of symptoms need to be present or certain key symptoms. Her reply was vague: "It all depends on – on the person."[196]

Polishchuk suggested that Cook's experience of battering was invaluable to her work with her clients. Cook agreed, saying that she learned from her clients as well. He then asked whether her capacity for objectivity in determining whether a woman was battered or experienced Battered Woman Syndrome was compromised by her personal experience. This she flatly denied: "No, I don't believe so."[197]

Cook was excused from the stand, leaving the lawyers to argue about whether she could testify as an expert. Labach then withdrew his application to have her qualified as an expert. Even had he persuaded the judge that she was both qualified and objective, her confused testimony might well have worsened Sorenson's prospects for acquittal. Unfortunately for Sorenson, Labach did not present another expert to replace the missing link of Battered Woman Syndrome. He closed the case for the defence with Sorenson as the only witness.

His closing address reviewed the response of Sorenson's mother to abuse: "She accepted it as part of being a wife and this twisted idea was passed on to Doreen."[198] He reminded jurors that Sorenson was a single mother by fifteen when her baby was threatened by her father with a gun. Labach recalled the extreme violence to which she was subjected by successive men, starting with Sam and ending with Lund. His focus was on her need to escape the house that night to avoid Lund's drunken, impending violence. After he blocked her exits, Sorenson grabbed the knife to try to hold him off so she could leave.

Labach warned the jury that the Crown would focus on minor inconsistencies in his client's evidence, but, he pointed out, this fight had evolved quickly. The Crown would suggest that she had other options, but Sorenson had no legal obligation to retreat: "A person under attack has to make decisions quickly and does not have time for calm and detached reflection as to what is the most proper course of action. Hindsight is a wonderful thing."[199] Sorenson was terrified of what Lund would do if he got the knife away from her: "Stabbing him was the only way to defend herself from being beaten or possibly killed herself. I know of no other way to describe it, ladies and gentlemen, self-defence."[200]

Labach told the jury: "If you do not agree with my assertion and you have a reasonable doubt that my client was acting in self-defence, then there is one other issue that I need to address you on."[201] He slipped here – in fact, if the jurors had a reasonable doubt that Sorenson had acted in self-defence, they were legally obliged to acquit her. Labach argued alternatively that she did not have the intent required for murder due to either the accidental nature of the homicide or her intoxication; he also submitted that she was provoked by Lund's racist slurs and his wrongful act of barring her exit. Any of these defences – accident, intoxication, or provocation – would at most make her guilty of manslaughter.

The Crown's summation acknowledged Sorenson's difficult life and violent relationships. However, asserted Polishchuk, Sorenson had managed to escape from these other relationships and had left Lund before. In fact, her first statements to the police suggested that Lund told her to leave.[202] She did not act in self-defence when she killed Lund: his chest wound was a stab wound, inconsistent with her description of waving the knife around in self-defence. His body had other unexplained wounds, some of which were possibly defensive wounds.[203] Sorenson was entitled to rely on legal advice to remain silent under questioning, but when she spoke she did not tell the police that she was afraid or acted to protect herself. Only in her last interview did she call the homicide an accident and say that Lund had kicked her.[204] Finally, Polishchuk disputed whether it really was an accident because Sorenson did not seek emergency aid and instead fled.

Justice Rothery charged the jury on 11 April on all three defences – self-defence, intoxication, and provocation – and raised the possibility of accident. Her charge on self-defence was bare bones. She provided an overview of each witness's testimony and the Crown and defence positions, but she did not relate the evidence of Doreen's experience of battering to the elements of self-defence in detail. Because there was no expert testimony through which Sorenson's actions could have been translated for the jury, it would have been difficult to insist on a more fulsome charge.

Two days later, on the morning of 13 April, the jury delivered its verdict: not guilty of murder but guilty of manslaughter. Labach asked to have the jury polled, requiring each juror to stand and individually state his or her verdict, in the hope that one juror might change his or her verdict and cause a mistrial. All affirmed that Sorenson was guilty of manslaughter.

At sentencing, Labach argued that Sorenson's eight years of abuse by Lund and her remorse ought to result in conditional imprisonment or "house arrest." Sorenson told the judge: "Forever I will feel the numbness that will never go away." She wept as she apologized to Lund's family in a "near-whisper."[205] Polishchuk asked for a jail term of five years. Justice Rothery acknowledged that Sorenson had found work, finished high school, sought counselling, and given up alcohol. Still, she rejected Labach's plea for leniency and sentenced Sorenson to three years of incarceration in a federal penitentiary. Lund's body bore several knife wounds, and Sorenson failed to seek emergency services after she stabbed Lund, explained the judge. Labach, later sworn in as a judge of the Saskatchewan Provincial Court on 1 May 2009, described the sentence as "certainly fair."[206]

A Fair Trial for Sorenson?

Why was Sorenson convicted of manslaughter on such strong facts for self-defence? Obviously, a trial transcript cannot answer all questions. The content of the four videotapes of her at the police station was not transcribed. Perhaps the tapes persuaded the jury that she was not defending herself. The Crown in closing did refer to the fact that she was largely silent, her head hanging low, and occasionally crying in the recorded interviews.

Is that behaviour inconsistent with self-defence? It might be equally consistent with what the Canadian Association of Elizabeth Fry Societies and the Native Women's Association of Canada describe as the "hyper-responsibility" that Aboriginal women take for their actions, whereby they assume responsibility far beyond that which is legally or morally justifiable.[207] Certainly, Fiddler reinforced her mother's hyper-responsibility when she insisted that her mother "confess," even without being certain of her involvement or the extent of her culpability.

It is also possible that the forensic evidence and Crown cross-examination of Sorenson revealed too many gaps and inconsistencies in her narrative of the unfolding altercation. Maybe she was not a credible witness to her jury. Her manifest remorse for Lund's death might have struck them as consistent with accident or intoxication, both defences more suggestive of a manslaughter verdict than with acquittal based on having acted to protect her life.

Yet, when compared with Heavenfire, Sorenson seems to have been better placed to advance self-defence. She had at least as much evidence from witnesses regarding the violence that Lund perpetrated against her. Unlike in Heavenfire's trial, all of the corroborating evidence of Lund's violence was provided by Crown, not defence, witnesses. Sorenson was not confronted with a list of white witnesses whose versions of the events needed to be directly addressed. Instead, she faced much less tangible presumptions that nonetheless required sophisticated lawyering.

Sorenson did not call 9-1-1 after she stabbed Lund, unlike Heavenfire when she fired the fatal shot. Still, jurors should have been able to imagine how difficult it would have been for her to call the Saskatoon police to turn herself in for stabbing her white male partner. Aboriginal people had every reason to fear the police. Saskatoon police were known by then, at least unofficially,[208] to have engaged in the deliberate removal of Aboriginal people from the inner city for "starlight tours." Several Aboriginal men died after they were driven by the police and dumped in rural locations miles from home and with inadequate clothing and means to survive.[209]

Not only might Sorenson have had good reasons to avoid the authorities, but also her flight from the site of the stabbing was neither legally nor factually inconsistent with self-defence. She was not accustomed to fighting back and must have been deeply shocked and shamed by the terrible consequences that ensued the one time she defended herself against Lund.[210] However, her jury might have viewed her failure to call for help as suggestive of a motive to kill or as inconsistent with their expectations about how a "real" battered woman would respond.

That Sorenson had never been violent toward Lund ought to have strengthened her case over that of Heavenfire. Not one witness saw Sorenson abuse or harm Lund, unlike the stream of witnesses who testified against Heavenfire. Was it possible that the jury was nonetheless persuaded that Sorenson was violent? Perhaps, in spite of the evidence of her daughters and friend Oktay that she was a gentle and loving person who was never violent, negative stereotypes about Aboriginal people as violent prevailed.

Or perhaps the jurors decided that, even if Sorenson did act in self-defence, she used excessive force and therefore could not be acquitted outright. Still, this conclusion ought to have been suspect in light of the very serious injuries that Lund had caused Sorenson in the past. Her vulnerability to male violence on the street was also on the trial record. Oktay testified as a Crown witness that all the "girls" whom he knew carried knives because the inner city where he and Sorenson lived was so dangerous.[211] This evidence could have been turned to her advantage to illuminate for the jury her precarious existence within a hostile environment, in which even her intimate partner could turn on her in an instant.

Yet, as Razack has written, male violence in the inner cities can be construed as "a natural by-product of the space and thus the social context in which it occur[s], an event that is routine when the bodies in question are Aboriginal."[212] This "naturalization" of white male violence against Aboriginal women is persuasive when the interaction can be characterized as consensual. The prosecutor emphasized that Sorenson had failed to leave Lund, placing her squarely within that category of women who assume the risks of male violence. Her homicidal act occurred in downtown Saskatoon, strongly associating it for the jurors with the violence and criminality that stick "to the Aboriginal bodies, entrenching a view that such bodies can be associated with little else."[213]

Beyond any suggestion that somehow Sorenson accepted the violence – both implicit and explicit – entailed in her relationship with Lund, where were the safe places to which she could have or, as Polishchuk suggested, should have escaped? Her options were even fewer than those available to women such as Bonnie Mooney. Sorenson had been systematically excluded by colonizing practices from being raised by a loving family, receiving an education, working productively, and living free of male violence. Every relationship that she had experienced had been unspeakably violent. She did not have a community or family to protect her. There was no reasonable possibility that the police or other justice institutions could have provided her with safety. What does "leaving" mean to a residential school survivor and battered Aboriginal woman living in Saskatoon? Where are the "safe spaces" for displaced and dislocated Aboriginal women?[214]

At the least, Sorenson's defence required a credible expert on Battered Woman Syndrome to render her acute endangerment and lack of other options as an Aboriginal woman in relationship with a violent white male comprehensible to her jury. Knowledge of the pitfalls for Aboriginal women of

Battered Woman Syndrome evidence and careful selection of the right expert to reinterpret this evidence to fit Aboriginal women's lives are critical to defending Aboriginal women who kill.

Could Sorenson have benefited from defence strategies aimed at exposing the role of colonization and systemic racism in her vulnerability to abuse, the particular form that Lund's abuse took, and ultimately her resort to self-defensive violence? Razack asks what it would mean "to deliberately introduce history and social context" into a murder trial.[215] In her analysis of the murder trial of two white men who killed an Aboriginal woman outside Regina, she showed how the men's lawyers "drew attention to their own ethnicity in a bid to represent everyone as equally raced."[216] This strategy, she argued, hid the racism of their clients' murderous attack on their Aboriginal victim.

Sorenson's defence might have benefited from social context evidence about how Lund's unlawful domination was reinforced by racism against Aboriginal women in Saskatoon. Her lawyer instead disputed Oktay's characterization of Lund as one of about fifty jealous Ukrainian men whom Oktay knew to be living with "Native" girls by asserting his own Ukrainian identity and daring Oktay to label him "jealous." Not only was Lund's whiteness shrouded by his Ukrainian ethnicity,[217] but also his racism slipped from view, and any racial bias possibly held – consciously or unconsciously – by Sorenson's jurors remained insulated from challenge and self-doubt.

Razack suggests that men like Lund who partner with Aboriginal women and also live at the margins in the inner city themselves become "racialized" and discreditable to criminal justice authorities.[218] In Sorenson's trial, Lund's "whiteness" was arguably in question, not only because Lund was Sorenson's partner but also because he was a marginal, alcoholic worker in downtown Saskatoon. His whiteness was arguably reprieved, however, when Labach inadvertently aligned himself with the deceased batterer and against his client.

Sorenson's defence required a sophisticated challenge to the "racelessness" of both Lund's violence and her prosecution for murder. The acquittal of Aboriginal women like Sorenson of husband killing – particularly when their husbands are white – demands passionate and strategic advocacy that in turn requires lawyers to recognize their own sex and race privileges and engage all available strategies to ensure that their clients receive a fair trial untainted by racist misogyny.

Labach's defence work for Sorensen was significant for his successful effort to extend the category of expert witnesses who can testify for battered women. *Lavallee* does not limit this category to psychiatrists and psychologists, allowing recognition of other forms of expertise. Labach also did not plead his client guilty, a far too common practice when Aboriginal women are charged with killing their abusers, as I discuss in the following chapter.

5

Donelda Kay, Denise Robin Rain, and Jamie Gladue

"Not a battered wife."[1]

In the early morning hours of her nineteenth birthday, 17 September 1995, outside a townhouse complex in Nanaimo, British Columbia, Jamie Gladue shouted "I got you, you fucking bastard," while "jumping up and down as if she had tagged someone."[2] That "someone" was Reuben Beaver, her twenty-year-old Aboriginal partner. She had "tagged" him in the heart with a large knife, and he died soon after. Gladue was charged with second-degree murder. Because Beaver had had sexual intercourse with Gladue's sister only an hour before and had called Gladue "fat and ugly," the Crown was willing to accept her plea of guilty to the lesser crime of manslaughter. Gladue was sentenced to three years in prison in February 1997 after a sentencing hearing that did not consider her Aboriginal background and did not explore in any depth her abuse at the hands of Beaver.

Gladue made legal history in Canada in 1999 when she appealed her sentence to the Supreme Court of Canada. Hers was the first case in which the Court interpreted section 718.2(e) of the 1995 *Criminal Code* reforms, which requires judges to consider all available sanctions other than imprisonment, with a particular focus on the circumstances of Aboriginal offenders.[3] The Court decided that, when sentencing an Aboriginal offender, the judge must consider the unique and systemic background factors that brought the offender to the crime and the appropriate sentencing alternatives in light of the offender's heritage. Ironically, while hailed as a victory for Aboriginal peoples in conflict with the law, the *Gladue* ruling simultaneously denied Gladue its benefit because her crime – manslaughter – was violent.[4]

In spite of the notoriety of her precedent-setting case, little is known about Gladue's background, beyond that her mother was Cree and her father Métis and that Gladue was a teenage mother of two very young children, five months pregnant with her third child. Little is also known about what brought her to kill Beaver. That is partly because Gladue pled guilty after a preliminary inquiry in which only the prosecution presented evidence but also because no one ordered a pre-sentence report, even though her act was characterized by the British Columbia Court of Appeal as a "near murder."[5] One might be forgiven for wondering whether sentencing a young Aboriginal woman for a violent crime was considered routine, rendering individualized justice superfluous?

The justice system resolutely refused to correct these omissions and hear about Gladue's circumstances on appeal. When her second lawyer attempted to introduce a psychologist's report describing Beaver's violence and its impact on Gladue on the night that she killed Beaver, the British Columbia Court of Appeal ruled that it was too late: this was "fresh evidence" that her first lawyer ought to have brought forward when she was sentenced. In any event, the sentencing judge knew of Beaver's conviction for assaulting Gladue while she was pregnant with their first child but had concluded that she was not a "battered wife."[6] Moreover, the appeal court said, the proffered report suggested that Gladue acted in self-defence, in conflict with the position of her first lawyer at the sentencing hearing. Unless she repudiated her guilty plea, Gladue was barred from offering this fresh evidence.[7]

On further appeal, the Supreme Court of Canada did not comment on the evidence that Gladue was indeed a "battered woman." The Court found that the sentencing judge had erred in failing to consider the individual and systemic features of her Aboriginal background that contributed to her offence as well as the available alternatives to imprisonment supported by her Aboriginal community or the larger community. However, since she had already been paroled and her offence was a "most serious" one implicating "domestic violence" by Gladue, the Supreme Court of Canada decided that no injustice had been done and refused to alter her sentence.

Was Gladue's outcome just? At the close of this chapter, I will re-examine her case to ask whether a guilty plea was inevitable or whether self-defence could have been asserted credibly. What can lawyers and the criminal justice system learn from her case and those of other Aboriginal women described in this chapter?

Donelda Kay

> "None of my business."[8]

Twenty-one-year-old Donelda Kay was charged with having committed, on 25 September 1993, in Regina, Saskatchewan, the second-degree murder of Dennis Noel Gordon by stabbing him once in the heart. Kay pled not guilty before a jury of seven men and five women. Her trial commenced on 6 June 1994 and was presided over by Justice Gene Maurice in the Court of Queen's Bench in Regina.

BL Dutka's opening address presented the case against Kay as open and shut. Kay was at a party in a Regina apartment where she argued sporadically with her partner, Gordon. None of the witnesses had seen Gordon touch Kay all evening. All would testify that she had done the pushing and hitting, escalating a silly argument into a homicide.

Dutka told jurors that they would hear that Kay asked Rebecca Bourassa, a young witness who had retreated from the party to an apartment across the hall, Apartment 3, for a knife. Kay then grabbed a knife from Bourassa's floor and charged into the next apartment and stabbed Gordon as he sat in a chair. "You will hear none of the Crown witnesses testify that they saw Donelda Kay being attacked by Dennis Gordon that night," Dutka declared. "You will not hear that she was being beaten ... You will not hear that she seemed afraid."[9]

Dutka thus tipped the jury to the possibility that Kay's lawyer, Don Worme, might advance self-defence. To achieve acquittal for Kay, Worme first had to establish an evidentiary basis for self-defence, to provide "an air of reality," and then to raise a "reasonable doubt" about whether she had acted in self-defence. Those accused of crimes need not "prove" defences: the presumption of innocence means that, if self-defence has an evidentiary basis, the Crown must disprove it beyond a reasonable doubt. An accused need only create a doubt that is "not based on sympathy or prejudice"; it must not be "imaginary or frivolous"[10] but instead "logically connected to the evidence or absence of evidence."[11]

The Crown's first witnesses were police constables AL Forster, Robert Peever, and Matt Fraser. Having attended the scene of the homicide, they described the premises, Gordon's body, the scratches, swelling, and marks on Kay's face and body, and the forensic evidence found at Apartment 2. Worme's cross-examination aimed to plant the seeds of reasonable doubt, forcing the police to acknowledge their failure to photograph a blood stain on the wall in the hall, which they did not test until days later.[12] They did not examine carefully the stairway outside the apartments for evidence.[13] The view from Apartment 3 into Apartment 2 was partially obstructed. The officers also agreed that the hand of the deceased bore swelling consistent with having punched someone[14] and was taped, as a boxer's hand might be.

Worme exposed the effects of a harsh life on the Aboriginal deceased. He asked Peever to describe Gordon's slash marks on his left forearm,[15] self-harm used by many survivors of childhood abuse to release their pain and suffering.[16] Peever had photographed Kay's body in ways "quite revealing."[17] When Peever said that Kay was "very co-operative," Worme made sure that the jury did not misapprehend the acute vulnerability that she experienced in the presence of uniformed male officers while her nearly naked body[18] was checked for old and new injuries: "She didn't appear to be enjoying it by any stretch of the imagination? ... She wasn't smiling? ... She wasn't looking very happy?" Peever replied: "No emotions at all, actually."[19] He took hair samples from Kay without resistance: "[S]he didn't say we couldn't and she didn't say we could."[20] Rather than arguing that her *Charter* rights had been violated,[21] Worme allowed the jury to absorb this picture of a resigned woman silently acceding to police authority.

Seventeen-year-old Bourassa was the chief witness for the Crown, the only person who claimed to have seen the stabbing. The source of the argument between Kay and Gordon was two pairs of Kay's pants – one in Bourassa's possession – "lent" by Gordon as "court pants"[22] for Bourassa. She relayed the argument between the couple as one sided, with Kay doing all the yelling, swearing, and slapping. After Kay grabbed a knife from her floor, Bourassa tried to get it away from her but failed. She said that Kay waved the knife and challenged Gordon – "come on, come on" – and then ran directly at him across the hall with the knife, stabbed him, and fled the building. Bourassa followed, alerting others in Apartment 2 that Gordon had been stabbed. Neither apartment had a telephone, so she ran to a pay phone to call 9-1-1.

Worme's cross-examination of Bourassa was prolonged, for hers was the main evidence standing between conviction and acquittal. Worme established that Bourassa, who was fifteen at the time of Gordon's death, commenced living with her twenty-seven-year-old boyfriend the day after he had a fight with his wife and left her and their three children.[23] She denied drinking at the party but admitted that she had a physical fight with Tracy Sebastien that night, retreated to her apartment across the hall, and then repeatedly slammed her apartment door until Dianne Pascal charged over and slapped her in the face to get her to stop. After that, Bourassa remained in her own unit, with the door open so that she could see into Apartment 2. Kay joined her in Apartment 3 until Bourassa told her that she had her pants. At that point, Kay crossed the hall to confront Gordon.

Worme asked Bourassa if she knew that "Dennis had given away virtually all of [Kay's] clothing."[24] She replied that she only knew about the pants and a silk shirt.[25] She testified that Kay asked her to go to Apartment 2 and tell Gordon that she was leaving, which she did. Kay went down the stairs to exit the building, but when Bourassa looked out her door Gordon and Kay were arguing in the hall. She heard hitting and slapping but did not see who hit whom.[26] When Gordon returned to Apartment 2, Kay came back to Apartment 3 to get the knife.

Worme forced Bourassa to admit that she did not see everything.[27] Beyond casting doubt on her capacity to observe all the events, Worme attacked her credibility. He dwelt on her many statements to the police and media that she was the only eyewitness to the stabbing, suggesting that she "got a lot of attention out of this."[28] He exposed her prior convictions for theft, over her objections.[29]

Through this witness, Worme introduced a theme to which he would return. He twice asked Bourassa whether she was concerned about the escalating argument between Gordon and Kay, or was it "none of your business?" She agreed that "it was none of my business."[30]

Dutka brought forward another four witnesses who had been drinking in Apartment 2. Darcy Longman said that he saw Kay punch Gordon in the head and push him backward into a wall.[31] Gordon's response, Longman testified, was just to laugh at Kay. Longman saw Pascal give Kay "a few shots" in the face when Kay returned to the apartment to approach Gordon as he lay on the floor after she stabbed him.[32]

Worme's first question of Longman cut to the chase. Worme asked whether the relationship between Gordon and Kay was a violent one. "Yeah," answered Longman. He saw Kay break a beer bottle over Gordon's head; Gordon then picked her up by the neck, strangled her until she was unconscious, dragged her body into another room, and left her there while they went out drinking.[33] Worme asked Longman whether he had spoken to Gordon about this. He replied: "Not my business."[34] Worme suggested that

Longman was not worried about the argument unfolding between Gordon
and Kay because he had "seen worse." "In fact," continued Worme, "you and
your girlfriend sometimes get into that kind of fight or argument?" "Yeah"
was the final word from Longman.[35]

In cross-examining the witnesses, Worme painted a picture of an out-of-
control drinking party where violence erupted on several occasions. Pascal
testified that she punched Kay in the face; she also slapped Bourassa when
she was throwing a temper tantrum. Sebastian testified to multiple fights
having occurred that night at the party: she too fought with Bourassa after
she slammed her door "up to 30 times."[36] Sebastian saw Pascal and Bourassa
fight and saw Gordon and Kay fight.[37] Joel Longman testified that he broke
up a couple of fights that night.[38]

Medical and forensics experts testified next. Under cross-examination,
Dr David Guerrero said that Gordon's arm had multiple non-medical needle
marks and that his right hand was swollen and bruised, "consistent with
having punched something or someone."[39] Dr MG Escanlar testified that
both the liver and the lungs of the deceased indicated that he was an IV drug
user[40] and a heavy drinker.[41] The tape on his right hand was possibly there to
prevent injury.[42] From Catherine McMillan, the jury learned that, though
most of the blood found at the apartment was Gordon's, some of it was un-
matched and could have been Kay's.[43]

The last Crown witnesses were the police officers who arrested Kay. To
Corporal Brian Tondevold, Kay said "[w]hy would I do this to him? I'm pregnant with his child."[44] She was stripped by Constable Elizabeth Gisborne
and placed in coveralls in a cell. Kay told Tondevold that she had a hospital
appointment for broken ribs.[45] He agreed that she was sobbing and distraught;[46] breathalyzer results showed that she was impaired.[47]

Worme turned the cross-examination to the subject of wife assault, repo-
sitioning Kay as a victim rather than an aggressor. He asked whether "it is
fair to say that in the majority of these cases the spouse being abused is the
woman?" When Tondevold said that the vast majority are women, Worme
pressed on: "The expression 'beaten half to death,' would that apply in many
cases?" "Yes," confirmed Tondevold.[48]

By getting the police to acknowledge the frequency of wife assault, the
potential lethality of husbands' violence against wives, that most such
crimes are unreported, and that women lie about their injuries and recant
their statements out of fear of further violence, Worme was anticipating
the Crown's response to Kay's claim of self-defence. Dutka would attempt
to convince the jury that they could draw a negative conclusion about the

severity of Gordon's violence and Kay's fear from the fact that Kay had not sought police intervention.

Gisborne, the next Crown witness, described the removal and cataloguing of the clothing that belonged to Kay: "She was very calm, very passive, and she hung her head a lot, and she was sobbing for most of it."[49] Unlike Tondevold, Gisborne hotly disputed Worme's proposition that the majority of spousal abuse victims are women: "Very often ... quite often it's the husband. I'm not an expert who can say it's 50/50, but it goes in reverse too."[50] The jury could not have known that in some police forces women constables like Gisborne are frequently subject to sexual harassment by male officers.[51] No wonder some like Gisborne try to conform and fit within its masculinist culture, sometimes by denying the gendered dimensions of spousal abuse. But Worme persisted, getting Gisborne to admit that she had been involved in cases in which women had been hospitalized with their injuries, that women often recant because they are afraid, and that in many instances – possibly the majority – women do not report spousal violence.[52]

Sergeant John Cavers testified next about Kay's police interview. Kay first said that she came from Apartment 3 to find Gordon in Apartment 2 with a knife in his stomach and did not know who had stabbed him.[53] When confronted with contrary witness statements, she admitted the stabbing but told Cavers that Gordon had been assaulting her:

> He kept kicking me around, in the stomach, he had broken my ribs before. He had this knife, he said "stab me, just do it." He handed me the knife and said "do it." When I had the knife he kept hitting me and saying, "Do it." He tells me I have to be tough ... He was beating me up. I told him I was going to call the cops, and as I was walking downstairs he pulled me up by the hair and made me sit on the couch.[54]

In the end, Kay agreed to the police version:

> Q: Actually what happened Donelda is that you got really angry, you took the knife and maybe he did tell you to stab him, but you took hold of the knife first, isn't that correct?
> A: Yes, you're right I did.
> ...
> Q: You were really angry about your clothes, weren't you?
> A: I wasn't angry about my clothes. I was mad about what he was doing to me.

Q: Why did he start to beat you?

A: He always does it when he's drunk. He hits for no reason, but I didn't me[an] to do it. I didn't think I got him that hard.[55]

Under cross-examination, Cavers explained that he had investigated hundreds of wife assaults over his career – on average one per week[56] – including two or three cases over the past four years in which the woman had been beaten to death.[57] He testified that battered women often provide other explanations for their injuries: he could not fathom why battered women stay with their abusers. He agreed that women constitute the "vast majority" of battered partners. At Worme's invitation, he explained "battered wife's syndrome" to the jury.[58]

Worme attempted to mitigate the effect of Kay's initial denials of her role in Gordon's death and her subsequent disclosure of his abuse by asking Cavers whether Kay became "increasingly comfortable" as the interview progressed. Worme proposed that "as the period wore on she, she became more comfortable with you enough to say that 'Yes, I did it'?" Cavers agreed, so Worme's last question was "[a]nd she reported to you at that point that she was the victim of such abuse, did she not?" "Yes," Cavers answered.[59] The Crown's case concluded, and the court adjourned for the weekend.

Worme had a difficult decision whether he would call Kay as a witness in her own defence. Would she be able to give testimony without detaching emotionally? Rupert Ross, a Crown prosecutor in the Ontario north, says that "Aboriginal witnesses often describe traumatic events in a flat emotionless fashion,"[60] which can be interpreted by non-Aboriginal judges and jurors as lacking credibility.

Her initial denials and her contradictory confession would also make Kay a vulnerable witness. The abuse that she experienced likely rendered her defensive. It is not uncommon for women who have experienced terrible violence to have internalized it as something that they deserved. Kay would be easily provoked if the Crown were to bait her with blame. If she were to expose her remorse, as a racialized woman and someone who might be seen as "rough," she would be vulnerable to a negative interpretation of her sincerity.

The transcript of Kay's police interview also revealed a pattern of what is known as gratuitous concurrence, the tendency to agree regardless of whether the question is understood or the answer is true. This communication strategy has been documented among Aboriginal Australians responding to non-Aboriginal speakers, particularly those in positions of authority.[61]

It can signal cooperation or hopelessness and resignation. Gratuitous concurrence is a serious barrier to fair trials for Aboriginal Australians because police and prosecutors can elicit contradictory answers or inculpatory statements, both of which can support inferences of guilt and lead to conviction. Although the Canadian legal system has not investigated gratuitous concurrence as problematic for Aboriginal accused, Kay's willingness to agree with various propositions advanced by the police must have been a concern for her counsel were Kay to be cross-examined by the prosecutor.

Yet self-defence requires some evidence of an unlawful assault against the accused, her reasonable fear of death or serious bodily harm, and her reasonable belief that she could not otherwise preserve herself. These are difficult elements to show without the woman's testimony. To keep his options open would require Worme to draw as much of Kay's account of the homicide from other witnesses as possible.

On Monday morning, Worme informed Justice Maurice that he would be calling a psychologist who would testify to Battered Woman Syndrome and Kay's state of mind at the time of the homicide. Worme requested permission for the doctor to remain in the courtroom to hear the testimony of his other witnesses, some of whom would be relaying what Kay had told them about her injuries. Dutka objected to the possibility that the expert would provide hearsay evidence. Worme explained that Kay's police statements raised violence by the deceased, which would be explored through the witnesses. Justice Maurice allowed Worme's request, cautioning that the weight of the expert's testimony would depend on whether the "facts" on which it was based were proven in evidence.[62]

In his opening address, Worme told the jurors that he would call a number of doctors, "not simply to go through every injury that Donelda sustained, not to call evidence of every traumatic beating that she received ..., but just to go through a representative sample."[63] Without this information, Worme said, they, like Sergeant Cavers, might wonder "why did she stay?" Worme told the jury that he would be calling psychologists to help them avoid the myths: "She likes it. It's her fault. She precipitated it. She wanted it. She can control it. She asked for it."[64]

His first witness, Randy Pipko, had been present at the party, but Dutka had declined to call him. Pipko said that the relationship between Gordon and Kay was "abusive ... [H]e kind of bossed her around." Once, when Pipko asked where Kay was, Gordon raised his fist and said "I put her out for the night." Pipko explained: "I gathered he knocked her out."[65] Was he concerned about Kay? "Maybe a little, but it was none of my business."[66]

The testimony of Kay's two psychologists, three physicians, and two shelter workers forced the jury to look at the violence that the Crown witnesses turned away from. Dr Josie Catania was qualified as an expert in children at risk and their teen mothers. Dr Catania met Kay after the birth of her first child in 1992 and learned that she had experienced maternal neglect and abuse. She was assaulted as a child by her uncle, then as an adolescent, and again by multiple male partners as a young adult. Some of these prior relationships were potentially deadly, such as that with Claude. He had AIDS, and when he swore that Kay would die with him Dr Catania consulted with Kay and her three sisters. They told her that Claude would beat Kay if she tried to leave.[67]

Her children had been used against her by successive abusers, and she had been unable to protect them from male violence. In consequence, one of her children had begun assaulting his younger sister.[68] Kay was thus a survivor of what Dr Catania called "multiple serialized battering," a term that she coined to capture the experiences of teen mothers, "where there are short-term relationships, and ... within that relationship there is abuse occurring."[69] Dr Catania testified: "[A] person exposed to multiple abuse and violence by different men would be more serious and more debilitating [because] if ... more than one person [is] abusing, each abuse constitutes a confirmation or a reinforcement of your value as a person, that each guy tells you, you are no good, you're not worth anything."[70] Kay, she said, "definitely" had the experience of multiple, serialized battering.

Dutka questioned Dr Catania's willingness to accept without investigation the history that Kay provided. Multiple, serialized battering had not been the subject of research, and Dr Catania's assertion about its consequences was speculative. A final point that Dutka drew was that Kay abused drugs and alcohol.[71] When Crown counsel completed her cross-examination, Justice Maurice warned the jury – his first of many such warnings – that Dr Catania had provided a great deal of hearsay evidence about Kay's experience of violence that was of no value unless those facts were proven before them.[72]

Kim Eklund, a worker at a battered women's shelter, said that Kay and her children sought refuge at the shelter in September 1991 and again in June 1993: "She was badly physically abused on her whole face. One eye, I believe it was the right eye, was completely shut. She had bruises all over her."[73] Eklund described Kay's emotional state as "withdrawn, not open, low self-esteem."[74] Kay opened up, Eklund said, as their counselling relationship and mutual trust deepened.

Kay also attended the Métis Addictions Council Centre for addictions and family violence specific to Aboriginal homes.[75] Diane Ozipko testified that Kay needed a month to stabilize before she could even enter the program in October 1993, after the homicide: "When she came in, she was quite distraught. She was very withdrawn, very suicidal, cried all the time, and didn't want to talk about too much at all."[76] The usual treatment program runs twenty-eight days, and though Kay attended for fifty-eight days she did not complete it due to relapses. Through cross-examination of Ozipko, Dutka discovered that Kay's relapse involved 222s,[77] pain relief that Kay sorely needed. Treatment centres and shelters need to enforce their drug policies strictly to ensure the integrity and safety of their facilities, but the impact on battered women like Kay who are facing multiple stressors[78] can be extremely harsh. Ozipko insisted: "I certainly feel she accomplished something."[79]

Kay's sisters described her childhood and adult experiences of abuse in ways suggestive of the "cycle of terror"[80] that Aboriginal women experience. Della Kay had witnessed her sister's rape by their uncle when Kay was five years old. She had seen Claude beat Kay. Della received a call from Kay on 22 September 1993 while Della was in a treatment centre. Kay was scared and begged Della to come and pick her up. "Why?" asked Worme. Before Dutka could object to hearsay evidence, Della answered: "She got beaten up."[81]

Shellyn Kay met Gordon when her sister brought him around in August 1993 and again in September when her sister's face was red from being hit. Shellyn observed the after-effects of Gordon's violence on many occasions: "[H]e'd come and look for her and she'd leave with him and then she'd come back a few days later, and she'd be, well, beat up. And I'd try to keep her with me again. I mean, they got worse, the beatings."[82] Shellyn described a night in September 1993 when her sister was dropped off by the police at her door. Kay had been badly beaten: "I felt sick in my stomach because she was, like, I could barely recognize her."[83] Her face was swollen, her lips were cut, she could not open her mouth wide enough to drink, and she was coughing up blood. She had bruises and welts across her back and legs and was moaning in pain. By this time, Dutka had given up objecting to hearsay evidence, so Shellyn freely said that she knew Kay had been beaten up by Gordon.

The day after, Shellyn helped Kay make her way to see her family doctor, Dr Varma. It took them twice as long to walk there because Kay could barely limp along, holding her head in her hands the entire way. Gordon spotted them on the street and caught up. He pushed Kay up against a wall, angry that she had left him and contacted the police. He threatened that, "[i]f she didn't go with him, ... something else is going to happen."[84] In the middle of the night of 22 September 1993, days before the homicide, Shellyn and Della received calls from Kay asking to be picked up.[85] They searched and called around but could not locate her. They feared the worst.

Kay's family doctor, Dr Varma, testified that Kay presented with multiple injuries on 1 September 1993. She had been beaten with a belt and kicked in the head, jaw, and neck by her boyfriend. She had bruises all over her face, neck, chest, and legs, and she had a fractured nose. Dr Varma saw her again the day before the homicide, when she had severe chest pain and was spitting up blood. Suspecting fractured ribs, Dr Varma scheduled an X-ray. Dr Varma saw Kay the next day at the hospital after she was arrested for the murder of Gordon. Blood was found in Kay's stool, which Dr Varma confirmed could have been "an indication of having been sodomized."[86]

Dr Kevin Schlamp, an emergency physician at the Regina General Hospital, examined Kay more thoroughly on 25 September. He found her depressed and silent. She kept her head down throughout his examination and limply allowed her body to be moved, like a doll.[87] She had scratches and abrasions on her face and back. The most significant injuries were tenderness on her stomach just below her ribs and on her back. Although X-rays ruled out fractured ribs, blood in her urine had been caused by severe trauma to her back. Worme lay before the jury the full range of Gordon's possible acts: "[W]ould it be consistent with it being caused by a physical beating? ... Kicking? ... Hitting with other instruments, other objects? ... Being thrown against something?"[88] Yes was the answer, over and over.

Dr John Richardson testified about Kay's blood alcohol levels, which placed Kay at close to double the legal limit for driving at the time of the homicide. Noting that Kay weighed only 100 pounds, she would have had problems with judgment and ability to control her impulses. Gordon had consumed more than double the legal limit, making his powers of judgment "severely restricted, if not absent."[89] His autopsy revealed traces of a drug that compounds the effects of alcohol, such that "the person would engage in violence that they would not otherwise."[90] Worme's last question hypothesized about the meaning of a threat to kill by a person in this condition. Dr Richardson answered: "[S]omeone with a history ... of behaviour patterns that were consistent with carrying through on these kinds of threats ... it would be consistent that that person would go ahead and do it."[91]

Worme then called to the stand his last expert witness, Dr Patricia Neilson. She previously worked in a battered women's shelter, but her practice focused on batterers. Unlike most experts who testify on behalf of battered women who kill, Dr Neilson did not dwell on whether Kay had a "syndrome," suffered from "learned helplessness," or mistakenly perceived herself to be "trapped." Instead, Dr Neilson focused on Gordon and his violence, educating the jury about the gendered nature of wife assault: "[T]hat's not to say that men never get hurt and that women can't be physically or verbally aggressive. But in most cases, and especially in cases of very severe violence, it's almost inevitably the man who is the offender and the woman who is the victim."[92]

Dr Neilson described the frequency and lethality of men's violence against their partners, explaining that women have different levels of tolerance and speaking to the "normalization" of violence in Kay's life: "[I]f you grow up, as Donelda did, in a lifestyle and have a whole history of experiences where you're surrounded by violence, when every person you know is violent and every relationship you've ever been in has been abusive, then I think that your acceptance of violence increases."[93]

Justice Maurice interrupted to remind the jury for the second time that Dr Neilson was speaking based on what she had been told by Kay and her family. This was hearsay evidence that Dr Neilson could rely on to form her opinion, but jurors should give no weight to matters not proven in court.

Dr Neilson explained that leaving a violent man is the most dangerous time for a woman because she is challenging his control.[94] She addressed the real limitations of promised protections for women who leave violent men.[95] She explained the cycle of violence but emphasized that, if unchecked, a man's violence against his partner escalates in frequency and intensity: "[A]ll the men I saw who had assaulted their partner, it always got worse."[96] She said that men use violence to get compliance from their female partners "because it works, and people get away with it."[97]

Dr Neilson defused the traps that can be set by prosecutors. She acknowledged that women sometimes provoke the man or initiate the physical altercation to get it over with and have some kind of control over when the violence happens. In the end, she said, they come out of it far worse than the man.[98] Dr Neilson turned around the "why didn't she leave?" question by asking "why didn't he let her go?"[99] She did not pathologize Kay as susceptible to male violence: "[I]f you want to predict empirically which relationships are going to be violent, you would look at the characteristics of the man."[100] In other words, "there's potential for any woman to be a victim of abuse."[101]

Dr Neilson was definite that Kay was battered and called hers the worst case of abuse that she had seen in her ten years of working with battered women.[102] The physical and sexual violence against Kay indicated that Gordon was "getting off on hurting someone else," making him "very dangerous."[103] Gordon attacked Kay in horrific ways: one time he kicked her with his boots, beat her until she was bleeding, sodomized her, then tied her up and left her. He also attacked her spirit, bringing his friends over to see her in this condition – "this is my old lady" – and to laugh at her.[104]

Again Justice Maurice interrupted. There was no proof before the jury of this assault or of its impact on Kay. He gave the jurors a third warning: "[Y]ou can't give any weight to any part of an opinion that's based upon statements like that where there's no proof whatsoever before us of that."[105]

Undeterred, Worme then led Dr Neilson through the diagnostic criteria for Post-Traumatic Stress Disorder (PTSD) and its subset, Battered Woman Syndrome, so that she could explain why both she and Dr Schlamp had determined Kay fit this diagnosis. She focused, however, on the real barriers to leaving. Fear of being murdered is reasonable, she said, when the batterer has acted on his other threats. The batterer's control can prevent the woman from seeing other options, especially when those around her accept the violence to which she is subjected. Most women have very limited resources: "Donelda is not the kind of person who can jump [on] a plane and go."[106] Her self-esteem was profoundly affected: "She lost her own sense of self, even now ... she's unable to look at herself in the mirror. She has this altered sense of perception which I think relates to kind of having lost her identity as a result of being so severely hurt."[107]

Dr Neilson referred to the police statement that Kay had tried to leave the party but Gordon had dragged her back up the stairs by her hair. Dr Neilson testified that the struggle that night between Gordon and Kay was not really about her clothes but about power and control, as her police statement indicated: "I wasn't angry about my clothes, I was mad at what he was doing to me."[108]

When Worme asked whether Kay had reason to fear for her life that night, Dutka's objection came too late.[109] Dr Neilson quickly replied:

Oh definitely. You know, if I didn't know anything about her, and I never asked her questions but simply knew the history of the abuse, I mean she tells me she was afraid for her life and thought she would die that evening.

But even if I didn't know that from her mouth, just knowing the history, I would predict she'd be dead by now.[110]

On that foreboding statement, Worme turned his witness over to the Crown.

Dutka secured a significant advantage in cross-examination when she established that Kay's relationship with Gordon was of very short duration. The testimony of Shellyn implied that the two began seeing each other in August, making theirs a six-week relationship. The research on Battered Woman Syndrome is based on much longer relationships of two to five years, Dutka said, in which women experience the full cycle of violence and become entrapped in the relationship.[111] Kay, she said, had not experienced the "honeymoon" phase of the cycle, which draws women back to the batterer, nor had she been involved with Gordon long enough to become entrapped or dependent.

Dr Neilson rejected Dutka's suggestion that the duration of a battering relationship is determinative of its consequences for the woman. Instead, what is important is the "frequency, the severity, and the impact it has."[112] A battered woman is one who has experienced the cycle of violence at least twice, which was certainly the case for Kay. Furthermore, Dr Neilson said, some batterers do not engage in "honeymoon" behaviour but alternate between the tension-building and the acute battering phases.

Dutka's attempts to get Dr Neilson to acknowledge that Kay's accounts might have been untrue and that the relationship was mutually violent failed. Dr Neilson replied that male batterers tell her stories about their female partners assaulting them and laugh – much as witnesses at the party reported Gordon laughing at Kay's efforts to push him away. Such men do not feel afraid, dominated, or humiliated, unlike women who are assaulted by their male partners.[113] Dr Neilson panned Dutka's reference to "mutually combative relationships." The power imbalances between men and women, the fact that sexual assault is a weapon used exclusively by men, women's fear, and men's physical power all make any claim to "mutuality" untenable, she testified.[114]

Dr Neilson also discredited the notion that "there are always two sides to a story." Although people usually think that "the truth is somewhere in the middle," this allowance should not be applied to wife assault: "My experience is that if he says this, and she says this, the truth is somewhere more extreme."[115] Battered women are so ashamed that they "invariably" minimize the man's violence as a coping strategy: "I've never had the experience … where a battered woman has totally exaggerated something."[116]

The Crown then proposed that Kay could have easily left this short relationship. Dr Neilson reminded Dutka of the phenomenon of "multiple, serialized battering." This experience is even more debilitating because of the repeat damage done to women's self-esteem.[117]

To the suggestion that Kay might have killed for other reasons, Dr Neilson insisted that context is everything: "[B]attering creates a whole atmosphere, a whole kind of surrounding environment of fear and control. And then it's within that, that whatever happens. So it's not like you feel afraid today, but then the battering stops, so you don't fear for your life. The fear is pervasive. It's always there."[118]

Dutka could not afford to let this point go. She rephrased her question. Suppose the woman acted aggressively to her partner all night, egging him on, and physically assaulting him. Isn't it possible that such a person is not acting out of fear? Dr Neilson was skeptical: "I would find it hard to believe that a battered woman who's been that beaten would be able to act like that ... But," she offered, "I suppose it's possible."[119]

Before Worme closed for the defence, he asked the judge to adjourn to enable him to take instructions from his client. He had a difficult decision to make. Would he call Kay to the witness stand? He returned on the morning of 15 June to announce that he was ready to make his final jury address. Kay would not testify.

Speaking to the jury, Worme said: "We trust you to use your common sense ... Donelda trusts you."[120] He focused on reasonable doubt, pointing to the gaps in the police collection of physical evidence as well as the many ways in which Bourassa's evidence was contradicted by other witnesses. This young woman, he said, was "very upset" that night, had engaged in several fights, and was described by others as "immature." She did not see everything that night: she did not see Gordon pull Kay back up the stairs by the hair; she did not see him assault or taunt Kay. The physical evidence of Gordon's hand and his drug and alcohol use, as well as Kay's injuries, corroborated her account, he said.

Worme reviewed the testimony of the doctors and Kay's sisters who had seen her injuries in August and September. "Is there any question who did this to her?" he asked rhetorically.[121] He told the jury that historically men were entitled to use force to "chastise" their wives as an aspect of women's status as chattel: "I hope you've changed that attitude. Women, the same as men. They don't have to run away if someone continues to beat them up. They don't have to leave the relationship if someone continues to assault them. That's an old way of thinking, although it's very common."[122] Gordon had "put Donelda out for the night," he commented; "that's not the way I kiss my wife goodnight."[123] He recalled her unrecognizable state when the police dropped Kay off at her sister's doorstep: "[W]hen was the last time you beat up somebody that bad?"[124]

When women have been repeatedly assaulted, Worme said, they cannot think about escaping – they are too focused on preventing the next attack. Not only does a woman lose the ability to see herself as important, but she is further entrapped when those around her accept the man's violence against her. Worme reminded jurors how others responded to Kay's victimization – "none of my business." He asked: "[I]s that how you'd expect your friends, the people that you turn to for help, is that how you would expect them to react?"[125]

Worme repeated Dr Neilson's evidence: Kay had experienced the worst abuse that Dr Neilson had ever seen and was "full of fear, anticipatory terror." "[K]nowing Donelda's history ... she predicted that she would be dead."[126] The issue, he said, was whether Kay thought that she had to do what she did: if jurors had a reasonable doubt, they must acquit her.

Dutka's summation emphasized the consistencies in the evidence from Bourassa, one of the few witnesses who had not been drinking.[127] Kay's explanation, Dutka said, only turned to self-defence once the officer contradicted her initial denials and asked Kay if she needed the knife to defend herself.[128] Her facial injuries were caused by Pascal, Dutka proposed, and her other injuries were too minor to be consistent with what she said Gordon had done to her.[129] Little weight should be accorded to Dr Neilson's opinions because no one gave evidence about the duration of the relationship or the frequency and severity of the abuse.[130] Her opinion was based on hearsay evidence not proven in court: in fact, Dutka suggested, much of it was inaccurate.[131]

Dutka proposed that Kay would have reported to the police if the abuse alleged were true. The accused had the capacity to leave Gordon and in fact was at the reserve away from him for a week at one point. Kay was aware of transition house options, having used these resources before. Dutka urged the jury to reject self-defence. Even Dr Neilson agreed, Dutka claimed, that "if the situation were, as I had described to her what the witnesses had relayed in testimony, ... then it would be hard to see how she could feel fearful."[132] Finally, Dutka cautioned, an acquittal would be "allowing [Kay] to commit murder in circumstances of revenge and anger."[133]

Justice Maurice warned the jurors – now for the fourth time – that they could not rely on the hearsay evidence provided by Dr Neilson for the truth about Gordon's violence. They should give little if any weight to the professional opinions to the extent that they were based on unproven claims. He instructed the jury on the defences of intoxication, provocation, and self-defence. He then cautioned them:

> [Y]ou may conclude that the deceased deserved killing, but that is not the test for self-defence. Whether a person deserves to be killed is not relevant where self-defence is raised by the evidence. You should not decide this case on your personal feelings towards the deceased. You must decide the issue of self-defence on the law as I have explained it to you.[134]

The jurors began deliberating the same day – 16 June. The next day they returned several times with questions for the judge. Could previous assaults by Gordon justify Kay's self-defence? The judge explained that assault need not be imminent to justify self-defensive violence. Past assaults and imminence were relevant to whether Kay had a reasonable apprehension that she faced grievous bodily harm or death that night. Jurors asked Justice Maurice to explain once more the meaning of manslaughter and the phrase "beyond a reasonable doubt." Once he had done so, they again retired.

The judge called the jury in on the evening of 17 June for an "exhortation." Justice Maurice urged them to reach a unanimous verdict to avoid the cost and waste of a mistrial.[135] He asked them to listen to one another and be open to reconsidering their verdicts. If they could not reconcile their verdicts, then they would have done the best they could do.[136] Court then adjourned until the next morning.

The jury continued deliberating the next day, but by lunchtime Justice Maurice exhorted them again: "Another Jury will not be in any better position to bring in a verdict than you are."[137] The jurors returned from lunch with another question: could Kay use self-defence if she had provoked Gordon that night? Justice Maurice advised them that the same right to use self-defence was available whether or not Kay had provoked the deceased.[138] They retired once more.

Ten minutes later the jury returned a verdict.[139] The foreman pronounced: "Not Guilty." The clerk of the court asked "not guilty of anything?" The foreman confirmed. The judge then repeated the question: "Just so I'm positive, Mr Foreman, your verdict is not guilty of anything?" Again the answer was confirmed. Justice Maurice persisted and asked the question for the third time: "Not guilty of murder and not guilty of the included offence of man-slaughter?" The foreman was curt: "Correct."[140]

The jury had been out for three days – the longest jury deliberation in Saskatchewan history.[141] Justice Maurice commended them on their con-scientious approach to their task: "[T]he questions that you asked me were some of the most difficult that I've ever been asked. And obviously you had considered these matters very carefully."[142]

Dutka was not persuaded. She asked that the jurors be polled individ-ually.[143] Only after each juror affirmed "not guilty" was Kay released from the prisoner's box. She reportedly "closed her eyes and appeared dazed." Her mother "let out a moan and began to sob." To reporters, Kay said that she was "very happy" about the verdict, smiling "shyly."[144]

Her acquittal was surely attributable in part to the tenacious and bril-liant defence work of Worme. He had done his homework: key passages in his opening and closing addresses drew on Greg Brodsky's addresses in his successful defence of Angelique Lyn Lavallee.[145]

As importantly, Worme brought his own valuable insights to Kay's de-fence. Worme was four years old when he witnessed the murder of his mother and his older sister by his sister's ex-husband in Saskatoon in January 1964. He managed to stay quiet through a terrifying ordeal in which his seven-year-old brother was struck in the head with a knife by his uncle and lay uncon-scious on the floor, while Worme's three-year-old cousin hid trembling under a table. Although Worme's brother survived, his head injury prevented him from testifying for the Crown. Worme instead carried that burden, making him one of the youngest eyewitnesses in a murder trial in Saskatchewan.[146]

Grandparents raised the two brothers on Poorman's Indian Reserve in central Saskatchewan. A member of the Kawacatoose First Nation, Worme was taught Cree traditions, spirituality, and treaty history of his territory by his grandfather. He attended law school at the age of twenty-one; his degree was in hand by 1985; and he was called to the Saskatchewan Bar the next year. His career has focused on seeking individual and collective justice for Aboriginal peoples.

By the time members of Kay's community approached Worme to repre-sent Kay, he was practising as a criminal defence lawyer and had served as the president of the Indigenous Bar Association from 1989 to 1991 as well as in many other organizations.[147] Kay's community held sway with Worme, for Kay too came from Poorman's Reserve.[148]

His experience with the dynamics of male violence allowed Worme to expose its "normalization" such that witnesses either did not "see" Gordon's violence toward Kay or did not consider it wrong. A significant aspect of many Aboriginal women's experience of intimate violence is its normalization as an "everyday" part of life. The twenty-six women interviewed by Anne McGillivray and Brenda Comaskey for their book *Black Eyes All of the Time* had, among them, experienced *thousands* of assaults by at least *100* perpetrators. Violence is perceived in some Aboriginal communities as "the community norm as well the relational norm."[149] In turn, "normalization" leads women and children to cope with violence rather than seek help,[150] especially in smaller communities where police and social services are unavailable, where the repercussions of disclosure can mean social isolation and rebuke, and where kinship networks can support men's denial of abuse. A further consequence of "normalization" of violence against Aboriginal women and children in isolated communities is that "thresholds – personal, familial, and community – tend to shift"[151] and thus to accommodate truly horrifying violence.

Worme used his examination of Bourassa, Longman, and Pipko to make vivid for the jury the community and relational "norm" of intimate violence. He asked Longman about his own violence against his female partner, and he asked others about the violence that they had seen in their lives. He reminded them that they had witnessed Gordon's violence against Kay. He asked them whether they had done anything about it, fully expecting the answer "nothing." He followed by asking "why?" and again receiving from each the same answer – "none of my business." In his closing address, Worme was thus positioned to remind jurors that there was no one to whom Kay could turn for assistance.

Worme tread carefully around the issues in his client's case. As an Aboriginal lawyer, he could hardly afford to name colonialism or racism as implicated in Kay's experience when even white lawyers fear the backlash. He also calculated that the dangers of calling Kay to the witness stand outweighed the benefits. She was thereby shielded from cross-examination by Dutka and possibly from jury antipathy. Worme left no stone unturned, calling seven expert witnesses who painted a picture of Kay's life that allowed the jurors to step into her shoes. The evidence of Dr Catania was a stroke of genius, for she was able to bridge the gap between Kay's six-week relationship and Battered Woman Syndrome, using "multiple, serialized battering." Dr Varma provided crucial details about Kay's injuries before and after the homicide, while Drs Schlamp and Richardson were willing to speculate on the nature of the force used by Gordon against Kay on the night of the homicide. Both the shelter and the addictions workers conveyed their unequivocal belief in Kay's story and their genuine empathy. Dr Neilson provided the strongest testimony on record for a battered woman charged with homicide. Worme knew that to understand the batterer was to appreciate the nature and degree of danger that his client faced.

Worme doggedly pursued every inconsistency in the evidence that he could mine for reasonable doubt, including the police failure to collect and handle the forensic evidence to professional standards. Rather than allow the jurors to rely on unarticulated and negative beliefs about a different world inhabited by Aboriginal women, he repeatedly asked them to measure Gordon's actions against their own: "[I]s that how you say goodnight to your wife?"

A less optimistic explanation for Kay's acquittal might lie in systemic racism and antipathy toward Gordon. Testimony from witnesses suggested that, from the moment the 9-1-1 call was placed, the emergency response was sluggish. The hospital was across the street from the apartment, but it took an ambulance crew from fifteen to twenty minutes to arrive, well after the police. As one witness testified, "we could have carried him across faster."[152]

The picture painted of Aboriginal violence by the evidence might have reinforced stereotypes and made Gordon's death less appalling to jurors in spite of the judge's admonition not to focus on whether the victim deserved his own death. His racialized identity could not have been overlooked; Gordon was described as a "male native" by the police officer who arrived at the scene.[153] That the Crown's chief witness was a young Aboriginal woman was not inconsequential: her evidence might have carried less weight in the first place and been diminished further when Worme exposed her prior criminal record and emphasized the self-importance that she claimed as "the only one who saw the whole thing."

In fact, Kay's acquittal might be explicable by the sad reality that Aboriginal peoples' lives and deaths remain relatively unnoticed by Canadian society. Sharon McIvor and Teressa Nahanee comment that, "[t]ypically, when victims and perpetrators are both Aboriginal, the courts allow us to treat each other like animals as long as we do not harm 'others.'"[154]

Thus, even criminal defence work informed by Aboriginal people's experience of colonization and racism can in practice devalue Aboriginal lives and communities. The decontextualized focus of Kay's criminal trial on the acts and omissions of Gordon, Kay, and the witnesses hides the role of the state in the ongoing practices of colonialism that continue to make Aboriginal women's lives so unsafe.[155] Aboriginal lands, resources, and communities experience ongoing encroachment by private interests wishing to exploit minerals, fish, water, and trees on their lands; by government expropriation of lands for military or other purposes; by the criminalization of unlicensed hunting, fishing, and gathering; and by the use of state force to quash Aboriginal efforts to protect lands through occupation and protest. The dependence and poverty imposed on Aboriginal communities whose lands can no longer sustain them, whose leadership was suppressed, and whose members were deprived of parenting and subjected to violence and abuse in residential schools remain unaddressed.

Denise Robin Rain

"The simplest case of this magnitude that ... I've ever dealt with."[156]

Denise Robin Rain killed her former common law partner in front of witnesses after an altercation that developed over the course of an evening involving heavy drinking. Donald Alexis died in Rain's trailer on the Duffield Reserve in Alberta on 22 January 1999 from a single stab wound to the heart. Rain was twenty-nine years old and had five children at the time. Her prosecutor proceeded with manslaughter instead of murder charges, enabling Rain to elect trial by judge alone rather than jury.[157] It is perhaps because she had a judge that she took the stand to testify, for she had a criminal record. Her counsel must have decided that the judge would not be prejudiced by her prior convictions for common assault, assaulting a police officer, and causing a disturbance.

In what could be seen as a casual approach to this prosecution, W Dunfield failed to call either a forensics expert or police officers to testify against the accused. As he explained to Justice Belzil of the Queen's Bench at trial in March 2000 in Edmonton, "[i]t is, Sir, without doubt, the simplest case of this magnitude that in my 27 years as a Crown I've ever dealt with."[158] He might have regretted these words by the end of the case.

The only official who testified was coroner Dr Dowling, whose evidence pointed to manslaughter, not murder. He was "of the opinion that not much force would be involved in inflicting this particular wound ... It was just a very unlucky stab."[159]

The main Crown witness was Duane Kootenay, Rain's brother-in-law, from Paul Band Reserve, west of Stony near Duffield. The night of the homicide he met Rain at a gas station, and she asked for a ride to his hockey game, where Alexis, from whom she was separated, was also to play. Neither man played hockey that night; instead, they drank with Rain, went to a casino, then stopped on the way home to purchase off-licence beer. Both Rain and Alexis insisted that Kootenay come into Rain's trailer with them for a beer, where the oldest daughter, twelve-year-old Shalanna, was sleeping with her four younger siblings.

Things turned ugly in the trailer, Kootenay testified. The two were "nit-picking," "cheap-shotting" each other. Alexis called Rain a bitch and was "pretty abusive" verbally. Kootenay observed Alexis crowding Rain, giving her no space. She pushed him away two or three times, finally pushing his chair backward, causing him to fall. Alexis began gesturing, pretending to hit Rain, "like, making a motion to hit her or making some quick gestures, and after she kind of flinches, he'd scratch his head and laugh." Alexis waved a closed fist and said "he was going to knock her out or something if she doesn't smarten up."[160]

The conflict escalated. Alexis put his arms around Rain's waist to restrain her: "[T]hey were kind of shuffling back and forth," and she was trying to push him away. Shalanna intervened and yelled at her father to leave her mother alone.[161] Kootenay tried to get Alexis out of the trailer and almost had him out the door, but when he turned back again both were at the kitchen sink. Alexis was moaning, staggering backward, and then he fell, bleeding. Rain ran from the trailer, only to return, grab the knife, stab herself, and lie down next to Alexis to die.

Kootenay attempted numerous times to get through to 9-1-1 but only received a recorded message. Finally, he called his wife to ask her to summon aid.

In cross-examination, Kootenay testified that Alexis "said that he'll floor her."[162] Seconds later "[h]e had her pinned against the counter."[163] Defence lawyer Alexander D Pringle, QC, put to Kootenay a death threat allegedly made by Alexis to Rain just before she stabbed him. Kootenay said that he did not hear it, but he acknowledged that he attempted to block out the conflict and did not hear and see everything.

Delores Rain, sister of the accused and wife of Kootenay, was also called by the Crown. She too could not get through to 9-1-1. She finally called the Stony Plain RCMP detachment. When asked whether they arrived promptly, she said: "Seemed like hours ... It took forever."[164]

Alexis and Rain had a thirteen-year relationship. Delores had witnessed Alexis's violence against her sister.[165] She saw Alexis attack Rain when she caught him in bed with another woman:

[He] chuck[ed] her around ... [and] held her against the wall ... He was throwing her around, just everywhere, just throwing her into the wall and just being real brutal to her ... [H]e started grabbing her by the neck ... with both hands[;] he was just pushing her and shoving [her] against the walls in that bedroom ... [H]er neck kept snapping back and the noise ... was really loud.[166]

Dunfield objected as Delores began to describe a second occasion of violence: what was the relevance of these events? Justice Belzil overruled, allowing Delores to recount how Alexis "just chucked her over my couch, like just literally threw her over my couch";[167] "he was pushing her hard, really hard," "[g]rabbing her by the arms and shaking her."[168] In cross-examination, the Crown attorney asked Delores if Rain was strong enough to keep him under control. Delores answered: "No."

Shalanna, the next Crown witness, described what she saw:

[H]e picked her up and threw her against the counter and then she was crying and saying, "Donald, just leave" ... I seen my uncle Duane try to take my dad out but he didn't want to go and they came back in and he said, "You f'ing bitch, you turned my kids against me" and he said "I should kill you now" ... [H]e was coming towards her from the door ... She picked up the knife and, well, he came towards her and she just – it happened real fast.[169]

Under cross-examination, Shalanna said that she had seen her dad throw her mother down the stairs, heave a chair at her, and then start throwing other things: "[B]y the time the cops were there, everything in the kitchen was just smashed."[170] She also saw him throw a punch at her mother and miss, smashing a hole in the wall,[171] and threaten her: "[I]f you guys try and leave I'll kill myself."[172] When she and her mother left, "he said he will shoot us and all this and we heard a gunshot when we were walking down the road and he came chasing after us."[173] She saw Alexis slam her mother against the wall, choke her,[174] throw her off the couch, and strike her.[175]

Rain then took the stand, testifying that she first met Alexis when she was fourteen and began a long-term relationship when she was seventeen: "I got shoved, slapped, punched, kicked. I got taken on fast car rides where he was going to kill us."[176] His first assault involved kicking her when she was seventeen and pregnant.[177] It is not uncommon for batterers' first attacks to begin or worsen during a woman's pregnancy: their jealousy and anger over the woman's reduced sexual and emotional accessibility and their sense of loss of control escalate.[178] Alexis assaulted Rain again when she was pregnant with their second child. His parents and sister did not intervene as he chased her and kicked her in the buttocks. The next morning she went into premature labour. Alexis threatened Rain and her babies with a gun that she managed to remove before calling the police. When she was pregnant with their fifth child, he threw her to the ground and said that he was going to kick "the little bastard out of her." She ended up "bruised and stiff."[179] After he smashed the house and the police took him away, she refused to cooperate with them.

Rain recounted many more acts of violence by the deceased, including an axe incident,[180] an occasion when he smashed her car window,[181] and another when he ripped her clothes off and tried to throw her out the window into the snow.[182] She left Alexis repeatedly. In explaining why she left him the last time, she said: "He's too unpredictable. He was too dangerous."[183] Many of her contacts with him while they were separated were regarding child support. Was he going to pay anything? Would he do anything for the children for Christmas?

Grabbing the knife on the night that she killed him was, Rain said, "an instant reaction, [I was] scared." After stabbing him, she ran from the trailer because he was going to hit her: "It was like an animal instinct where there's fear, you just react and that's what I did, and I never meant it to be fatal or anything."[184] She testified that she had a sore back from being thrown or shoved against the counter by Alexis that night. Rain repeated his threat to kill her made after Shalanna intervened. She claimed to have used the knife to scare him so that he would not hurt her: "I drew the knife, brought it forward and at the same time that he came at me."[185]

Dunfield tried to get Rain to admit that she was angry about being called names and pushed around by Alexis. Characterizing her as angry would serve two functions. Had she stabbed him in anger, it would suggest that she killed under provocation, justifying a conviction for manslaughter. Battered women do experience anger,[186] but it is an "outlaw" emotion for women, seen as inconsistent with being a "real" battered woman.[187] As one African American woman who was originally convicted for killing her batterer explains, "[p]eople don't expect battered women to be angry. The fact that I wasn't meek and mild really hurt me at my [first] trial."[188] When members of subordinated groups express anger, they lose credibility and are seen as unreasonable.[189]

Rain insisted that she was hurt and afraid, not angry. Dunfield proposed that she was not in danger because Alexis usually hit her only when they were alone, and Duane was there.[190] Rain protested: Alexis refused to leave.

She also feared that he would beat up Duane if he tried to intervene. Dunfield quoted her RCMP interview where she was asked what she meant by "we were fighting." She answered: "He pushed me so I pushed him back."[191]

Dunfield confronted Rain with her police interview where she told the police that Alexis said nothing before she stabbed him. She explained that she remembered the threat months later when she was seeing a psychologist. Dunfield queried why she used a legal term, suggestive of coaching by her counsel, when stating that she used "not excessive force" in wielding the knife. Rain responded that she used this phrase in everyday parlance. Dunfield pointed out that she used the same words as Shalanna. Rain acknowledged that she and her children discussed what happened, using those very words.[192] Dunfield interjected, rather sarcastically, "[o]r she may have a remarkable memory."[193]

He sparred with Rain, suggesting that she had no fear when Alexis was walking out the door – "he's got his coat on, his beer in his pocket, Duane's waiting for him, he's on his way. Right?" She explained her fear by reference to his intoxication. Dunfield retorted: "[A]nd yet you bankrolled his whole drinking binge that night, start to finish?"[194] Rain acknowledged that she "was always hoping that things would be different."[195] But was there any reason to think that Alexis was a changed man? "He admitted to his addictions and how he was going to stop,"[196] she explained. If so, why was she buying him booze? "He was ordering and he had no money so I didn't want him to get in trouble,"[197] she replied. Rain said that she was not angry that he spent her sixty dollars on his rounds because she was going to the casino to win money. Dunfield responded with incredulity to what he called her "extra-lucky casino ability": was she clairvoyant?[198]

Dunfield asked why Rain gave Alexis money to pick up more beer on the way home: "[D]id you say you've had enough? Or ask Duane to take him home?"[199] He returned to her emotional state: was she not angry when she pushed him off his chair?[200] Rain said that she cried out of both hurt and anger but denied that she was still angry minutes later when the stabbing occurred. When Alexis was holding her in a grip and they shuffled back and forth in the trailer, what was running through her mind? "Come on," he replied when she said that she was afraid. "You weren't scared at that point. I mean he was just holding on to you? ... [Y]ou were just being restrained?"[201] "No. No, that's not it," she answered. "He had me and he was trying to throw me around, and I was trying to resist him, trying to push him away."[202]

Dunfield concluded his cross-examination with an apology: "Ms. Rain, forgive me if I've been persistent in my questioning. This is a serious matter;

a man's life was lost. I know that your loss has been tremendous and that of your children. My apologies if I've seemed abrupt."[203]

Darlene Rain, another sister, was the last defence witness. She called the police when Alexis hit Rain on the jaw with enough force to knock her head sideways, calling Rain a "black cunt, black hole."[204] Darlene kicked Alexis out of her car, and her spouse got out to calm him. Alexis punched him in the face.

In cross-examination, Dunfield suggested that Rain was "giving" as much as "getting" in these arguments. This characterization Darlene denied, but then he asked whether her sister ever got angry. She replied: "About her inability to support the family away from social assistance, about her – at one point her inability to have a home to raise her children." Eagerly, Dunfield asked, "she blames Donald?" "No," said Darlene, "she blames society, the community agencies. She would apply for jobs and she wouldn't get them."[205] She declared: "I've never seen her in a state that you're trying to state." Again Dunfield resorted to sarcasm: "Well, I think the word I used is a-n-g-e-r, anger."[206]

Pringle urged Justice Belzil to acquit Rain on the basis of self-defence. He referred to Alexis's violence against Rain, even in the presence of other adults. Alexis terrorized Rain that night by pretending to hit her, grabbing her to throw her, and abusing her verbally. His final rush threw her against the kitchen counter, where she happened to find a knife behind her. Pringle characterized her reaction as instinctive or instantaneous, a reasonable attempt to scare the deceased and stop his threatening behaviour.

Dunfield's closing emphasized the discrepancies between Rain's account to the police and her testimony, particularly her more recent recollection of Alexis's threat to kill her. Rain had been aggressive physically toward Alexis all evening and had become increasingly angry, Dunfield suggested. He pointed to her criminal record as well as her admissions that they were "fighting" to suggest that at best she drew the knife in reaction to extreme provocation, which would support a manslaughter conviction: "[S]he was ready to participate in this climate of violence at least to a certain extent ... I don't buy the notion that she's just cowarding [sic] in the corner. In response to his activity, she takes an aggressive posture and responds herself."[207] Rain had been the aggressor: "She wasn't a retiring, passive person." Dunfield minimized the violence of Alexis: "[I]n all the years that they were together though we did hear of some pretty nasty things happening, there's never any grievous bodily harm."[208] "Well he picked up an axe on one occasion and fired a rifle,"[209] interrupted the judge. Dunfield responded that there were no witnesses, forgetting perhaps that Shalanna had also testified about her father firing the gun. Dunfield argued that "[i]t simply raises the question in my mind would any reasonable person who was subject to a gun being fired at them in any circumstances wouldn't report it at least to someone for some intervention."[210] He continued: "[T]he background and summaries of the assaults that he was convicted of in relation to her [were] much less serious than the one that she described with either the axe or the gun. So why the inconsistency, I don't know."[211] The judge mused: "Or is that [an] indicia of a dysfunctional relationship?" Dunfield replied: "Maybe. You know, we didn't have any expert witness to assist us in that regard."[212]

Justice Belzil found Rain and the other witnesses credible.[213] He reviewed Alexis's criminal record of five assault convictions, two for assaults against Rain, and the testimony from numerous witnesses regarding his attacks on Rain, calling it a "significant criminal record for offences involving violence."[214] The only conflict in the evidence was whether Alexis threatened to kill Rain seconds before she stabbed him: Rain did not recount this in her statement to the RCMP, and Kootenay did not recall hearing these words. However, since Kootenay did not deny that this threat was made, Shalanna's testimony persuaded the judge that Alexis uttered this threat. Justice Belzil acquitted Rain because he had a reasonable doubt whether she acted in self-defence.

Rain's acquittal is surprising, especially when compared with Doreen Sorenson's conviction. After all, Rain and her daughter admitted having discussed and together recalled Alexis's threat to kill Rain months after their initial police interviews, potentially undercutting their credibility. The defence also took a serious risk in not calling expert testimony to support self-defence, as illustrated by Sorenson's conviction. Dunfield attempted to capitalize on this omission by pointing out that inconsistencies in Rain's testimony had not been explained by an expert. Perhaps Pringle was confident that the judge was open minded and able to avoid the myths about wife battering that impede fair consideration of self-defence.

However, Rain's position as a "battered woman" might have been more precarious than Sorenson's because Rain could be portrayed by the prosecutor as aggressive. Unlike Sorenson, Rain had witnesses, but Shalanna's testimony carried a hint of collusion, and Kootenay's presence could have cut either way. Kootenay claimed not to have heard Alexis's threat, and the judge might have ruled out self-defence on the basis that help was at hand should Rain have needed it.[215]

Rain's trial record, like Sorenson's, also failed to register how few options she had. Dunfield questioned her veracity and her endangerment because Rain had reported assaults less violent than those to which she testified. Justice Belzil attributed her inconsistent reporting to a "dysfunctional relationship." But emergency and police services for Aboriginal communities are highly unreliable and shelters and services for battered women almost non-existent in smaller locales.[216]

Rain's acquittal against all of these odds might speak to her strength of character and her credibility. It might also suggest an experienced trial judge who has seen enough wife battering to appreciate the risk of intimate femicide that Alexis's behaviour presented. Yet the possibility remains that Rain was acquitted because the Crown attorney did not invest resources in a murder prosecution and because she "only" killed another Aboriginal person.

Jamie Tanis Gladue

Gladue's guilty plea is in fact a far more typical outcome for Aboriginal women than the trials profiled above. Most battered women plead guilty to manslaughter, as discussed in Chapter 3, but Aboriginal women are even more likely to do so. My files revealed that twenty-five of the thirty-seven identifiably Aboriginal women entered guilty pleas to manslaughter – half of the total number of guilty pleas (fifty) in my study.

Furthermore, Gladue was sentenced to the same three-year term of federal imprisonment that Doreen Sorenson received after a trial in which self-defence failed. Their sentences were more punitive than the average for manslaughter by a woman of a male partner in Canada, which is two years less a day in a provincial institution or less.[217] The Aboriginal women in my study tended to receive longer sentences, making Sorenson's and Gladue's three-year sentences the average for Aboriginal women who kill. The two longest sentences for manslaughter among my files, of eight years each, were meted out to Aboriginal women.[218] Some can arguably be explained by these women's prior criminal records for violence, but neither Gladue nor Sorenson had any such record.

The *Gladue* decision held the promise of alternatives to incarceration for Aboriginal women convicted of crimes.[219] However, the main beneficiaries of these alternatives are non-Aboriginal offenders – Aboriginal incarceration rates have only increased since the *Gladue* decision.[220] Toni Williams argues that Aboriginal women, who experience both racism and misogyny, have fared particularly badly. She explains that "sentencing courts respond to ... Aboriginal women with a simple narrative that constructs Aboriginal families as incubators of risk, Aboriginal communities as containers of risk and the prison as a potential source of healing intervention in the defendant's life."[221] In fact, Aboriginal women's experience of incarceration has been brutal, particularly for its replication of the violence that shapes their lives.[222] Patricia Monture-Angus has argued that prisons have replaced residential schools as a tool enforcing colonial relations.[223] As Fran Sugar and Lana Fox comment, "prison is an extension of life on the outside and because of this it is impossible for us to heal there."[224]

Was Gladue well advised to forgo her right to trial in return for a three-year sentence? Donelda Kay's case bore a close resemblance to Gladue's. Both women were extremely young – Kay twenty-one and Gladue nineteen – when they killed their partners; both had small children; and the evidence showed that both had been assaulted on previous occasions by the men whom they killed. Although little evidence of Beaver's past violence was on record because there was no trial at which such testimony could have been aired, his criminal record for assaulting Gladue during her first pregnancy was introduced at sentencing. Both women identified their injuries while in police custody: Kay stated that she was missing a hospital appointment for broken ribs, and Gladue had bruising that the police photographed. Gladue was five months pregnant, while Kay thought that she was pregnant at the time.[225]

Both homicides took place after extended drinking parties, and both women were described by witnesses as the aggressor in the confrontation. Although no one saw Gordon either strike or threaten Kay that night, several saw her slap him, call him down ("come on") with a knife, and push him. In Gladue's case, witnesses reported that Gladue became increasingly agitated over the course of the evening as Beaver repeatedly disappeared from the party. Gladue told Georgette Atleo that he had fooled around on her before and that she would kill him if he did it again.[226] The chief witness for the prosecution in each case claimed to have witnessed the accused woman stab the deceased, seemingly deliberately. While in Gladue's case that witness was a stranger to the accused – a mature, male neighbour named Anthony Gretchen – in Kay's case the young Aboriginal witness had been part of the evening's events. Despite the difference in age, sex, and origin of these two key witnesses, from the Crown's point of view, both cases must have looked like straightforward prosecutions.

That confidence could only have been enhanced by the fact that neither woman's police statement was consistent internally or with the versions of other witnesses, and neither statement was entirely exculpatory. Gladue was described at her sentencing hearing by the prosecutor as "a somewhat enigmatic individual." She told police: "We argued but I did not do nothing to him"; "[h]e was passed out on the bed, I started to talk to him, then he left out the front door"; "[w]e fight and I hit him but I would never kill him"; and "I did not do nothing to him." Kay too first denied both her involvement and that she and Gordon had argued: "He can't be dead. I never did nothing though."[227]

In some ways, Gladue should have had a better chance at acquittal than Kay. After all, she had been in a common law relationship with Beaver for almost three years, making it probable that, since he had assaulted her while she was pregnant, his violence was already well out of control.[228] In addition, by the time of Gladue's sentence appeal, her lawyers had in hand an expert report suggesting that Gladue had experienced Battered Woman Syndrome, which would have buttressed her self-defence argument. Kay, on the other hand, had been involved with her boyfriend for six weeks. As well, Gladue did not have a criminal record of violence and might have been able to testify in her own defence.

The transcript from Gladue's preliminary inquiry reveals further evidence that strengthened her case over Kay's and might have facilitated acquittal. Atleo saw Gladue and Beaver outside Gladue's sister Tara Chalifoux's unit. Beaver was grabbing Gladue, who was trying to push him away.[229] Gladue was yelling: "Leave me alone, leave me alone."[230] Furthermore, unlike the chief witness in Kay's case who denied hearing any sort of fight between Gordon and Kay prior to the stabbing, the eyewitness Gretchen heard a physical fight in process before Gladue and Beaver emerged from the townhouse. He overheard a female voice swearing, loud banging, and the sounds of furniture being slammed and pushed.[231] At the sentencing hearing, the Crown introduced photographs showing the bruising on Gladue and acknowledged that Beaver might have been threatening her and her fetus. However, he said, "even accepting everything that my friend said yesterday about the assault inside the premises, when Mr. Beaver left the home, there was no longer any threat to the accused or the fetus."[232]

The preliminary inquiry also revealed that Gladue was not simply "jealous" of Beaver's behaviour toward her sister. Chalifoux testified that she left the party because she had had too much to drink. At home, she vomited and then crawled into bed. She became aware of Beaver watching through her bedroom window. He then entered through her kitchen window, approached her in her bed, and began kissing her. She rejected him at first but then kissed him back. However, when he took off her pants and tried to have intercourse, she pushed him away. They heard banging at the door. He jumped up, dressed, and left the room. Gladue entered her bedroom minutes later, looking for Beaver. Gladue said that "she had a feeling that he'd come over here because he always goes after women who are drunk."[233] After Gladue left, Chalifoux found Beaver gone too. Only then did she begin crying.

The defence lawyer on cross-examination explored her feelings about what Beaver had done. Chalifoux was crying because of how he had treated her: "It brought back bad memories" related to abuse.[234] She agreed that Beaver had followed her because she was drunk.

Gladue and Chalifoux's father, Lloyd Chalifoux, testified that Beaver engaged in predatory sexual behaviour. Lloyd raised nine children between the ages of thirteen months and twelve years on his own, fighting social services the whole way. He was present at the party that night and several times in testimony said that he was very protective of his children. He recalled that, when his kids were younger, he had been suspicious of Beaver's motives:

> One of the things I had noticed that when I'd pick them up in the morning to take them to school they had their sister baby-sitting, Tara most of the time. And they'd get in the car but then Reuben would always go back sometimes when my daughter was there baby-sitting. He'd go back in for a few minutes and then come back out ... [W]ell, he acted like he forgets things, but most of the time he didn't have anything ... [T]hat kind of bugged me in a way because I was thinking that maybe he was hitting on my girls ... [A]ll Tara said was, "Yeah, he does that sometimes."[235]

The racism that might have shaded the witnesses' observations and testimony was only briefly visible in the preliminary inquiry. The Crown prosecutor asked witnesses to identify whether others whom they observed were "Caucasian" or "native" throughout the hearing. Lloyd responded, gently correcting him: "The impression I got was that they weren't First Nations, no."[236]

Aboriginal Women and the Guilty Plea

All battered women experience enormous pressures to plead guilty, but for Aboriginal women there are additional factors. The *Report of the Royal Commission on Aboriginal Peoples* explains:

It appears that they have little understanding of their legal rights, of court procedures, or of resources such as legal aid and most Indian people enter guilty pleas because they do not really understand the concept of legal guilt and innocence, or because they are fearful of exercising their rights. In remote areas the Aboriginal people appear confused about the functions of the court, particularly where the Royal Canadian Mounted Police officers also act as Crown prosecutors, or where the magistrates travel about in police aircraft.[237]

Additional pressures include linguistic and cultural differences that make "guilt" versus "innocence" foreign concepts for some Aboriginal people; the fact that Aboriginal people are more likely to be denied bail pending trial and to spend longer periods incarcerated pretrial, increasing the pressure to plead; reduced access to legal representation for Aboriginal people, particularly those in remote areas; and the fact that Aboriginal people are notably intimidated by court processes, leading them to plead guilty just to "get it over with."[238]

Gaining access to lawyers who can communicate with and gain the trust of Aboriginal clients is another serious barrier to going to trial with a viable defence. As one federal government report notes,

[d]ifficulties in cross-cultural communication are believed to have an impact on the quality of service delivery. The legal system is based on premises that are, to a large extent, foreign to Inuit and Aboriginal culture. As a result, the legal system is not necessarily clearly understood by accused of Aboriginal ancestry, and it is very difficult to translate legal terms into Aboriginal languages. In some cases, as a result of these difficulties in cross-cultural communication, the extent and quality of communication between the accused and counsel may be limited to the point where the accused is under-represented.[239]

The legal "underrepresentation" of Aboriginal persons accused of crimes can lead to inappropriate guilty pleas, particularly for those who are both female and Aboriginal. For example, in Australia, Aboriginal women are recognized as "the most legally disadvantaged group" in the country.[240] One study found that 80 percent of Aboriginal women charged with the homicides of their male partners pled guilty, and overall 100 percent either pled guilty or were found guilty, compared with 67 percent of non-Aboriginal women.[241]

The wrongful conviction of Robyn Kina, an Aboriginal Australian woman, illustrates the problem. She was convicted after a murder trial in which she did not testify and in which no evidence was offered in her defence. Although Kina conveyed to her lawyers and others the deceased's violence, preceding and at the time of the homicide, none of this evidence was investigated or presented at trial. Counsel discouraged her from giving evidence in her own defence. Her lawyer explained:

> In my experience, Aboriginal clients were generally very reluctant to give evidence, unless they were given considerable support and encouragement to do so. I recall that the appellant would have needed considerable positive encouragement to make a decision that she wished to give evidence in this matter. I did not provide any such encouragement.
>
> I did not think that the appellant should give evidence. One of my main concerns about the appellant giving evidence was the fact that, at that time, she was still in a depressed and remorseful state, and seemed to blame herself, rightly or wrongly, for everything which had occurred.[242]

The appeal court set aside Kina's conviction because a miscarriage of justice had occurred: had this evidence been introduced, it would have raised a significant possibility of acquittal based on self-defence or a manslaughter verdict based on provocation. Crown counsel did not reprosecute Kina. Although the court was careful not to condemn her lawyers, they missed information critical to her defence.[243]

In the Canadian context, the Canadian Association of Elizabeth Fry Societies and the Native Women's Association of Canada describe an Aboriginal woman who pled guilty to a homicide committed by her nephew, taking responsibility for his act because she had given him alcohol.[244] According to the authors,

> individualized systems of legal responsibility (such as those that provide the foundation for Canada's criminal law) may not be well understood by individuals who come from community-focused and collective cultures. When such persons offer advice that might be appropriate in a collective culture (e.g. accept responsibility or heal the family), the woman accepting such advice might become more vulnerable in the courts.[245]

Sugar and Fox also document wrongful convictions of Aboriginal women:

There are several reports in the interviews by women who had neither believed that the court system would treat them justly nor trusted the lawyer who was supposed to act on their behalf. Since they felt powerless and had no trust in or understanding of the process, some acquiesced. They accepted an unfavourable plea bargain, or remained silent, refusing to offer evidence that either exonerated them or implicated others in the more serious features of the crimes with which they had been charged. They endured being sent to prison in the same silence with which they had greeted past victimization.[246]

Another difficulty is that Aboriginal women's linguistic usages can be misunderstood by police, prosecutors, and defence lawyers. Gratuitous concurrence was discussed earlier regarding Kay's police interview, but socio-linguists have documented many other linguistic barriers to fair trials for Aboriginal Australians.[247] The risk of miscommunication is heightened in exchanges in which there is an "illusion of communication," in which Aboriginal and English speakers "engage in apparently intelligible conversations without conveying the intended meaning."[248] Australian human rights commissions and courts have recognized the problem in Australia and have catalogued strategies to address the unfairness.[249]

Canadian researchers have not yet examined this issue, but McGillivray and Comaskey found in their interviews with Aboriginal women who had experienced intimate partner violence that "[m]any respondents used the term 'fighting' in depicting physical abuse, an expression rarely used by women who are not Aboriginal. They used the term to describe incidents in which a respondent argued, fought back, or otherwise felt herself to be a participant, even if an unequal one, in the altercation."[250] McGillivray and Comaskey speculate that describing intimate partner assault as "fighting" can serve "a normalizing function by placing intimate violence on a par with more accepted male-male violence. It may give a woman a sense of strength, of being able to survive. Certainly, it masks the power differential in intimate violence."[251] But police, lawyers, and jurors might see "mutual violence," not wife battering, when an Aboriginal woman in custody makes these kinds of statements. Certainly, when judges describe violence in relationships as "fights," it "work[s] to emphasize the participation of the accused in the dysfunctional relationships rather than foster sympathy for a battered woman."[252] The term "fighting" was used by Sorenson, Rain, and Gladue, but only in Rain's case was the meaning pursued.

Another factor contributing to the pressure to plead guilty is the fact that, like all battered women,[253] Aboriginal women's survival strategies in the face of male violence include alcohol and drug use to numb physical and psychic pain. Substance use is also strongly related to the experience of childhood sexual abuse,[254] a harm to which Aboriginal women have been disproportionately exposed through the practices and effects of colonization, including residential schools.[255] A dangerous and escalating cycle is generated whereby women who misuse substances to alleviate suffering are at increased risk of further and more debilitating male violence, both physical and sexual.[256]

Women who experience blackout from drugs or alcohol cannot account for the events leading to the fatality, handicapping a self-defence claim. Aboriginal women can face not only these challenges to a trial on the merits but also the effects of discriminatory stereotypes about Aboriginal people and substance abuse.[257] In Ontario, the police are more likely to report that alcohol is involved in Aboriginal homicides,[258] but this does not tell us whether these records are accurate. For example, dissociation caused by blows to the head or psychological trauma might be mischaracterized by the police as alcoholic blackout, such that the woman might not receive emergency medical treatment or protection.[259]

Like Heavenfire, Sorenson, and Kay, Gladue was intoxicated when she killed her abuser. Intoxication is a defence to murder but not to the included offence of manslaughter, which does not require proof of intention to kill. There is a remote possibility that defence counsel can prove on a balance of probabilities the defence of "extreme intoxication," a complete defence to manslaughter, if the accused was so intoxicated that she did not have the capacity to control her physical movements or her intentions.[260] However, this defence is now barred under *Criminal Code* section 33.1, in part due to lobbying by the women's groups, including Aboriginal women.[261]

Gladue's intoxication could have reduced her murder charge to manslaughter on the basis that Gladue did not intend to kill Beaver. Even then a jury can reject intoxication, which can be a particular risk when the accused is an Aboriginal woman. Far from mitigating the crime, intoxication can aggravate the offence in the minds of some, particularly if they associate intoxication with an accused's social, economic, or cultural background. For example, Sheila Noonan has argued that "judicial narrations [of Aboriginal women's violent acts] reinforce stereotypical assumptions about Aboriginal drunkenness, violence, and intra-racial quarrels."[262] At the sentencing stage,

Aboriginal women's alcohol use might receive more attention than the male violence to which these women were responding.[263]

Lawyers advancing intoxication defences for Aboriginal women would want to contextualize alcohol or drug abuse as a consequence of colonization, past[264] and present, and of exposure to violence and abuse. Failing to do so can encourage jurors to consider addiction as inherent to Aboriginality.[265] Conceptualizing substance use as psychic self-defence or even as deliberate resistance to the forced assimilation of Aboriginal peoples[266] can assist jurors in setting aside judgmental attitudes and recognizing the woman's humanity.

A prior criminal record can also contribute to Aboriginal women's choice of guilty plea over trial. A number of Aboriginal women in my files had prior convictions that might have affected counsel's evaluation of the strength of the defence. This is because the woman can be cross-examined on her prior convictions if she takes the witness stand to testify. This information might suggest to the jury that she is "criminal," violent, and untrustworthy as a witness. No studies compare Aboriginal and non-Aboriginal women's criminal records when these women are charged with homicide, but Aboriginal women as a group face much higher rates of criminalization, incarceration,[267] and maximum security classification in federal institutions.[268]

Beyond these many barriers to a fair trial on the merits, the greatest challenge for Aboriginal women is that they are invariably described as the aggressors. Witnesses, prosecutors, and judges state emphatically that the accused Aboriginal woman is not a battered woman or not a *real* battered woman. This characterization flies in the face of the available systemic data reviewed in Chapter 4 regarding Aboriginal women's experience of intimate partner violence. It is also inconsistent with the facts in the individual cases. In all of the prosecutions detailed in these two chapters on Aboriginal women, there was ample evidence that the woman had been assaulted by her male partner. In fact, all of the Aboriginal women's cases in my files have corroboration of the male violence perpetrated against the women, partly because of the extended kinship and community networks that witness much of this violence, but also because Aboriginal women are more likely than others to seek police intervention.[269] Furthermore, unlike the cases of non-Aboriginal women who killed men who were asleep or passed out, the Aboriginal women in my files, almost to a woman, killed in the course of an ongoing altercation, usually a violent one. Self-defence looms on the horizon of each Aboriginal woman's homicidal act.

On average, Aboriginal women ought therefore to have a better shot at acquittal than other women. In fact, the acquittal rate of those Aboriginal women who refused to plead guilty in my study is quite high: of the ten Aboriginal women who went to trial, seven were acquitted and three convicted. There is thus reason to worry that guilty pleas by Aboriginal women might not fairly allocate their responsibility.

How did the lawyers and judges involved in Gladue's case reach the conclusion that Gladue was not a battered woman? Was this a factual claim or a moral one? Was the claim that Beaver did not batter Gladue or that she did not experience Battered Woman Syndrome? The difficulty is that his prior conviction for assaulting her was before the court, and there was no evidence introduced at that point about whether she had been diagnosed. Was the claim rather that her behaviour – her alcohol consumption, jealousy, anger, or aggression – surpassed the moral boundaries of a "battered woman"?[270] For women like Gladue, it seems that their very womanhood is on trial.

Consider what a lawyer who was more knowledgeable about Aboriginal women's realities would have done with Gladue's statements to the police, her injuries, the evidence about the confrontation that preceded the homicide, and the other available information about Beaver. The fact that Battered Woman Syndrome evidence might not be a simple fit for Aboriginal women cannot mean that they are not entitled to invoke self-defence. Heavenfire's expert was able to frame her actions using Battered Woman Syndrome, incorporating her experience of racism into the framework; Kay's experts recast her experience of male violence as multiple, serialized battering. What other forms of expert evidence are available to help lawyers avoid guilty pleas and represent their clients' self-defence claims? In the next chapter, I will explore one such possibility while demonstrating that Aboriginal women are not the only women for whom Battered Woman Syndrome is an inadequate theory.

6

Lilian Getkate

"Their perceptions become ... so warped that they believe they are unable to escape the violence."[1]

Lilian Getkate called 9-1-1 at 4:53 a.m. on 8 December 1995 from her home in suburban Ottawa. Her husband, she gasped, was lying in a pool of blood. Sobbing, and almost unintelligible,[2] she said that she heard a loud bang and footsteps on the stairs. Could the police come quickly?

Officers arrived and escorted Lilian and her small children, Dara and Kevin, shivering in their pyjamas, to a police cruiser while they searched the house. Lilian blew kisses to her children in the back seat through the glass that separated her in the front seat, where she sat with an officer. Inside the house, the police found Marinas (Maury) Getkate dead, two gunshot wounds to his head. His apnea machine, which he wore to sleep, was still on his face, though the pump was turned off. They found no sign of forced entry and no footprints in the fresh snow on that bitterly cold night.

The police interrogated Lilian at the station while her children were kept in a separate room. She was arrested for murder by 11:15 a.m. and was advised of her right to remain silent and to retain counsel, prompting her to ask repeatedly to phone a lawyer. However, the officers diverted her from contacting counsel. Sergeant Wisker told her that

no matter what happens and no matter what you think of me, I can assure you of one thing. Is that if there's a burden inside of you now, it's never going to go away.

...

That causes me more concern about you and your children. What happened to Maury is over and done. There's no reason why you or your children should have to go through more down the road. Whatever it is you're afraid of now, and I can understand what that might be, but ... we can get past that point here and move on. Whatever I can do to make life easier for you, if there's anything I can do that will ensure you for your children, I'll do whatever it is you want me to do or that I can do.[3]

Within six hours, Lilian confessed to the homicide. She was unable to provide details, beyond the location of the gun, due to gaps in her memory. Her apology to the officers for lying to them in her original statements[4] was icing on the cake. For the police investigators, abused women like Lilian make for easy pickings: they summon the police themselves, quickly confess their crime,[5] and usually provide the weapon.[6]

Battered women's cooperation with police investigators is not surprising. A woman confronted in an interrogation room by the sheer size and masculine authority of police officers can be easily intimidated – more so if she has experienced male violence. Some police take advantage of this and run roughshod over the constitutional rights of women charged with the murder of their husbands.[7] Women's vulnerability is increased when their children are also present at the station and especially when officers offer "help" or "protection." Lilian's admissions were later excluded from the trial because of the inducements offered by the officers and because Lilian had been denied her right to contact counsel without delay.[8]

Police searches of the Getkate home turned up the gun in the basement, under a pile of clothes, where Lilian told the police to look. They also found many other weapons, months of doctored financial records hidden in bags in the basement, and a note in the dining room buffet. This note was relied on to charge Lilian with first-degree murder.

Self-defence would be a challenging defence: not only had Lilian lied to the police at first instance, but also she was unable to fully recall the homicide and so could not easily create the evidentiary basis for the need to defend herself. She had shot a sleeping man and had not disclosed abuse by her husband to anyone. Not to police, doctors, friends, or even her mother.

The criminal prosecution of a battered woman furthers her subordination by perpetuating the deprivation of her liberty that the batterer pursued. What is said to and about the woman by the prosecutor, the expert witnesses, and the judge during a trial can echo and thus reinforce the battering

process. James Ptacek[9] has examined the attitudes of judges and the ideological messages conveyed by judicial responses to battered women seeking
protection orders in the Massachusetts courts. He argues that these messages can replicate the strategies of batterers and further entrap the woman.
For example, judges can minimize or deny the woman's experience of violence, "mirroring batterers' actions by making light of the abuse, saying the
abuse didn't happen, saying she caused it, making her feel guilty, saying it's
just a 'lovers' quarrel ... They may intimidate her through patronizing dis-
plays of authority or harsh remarks."[10] Such responses affect the woman
seeking protection concretely in terms of whether she gets her order and
psychologically by reinforcing what the batterer has already told her: you
are exaggerating. It's your fault. No one will help you.

Ptacek's work raises the question of whether the prosecution of battered
women also serves to maintain violent men's power over their wives. Do
battered women's murder trials constitute a significant component of patriarchal authority? The judge will normally – with rare exceptions[11] – avoid
expressing an opinion about the accused and her guilt or innocence in front
of the jury. Judges might reveal their views more subtly through their communication with counsel and the witnesses, and they might express their
opinions more directly after the verdict and during sentencing. No doubt
judges' rulings on matters of admissibility of evidence and matters of law
during a murder trial affect the outcome by expanding or contracting the
"facts" available for consideration and available defences, for example. Yet,
overall, judges' influence on the verdict and on public opinion is relatively
circumscribed in a jury trial.

Instead, prosecutors play a stronger ideological role in the murder prosecutions of battered women. Crown offices across Canada have instituted
policies requiring vigorous prosecution of wife assault,[12] even if the only
evidence is the woman's testimony. This stance constitutes good public
policy given how hard batterers work to keep their crimes secret and how
difficult it is for women to disclose their partners' violence.

Implicit in these policies is a commitment to support and encourage
women to report wife assault – no easy task. Angela Browne explains:
"Because society's standards on violence against wives are ambiguous, and
because abused women rarely discuss their victimization with others,
most battered women are quite dependent on ... 'internal' anchors to determine the latitude of behaviours they will accept."[13] It therefore becomes
critical for police, prosecutors, and judges to set clear prohibitions around

wife assault and to foster women's trust that their reports will be treated seriously.

Yet these same policies might motivate Crown attorneys to insist on prosecuting battered women who kill. Cheryl Hanna suggests that prosecutors might proceed against women who kill batterers to "legitimate and reinforce state intervention" against batterers. Battered women who kill rather than seek police intervention undermine the state's role as "liberator."[14] Prosecutors draw a firm line between "offender" and "victim" daily, leaving no room for a woman who has killed to also be a victim of her victim. But can black-and-white thinking used to justify the vigorous prosecution of abused women who kill help Crown attorneys respond effectively to the far more common and deadly crime of wife battering? This is an especially problematic approach when many women themselves must commit acts of violence to survive. Is the goal of encouraging women to report wife assault compromised when the Crown prosecutes a woman who asserts that she killed her battering husband in self-defence?

"I couldn't take it anymore, and he was starting to get after the kids"[15]

Lilian was released after a two-day bail hearing on 19 and 20 December.[16] But first her lawyer agreed to something that most criminal defence lawyers would never consider.[17] A general practice lawyer with limited criminal law experience, Frank Armitage represented his wife's friend – Lilian. It is ordinarily considered a conflict of interest to represent a friend, but he was the only lawyer whom she knew, and she was desperate to have him. Armitage agreed to have Lilian examined by a psychiatrist chosen by the Crown attorney in the hope of reducing the murder charges. At a minimum, he hoped to secure her release on bail.[18] However, his decision also endorsed an untenable thesis that Lilian was possibly mentally ill and placed her within the realm of psychiatry.

The Crown engaged Dr John Bradford to assess whether Lilian was "fit to stand trial" and whether a "mental disorder" finding under section 16 of the *Criminal Code* might be appropriate. This justification was thin in legal terms. "Fitness" for trial is a minimal capacity test: is the person capable of understanding the legal jeopardy that he or she is in, and can he or she communicate with the lawyer?[19] The bar is set very low here so that persons charged with a crime do not languish in institutions, their guilt or innocence made irrelevant by their continued detention. A "mental disorder" defence was at that point at least as remote. Mental disorder requires proof on a balance of probabilities that the person suffered from a disorder depriving her or him of the ability to know right from wrong.[20] The only possible basis for either claim was Lilian's incomplete memory of the homicide. This is far from an evidentiary basis for either issue.

Armitage succeeded in getting Lilian bail, but the Crown refused to abandon or downgrade the charges. If anything, Dr Bradford's report, summarized in the bail decision, strengthened the Crown's resolve to prosecute her to the full extent of the law:

> He had interviewed the accused for some three hours on December 14th, 1995 and concluded that the accused did not suffer from any major mental illness and found no evidence of any further or present psychiatric disorder, nor was she suffering from any drug or alcohol abuse. He found the accused to be in a depressed mood, but that this was reactive to the event rather than pre-existing. He further stated that it was too early to determine whether a s. 16 issue was present or not. He did not find her to have any personality problems. The accused had described to Doctor Bradford that she had a difficult relationship with her husband, that he was demanding and dominating and that she had suffered some physical abuse, mostly by shaking and grabbing, but mainly in the nature of verbal abuse.[21]

Her statements to Dr Bradford were found to be voluntary and admissible as evidence against Lilian in the trial[22] because she agreed to the interview based on advice from her lawyer. Her trial counsel, Patrick McCann, argued that Armitage's decision to allow her to be interviewed one week after the homicide while in detention amounted to "ineffective assistance of counsel," in violation of her sections 7 and 11(d) *Charter* rights. The judge dismissed the argument while conceding that "[t]here is no question that other counsel probably would have taken a different position."[23]

Dr Bradford's conclusions would come back to haunt the defence and arguably served a broader function – to stabilize and reinforce male violence in the home. As Frances Cobbe argues, condemning "only the worst incidences of wife torture ... implicitly set[s] a standard of toleration for 'normal' wife beating, thereby actually increasing the average level of women's misery to be officially permitted, particularly in those cases where intimidation rather than persistent brutality [i]s the primary means of control."[24] Expert evidence like Dr Bradford's and prosecutorial statements that minimize forms of wife battering normalize – legalize even – much of men's physical, psychological, and sexual domination of their wives.

Crown Attorney Julianne Parfett believed that Lilian was not a "battered woman" but a murderer who deserved criminal condemnation. Her opening address to Lilian's jury of ten men and two women in September 1998 briefly outlined the evidence that she would present. Parfett provided no motive, though she referred to Lilian's statements to others about their "financial problems."[25]

McCann, with Parfett's acquiescence and Justice James Chadwick's agreement, was permitted to present his opening address immediately after that of the Crown, enabling jurors to appreciate the nature of the defence early on. McCann said that he would reveal the "secret life" of the Getkates, including Maury's obsession with weaponry, explosives, and survivalist literature and methods; his psychological, sexual, and physical abuse of Lilian; and his ability to convince her that she could not leave him because, as a civilian member of the RCMP with both the knowledge and the means to do so, he "would find her, take the children, and disappear without a trace."[26]

On the night of the homicide, McCann said, Maury brutally raped Lilian outside Dara's bedroom, raising her fear that Dara would be his next victim. She would testify about her "disembodied recollection" of loading and firing the weapon: "Eventually she came to the realization that she had done the shooting."[27] McCann told the jurors that they would hear from Lilian's family doctor as well as two psychiatrists who specialized in domestic violence. Dr Glancy would testify that Lilian suffered from Battered Woman Syndrome and would explain how women become helpless, "[t]heir perceptions ... so warped that they believe they are unable to escape the violence."[28]

Parfett's first witnesses were the police who retrieved evidence and questioned Lilian. Sergeant John Copeland described bullets found in Lilian's coat pocket and the recovery of the murder weapon from the basement – a rifle with a flash eliminator. He detailed the shotgun in the master bedroom closet – a closet that ran through the top floor to join a child's bedroom – loaded, cocked, and ready to fire[29] as well as "a collection of weapons and barrels and ammunition"[30] removed from the same closet.

McCann in cross-examination asked Copeland about the live explosive device found in the basement. Copeland had not risked photographing the device because it had appeared unstable. It was a glass cylinder, with a stopper on one end, a crystallized substance inside, and wires connected to the stopper. The RCMP removed it and confirmed that it was an IED, an improvised explosive device. They detonated it, reporting the powder as "very sensitive to impact, heat and friction. It is incompatible with metals and has poor storage qualities."[31] The only further question that McCann asked was about the nature of the explosion it caused when detonated. Copeland's answer was terse: "It was a high explosive."[32]

Police Constable Steve Kerr described three boxes of weapons and books seized from the residence. Their subjects were booby-traps, sniping, infiltration, lock picking, money laundering, the criminal use of false identification, surveillance, improvised explosives, the manufacture of concealable weapons, exotic weapons, weapons modification (including materials suggesting that Maury had modified the murder weapon by adding the flash eliminator), the manufacture of guns such as machine guns, SWAT tactics, surreptitious entry, applied surveillance photography, methods of disguise, how to track and find missing persons, night movements, intercepting communications, principles of a quick kill, mercenary manuals, smuggling, incendiary manuals, and a book called *Without a Trace*, a manual on how to commit crimes leaving no evidence.

Under cross-examination, Kerr listed the weapons: eight guns, machetes, knives, throwing knives, daggers, bayonets, martial arts weapons known as ninja claws and nunchuks, and switchblades – all prohibited weapons in Canada. Parfett minimized the relevance of the books by having the witness date them back to the 1970s and 1980s.

Detective Paul Holland testified about bags of unopened and doctored bills found hidden in bags of clothing scraps in the basement. The unopened mail was from creditors such as utilities and credit card companies. The doctored bills had been altered by cutting, pasting, and whiting out to convey that amounts had been paid and received when they had not. He speculated that Lilian was spending money elsewhere and did not want Maury to know.[33]

Constable Dan Berrea described her demeanour while she waited in the police car and at the station. Lilian appeared neither confused nor suffering from a mental problem.[34] She broke down and wept sporadically but tried to comfort and distract her children throughout.[35]

Maury's former co-worker and friend Travis Gee testified that Maury and Lilian had "more traditional roles" in their marriage: he worked, and she was a stay-at-home mom. Lilian managed the finances, as did Gee's wife: "[Maury] and I both perceived that we had married a good manager who would be able to take care of things while we were out on our more abstract tangents."[36] Gee once observed Maury "plead" with Lilian for money to buy a book at a book fair.[37] Maury was "extremely intelligent" and enjoyed figuring out how things worked. He left work punctually "to be with his family and children."[38]

Gee had never heard Maury lose his temper – "I have seen more illtempered teddy bears"[39] – or voice an interest in weapons. When McCann asked him if he would be surprised to know that Maury had a collection of prohibited weapons, Gee exclaimed: "Are you sure they weren't hers?"[40]

Parfett called Dr Bradford, a well-known expert in the Ottawa courts who worked with male sex offenders, to the stand. His qualifications to testify as a forensic psychiatrist were not challenged by McCann. He was permitted to testify about Battered Woman Syndrome even though he had neither researched nor published in the area and had seldom been accepted by the courts as an expert for this purpose.[41] Dr Bradford met Lilian while she was in police custody six days after the homicide for a two- to three-hour interview. He ruled out mental disorder but testified that Lilian might have been genetically disposed to depression.[42]

Dr Bradford described Lilian as unhappy because Maury was not home enough and said that the Getkates experienced financial hardships. When Maury pursued a master's degree and then a PhD, Lilian supported the family with several jobs, working up to sixty hours a week and going without meals so that there would be enough food for her first child and Maury. Gee's understanding of Lilian as a "stay-at-home" wife was based on the image John preferred to project as a "traditional," male bread-winner family, ignoring the fact that his degrees had been financed by her labour.

Dr Bradford rationalized Maury's abusive behaviour, pointing to his apnea[43] and his stress over his doctoral dissertation.[44] Lilian was working nights to support them, but Maury would telephone her during the day and wake her, seemingly unconcerned about her sleep. He became physically abusive, grabbing her, pushing her against walls, and speaking in a controlling voice.[45] Given that Maury was six foot two and over 200 pounds while Lilian was five foot one and 120 pounds at most, these acts were "significant," according to Dr Bradford.[46] Maury had dragged Lilian upstairs by the hair on one occasion, held her over the top of the stairs on another, threatening to drop her, and pinned her to the floor, his knee in her back, cutting off her breathing and instilling in her the fear of death.[47] Dr Bradford said that the "grabbing and pushing" occurred more frequently and that the extremely frightening attacks occurred only once.[48]

Lilian tried to get Maury, an industrial psychologist for the RCMP, to go to counselling, but he refused, Dr Bradford said, because he was "professionally threatened."[49] She proposed returning to work part-time to ease the financial pressures, but this Maury also adamantly opposed, leading to "further pushing and shoving and verbal abuse, and she was afraid at that time, but not afraid of being hurt seriously," Dr Bradford testified, "but afraid of the future and the abuse that was going on."[50] Lilian proposed separation, but told Dr Bradford that Maury threatened that "he would take the kids and live somewhere where she wouldn't be able to find them."[51] After he completed his PhD, he continued to assault Lilian, pinning her to the floor. The children began to fret about the loud arguments, and Maury started closing windows so that neighbours would not hear them.

Dr Bradford referred to "tension in their sexual relationship." Lilian's interest had deteriorated in light of their difficulties, but Lilian denied sexual abuse to Dr Bradford. Perhaps it is not surprising that he would not gain her confidence only days after the homicide and while she was incarcerated. Sexual assault is one of the most "risk-free" acts of violence that a man can engage in and is frequently committed repeatedly – not as an isolated act.[52] It is also the most difficult form of abuse for battered women to disclose;[53] the legal system responds notoriously poorly to sexual assault allegations;[54] and marital rape is particularly resistant to successful prosecution.[55]

Dr Bradford said that Lilian had lost weight, cried uncontrollably, could not eat, and had insomnia, suggesting a "major depressive episode."[56] If her depression was not hereditary, then it was linked to "interpersonal stress" or "marital discord."[57] Of the abuse, he said: "Certainly when people end up in marital discord and there are arguments and emotions run high, pushing and shoving is not uncommon."[58] Although he did label "being held" and having "difficulty breathing" as "unusual," he testified that there did not appear to be hitting, punching, or attempted strangulation. Because Lilian had not sought medical attention, he concluded that "the injuries were not sufficient for that."[59]

On the night of the homicide, Dr Bradford said, Maury was annoyed that Lilian did not come to watch TV with him and instead tended to the children. He became annoyed again when she did not join him in bed right away. In spite of the "tension," Dr Bradford said that they did have intercourse. When Dara later called out in the night from a bad dream, Lilian went to her room to comfort her. Maury came after her, angry that she had not returned to their bed. Lilian dozed, then awoke, loaded the gun, and pointed it at her husband, "and a shot went off and then another shot."[60] She then heard her daughter cry out again, so she put the gun in the basement, comforted her daughter, then turned on the bedroom light and discovered blood everywhere. She called 9-1-1, but "didn't believe that she had done what she had done."[61]

Parfett asked Dr Bradford whether Lilian fit the criteria for Battered Woman Syndrome. Some aspects matched, such as depression, memory problems, and cyclical abuse, but "essential" elements were absent. Lilian had not been sexually abused, most of the abuse had been verbal, she had not been socially isolated by her husband, she had not described any escalation of abuse prior to the homicide, and she had not indicated that her life was in danger that night.[62]

In cross-examination, McCann squeezed a few concessions out of Dr Bradford. The room in which he interviewed Lilian at the detention centre was not an ideal place to talk to someone who was emotionally upset.[63] He might not have accurately recorded everything that she said.[64] Dr Bradford accepted that battered women often downplay the violence that they have experienced, especially sexual violence, which takes time and careful questions to elicit.[65]

McCann contrasted Dr Bradford's conclusions with the reports written by his experts, Dr Wendy Cole and Dr Graham Glancy. They discussed Maury's sexual violence, his threats to harm her family if Lilian left, and two rapes on the night of the homicide, the second in front of her daughter's door. The last attack convinced Lilian that Maury was no longer keeping his violence in check.[66]

Parfett dismissed the discrepancies as based on "substantially different accounts"[67] by Lilian. In re-examination, Parfett pointed to Dr Cole's note that Lilian pursued volunteer interests (assisting at her children's school and acting as a Brownie leader), which allowed her to develop a network of friends. She had consulted Armitage about a separation. She did the bookkeeping for the family finances. Dr Bradford said that these activities showed that she was not controlled by Maury and had avenues of support and escape. Although women might be reluctant to disclose sexual abuse, he said that it would be "unusual" for a woman to flatly deny it if asked directly.[68]

Yet US expert Evan Stark states that battered women have a propensity "to recall abusive episodes they initially denied" and that this is "a sign of recovery from trauma."[69] Advocates who work with incarcerated battered women seeking clemency report that "often the most horrific details would come out in interviews with others and would then be confirmed by the client. But the client would not herself bring up these details even when doing so could only help in the preparation of her clemency petition."[70]

Parfett's re-examination had strayed from its proper scope,[71] entitling McCann to cross-examine Dr Bradford again. McCann suggested that Lilian was still largely under Maury's control since her volunteer activities involved the children and all financial transactions were reviewed and approved by Maury. Dr Bradford said that this went to the degree of his control. McCann asked whether the liberating potential of Lilian's consultation with a lawyer "boils down to the type of advice she is getting from the lawyer?" Dr Bradford responded: "I hope most lawyers give good advice."[72]

June Fuller, Lilian's mother, was the next Crown witness. Much of her testimony pointed to Maury's control over her daughter. Lilian had to "check in" with Maury regularly: "She had to have permission and she basically didn't do really anything without his consent."[73] Lilian was not permitted to return to part-time work because no wife of his would work as a cashier.[74] Her extreme anxiety about ensuring that her newborn second child did not disturb Maury in his studies was apparent.[75] When Parfett suggested that Maury wanted the best for his wife, Fuller disagreed: "Any conversation I ever had with Maury was about Maury."[76]

In the week before the homicide, Fuller tried repeatedly to contact Lilian. When she finally reached her, Lilian begged off with a headache: "She had never ever spoken to me in that tone, she just sounded beaten ... beaten down mentally."[77]

Parfett elicited from Fuller her rueful acknowledgment that, though Lilian was deeply unhappy, she had never disclosed abuse to her. Parfett broached the topic of Kevin as a "difficult child," another possible "cause" of Maury's irritability, but Fuller resisted: "He is a wonderful child, but spirited."[78]

In cross-examination, Fuller described Lilian as a quiet, passive person devoted to her children – "not a mean bone in her body."[79] Fuller had last seen her in 1994 and wondered "when did my daughter get so old? She was so thin and her eyes were old."[80] Maury would not allow Lilian to visit her mother in British Columbia in the summer of 1995 even if she took the children with her and Fuller paid for the tickets. Lilian was broken-hearted, as was her mother.[81] About her last conversation with Lilian before the homicide, she said "I became very, very concerned as to her state of mind and her situation as she was very out of character."[82]

Maury's brother John testified that Maury was a smart kid who enjoyed electronics, magic, guns ("a natural pastime for anybody from southern Alberta"[83]), survivalist groups, paramilitary activities, explosives, and intelligence. Maury almost blew up the bathroom once with a home-made device[84] but later "lost interest" in these activities.

This sweeping statement was qualified through cross-examination. McCann read aloud a 1993 letter from Maury requesting a new catalogue of books on his "hobbies." He also introduced Maury's application for a pardon for breaking into a storage unit by lock-picking.[85]

Parfett called Anne Breakeyasmus, Lilian's good friend, to the stand. She testified that Lilian could never accept invitations without Maury's approval. Lilian would glance at Maury, he would remain silent, and then she would say that they would talk it over at home and get back to Anne. Even in his absence, she never committed to anything; she always had to ask him. Lilian claimed that she could do what she wanted, "but I never saw her do the things that she said she could without any complaints."[86] The two friends went "fairly regularly" to garage sales, ate lunch at McDonald's, and "shopped" at the Salvation Army Thrift Store – where Lilian bought her and the children's clothing while denying a money problem.[87]

Breakeyasmus testified that Lilian never spoke of abuse, but there was something very odd about their relationship: "She was always looking at him to make sure, like a dog when you are walking it, and they always want to make sure they are pleasing you."[88]

In cross-examination, Breakeyasmus described Lilian as gentle and thoughtful: "[S]he was always helping somebody." She had "the patience of Job, I would say, with children."[89] Lilian frequently declined lunch at McDonald's. Breakeyasmus realized that she had no money for even a frugal lunch, so she treated her on many occasions. She tried to get Lilian to open up about the obvious problems in her marriage and asked her whether she had her own bank account and money. Lilian swore that she did but so defensively that Breakeyasmus was convinced she did not.[90] Three days before the homicide, Lilian desperately tried to get Breakeyasmus to come for lunch to talk. Lilian suddenly began talking about getting a mature dog "for protection."[91] She told her friend that she was worried about break-ins but later when testifying said that she wanted protection from Maury: "I felt that he was seriously going to hurt one of us soon."[92]

Lilian's friend Christine Paul helped to clean up the Getkate home after the homicide. She was struck by Maury's impressive wardrobe: rows of expensive suits hung with matching shirts and ties.[93] Lilian had few things; her only good dress she gave to Paul.[94]

Dianne Noel, Lilian's friend, was called next by Parfett. Noel too acknowledged that Lilian had never disclosed abuse. After her arrest and while detained, Lilian repeatedly told her that "I couldn't take it anymore, and he was starting to get after the kids."[95] Noel said that Lilian "didn't even look like herself. I didn't even think she knew what she was saying at that point."[96] Noel testified to escalating tension between Maury and Lilian in the months preceding the homicide, Lilian's statement that "Maury is getting worse,"[97] and her own observation that Lilian had become afraid of Maury.[98]

In cross-examination, Noel said that Maury was domineering and monopolized the conversation, speaking only about himself, while Lilian served him and occupied the children.[99] She tried to see Lilian for coffee in the evenings but gave up in disgust. Lilian would cancel at the last minute because Maury would not watch the children. Or, if the children were already in bed and they did go, Lilian would have to call home to "check in":

> I found it quite unusual that a, you know, a grown woman would go out for coffee with a friend, we always went, we went to a place a block and a half from home, and when we would arrive she would have to call her husband, and she said, don't you have to call your husband? I said, why would I have to call my husband, I'm having coffee out. I thought it strange that she wondered why I wouldn't have to call home to say what, that I arrived[?] ... [A]nd usually she would be on the phone, those three times that I remember, she was on the phone at least ten minutes while I was sitting with our coffee.[100]

The calls did not leave much time to chat because "she was only allowed to be out maybe an hour, an hour and a half maybe. It was usually timed."[101] Lilian never had money or bought anything new – only clothing from garage sales and the Salvation Army. Maury wore $1,000 suits and spent a great deal of money on his book collection, his brief case, and his tie rack. Noel once saw Dara walk up to her father, who was reading the newspaper in the living room, to ask him a question: "[H]e turned around and hit her as hard as he could ... across the back, on the buttocks."[102] On another occasion, she saw Maury grab Kevin roughly, and "Lilian ran over, she physically ran over when she saw him pick him up that firmly."[103] Noel's daughter, who played with the Getkate children, told her that Maury's yelling frightened her. Apparently, Dara told her not to be afraid – "it happens all the time."[104]

Lilian called Noel at home daily in the late afternoons in the months before the shooting. Noel was trying to get dinner ready for her own family but sensed that something was not right and stayed on the telephone out of concern. Lilian sounded "extremely nervous" and would suddenly hang up the phone without even a "goodbye" – just "here comes Maury, I have to go."[105] Then she suddenly stopped calling. Lilian had become even thinner, she had not had a haircut in months, and "her face was almost a gray colour."[106] She also stopped returning Noel's calls and going to church – "that was rather odd because she really enjoyed church."[107]

Noel's last words described Lilian's appearance before and after the homicide: "I can't believe the difference in her. She holds herself straighter, she looks like she has confidence now ... She doesn't look so frail and sickly and all hunched over and just sort of, you know, timid."[108]

McCann's first witness was Gordon Taylor, a private investigator hired to go through the house after the police. He found another six boxes of materials, mostly books and manuals on martial arts and militia tactics, ninja fighting, hand-to-hand combat, hypnotism, phone tapping, assassination, the art of invisibility, camouflage, techniques of stealth and concealment, hacking into telephones and computers, and many others. He also turned up handcuffs, locks, a machete, and a vibrator.

The following day the judge ruled on an issue argued in the absence of jurors. McCann won a directed verdict of acquittal on the first-degree murder charges because Parfett had failed to introduce sufficient evidence of "planning and deliberation." There was no financial gain by Lilian, especially since Maury no longer had life insurance. The note found in the buffet, which read "[p]ension $2,100, back pay two wks. Vacation time 12 days. If Maury dies, plus pension – submit a claim for myself plus kids,"[109] could not alone support a scheme or plan. Nor did the fact that Lilian acquired, loaded, and fired the gun: these acts could be quickly accomplished by someone knowledgeable about firearms.[110] Lilian was left to stand trial on second-degree murder.

Called to the witness stand, Lilian told the story of her relationship with Maury. Her voice frequently dropped to a murmur, causing jurors to strain to hear her.[111] They met on a blind date when she was eighteen and he was twenty. He was the first man to pay any attention to her, and she found him "exciting."[112] She was a follower, so his insistence on being the leader attracted her. She adopted some of his interests, going on car rallies and learning to shoot at a gun club. He practised ninjitsu with his friends and played with explosives, one time setting off a device in their bathroom.[113] She found his interest in poisons and how to kill someone using pressure points unsettling.[114] His habit of yelling at women on the street from his car was hurtful and distasteful.[115]

They lived together for four years, Maury refusing to accede to Lilian's dream of marriage. Then, when his brother announced his upcoming wedding, Maury abruptly told his parents that he and Lilian too were marrying: "He never asked me or anything ... [H]e just told them."[116] His abuse began in earnest when Lilian became pregnant two years later. She had to stop work at seven months because of health problems, and Maury was unhappy about the lost income and his decreased access to sexual intercourse.[117] Dara's birth and the disruption of a new baby increased his anger. He would yell at Lilian to keep the baby quiet – he objected to any noise at all – and complained that he was not getting her attention: "[H]e told me I was spending too much time with her."[118] Lilian was back at work, running a Mac's Milk store, doing all the childcare, cooking, and housework, and typing all of his course work. Maury began monitoring her at work, coming to her store to sit and watch her, to make sure, he said, that she was really working. He began calling her a "dumb bitch," "lazy," and a "dumb c**t."[119]

Maury began to push Lilian around, sometimes grabbing her arm and pulling her back when she tried to walk away from an argument. He yelled so much that neighbours complained.[120] When Kevin was born four years later, Maury decided to return to school for his PhD. He became more aggressive, shoving Lilian against walls, forcibly sitting her down and making her listen to him, and dragging her up the stairs by her hair. He was unhappy about everything – where they were living was not good enough, the people were not smart enough, the children were too noisy, he did not like what she cooked. He told Lilian that "he could end it" for her,[121] then pushed her face into a mattress while he put his weight on her back. It was her fault that he got so angry, he said, her fault that they did not have enough money, her fault that she did not meet his sexual needs, her fault that the children did not meet his standards.[122]

He began forcing intercourse on her, Lilian recounted, blinking back tears.[123] "[H]is words were that I was his wife and it was my duty and if I was too tired and I didn't want it or whatever, that wasn't good enough, and he would take it anyway."[124] Maury bought her a garter belt and crotchless underwear and demanded that she wear them out to dinner. After the meal, when they returned to the car, he took her to the top of the parkade, which was blocked off:

> [H]e leaned me up against a railing so I was facing down. We were up about four or five flights, about that, and there was a ledge there. He told me to stand on that and he lifted up my dress and had sex with me there, and when he was done he looked over the edge and he said it would take nothing

to just push you over, and I didn't know what I had done to deserve that. We hadn't argued or anything during supper ... I don't know what I did ... I felt used, I felt degraded, scared, sick.[125]

Another time at the top of the stairs in their home, Maury lifted Lilian and said that he could throw her down the stairs. He also put his hand under her chin and lifted her up against the wall by her throat. Lilian suffered from back pain, migraines, and the helplessness of watching Maury spank Kevin hard and hit his legs and head.

They moved to Ottawa in 1993, and for a while Maury seemed happier. But as student loans became due and finances became tight, he resumed his verbal and physical abuse. He criticized everything about Lilian and told her to "learn to listen and you won't get treated this way." He would become very angry, his eyes hard and cold, which frightened her because it seemed that he did not care at all anymore. He deliberately tripped her when she walked away, humiliated Dara about her learning disabilities until she was in tears before school in the mornings, and assaulted Kevin such that Lilian would never leave him at home with his father.[126]

By 1994, Maury was complaining of sexual boredom. He bought a vibrator for Lilian to insert into his anus, and then he would penetrate her with it – at first changing condoms on it but later not bothering – which was "disgusting" for her.[127] He began ripping off her clothes and pinning her down when she refused sex because the children were just outside in the yard. He seemed to get more pleasure if she struggled, she testified. He called her names, including "fat cow," even though she weighed only 118 pounds. He would wake her in the middle of the night with his hands on her throat: "[H]e would tell me, all he would have to do is push one certain spot and I would be gone. No one would be able to detect how I died."[128] He also began demanding sex in the night after he woke her up by squeezing her neck.

In 1995, Maury started working for the RCMP. He finished his PhD but then started writing a book – another project that caused him great stress. His aggression increased; he rarely apologized anymore, which frightened Lilian. A batterer's contrition ends when his victim no longer believes it and he knows it. When contrition is abandoned, her fear increases as she realizes that she has become nothing to him – expendable.[129] Maury began leafing through his weaponry books again, and Lilian worried about the kids seeing these materials. He took his gun collection out and cleaned his weapons in front of the children. He would point a gun at her, telling her that she would never know if there was a bullet in it, and then pull the trigger. "I was really scared. I would shake. I would cry. I couldn't move. I was afraid if he had a bullet in there and I moved, he would really shoot me."[130] He would smile when he did this, looking past her: "It was a funny smile."[131]

Lilian was not aware of the live explosive device found by the police in their basement, but she testified that Maury "told me there was an explosive that he could put into the plug, into the socket, that would blow, it was strong enough that it would probably blow the top floor of the house off, that side of the house apart, and it would be undetectable how it happened."[132] He told her that if she left he would kill her family members. He would track her down and find her, using RCMP resources. He would take the kids and disappear by relying on all that he had learned from his paramilitary training: "He wasn't one to make idle threats. Generally, he carried through."[133] Maury also said that she would not have a chance in a custody fight. He earned the money – she would not get a cent. He was a member of Mensa and much smarter than Lilian, who had not graduated from high school. She was a poor housekeeper. She was not taking care of the bills properly. She was not a good mother.

At one point, Lilian completed her high school equivalency and audited university-level courses, but Maury said that she "would never make it in university."[134] She took a "get back into the workforce" workshop for which she had to write a paper on "what we thought we could do." She wrote that she would like to attend university and become a genetics counsellor. Maury denounced her for being untruthful, threw her essay into the fireplace, and prevented her from retrieving the burning pages.[135]

Lilian was anxious that Dara would bear the brunt of his rage if she left because he had started to rub nine-year-old Dara's body, stroking her back and between her legs. Maury asked Lilian when Dara would begin to develop breasts and whether she already had pubic hair.[136] He told Lilian that she was not satisfying him sexually but said that it did not matter because he had "up and coming prospects." She took this to mean Dara.[137]

Lilian also testified that she was in charge of the banking but never paid a bill or withdrew money without Maury's approval. She used their credit cards for socks and underwear – things that she could not buy second hand – and for birthday gifts. Maury spent freely on his books and journal subscriptions as well as on his clothing and other personal items. To avoid his wrath, she began altering the bills when she could not pay them. She attempted to pay them off in small increments by spending less of her monthly grocery allowance on food. At the time of the homicide, the credit card bills totalled around $2,000.[138] A rent cheque had bounced.[139]

Lilian described "meetings" at the kitchen table where she would have to listen to Maury review the finances and areas that she needed to improve. One of these "meetings" produced the note tendered by the prosecution. Maury made her write out "how much he was really worth" when he brought home his benefits statement one day.[140] One bill that Lilian was unable to pay was for life insurance on Maury. He was not upset when he opened the notice of cancellation from the company. Lilian recalled his ominous words: "Something to the effect I wouldn't be needing it anyway."[141]

In the three weeks prior to the homicide, there was no respite: Maury was angry all the time. He "would come storming through the door right after work; he would leave banging the door."[142] He escalated his sexual demands, waking Lilian in the night by applying pressure to her throat. She slept only a few hours a night, trying to avoid him; she ate only bites at dinner; she stopped going to Brownies; she stopped showering and grooming herself; she stopped going to church; she stopped answering the telephone and returning calls: "I was very tired ... I just didn't care."[143]

On the night of the homicide, Maury told Lilian that he would be taking the next day off work, which was highly unusual – he never even took holidays. After she put the children to bed, she twice did his bidding to bring him to orgasm. After the second time, he told her that "it was the worst piece of ass he ever had," put his apnea mask on, and went to sleep.[144] She had a difficult time sleeping – she felt "really dirty" and worried about infections. She went to Dara's bed around 4 a.m. when Dara had a nightmare about snakes, then fell asleep.

Lilian was awakened by Maury at the doorway. He demanded that she take off her clothing, saying that her place was with him, not the children. He leaned her over the couch and told her that "he was going to fuck [her] like a dog." She wept and told him that he was hurting her, but he would not stop. When he finished, he said "there, that will teach you. You are supposed to be upstairs with me."[145] Lilian was frightened; she wondered "what would have happened if Dara would have come out, what he would have done."[146] She lay there for some time, and the next thing that she knew she heard creaking on the stairs, then "a couple of sharp noises."[147] She heard Dara call out, went to comfort her, and then turned on the light in the bedroom to find a bloody scene.

The memories came back to Lilian at different times. During her detention at the police station, she remembered hiding the gun in the basement; a few months prior to trial while in a counselling session, she recalled placing the gun in the hall corner before entering Dara's room.[148] Lilian disclosed Maury's sexual abuse by writing it out on paper for Dr Glancy – the only doctor to whom she conveyed this information.[149] By the time of her trial, she had received counselling from Dr Cole, joined several groups for abused women, became a member of Co-Dependents Anonymous, taken parenting courses, and started karate: "I still fight the voices a lot of times, but I know I'm not the things that he has told me."[150] But in the days before the homicide, "the way things were going I felt that he was going to do something to me where I would end up dead ... Things had intensified so much I thought it was going to be soon."[151] Lilian felt safe for the first time in years at the detention centre: "I realized that no one could get at me ... I knew my kids were safe. I felt protected."[152]

Parfett's first tactic was to blame Lilian for not disclosing Maury's abuse. When she began to have serious concerns, "you didn't do anything about them; right? ... You didn't talk to any of your friends and family?"[153] Of her failure to tell a neighbour and good friend in Guelph of the abuse, Parfett commented: "But you didn't bother to tell her?"[154] Lilian was terrified that Maury would find out: "He would have known if she would have slipped and said something or her actions would have been different towards him."[155] He was highly attuned to subtle changes and would have known. But Parfett asked her again: "You can't even express so much as a concern to this neighbour?" "You don't say a word?"[156]

When the violence in Guelph became more deadly, according to Lilian, Parfett was incredulous: "So, once again you made no effort to help yourself?"[157] She had seen a counsellor in Guelph for help with depression, to which Parfett responded: "And once again you fail entirely to tell this person the extent of the problem that you are dealing with?"[158] "There is your golden opportunity to tell someone, I am being physically abused, I am scared, I need help, but you don't bother?"[159]

Parfett's second tactic was to portray Maury's actions as reasonable. Maury insisted that Lilian follow him to Guelph, while she thought that time apart might stop his abuse. She wanted to keep her job, her community, and the children in Lethbridge and instead commute for his two-year study program. Parfett said: "This is quite a series of legitimate concerns and a perfectly understandable position to take where a young family don't want to go half way across the country without you. I want to keep us together. What is there to criticize in this?" When Lilian said she was pushed into going, Parfett queried: "He didn't exactly hold a gun to your head?"[160]

Parfett's third tactic minimized Maury's violence: "[A]ll that had happened is a little bit of pushing and shoving and a little bit of grabbing."[161] When Maury resumed his abuse in Ottawa, was it not "in essence just a repetition of everything that you have gone through already in Guelph?"[162] Lilian disputed this: Maury began pulling out guns, he renewed his interest in his books, and the frequency of his attacks and the intensity of his anger increased. But Parfett asked: "All he is doing is cleaning those guns?" Lilian replied: "He is also pointing it at me. He was also showing Dara the guns."[163]

Of Maury's increasingly frightening behaviour, Parfett asked, rhetorically, "he never did push you down the stairs; did he?" "He never ever did push you over a railing or anything of that sort; is that correct? ... [H]e always let up when he had you [pinned face down] on the mattress; is that correct? ... So, in essence, although he made these threats, he never once carried anything out?"[164] Lilian replied, "I wouldn't be here if he had."[165]

Parfett's fourth tactic focused on normalizing Maury's sexual behaviour. Lilian testified that there were times when she initiated sexual relations with her husband, leading Parfett to engage in cross-examination that could easily have come from a defence lawyer cross-examining a female complainant in a sexual assault prosecution:

Q: [O]n these times when you were interested and you wanted it, were you the one putting on the lacy nightgown?

A: No, I didn't.

Q: You never put on a lacy nightgown for him?

A: No, I didn't have one until Ottawa.

Q: In Guelph you got the crotch-less panties?

A: Yes.

Q: You put those on for him?

A: No.

Q: Never put those on for him?

A: No.

Q: Never put on a garter belt for him?

A: Only at his insistence.

Q: Never dressed up nice for him?

A: I dressed in a nice dress and we would go out for supper, but I wouldn't put a garter belt and crotch-less panties on.

Q: You wouldn't do anything along those lines?

A: No.

Q: To make him happy?

A: No.

Q: That wasn't what you were interested in; was it?

A: No.[166]

Later, in cross-examination, Parfett returned to Maury's sexual abuse. Lilian had, in the weeks before the homicide, tried to avoid sexual contact by going to bed long after Maury was asleep and getting up and leaving the room before him in the morning. This, said Parfett, showed that "[t]he bottom line is you are in control here?"[167] As for her fears about Maury's use of the vibrator, Parfett asked: "And can you tell me Ma'am, whether or not you ever got any kind of vaginal infection?"[168] Lilian replied that she had yeast infections. Parfett pressed on – "urinary tract infections?" Yes, those too.

Parfett circled back to sexual abuse for a third time, characterizing the evening of the homicide as "a very quiet, calm, peaceful night?"[169] Lilian agreed that the early part had been calm. Parfett then suggested that she went upstairs when Maury asked her to, "knowing" that she was going to have sex with him: "I suggest to you that you wanted it that night, too." Lilian protested, but Parfett continued: "If you wanted to avoid it that night, you could have done what you have done in the past, and that is stay downstairs."[170]

Lilian had not disclosed the multiple rapes to Dr Bradford. In a series of questions evoking the now discredited notion that if a woman failed to raise "hue and cry" and disclose rape at the earliest opportunity she must have fabricated it,[171] Parfett asked:

Q: This is the first opportunity to tell somebody why it [the homicide] happened; right?

A: That's right.

Q: But you don't ever mention the sexual assault that you are alleging occurred in the living room?

A: No, I didn't.

Q: Never mentioned it once to him?

A: No, I didn't.

Q: Skipped right over that; right?

A: I didn't mention that to him.

...

Q: There is never any doubt, you are telling us now, ... in your mind about that having occurred at the base of the stairs?

A: That's right.

Q: But you don't bother to tell Dr Bradford?

A: No, I didn't.

Q: I suggest to you that doesn't make a whole lot of sense, because you are telling us now that it was that event, that allegation of the sexual assault that was the triggering event as to what happened afterwards; right?

A: Yes.

Q: The critical, the most important item in what you are telling us now?

A: That's right.

Q: When you get the first opportunity to tell that story, you don't do it?

A: I told you previously I couldn't tell anybody.[172]

All Lilian had to do was give Bradford a simple "yes" when he asked her directly about sexual abuse, Parfett said. Lilian replied, "I have had a man telling me all those years that I was his to use, that I was his. It was my duty."[173] Parfett continued – Maury was dead now and could no longer silence her: "[T]he real reason why you ... denied any sexual abuse whatsoever to Dr Bradford was because there never had been any?" "There was lots," Lilian insisted.[174]

Parfett mined Lilian's accounts of Maury's abuse to Drs Bradford, Cole, and Glancy as well as her testimony for discrepancies in what Lilian had disclosed and the relevant dates: "This is an issue of you not being able to tell two people the same story."[175] Again Lilian defended herself: "I knew the court would see Dr Cole's report. So why wouldn't I stick with that?" Parfett retorted: "Mrs Getkate, you do seem to have trouble sticking to a story."[176]

Lilian's difficulties in recalling the sequence of events over a decade of abuse are not uncommon for battered women who are overwhelmed by terror. Crushing anxiety, fear of obliteration, and the inability to sustain a sense of security and safety in turn affect one's "sense of the '*world as meaningful*,'" according to Donald Alexander Downs.[177] In consequence, "[t]ime may be comprehended as a series of discrete moments, each of which severs prior experiences from subsequent ones in such a way that no continuous 'narrative' can be sustained."[178]

Lilian explained that she might have miscommunicated, but "[i]t takes a long time to get over this kind of abuse, and it is still very difficult ... for me to talk about."[179] Parfett insisted: "[I]t didn't happen the way you say it happened."[180]

Parfett turned to Lilian's failure to protect her children: "Yet when they start being abused, you still do nothing?" Lilian got between Maury and the children: "That is what I did to protect them." "You did nothing to stop it on a permanent basis? Nothing?"[181] Parfett asked the same questions repeatedly: "You simply leave them in the situation?"[182] Of the loaded gun kept by Maury in the bedroom closet, she asked: "And you do absolutely nothing about it?"[183] Lilian said she ensured that they were never upstairs alone.

She failed to tell her lawyer Armitage about Maury's abuse of the children, the loaded gun, or Maury's sexual interest in Dara. Parfett asked: "So you go to this person to find out how to get yourself away safely and you don't give him any of the information he needs?"[184] "[Y]ou don't bother to tell Mr Armitage about this?"[185] Armitage had advised her to go to a women's shelter, leave the children with Maury, then go to court to seek custody and support. But, said Parfett, Lilian did not follow up on her lawyer's advice. She defended her decision: "He didn't know Maury."[186]

Parfett arguably offered evidence on the likely legal response – something that McCann could have challenged. She said:

> I suggest to you that if you had told him anything about the physical abuse, the sexual abuse, the physical abuse of the children, the possible sexual interests in Dara, the presence of guns in the house, the advice would have been pretty short and simple, get out, get out with the kids, and we'll take care of it, and there is not a hope in heaven that Maury will ever see those kids again?[187]

Women escaping abusers cannot just "get out." As Cynthia Gillespie explains, "the victim's chances of being killed increase significantly each time she attempts to do what we socially expect and require her to do to end the battering."[188] That Maury was a member of the RCMP, albeit a civilian member, undoubtedly affected Lilian's options. He threatened her with his access to RCMP computer databases. Reporting men who are affiliated with the police to the police can be extremely dangerous.[189] And no lawyer can promise a client that she will get custody or that her ex will not be permitted to see his children. Far from it.

Maury put away his books "after much yelling and arguing." Parfett seized on this – "Maury listened to you and put them away in the crawl space?" She extrapolated: "[W]hen you felt strongly enough about an issue to push it ... you would push your point,"[190] condemning Lilian for not dealing with the bigger threat to the children posed by the loaded shotgun in the adjoining closet. Lilian protested that Maury had loaded the gun only the week before he died. Parfett asked: "Up to around February of 1995, you're still capable of achieving anything that you, of achieving when you find something that bothers you enough you can deal with it?"[191] Yet, she said, Lilian did not "bother" to tell Armitage that Maury was "dry firing" guns at her.[192]

Parfett suggested that Lilian controlled household finances: she prepared monthly budgets, banked with her ATM card, and paid the bills. She did these tasks only with Maury's approval, but Parfett said: "So what you would have us believe, Mrs Getkate, is that he had complete control over all aspects of the finances?"[193] Lilian hid bags of unopened bills in the basement, had not fully paid the bills over a six-month period, had falsified the bank statements, and had altered credit card bills to suggest that payments had been made: "[W]e are dealing with this remarkably intelligent man, you are telling us that he doesn't notice the difference between a photocopied bill and a real bill?"[194]

Parfett suggested that Lilian's real complaint was that Maury didn't have time to spend with her. Lilian countered: "I did not look forward to the time that he was going to spend with me."[195] Parfett changed direction, saying that Maury was a very busy man, working full time, coming home to work evenings and weekends on his book, so he did not have time to commit all the acts of abuse that Lilian recounted[196] or to handle the money: "That was your job."[197] He could not possibly have had the financial control: "You're the one who is deciding how and when those bills are going to be paid?" Lilian flashed back: "Then why did I cut and paste them?"[198] Parfett introduced her handwritten budget notes, which indicated $600 per month for groceries, and pointed out the discrepancy with her testimony that she had only $400 per month: "Month after month, you are setting out budgets that were far greater than what you told us you were budgeting for?"[199] Lilian explained: "That budget was not put through."[200]

Parfett broached the subject of the nightly after-dinner "meetings": "[T]hat was your time together ... when you would discuss things; is that correct?" Lilian contradicted her: "It would be more him telling me what went on during his day and that sort of thing. He generally didn't ask me too much what went on in my day ... I was to sit there and listen to him."[201] Reviewing Lilian's notes from one of these meetings, Parfett suggested that Maury used this time to identify problems and try to improve their relationship. Again Lilian disagreed: "No. That is not what he was doing. He was telling me that those are my problem areas."[202] Parfett suggested that Lilian "tuned out" Maury during these meetings, when "this man tries to sit down and discuss with you the problems in the relationship." She continued: "It wasn't convenient for you to talk about it?"[203]

Parfett returned to Lilian's failure to disclose Maury's abuse. Lilian explained: "I had said a couple of things to Ricky [Armitage] at one point, and she treated Maury with a real cold shoulder, and that is what I was afraid of, and he picked up on it."[204] Her efforts to seek help from Ricky and her husband might seem inadequate, but each effort, no matter how small, augmented her endangerment.[205] Robbin Ogle and Susan Jacobs comment that, if battered women defend themselves with violence, "the law provides the 'final beating' by requiring *substantial evidence* of battering which the batterer has fought hard to prevent all along."[206]

Parfett continued: "You're trying to tell us that it was safer for you and the kids to not try to do anything about it than for you to break the silence and talk to friends?"[207] Lilian said: "It was safer for me to stay with Maury than to leave because he had threatened our lives and I believed he would carry it out."[208] Parfett challenged Lilian: she did not tell her friends or Armitage about the abuse "because there wasn't anything to tell them."[209]

Parfett disputed that Maury was not interested in his children by producing a photograph of him taking birthday candles off Dara's cake and another of him with Kevin "cuddled up" on his lap. Lilian contradicted her: "He is sitting straight up on my husband's lap."[210] Parfett produced Maury's day timer, which listed the children's activities. When Lilian explained that Maury did not take the children to these activities, Parfett remonstrated: "This is a man you are telling us has little or no interest in their [sic] children's lives, but he is keeping track of their Brownies' times, their Beavers' times, their appointments, their registrations?"[211] A notation in Maury's diary, "get Lil's present," and an unsigned Christmas card for Lilian found in his briefcase Parfett used to suggest that Maury did have feelings for Lilian.

In re-examination, McCann asked:

[H]ow long did it take him to drag you upstairs by the hair, push your face into the mattress? ... How long did it take him to trip you up and put his foot in your back on the floor? ... How long did it take him to point the gun at you and pull the trigger? ... How long did it take him to hold you at the top of the stairs and threaten to throw you down the stairs? ... How long did it take him to whack the kids?

"Minutes," Lilian answered.[212]

Maury continued to have a hold on Lilian long after his death. She experienced nightmares about him and woke up startled, fighting for her life, feeling that she was being strangled by him.[213]

"They should just lock me up and throw away the key"[214]

Lilian expressed deep remorse and anguish to Dr Graham Glancy, the psychiatrist who spent two full days assessing her five months after the homicide. An expert on Battered Woman Syndrome, Dr Glancy had experience working with female offenders, the vast majority of whom experienced male violence. He had testified as an expert on Battered Woman Syndrome in eight previous cases and had published articles on Battered Woman Syndrome in professional journals.[215] Parfett did not contest his expertise.

Dr Glancy described types of batterers, focusing on social conformists like Maury, who present one face to the world and another to their families, who appear egotistical but are actually fragile emotionally, and who have a deep need therefore to control the relationship, their partner, and their children.[216] Dr Glancy told the jury that any woman can get into a relationship that turns violent, but those who marry young, have little previous experience with men, and hold conventional and religious views about marriage might be more likely to internalize abuse and find it harder to escape.[217] Memory problems, difficulties in concentration, and "spacing out" are commonly experienced by severely abused women.[218] Many fantasize about the abuser's death[219] and continue to feel panic, fear, and anxiety once they have escaped, even when the man is deceased.[220]

Women do not "break the silence" for many reasons, Dr Glancy testified. Shame, especially regarding sexual abuse, self-blame, commitment to marriage as a religious institution, and fear of retaliatory violence constrain women's ability to disclose abuse:

> [E]very so often there is a highly publicized case where a woman leaves a man and he goes after her and kills her, and every time one of those happens, and there is intense publicity, this serves to keep a lot of women trapped because they think, well, if that can happen to that one woman ... it could happen to me.[221]

Moreover, he said, one of women's most crippling fears is of losing custody of their children: "[W]e know that 50% of men who abuse their wives also abuse their children."[222]

Dr Glancy affirmed that psychological and sexual abuse are more destructive than physical abuse[223] because they are aimed at degrading the person and destroying self-confidence and, essentially, the self. Constant monitoring of another person, efforts to control all aspects of her life and behaviour, and threats to harm or kill her, her children, or others whom she loves disempower the woman and thwart her efforts to escape. In fact, Dr Glancy said, "sometimes there doesn't need to be very much physical abuse as long as there are threats of physical abuse there, which serve to control the woman, keep her in her place."[224]

Lilian continued to "rationalize" Maury's abuse to some extent. For example, Dr Glancy noted, she identified "financial stress" and "Kevin was a difficult baby" as "causes" of Maury's violence.[225] These are the kinds of rationalization that society reinforces, as did Dr Bradford and Parfett. Furthermore, Dr Glancy said, Lilian only came gradually to see behaviours such as pushing as abuse, and her confusion about the precise chronology of her husband's abuse over a ten-year period is typical of battered women – but also "very difficult to do for almost anybody."[226] Psychiatric interviews are geared not to finding out who did what, when, and how, he said, but to diagnosing behavioural patterns and initiating appropriate therapy. Psychiatrists are not trained to assess the veracity of patients or record details and minute discrepancies as are police and lawyers.[227]

Dr Glancy retold Lilian's story, explaining that, when Maury tossed her essay on her career aspirations into the fire and burned it, he attacked her self-esteem, calling her dreams a "lie." He also concretely stopped Lilian from passing her course and gaining some independence by stepping out.[228] Armitage's legal advice, even though based on incomplete information provided by Lilian, nonetheless exposed a lack of options: she would have had to trust that her children would not end up in Maury's hands, and "she was aware that shelters had been cut by the government and wasn't sure how to access a shelter or whether there were really any shelters."[229] Moreover, Dr Glancy continued, women who leave violent men are at a heightened risk of being murdered for up to two years after they separate.[230]

Lilian suffered from chronic depression (dysthymia); she experienced depersonalization at the time of the homicide, compromising her ability to conceptualize other options but also to form the intent to kill; and she suffered from PTSD, more specifically Complex PTSD, the "new diagnosis" proposed by Dr Judith Herman. Dr Glancy explained that Complex PTSD captures more closely battered women's "idealisation of the abuser," "attention memory problems," "dissociative episodes, and the depersonalization."[231] Neither Complex PTSD nor Battered Woman Syndrome appears in the fourth edition of the *Diagnostic and Statistical Manual of Mental Disorders*,[232] but "many of the symptoms of battered woman syndrome generally come under those two diagnoses, dysthymia or chronic post-traumatic stress disorder."[233] Even though Dr Glancy diagnosed PTSD, his testimony was anchored in the language of Battered Woman Syndrome as interpreted by lawyers, whereby nuanced and sophisticated diagnostic considerations are reduced to simplistic, rigid requirements.[234]

Dr Glancy affirmed that Lilian apprehended being killed and that her daughter would be sexually abused. These fears were reasonable given Maury's behaviour, his threats, and her ability to predict the escalation in his violence. Dr Glancy also said that her perception that she had no options was reasonable: she could not contact the police, given Maury's employment with the RCMP, and she could not devise a safe plan to escape and protect her children.

Unfortunately for the defence, Dr Glancy went further. He clarified that Lilian feared she would "eventually" be killed and Dara would "eventually" be sexually assaulted by her father.[235] He noted that "she did not believe that he would kill her imminently right then ... [T]he jury should be aware she did not believe that he was on his way down to kill her right at that time."[236]

McCann asked whether Dr Glancy could plausibly offer any other explanation for why this "meek, mild, non-violent, loving individual would between 4:00 and 5:00 in the morning ... suddenly shoot her husband."[237] The doctor ran through the possibilities, crossing them off – no delusions or hallucinations, no history of violence or aggression, and, though there were some financial difficulties, a planned murder while the children slept downstairs, hoping to get away with it, was improbable. Lilian "seemed sincere and genuine and honest."[238]

Parfett's cross-examination aimed to undermine Dr Glancy's conclusion that Lilian was a battered woman and suffered from Battered Woman Syndrome. Parfett secured Dr Glancy's acknowledgment that it was possible, though unlikely, that Lilian's PTSD and dissociation could have been caused by the homicide itself.[239]

Dr Glancy resisted Parfett's claim that "a lot of women break the silence." Many more women do not disclose abuse, he reminded Parfett.[240] It might have helped the jury to know that research indicates that at most one in ten women disclose abuse; on average, women are assaulted thirty-five times before they first contact police.[241]

Dr Glancy rejected Parfett's characterization of Maury's holding Lilian over stairs and threatening to drop her or pressing her neck as not "battering incidents." These are assaults, but more importantly "the most serious part is the threat."[242] With the exception of the choking incidents, Parfett proposed, "all of the physical abuse that she alleges falls within that low level, that is consistent with 15% to 35% of all couples who experience physical abuse in a relationship?"[243] Dr Glancy countered that physical assaults in conjunction with psychological abuse, threats, and sexual abuse are not "low level" abuse.

Parfett continued her attack on Dr Glancy's evidence. Lilian did not meet the criteria for Battered Woman Syndrome laid out in his own publications, in which Dr Glancy wrote that enforced social isolation, totalitarian control, and financial abuse are its hallmarks. Lilian was not monitored during the day by Maury while he was at work, she had friends, and she had the car during the day. Dr Glancy retorted that Lilian had to report back to Maury on her activities and on the banking, he vetted her friends and expenditures, he told her what to wear, and he refused to allow paid employment. Moreover, the indicia for Battered Woman Syndrome need not all be present for a diagnosis. Even the Supreme Court of Canada had cautioned against generating a rigid stereotype of the battered woman, he chided.[244]

Parfett challenged Dr Glancy's conclusion that Maury had committed sexual sadism. She inadvertently opened the door to the evidence that Lilian had told Dr Glancy that Maury had locked handcuffs on her wrists six or seven times during sexual intercourse. Parfett tried to block this evidence, protesting that Lilian had not testified about this practice, but Dr Glancy continued: "I think His Honour will tell us that psychiatrists can use hearsay which may go to the weight of his evidence."[245]

Parfett then attacked Dr Glancy's conclusion regarding the threat posed by Maury because he had not "practiced" any of these "arts" such as ninja or night stalking for twelve years. Dr Glancy astutely answered: "I'm not sure there is evidence before the court that shows that if you don't practice killing people ... the expertise goes away."[246]

Parfett also questioned whether Lilian faced an escalation in the abuse prior to the homicide and whether that night Maury presented a new or heightened threat. Can escalation be established when the chronology cannot be documented? Many aspects of his behaviour on the fatal night – use of the vibrator, non-consensual intercourse, anal penetration, and the risk that the children might interrupt them – were nothing new and presented no "lethal aspect."[247] Dr Glancy responded:

> [W]hat made her believe that is an accumulation of the history of repeated abuse and then the change in him that night which included the fact that he just didn't seem to care any more, that it was particularly sustained and

intense that night, suggested to her that the belief she had had some time, that he would take the kids, he would sexually assault the kids, and he would kill her at some time, brought it all to a head.[248]

Parfett asked whether Lilian feared that it would be that week, month, or year. Dr Glancy repeated: "It was not imminent."[249]

When a marriage is disintegrating, Parfett asked, is it not usual for threats about custody and support to be made? Dr Glancy agreed but refuted her proposal that it is not uncommon for people to say "I'll kill you."[250] Nor would he accept her proposition that, because there was no evidence that Maury was a pedophile, his risk to Dara was negligible. Most incest offenders are not pedophiles: this crime is better understood as "surrogate behaviour," in which the man sees his daughter rapidly approaching puberty and considers her a surrogate for his wife.[251]

Parfett asked Dr Glancy whether he was surprised that Dara and Kevin had only heard yelling and not witnessed acts of violence by their father. Dr Glancy agreed that he was somewhat perplexed by this.[252] But in re-examination, Dr Glancy said that the children described to the police weekly fights they heard from the basement and then, the day before the homicide, a "really big fight" that was "really scary." The two children clung to each other in the basement, listening to their father bellowing and their mother sobbing, hearing glass breaking and things being thrown. They peeked upstairs and saw potted plants and dirt strewn all over, but their mother rushed over. As Dara told the police, "[m]y mom said, can you stay in the basement? She was crying."[253]

Dr Wendy Cole was the next witness to be qualified as an expert specializing in psychiatry and domestic violence. She described Lilian in January 1996, almost two months after the homicide, as "profoundly depressed": "She could hardly speak. She spoke in whispered tones. She spoke with very slow speech, and she was having some difficulty with concentration. She felt generally unwell, she was very fatigued, she had low energy, she had very little interest in her personal appearance, personal hygiene, in day-to-day activities."[254]

Dr Cole treated Lilian over a six-month period and prepared an assessment but not a full forensic report. She diagnosed depression and chronic PTSD resulting from domestic violence. To Dr Cole, Lilian also said that "they should lock me up and throw away the key." She never attempted to justify her actions, according to Dr Cole.[255]

McCann asked Dr Cole to comment on Battered Woman Syndrome, bringing Parfett to her feet to object: Dr Cole had not been qualified as an expert in this area, and she must be limited to "domestic violence." Justice Chadwick intervened: "[F]rom what I have heard of Dr Glancy, I would think battered woman syndrome is part of domestic violence; if not, we have wasted three weeks."[256]

Dr Cole testified that Lilian fit the syndrome: "[A]s a result of [profound depression], she had genuine cognitive and emotional impairment."[257] Dr Cole referred to Maury's interest in explosives and Lilian's belief that Maury "would make a device that might actually harm her parents."[258] Dr Cole said that women like Lilian cannot leave their children behind, and shelters and community resources are "poor, poor options."[259]

Dr Cole then rationalized the differences between what Lilian told Dr Bradford six days after the homicide and what she told her nearly two months later. Her profoundly distressed and depressed state would have prevented her from telling a complete story. The differences between her assessment report and Dr Glancy's report four months later she explained by Lilian's improved condition. Dr Cole added that, when abusive events are so common that they are simply part of one's life, it becomes very diffi-cult to recall specific events and dates.[260]

In cross-examination, Dr Cole said that Lilian might not have disclosed sexual abuse to Dr Bradford because women with limited relationship ex-perience might not like what is happening, but

> they truly don't recognize that society would consider it abusive. They don't know what goes on in other relationships. They are not aware ... that, for example, sexual acts should be mutually consenting and mutually pleasur-able to both ... [Y]ou have people who will be in a relationship and simply accept that it is their duty, that it is the expectation of this marriage that certain acts will go on.[261]

Parfett suggested that Lilian's remorse was consistent with her guilty rec-ognition that "there was no excuse for what had happened." Dr Cole cut her short: "I think that is why we are all here today. That is for the court to decide."[262]

McCann's closing address told the jurors that self-defence was key to Lilian's defence. Later McCann referred to Dr Glancy's evidence that Lilian did not have the capacity to form the requisite intent for murder.[263] She fit the Battered Woman Syndrome criteria and killed Maury believing that the sexual and physical abuse would not stop and that he would "eventually" kill her and harm her children.[264]

McCann referred to the live explosive device: "He said he could blow the top off the house, get rid of her any time he wanted." He asked the jurors to "imagine living ... in a home where there is talk about explosives and where ... there was a very powerful, very unstable explosive found by the police at the house."[265]

Lilian was "a timid, quiet, unassuming doormat sort of a person at the time. She is not now, but she was then."[266] She was "the perfect sap for an abusive, brutal husband."[267] What would have caused her to shoot her sleeping husband? McCann said: "There is only one possible explanation that makes any sense; isn't there? Only one thing that sort of fits with our human experience, the way people act, and that is if you accept the explanation that was given to us by Dr Glancy and Dr Cole, that she could not see any other way out from this nightmare."[268]

Parfett said in closing that Lilian killed her husband because she could see no way out of a bad marriage. At most, she experienced "moderate abuse" – minor pushing and shoving. She was neither violently attacked nor threatened with death; she was not subjected to "totalitarian" control or psychological abuse; and her children were not endangered. Her claims were not corroborated. If there was escalating abuse, friends would have seen the bruising, and the children would have witnessed the violence.

In dismissing Lilian's allegations of sexual assault, Parfett again drew on the rhetoric used by defence lawyers in sexual assault cases: "These allegations are the easiest to make and the hardest to disprove, unless there are injuries or complaints to someone outside of the relationship they can't be disproved."[269] She continued that "what does come through loud and clear when you listen to Lilian Getkate's evidence is that the real problem was that Lilian Getkate in all hunger wanted to have sex with her husband and that all sex with her husband was done reluctantly."[270]

The most accurate account of Lilian's marriage and the homicide was that provided to Dr Bradford, before Lilian was "cued" to shape her story to fit Battered Woman Syndrome, according to Parfett. She reviewed every last discrepancy in Lilian's evidence: the only credible explanation for the homicide was that Lilian hoped to get custody, escape from financial difficulty, and rid herself of Maury. Furthermore, Parfett said, Lilian must have felt angry that night after being profoundly insulted by her husband. Coupled with her depression and her desperation to exit the relationship, his acts and words led her to resolve to kill him that night, making her guilty of murder.[271]

Justice Chadwick charged the jury that, since Lilian had admitted the killing, they need only consider self-defence, provocation, and no intent to kill. First, he told them, consider self-defence. If Parfett had not persuaded them beyond a reasonable doubt that Lilian had not killed in self-defence, they must acquit her. She must have faced an unlawful assault, but it need not have been an actual assault if she "reasonably believed in the circumstances that she was being unlawfully assaulted."[272] Justice Chadwick referred to Lilian's evidence of the sexual assault perpetrated by her husband that night and her fear that he would "ultimately" further abuse Lilian and sexually assault her daughter as possible "unlawful assaults."

The next element of self-defence, reasonable fear of death or grievous bodily harm, must be assessed from the standpoint of Lilian's experience, if the jury accepted her evidence, of escalating control and violence. The anticipated harm need not be "imminent"; rather, "imminence" is one factor to consider in assessing the reasonableness of her fear: "[Y]ou will look at the cumulative effect of all of these years of abuse as to whether she apprehended the risk of death or grievous bodily harm."[273]

The jurors were then to ask whether Lilian reasonably believed that she could not otherwise preserve herself. The judge reviewed the evidence of the psychiatrists, advising jurors to consider whether Lilian fit Battered Woman Syndrome and the impact of Maury's behaviour on her state of mind and her ability to seek other options: "The perception of Maury Getkate in the eyes of Lilian Getkate according to her evidence was that he was all powerful, both in physical strength and what he could do. There was a constant threat of taking the children away from her, disappearing with them, harm to her parents if she separated at any time."[274]

Justice Chadwick told the jurors that, if they found that the Crown had disproved self-defence beyond a reasonable doubt, they must then consider whether Lilian was provoked by Maury's wrongful sexual assault or the insult that Maury delivered to her. If so, then would the reasonable person in her shoes, who had undergone her experiences, have lost the power of self-control? Furthermore, was Lilian actually provoked by Maury, and did she react "on the sudden," before her "passions" could cool? Justice Chadwick commented that there was a period of time between Maury's acts and insults and Lilian's reaction, but he told jurors to "take into account subjective factors, that is evidence of Lilian Getkate's mental condition, her temperament, the cumulative effect of physical, verbal, and sexual abuse."[275]

If Parfett had not persuaded them beyond a reasonable doubt that Lilian was not provoked, then they must acquit her of murder and find her guilty of manslaughter.

Finally, if they determined that provocation did not apply, then they must ask whether Lilian had the intent to kill in light of her dissociation and the medical opinion of Dr Glancy. If they had a reasonable doubt about her intent, then they must acquit her of murder and convict her of manslaughter.

The jury retired to consider their verdict just before noon on 1 October 1998. When they returned almost four days later, on 4 October at 10:35 a.m., Justice Chadwick commented, "[f]or a while I thought I would never see you again."[276] The foreman quickly delivered their verdict – not guilty of murder but guilty of manslaughter. The judge thanked the jurors:

> The battered spouse syndrome that we heard so much about is not an easy concept, and that is why we had the experts to try and help us through and to understand some of these things, and I'm sure that it may have caused you great concern to think that a person who has taken another person's life would go free as a result of this.[277]

Another Ending?

Could Lilian have avoided a manslaughter conviction by not relying on what Justice Chadwick called "the battered spouse syndrome"? It seems that her counsel was not expecting acquittal based on self-defence. McCann wrote later that "Getkate never claimed to be acting in self-defence, but testified to recalling only bits and pieces of the shooting."[278] He used Battered Woman Syndrome to show that she had no intent to kill because she was in "a depersonalized state": "Women who fit the criteria are also psychologically disturbed."[279]

Lilian's manslaughter verdict – like women's guilty pleas to manslaughter – is part of a pattern of verdicts in which battered women are "excused" by reason of their psychological frailties or provocations, but they are not "justified" or vindicated by acquittal based on self-defence.[280] McCann did not press self-defence for Lilian, so perhaps the verdict is not surprising. Nonetheless, this pattern of manslaughter verdicts is especially striking for women who kill sleeping or incapacitated batterers. Jane Hurshman's jury acquittal for shooting Billy Stafford when he fell into a drunken stupor was exceedingly rare. Only one other woman in my study was acquitted in similar circumstances, but not by her jury.[281]

Yet the jury could have acquitted Lilian even if the law was against her. Juries have the inherent authority to engage in "jury nullification" by returning a "perverse verdict" that flies in the face of the law. This power derives from the historical role of the jury as the guardian of community morality and the bulwark against abusive state power. Regina Schuller's work studying mock jurors suggests that expert testimony in support of battered women's self-defence claims has its greatest impact when jurors are released from a strict application of the law.[282]

Canadian law recognizes the jury's power to nullify: judges cannot order juries to convict;[283] they must, absent specific circumstances,[284] leave acquittal as an option for the jury; and jurors cannot be called on to explain their verdicts.[285] At the same time, Canadian law forbids defence lawyers from informing juries that they possess this power on the theory that chaos would ensue if juries were to refuse to apply the law.[286] Defence lawyers are permitted to urge juries to acquit on this basis in some US states,[287] but in Canada defence counsel must find other ways to impress on jurors that the woman acted to save her life even if that act does not fit the strict letter of the law.

Getkate had distinguished counsel and a sympathetic judge,[288] yet her self-defence case might not have been presented compellingly. Possibly, her jury needed more information about the explosive device in the basement. What could have triggered an explosion? What damage to life and property would it have caused if detonated? Was the device evidence of a criminal offence by Maury? Not a single witness linked the improvised explosive device to Lilian's need to use violent self-defence; in fact, her expert witness, Dr Glancy, emphatically told jurors that the danger to Lilian and her children was not imminent. Neither was this link between the IED and self-defence made by McCann or Justice Chadwick. The jurors needed to be told that Lilian's fears of grievous bodily harm or death were objectively reasonable in light of the discovery of Maury's device: the risk was both ongoing and imminent.

Arguably, Battered Woman Syndrome was not the ideal strategy for Lilian's defence given the lack of corroborated evidence of extreme violence by Maury. Evan Stark, a long-time advocate for battered women and an expert who has written and testified extensively on using Coercive Control as an interpretive framework for women on trial, explains that "BWS and PTSD require proof of severe traumatic episodes, proof that may be impossible in cases characterized by repetitive, but minor acts of abuse embedded in an ongoing pattern of control."[289] Maury's use of physical violence was strategic; Maury predominantly relied on subtle threats, psychological terror, and sexual abuse to dominate Lilian.[290] Parfett might have persuaded the jurors that any violence Lilian suffered was minor, such that she could not have developed a syndrome or been hindered in seeking outside help.

It was also difficult to show the sharp escalation in her endangerment on the night of the homicide. The notion of a catastrophic choice of kill or be killed is the premise on which self-defence is based, and Battered Woman Syndrome evidence is used to make visible for the jury the serious threat that the woman faced. Here Lilian had no corroborated evidence of Maury's pattern of extreme violence, no memory of what precipitated her act, and no claim that she faced deadly violence.

Another problem was that the Lilian who testified at trial was not the same Lilian who killed Maury. As Stark explains, the Battered Woman Syndrome narrative "is designed to elicit the court's sense of outrage by imagining the woman who is no longer there"[291] – that is, the stereotype of the fearful, passive, and dependent battered woman. Witnesses commented on how much more confident and healthy Lilian appeared at trial. Parfett might well have convinced jurors that Lilian was not "helpless" in light of her other activities, her strategic decisions,[292] and her ability to defend herself in the witness stand, even under Parfett's gruelling cross-examination.

Coercive Control

In contrast, there was ample evidence of Maury's "Coercive Control,"[293] much of it from Parfett's witnesses. Coercive Control denotes the range of behaviours used by the man to limit the freedom of his female partner, curtail her liberties, exploit her resources, and subjugate her to his will. This theory shifts the focus away from his discrete acts of violence and toward the pattern of psychological domination and continuous abuse perpetrated by him "to secure privileges that involve the use of time, control over material resources, access to sex, and personal service."[294]

Coercive Control attempts to capture battered women's experience, in which physical violence is not the most crippling aspect of battering. This theory has been developed by feminists who staff women's shelters and advocates who see the patterns in men's abuse of their partners. They recognize that actual violence is only one aspect – and often not the most damaging one – of a man's abuse. Women consistently report that the more difficult thing to recover from is the deep impact of psychological abuse, sexual humiliation, and denigration.[295]

Coercive Control, like Battered Woman Syndrome, can ground self-defence. Coercive Control theory was used successfully in US battered women's defence work starting in the early 1990s, but it was not advanced by Canadian defence lawyers until almost two decades later.[296] A man's deployment of Coercive Control is more predictive of intimate homicide than the severity or frequency of his physical violence. Coercive Control is a more significant risk factor for lethality, especially when combined with separation or the threat of separation.[297] One US study reports that a "'highly controlling' abuser was one of two risk factors that increased a victim's risk of fatality ninefold."[298] The Battered Woman Syndrome model facilitated Parfett's insistence on identifying discrete acts of life-threatening violence and pinpointing when the threat would materialize. But as Robbin Ogle and Susan Jacobs argue, battering is "a slow, homicidal process."[299] Every move that the woman makes toward freedom is matched by an escalation of threats and control: "The situation is constantly potentially homicidal."[300]

An expert in Coercive Control would have mapped out for the jury the subjects and methods of Maury's control over Lilian's life.[301] Stark writes that "[t]he main means used to establish control is the micro-regulation of everyday behaviors associated with stereotypic female roles, such as how women dress, cook, clean, socialize, care for their children, or perform sexually ... These dynamics give Coercive Control a role in sexual politics that distinguishes it from all other crimes."[302]

In Lilian's case, an expert might have testified that it was Maury's decision whether and when the couple married, where they lived, how much money they spent, what they did socially, when and how they had sexual relations, whether Lilian worked, whether she returned to school, what she wore, which friends she saw, whether she was allowed to visit her family in British Columbia, how the children were disciplined, and even what she was allowed to dream for herself – "a lie," Maury declared, when he threw her essay into the fire. He also engaged in "tangential spouse abuse," an extension of Coercive Control.[303] By using force against Kevin and touching Dara sexually, by telling Lilian that he would hunt them all down if she fled or secure child custody were she to separate, he paralyzed her and ensured her compliance.

Every witness, apart from Gee, saw Lilian's subservience to her husband, the way in which Lilian watched him constantly for signs of disapproval, how he dictated their social engagements, his use of force against his children, and her evident fear of him. The testimony of her friend that she was shocked when Lilian asked whether she needed her husband's permission to go out for coffee and her anxiety that Maury would know if she disclosed his abuse conjure up an "unreal world"[304] in which he was a dictator, in which his power was so omnipresent that Lilian no longer questioned it. In fact, his power became almost agentless in her evidence about her family budget when she told Parfett "that [the] budget didn't go through," that "it wasn't approved."

Maury monitored Lilian through his after-dinner "meetings" in which he reviewed the finances and had her record her own failures as a wife and mother. His insistence that she call him and talk to him whenever she tried to go out with friends in the evenings demonstrated his authority even in small matters. His diary, where he recorded her movements through the children's activities, could have been read as another manifestation of his control,[305] refuting the prosecution's claim that it showed he was an involved father. His use of weapons, his reminders to Lilian of his power (Maury was the smart one, the one with a PhD, the Mensa member, the RCMP employee who would be believed over her, who would have access to resources to find her should she flee, and who would fight her should she hope for custody of the children), and his veiled references to Dara's coming puberty – all enforced his omnipotence and her helplessness. As Lisa Goodman and Deborah Epstein explain, "[e]ven nonviolent control tactics take on a violent meaning through their implicit connection with potential physical harm."[306]

When battered women testify with confidence or display anger over the abuse, Stark explains, they can seem defensive, and their accounts can sound exaggerated or manipulative. The woman's demeanour might be measured against the stereotypes associated with Battered Woman Syndrome, allowing prosecutors to persuade jurors that the woman wasn't really battered – or, if she was, that it was not that bad. To counter these problems, Stark asks jurors to imagine, looking now at this strong and capable woman testifying in her own defence, what it would have taken to deprive her of her most fundamental liberties and dignity.[307] This strategy would have required jurors to refocus on Maury's calculated course of conduct aimed at subjugating Lilian and explained why she might have reacted defensively to cross-examination that minimized and denied his abuse.

Coercive Control also would have allowed McCann to refute directly Parfett's theory that Lilian ran the finances and could have managed Maury's risk to her and their children. In presenting her experience of his Coercive Control to a jury, an expert would have highlighted how Lilian struggled for control over her life and the consequences that befell her when she overtly opposed Maury's will. Stark argues that battered women exercise "control in the context of no control" by finding small and often invisible ways to resist and thwart their batterers.[308] So, for example, rather than showing that Lilian really was in control, as urged by Parfett when she pointed to her strategies for avoiding sex, protecting her children from a loaded gun in the closet, or hiding the finances from Maury, these acts would be described by a Coercive Control expert as her efforts to assert herself, to somehow live with her anxiety about her children's safety, and to maintain a measure of her own humanity by resisting.

Stark says that this concept of "control in the context of no control" helps the jury to see that, while such acts might have helped to "control individual episodes," ultimately they have failed to protect the woman from ongoing and escalating danger. The jury can then see the woman's ultimate homicidal act as a "culmination of a rational strategy of defense, not an act of insanity or vengeance."[309]

Coercive Control as a defence theory for Lilian would have been able to capture for the jury the undisputed intimidation and control that Maury used to entrap her. His acts were unwittingly supported by a social, economic, and legal system that simply could not guarantee her safety, custody, or economic means to support herself and her children. And Lilian knew it. As a theory that looks at the pattern rather than discrete incidents, Coercive Control might have been better able to reveal the escalation of Maury's sexual abuse and the imminence of the threat to the lives of Lilian and her children.

Most importantly, Coercive Control might have been her best shot at acquittal. The theory explains that women survive by hiding their true selves from their abusers and suppressing their rage. Lilian might have been overwhelmed by fear and anger – emotions that she could then neither acknowledge nor display – triggering her dissociation and her homicidal act. That Maury had evidently revived his interest in paramilitary weapons and had constructed a live explosive device in the basement comprised hard evidence that her increasing dread was grounded in a terrifying reality: he had taken his threats to a new level, and every minute in that house was potentially lethal.

The Media

McCann told news media that the jurors accepted that Lilian was a battered woman, "to some degree," calling it a possible "compromise verdict."[310] Her mother commended the jury's fairness: "An acquittal would have been nice

... [but] we're very relieved."[311] Parfett claimed that the verdict "rehabili-tated" Maury's reputation: "[Maury] was not the monster his wife made him out to be."[312] The Getkate family members who sat through the trial were angry and hurt, calling Lilian's testimony "a crock."[313]

Justice Chadwick sentenced Lilian on 10 November 1998 on the basis that the jury found that she was an abused woman but "not to a degree where the death could be justified at law."[314] Still, he rejected Parfett's argu-ment that Lilian experienced a very low level of abuse, instead finding that she fit fairly high "up the scale." He ordered her to serve two years less a day on house arrest in the community of Maple Ridge, British Columbia, where her children were residing with their grandmother.[315] She was to continue attending Co-Dependents Anonymous and counselling sessions, perform 200 hours of community service, continue her part-time employment, and maintain contact with her family. Justice Chadwick also urged her to allow her children to connect with their father's relatives.[316]

Parfett contested this sentence. She took the unusual step of speaking to news media, calling the sentence "an appalling message to send to the public" and claiming that there was no corroborating evidence that Lilian was abused: "All of the evidence came from Mrs Getkate herself. No one could corroborate it. Not a bruise, not a hospital record, not a police report. Nothing ... We simply say, 'Yes, you were abused. Fine. You walk.' That's what this sentence is all about."[317] This claim ignored the testimony of Crown witnesses who saw Maury's control over Lilian and his assaults on the chil-dren, the weapons collection, and the IED in the basement.

Parfett noted that, as of January 1996, just three weeks after Maury's death, a new mandatory minimum sentence was introduced to require a jail sentence of at least four years for manslaughter committed with a firearm.[318] She called the timing "ironic"[319] and announced her desire to appeal the sen-tence, even though no other battered woman convicted of manslaughter using a gun would in future receive house arrest. Although ultimately the Attorney General's office refused permission to the Ottawa office to appeal the sentence,[320] Parfett's public remarks added fuel to the backlash against Lilian and other battered women.

Journalists and news media strive for objective and informed reporting, but "newsworthiness" nonetheless shapes content and presentation. How the media report wife battering and intimate partner homicide affects pub-lic attitudes and the lives of individual men and women. Studies have docu-mented the ways that language choice, use of the passive construction, and selectivity regarding which information is presented in accounts of wife battering and intimate femicide subtly shape our understandings of blame-worthiness and responsibility.[321] Batterers use news reports of other men's violence and court rulings exculpating violent men to threaten and intimi-date their partners.[322] As Dr Glancy testified, battered women monitor such news items and their partners' reactions as they attempt to assess their level of danger.[323]

The murder trial of a woman who kills an alleged batterer creates op-portunities for journalists, editors, and citizens to pronounce judgment, directly and subtly, on battered women. Media accounts might adhere rigor-ously to strictly factual accounts of the trial and evidence, but others shade, explain, or minimize the evidence, supporting or condemning the accused woman. Media studies have reached different conclusions about whether men's and women's homicidal acts receive comparable or informed news reporting,[324] but Lilian's case provided countless examples of overt and co-vert bias. Not only was Lilian vilified, but also Parfett's remarks and the media coverage arguably contributed to the entrapment of other battered women by overemphasizing the need for corroboration and ignoring the proof on record in Lilian's case.

Both the *Ottawa Citizen* and the *National Post* howled in protest over Lilian's sentence, echoing Parfett's words and misrepresenting the evidence. Throughout the trial, the *Ottawa Citizen* chose provocative headlines, some supportive of the defence,[325] many favouring the Crown.[326] Its headlines frequently described Lilian as the "wife," while Maury was the "psycholo-gist,"[327] positioning her as defined by her sex and marital status and him by his profession. The *Ottawa Citizen* titled its editorial "An Insult to Our Sense of Justice," repeating Parfett's words almost verbatim, and reiterated her claim that nothing substantiated Lilian's abuse.[328] The editorial provided misleading information to the community and especially to battered women by asserting that, "[h]ad Mrs Getkate dialled 9-1-1 and repeated those alleg-ations, police would have quickly taken her husband away."[329] Bonnie Mooney's case shows how dangerously mistaken that claim is.

The *National Post* editorial, "Battering Justice,"[330] incorrectly claimed that *Lavallee* elevated Battered Woman Syndrome to "an absolute defence" in homicide trials, accusing feminists of misleading the public that *Lavallee* would not erode the legal prohibition on murder. The *National Post* sug-gested that "the mere presentation of the 'battered woman' claim ... had been enough to win the day,"[331] implying that Lilian had been acquitted and wrongly suggesting that Battered Woman Syndrome testimony was the only evidence supporting her story. The opinion accepted that prior abuse should mitigate the sentence but then suggested that Lilian had received the "functional equivalent" of an acquittal. The concluding paragraph derided the syndrome, the expert, and widely published research: "Pseudo-scientific defences introduced by partisan psychiatric 'experts' during the trial give a patina of respectability to bizarre theories that should remain in the unpublished doctoral dissertations where they were born."[332]

Other news articles were more subtly inflammatory. Ron Corbett wrote that Lilian had spent "a grand total" of eleven days in jail, had seen her children "almost daily after killing their father," and had been found "guilty only of manslaughter for pumping two bullets into her husband while he slept."[333] In another piece, Corbett mused: "There will always be something ambiguous about this story, something transitory and unfathomed. Was Mrs Getkate a battered wife? There will always be debate on this subject."[334] Yet the three psychiatrists disagreed only on the extent and the impact of the abuse – not whether Maury abused Lilian.

Peter Hum's article, "Killer's 'Stay-at-Home' Jail Term Pushes Crown to Request Appeal,"[335] quoted extensively from Ottawa's head Crown Attorney Andrejs Berzins. Berzins stood behind Parfett's effort to appeal the sentence. Blurring the distinction between men who kill their wives and women who kill their abusive male partners, he asked: "Is a conditional sentence ever appropriate in a homicide case, especially domestic homicide?"

The *National Post* wrote several pieces using "husband-killer" in the headlines,[336] while British Columbia's *The Province* labelled Lilian a "killer mom."[337] In fact, the *Ottawa Citizen* revisited her sentence in an editorial published months later criticizing another sentence of house arrest. The newspaper referred to Lilian as serving her sentence in "her home in temperate British Columbia" and claimed that "light sentences fuel the agitation of law-and-order politicians who start calling for minimum jail sentences for certain crimes."[338]

Citizens wrote angry but often misinformed letters to the editors.[339] A prolonged rant by CFRA-AM host Lowell Green two days later targeted Lilian's case. Women could now take out "huge insurance" policies on their husbands, "plug" them full of "brain holes," and then tell everyone that their husbands were beasts – "don't worry that you've never told anyone about this ... [for] your word is all you'll need" – so that they can become rich widows. He sang a refrain, "[i]t's men bashing time," telling listeners that "it is now safe for women to plug their husbands in the bedroom and walk. What a joyous day for the femi-Nazis."

The Canadian Broadcast Standards Council (CBSC) received complaints that his broadcast grossly misrepresented the facts in the case, mocked the serious problem of wife battering, and promoted hatred against women, thereby increasing the risk of male violence. The CBSC dismissed the complaints, saying that Green did not make discriminatory comments about an identifiable group but merely commented on a judicial decision and the political opinions of "certain feminists."[340]

Lilian's lawyer tried to stem the backlash with his own letter to the *Ottawa Citizen.*[341] Its editorial, McCann wrote, demonstrated "a complete lack of understanding" of the trial, based on "the intemperate remarks of the assistant Crown attorney who has twice in the past two years failed in her attempts to obtain murder convictions against abused women who have struck back at their abusers."[342] McCann corrected the misperception that Battered Woman Syndrome is a defence on its own. He pointed out that people are convicted all the time based on uncorroborated evidence, but that simply was not the case in Lilian's trial – her allegations were supported by other evidence.

McCann commented on the implications of insisting on corroboration from battered women: "If only women who call police or complain to friends can claim to be abused, then the most seriously abused women will be eliminated. Any expert on the subject and anyone who has worked with the most severely abused women will tell you they never complain and rarely go to emergency wards. They are just too afraid." Finally, he wrote, the editorial's claim that Lilian's sentence represented a "licence to kill" was uninformed by the many legal precedents supporting the outcome.[343]

Other citizens waded in. Suzanne Vezina, for example, wrote that the *Ottawa Citizen*'s editorial claim that all Lilian had to do was call 9-1-1 "[s]ounds familiar. That's exactly what the late Arlene May of Collingwood did, numerous times – before her ex-boyfriend Randy Iles shot her to death. The courts are finally coming around to the realization that the only sure way an abused woman can guarantee her safety from her abusive partner is by killing him before he kills her."[344]

Donna Johnson wrote an opinion piece, arguing that "[w]hen a woman shoots her abusive husband you can be quite certain that a terrible series of events has driven her to this act."[345] Lilian should not have been prosecuted at all: "[W]hy are we prosecuting women we might otherwise be burying?"[346]

Lilian handled the media glare and public backlash with dignity and humility. She told reporters that she had packed her suitcase in anticipation of a three-year jail sentence and was startled by Justice Chadwick's ruling: "I took someone's life and I'm not going to jail. Of course I'm surprised by that."[347] She was also shocked and angered by the media attack that labelled her a "killer mom" in *The Province*.

Lilian invited *Ottawa Citizen* reporter Corbett to visit their home to see how the kids were doing. There she told him that her children had seen the articles and had in fact taken news clippings to school to explain what had happened to their classmates and teachers. Lilian spoke about her hopes to upgrade her education and eventually to work with other battered women. "I just want to live quietly with my children," she said. "Those people who are saying all those things about me, unless they've walked a mile in my shoes, why would they want to judge me?"[348]

The Prosecutor ... and the Judge

Parfett's interest in Battered Woman Syndrome did not end with the Getkate trial. In a paper that Parfett published in 2001, she argues that Battered Woman Syndrome should be abandoned because it is scientifically unsound:

> It is also important to note that, in his experiments with dogs, Martin Seligman discovered that dogs do not always develop learned helplessness. In fact, the only dogs who developed learned helplessness, were the ones that had been initially shocked while they were confined in a hammock and did not have a method of escape. The dogs that were not subjected to this initial shock, *never* developed learned helplessness and always escaped when a way out was offered to them. Again, when the analogy is drawn between Seligman's experiments and women in abusive relationships, one would expect that a woman would respond like the second group of dogs and would leave the relationship, since she would not develop any psychological barrier to leaving.[349]

Parfett appears to suggest that battered women are not as "confined" as dogs in a hammock when their batterers first attack them and that they therefore do not develop "learned helplessness." She also argues that Battered Woman Syndrome amounts to "political ideology" that seeks to excuse women of responsibility for their crimes. Ironically, given how she deployed the syndrome against Lilian, Parfett criticizes Battered Woman Syndrome for reinforcing sex discriminatory beliefs about women.

Battered Woman Syndrome, Parfett writes, is unnecessary after the *Lavallee* decision. Battered women's own testimony about their abuse can be used to show all the elements of self-defence, without resort to Battered Woman Syndrome or the need for an expert witness. For those women whose actions do not fit self-defence, she proposes the defences of mental disorder and provocation, with some modifications.[350] Paradoxically, Parfett seems to prefer Coercive Control theory over Battered Woman Syndrome while noting that it was not yet considered by Canadian courts.[351]

Lilian's manslaughter conviction, her pre-trial incarceration, and her conditional imprisonment were not her only punishments. Lilian was verbally and publicly chastised in and out of court. Her experience of abuse and that of her children were denied, minimized, and justified. The furious backlash against battered women washed over her for months after her sentence. In fact, her name and case continue to be the subject of online misinformation, distortion, and hate. Her murder trial raises the question of whether the rhetoric of prosecutors, the opinions of experts, or the editorial opinions of newspapers reporting on murder prosecutions of battered women themselves contribute to the entrapment of women on trial by re-enacting the experience of abuse. What roles do these pronouncements about men, women, and wife battering have beyond the courtroom doors? Do they shape public opinion, limit the availability of other support systems, or affect other battered women's ability to disclose, to seek help, to break free?

The Getkate case offers food for thought for Crown attorneys committed to prosecuting wife battering and lessons for defence lawyers in their choices of experts and theories. One issue left unexplored, however, is the impact on self-defence of Lilian's memory loss at the time of the homicide. This is not a rare problem for battered women, as the next chapter will discuss. It is one, however, that requires informed and creative lawyering.

Julianne Parfett was appointed to the Superior Court of Justice of Ontario in January 2007, the court that has jurisdiction over murder trials in Ontario.

7

Margaret Ann Malott and Rita Graveline

"She was defending not only herself, but her psychological self."[1]

Margaret Ann Malott shot her husband, Paul Malott, six times in his car on 23 March 1991 in Kingsville, Ontario. She then took a taxi to a trailer park, where she tried to kill Carrie Sherwood, Paul's girlfriend, by shooting, stabbing, and bashing her head. After a struggle, Margaret lay bleeding from head and chest wounds, while Sherwood escaped to a neighbour's. Margaret managed to find a telephone in the trashed trailer and called 9-1-1. In a rambling call, she said:

> Is someone coming ... ? I tried to shoot somebody and I'm stabbed and everything. I'm the one to blame ... I'm really fucked up on pills ... I shot my husband Paul. He's someplace. I can't remember where I shot him. He's in Kingsville someplace, but he tried to strangle me and he started saying things about me. I'm not normal. I'm under psychiatry ... I'm pretty buzzed up on pills ... I just want to go to the hospital and go to jail and get out of here.[2]

Margaret was charged with first-degree murder and attempted murder. She claimed self-defence for shooting Paul but had little memory of and no explanation for her attack on Sherwood.

On 11 August 1999 in Luskville, Quebec, Rita Graveline played darts with her husband, Michael Graveline, in a pub. They were dropped home by her daughter-in-law and son. Michael went to bed while Rita played solitaire and drank a glass of beer. Some time later she shot and killed him with his hunting rifle, then called 9-1-1, saying "I just killed my husband."[3] She asked at least ten times for the ambulance to "please hurry" to see if her husband was okay. When the police arrived, she came out in a T-shirt and underwear. She was handcuffed and placed in the police car while the police searched the house. At the station, she asked: "Did I kill my husband?"[4] When told that he was dead, she sobbed: "No, no, no." Like Margaret in her attempt to murder Sherwood, Rita drew a blank about how she came to shoot her husband. As she whispered to the police in her videotaped statement, "[i]n my heart I did something wrong and I don't know why!"[5] She was charged with second-degree murder.

Both women were middle aged – Margaret was forty-six, and Rita was fifty-one[6] – having endured at least twenty years of brutality and countless blows to the head, face, and neck. Margaret and Rita shared memory loss or dissociation at the time of the criminal act. They also shared the distinction as battered women of having their cases litigated all the way to the Supreme Court of Canada, the first such cases since *Lavallee* in 1990. Along the way, their lawyers attempted to expand defences for battered women who kill by reshaping self-defence and provocation, and advancing intoxication and automatism.

Margaret Ann Malott

"His guns was his life."[7]

Margaret's lawyers were unable to get her charges of first-degree murder and attempted murder treated in separate trials,[8] reducing her chances of acquittal. Even were the jury inclined to be sympathetic to self-defence in Paul's death, they would hear about her attack on Sherwood, a woman who could not be painted with the same brush as Paul. This evidence could damage Margaret's credibility and undercut self-defence.

Margaret pled not guilty to both charges before a jury of eight women and four men on 21 May 1992 in Windsor, Ontario. Knowing that the trial would be lengthy and the stakes high, one of her lawyers, Tim Zuber, tried to persuade Justice Carl Zalev to allow him to make an opening statement to the jury immediately after that of the Crown attorney.[9] Justice Zalev refused: "While it may be said that it might be fairer to allow the defence to open immediately after the Crown, it certainly cannot be said to be unfair."[10]

Crown attorney Denis Harrison opened, saying that "the accused decided to shoot, to kill her husband and Sherwood. She planned it, obtained
the gun and ammunition."[11] His first witness was medical examiner Dr
George Yee. He described the deceased as big – over six feet and 285 pounds.
Six bullets entered Paul's body, including his forehead. That one, Dr Yee
testified, was fired from approximately eighteen inches away. Some of the
bullets seemed to have travelled from left to right in Paul's body, whereas
others seemed to have come from the right side.[12]

Constable Ronald Middel searched the house where Margaret was living
with her mother-in-law and daughter Jody. In the basement, he found a
padlocked room whose door hinges had been loosened. He pulled the hinges open using a screwdriver and entered a room full of rifles, handguns,
bayonets, ammunition, and other weaponry. A glass gun cabinet had been
pried open, and one gun was missing. Margaret's other counsel, Duncan
MacIntyre, asked Middel whether he knew that over 100 firearms were in
the home? Had he noticed the whip and the large swastika?

At Sherwood's trailer, Ontario Provincial Police (OPP) officer Gary
Shurgold said, blood was smeared and spattered at the doorway; bullet
holes were in the walls, doors, and furniture; two windows were broken;
and the living room was in disarray: a table was knocked over, broken glass
was everywhere, and furniture was smashed. He recovered a handgun, its
one unspent bullet jammed. A bloody, twenty centimetre knife was in the
trailer, as was Margaret's purse, containing prescription pills, including
Halcion, three rounds of ammunition, and a spent cartridge. Eleven other
guns, swords, a spear, a bow and arrow, and a large quantity of ammunition
were in the trailer.

Kingsville police constable Gregory Hutton found Sherwood covered in
blood, shaking, and sobbing. He noticed another woman lying half out the
door of the trailer next door. As he approached her, the woman said: "It's
my fault. I shot her." Her hair and shirt were matted with blood. She told
Hutton: "Carrie stabbed me in the chest. It's my fault. Is Carrie all right?"
Then, calmly, she said: "I shot my husband. He's dead."[13]

Hutton found Paul's car but could not open the driver's door. The passenger window was open seven inches, and blood was dripping inside the driver's window. Paul's body was in a seatbelt, slumped toward the passenger
seat. A sheathed knife was removed from his body.[14] Hutton recognized
Paul through "several occurrences ... He's a formidable man in size and he's
not one somebody forgets."[15]

Dr William Poloski examined the deceased, Margaret, and Sherwood at Leamington District Hospital. He pronounced Paul dead, then treated Sherwood, who had an entry bullet wound near her ear and an exit wound through the back of her skull, another bullet hole through her hand, and lacerations on her shoulder and lower back.

Margaret had cuts on her face, scalp, and chest. She was alert and calm, with no signs of drug or alcohol use. Dr Poloski ordered a drug screen, which showed no significant drug consumption. MacIntyre focused Dr Poloski on Halcion, banned in several countries for its hypnotic effects, links to bizarre behaviour, and amnesia. The hospital had no capacity to screen for this drug, so the doctor could not rule out the possibility that Margaret had ingested it.

Paul's friend Donald Bailey testified that he ran into Margaret the week before Paul's death. She told him that Paul was living with "a young whore or a hooker in Kingsville." "[S]he's got him for now," he quoted her as saying, "but she won't have him much longer."[16]

MacIntyre accused Bailey of telling someone else that "he was going to sink Margaret."[17] This Bailey flatly denied. When MacIntyre asked about her condition when she made that statement, Bailey said that it was not rough, but "like her appearance, her face and everything else wasn't, you know, normal. Her hair was like a rat's nest and it wasn't the most appropriate clothing to be going out for a Sunday stroll, okay."[18] Dissatisfied, MacIntyre pulled out his answer from the preliminary inquiry. Bailey's earlier statement was read out: Margaret "[l]ooked like she was dragged through a knothole backwards. She was in pretty rough shape."[19]

Bailey denied knowing that Paul was a drug dealer, a police informant, or a wife beater. He once saw Margaret with a bandage on her nose, "but I don't know how she got it."[20] He knew that Paul had once been charged "for something," but he never inquired further. Bailey had seen Margaret "stoned on prescription drugs" on the streets. Some days she would walk by him without "seeing" him or even hearing his greeting.[21] He claimed that Margaret "beat up" Paul by giving him "a couple of shots to the head, gave him a boot in the private area of the body a couple of times, buckling him over." MacIntyre was incredulous – "you honestly believe that?" Bailey insisted that he had seen it himself.[22] MacIntyre reproached him: "I'm suggesting to you you're prepared to say almost anything you have to to put my client in jail?" Bailey answered: "And I'm prepared to tell you you're a liar."[23]

Paul's mother, Mary Featherstone, heard loud pounding from the basement on the day of the homicide. She later surmised that it came from

Margaret's effort to get at the guns in the locked room, to which only Featherstone and Paul had a key. "His guns was his life,"[24] she declared. After Margaret left in Paul's car to buy groceries on the afternoon of the homicide, Jody answered the telephone: "She cried and screamed and said you're not my mother, then she dropped the phone. I picked up the phone. I asked [Margaret] what was wrong and she said Paul is dead ... I shot him."[25]

Featherstone denied that Margaret was forced to cook meals for Paul and Sherwood or that Paul sat Sherwood on his lap at the dining table.[26] She denied that Paul beat Margaret. She had never seen a mark on Margaret over their twenty-year marriage.[27] She denied encouraging Paul to beat Margaret. Rather, Paul told her, Margaret woke him up by hitting him in the face with a frying pan.[28] Featherstone had given Paul some of the guns in his collection because he was her only son. "[G]irls don't need guns," she pronounced.[29]

Featherstone scoffed at Margaret's claim that Paul forbade Margaret from seeing her five children from her prior marriage: "That I do not believe sir. If you were any kind of mother sir you would go to see your child regardless."[30] She denied knowledge of Margaret's suicide attempts; she had never heard fighting or arguing; she had never seen Margaret in a "glazed" state. Featherstone admitted that her daughters had flushed Margaret's medications down the toilet after the homicide, possibly her Halcion, not because they did not want police to find them, she claimed, but because there were small children in the house.[31] When asked if her son was a drug user, she answered: "At times sir, but he reformed."[32]

Taxi driver Tracy Tillotson, who took Margaret to the trailer park, testified that after asking for a taxi she twice asked "could we hurry up a little bit?" Tillotson chatted about the weather, but she did not answer him. At the trailer, she asked him to wait. He fidgeted, becoming more nervous as the minutes passed. He heard noises from the trailer – the sounds of screaming, bodies hitting walls, and finally glass breaking. In a panic, he called dispatch. He was told to leave the scene while his boss called the police. Tillotson described Margaret as a "normal day passenger," but MacIntyre reminded him that at the preliminary inquiry he had testified that she was "like in a daze."[33]

Sherwood testified next. She was a "petite, soft-spoken woman"[34] described by neighbours as "a very quiet girl, babyish in her looks, ... [who] seemed to prefer older men," referring to her recently deceased fifty-two-year-old husband and Paul, who was forty-two at the time of his death.[35] She was twenty-two.

Margaret called the trailer earlier that afternoon, just after Paul left to pick her up to go grocery shopping. Margaret asked Sherwood if Paul had left yet and why she was not with him. Sherwood explained that she was not feeling well, ending the call.[36] She fell asleep only to be woken by knocking. When she opened the door, Margaret asked her "[w]here's Paul?" Sherwood was confused by the quizzical look on Margaret's face and her "weird" demeanour. She ushered Margaret into her living room, where Margaret pulled a handgun from her purse, saying "I've got something for you." She began firing the gun, then asked "[c]an I see your snake?"[37]

Sherwood inched closer to seize the gun. Margaret pulled the trigger, blowing off the base of her finger. Margaret grabbed a pillow and pulled it over Sherwood's head. She fired the gun again, grazing the base of Sherwood's skull. Margaret reassured Sherwood that the bullets were not real,[38] then tried to fire the gun again, but it jammed.

Margaret hit Sherwood on her head with the gun and told her not to worry: she had called an ambulance before she arrived. Sherwood struggled against unconsciousness but managed to get the gun. Margaret said that "she wasn't going to hurt me anymore,"[39] but then she grabbed a knife, stabbing Sherwood in the nose and near her left eye.

Sherwood ran to her bedroom and slammed the door. Margaret heaved against it, pushing it open, and tried to stab her through the opening. Sherwood smashed a window and threw the gun outside, hoping to attract attention. Margaret stabbed her in the waist. Sherwood grabbed the knife and tried to hold on to it, then ran back through the trailer with Margaret on her heels, stabbing at her back.

Margaret cornered her in the kitchen with the knife and used her body to thrust it at her. Again Sherwood seized the knife with her hands to protect herself. Fingers slashed and bleeding, she held on. "[A]t the spur of the moment, the only thing I could do was put my fingers in her eyes. She tried to back away quickly but I went with her with my fingers. I said these fingers aren't going anywhere until you let me have the knife."[40]

Margaret let go of the knife but seized a bottle and tried to smash it over her head. Sherwood repelled it with the knife, and glass shattered above her. She began stabbing Margaret in the head "to tire her out." But Margaret picked up another bottle and again tried to strike her head. This bottle Sherwood seized and threw at the front window, breaking more glass. Margaret collapsed in exhaustion on the couch, and Sherwood ran from the trailer.

In cross-examination, Sherwood said that Paul brought many weapons to her trailer – "he had them all over the house."[41] She denied sitting on his lap or that Margaret had been forced to cook for them: "[S]he offered us lunch."[42]

John Jacobs, an ambulance attendant, testified that Margaret told him that her husband was dead. She elaborated: "At least he should be. You know I shot him five times."[43] She told Jacobs that she had swallowed a handful of pills; he found her pupil response sluggish.

Sue Matthews, the registered nurse in emergency at Leamington Hospital, agreed that Margaret's responses were slightly slow. Margaret told her that she had taken "sleeping pills, nerve pills and some little white pills."[44] She was calm and asked "[w]here's Paul?" and whether "Carrie" was okay. She also said "she's so young ... [W]hat does he see in her? ... [H]e shouldn't have come back."[45]

Ismail Moftah, a forensic toxicologist, explained Margaret's blood work. The tests showed traces of barbiturates and salicylates (pain killers such as aspirin). Lorazepam (Ativan) and Halcion, prescription bottles found in Margaret's purse, cannot be detected unless present in large quantities. MacIntyre focused on Halcion's dangerous side-effects, such as confused states, memory impairment, and violence, and why testing might not con-firm its ingestion.

MacIntyre opened his case dramatically: Margaret was justified in killing Paul: "[H]e earned every one of those six bullets that were put into him that day."[46] She told the 9-1-1 operator that her husband had been choking her.

Paul was a drug dealer, a weapons collector, a thief, a pimp, a fence, a close associate of several motorcycle gangs, and a violent abuser, MacIntyre said. He had been involved in a murder conspiracy culminating in the death of Hannah Buxbaum,[47] and he was on the OPP's payroll as an informant. It was perilous for Margaret to ask for police aid or leave Paul.

"I don't think there's a member of this jury that's not going to be filled with loathing and disgust when you hear about it," MacIntyre cautioned. "You're going to hear about whippings. You're going to hear about objects being inserted into vaginas, specific incidents [of] bondage ... I'm not talking about for fun. Forced anal intercourse."[48] His expert would testify that this was "one of the most severe cases of the Battered Wife Syndrome that he'd ever seen."[49] Turning to Margaret's violence against Sherwood, MacIntyre told jurors that Margaret was a "slave": Sherwood and Paul "flaunted" their relationship, making Sherwood an "instrument of abuse."[50] He would call evidence about "the kind of help she got from doctors. They prescribed a bunch of pills."[51]

A few days before the homicide, MacIntyre continued, Margaret begged Paul to come back. Instead, he laughed, calling her

a pig, a slut, a bitch. He never used her name most of the time. What happens when they're treated like that? Is there anything left? Is there anything left of them except one great big ball of pain and fear[?] ... This woman's destroyed psychologically. She was defending herself that day. She was defending not only herself but her psychological self. What was left of it?[52]

MacIntyre was trying to convey to the jury the enormity of what Paul had done to Margaret, highlighting the turning point at which the woman recognizes a fundamental threat to her psychological self, "those psychological functions, attributes, processes, and dimensions of experience that give meaning and value to [our] existence."[53] A woman who fails to act in these circumstances is reduced to "a state of virtual nothingness tantamount to psychological death."[54] Obviously, there must have been something left of herself for Margaret to defend if this theory were to hold. The question, of course, was whether the law permits women to kill in "psychological self-defence."

MacIntyre's first witness was Margaret's mother, Eva King, who saw and experienced first hand Paul's violence. King once tried to call the police because Paul was assaulting Margaret. He yanked the phone away; then "he picked me up and he threw me all the way from the kitchen, through a hall and into a living room."[55] King saw Paul hold a gun to the head of Margaret and their son Colt when he was a baby. Paul ordered King to leave at gunpoint. She did not call the police because she was terrified that he would harm Margaret and the baby. She heard Paul threaten to kill family members if Margaret did not follow his orders.

In cross-examination, Harrison established that King had seen evidence of Paul's abuse only twice in recent years. She explained that Paul prohibited contact. She recounted Margaret weeping on the telephone days before the homicide because she had to wait on the new couple while Sherwood sat on Paul's lap "making love" in front of her.

Margaret's older sister Marilyn Reneau testified that Paul prohibited her contact with Margaret as well[56] and had threatened to kill her.[57] She observed cuts on Margaret's arms[58] and bruises on her legs. She saw Margaret at the hospital after the homicide: her speech was slurred and incoherent, and "she drifted in and out."[59]

Margaret's seventeen-year-old daughter, Jody, testified that Bailey called at the house where she lived with Featherstone, her grandmother, a few months before the trial. He told her "[d]on't worry, I'll have [Margaret] put away like for life and she'll never walk the streets again."[60]

Jody's father was arrested for trafficking in drugs when Jody was nine. She and her mother were taken to the station, searched, and held all night. Another time they had to sleep in the basement because Paul thought that someone was coming to shoot at the house. She heard her father berate her mother that "she was crazy and he didn't like ... the way she looked."[61] Her father accused Margaret of disobeying him and sleeping around, even though he frequently cheated on her.[62]

Jody helped her mother with her medications because she was too confused to take them properly. One night her mother was so disoriented that she fell and had to be taken to the hospital. Her medications were cut back, but then, Jody testified, "they started giving her a whole bunch again."[63]

Harrison wanted to know why her father raged against the way her mother looked – was it "her hair and that sort of stuff?" Jody's father was unhappy with her mother's clothes and her weight,[64] common complaints by batterers, who have rigid sex role expectations of their partners' bodies and self-presentation.[65]

Margaret's niece, Denise Gaffan, told jurors that when she was growing up her parents tried to keep the kids away from Paul. She recalled a night when her aunt Margaret came to the house bleeding from her mouth and crying. Paul arrived, and she, her grandmother, and Margaret used their combined weight to bar the bedroom door. In future, she avoided Paul: "I was afraid of him."[66]

Constable Mike MacKinnon testified that in April 1974 police confiscated a bow and arrow after being called for a "dispute with wife." They arrested Paul for breach of the peace. In July 1978, Paul was in court for another unknown charge, which was withdrawn on his promise to keep the peace. In August 1978, he was again arrested for breach of the peace for "fighting with his wife."[67] This charge was also withdrawn.

Dr Walter Joseph Cassidy referred to his March 1992 report that drew on the records of one local pharmacy, the blood-screening results, nurses' notes from the hospital, and a ninety-minute interview with Margaret eight months after the homicide. She held prescriptions for Ativan, Doxepin, Seconal, and Halcion, among others. She was taking Halcion in quarter doses twice a day, but she consumed a handful of pills the morning of the homicide: "[S]he was regularly taking a variety of psychotropics and had

increased them in an unorganized fashion ... [S]he was compulsively pop-
ping pills which I believe have an effect in terms of assessing her com-
petency and ... her ability to form the intention for some of her actions."[68]

Dr Cassidy explained that the hospital blood screening was not designed
for medical-legal issues but was geared to detecting life-threatening doses.
Halcion is absorbed quickly, so patients easily overdose by taking it repeatedly, at the risk of delirium and dream-like states. "It would," he said, "affect
her ability to process information to control her behaviour. It would make
her more likely to act out in unpredictable ways. She was a distressed person, so it would make her more likely to be suicidal or homicidal."[69] Her
history suggested Battered Woman Syndrome. She was a passive woman who
could not express anger.

Under cross-examination, Dr Cassidy said that none of the doctors – her
family doctor, her gynecologist, and two psychiatrists – would have written
prescriptions had they known of her other prescriptions.[70] This comment
highlighted the serious compounding effects of these drugs but also implied
that Margaret engaged in "double-doctoring," a criminal practice of fraudu-
lently obtaining prescriptions from multiple doctors.[71]

Harrison confronted Dr Cassidy with an earlier report following his
examination of Margaret in 1987. His notes recorded that she got along
well with her husband, was experiencing distress over an abortion, could
not hold a job because "she feels that people talk about her and she feels
centred out,"[72] and liked to hurt people emotionally and physically.[73]

Harrison then asked Dr Cassidy to produce his notes from his interview
with Margaret post-homicide. Dr Cassidy wrote that "she got the gun with
the intention of shooting her husband,"[74] which contradicted his evidence
that she was unable to form the intent to kill. He also recorded that Paul
"was yelling at her again and had just stopped yelling and he opened the
door and she just shot him." She then "went off to shoot the girlfriend ...
although she really didn't think that one over."[75] He indicated that Margaret
said that twenty years earlier her husband had throttled her so badly that she
had coughed up blood, but "since that time she was not afraid of him killing
her."[76] Dr Cassidy agreed that one can form the intention to commit an act
even if a drug lowers one's inhibitions.[77]

Margaret's twenty-year-old son Colt told the jury that he had seen his
mother with a "bloody nose or her mouth ... bleeding" perhaps ten to fifteen
times,[78] but his father slapped, criticized, and swore at her incessantly. His
father visited him with Sherwood before his death, bringing cocaine to use
and sell. Colt confessed that he started pushing his girlfriend around: "I

started to be mean and always being hard on [her] and always giving her heck for stupid little things and not trusting her."[79] He had since begun seeing a psychiatrist.

Harrison's cross-examination forced Colt to admit that he had last seen his father assault his mother years before. However, Colt had left whenever an argument started: "I just couldn't stand it anymore. It was like watching a rerun."[80]

Margaret's younger sister, Glenda Nagypal, testified that Paul had said, after living with Margaret only six weeks, "she's so fucking stupid I should have her mind in control in no time."[81] He ordered Margaret, "bitch get me a glass of water and I said now ... or you know what happens."[82] She was to remove his cowboy boots whenever he entered a home.[83] He called her "bitch, wench, witch or Maggie May. He never ever called her by her real name. Later on it ... turned into fucking slut, c**t and whore."[84]

When Nagypal asked about black circles under Margaret's eyes, Margaret said that Paul badgered her all night for information to drive a wedge between her and her sister. He began harassing Margaret in front of Nagypal to tell her "what you said about her." When Margaret told him to be quiet, he flew into a rage and attacked her, dragging her by the hair while she screamed. Nagypal's husband waved a rifle to remove Paul, but he threatened that if Margaret did not come too "he would be back and all hell would break loose."[85]

After that, the sisters saw each other less frequently as Margaret withdrew, looking more tired, drained, on edge, "looking around like if she did something wrong, what was going to happen?"[86] Nagypal saw Paul whip her sister at a family picnic with his belt. He threatened Nagypal with the belt, and she ran to call the police from a pay phone. When she came back, Margaret was wildly trying to get the kids into the car: "If the cops show up at my house, I'm dead."[87]

Nagypal's daughter, Susan Jordan, lived with Paul and Margaret off and on as a young girl of eight or nine because she did not get along with her stepfather. Paul often disappeared for days and left them with no groceries or money. Jordan would steal food from her family's freezer so that they could eat. Paul called Margaret a douche bag, c**t, slut, and pig while playing with his knife, "letting her know it was there and he'd use it."[88] He would get Colt to abuse his mother: "[G]o tell your Mom to shut up ... [G]o tell your Mom she's a bitch ... [A]nd he thought it was funny for Colt to do this."[89]

Jordan was sent home when Paul's anger escalated, but she saw the bruising on Margaret's arms and legs when she returned. She heard Paul threaten to kill Margaret and her mother if her mother ever returned to the house; she also saw him wave a gun and tell Margaret that he could "blow her head off."[90] At a wedding, she encountered Paul strangling Margaret against a wall. The next day Margaret acted as if nothing had happened, which Jordan found confusing. In fact, Margaret could not recall this assault in her trial testimony.[91]

Detective Gary Clark of the OPP Intelligence Branch said that Paul was a paid informant from 1986 to the date of his death. He had criminal records for break, enter, and theft, assaulting the police, possession of stolen property, drug trafficking, impaired driving, and causing a disturbance, but he was never convicted for assaulting Margaret. Paul associated with "criminals" and provided information to Clark. Clark knew that he had used speed and by March 1991 suspected that he was "sliding back to his old habits."[92] Clark testified that Margaret had never complained of abuse or said that she was afraid. Paul had been a reliable and helpful informant who had not, to Clark's knowledge, engaged in criminal acts while being an informant.

Clark's files noted a series of exchanges between Margaret and Clark beginning 14 March, when she reported that Paul had moved to his girlfriend's trailer, taking with him a gun and ammunition. Margaret thought that he was using drugs again and involving Colt in trafficking. She asked Clark not to let Paul know that she had called, but Clark called Paul to say that he needed to move his gun collection with him to the trailer; Margaret called Clark back, accusing him of having "squealed."[93]

She called again on 18 March, complaining that Paul had brought his new girlfriend to the house and was using and trafficking drugs. Clark asked a drug squad officer to put surveillance on Paul, but noted that Margaret had a history of "mental illness" and "wasn't to be considered very reliable as she was a woman scorned by her husband who had left her for a younger woman."[94]

Margaret called Clark the next day to say that she had had to cook supper for Paul and his girlfriend and that they had smoked hash together. She said that she was taking medications for her mental illness and was having a rough time.

Margaret called Clark one last time on 22 March, two days before the homicide. He did not return her call.

Her acute vulnerability must have been apparent to jurors from the moment that she took the stand. Her counsel had to ask her to speak up as she told the jury that she left school midway through grade eight when her parents separated and her mother had a nervous breakdown and attempted suicide. Margaret sought love and security from her first abusive boyfriend that year – she was thirteen, and he was seventeen.[95]

She disengaged emotionally from that relationship by attaching to Don Bruner when she was eighteen. She bore five sons in seven years. He was a gambling addict who was extremely violent. He punched her in the face and kicked her pregnant belly, causing her to spot blood. She obtained peace bonds, but he simply shredded them in her face.

Margaret left Bruner when she was twenty-five but fell immediately into the arms of Paul, who told her the very first night that he could control her mind in ways that she would not even know. He demanded to know everything about her so that he could help her to work on her "weakest parts." He began timing her when she ran errands and limiting her contact with other people. She would wake up in the night to find him staring at her over a lit candle, playing strange music, making odd sounds, and saying "I can sense your next move."[96]

Paul became enraged when one of her toddlers touched her breast: "[H]e ... slapped me across the head and told me if I ever let my kids touch any part of my body that I would get the same again."[97] Margaret was required to get fully dressed before her children saw her in the morning, and she was not permitted to cuddle them, even her six-month-old baby: "I was not allowed to pick him up. I had to feed him with his bottle laying down ... I was not allowed to pick him up."[98] Her five boys were confined to the bedroom by a board that Paul put up against the door. They had to eat, play, and sleep caged in one room because Paul "was teaching them survival."[99] He told her that "they've got to grow up tough. Let them go."[100]

Margaret surrendered custody of her boys in 1970 to her mother when Paul decided that they would travel the province doing seasonal work. He then began preventing her from even seeing her children because, according to him, "[w]hen I left with him, I left my past behind. I was starting anew."[101] Her mother sometimes brought her children to visit, but Margaret was forced to push away any child who came to be hugged.[102] When she was pregnant with Colt, Paul punished her for allowing one of her children to touch her belly.[103] He accused her of having a sexual relationship with her son Mike,[104] a recurrent theme that mortified her.[105]

Margaret usually obeyed his many rules because, she said, Paul was much smarter than her – he knew what he was doing.[106] He forbade her from leaving the house without him or wearing makeup outside the house. He demanded that she wear a padded bra to conceal her breasts. She never did anything right: "He always condemned everything I did. I never did it right ... [W]hat I said was always wrong. I had a wrong judgment."[107]

Paul used sleep deprivation to force Margaret to reveal every detail about her life and thoughts: "If he found out something that I had left out in my telling him my life, he would bring up the subject constantly like until like I was exhausted. I couldn't take care of my kids because I wasn't getting sleep."[108] This information he then used to alienate her family and friends and to control her. She was forbidden from seeing her sisters; her mother was barred from their home.

Paul's sexual abuse of Margaret reached the level of what is called sadistic or obsessive marital rape.[109] Paul pinched and twisted her nipples – sometimes during sex and sometimes as pure punishment – until she fell to her knees and almost passed out with the pain. On one occasion, her agony was so overwhelming that she grabbed his testicles. He reared back and punched her in the face, breaking her nose.[110] He forced her to have sex all night, to stay on top of him without moving while he slept. He inserted bottles and baseball bats into her vagina; he penetrated her anally even though it caused her such pain that she could hardly walk afterward.[111] Paul made Margaret wear a bridle[112] while he handcuffed and whipped her. He flaunted his many relationships with other women, explaining that he did this to punish her for touching her kids or some other infraction. He gave away her rings, including a special one that he had given to her, to one of these girlfriends.[113]

Knowing that Margaret was highly claustrophobic, Paul locked her in closets and threw lit matches at her. He held pillows over her face until she was on the verge of asphyxiation, tied her naked to beds to watch her thrash about, and squeezed pressure points on her neck until she blacked out. Then, when she was terrified and weeping, he would insist on sexual intercourse. When Margaret was a few months pregnant with Colt, Paul choked her until she coughed up blood and kicked her as she lay on the floor spitting up. She was prohibited from seeking medical aid and dared not tell anyone because she would be endangering that person.[114]

Margaret rarely reported the abuse to the police because it was too risky. On one occasion, however, when Paul dragged her by the hair outside and began kicking her, she ran to a neighbour's to call them. They came and warned him, but after they left he threw knives at her feet. As she tried to leave the house, he fired an arrow at her head, missing it by inches. After her second call, the police took away the bow and arrow and arrested him.[115] The charges were withdrawn when Margaret failed to testify: Paul had warned her that there would be hell to pay if she did.[116] She called the police another time when he was beating her up. He screamed that he would get even with her as he was hauled away. That night one of his friends came banging on her door. When she peeked out, she could see a man with a handgun. She refused him entry. When Paul came home from jail in the morning, he attacked Margaret so violently that the landlord tried to intervene. Paul told him to mind his own business.[117]

Life with Paul was chaotic. He regularly disappeared, sometimes for months. When Margaret saw him on the streets, he would be high, ragged, and unwashed.[118] She tried to send messages because he left her and the children with nothing to eat and no money to buy groceries. He was once out of contact for so long that she moved while he was away, incurring his wrath. During another prolonged absence she left a message with the police asking them to tell Paul that he had given her gonorrhea and needed treatment.[119] While he was away, he would send his sister, aunt, or friends over to monitor her.[120]

Over the twenty years, they moved constantly – at least twenty-three times based on her testimony – making it hard for Margaret to tell a consistent narrative. There were periods of homelessness when they slept on other people's couches or in a car for months.[121] They were evicted at least four times due to the disturbances caused by Paul's lifestyle, including police raids and property damaged by Paul.[122]

Margaret described what her home was like when Colt was a child: "People were coming at all hours of the night to buy speed. They would come there and sit at the table and fix it up, go into the bathroom and puke and go right back for more. This happened all night long."[123] They would bring money and goods obtained by crimes to buy drugs from Paul. On one occasion, when Margaret was home alone with Colt and Jody, a man owed money by Paul fired shots through the front window.[124] In the morning, she found her tires slashed and the car door kicked in. They were asked to move out in a letter signed by the landlord and neighbours.

Margaret accepted Paul's authority: "[H]e was taking all my privileges away,"[125] but "I'm not saying he was a bad person."[126] She was not allowed to keep her money, but she agreed with his decision because she never knew how to handle money.[127] Her testimony used words and phrases – "our disagreements"[128] – that gave her equal responsibility for his violence and control. So desperate was Margaret for Paul to believe that she had never cheated on him that she took a lie detector test, went to a hypnotist, and allowed Paul to inject her with speed, which he claimed was a "truth serum."[129]

Paul harangued Margaret about her faithfulness while openly bringing women to their bed. He sent his friend Pete Wexler – who once set their dog on fire[130] – over to "test" her. She tried to keep him out, but Pete kicked in her door and then handcuffed her to a chair. He told her he was there to rape her; when he released her, she fled to a neighbour's and called the police. After Pete was taken away, Paul just laughed: "He said well I sent him there to see if he could get anything out of you."[131] Pete also loaded, pointed, and "flicked" the trigger of a firearm at Margaret, to Paul's amusement.[132]

Like so many battered women,[133] Margaret had been subjected to torture. The legal definition of torture requires its commission by state officials, but Paul undoubtedly committed this crime as defined more expansively by the World Medical Association: "Torture [is] the deliberate, systematic, or wanton infliction of physical or mental suffering ... to force another person to yield information, to make a confession, or for any other reason."[134] Paul demanded that Margaret confess to having committed adultery, which she never yielded, but above all he sought utter dominion over her. Between men, this objective has long been understood for its lethal potential. John Locke wrote in 1697 that "he who attempts to get another Man into his Absolute Power, does thereby put himself into a State of War with him; It being understood as a Declaration of a Design upon his Life."[135] Frances Cobbe wrote in 1878 that "[w]ife-*beating* is the mere preliminary canter before the race ... Wife-*beating* in process of time, and in numberless cases, advances to Wife-*torture*, and the Wife-torture usually ends in Wife-maiming, Wife-blinding, or Wife-murder."[136]

Beyond physical torture, Paul also deployed "psychological torture," defined by Amnesty International as (1) enforced isolation; (2) monopolization of perception (e.g., the induction of altered states of consciousness through the administration of drugs and hypnosis); (3) induced debility – exhaustion (through sleep deprivation); (4) threats; (5) occasional indulgences (Margaret's "privileges"); (6) demonstrating "omnipotence"; (7) degradation; and (8) enforcing trivial demands.[137] Psychological torture causes as much mental and traumatic stress as physical torture,[138] and it amplifies brain injuries, making it more difficult to treat for depression and anxiety those who have experienced both.[139]

Psychological torture can be committed with impunity apart from those forms that amount to the criminal offences of assault, unlawful confinement, threatening, or what is now called criminal harassment or "stalking."

Even had Margaret committed suicide as a result of psychological torture, Paul would have escaped criminal liability. The criminal law does not recognize killing by "influence of the mind" alone, except in the case of wilfully frightening a child or sick person.[140]

So defence counsel tried to keep Margaret focused on tangible abuse – physical and sexual assault. "I wonder if I could direct you a little – try and focus you a little more. I'm talking in terms of you and Paul and what you would feel prior to your getting actually physically assaulted?"[141] MacIntyre insisted on numbers. During a three-year period, she estimated, Paul had raped her maybe ten times.[142] How many times had she been beaten up while she lived at a particular address? She answered fifteen to twenty times.[143] On how many occasions did Paul insert objects into her vagina?[144] What about this tying up and whipping?[145] How often was she locked in a closet?[146]

MacIntyre tried to explore her injuries, but Margaret minimized them. She said that she was "just sore"[147] or that the result was "just some bruises."[148] She explained: "It's hard to remember some of the thing[s] that you have to forget – try to forget."[149] She attempted suicide and was hospitalized twice for a nervous breakdown.[150] She never disclosed the source of her suffering to doctors for fear that Paul would find out.

Even after Paul left Margaret, he came to the house daily for her to dress, groom, and feed him, monitor her movements, and wake her throughout the night.[151] She experienced sleeplessness, constant shaking, vomiting, nausea, confusion, and anxiety. She began doubling and tripling her medications. Her doctors, she said, neither warned her about side-effects nor asked her about other medications: "I thought the doctors kept in touch with each other over knowing that I was under the treatment, but they didn't."[152]

Paul first brought Sherwood to the house three weeks before his death; this became a daily ritual in the weeks before he died. Margaret testified that she had sex with Paul the week before his death. He laughed in her face and called her a fool – he was not coming back to her. The day before the homicide, Sherwood sat on his lap in the dining room, where they kissed in front of Margaret. Sleepless, Margaret took her medications three times to knock herself out. In the morning, she removed the hinges from the gun room and took out a gun and some bullets. She had fantasized his death: "I would never be free as long as he was alive, no matter whether he was with me or he wasn't. I had no way out. Many times I left, he followed. As long as he was alive my life was in hell."[153]

That morning Margaret was frightened because Paul had ordered her to leave him alone, and if she did not "he would take care of it."[154] She took more pills as she waited for him to pick her up to do the shopping for his mother: "I was very upset. I was very scared. Hoping that these pills would get me through ... the day."[155] She feared that something might happen to her, so she took his gun and ammunition. He always had a shotgun in the back of the car and a knife strapped to his body. In the car, Paul argued about who would claim Jody for income tax purposes and grabbed her shirt threateningly. They arrived at a medical centre, where Margaret was to fill a prescription so that he could use the pills to mix with speed to sell. He undid his seatbelt, according to her, and glared at her. He started choking her, saying that she had better start listening to him.

Margaret found the medical centre closed. As she returned to the car, she saw his door open and his leg emerging. She began firing the gun, then reached into the car, turned off the ignition, and took the keys: "I was afraid that he was still going to come after me."[156] She remembered hailing a cab to the trailer but thereafter recalled only bits of her prolonged effort to kill Sherwood. She denied intending to kill Paul or any grudge against Sherwood: "I'm not a violent person."[157]

Harrison ignored the majority of Margaret's testimony about the years of violence and degradation. Instead, he zeroed in on the last six months of Paul's life, suggesting that Paul rarely assaulted Margaret in that time and putting her on the defensive:

Q: Let's try again. The fall of 1990 he was living at his cousin Lloyd's. Right?
A: Not all the time, no.
Q: Well as you described it?
A: No, he was living at his mother's still a year before the accident.
Q: What accident?
A: What happened on the Saturday.
Q: You shot him six times. Are you calling that an accident?
A: Sorry.[158]

Margaret said that Paul slapped her face when she touched his arm and begged him to come home after he started living with Sherwood.[159] Harrison suggested that Paul was disengaging in those final three weeks – "he wasn't talking to you very much. Had nothing more to do with you?"[160] Margaret denied this, but Harrison continued: "And there's no more slapping – no more physical fighting at all, was there?" She answered: "No it was the way he talked about me."[161] Paul continued to threaten her and punish her with sleep deprivation.[162]

Harrison disputed that Margaret cooked supper for Paul and Sherwood the night before the homicide since she called Clark about it three days earlier. Margaret denied that she planned to kill Paul: "I had no control of what I was doing ... [T]he medication I was taking was way too much,"[163] she explained. She agreed that she got the gun thinking of shooting Paul and herself[164] but then said "I really didn't intend to shoot him, no[t] until things went on on the way up there and when we got there."[165]

Harrison took Margaret through the actions that she performed to obtain and load the gun, make the calls to arrange the shopping trip, choose the medical centre (a destination that he accused her of knowing would be closed and deserted[166]), place the gun and shells in her handbag, shoot Paul at the centre, reload the gun, and then travel to Sherwood's address. Harrison said: "You had decided to end it. Is that correct?" Margaret replied: "Not permanently, no." He was incredulous: "Not permanently? How were you going to end it by shooting him not permanently?" She answered: "I had no intentions of really shooting him. I was afraid. That is why I took the gun because I could not accept what was going on. He could not be bothered with me."[167] But Harrison quickly returned to her earlier admission: "[Y]ou've agreed with me clearly that you got the gun and were going to kill him and kill yourself. Am I right there?" "Yes." "That's correct?" "Yes."[168] Minutes later Margaret was again denying that she got the gun with the intention of killing Paul.

Harrison questioned whether Paul had choked her in the car: "Were you injured? ... Did you complain to the doctor at the hospital about being strangled?"[169] Strangulation injuries manifest in only half of cases[170] since much of the damage is internal, such as aspiration pneumonia and subconjuctival hemorrhage.[171] Even the milder injuries such as bruises might not appear until twenty-four hours later or more. Margaret had told the 9-1-1 operator that Paul had choked her but had no memory of her statements to 9-1-1 or to hospital personnel.

Harrison suggested that she shot Paul between the eyes from within the vehicle. He claimed that the bullets travelled from Paul's right to left,[172] placing Margaret in the front seat when she fired the gun, not outside on the sidewalk near the driver's door. She denied this scenario.

Harrison also disputed whether Paul was stepping out of the vehicle when Margaret shot him, with his leg and foot already out of the car door.

The seatbelt was still on the body and allowed for little movement. She must have aimed very carefully to have fired, from a distance of four to six feet, to strike his body without once hitting the door or window. She claimed that she fired the gun, "just blazing." She must be a "good shot," Harrison mused.[173]

Margaret denied that she went to the trailer park to kill Sherwood, but she admitted that she was not afraid of her.[174] Harrison thundered: "You didn't go there to tell her how sorry you were for just shooting her boy-friend?" This caused MacIntyre to object that he need not shout.[175] Margaret had no memory of attempting to kill Sherwood. When Harrison asked "[s]he put up a big fight, didn't she?" Margaret replied "I'm glad she did."[176] Sherwood had tired her out and was then able to get away. Margaret said: "Oh yes, I'm glad she did do that, yes."[177]

Harrison closed with Margaret by revisiting the question of her intent. Again she capitulated:

> Q: You wanted to end it as you told me earlier by shooting him and shoot-
> ing yourself, correct? Correct?
> A: No.
> Q: No, that's what you told me earlier. Are you changing that again?
> A: No.
> Q: Is that correct?
> A: Not in a sense that you're taking it. Yes I said that but ...
> Q: You said that and what you meant by that is that you wanted to end it by
> killing both of you. That's not complicated, no?
> A: No.
> Q: And that's what you meant?
> A: Yes.[178]

Dr Peter Jaffe was the final defence witness. MacIntyre presented his credentials as an expert in domestic violence and battered women to en-sure that the jury weighed his evidence with care. Dr Jaffe had testified as an expert witness on Battered Woman Syndrome at all levels of court in Ontario in what he called the far more usual murder prosecution – "after someone like Margaret Malott has been killed."[179]

Dr Jaffe and his staff had interviewed Margaret five times. He had also interviewed Jody and Colt and consulted the other available reports on Margaret. Of the hundreds of women whom he had assessed, Margaret was "one of the most severe cases because of the severity of the violence, the frequency of the violence, the pattern of years ... Paul Malott basically did everything to Margaret short of killing her and he came close to doing that on several occasions."[180]

Margaret began to tolerate higher and higher levels of violence and to internalize the abuse from Paul as what she deserved as a worthless person "because he bragged that other women would accept almost anything that he did."[181] He abused her psychologically by threatening her and her family, monitoring her movements, controlling her behaviour, and destroying her other relationships. Her children told Dr Jaffe that they had several times been introduced to their father's girlfriends and told that they would make better mothers.[182]

Margaret believed that Paul was all powerful, a belief reinforced by his use of brainwashing techniques, his work as a police informant, his connections with gangs and violent criminals, and the fact that many others were afraid of him. His forms of abuse were cumulative and so intertwined that any one would trigger a traumatic memory and reinforce the violent threat that he posed: "[T]he psychological and emotional abuse gets linked into the physical abuse and can [e]ngender the same kind of fear and reaction in a victim ... [Y]ou always have a sense of being in danger when you're in contact with the batterer."[183]

Dr Jaffe testified that it is common for battered women like Margaret to fantasize about the deaths of their tormentors. Her confusion – describing the homicide as "an accident" – and her inability to tell a linear story about when Paul committed which acts of abuse were also normal:

> [W]hat happens is when you've had 20 years of terror in your life and you've experienced hundreds of acts of physical, sexual violence and you've also experienced the emotional and psychological abuse, I think after a while it's hard to separate one incident from the other and when you start to talk about the incidents they'll trigger other kinds of memories.[184]

More than a year after Paul's death, Margaret continued to experience flashbacks, nightmares, and fear that Paul would "still come after her somehow."[185]

Dr Jaffe said that Margaret had been overmedicated by doctors who had responded to her anxiety and depression by prescribing tranquillizers and anti-depressants rather than attending to the underlying cause. He indicated that this is a common pattern. Doctors identify only one in ten abused women who seek their help because either they do not ask the right questions or they "are not open to the information." This approach further incapacitates women who become addicted and who might then engage in "double-doctoring" to maintain their addictions.[186]

Dr Jaffe spoke from a strong research base showing that, when battered women show up in emergency rooms, clinics, and offices, physicians fail overwhelmingly to identify battering as the cause of their injuries.[187] Yet the same women are treated with tranquillizers and pain medications at a far higher rate than non-battered patients who present with injuries.[188] Using such drugs to treat battered women is dangerous both because they present a high risk of attempted suicide and alcohol and drug abuse[189] and because they might well have undiagnosed brain injuries for which medication is contra-indicated.[190] Battered women have a good chance of leaving a medical consultation with a psychiatric label such as "neurotic," "hysteric," "hypochondriac," or "well-known patient with multiple vague complaints" and being referred for psychiatric treatment.[191] One study reports that "battered women were an otherwise normal population who developed a complex profile of psychosocial problems subsequent to the presentation of an initial episode of domestic violence at the hospital."[192]

The psychiatric and prescription drug approaches contribute to the social entrapment of battered women like Margaret. The patient misses an opportunity for assessment of her endangerment. Moreover, drug use can disable the woman further by allowing her to tolerate what might otherwise be unbearable suffering[193] and clouding her judgment and capacity to think clearly about her options and the possibility of escape. Her abilities to secure or keep employment, reduce her isolation by maintaining contact with friends and family,[194] and keep her children should she try to leave are all undercut by psychiatric labelling and drugging. So too is her credibility should she seek police intervention, as evidenced by Detective Clark's response to Margaret.

Most importantly, drugs and psychiatric labels define the problem as the woman's, affirming her batterer's claim that the woman is both crazy and responsible for his violence, thereby reinforcing his power over her. Evan Stark and Ann Flitcraft explain: "Now, like her physician, she may perceive her life with an abusive male as symptomatic of an underlying pathology, dependency, and helplessness."[195]

In the weeks before Paul's death, Margaret felt herself disappearing. Dr Jaffe said: "There was nothing left of her because she had put up with so much."[196] Her desperation and pain became intolerable, so she self-medicated, abusing her prescriptions.

Margaret told Dr Jaffe that Paul threatened and struck her in the car en route to the medical centre. She experienced "an increasing sense of pain ... fear and threat."[197] Dr Jaffe also testified that, when Margaret hailed the taxi, she felt that "Carrie was an extension of Paul ... What she described was ... the feeling of wanting to eliminate Carrie and then kill herself and just end everything."[198] She was "trying to somehow erase Paul and erase Carrie from her life ... to protect herself ... She describes just trying to be safe."[199]

Harrison's cross-examination proposed that Paul's violence had petered out. Dr Jaffe countered that his violence was ever present due to his threats and psychological abuse. Well, then, Harrison continued, the experts agree that battered women who kill in self-defence typically face escalating violence immediately prior to the homicide, often an "uncontrollably savage, acute incident."[200] Jaffe again disputed Harrison's definition of violence.

Harrison turned to his final attack, asking how many women kill their husbands after they have left and taken up residence with another woman. Dr Jaffe acknowledged that this would be rare. Harrison pressed on: "Ever, how many? Do you recall any?" Dr Jaffe answered: "Maybe two or three. I think it's uncommon." Harrison continued: "And how many of those ... did the woman arrange for the husband ... to come and get her, to take her in a car?" Here he held up his fingers in a "0." Dr Jaffe acknowledged that "I can't tell you any – are you holding up a zero? Yes zero." Harrison then asked: "How many cases did the woman who arranged for her husband to come and get her, get a gun with the intention of killing herself, her spouse and the girlfriend?"[201] "It's very uncommon," Dr Jaffe answered. Harrison asked whether Margaret intended to kill Sherwood as well as Paul and herself. Dr Jaffe replied: "It was all three of them."[202]

In his closing, MacIntyre urged the jurors to "affirm that a battered woman 'has a right, as we all do, to act in self-defence.'"[203] He reminded them of the years of brutality that Margaret endured at Paul's hands, culminating in his "flaunting" of his new relationship while continuing to dominate and terrorize Margaret. MacIntyre asked the jurors to use Battered Woman Syndrome to find that Margaret acted in self-defence: "The battered-wife syndrome isn't something that you catch like a cold," MacIntyre said. "It's imposed on you. It's imposed by a brutal, battering, sadistic husband in this case."[204]

MacIntyre further argued that Margaret did not have the necessary intent to attempt the murder of Sherwood given her confused and intoxicated state. Margaret experienced "involuntary intoxication" because she did not know the effects of the drug combinations. This, he argued, would provide a complete defence. Alternatively, Margaret was provoked into killing Paul, reducing murder to manslaughter. But MacIntyre maintained that he was not seeking a manslaughter verdict: "I want you to set her free."[205]

Harrison told the jury: "This is not a public inquiry into the issue of battered women."[206] Some battered women kill out of "anger, revenge, wanting to end it all, jealousy."[207] Margaret did not face a threat to her life when she killed Paul, his violence having abated since he moved out. She was hurt and angry and could not cope with his abandonment.

The physical evidence did not support the story told by Margaret: "How could it happen the way she said?" Harrison said: "Do you accept that she was firing away, blazing away, half a car length away?"[208] There was negligible evidence of drug intoxication, insufficient to displace her admitted intention to end her pain by killing these two people. Margaret formed a clear plan to end it all and executed it "with determination."[209] He asked the jury to convict her on both charges.

Justice Zalev charged the jury, reviewing the evidence – medical, physical, and testimonial – for and against self-defence. He did not review Paul's violence over the years but told the jurors that this evidence was "of the greatest importance": they should study a chart prepared by Dr Jaffe documenting Paul's abuse of Margaret "in detail."[210] He continued: "Bear in mind that day he had a knife on his belt and her evidence was that he usually kept a gun in the car and you will recall her evidence about his collection of knives, guns and whips and you also have photographs."[211] Justice Zalev said that Paul's past abuse went to his propensity for violence, her ability to gauge her level of danger, her belief that she had no way out, and her deteriorated mental state caused by the cumulative effect of his abuse.

Justice Zalev said that, if the jurors were not satisfied beyond a reasonable doubt that Margaret had the intent to kill, whether because she was so intoxicated by the pills that she lacked the capacity to form the intent to kill or because of "her mental state," they must acquit her of murder and attempted murder. She would still be liable to manslaughter and assault with a weapon because these crimes do not require proof of the same degree of intentionality. If, on the other hand, they found that she had the intent to kill Paul and Sherwood, then they must also consider whether she had the capacity to "plan and deliberate" his death in light of the evidence of her mental condition and drug use. Finally, Justice Zalev told the jury that provocation was not available, nor was the defence of "involuntary intoxication." He left them with four possible verdicts regarding Paul's death (not guilty, manslaughter, second-degree murder, first-degree murder) and two possible verdicts for the attack on Sherwood (attempted murder, assault with a weapon).

When the jury retired on 6 October, Margaret's lawyer Zuber submitted four objections to the charge. First, jurors had not been left with the option of an acquittal regarding Margaret's attack on Sherwood. Second, he invoked a creative interpretation of self-defence. Referring to the legal requirement that the accused face death or "grievous bodily harm," Zuber asked the judge to read the latter phrase broadly, to include the risk of psychological harm. He relied on a Supreme Court of Canada decision[212] that threatening to rape a woman amounted to the crime of threatening to commit "serious bodily harm" because rape is likely to have serious psychological effects and can have serious physical effects. Paul's psychological abuse of Margaret had, if anything, escalated prior to the homicide. Given Dr Jaffe's evidence that his psychological abuse was entwined with his physical and sexual abuse and triggered Margaret's intense anxiety and fear, this argument would have made self-defence more compelling.

Zuber's third and fourth objections related to Justice Zalev's decision to withhold involuntary intoxication and provocation from the jury. Zuber tried to persuade the judge that Margaret had involuntarily become intoxicated by drugs because she did not understand their compounding effects, entitling her to a possible acquittal as opposed to a manslaughter or assault with a weapon conviction. With respect to provocation, the threatening words spoken by Paul in the car and his act of choking Margaret constituted a "wrongful act or insult" that would have caused an ordinary woman standing in her shoes – here a battered woman – to lose self-control. This was another creative effort to urge the court to take into account the experiences of battered women. Justice Zalev rejected Zuber's objections without providing reasons.[213]

Over the next three days and two nights, the jury returned to the courtroom eight times with questions for the judge. On the third day, they asked whether they could make a recommendation when they returned a verdict. Justice Zalev replied that they were free to make a recommendation but that he would not be bound by it.

At 3:30 that afternoon, the jury finally delivered a verdict. Margaret stared straight ahead as they pronounced her guilty of second-degree murder and attempted murder. One of the women jurors "fought to hold back tears."[214] Nonetheless, all of the jurors affirmed their verdict when MacIntyre asked that they be polled individually.

With their verdict, the jury provided a written recommendation: "The evidence of the severity of the Battered Woman Syndrome in this case was such that we wish to recommend the minimum sentence allowed in this case and suggest that she receives all the therapeutic assistance needed to overcome the psychological scars associated with this syndrome."[215]

Because her murder conviction meant that Margaret would serve a life sentence, the only discretion afforded to Justice Zalev was to set her parole ineligibility for a period between ten and twenty-five years, taking into account the jury's advice on parole. The judge asked the jurors whether their recommendation supported setting her parole ineligibility at the lowest possible level. No one in the courtroom voiced disagreement. Margaret was sentenced on the spot, without submissions of either counsel. She was ordered to serve a life sentence for murder, with parole ineligibility set at ten years and a concurrent sentence of four years of imprisonment for her attempt to murder Sherwood.

Harrison praised the jury for being able to "separate the legality of her guilt or innocence on the murder but recognize that she should get some consideration"[216] for the abuse that she had suffered. He speculated that they found her not guilty of first-degree murder because "they were able to give her some benefit on the planning and deliberation in light of the abuse and her state of mind."[217] He emphasized that "[t]here are other options. If you do kill, the community expects you to be charged, prosecuted and let the courts decide."[218]

Dr Jaffe told reporters that legal progress for battered women was slow: "The justice system was designed by men for men ... It's easy for a man to judge a woman and say 'I wouldn't have stayed.' But if you understand what a woman goes through, you can understand why she was driven to kill."[219]

MacIntyre told the media that the verdict demonstrated society's refusal to accept Battered Woman Syndrome: "I think this whole thing is based on fear," MacIntyre said. "Fear of women killing men."[220] He criticized the judge's refusal to put provocation to the jury: "The definition of provocation has to be extended to battered wives ... It's not a spur of the moment thing, it's a slow burn cumulative effect."[221]

MacIntyre criticized politicians for sending mixed messages by launching campaigns to educate the public that wife assault is a crime while sending battered women to jail. Prosecutors, he said, "have to take some responsibility. They don't always have to go after a charge of first- or second-degree murder."[222]

Margaret's Appeal to the Ontario Court of Appeal

Intoxication

Margaret's convictions were appealed to the Ontario Court of Appeal on three grounds. Michelle Fuerst, counsel for Margaret, argued that the trial judge erred in the intoxication instruction by focusing on the abstract question of whether Margaret had the capacity to form the intent to kill over whether she actually formed that intent.[223] This ground was dismissed: the judge mentioned capacity but told the jury at several points in his charge that they must acquit her if they had a doubt about whether she intended to kill. In any event, the appeal court said, intoxication should not have been put before the jury because there was no evidentiary basis for it; thus, "no substantial wrong or miscarriage of justice" occurred.[224]

Yet two of the medical witnesses described the side-effects of the drugs that Margaret had been prescribed and the inability of screening to detect these drugs. She testified to her drug consumption, supported by her words to 9-1-1, the observations of emergency personnel that her pupils were somewhat dilated and her reactions slowed, and the testimony of the taxi driver and Sherwood, whose descriptions of Margaret's words and behaviour were consistent with drug-induced intoxication. Surely, there was some evidence to support an intoxication defence.

Provocation

Fuerst argued that provocation should have been left for the jury's consideration because the question of whether there was a "wrongful act or insult sufficient to cause the ordinary person to lose the power of self-control" should be assessed on the basis of one with Margaret's experiences. Drawing on a UK campaign[225] and legal precedent,[226] Fuerst argued that the "ordinary person" must include battered women and that the defence of provocation ought to encompass "cumulative provocation," in which a final, seemingly insignificant, act or insult by the deceased triggers a battered woman's violent reaction.

Even though on the evidence mere minutes, at most, separated these events, Margaret's appeal judges said that Paul's act of choking was "relatively distant in time from the shooting, which cannot be said to have followed 'on the sudden,'"[227] implicitly rejecting the "slow burn" provocation argument.

The Ontario Court of Appeal also noted that Margaret did not testify that she was actually provoked:

She gave no evidence that, in shooting her husband, she was acting on the sudden and shot him in a fit of passion. On the contrary, she had much earlier taken some pains to get a gun from locked premises, loaded it, and put it in her purse. The appellant's behaviour following the shooting was characterized by a lack of passion.[228]

This begs the question of what "passion" looks like for battered women who kill. Is a woman who has been psychologically damaged and numbed by violence, who appears to be emotionally detached, necessarily showing "a lack of passion"?[229]

The *Malott* decision remains anomalous and arguably discriminatory in the realm of provocation cases. Jealous husbands[230] and abandoned husbands,[231] even those who bring weapons to confrontations and take deliberate steps to conceal their crimes, can secure access to provocation. Currently, provocation is less persuasive for jurors when men kill their wives than it has been,[232] but these cases remain troubling.[233] Provocation as a defence is rooted in our history, whereby women were the property of their husbands, as were sons and daughters. Originally, only self-defence would excuse murder, but an exception evolved by which a man who came upon his wife engaging in adultery or his son being sodomized would be convicted of the lesser crime of manslaughter if he lost the power of self-control and killed in a "fit of passion." The provocation defence has, over time, expanded further to include any "wrongful act or insult" that would cause the "ordinary person to lose the power of self-control."

Provocation has also evolved to potentially include women claimants. Among my case studies are two women whose guilty pleas to manslaughter were accepted by the Crown in part based on provocation[234] and two jury verdicts of manslaughter that might have been predicated on provocation.[235] Women's provocation defences are rare not only because women do not generally describe themselves as "losing control" and acting out of anger but also because it would be the unusual woman who could spontaneously attack and kill her male partner. Since men can use their bare hands to kill women by beating them to death or strangling them, they can effect death "on the sudden" when enraged by their partners' behaviour – often their decision to leave the relationship. Women must secure weapons and bide their time before they can act out homicidal rage – which can undercut provocation.

But men also use weapons to kill their spouses under alleged provocation. Consider Bert Stone, who used a knife to inflict forty-seven stab wounds on his wife, Sharon Stone. Although Bert had earlier been charged with attacking Sharon in a public place, and she had confided to her siblings that he was abusive and that she wanted to leave him,[236] his uncorroborated account of the homicide was that she launched a verbal attack on him,[237] which caused a "whooshing sensation" to wash over him. The jury accepted that Bert was provoked and convicted him of manslaughter. In turn, his sentence was mitigated by her "provocation," and he was sentenced to seven years of imprisonment.

Perhaps the most telling comparison to Margaret's case is that of Norman Thibert, a man who had pursued extramarital relationships and whose wife had left him for her co-worker Alan Sherren. Thibert requested that his wife meet with him so that he could plead for her return. This request she refused, so, with a loaded gun in his car, he drove to her place of work, "thinking he might have to kill [Sherren]."[238] He changed his mind while driving and decided to use the gun as a bluff to get his wife to agree to talk to him alone. He intercepted her outside the bank where she worked, telling her that he had a high-powered rifle in the vehicle and asking her to go somewhere with him to talk. Sherren emerged from the bank to lead her back inside. Thibert stopped them by pulling the gun from his truck:

> [T]he deceased began walking towards him, with his hands on Mrs. Thibert's shoulders swinging her back and forth, saying, 'You want to shoot me? Go ahead and shoot me,' and 'Come on big fellow, shoot me. You want to shoot me? Go ahead and shoot me.' At some point, Mrs. Thibert either moved, or was moved aside. The appellant testified that the deceased kept coming towards him, ignoring the appellant's instructions to stay back. The appellant testified that his eyes were closed as he tried to retreat inward and the gun discharged.[239]

Thibert advanced provocation, but the jury convicted him of murder. Three of the five justices of the Supreme Court of Canada who heard his appeal ruled that his judge had been right to instruct the jurors on provocation. An ordinary person in Thibert's shoes, denied access to time alone with a wife who has left him and who is upset and sleep deprived, would have lost the power of self-control upon being "taunted" by his wife's lover and seeing his wife handled in a "proprietary manner." Because the trial judge had improperly instructed the jury on the burden of proof for provocation, Thibert was entitled to a new trial, at which the judge accepted provocation and convicted him of manslaughter.[240]

More recently, the Supreme Court has somewhat limited the reach of the provocation defence by ruling that "a wrongful act or insult" and its effect on the ordinary person must be interpreted in light of "contemporary norms of behavior, including fundamental values such as the commitment to equality."[241] The Court said that neither "antiquated beliefs such as 'adultery is the highest invasion of property'" nor "inappropriate conceptualizations of 'honour'"[242] can be ascribed to the ordinary person for the provocation defence. It did not, however, retreat from its decision in *Thibert*. While recognizing that spouses have the right to leave a relationship, it said that "the means by which that spouse communicates this decision may amount *in fact* to an 'insult'" that could, if sufficiently grave, cause the ordinary person to lose the power of self-control.[243]

If men invoke provocation for the frenzied stabbing of an alleged "nagging wife" or for shooting a rival, then surely Margaret deserved the opportunity to present provocation to her jury. Of course, provocation is no panacea for battered women, whose "provocation" is on an entirely different scale from that of men such as Bert Stone and Norman Thibert. As long as this defence remains on the books,[244] should it not equally recognize the circumstances in which battered women like Margaret kill?

Self-Defence
Fuerst argued that Justice Zalev failed to present self-defence fairly on two grounds. First, it was not offered as a defence to the attempted murder charge, whereby Margaret saw Sherwood as an extension of Paul's abuse. The Ontario Court of Appeal responded: "This theory, tortured from isolated passages of Dr Jaffe's expert testimony, trivializes the battered woman syndrome as a component of self-defence. Self-defence hardly embraces the actions of the appellant who, after killing the partner who was her abuser, reloaded her firearm, hailed a taxi, directed it to Sherwood's trailer home, and attempted to kill her."[245]

Second, Fuerst argued that the self-defence instruction on the murder charge was inadequate because Justice Zalev should have summarized the evidence of Paul's abuse of Margaret and related Dr Jaffe's testimony on Battered Woman Syndrome to each element of self-defence. On this point, the Court of Appeal decided that the judge had dealt fairly with self-defence, particularly when Dr Jaffe's testimony was not completely favourable and the judge had not highlighted its frailties.[246]

Justice Rosalie Abella disagreed with Justices George Finlayson and Allan Austin on the adequacy of the self-defence instruction. She criticized the trial judge for failing to tell the jury which of the facts described by Margaret could have amounted to an "unlawful assault" and for referring only briefly to Battered Woman Syndrome without explaining the concept to the jury or how it related to self-defence. The judge did not "sufficiently recite the expert evidence on the potential effect of years of battering to the reasonableness of Margaret's apprehensions about the degree of danger she was in, and about what she felt she had to do to eliminate the danger."[247] Noting the number of questions that the jury asked, their finding that the crime was not planned and deliberate, and their recommendation for the minimum sentence, Justice Abella concluded that, "had they been properly charged, they may have come to a different verdict."[248]

Margaret's Appeal to the Supreme Court of Canada

Justice Abella's dissent on this question of law entitled Margaret to a further appeal to the Supreme Court of Canada on self-defence. All justices of the Supreme Court agreed that Justice Zalev's self-defence instruction was adequate. Justice John Major explained:

> [I]t could be argued that it may have been desirable for the trial judge to have instructed the jury to a greater extent in making the connection between the evidence of battered woman syndrome and the legal issue of self-defence. However, in reviewing the trial judge's charge as a whole, I am satisfied that the jury were left with a sufficient understanding of the facts as they related to the relevant legal issues.[249]

Justice Claire L'Heureux-Dubé and Chief Justice Beverley McLachlin wrote that women must not be held to some rigid stereotype of "battered women":

> To fully accord with the spirit of *Lavallee* ... a judge and jury should be made to appreciate that a battered woman's experiences are both individualized, based on her own history and relationships, as well as shared with other women, within the context of a society and a legal system which has historically undervalued women's experiences ... [A]ll of this should be presented in such a way as to focus on the reasonableness of the woman's actions, without relying on old or new stereotypes about battered women.[250]

None of this was any help to Margaret, however, since they agreed that her self-defence instruction was adequate. She was left with a life sentence of imprisonment and the weight of her prolonged traumatic experience.

Rita Graveline

> "I thought if anything it would be my father who would have
> shot my mother."[251]

According to friends and neighbours who spoke to reporters after Rita Graveline's arrest for second-degree murder on 12 August 1999, Michael Graveline "hounded" his wife, "often yelling at her in public places."[252] Her daughter and son were convinced that if anyone died it would be their mother. Yet, when it came to her trial, Rita was unable to testify to having killed in self-defence because she experienced complete blackout.

The Crown prosecutor, Martin Côté, told the jury of eleven women and one man[253] in a Hull, Quebec, courtroom in February 2001 a simple story in his opening address. He would establish that Rita had killed her husband that night, while he slept, with one shot from a rifle.

Her counsel, Marino Mendo, persuaded Justice Martin Bédard to allow him to address the jury directly after the Crown prosecutor. Mendo said that Rita admitted shooting the deceased but that she had a valid defence, Battered Woman Syndrome.[254] His client had experienced thirty years of "duress" caused by her late husband. Justice Bédard interrupted to say that Battered Woman Syndrome is not a defence, "but it's a context that will be given to you which leads to the defence of self-defence, okay?"[255] In fact, Mendo never breathed the words "self-defence" in his opening address or even in his closing address. That he left to Justice Bédard.

Côté first called Peggy Graveline-Proulx, sister of the deceased. She said that the only injuries she ever saw had been attributed by Rita to accidents. She described Rita as a "happy-go-lucky ... prankster"[256] but was aware that she had been on medical leave the year before for depression. In the weeks before the homicide, Rita was tired and poorly groomed.[257] Graveline-Proulx was not close to her brother because he drank excessively and caused "friction." She had seen Michael "backhand" Rita once but had never asked Rita about abuse: "Everything in my house stayed at my house and what was in her house stayed at her house."[258]

Mary-Lou Pomainville, a family friend, had seen Rita wearing sunglasses to cover black eyes and swollen cheekbones when Michael had injured her in 1992 and 1997. She explained: "She had her days of being very afraid of him."[259] Pomainville was at the pub the night of the homicide, where "something was brewing."[260] "Mickey was sitting down with his long face, you know, his mad face."[261] There was, she said, "something mean about him."[262] Rita was the opposite of Mickey: "a wonderful person," "funny," not a bad bone in her body," "a gentle, respected lady."[263]

Kim Wilson, Rita's daughter-in-law, said that she saw her own child cause one of Rita's injuries and witnessed Rita fall and break her ankle. Her husband was twice attacked by his father. They had to keep Michael's guns at their house while Michael was denied access to weapons under court order. Mendo asked her to repeat the names that Michael called Rita in public, usually when he was drunk, at least three to four times a week – "a whore, a bitch, a c**t, a good for nothing."[264] Her husband was over at his mother's house regularly to check on Rita, but Wilson insisted that he was concerned for the safety of "both of them."[265] Mendo expressed surprise that her one-year-old child had caused his grandmother a black eye. "Yes," Wilson affirmed.[266]

The forensic witnesses testified that the deceased was found covered in a comforter with a bullet hole from a shot fired from more than six feet away. The lightbulb in the room where his body lay was missing. Côté introduced Michael's three criminal records for drunk driving, one that caused someone bodily harm, and his charge for assault causing bodily harm, dismissed when Michael entered into a peace bond. At the time of his death, Michael had over twice the legal level of alcohol for driving.[267] When Côté began to show the jury the videotapes of Rita's statements to the police, Mendo requested that Rita be excused: "[S]he finds it too unbearable."[268]

Mendo then began to call his witnesses. Gail Findlay, Rita's neighbour, testified that in 1991 Rita pounded on her door for help, having been "roughed up." Rita went to hospital and Michael to jail, but Findlay could not recall a more recent incident. Denise Robataille, a summertime neighbour at their campsite, witnessed several assaults by Michael, saw bruising on Rita's body when Rita wore a bathing suit, and heard screaming and weeping from their camping trailer. "And she also told me that ... he seldom hit her in the face because if he would hit her in the face she couldn't go to work."[269] Côté pinned Robataille down on the dates, forcing her to acknowledge that these events took place between 1989 and 1992.

Dr Gilles Chamberland, a psychiatrist who practised out of Montreal, evaluated Rita post-homicide. Rita, he said, came from a family of ten children with a father who was gentle when sober but violent to her mother when drunk. Rita was forced to leave school in grade ten to support her family because her alcoholic father could not provide for them. She met

Michael when she was eighteen and became pregnant. He asked her to marry him, and she hesitated. He said that, if he could not be the father of her child, no one would, and he accelerated the car to dangerous speeds. Rita was frightened but decided this meant that he really loved her, so she accepted his proposal.[270]

Michael began to isolate Rita and displayed obsessive jealousy, barring even her women friends from their home. She quickly "learned not to show resistance to the [sexual] advances of her spouse."[271] She recounted lacerations, fractures, black eyes, and an occasion when he threatened her and her daughter with a gun, which resulted in police intervention. Rita coped by minimizing and repressing Michael's abuse. Her son described terrible violence – his father breaking a bottle over his mother's head – that Rita could not recall.[272] Dr Chamberland testified that Rita had fled with her children once to her sister's home in Ontario. Michael tracked her down the next day; she never tried to escape again. The doctor added that Rita had told him that she had not been beaten by the deceased over the past three years.[273]

Dr Chamberland described her history of depression, which necessitated a "non-suicide pact" with her treating doctor,[274] and said that the high dosage of Paxil (in addition to another anti-depressant) that Rita was receiving was "exceptional."[275] She stopped taking her medications because her husband complained that they diminished her sex drive. At the pub on the night of the homicide, Rita experienced several conflicts with her husband: he was angry that she requested money from others to buy a glass of beer. When she kissed an elderly man on the cheek to wish him luck in the darts game, Michael announced to all present that his wife was unfaithful. Upon reaching the front door of their home that night, Rita struggled to find the key. When she located it and opened the door, Michael pushed her inside, calling her a "fucking idiot."[276] He went to bed, and Rita stayed up playing solitaire while she drank another glass of beer. Michael came downstairs briefly to insult her again. She sat crying, then headed upstairs. After that, she recalled nothing – "as if there were a black hole" – until she heard a loud bang and found herself standing in the bedroom holding his rifle.[277] She let the weapon fall, descended, and called 9-1-1.

Dr Chamberland diagnosed Rita with "dissociative amnesia," a condition that makes it hard to retrieve memories because she was not herself.[278] Her answers to his questions were "naïve," leading him to conclude that she spoke with "candour."[279] His second diagnosis was that Rita had a "dependent personality."[280] And, though it is not strictly a psychiatric "diagnosis," he also testified that Rita experienced Battered Woman Syndrome.[281] She withdrew from conflict with her husband, bottling up her resentment, suffering, and sadness, which ultimately led to her break from reality, he said.[282] Judith Lewis Herman reports: "People in captivity become adept practitioners of the arts of altered consciousness, through the practice of dissociation, voluntary thought suppression, minimization, and sometime outright denial; they learn to alter an unbearable reality."[283]

People can also react in an automatic manner when pushed by their accumulated and repressed urges; they dissociate because their behaviour is at the extreme of their own values.[284] Dr Chamberland testified that Michael was escalating the conflict that night, but Rita had no means to extract herself and no control over her actions. She was "absolutely unconscious."[285] He emphasized: "Mrs Graveline was unable to show any kind of opposition to her husband ... and this is how come the urge had to manifest itself ... in an unconscious manner ... in a state of dissociation."[286]

His assessment of Rita's psychological state is supported by the work of Dr Lenore Walker, the originator of Battered Woman Syndrome. She explains that, by the time homicide occurs, the woman's ability to defend herself psychologically is "unravelling," even though the woman is not consciously angry: "The ... descriptions of the final incident indicate that they separate those angry feelings by the psychological process of a dissociative state ... They fear showing anger will cause their own death, as indeed it could, as batterers cannot tolerate the woman's expression of anger."[287]

Dr Chamberland acknowledged that in the past few years Michael's aggression had been verbal, not physical – Rita did not believe that Michael wanted to harm her.[288] Dr Chamberland said that she had a tendency to excuse her husband, believe the best of him, and attribute his violence to alcohol.

Côté asked whether Rita could have been afraid on the night of the homicide given that Michael's extreme violence had ceased years before and she faced "only insults" and pushing.[289] Dr Chamberland replied that Rita was living in fear related to Michael's earlier violence. Her dissociation was triggered by his escalation of aggression.[290] But, since she was unconscious, the doctor conceded that she was not defending herself when she shot her husband.[291]

Research demonstrates that Dr Chamberland was right to stand his ground regarding the legitimate fear that Rita might have felt in response to what might appear to be "only" psychological abuse or slapping, pushing, and shoving. "Minor" violence is a predictor of severe injuries in battered women, as is psychological abuse by the perpetrator.[292]

Dr Chamberland refuted the proposition that Rita might have suffered from "hysterical amnesia" after the homicide. She did not have a hysterical personality, nor was she a sociopath.[293] The Crown then produced a study reporting that between 25 percent and 45 percent of persons accused of homicide claim amnesia at the time of killing[294] and another study describing a particular diagnostic test for dissociative amnesia.[295] Dr Chamberland was unaware of these studies but maintained that the diagnostic tool was used only by researchers; he knew of no psychiatrists who used it.[296]

In re-examination, Mendo asked Dr Chamberland why Rita did not believe that her husband wished to harm her. This is a defence mechanism "which protects the [battered woman] from a form of suffering and before we undo this we must be careful,"[297] he explained.

Lilian Kluke, Rita's younger sister, testified that when she was twelve she babysat Rita's child. She was terrified of Michael and saw him scream obscenities at Rita and drag her by the hair.[298] Rita fled, but he would call her parents' home to say that he was coming with a gun to blow all of their heads off unless Rita returned.[299] Kluke saw many injuries on her sister: a broken arm, black eyes, bruises. To Michael, "you weren't human, you were his and that's it,"[300] she testified. He was "just like a snarling dog," on whom her family had placed restraining orders to keep him away from their home.[301]

Under cross-examination, Kluke insisted that Rita had been assaulted by Michael in the past two years before his death. She knew that he had slapped her around in 1998 and 1999 because her mother had stayed at Rita's at that time and had told Kluke about it.[302] Justice Bédard interjected: this was hearsay that the jury must disregard. Côté suggested again that the deceased had not been violent to Rita "apart from the occasional shove" since 1997. Kluke stood firm: "Knowing Mickey the way I do, I would disagree."[303]

Kelly Graveline, daughter of Michael and Rita, echoed Kluke: "[W]e were not people, we were his possessions and he didn't want anybody else to come in to make family contact."[304] She continued: "[E]very comment that came out of his mouth had swear words in it all the time and ... if he called her a name it was 'you're a fucking c**t.'"[305] Kelly recalled an attack in which her father repeatedly smashed her mother's head onto a brick countertop, necessitating stitches.[306] She once stepped in to protect her mother, and he punched Kelly in the face. "[O]f course he laughed,"[307] she said. Her mother was slapped, pushed into furniture, punched, pushed; Michael threw items at Rita and smashed the dishes; he threatened to shoot them with a shotgun. Her mother's efforts to call the police or flee were thwarted by Michael pulling the phone out of the wall and blocking the door.

Côté wanted Kelly to affirm that she was unaware of any violence by her father toward her mother in the past two to three years. When she balked and said that she had received calls from her mother complaining that he had assaulted her at least twice in the past few years, Côté confronted her with both her police statement and her evidence at her mother's bail hearing, where she had testified that she was unaware of any violence in the prior three years.[308] Kelly was too overwhelmed to think straight at the police station and the bail hearing,[309] she said. In re-examination, Mendo asked her to expand on her bail evidence that her mother had asked to stay with her in the winter of 1999. Kelly explained that her mother was afraid to go home.[310]

Michael Graveline Jr also testified about his father's violence. At age five, he saw his father break a beer bottle over his mother's head,[311] and he recalled his father saying that if Rita tried to leave he would find her and kill her.[312] He described constant verbal and psychological abuse of his mother and frequent physical abuse, when he and his sister were wakened by their father's screaming and smashing of furniture and dishes.[313] He first stood up to his father at age fifteen and removed a loaded gun from him. His father called him a "bastard," claiming that he was someone else's son. Michael Jr began intervening at age seventeen to protect his mother, describing himself as a "watch dog."[314] After he left home, his mother would continue to call him for help: "[W]hen I arrived at the house her shirt would be ripped and glasses would be broken on the floor and ... the telephone would be ripped out because he didn't want her calling me a second time."[315]

His mother was a "very loving" person, easily intimidated.[316] She was deprived of friendship by his father, who was jealous of everyone. Michael Jr saw his mother try to push his father away twice but otherwise never saw her use force. In 1998, he saw his father slap his mother across the face in a bar, and in 1999 she called him sobbing. He said that "a lot of times she didn't want to tell me what was happening because she knew if she did tell me I'd be down there right away and then, when she did mention on the phone, yes, he hit me and he's breaking things and – I'd be down there."[317] Michael Jr witnessed a fight ten days before the homicide. His father was angry because his mother had been out all day buying him a birthday present.

Michael Jr saw his father glowering at the darts game in the pub the night of the homicide. His father was furious because his mother had spent five dollars on a lottery machine in the pub. At the conclusion of the darts competition, his father was eerily silent, which was "very scary." Michael Jr elaborated: "[W]hen he was quiet ... the temper was brewing and, you know, it was just going to escalate ... [H]e would explode, so it wasn't ... good to see him when he was quiet."[318] Michael Jr knew that his father was angry because, when they pulled up, he left the car without a word, had a look that showed he was angry, and walked straight to the front door without a backward glance. Like his sister, Michael Jr said that, when the police came to his door, "I automatically figured it was my mother who was shot."[319]

Coté accused Michael Jr of "accentuating" his father's "problems"[320] compared with his police statements and evidence at his mother's bail hearing. Michael Jr conceded that he witnessed less physical violence by his father from 1993 and on,[321] but said his mother often called, even in the week before the homicide, to complain that his father had hit her. Côté pointed out that at the bail hearing Michael Jr said that the last time he remembered such a call was six months earlier. In re-examination, he explained: from the homicide on 11 August to the bail hearing six days later, he was the family member in charge of everything – the funeral, the house, and getting his mother out on bail. He had his mind "on other things."[322]

Rita testified next. Reporters said that her testimony "often wandered,"[323] like that of Margaret. Her husband was physically violent over their thirty-two-year marriage. When asked by Mendo to provide details, tears began to roll down her cheeks.[324] "It's so hard for me because I tried to cover up so much and I'm so embarrassed to tell."[325] When Rita tried to flee hitting, shoving, and verbal abuse, Michael would either dismantle the car's wiring or pull her from the vehicle. Mendo pressed her for details – "your whole life madam, go through 30 years if you have to."[326] But as she began to recount abuse, she exclaimed "God! I'm slipping years, I'm going up and down."[327]

Rita struggled on, describing how Michael isolated her from friends and family when he moved her to Luskville.[328] Her husband assaulted her every week, sometimes causing a broken arm, black eyes, bruising, a dislocated hip, and a wound on her head requiring stitches. He frequently threatened Rita with firearms, most recently in August 1999, when he threatened to get his gun "to get rid of two stupid people at once,"[329] referring to her and her mother, a seventy-nine-year-old woman in a wheelchair.

Rita usually lied about her injuries: "I didn't want them to hate him, to brand him. One of Paul's [her daughter's boyfriend at the time] brothers had already beaten him ... because he beat me up, I didn't want to see him beat up."[330] Michael also threatened that, if she ever charged him, "when he was through with me, I'd never put a charge on anyone else."[331] After the one time that she fled to her sister's, he told her that he would kill her if she ever did that again.[332] Nonetheless, she loved him. When he was not drinking and gave her a hug, "I would want to crawl right inside him, that's how much I cared."[333] Rita never considered divorcing him because she had been raised Roman Catholic, and no one in her family ever divorced. Instead, she had to "[m]ake the best of it, try."[334]

When Mendo asked whether Rita had been sexually abused by Michael, Coté questioned its relevance, "considering that the battered wife syndrome is not an issue for the Defence." Justice Bédard disagreed: "I'm not aware that the battered syndrome [sic] is not an issue anymore. It surely could be relevant."[335]

Rita submitted to sex even though it became painful as she entered menopause and she often suffered for days after. If she declined, her husband would work himself into a jealous fit, accusing her of "getting sex elsewhere."[336] He insisted that she stop taking anti-depressants, believing that they caused her failure to "perform." She lost interest in life, in cooking, in caring for herself. She had only one friend, Claire, who, Michael warned, was not welcome in their home. Rita stopped cleaning the house because the only guests were his friends, who came to drink, leaving bottles, glasses, and ashtrays everywhere.

Rita described an incident on 31 July, days before she shot her husband, when she came home from shopping for a birthday gift for him. She returned to find him drinking with a friend in the garage. He asked her "who did you fuck today?" Rita was mortified and returned to the house to prepare dinner. He came into the kitchen, took raw hamburger meat, and smashed it in her face. She handed him his present, which he threw in her face, telling her to shove it up her ass – he did not need anything from her anymore. When she bent to retrieve the gift, he pushed her head into the floor, holding her there. "I just backed away on my hands and knees and I went upstairs and I stayed there and I just literally cried all day."[337]

On the night of the homicide, Rita testified, she knew that Michael was angry about something on the ride home. He could not find his key for the front door, so she dug a spare key out of her purse and opened the door. He gave her "a little shove," and she responded by saying "you fucking idiot, don't start this again."[338] Michael called her "some filthy names," went upstairs, and then returned and "told [her] that he was totally fed up with [her] nonsense and we were going to see about this."[339] She sat to drink her fourth glass of beer that night and to play cards, crying. She recalled going upstairs, but the next thing she knew she was standing in her underwear with a gun that had just been discharged. Rita said that she "had been searching and searching for a whole year to try and remember."[340] She had no recollection of how she came to shoot him or where her slacks were.

The medical notes of Dr Busing, who treated Rita's recurring depression, were introduced through cross-examination by Côté. In August 1997, Dr Busing indicated, her depression arose out of her husband's abuse, but Rita had not experienced further abuse since 1991 or 1992. In another entry, from September 1999, Dr Busing recorded that Michael stopped his physical abuse in that time frame. His hitting and shoving continued, but he was not as violent as he had been, she explained, and there were "[n]o further incidents with him cutting me or hitting me in the head."[341] But Côté reminded Rita that she had testified to being threatened with a gun, punched in the head, and having her arm broken between 1992 and 1999: "Why are those incidents not there?"[342]

Côté then confronted Rita with Dr Busing's notes from a therapy session post-homicide. Dr Busing wrote that she recalled walking up the stairs while holding the gun, in contrast to her trial testimony.[343] She felt "very angry" about her husband's accusations of infidelity.[344] Reviewing the videotape of her police interview, Côté said that, when officers asked Rita whether Michael hurt or threatened her that night, she shook her head "no."[345]

Côté also cross-examined Rita on statements that she made to Dr Gagné, a psychiatrist retained by Côté. To him, she said that she hoped Michael would die, "but I never planned to kill him, I still loved him, I was never concerned that he would kill me."[346] Rita could not recall having made these statements to Dr Gagné in April 2000.

She also told him that Michael had not physically abused her in the past few years, but she explained in court that she thought he was asking her about "really being hurt and stitches."[347] She recounted the fight with Michael the day before his birthday but did not tell the doctor that Michael had smashed raw meat in her face, thrown his gift at her, or pushed her head to the kitchen floor. Rita explained: "I didn't have no marks from him pushing me on the floor, because I didn't hurt my face or anything else. I crawled away."[348]

Her explanation underscores a compounded challenge for defence lawyers. First, there is no widespread social understanding of what constitutes "abuse," "violence," or "battering." The legal definition of "assault" is simple – the non-consensual application of force to another person or the threat to do so[349] – yet men's assaults on their female partners are not always treated as such. Michael was charged for threatening Rita and Kelly with a rifle, but this charge was resolved by a "peace bond," not a conviction. Media commentary often conveys the message that minor assaults within relationships are "normal," "mutual," or not "real" domestic violence.[350] Rita might be forgiven for thinking that pushing is not "physical abuse."

Second, women survive violent relationships by minimizing, denying, and "forgetting" the abuse.[351] Counselling and distance are needed before women can necessarily recognize all the ways in which they have been abused. Even when they do disclose abuse to those whom they trust and while in recovery, women often leave out many incidents, even the "worst" ones, sometimes to spare others.[352] Women's advocates advise that women must be asked specific questions about abuse, just like sexual assault, in order to elicit the information.[353] Our muddled understanding of what "abuse" is together with battered women's psychological survival strategies make it easy to discredit their accounts for their inconsistencies regarding whether, when, and how they were "abused."

Côté challenged Rita's evidence by referring to her statements to Dr Morissette, a psychiatrist not called by the defence, in January 2001. To him, Rita said that there had been no physical violence in the past two or three years and that, as she sat crying at the kitchen table the night of the homicide, she told herself that she would not accept being assaulted and treated like a dog.[354]

Côté accused Rita of having "remembered" the assault in the kitchen "to cover up for Michael [Jr]'s change [in testimony]."[355] Her voice breaking,[356] she said: "I've been so embarrassed of this abuse all my life, I don't tell nobody about it ... And maybe it's wrong, but – my lawyer told me I have to, my children told me I have to, and it's still hard for me to say it because I am so embarrassed."[357]

Côté suggested that Rita first removed the lightbulb from the only lamp in the bedroom because a crushed bulb was found on the floor in the spare room. She took the gun out, found the bullets, and loaded it. She then, he proposed, pulled the covers up to cover her husband's head, stood back at the door of the bedroom, and fired the gun once. Rita responded: "No. No. I wouldn't do that. No. I don't remember that far."[358] Côté then challenged her on why she told 9-1-1 that she had just killed her husband. How did she know that she fired the gun? How did she know that he was dead? Did she stop to see if he moved? "It's because you knew you had shot him," he declared.[359]

When Rita stepped down from the witness stand, Mendo told her: "It's over." "It's over?" she asked, momentarily confused. The judge clarified – she could sit down now. Mendo added: "You can rest now."[360]

Côté was not taken by surprise by the defence, but he was nonetheless permitted to call Dr Gagné in reply.[361] Dr Gagné interviewed Rita in April 2000. He said that she experienced dissociative amnesia triggered by her homicidal act. She had experienced no other traumatic event to trigger dissociation; she had frequently been verbally abused by her husband and had endured minor shoving in the past, but these events could not have instigated her memory loss.[362] Dr Gagné agreed that Rita was a battered woman but said she did not experience Battered Woman Syndrome. She was not in fear of her life, which he claimed was a fundamental feature of Battered Woman Syndrome.[363] Furthermore, Dr Gagné said, dissociation or amnesia was not identified as a feature of Battered Woman Syndrome in the literature.[364] On both of these points, he was simply wrong.

In cross-examination, Mendo asked him to identify where in the literature it says that a woman must fear for her life before she is recognized as suffering from Battered Woman Syndrome.[365] Mendo suggested that, since Dr Gagné wrote his report four months after interviewing Rita, his assessment might have been less than accurate.[366] Mendo secured the doctor's agreement that, to survive mistreatment, battered women might try to forget the "bad" and cling to the "good" memories. Dr Gagné also agreed that, since Rita had been battered for over thirty years, had experienced three major depressions, and had stopped taking her medication, "those factors ... are all symptomatic of a psychological trauma that itself can cause amnesia."[367] Mendo asked whether the doctor could exclude a diagnosis of dissociative amnesia? The doctor responded: "Not at all ... [I]t's a true amnesia of the psychological type."[368]

Mendo's closing reminded the jurors that Rita called 9-1-1 for help but that the police priority was her arrest over rendering aid to Michael. Mendo pointed out problems in the collection of evidence: her 9-1-1 call was not recorded,[369] and the police handled weapons at the house before they were photographed. Mendo asked "what's the relationship with these mistakes in regards to the case of Mrs Graveline when I admit that she killed someone?" "Well," he explained, "Mrs Graveline made some mistakes in her testimonies or in her statements."[370] He said: "She made mistakes. Police made mistakes. I made mistakes."[371] He then described Dr Gagné as "a good man, he's a nice man – he's probably a good doctor, but Dr Gagné, with all the respect I have for him, he's too busy. He did a haphazard job in this case."[372]

Of the evidence from Rita, Mendo said: "If she's putting on a show, well, give her an Oscar, because she did a good show ... Don't you think it would have been easier for her to simply say, listen. He was coming towards me. There was no way out and I shot him."[373] Although Mendo admitted that Rita did not claim self-defence, he nonetheless said that "maybe you can look at that too, I don't know. I have no idea of that. You can always examine all the facts. That's what I'm asking you, examine all the facts."[374]

Regarding her minimization of Michael's violence, Mendo said: "She doesn't want to say it. You saw it. I'm her lawyer. I want her to speak. I want my Defence. I want her to give us everything. You saw what I had to do to get it out of her?"[375]

Mendo expressed disbelief – "come on!" – as he reviewed the evidence, such as Rita's story of getting a black eye from a one-year-old baby.[376] Michael controlled Rita all the time, Mendo told the jury: "It's total control, total humiliation."[377] He also talked about her pride in being a tidy house-keeper and good cook and contrasted this pride with the mess of her home as shown in police photographs – the disarray caused by depression. He commented: "We're at the end of our consciousness."[378]

Mendo asserted that, on the night of the homicide, something must have happened when Rita went up to get ready for bed.[379] "We don't know what happened,"[380] he said, but Michael pushed Rita and called her abusive names earlier: "That was brutality also."[381] Mendo concluded with a plea: "I'm asking you today, tell her it's not her fault. Tell her that what happened she has nothing to do with consciously speaking. Acquit her."[382]

Côté mocked the rhetorical tactic employed by Mendo. "[T]here is no defence in law that you can describe as saying, 'come on!' [I]t doesn't exist. There's no defence, well, 'come on!', and my colleague repeated that to you a few times ... and said well, 'come on!', well, that's not a defence."[383]

Like the Crown prosecutor in Margaret's case, Côté did not contest Michael's battering, but he said that some of Rita's evidence was just not credible. Like Margaret's Crown prosecutor, he also claimed that Michael's abuse had abated prior to the homicide. There was only "the occasional slap or shove," said Côté. Self-defence was unavailable because Rita had told Dr Chamberland that she did not think Michael meant to harm her.[384]

Côté said it was implausible that Rita could have loaded and fired a weapon that she claimed never to have used, all while unconscious. She must instead have dissociated after she realized what she had done. He repeated the "slips" in her evidence, such as when she said that she waited for a moment to see if her husband moved.[385] "Why would someone ... wait, wait to see if he would move? ... This is Rita Graveline ... the woman who loves her husband ... Doesn't even go to see him."[386] Côté concluded: "[Y]ou are not to determine that Mr [Michael] Graveline is a sad pathetic person and deserved it ... As much as I think that Mrs Graveline is a good person, it doesn't mean she's allowed to shoot him."[387]

The jury was then excused to allow counsel to discuss with the judge which defences should be considered. Côté argued that automatism and self-defence were fundamentally inconsistent because self-defence involves an intentional use of force, while automatism is a state in which the person exhibits no conscious will: therefore, self-defence should not be offered to jurors. Mendo did not plead self-defence before the jury, but Justice Bédard said that his jury address would "address all the possibilities the jury might have to face deriving from the evidence."[388]

When they returned, the judge instructed the jury first on automatism, a term describing "the state of a person who though capable of action, is not conscious of what he or she is doing."[389] It is classified as either mental disorder ("insane") or non-mental disorder ("non-insane"). The first results in a mental disorder disposition, whereby the person is kept in custody and assessed for dangerousness, while the latter results in acquittal. Because all the experts agreed that Rita displayed no signs of mental illness, only non-mental disorder automatism was at play, Justice Bédard said.

After reviewing key elements of the testimony of all the witnesses, including Rita's evidence that when he drank Michael became verbally and physically aggressive, "perhaps even sexually abusive,"[390] Justice Bédard discussed the expert evidence. Even Dr Gagné's report excluded a murder verdict because Dr Gagné said that Rita was conscious in his view but that her mental state "limited her capacity to consider the long-term consequences of her act."[391] Justice Bédard repeated Dr Gagné's words under cross-examination: Dr Gagné "believed ... that she suffered from amnesia, from the point to when she was climbing the stairs, up to the time that she heard the gunshot."[392]

The defence of automatism, Justice Bédard continued, must be proven on a balance of probabilities: it must be more likely true than untrue that Rita experienced this state. The defence said that she experienced an emotional blow caused by the interruption of her medications, the beer that she consumed, the accumulation of abuse, her depression, and Michael's words and actions that night.[393] It was up to the jurors to determine whether her "cable snapped."[394]

Justice Bédard reviewed the conflicting evidence about whether Michael abused Rita violently over the past three years before the homicide but reframed the question: "[H]as Michael Graveline ever changed, has he ever stopped being abusive, verbally, psychologically, physically?"[395]

If the jurors rejected automatism, they should consider whether Rita acted in self-defence. If they were left with a reasonable doubt that she suffered from Battered Woman Syndrome, then they could use this evidence to support self-defence, but the judge also told the jurors that "the defence of automatism is totally at the opposite of ... self-defence."[396]

Justice Bédard then charged the jury on provocation, saying that Rita might have been provoked and lost the power of self-control by virtue of Michael's acts or insults that would have caused the ordinary person to lose self-control. If so, did she actually lose self-control, and did she react suddenly? A reasonable doubt on provocation, he told them, would result in a manslaughter conviction.

After this charge, Côté asked the judge to repeat his expert's position that Rita's amnesia was triggered by the shooting of her husband. The jury needed to focus on when and what triggered the accused's dissociation. He also objected to the judge's reference to Rita having experienced "sexual abuse" given her equivocal evidence. The judge disagreed: "[I]f one puts pressure on one's partner to stop taking medication in order to allow intimate relations ... to be more easily performed or more satisfactorily performed, that could be considered as sexual assault ... [where] her testimony as a whole [was] that she felt she had no choice."[397]

Justice Bédard acceded to Côté's first complaint and brought the jury back to clarify Dr Gagné's position on the cause and timing of the dissociation. The jury then retired to deliberate and returned eighteen hours later to deliver a "not guilty" verdict. Rita was clutching Mendo's hand as she burst into weeping upon hearing the verdict.[398] Justice Bédard was reported as "visibly moved" when he told her that "you are a free woman."[399] Rita responded: "I have no legs ... [T]hey're like Jell-O."[400] To the reporters, she appeared to be "[o]verwhelmed by a mix of elation and relief."[401] She said: "I didn't know what to expect ... I'm just so happy."[402]

Mendo speculated that the verdict was based on the automatism defence, but "we will never know."[403] The acquittal would not "open the floodgates," he explained – "sane" automatism "is one of the hardest [defences] to prove."[404]

The *Ottawa Citizen*'s editorial disparaged the verdict, calling it "therapeutic jurisprudence," whereby "crime is a state of mind. And this is not a place Canadians want their judicial system to inhabit."[405] "[O]dd psychological belief systems" have "colonized" the criminal justice system, the editors claimed, contributing to a "mentality of non-responsibility."[406] Margaret Wente for the *Globe and Mail* put an anti-feminist spin on this theme:

> We're appalled when rape cases are argued by putting the victim on trial. I guess there's another standard when the sexes are reversed. I guess that when some submissive, mild-mannered woman does something violent and completely out of character, we've got to reach for voodoo diagnoses to explain it. We'd rather judge her on her mental state (assuming we can know it) than judge her on her actions. We'd rather hold a woman's deeds to a lower moral standard than a man's.[407]

Côté told reporters that the verdict did not surprise him,[408] but he objected to it because self-defence ought not to have been presented to the jury along with automatism: "You can't be a robot, not knowing what you are doing, and then at the same time be defending yourself from your husband. They're contradictory."[409]

The Crown's Appeal to the Quebec Court of Appeal

Automatism

The Crown filed an appeal to the Quebec Court of Appeal alleging two legal errors. One was that the judge had not properly instructed the jury on the legal requirements for the automatism defence. In the *Stone*[410] decision of 1999, the Supreme Court held that Bert was denied access to automatism: Sharon's alleged "nagging" might have supported provocation, but it did not qualify as a cause of psychological shock.

Rita's acquittal on the basis of non-mental disorder automatism was extremely rare for a battered woman.[411] Non-mental disorder automatism can be caused by a physical or psychological blow. Some battered women have been acquitted when they have entered dissociated states after blows to the head,[412] but "psychological blow" automatism is even more remote.

The criteria outlined for automatism by the *Stone* decision in 1999 seemed to make it even harder for a battered woman to invoke this automatism. At that time, *Stone* seemed to require that the judge weed out feigned claims by determining first whether the evidentiary basis for the defence is met by reference to the accused person's account, psychiatric evidence, eyewitness testimony, or any other corroborative evidence and second whether there was a motive for the crime.[413] If the person who triggered the dissociation was also the target of the accused's violent act, the Supreme Court warned, this suggests motive and undermines the claim of dissociation. One can see readily that, if a battered woman has killed her abuser, her claim to non-mental disorder automatism might be suspect by reason of her possible motive to kill and the fact that the trigger was also the victim.

Stone also required that, if there is evidence of automatism, the judge should presume that the person suffered from mental disorder automatism, which precludes acquittal.[414] To displace that presumption, the defence must show that the accused was not suffering from a mental disorder. Battered women who have been diagnosed with psychiatric conditions might be relegated to the mental disorder defence, though the question of whether a given condition amounts to a mental disorder is a question of law for the judge.[415]

Stone distinguished between internally caused automatism (mental disorder) and externally caused (non-mental disorder) automatism based on whether the person was subjected to "an extremely shocking trigger" to which a normal person might have reacted by dissociating. The "normal" person is one who has had the same experiences as the accused but not her "subjective psychological make-up."[416] This limited understanding of the "normal" person can keep some battered women from the defence if, for example, the woman suffers from Battered Woman Syndrome. Experts for the defence could emphasize that Battered Woman Syndrome is a normal response to traumatic experiences, but another problem for battered women here might be that the triggering event is one among many verbal or physical assaults and can even appear to be far less "shocking" than previous ones. This was indeed argued by Dr Gagné for the Crown in Rita's case.

Stone also distinguished mental from non-mental disorder automatism based on whether the person continues to present a danger to others, especially in light of the likelihood of recurrence of the trigger. Battered women might fare better on this test because the batterer's death will normally remove the trigger. Once the judge decides which form of automatism is to be put before the jury, they will then be told to decide whether the defence has been established.[417]

Rita managed to pass these numerous hurdles because her case was exceptional. The Crown's expert supported her claim to have dissociated and rejected the possibility that she was feigning. This meant that the evidentiary foundation was easily met without regard to whether Michael was both the trigger and the target of her homicidal act. The Crown's expert also declared Rita free from mental disorder, as did her own experts, making it easier for the judge to shift her claim to the non-mental disorder category without deciding whether she experienced an extremely shocking event.

On appeal, Denis Pilon for the Attorney General of Quebec argued that Justice Bédard had failed to instruct the jury that an extremely shocking blow was needed to find automatism. This demand for a significant triggering event can be particularly problematic for battered women who have survived by dissociating but who might not even be aware that they have deployed this mechanism of psychological self-defence. However, Rita's appeal judges rejected the argument because the Crown had conceded that her claim met the evidentiary threshold.[418] Furthermore, the judge had offered to the jury the opposing theories regarding the cause and timing of Rita's dissociation, including the Crown's position and the defence theory that "automatism can result from the build-up of events over a period of time which have a cumulative effect and then another further event(s) of an abusive (but not necessarily shocking) nature can trigger the non-mental disorder automatistic state."[419]

Self-Defence

Pilon met with success on his self-defence argument. The Quebec Court of Appeal in a 2-1 decision agreed that the trial judge had been in error in leaving self-defence with the jury since there was no evidentiary basis for it and since it was in conflict with automatism. Because Mendo had announced an intention to argue Battered Woman Syndrome in his opening address and the jury would have then listened to the evidence through the lens of self-defence, the majority found that the verdict would not necessarily have been the same had self-defence not been offered by the judge.[420] They ordered Rita back for a new trial.

One judge disagreed on the self-defence issue. Justice Thérèse Rousseau-Houle found that, since the defence experts testified that Rita suffered from Battered Woman Syndrome, which has been developed legally in the context of self-defence, it was not an error for the judge to explain self-defence to the jury.[421] It was also important to tell the jurors about the criteria for self-defence because Justice Bédard had been forced to tell them that Battered Woman Syndrome was not a defence, but self-defence was, after Mendo's opening address. More importantly, she noted that the evidentiary basis for self-defence need not come from the accused herself. Rita's children were in fear for her life; there was ample evidence that Michael had caused serious injuries and made death threats in the past; and the experts said that her repressed fear and her inability to find a way out caused her automatism.

Rita's Appeal to the Supreme Court of Canada

This dissent permitted Rita, like Margaret, to appeal to the top court. The Supreme Court of Canada, in a 6-1 decision, reversed the court below it. Justice Morris Fish for the majority accepted that self-defence and automatism are "incompatible in theory, though perhaps not always in practice,"[422] leaving open the possibility that battered women might be able to argue these defences in the alternative. Even if the trial judge had been wrong in law to put self-defence to the jury, the Crown had not met the heavy burden to show that the error had led to the acquittal: "In effect ... we are urged ... to find that the jury acquitted on what the Crown characterizes as an unreasonable basis rather than on the reasonable basis that is recognized by the Crown to exist."[423]

Rita's seven years of criminal litigation ended with the Supreme Court decision to reinstate her acquittal on the presumed basis of automatism.

Battered Women and Automatism

Rita's acquittal ought to encourage lawyers to consider automatism for women who experience memory loss when they kill abusive partners. However, automatism supported by Battered Woman Syndrome as a defence for other battered women is challenging: the burden of proof is high, and its use risks a finding of not criminally responsible on account of mental disorder.[424] Feminist commentators are wary of such "no intent" defences because they focus on the woman's internal emotional or mental state rather than the danger she faced.[425] But when the alternative is conviction, lawyers might have little choice.

Dissociation and flashbacks are symptoms of PTSD, Complex PTSD, and Battered Woman Syndrome, and they can be triggered by sensory experiences that resonate with the trauma. When women have experienced repeated trauma over years, many possible triggers can initiate dissociation because battered women are constantly exposed to stresses from their abusers. Blows to the head, previously inflicted brain injuries, or psychological shocks increase the chances of dissociation and thus warrant investigation by counsel as possible supporting evidence.

The Role of Head Injuries

One issue left unexplored in the trials of Margaret and Rita was the role that head injuries might have played in their dissociation. The long-term effects of concussions on professional male athletes have only recently become the subject of study and public concern, as reflected by media reports;[426] lesser known is that female athletes are at higher risk of concussion and experience more difficulty in recovery.[427] Women's experience of traumatic head injuries is poorly understood, according to Kathleen Monahan and K Dan O'Leary: "[T]he vast majority of head injury literature remains focused on the difficulties of men with head injuries and subsequent family disruption and adaptation."[428] Yet batterers are known to target women's heads[429] by slapping and punching their faces, kicking and slamming their heads into objects, shaking women violently, pulling their hair, and strangling them.

Traumatic brain injuries can usually be detected by a CT scan, but mild traumatic brain injury (MTBI) might not be discernible. The risk that MTBI will develop into post-concussive syndrome (PCS), "a complex set of physical, cognitive, behavioural and affective complaints observed in some MTBI patients,"[430] increases with successive concussions, family and social stress, and pressure to return early to pre-injury activities, among other factors.[431] When MTBI is not diagnosed, the chances of further brain injury are heightened because the person might engage in or be subjected to the same head trauma before her brain has time to heal.

While concussions and brain injuries in professional athletes are notoriously undiagnosed,[432] those of battered women are more so because they rarely seek medical treatment, especially when they "may not recognize their symptoms to be the result of their injuries."[433] Battered women thus commonly experience repeated head injuries,[434] increasing their risk of chronic brain trauma and cognitive losses.[435]

The cognitive, behavioural, and affective symptoms of PCS might appear weeks or even months after the trauma, making it difficult to connect the symptoms with the cause. Complicating diagnosis, these symptoms appear similar to and often overlap with those of PTSD, also experienced by battered women. The common symptoms include fatigue, sleep disturbance, headaches, dizziness, flashbacks, amnesia, dissociation,[436] and anxiety.[437] Almost half of battered women report having lost consciousness during a battering incident,[438] and from 35 percent[439] to 100 percent[440] of those who suffer head trauma display symptoms of MTBI or PCS. The resulting cognitive deficits include confusion, difficulties with concentration and abstract thinking such as projecting into the future and processing information, difficulties with retaining information and following directions, and emotional changes such as increased irritability, agitation, depression, and volatile mood swings.[441]

For battered women, the implications of brain injury might be threefold. First, their ability to make "informed, consistent choices of whether to leave or return to the batterer may be compromised," as might their ability to engage in safety planning and organize the resources needed to escape.[442] Second, the affective changes associated with PCS can lower the barriers to homicide when, for example, women experience dissociation, the inability to control their impulses,[443] and increased feelings of aggression.[444] Antidepressants prescribed to battered women can exacerbate these risks.[445] Third, although MTBI is often a hidden deficit, the symptoms of PCS can become evident when the person is under a severe stress,[446] such as that generated by a murder trial. Confusion, anxiety, and amnesia interfere with a woman's ability to instruct counsel and to testify coherently and credibly in her own defence.

Margaret and Rita both experienced dissociation at the time of their respective homicides, but evidently neither was screened for MTBI or PCS. There are certainly risks for women of being diagnosed with brain injuries, such as losing custody of their children,[447] but treatment can ameliorate these injuries, and in a murder trial the consequences of conviction can outweigh other risks. The testimony of Margaret and Rita was confused, disjointed, and frequently undermined by contradictory statements that they had made to psychiatrists and on the witness stand. Both women experienced "nervous breakdowns" and were prescribed anti-depressants and anti-anxiety medications over lengthy periods of time. Each had memory loss regarding very serious attacks to their heads that were observed and recalled by others. Expert evidence on the cumulative effects of multiple assaults to the head and prescription medications might have helped to explain the inconsistencies in the women's evidence and might have enhanced the legal defences available to these women.

Rita's acquittal raises the question of whether Lilian Getkate or Margaret Malott could have advanced automatism.[448] Lilian had no memory of shooting her husband while he slept, and this issue remained unexplored by her defence. She too was dragged by her hair, lifted by her neck, and throttled. Maury's attack on Lilian outside her daughter's bedroom would arguably qualify as a "psychological blow," but her lawyer might have worried that her confused claim that she heard someone in the house damaged her credibility. Margaret had no recall of her attempt to kill Sherwood, but the physical and psychological blows comprised by Paul's attacks to her head and neck, her drug use, and her homicidal act could have caused her dissociation. No doubt both women would have needed expert evidence like that offered by Dr Chamberland to identify dissociative amnesia and to link that state to their legitimate fear.

Rita's case also provides some support for advancing self-defence even in cases in which the woman has no conscious memory of the homicide. To exclude such a possibility outright fails to account for battered women's experiences.[449] Lenore Walker says that battered women repress fear to survive: "Most women who killed their batterers have little memory of any cognitive processes ... This desperate attempt at remaining unaware of their own unacceptable feelings is a measure of just how dangerous they perceive their own situation."[450] Mendo's strategy of using Battered Woman Syndrome in support of automatism implicitly suggested a motive of self-defence, supported by the testimony of Rita's children and experts.

Unlike Rita, Margaret will remain under life sentence for the rest of her days even though paroled. Paul attacked, threatened, and degraded her with impunity for years, causing injuries, addictions, and psychological impairments. Yet her culpability was assessed without regard to the many others who turned a blind eye to her endangerment and with a narrow focus on the few hours preceding her crimes. Her lawyers, like Rita's, fought for advances in defences for battered women. They argued for psychological self-defence, cumulative or slow burn provocation, and involuntary intoxication, all strategies whose potential remains to be explored by lawyers in future cases.

Conclusion

This book has profiled the civil litigation of Bonnie Mooney – a woman who did not kill – and the criminal trials of ten women who did. Mooney's case challenges many of the misperceptions about batterers and battered women and shows the stark choices that women face when men will not let them go. The acquittals allow glimpses of dilemmas that arise in these trials and the successful strategies of their respective counsel. Jamie Gladue's guilty plea was only one of the many such pleas in my sample where self-defence was plausible on the facts. Her case illustrates the biggest barrier to justice for battered women – the systemic disincentives to proceeding to a trial on the merits – even when women seem to have a case for self-defence.

Margaret Malott's murder conviction and the manslaughter convictions of Doreen Sorenson and Lilian Getkate show some of the outer limits of our legal system's ability to respond to the use of violence by battered women to free themselves. Jane Hurshman's jury acquittal from thirty years ago remains a high-water mark for battered women who kill. The *Lavallee* decision repudiated any "imminence" requirement for self-defence and suggested that the Nova Scotia Court of Appeal's decision overturning Hurshman's acquittal was no longer good law. Yet, among the nineteen women in my study who killed in non-confrontational situations, only two were acquitted at trial and not on self-defence.[1]

Women in my study whose convictions might be unjust, either because they pled guilty when they had arguable self-defence cases or because their trials were in some way unfair, might have (or have had) individual remedies. They include appeals[2] and applications under section 696 of the *Criminal Code* for conviction review by the Minister of Justice. Once a trial or guilty plea has concluded with a guilty verdict, however, the presumption of innocence is expended. Thus, appeals and ministerial reviews require the convicted person to carry the burden of persuading the decision maker that there was a legal error that likely affected the outcome. Furthermore, legal aid for appeals and section 696 applications is discretionary.

If a legal error is not identifiable, then the window for successful appeal becomes smaller. For example, the person cannot introduce new evidence if, by due diligence, it could have been adduced at trial.[3] In other words, women who end up in jail because of tactical decisions made by their lawyers cannot seek relief, unless their lawyers are judged to be incompetent. In my study, only four battered women succeeded in their appeals; two of these resulted in court-ordered acquittal or acquittal at the second trial.[4]

We therefore cannot count on the legal system to fix the wrongful convictions of battered women. We are also unlikely to see again an en bloc review of battered women's cases like Judge Ratushny's *Self-Defence Review*. The presumption is that lawyers and judges have now adjusted to the *Lavallee* decision and that women are receiving its benefits. A convicted battered woman is unlikely to have access to "innocence" initiatives that advocate for the wrongfully convicted for the simple reason that these projects use factual innocence as their criterion.[5] Battered women usually admit that they killed but challenge whether their act was morally or legally culpable. In this context, US advocates have compared individual executive clemency applications – the equivalent of ministerial reviews – to using a small bucket to bail unjustly imprisoned women from a rusty, sinking vessel. There are "holes in the hull" of the vessel caused by backlash against battered women, harsh sentencing policies, and legislative retractions of parole eligibility: "The best criminal justice boat imaginable will need bailing. The boat we are in has sizeable holes in the hull. The holes are bad criminal laws and policies. The boat will sink unless the hull is repaired."[6]

The transcripts of these eleven women's cases suggest the need for change to make a trial on the merits a more viable option so that women's self-defence claims can be fairly judged, especially those of Aboriginal women. Reforms to the criminal law governing homicide trials are needed to reflect women's experiences and resources are needed to assist defence lawyers in representing battered women. Finally, changes to policing and the social welfare system to enhance women's escape as an alternative to self-defensive violence must be pursued on an urgent basis.

Promoting Women's Access to a Fair Trial on the Merits

One might be forgiven for asking what is so bad about the fact that the majority of battered women plead guilty to manslaughter when many receive relatively light sentences? For example, among the forty-nine battered women who pled guilty to manslaughter or conspiracy to commit murder, eighteen received suspended sentences with probation or conditional sentences with "house arrest." Apart from the potential for a lighter sentence, some women will plead guilty regardless: some will do anything to avoid testifying and exposing their lives and those of their children and loved ones to the public glare of a homicide trial.[7] Others might wish to accept responsibility for the death and will plead guilty no matter how comprehensive any reforms might be.

Yet, even for those who receive suspended sentences or conditional imprisonment (house arrest), a criminal record has devastating consequences on the ability of women to support themselves and their families through employment. Moreover, the majority of women in my study who entered guilty pleas in fact received at least provincial jail time of less than two years. Twelve women were so sentenced, and another nineteen received federal sentences. Twelve of those nineteen given federal sentences, some as long as eight years, were Aboriginal women. Furthermore, fewer and fewer battered women are receiving compassionate sentences. This is because since 1995 anyone who uses a firearm to kill faces a minimum sentence of four years of incarceration if convicted of manslaughter,[8] making provincial sentences and conditional imprisonment unavailable. In fact, since 2008, conditional imprisonment has been unavailable to anyone convicted of a "serious personal injury offence,"[9] which includes manslaughter committed by a battered woman with a knife, for example.

Prison is a dehumanizing and destructive experience for anyone. Women who have survived intimate partner violence by resisting a man's dominion have a particularly hard time in prison because their defensiveness and "highly combative reactions" can be read as defiance and punished harshly.[10] Rather than rebuilding the woman's self-image, confidence, and sense of safety in the world, prison experiences such as being strip-searched can "break" a woman who steadfastly resisted being broken by her abuser.[11] In fact, some sentencing judges refuse to send battered women to jail precisely because they have already suffered the loss of liberty for years.[12]

For Aboriginal women, imprisonment perpetuates the experience of colonization, including the loss of their children.[13] Aboriginal women are more likely to be classified as maximum security once incarcerated, making their experiences particularly brutal.[14] When they emerge from prison, many battered women struggle to reunite with their children and survive at the margins of society,[15] even though most avoid future abusive relationships[16] and have negligible recidivism rates.[17]

Reducing the Pressure to Plead Guilty

When the stakes are this high for battered women, and when they are giving up their right to argue self-defence and the possibility of an acquittal, the "bargain" must be struck under the fairest conditions possible. Judge Lynn Ratushny called battered women's guilty pleas "worrisome" because "they are influenced in whole or in part by forces extraneous to the merits of the cases."[18] She made several recommendations to address what she perceived as the most significant contributor to battered women's guilty pleas – the mandatory life sentence for murder. Her recommendations remain urgent priorities.

Charge Battered Women with Manslaughter, Not Murder

Judge Ratushny recommended that Crown prosecutors prepared to accept a guilty plea to manslaughter downgrade murder to manslaughter if the woman's plea is "equivocal." A guilty plea is equivocal when the woman at the same time claims facts supporting a complete defence such as self-defence. This change would require provincial Attorneys General to implement new guidelines for prosecutors. It is true that charging battered women who kill with manslaughter rather than murder might require more resources because some women will go to trial if they are not faced with murder's mandatory life sentence. But if a manslaughter conviction is secured after the accused has rejected a Crown attorney's plea offer for manslaughter, then the Crown might argue for longer incarceration.[19] More importantly, a new norm of charging manslaughter rather than murder in these circumstances would go some distance toward removing from the criminal system what are arguably false guilty pleas or wrongful convictions.[20]

My study supports a bolder recommendation. Women living in violent relationships experience ongoing threats and unpredictable dangers. It might be impossible to pinpoint a final, fatal threat, yet the woman might well have been at risk for intimate femicide. As Dr Neilson testified in Donelda Kay's trial, "battering creates a whole atmosphere, a whole kind of surrounding environment of fear and control. And then it's within that, that whatever happens. So it's not like you feel afraid today, but then the battering stops, so you don't fear for your life. The fear is pervasive. It's always there."[21] Prosecutors should therefore consider eschewing murder charges in favour of manslaughter charges whenever there is evidence that the woman experienced battering, whether or not the facts that she alleges support self-defence.

Refrain from Charging Battered Women with First-Degree Murder

Another recommendation emerging from my study is that prosecutors should refrain from charging first-degree murder when battered women are on trial. With the possible exception of contract killings, there is no reasonable prospect of conviction for first-degree murder in these cases in Canada. Judges and jurors exposed to the horrors of battered women's lives rarely return first-degree murder verdicts. In fact, they rarely return even second-degree murder verdicts.[22] Laying first-degree murder charges functions only to put unbearable pressure on women to plead guilty to homicide to avoid the prospect of twenty-five years in prison without eligibility for parole.

Enact Judicial Discretion for Sentencing Battered Women Convicted of Murder

Judge Ratushny also recommended that Parliament enact an "escape hatch" for sentencing second-degree murder[23] when the person killed in response to aggression, whether or not the act fits within self-defence. The jury would be able to recommend, "in exceptional circumstances, that a person convicted of second degree murder be considered for leniency."[24] The judge would then have discretion to impose an appropriate sentence, with life imprisonment as the maximum, not the minimum, sentence. Judge Ratushny surveyed eleven other jurisdictions[25] and concluded that Canada's mandatory life sentence is "relatively severe."[26] For example, US federal sentencing guidelines and those of California, Florida, Kentucky, and Minnesota permit judges to depart from the mandatory sentence when the victim was the aggressor.

Judge Ratushny's recommendation received widespread support, even from victims' rights groups.[27] It should be pursued as a law reform effort but in a broadened form to include first-degree murder (see the discussion below) and any homicide offence carrying a mandatory sentence, such as the four-year mandatory prison sentence for manslaughter using a firearm.[28]

Because women need to use weapons to defend themselves, mandatory jail sentences for weapons use arguably has a discriminatory impact on women.[29]

There is reason to believe that battered women would indeed benefit from jury recommendations. Margaret Malott's jury took it upon themselves to call for a merciful sentence; Lisa Ferguson's jury handed a letter to the judge urging that wife assault be treated more seriously by the criminal justice system.[30] A bill proposed by Senator Mobina Jaffer that would enact a similar reform warrants public debate and support.[31]

Address Systemic Inequalities Faced by Aboriginal Women

The additional pressures on battered Aboriginal women to plead guilty demand special attention. Reducing these women's guilty pleas is a complicated problem because of the systemic issues facing Aboriginal people in the justice system. Nothing less than recognizing Aboriginal sovereignty, fairly resolving land claims, and redressing the wrongs of colonization will do. Justice Ratushny's recommendation that murder charges be downgraded to manslaughter when the Crown is willing to contemplate a guilty plea to manslaughter ought to apply with particular force to Aboriginal women. A generous approach to Aboriginal women who kill would acknowledge the roles that criminal law and colonization have played in producing the chaos and endangerment that sets the stage for women's homicidal violence. This approach would also respond to the systemic failure of emergency services for Aboriginal communities identified in several of the files in my study as having played a role in the demise of the victim.[32]

Furthermore, some Aboriginal women in my study had criminal records of prior violence,[33] often against the men whom they ultimately killed. Yet these prior convictions might also have resulted from guilty pleas by women not represented by counsel. There is no constitutional right to state-funded counsel to defend against charges that do not carry a substantial possibility of jail time.[34] The Manitoba Justice Inquiry pointed out the implications of such policies for Aboriginal people: when they are denied legal aid for minor offences, they tend to plead guilty and thereby accumulate criminal records that will, for future offences, result in incarceration.[35]

Given the violent milieu in which so many of these women committed assaults, and the failure of arrest and charging policies to distinguish between primary aggressors and women who defend themselves, the criminal records of Aboriginal women might unfairly represent them as "violent" or "criminal." The consequences of an assault conviction for a battered woman might not necessarily be jail, but they are nevertheless deadly serious because criminal conviction contributes to her entrapment in a relationship with a potentially lethal outcome.[36] A criminal record interferes with her ability to call for police intervention in future, with her ability to retain custody of her children should she escape, and with her murder trial should she kill in self-defence. A homicide trial is not the place to contest the fairness of earlier convictions, yet a woman's credibility can be undermined dramatically when the woman is questioned about her record should she take the witness stand to testify.

All of these consequences of criminal conviction are heightened for Aboriginal women because they face greater obstacles to police aid, higher exposure to extreme violence, and more negative stereotypes as women on trial for homicide. One way to address this problem is for provincial legal aid schemes to broaden their interpretations of "serious" offences to include charges of violence levied against women in abusive relationships, particularly Aboriginal women.

Improving Trial Fairness

There are other structural reforms to be undertaken to address prosecutorial practices and legal ambiguities identified in this study that might misinform the jury or unfairly prejudice a woman's trial.

Generate Ethical Constraints for the Prosecution of Battered Women

Mary Becker, a US lawyer who works with incarcerated battered women, argues that many of the questions and strategies pursued by prosecutors of battered women ought to be prohibited based on their unfair and misleading effects. If at a pre-trial hearing a judge finds evidence of abuse of the accused by the deceased, then the prosecutor should not be permitted to tell the jury that she was not a "real" battered woman because she had a job or friends or describe hers as simply an unhappy marriage.[37] Likewise, the fact that a woman has denied or minimized abuse in the past should be inadmissible as evidence of no abuse,[38] and her anger should be inadmissible to show that she was not afraid and therefore could not have acted in self-defence.[39]

According to Becker, battered women should be entitled to corrective instructions by judges to their juries to inform them, contrary to assertions by prosecutors, that "inconsistencies in memory about the shooting are normal for women who kill their abusers."[40] Prosecutorial "experts" who do not have significant training or experience with domestic violence and who are unfamiliar with the literature in the area can mislead the jury and distort the fact-finding process. Becker suggests that proposed experts must be carefully scrutinized to ensure that they are "truly qualified, with real knowledge and experience in the field."[41]

Many prosecutors in my study used the same strategies and arguments in spite of the admonishment by Justices McLachlin and L'Heureux-Dubé in *R v Malott*[42] that battered women must not be judged against a generalization or prototype. Furthermore, Crown experts with little or no experience with domestic violence testified as Battered Woman Syndrome experts. Two such experts provided testimony about the syndrome that was simply wrong. Most concerning, however, are the examples that my study provides of aggressive and demeaning prosecutorial treatment of battered women on trial. The worst such instance that I came across was that of Peter Barnes, who prosecuted Jean Millar at her second trial. He was disciplined for mocking Millar during her trial by setting up a "contest" in a nearby tavern. He invited police officers, the bar's owner, and bar patrons to submit questions to him to use in cross-examining Millar, for which he awarded prizes of coffee mugs.[43]

I support Becker's recommendations to curtail misleading Crown arguments even though in some of the cases in my study the jury did not succumb to them. Crown attorneys who prosecute battered women take on a difficult ethical role in which they face conflicting pressures regarding the public interest. Fair practices must be carved out in such a specific and highly charged area of prosecution. My study reveals other unfairnesses, whereby Crown objections to hearsay evidence and to leading questions can keep from the jury essential evidence that is difficult to extract otherwise from battered women.[44] These rules should be revisited by provincial Attorneys General responsible for prosecutorial guidelines for Crown prosecutors.

Reforming Criminal Law

My study suggests that the prior version of section 34 of the *Criminal Code* was a good law from the point of view of women who kill their abusers, though some issues required clarification. The 2012 reform of section 34, which came into force 11 March 2013, contemplates a broad notion of self-defence that can be invoked for any crime; it also abandons the language of "justification," arguably widening its scope. Section 34(1) now requires that the accused reasonably believe that force or threat of force is being used against her or another person; the act committed must be committed for the purpose of defending or protecting herself or another; and the act committed must be reasonable in the circumstances. Section 34(2) directs the court to assess the reasonableness of the accused's act by reference to, but not limited by, a list of factors, including the nature of the force or threat; its imminence; the availability of other means to respond; whether a weapon was used or threatened; the age, size, and gender of the parties; the nature and duration of the relationship, including prior interaction, communication, force, or threat; the proportionality of the person's response; and whether the anticipated threat or force was known to be lawful.[45]

This new defence will resolve some of the legal uncertainties revealed in my case studies. It will not, however, put to rest all the issues, and it will not diminish the continued relevance of the stories from the transcripts and the insights that they offer. Like all statutory reform, the new section 34 requires advocacy and judicial interpretation to implement it. Its application will be shaped by the prior case law because it relies on many of the same concepts and principles as did the former law.[46] As I review my recommendations on the law of self-defence, I will comment on whether and how the new law measures up.

Neither version of section 34 imposes a formal duty to retreat before using lethal violence, and this is critical for women: they need not leave or attempt to leave the relationship before resorting to homicide, and they need not exit their homes in anticipation of an attack. To disqualify women from self-defence because they failed to exit the relationship would amount to a duty of "pre-retreat" imposed on no others.[47] Thus, "why didn't she leave?" is not a legal question, making it critical that lawyers and judges tell the jury that it is legally irrelevant.

Neither version of section 34 carries a strict proportionality requirement, allowing, for example, a woman to kill to avoid further violence that risks force even if lethality is not necessarily anticipated. Although proportionality is relevant to reasonableness, abused women need not identify a new or increased threat to their lives: the law permits them to kill to avoid repetition of the everyday brutal attacks that many women in this study endured.[48] Besides, how could it be otherwise? Strangulation, head banging, and gun pointing by a batterer can all end fatally: it is entirely fortuitous whether these acts produce a woman's death.

Section 34(2) also permits resort to pre-emptive violence when force is threatened – the old version required threat of "grievous bodily harm," while the new version refers only to force or threat of force. Both versions theoretically permit a woman to kill a sleeping or unconscious partner. Canadian courts have ruled that imminence is relevant to but not determinative of whether the woman reasonably believed that she faced serious harm and whether she could not otherwise preserve herself.[49] The new law similarly deals with imminence as a component of "reasonableness." Some might find it troubling that a woman might kill before the onslaught of an attack by her incapacitated partner. US authors have made the analogy to international law principles authorizing pre-emptive strikes to avoid devastating loss of innocent lives:

> If a state has developed the capability of inflicting substantial harm upon another, indicated explicitly or implicitly its willingness or intent to do so, and to all appearances is waiting only for the opportunity to strike, pre-emptive use of force is justified. Admittedly, that line is not bright. Mistakes may be made. It is better, however, that the price of those mistakes be paid by states that so posture themselves than by innocent states asked patiently to await slaughter.[50]

As these authors have argued, why should women live in anticipatory dread and hypervigilance?[51] Is it not just to shift the risk of death to those men whose aggressions have created such dehumanizing fear in their female partners?[52]

Section 34's continued use of a mixed subjective-objective test to assess whether force was used or threatened and the reasonableness of the accused's response in the circumstances is also appropriate. Women's moral culpability is assessed not only against what women actually feared but also against what they reasonably feared, permitting the introduction of evidence about their group experiences and holding them to social expectations of reasonable restraint. I maintain that Canadians would not be well served by moving to a purely subjective test for self-defence. Batterers who kill their victims might be able to persuade jurors that they feared for their lives, while battered women's testimony unaided by objective expert evidence might not be as persuasive.[53]

In spite of the many strengths of Canada's self-defence law, there are some murky areas revealed by my study, some of which have arguably been resolved by the new law. One direction that Canada should not take, however, is that taken by two Australian states that have created either a new offence of "defensive homicide" or a defence of "killing for preservation in the context of an abusive relationship," which extends to killing in a non-confrontational situation.[54] Although both initiatives were motivated by the injustices faced by battered women, if successful they result in a manslaughter conviction rather than acquittal. Not only do these reconceptualizations fail to provide an advance for Canadian women, but also, in the case of "defensive homicide," the results thus far suggest that it is being taken up successfully by men who kill other men (twelve of the first thirteen cases[55]), thereby arguably resurrecting the provocation defence that Victoria had abolished.[56] In the defence of killing in the context of an abusive relationship, this new law can actually undo progressive results such as acquittals for battered women.[57]

Clarify the "Excessive Force" Rule for Self-Defence

An initial problem is that, if a woman is judged to have used "excessive force" in defending herself, she will be disqualified from self-defence and convicted of murder.[58] The law does allow some leeway here, because courts have said that a person afraid for her life need not measure "with nicety" the precise degree of force needed to repel the attack.[59] However, Judge Ratushny identified the "excessive force" cut-off as the stumbling block for some women in the *Self-Defence Review.*[60] Women in my study possibly either entered guilty pleas to manslaughter or were in fact disqualified from self-defence by their juries on this basis, as Margaret Malott might have been.

The new law does not address this issue directly. Codification of the excessive force rule is needed to ensure consistent application of the principle, with the proviso that those who overreact out of reasonable fear or confusion should be excluded from its reach.[61] Furthermore, we might consider adopting the defence of "excessive self-defence," as have three Australian states.[62] However, while this defence permits a halfway verdict of manslaughter if successful, there is a risk that jurors who might otherwise acquit a battered woman, even if her use of force is "excessive," will be tempted by this compromise verdict.

Identify Sexual Assault as "Grievous Bodily Harm"

The new law of self-defence makes it clear that women can kill in anticipation of marital rape, because section 34 is available to defend against any form of "force." None of the women in my study explicitly claimed that she killed her abusive partner to avoid rape, yet many of them experienced terrifying sexual violence from their abusers. For most if not all of them, marital rape was a fact of life – their lot as women and wives. Marital rape has been a crime for almost three decades in Canada, but multiple factors combine to immunize it from social condemnation and the scrutiny of criminal law.[63]

Canadian law was unclear on whether "grievous bodily harm" includes sexual assault. On the one hand, it must be "very severe or serious" bodily harm or injury, even if it is not permanent or life threatening.[64] On the other, "bodily harm" for the purposes of other offences in the *Criminal Code* is defined as "any hurt or injury, whether physical or psychological, that interferes in a substantial way with the integrity, health or well-being of a victim."[65] Consequently, a threat of rape has been held to amount to a threat to commit "serious bodily harm."[66] But is it "grievous bodily harm" for the purpose of self-defence?

Rita Graveline's judge understood that her husband's sexual abuse was relevant to her self-defence claim even though he did not frame it as "grievous bodily harm." No doubt, in some forms, such as those experienced by Donelda Kay and Margaret Malott, marital rape clearly causes "very serious" physical harm. But in most cases the real harm of marital rape is the profound psychological harm that women endure in consequence. The jurisprudence on self-defence claims when women have stabbed men non-fatally who tried to sexually assault them is mixed.[67]

Although the new law does not circumscribe the kind of force entitling a woman to use self-defensive violence, the question of proportionality and the availability of other options will still be relevant to whether her homicidal act was reasonable. Clear judicial interpretation must settle whether, in all humanity, women are entitled to kill to avert sexual assault, including marital rape.[68]

Self-Defence Must Be Available for First-Degree Murder

Another question is whether self-defence is available for premeditated or contract murder. The main objection is that such murders are particularly heinous and deserving of denunciation: who has the right to take the law into his or her own hands and plan or purchase another's demise? Self-defence is also said to be counterindicated by detached contemplation or planning.[69] On the technical side, however, self-defence was not and is not now precluded by section 34 for first-degree murder. A woman might reasonably fear force and might fairly conclude that she has no other option that guarantees her safety. Now that self-defence is no longer cast as a justification, any last barrier to its use for first-degree murder has been removed.[70]

A number of women in my study were charged with premeditated murder and still argued self-defence, some successfully. No judge whom I am aware of instructed jurors that, if they found that the murder had been "planned and deliberate," self-defence would be unavailable. It seems the expanded understanding of self-defence to encompass pre-emptive killing can include premeditated homicide. None of the women in my study who were involved in contract killing went to trial on self-defence, so there is no clear law one way or another on this point. But this might be the only way to save their lives or those of their loved ones for women like Bonnie Mooney, who are told that the most the legal system can do is jail her threatener for a few months. Our law should affirm clearly that self-defence is available for all forms of homicide.

Self-Defence Should Be Available for Protecting Children and Others

Women who kill to defend their children or others are now, theoretically, granted the same right of "self-defence" as those who defend their own lives, according to the new section 34. Both Kim Kondejewski and Lilian Getkate acted in defence of their children, but the former defence in section 37 of the *Criminal Code* was more narrowly cast than self-defence. It required strict proportionality between the threatened harm and that caused, leading their lawyers to back away from "defence of others" and instead rely on self-defence. Self-defence worked for Kondejewski but not for Getkate. And even in Kondejewski's case, defence of her children seemed to be her true motivation. Another limit of section 37 was that it would not have helped Mooney had she defended Hazel against Kruska's murderous rage since it was confined to the defence of those under one's "protection." The new section allows for protection of others without qualification; it will be up to defence lawyers to advance it for women who kill to protect their children, family members, or friends and to argue that it must be informed by a battered woman's experiences and perceptions.

Consider Reconceptualizing Self-Defence

A related question is whether battered women are entitled to kill in psychological self-defence, as asserted by Malott's lawyer and argued by psychologist Charles Ewing. The legal answer to this question again depends on how "force" is interpreted. As discussed, "psychological injury" is a form of "serious bodily harm" that arguably could ground self-defence. When the imminent psychological destruction of another is occasioned by a pattern of threats and coercion, or when it has been hastened by traumatic brain injury caused by the abuser, should criminal law condemn the woman who kills to preserve the last shred of her personhood? The law of self-defence can potentially encompass psychological self-defence, though there are clear difficulties in assessing the degree and certainty of the psychological destruction of another person, for this concept is dependent on somewhat abstract and elusive understandings of the "self."[71]

What about the situation in which a woman kills her abuser to achieve her liberty? The deprivation of another person's freedom by physical restraint is a crime, but is it "force" as understood by the law? Captivity by Coercive Control in the absence of force is not itself a crime, though Evan Stark argues that it should be.[72] A man's use of Coercive Control is strongly indicative of potential lethality, especially when combined with separation or the threat of separation and an available weapon. It has been used in support of claims that women killed to avoid death or serious bodily harm, though it does not seem to have been used successfully as a stand-alone defence. A change in the law of self-defence might be unnecessary to permit women to argue that they killed in psychological self-defence or to escape a man's Coercive Control; nevertheless, additional reforms in the law might usefully clarify the legitimate boundaries of self-defence. For example, five of the Australian states permit the use of self-defence for acts taken to "prevent or terminate the unlawful deprivation of liberty," though one of these states permits this form of self-defence only for manslaughter, not murder.[73]

Sharing Successful Defence Strategies
The selected transcripts reveal strokes of genius by defence lawyers and creative strategies that can serve other lawyers who represent battered women. Both Greg Brodsky and Don Worme made the difficult decision not to put their clients on the stand, yet they prevailed. Alexander Pringle secured acquittal for Denise Rain without calling an expert witness to interpret her actions.[74] Defence lawyers argued (unsuccessfully) for their clients to sit at the counsel table instead of in the prisoner's box. More likely to persuade trial judges was the oft-made argument that the defence should be permitted to open its case to the jury immediately after that of the Crown in light of the complexity of battered women's defences. Richard Wolson persuaded

Kim Kondejewski's judge to allow him to make additional closing remarks to the jury after the Crown closed.

Other defence strategies revealed by the transcripts that might be pursued in additional studies can be briefly mentioned here. For example, both Marino Mendo for Rita Graveline[75] and Leonard Shore, counsel for Lisa Ferguson,[76] succeeded in arguing that they should be entitled to challenge potential jurors for cause on the basis of myths and stereotypes about wife battering and battered women. If nothing else, this strategy alerts jurors to the influence of biases and misconceptions, whether conscious or unconscious, especially important given the prevalence of wife battering and the strong possibility that actors in the trial have experienced, perpetrated, or witnessed wife battering.[77] Fagie Fainman, counsel for Mary Ann Keeper, persisted through Saskatchewan's longest sentencing hearing on record (twelve days and fifteen witnesses), over the objections of the prosecutor and a very frustrated trial judge, to challenge the rules of evidence repeatedly so that she could get before the judge the full context of Keeper's act of homicide.[78] Victoria Seddon's lawyer, John Buchanan, managed to secure his client's acquittal on the basis of self-defence by relying on the physical evidence that his client was dissociated at the time of the homicide and had no account to provide of her actions.[79]

Vigorously Protect Women's Rights to Counsel and to Silence

Most of the women in my study succumbed to police pressure to confess and/or to answer questions about the abuse that they had experienced at the hands of the deceased. Their answers were invariably used to discredit and confuse them at trial. Clients who confess or whose accounts change over time are, of course, perennial problems for defence lawyers. The problem is more acute for battered women who are not only easily intimidated by males in authority but also still in trauma, might never before have broken the silence, and have repressed much of their suffering to survive. It is unreasonable and unfair to expect such a person to give an airtight account of the homicide and decades of battering in the hours, days, or even weeks after the homicide.

Lawyers should get to the police station when a woman is arrested for murder to try to prevent her from answering police questions as best they can within the narrow window afforded to them.[80] They must also get their clients released on bail urgently, because the longer they remain in custody the more damage can be done to available defences. Lawyers should avoid offering their clients for evaluation by a Crown expert at this point.

Seek Support for the Woman to Promote Disclosure and Recovery

Once the woman is released and awaiting trial, a defence lawyer can assist her in disclosing painful information by asking her to write out her story in the privacy of her own home, keyed by questions prepared by counsel. Jane Hurshman's story emerged through a stack of notebooks that Hurshman filled for Alan Ferrier, as did Margaret Malott's. This kind of written record can also assist any experts who interview the woman and her trial lawyer in keeping the basic narrative of her life straight. In many of the transcripts, confusion and contradiction plagued the women's accounts, allowing the prosecutor to challenge the woman's veracity and unfairly cast her evidence as unreliable.

In preparation for trial, battered women need a counselling relationship to safely process the abuse that they have survived so that they can testify in their own defence. Cases can be lost on the basis that the accused woman is simply too traumatized or drugged to properly assist in her own defence.[81] Women who have received counselling can be accused of having been "primed" to present themselves as battered women or as having acted in self-defence.[82] However, if a woman has not had the opportunity to reflect with counselling support, she might still be grieving her partner's death and engage in self-blame, making her an easy target for cross-examination. There is also the risk that she will fail to recall helpful information for her defence. Women who have not had the opportunity to work through the aftermath of battering can also make poor witnesses if a prosecutor can easily trigger them into a defensive stance in front of the jury by, for example, accusing them of exaggerating the abuse.

Consider Screening for Traumatic Brain Injury

If their clients have endured blows to the head or strangulation, defence lawyers should have them screened for traumatic brain injury.[83] Confirmed brain injury can assist the woman in understanding her limitations and indicate the need for rehabilitative services.[84] Brain injury can point to an automatism defence, whether based on an immediately preceding physical cause or a psychological blow. It can also signal to defence counsel the need for expert testimony to contextualize for the jury the woman's memory or cognitive difficulties. No doubt women's lack of recall of the homicide plays a significant role in the decision to plead guilty and avoid trial. As this book has shown, women experience blackout or memory loss from many causes – psychological distress, alcohol or drug abuse, and traumatic brain injury.

It is daunting to defend a woman who cannot recall the homicide, but the trials of Gladys Heavenfire and Rita Graveline[85] show that it can be done.

Consider Alternative Forms of Corroboration and Expert Evidence
Defence lawyers must anticipate that the effects of long-term abuse inevitably include repression, memory loss, minimization, and confusion about what happened and when. In this context, lawyers will want to identify all possible sources of corroboration, whether by witnesses, diaries, medical and psychological records, photographs, and phone records, among other sources, to shore up the woman's testimony or indeed supplant it.

Expert evidence must be called to address the specific deficiencies in the woman's evidence and to situate those deficiencies in the context of battered women's experiences. The woman's counsellor might not be the most appropriate person to prepare an expert report and testify on her behalf. Considerations include whether the person has the professional credentials needed to qualify as an "expert" in the area that will be used to frame the woman's evidence; whether the person will be a credible expert in front of a jury; whether the witness's neutrality will be challenged by reason of the counselling relationship; whether the expert can assist with problematic aspects of the woman's testimony; and whether the woman can endure a trial without the ongoing support of her counsellor, who will be unable for a time to discuss the trial and her evidence with her.

Defence lawyers need to select the right form of expert testimony to support their cases, whether it is delivered in psychological terms or as social context evidence about battered women's realities and the available alternatives. Juror studies predict that women are more likely to be acquitted or convicted of manslaughter rather than murder when either form of expert testimony is used.[86] In choosing a theory and the expert who will deliver it, defence lawyers will want to carefully weigh the advantages and disadvantages of using Battered Woman Syndrome, Complex PTSD, social context evidence of battering, or Coercive Control.[87] Battered Woman Syndrome remains a compelling theory because it is better known to lawyers, judges, and laypersons and because it is specifically aimed at the problem areas for battered women of demonstrating their ability to predict their partners' violence, their reasons for staying, and their lack of reasonable alternatives.

Feminist legal analysts have advanced social context evidence about the effects of battering and the realities of women's alternatives as a preferable alternative to psychology-based defences for many reasons.[88] It has been argued that social context evidence avoids individualizing the experience of social entrapment of battered women and pathologizing the woman as suffering from a psychological condition. Regina Schuller's research supports this analysis; although her juror studies found that jurors render more lenient verdicts regardless of the form of expert evidence, those hearing Battered Woman Syndrome evidence were more likely to find the woman not guilty on the basis of insanity than those who heard social context evidence.[89] Social context evidence can also facilitate a broader inquiry into the impacts of women's inequality and the systemic forces that entrap battered women.

When there is little evidence of physical violence, or when the woman cannot, for whatever reason, conform to the stereotypes associated with Battered Woman Syndrome, either Complex PTSD or Coercive Control can be more compelling theories. These theories describe how men capture women without necessarily resorting to extreme violence, and they focus on abusive men's strategic behaviours to hold women in captivity. By analogizing to other forms of captivity not charged with gender, Complex PTSD allows jurors to see how the deceased deliberately "broke" the accused, a woman who was not prepared mentally or physically as a soldier or a political activist for prolonged isolation and torture. Both this theory and Coercive Control defuse the question of whether the accused is a "real" battered woman, a good mother, or a wholly "innocent victim" by showing that any woman can be "captured" in the right circumstances and that abusers tailor their strategies accordingly. Aboriginal women can be subjected to racist abuse and forced to give up their children, as was Gladys Heavenfire; Asian women can be prohibited from cooking their food or displaying pictures of their families;[90] women can be tormented through their phobias or required to betray those whom they love.

Complex PTSD and Coercive Control might be preferable when it is hard to pinpoint a final or catastrophic threat, when women kill essentially to free themselves from captivity and perpetual dread. Complex PTSD and Coercive Control are also more amenable when the accused does not present as a "victim," either because she has recovered her health and confidence prior to trial or because she is defensive or verbally assertive.

Lawyers defending Aboriginal women must ground their defences in an awareness of the impacts of colonial history and racism on their clients' lives and on potential jurors.[91] Lawyers who attempt to run a "race-neutral" defence might be condemning their clients to conviction. Aboriginal women need experts who are knowledgeable about Aboriginal women's experiences, who can provide culturally appropriate interpretations of the woman's actions so that they fit within whatever theory counsel is presenting to the jury. Without this assistance, defence lawyers might miss the meanings of Aboriginal women's words,[92] be unable to convey the cumulative effect of multiple abuses on a woman's perception of danger, not realize that there is no safe place for Aboriginal women to escape to, and not appreciate that the woman has learned the hard way that no one is going to help her.

Develop a Strong and Consistent Defence Narrative
Some lawyers and judges, in the cases that I studied, have referred to the "battered spouse syndrome." Defence lawyers have nothing to gain and much to lose by slipping into gender neutrality. Acknowledging that women are capable of violence and that some men experience abuse from their female partners is a far cry from the proposition that men are subject to escalating endangerment and are socially, economically, and politically entrapped. Furthermore, there are no large-scale studies of "battered men" to draw on to assess whether and to what extent men's experiences might be similar to women's.

When lawyers use gender-neutral terms, they implicitly suggest to jurors that men's and women's experiences are interchangeable. Jurors in turn can minimize the violence to which the woman was subjected and overestimate her avenues of escape. Similarly, introducing expert evidence on "battering and its effects" without a gendered or feminist analysis of women's group experiences is risky. By failing to challenge the male-centred paradigm that shaped the law of self-defence and the sexist beliefs and stereotypes about "good" women and mothers that condition the police and criminal justice system response to battered women, this type of evidence can fall short of putting a woman's homicidal act in full context.[93] Gena Rachel Hatcher cautions that this form of evidence can fail to capture "how the experiences of sexism, subordination and certain societal pressures and assumptions are reflected in the perceptions and behaviours of a battered woman."[94]

The successful lawyers in my study were those who advocated tirelessly and fearlessly throughout the woman's trial and conveyed unequivocal belief in her innocence. Those who developed a strong narrative and made use of rhetorical devices seemed to persuade the juries. None of these lawyers used neutral language in the opening or closing address.

Safety and Freedom for Battered Women

Experts on men's use of battering and Coercive Control are the front-line workers of the independent women's movement. These are the feminist activists whose collective experience of more than forty years in rape crisis centres, women's shelters, and transition homes has informed a sophisticated analysis of male violence against women, the criminal justice system, and which steps must be taken if we are to free women.[95]

On a daily basis, front-line women listen to women's accounts of male violence and help these women to strategize for their own safety. They intervene with the police and prosecutors to persuade them to follow the protocols that they pressured these institutions to adopt in the first place. They attend court with women, standing with them, and supporting them through brutal processes. They assist women in finding homes, child care, and social welfare. They grieve when women are unable to escape and when they are murdered.

The problems identified by feminist activists are crystal clear. Over and over, they expose and condemn women's inequality, discriminatory police and prosecutorial responses, and the inadequacy of our social welfare system as significant barriers to battered women's safety. We do not have the legal mechanisms to keep dangerous abusers incarcerated and away from the women and children whom they are bent on harming, even when the criminal justice system is functioning at its best. We have yet to create consistent police responses to battered women who ask for intervention, so their endangerment is escalated when they ask for but are denied police aid. We also have no mechanisms of accountability for police and prosecutors who fail women by not following those protocols in place, even when their actions amount to legal negligence and grave harm results. Although the police have suffered serious losses of public confidence in the past decade as abuses and police failures have come to light, they continue to resist civilian-based accountability mechanisms. Women's demands for a robust, liveable guaranteed minimum income and a national day care program have been ignored by politicians.

So we can expect to see cases every year in which, even with our best efforts, battered women – and sometimes their children, family members, and friends – are murdered by men who will not let them go. It will take ordinary Canadians to insist that we find ways to stop violent men, that the police and prosecutors follow rules, and that, when they breach them, they be held accountable – like everybody else. Batterers know that they are mostly above the law and act with impunity.

Support the Independent Women's Movement and Invest in Women's Shelters, Housing, Social Welfare, and Access to Child Custody
The most important thing that we can do to improve battered women's safety is to respect the leadership of the independent women's movement on these issues, which means seeking their views in the media, prioritizing their reform proposals, and funding their organizations and research. The results of a global study of seventy countries over forty years indicate that the most important factor in promoting change with respect to male violence against women is not the wealth of a given nation, the election of more progressive governments, or the number of women elected to political office. Rather, the presence of a strong, automonous women's movement, "able to articulate and organize around their top priorities as women, without having to answer to broader organizational concerns or men's needs," was the key to social, legal, and political change regarding violence against women, as demonstrated by data of "unprecedented" scope.[96]

We require a massive investment in shelters and transition houses to address the inability of existing shelters to meet the crushing need. The rate at which women kill their male partners has declined where escape routes such as shelters have been created.[97] While intimate femicide has declined, it has done so at a far lesser rate than that of male partners. The most recent Canadian data indicate that the disproportionate rate at which men kill their female partners as opposed to women who kill their male partners now stands at 6:1. Statstics Canada has reported that, for the period 2010-11, the number of intimate partner homicides has remained stable but that the data show significant changes by sex: "The rate of intimate partner homicides committed against females increased by 19%, the third increase in four years, while the rate for male victims declined by almost half."[98]

We also need humane social welfare and public housing policies to allow women and their children to live free of violence and with dignity. Welfare rates and policies must not further women's social entrapment by shaming women, coercing them, or forcing them back to abusers to survive. We need child custody principles that respect women's caregiving roles by ensuring that children stay with their primary caregivers as a rule and that take seriously the impacts of men's abuse on their children as well as their former partners. As early as 1878, Frances Power Cobbe argued for a bill whereby "the injured wife would have the *very thing she really wants*, namely, security against further violence, coupled with the indispensable custody of her children (without which, no protection of herself would offer a temptation)."[99] Battered women need to know where they stand legally before they decide how to protect themselves and their children, and they need to have some confidence in their safety if we are to prevent homicide as a last resort.

Reconceptualize the Crime of Battering

Criminal laws must attempt to capture battering as an ongoing crime of illegal domination as opposed to one focused on discrete incidents of serious assault.[100] The criminal law of assault as currently constituted cannot respond adequately to minor and frequent assaults, marital rape, threats, and psychological abuse deployed as part of a pattern of Coercive Control and intimidation.[101] A crime of Coercive Control, as proposed by Evan Stark, would be one way forward. This offence would recognize the harm of "captivity," including its lethal potential, beyond broken bones or black eyes. It would treat Coercive Control as a crime against women's liberty rights, akin to kidnapping,[102] and would carry much more serious sentences than those currently imposed for wife assault. France has enacted a criminal offence of "mental harassment" aimed at forms of psychological abuse such as repeated humiliation, verbal abuse, or enforced isolation,[103] though this new crime is not yet rigorously prosecuted by authorities.[104] The details of any new crime would need to be worked out,[105] but the idea of trying to reconceptualize wife battering deserves attention and debate.

Develop and Enforce Police and Prosecutorial Protocols for Wife Battering

Prosecutors and the police need arrest, charging, and prosecutorial policies that eschew "gender neutrality" and instead recognize the gendered nature of battering.[106] Decisions regarding bail and sentencing must be informed by the best risk assessment tools available to predict the level of danger that the woman faces.[107] The police must adopt arrest policies that target the primary abuser;[108] they must stop arresting battered women who seek their aid; and they must follow through with charges that reflect the seriousness of the man's actions. When men strangle their partners to the point of unconsciousness, attempted murder ought to be the charge. When women try to withdraw charges, the police and prosecutors need to assess the reason for the withdrawal and whether there is anything that can be done to protect the woman and her family.[109] If not, they need to tell Canadians loudly and clearly that the criminal law as currently cast cannot protect women from their batterers. Their experience and political clout are critical to supporting front-line workers, educating the public, and demanding new solutions.

Promote Women's Equality

Most importantly, women's equality – economically, politically, legally, and socially – is a necessary condition for the elimination of male violence and women's need to resort to homicide to extricate themselves. In a speech given to the Canadian Bar Association a year after the *Lavallee* decision was released, Justice Wilson said that "[t]he economic, political and social inequality of women both fuels and justifies violence against women in society which values power over all else." As long as women are systematically subordinated to men, "they will suffer, at the minimum, ongoing physical domination and, at the maximum, physical and sexual abuse."[110]

Evan Stark and Anne Flitcraft argue that we must do more than protect women's safety, for what is safety without freedom? They state that "enormous hazards lie ahead if shelter is promoted as a concealed refuge from the violence of male-dominated family life, shelter occupants are defined as victims rather than as survivors, safety is emphasized over liberation, and a simulation of community is offered in lieu of direct challenges to existing community power structures."[111] It is indisputable that societies in which women enjoy greater equality also record lower rates of male violence.[112] We simply cannot expect to reduce or eliminate wife battering through criminal justice initiatives: we must support women's aspirations for freedom and equality and reshape our social, economic, legal, and political policies accordingly. There is no shortcut.

Believe Battered Women

Moral courage is required all around: from the police, who need to make decisions about whom to arrest; from prosecutors, who must insist on charges that reflect the full brutality of some men's acts; from politicians, who should support unpopular welfare programs and equality initiatives for women; from all of us, whose most important political act is to believe women.[113] Believe battered women when they say that they are in danger. Believe them when they fear for their children's safety. Believe them when they tell us that they had no other option than to kill. As Elizabeth Dermody Leonard argues, "[a] woman who is told 'If I can't have you, nobody can' and who manages to survive that final deadly assault by her male intimate is the closest voice we have to the many women who do not live through that last violent assault. The more we learn from their lives, the more lives can be saved."[114]

Battered women's moral courage deserves our respect. While other vigilantes might escape criminal condemnation and are often seen as folk heroes, battered women are rarely treated in this manner.[115] Elisabeth Ayyildiz argues that a battered woman should be hailed as "a defender of justice, one repairing the moral order when the state has failed to do so."[116] When women kill to save their own lives, they assert that they matter, that their lives count – even more than the lives of their abusers. After everything that their batterers have done to them, told them, and called them, after their own efforts to please, to placate, to abnegate themselves to meet the unreasonable demands of petty tyrants, they have somehow taken a stand for their own humanity and saved themselves. And for this we should also be grateful.

Appendix

Women's homicide cases in which there was evidence of prior abuse, 1990-2005

Name (Year/ Location)	Charges laid	Outcome	Sentence	Prior abuse	Alteration at time	Member of racialized group	Defence argument/ basis for mitigation of sentence	Source
Mary Altenhofen (1993/ Calgary, AB)	MANS	A	None	Y	Y	Aboriginal	Self-defence/BWS	"Battered Wife Acquitted in Spouse's Death," *[The] Vancouver Sun* (23 September 1993) A8
CMA (2005/ Whitehorse, YK)	N/A	GP-MANS	5 years in prison	Y	Y	Aboriginal	Remorse/ rehabilitation	*R v CMA*, 2005 YKSC 58
Jocelyne Bennett (1993/ Ottawa, ON)	2nd DM	GP-MANS	Suspended sentence: 3 years' probation	Y	N	N/A	Spousal abuse/BWS	*R v Bennett*, [1993] OJ No 1011 (Ct Just)
Jessica Bigstone (2004/ Edmonton, AB)	2nd DM	GP-MANS	5 years in prison	Y	Y	N/A	She had an "utterly tragic life, growing up in an alcoholic family with an abusive father."	Gordon Kent, "Mom Gets Five-Year Term for Killing Husband," *[The] Edmonton Journal* (5 May 2004) B2
Bernice Bird/Bryd* (2005/ Winnipeg, MB)	2nd DM	GP-MANS	Conditional sentence: 2 years less a day	Y	Y	Aboriginal	Spousal abuse/remorse; she was "justified in taking defensive action" but force used was excessive.	*R v Byrd*, [2006] MJ No 102 (QB)

Name (Year/Place)			Sentence					Citation
Peggy Bone (1996/Fort McMurray, AB)	2nd DM	GP-MANS	4 years in prison	Y	N/A	Aboriginal	N/A	R v Bone, [1996] AJ No 1306 (QB); Fort McMurray Court Registry File No 9613-007c00101 (oral communication 2009)
Bonnie Jean Boyd (1998/Fort McMurray, AB)	1st DM	C-MANS	Conditional sentence: 18 months	Y	Y	N/A	Spousal abuse/BWS	"Conditional Sentence in Abuse Slaying," [The] Edmonton Journal (17 January 1998) A5
Emily Bradford* (1995/Lancer, SK)	2nd DM	A	None	Y	Y	N/A	Self-defence/BWS	R v Bradford, Transcript of Charge to the Jury, QB No 922 Saskatchewan Court of Queen's Bench, Swift Current, 19 February 1996; Dan Zakreski, "Swift Current Mayor at Centre of Bizarre Case: Millionaire Cattleman Charged in Suspected Plot against Official," The [Saskatoon] Star Phoenix (28 October 2001) A1
Camellia Britt (2002/Kirkland Lake, ON)	1st DM	GP-MANS	Suspended sentence: 18 months in substance abuse treatment; 3 years' probation	Y	Y	Aboriginal	Spousal abuse/BWS	Canadian Press, "Northern Ontario Woman Sentenced to 18 Months Drug Treatment for Manslaughter" (22 January 2002) newswire; R v Britt, [2000] OJ No 4742 (Sup Ct)

Abbreviations used in this Appendix are listed on page 336.

Name (Year/Location)	Charges laid	Outcome	Sentence	Prior abuse	Alteration at time	Member of racialized group	Defence argument/ basis for mitigation of sentence	Source
Emily Brown (1991/Oak Lake Reserve, MB)	MANS	GP-MANS	Suspended sentence: 3 years' probation	Y	Y	Aboriginal	Spousal abuse/BWS	Nilu Balsara, "Killed Abusive Husband, Manitoba Woman Freed: Judge Ruled Justice Would Not be Served by Jail Sentence," *The Globe and Mail* (12 August 1991) A5
Maura Silvana Cabrera (2003/Welland, ON)	1st DM	GP-MANS	Conditional sentence: 2 years less a day	Y	N	Guatemalan	Spousal abuse	*R v Cabrera*, [2003] OJ No 4510 (Sup Ct Just)
Donnaline Caplette (1995/Vancouver, BC)	2nd DM	GP-MANS	Suspended sentence: 1 year probation	Y	N	Aboriginal	Spousal abuse	*R v DEC*, [1995] BCJ No 1074 (SC)
Melissa Cattleman (2005/Calgary, AB)	2nd DM	GP-MANS	6 years in prison	Y	Y	Aboriginal	None accepted	Daryl Slade, "Tearful Wife Jailed for Fatal Stabbing," *[The] Calgary Herald* (20 December 2005) B3
Linda Côté (1995/Morin Heights, QC)	MANS	A	None	Y	Y	N/A	Self-defence/BWS	Marie-Claude Girard, "Même après avoir tué son mari, Linda Côté vivait dans la terreur," *La Presse* (5 July 1995) A3

Name (year/location)	Charge	Plea	Sentence				Defence	Citation
Nancy Cowley (1995/Kenora, ON)	2nd DM	GP-MANS	7 months in prison	Y	Y	N/A	Spousal abuse/BWS	R v Cowley, [1995] OJ No 592 (Ct Just)
Merna Joyce Crowchief (2004/Calgary, AB)	2nd DM	GP-MANS	3 years in prison	Y	Y	Aboriginal	Spousal abuse	R v Crowchief, 2005 ABCA 92
Mary Deschenes (2001/Iqaluit, NU)	2nd DM	C-MANS	Conditional sentence: 9 months	Y	Y	Aboriginal	Self-defence	Greg Younger-Lewis, "Iqaluit's Mary Deschenes Dies at 44," [The] Nunatsiaq News (4 June 2004) online http://www.nunatsiaq.com
Angela Drake (1995/Niagara Falls, ON)	2nd DM	GP-MANS	Suspended sentence: 3 years' probation	Y	Y	N/A	Spousal abuse/BWS	R v Drake, [1995] OJ No 4375 (Ct Just)
Wanda Lee Dunlap (1991/Truro, NS)	2nd DM	GP-MANS	1 year in prison	Y	Y	N/A	Spousal abuse: "she was in fear that the deceased was going to attack her and cause serious harm to her."	R v Dunlap (1991), 101 NSR (2d) 263 (SC(AD))
Lisa Ferguson* (1997/Woodlawn, ON)	2nd DM	C-MANS	Conditional sentence: 2 years less a day	Y	N	N/A	Self-defence/BWS	R v Ferguson, [1997] OJ No 2488 (Ct Just)
Rachael Fisher (2003/Thunder Bay, ON)	2nd DM	GP-MANS	8 years in prison	Y	Y	Aboriginal	None accepted	R v RE [2004] OJ No 544 (Sup Ct Just)

Name (Year/Location)	Charges laid	Outcome	Sentence	Prior abuse	Alteration at time	Member of racialized group	Defence argument/basis for mitigation of sentence	Source
Kerri-Lee Foy* (2002/Toronto, ON)	1st DM	GP-MANS	6 years in prison	Y	Y	N/A	Remorse/spousal abuse	R v Foy, [2002] OJ No 4004 (Sup Ct Just)
Lilian Getkate* (1998/Ottawa, ON)	1st DM	C-MANS	Conditional sentence: 2 years less a day	Y	N	No	Provocation; no intent; self-defence	R v Getkate, [1998] OJ No 6329 (Ct Just)
Victoria Wynter Gil (2003/Windsor, ON)	2nd DM	Charges stayed	None	Y	Y	N/A	No reasonable prospect of conviction/Gil earlier acquitted for assault against same man based on self-defence.	Jake Rupert, "Gil 'Relieved' as Crown Drops Murder Charge," The Ottawa Citizen (8 August 2003) B1
Arlene Rosa Gilpin (2002/Anaham Reserve, BC)	N/A	GP-MANS	Conditional sentence: 2 years less a day	Y	Y	Aboriginal	Remorse/rehabilitation/spousal abuse	R v Gilpin, 2002 BCSC 1876
Jamie Tanis Gladue* (1997/Nanaimo, BC)	2nd DM	GP-MANS	3 years in prison	Y	Y	Aboriginal	Remorse/victim provocation	R v Gladue, [1999] SCR 688
Kathleen Gonzales (1992/Courtenay, BC)	MANS	A	None	Y	Y	N/A	Self-defence/BWS	Canadian Press, "Battered Wife Cleared of Man-slaughter," The [Toronto] Star (30 January 1992) A12

Evelyn Rose Graff (1993/Medicine Hat, AB)	1st DM	GP conspiracy to M	10 years in prison	Y	N	N/A	Spousal abuse	Kim Lunman, "After the Abuse, a Prison Term," [The] Edmonton Journal (14 February 1993) A5
Rita Graveline* (2001/Gatineau, QC)	2nd DM	A	None	Y	N	No	Automatism/self-defence/BWS	R v Graveline, 2006 SCC 16
Suzanne Hay (1998/Wetaskiwin, AB)	1st DM	GP-MANS	4 years in prison	Y	N	N/A	Spousal abuse/victim provocation	Gordon Kent, "Battered Wife Gets Four Years in Jail," [The] Edmonton Journal (24 November 1998) A1
Gladys Heavenfire* (1991/Calgary, AB)	2nd DM	A	None	Y	Y	Aboriginal	Self-defence/BWS	Monica Zurowski, "Woman Found Not Guilty of Murdering Husband," The Calgary Herald (25 June 1991) A1
Marilyn Howard (1991/Gitsegukla Reserve, BC)	2nd DM	GP-MANS	5.5 years in prison; reduced to 2 years on appeal	Y	Y	Aboriginal	Spousal abuse	R v Howard, [1991] BCJ No 3780 (CA)
Shannon Deanne Hanuse (1996/Edmonton, AB)	2nd DM	A	None	Y	Y	N/A	Self-defence/accident	Florence Loyie, "Stabbing Ruled Accidental," [The] Edmonton Journal (29 June 1996) B4
Valerie Kahypeasewat* (2004/Saskatoon, SK)	N/A	GP-MANS	Conditional sentence: 2 years less a day	Y**	Y	Aboriginal	Spousal abuse/BWS	R v Kahypeasewat, 2006 SKPC 79

Name (Year/ Location)	Charges laid	Outcome	Sentence	Prior abuse	Altercation at time	Member of racialized group	Defence argument/ basis for mitigation of sentence	Source
Donelda Ann Kay* (1994/ Regina, SK)	2nd DM	A	None	Y	Y	Aboriginal	Self-defence/BWS	"Battered-Woman's-Syndrome Defence Advanced by Regina Woman's Acquittal," The [Saskatoon] Star Phoenix (22 June 1994) C9
Patricia Kay (2002/ Regina, SK)	2nd DM	GP-MANS	5 years in prison	Y	Y	Aboriginal	Spousal abuse/BWS	Barb Pacholik, "Five Years for Manslaughter," The [Regina] Leader Post (14 December 2002) A7
Mary Ann Keeper* (1993/ Little Grand Rapids Reserve, MB)	2nd DM	GP-MANS	Suspended sentence: 3 years at Hollow Water	Y	Y	Aboriginal	Spousal abuse/BWS	Kevin Rollason, "Battered Woman Spared Jail Term," The Winnipeg Free Press (3 June 1993) B1
Theresa Kneiss (1992/ Edmonton, AB)	2nd DM	A	None	Y	Y	Taiwanese	Self-defence/BWS	"Battered Wife Bursts into Tears after Being Acquitted of Murdering Husband," The Vancouver Sun (4 June 1992) A4
Kimberley Kondejewski* (1998/Brandon, MB)	1st DM	A	None	Y	Y	No	Self-defence/BWS	"Abused Woman Cleared in Husband's Killing," [The] Edmonton Journal (23 May 1998) A3

Case	Charge	Conviction/Outcome	Sentence			Aboriginal	Defence	Citation
Lydia Koosees* (1999/ Kashechewan, ON)	1st DM	GP-MANS	20 months in prison	Y	Y	Aboriginal	Spousal abuse	*R v Koosees*, File No 10201/99, Ontario Superior Court of Justice, 16 September 1999, Cochrane, ON
Joanna Laurel Linklater (2005/ Pelican Narrows, SK)	2nd DM	GP-MANS	Conditional sentence: 2 years less a day	Y	Y	Aboriginal	Spousal abuse/BWS	Canadian Press, "Woman Convicted of Killing Common-Law Husband Gets Conditional Sentence," *Prince Albert Daily Herald* (23 January 2005) QL
Sylvia Machiskinic (2004/ Rose Valley, SK)	2nd DM	GP-MANS	2.5 years in prison	Y	Y	Aboriginal	Spousal abuse/remorse/ rehabilitation	*R v SM*, 2004 SKQB 358
Penny Maikantis (1996/ Toronto, ON)	2nd DM	GP-MANS	4.5 years in prison	Y	N	N/A	Spousal abuse	Gary Oakes, "Woman Is Jailed for Killing Her Lover," *The [Toronto] Star* (16 October 1996) A14
Margaret Ann Malott* (1991/ Kingsville, ON)	1st DM and attempted murder	C-2nd DM and attempted murder	Life in prison; no parole eligibility for ten years	Y	N	No	Self-defence/BWS	*R v Malott*, [1998] 1 SCR 123
Monica Elizabeth Manton (1996/ Winnipeg, MB)	1st DM	Charges stayed at the preliminary inquiry	None	Y	Y	N/A	Self-defence/BWS	David Kuxhaus, "Wife's Murder Charge Stayed," *The Winnipeg Free Press* (12 September 1996) A1

Name (Year/Location)	Charges laid	Outcome	Sentence	Prior abuse	Alteration at time	Member of racialized group	Defence argument/basis for mitigation of sentence	Source
Lorraine Massettoe (1993/Fort Ware, BC)	N/A	GP-MANS	One year in prison	Y	Y	Aboriginal	Remorse	R v Massettoe, [1993] BCJ No 585 (Prov Ct)
Helen Mayo (2001/LaSalle, QC)	MANS	A	None	Y	Y	Aboriginal	Self-defence	George Kalogerakis, "Woman Freed in Abuser's Death: A Judge Said the Woman, Who Endured Frequent Beatings, Acted in Self-Defence When She Stabbed Her Ex-Boyfriend as He Bashed a Frail Neighbour Who Was Trying to Defend Her," The [Montreal]Gazette (25 May 2001) A1
Bonnie McAuley (1995/Ottawa, ON)	1st DM	C-1st DM	Life in prison; no parole eligibility for 25 years	Y	N	N/A	Jointly tried with her son – he argued self-defence, and she argued no role in the murder.	R v McAuley, [2003] OJ No 1155 (CA)
Gail Alice McDow (1995/Dartmouth, NS)	2nd DM	GP-MANS	2 years less a day in prison; raised on appeal to 5 years	Y**	Y	N/A	Spousal abuse	R v McDow, (1996), 147 NSR (2d) 343 (CA)

Agnes McMaster (1990/ Calgary, AB)	MANS	Discharged after preliminary inquiry	None	Y	Y	N/A	Self-defence	"Wife Cleared in Stabbing Death of Husband Who Was Beating Her," The [Toronto] Star (22 August 1990) A26
Jean Millar* (1992/ Foresters Falls, ON)	1st DM 1st trial; 2nd DM 2nd trial	C-2nd DM 1st trial; C-MANS 2nd trial	4 years in prison	Y	N	No	1st trial: denial; 2nd trial: self-defence/BWS	Canadian Press, "Woman Jailed 4 Years for Killing Abusive Husband," The [Montreal] Gazette (10 December 1992) B5
Roxanne Murray (1991/ Grand Forks, BC)	2nd DM	Charges stayed	None	Y	Y	N/A	Self-defence/BWS	Ken MacQueen, "Family Tragedy: Abused Wife Pulls Trigger to End Beatings," The Calgary Herald (3 March 1991) C2
Jessie Neckoway (1999/ Winnipeg, MB)	MANS	A	None	Y	Y	N/A	Self-defence/BWS	"Jury Acquits Woman," The Winnipeg Free Press (6 May 1999) A9
Susan Neyelle* (1992/Fort Franklin, NWT)	2nd DM, MANS after preliminary inquiry	C-MANS	2 years less a day in prison	Y	Y	Aboriginal	Spousal abuse	R v Neyelle, [1992] NWTJ No 184 (SC)
Karen Oertel (1992/ Brandon, MB)	2nd DM	GP-MANS	6 months in prison	Y	Y	N/A	Spousal abuse	R v Oertel (1992), 18 WCB (2d) 36 (Man QB)

Name (Year/Location)	Charges laid	Outcome	Sentence	Prior abuse	Altercation at time	Member of racialized group	Defence argument/basis for mitigation of sentence	Source
Eileen Paliska (1998/Welland, ON)	N/A	GP-MANS	Suspended sentence: 1 month probation	Y	Y	N/A	Spousal abuse	Canadian Press, "Woman Who Killed Husband Gets Probation," The [Toronto] Star (21 August 1998) A11
Tammy Lyn Papin (1990/Kingston, ON)	2nd DM	A	None	Y**	Y	Aboriginal	Self-defence/BWS	Murray Hogben, "Jury Rules Self-Defence: Woman Found Not Guilty in Stabbing Murder," The Kingston Whig-Standard (15 November 1990) 1
Linda Paquette (1996/Montreal, QC)	MANS	A	None	Y	Y	N/A	Self-defence/accident	Presse Canadienne, "Femme-acquittement," Nouvelles générales du Québec (6 septembre 1996) newswire
Mary Bernadette Parker (1994/Mississauga, ON)	MANS	GP-MANS	Suspended sentence: 3 years' probation	Y	Y	N/A	Spousal abuse	Farrell Crook, "Battered Woman, 61 Gets 3 Years' Probation for Stabbing Husband," The [Toronto] Star (21 September 1994) A8
Skeeter Paul (1991/Waterhen Reserve, MB)	N/A	Charges stayed	None	Y	Y	Aboriginal	Self-defence	Sean Fine, "Crimes of the Hearth: In Anticipation of Violence," The Globe and Mail (31 October 1992) D2

Case	Charge	Plea/Verdict	Sentence			Background	Defence	Citation
Gloria Phillips (1992/North York, ON)	2nd DM	GP-MANS	2 years less a day in prison	Y**	Y	N/A	Spousal abuse/BWS loss	*R v Phillips*, [1992] OJ No 2716 (Ct Just)
Valentina Potseloueva* (1996/North York, ON)	MANS	A	None	Y	Y	Russian refugee	Self-defence	Gary Oakes, "Abused Woman Cleared in Man's Stabbing Death," *The [Toronto] Star* (13 March 1996) A7
Wanda Quewezance (2005/Kamsack, SK)	2nd DM	GP-MANS	4 years in prison	Y	Y	Aboriginal	Abuse/remorse	*R v WLQ*, 2005 SKQB 10
Denise Robin Rain* (2000/Edmonton, AB)	MANS	A	None	Y	Y	Aboriginal	Self-defence	*R v Rain*, File No 9901242980I, Alberta QB, 27 March 2000, Edmonton
Jessie Redhead (1993/Shamattawa, MB)	2nd DM	A	None	Y**	Y	Aboriginal	Self-defence	Justice Linda Giesbrecht, *Report by Provincial Judge on Inquest Respecting the Death of: Patrick Norman Redhead* (Winnipeg: Manitoba Courts, 2003) at 49.
Suzanne Riley (1996/Walpole Island, ON)	N/A	GP-MANS	Suspended sentence: 3 years at Healing Circle	Y	Y	Aboriginal	BWS	"Woman Sentenced to Healing Rituals for Killing Boyfriend," *[The] Edmonton Journal* (21 December 1996) A12

Name (Year/Location)	Charges laid	Outcome	Sentence	Prior abuse	Alteration at time	Member of racialized group	Defence argument/ basis for mitigation of sentence	Source
Rachelle Kathryn Robertshaw (1996/Hamilton, ON)	2nd DM, MANS after preliminary inquiry	A	None	Y	Y	N/A	Self-defence/accident	Barbara Brown, "Jury Acquits Woman of Killing Husband: Picked Up Knife to Fend Off Attack, Court Heard," The Hamilton Spectator (17 April 1996) B3
Terena Ross* (1997/ Vancouver, BC)	MANS	Charges stayed	None	Y	Y	Aboriginal	BWS	Kevin Griffin, "Manslaughter Charge Stayed," The Vancouver Sun (24 March 1997) B12
Charmaine Susanna Rusaw (1996/Creston, BC)	N/A	GP-MANS	Suspended sentence: 3 years' probation	Y	Y	N/A	BWS	Jody Lamb, "Judge Spares Abused Wife Time in Jail," The [Vancouver] Province (7 March 1996) A11
Thérèse Saint-Denis-Bennett (1995/ Calumet, QC)	1st DM	C-1st DM	Life in prison; no parole eligibility for twenty-five years	Y	N	N/A	Self-defence/BWS	Jean-Paul Charbonneau, "Thérèse Saint-Denis-Bennett condamné à 25 ans pour avoir assassiné son mari," La Presse (2 décembre 1995) online http://www.lapresse.ca
Victoria Seddon* (1993/ Nanaimo, BC)	MANS	A	None	Y	Y	N/A	Self-defence/BWS	Judy Swanson, "Battered Woman Acquitted in Stabbing," The [Vancouver] Province (20 January 1993) A19

Marlene Smith (1990/ Etobicoke, ON)	2nd DM	GP-MANS	2 years less a day in prison	Y	Y	N/A	Spousal abuse/BWS	Gary Oakes, "Stabber 'Battered Spouse' Court Told," The [Toronto] Star (1 December 1990) A19
Doreen Sorenson* (2003/ Saskatoon, SK)	2nd DM	C-MANS	3 years in prison	Y	Y	Aboriginal	Spousal abuse	Janai Gopal, "Woman Receives Three Years in Prison for Stabbing Death," The [Saskatoon] Star Phoenix (18 May 2006) A3
Constance St-Hilaire* (1996/ Charlesbourg, QC)	2nd DM	GP-MANS	2 years less a day in prison	Y	Y	N/A	Spousal abuse	R v St-Hilaire, [1996] JQ No 597 (CS)
Melissa Stewart (1992/ Dartmouth, NS)	1st DM, reduced to 2nd DM after preliminary inquiry	C-MANS	Six years in prison	Y	N	N/A	Self-defence	Cathy Nicoll, "Car Death Woman Gets Six-Year Term: Crown May Appeal Case Called 'Closer to Murder'," The [Halifax] Daily News (21 August 1992) 6
Norma Grace Taypayosatum* (1998/ Nipawin, SK)	2nd DM	GP-MANS	8 years in prison	Y	Y	Aboriginal	None accepted	R v Taypayosatum, Transcript of Plea and Sentencing, QB Cr 1215, Saskatchewan Court of Queen's Bench, Melfort, 20 May 1998
Annette Thandi (1995/ Newton, BC)	1st DM, conspiracy to murder	GP to conspiracy to murder	2 years less a day in prison	Y	N	N/A	Spousal abuser	R v AT, [1999] BCJ No 1219 (SC)

Name (Year/ Location)	Charges laid	Outcome	Sentence	Prior abuse	Altercation at time	Member of racialized group	Defence argument/ basis for mitigation of sentence	Source
Yu-Ming Tran (1991/ Toronto, ON)	2nd DM	GP-MANS	1 year in prison	Y	Y	Cambodian	Spousal abuse/BWS	R v Tran, [1991] OJ No 2052 (Ct Just Gen Div)
Myrtle Trimble (1990/ Mississauga, ON)	MANS	C-MANS	Suspended sentence: 3 years' probation	Y	Y	No	Self-defence	Kellie Hudson, "Battered Wife Gets No Jail in Slaying," The [Toronto] Star (10 May 1990) A1; R v Trimble, [1992] OJ No 3287 (CA)
Elaine Trombley* (2000/ Windsor, ON)	2nd DM 1st trial; MANS 2nd trial	C-MANS 1st trial; A 2nd trial	7 years in prison; none after second trial	Y	Y	N/A	Self-defence/BWS	R v Trombley, [1999] 1 SCR 757; Donald McArthur, "Windsor Woman Found Not Guilty of Manslaughter: Wife Said She Feared for Her Life When She Stabbed Husband," The National Post (21 March 2000) A8
Peggy Turato (1991/ Vancouver, BC)	Crown did not lay charges	No charges	None	Y	Y	N/A	Self-defence/BWS	Mary Lynn Young, "Battered Woman Not Charged: Killed Her Husband after Years of Abuse," The Vancouver Sun (28 June 1991) A14

Annie Turbide (2005/ Longueuil, QC)	MANS	GP-MANS	Conditional sentence: 2 years less a day	Y	Y	No	Spousal abuse/BWS	R v Turbide, [2005] JQ No 4266 (CS)
Micheline Vaillancourt* (1996/ Vanier, QC)	2nd DM	C-2nd DM; A on appeal	None	Y	N	No	Self-defence/BWS	R c Vaillancourt, [1999] JQ No 571 (CA)
Micheline Veilleux (2003/Quebec City, QC)	2nd DM	A	None	Y	N	N/A	No factual causation	Nouvelles Télé-Radio, "Micheline Veilleux est acquitée du meurtre de son ex-conjoint" (11 novembre 2003), infomart
LMW (2004/ Chilliwack, BC)	N/A	GP-MANS	Conditional sentence: 12 months	Y	N	Aboriginal	Prior abuse/sexual assault attempt while she was unconscious	R v LMW, 2004 BCSC 1792
Cherie Pearl Wasicuna (2002/Sioux Valley Dakota Nation, MB)	2nd DM	GP-MANS	30 months in prison	Y	Y	Aboriginal	Spousal abuse/remorse	R v CPW, [2002] MJ No 541 (Prov Ct)
Betty Ann Whitehead (2001/ Saskatoon, SK)	2nd DM	GP-MANS	2 years less a day in prison	Y	Y	Aboriginal	Spousal abuse/BWS	Lori Coolican, "Woman Gets Two-Year Sentence for Stabbing Abusive Husband," The [Saskatoon] Star Phoenix (27 January 2001) A4

Name (Year/Location)	Charges laid	Outcome	Sentence	Prior abuse	Alteration at time	Member of racialized group	Defence argument/basis for mitigation of sentence	Source
Geraldine Whitten (1992/Dartmouth, NS)	2nd DM	GP-MANS	Suspended sentence: 3 years' probation	Y	Y	N/A	Spousal abuse	R v Whitten, [1992] NSJ No 105 (SC)
Beatrice Rose Whynot (1996/Liverpool, NS)	2nd DM	GP-MANS	5 years in prison	Y	Y	N/A	Self-defence	R v Whynot, [1996] NSJ No 12 (CA)
Ruth Wolfe (1997/Toronto, ON)	2nd DM	GP-MANS	2 years less a day in prison	Y	Y	N/A	Spousal abuse	Gary Oakes, "Woman Jailed for Killing Boyfriend: Judge Tells Her to Take Advantage of Lenient Sentence," The [Toronto] Star (25 June 1997) A24
Darlene Alice Young (2003/Falkland, BC)	1st DM	C-2nd DM first and 2nd trial; GP-2nd DM	Life in prison; no parole eligibility for 10 years	Y	N	N/A	Self-defence	R v Young, 2003 BCSC 1751; Castanet Staff, "Falkland Woman Confesses to Murder" (5 November 2009) online http://www.castanet.net

C   Convicted
A   Acquitted
GP   Guilty plea
N/A   Information not available
*   Transcripts obtained by author
**   Prior abuse but not necessarily by deceased

Notes

Introduction

1 *R v Lavallee*, [1990] 1 SCR 852.

2 Linda Gordon, *Heroes of Their Own Lives: The Politics and History of Family Violence* (New York: Viking, 1988) at 256. See also Elizabeth Pleck, *Domestic Tyranny: The Making of American Social Policy against Family Violence from Colonial Times to the Present* (New York: Oxford University Press, 1987).

3 *Hawley v Ham*, unreported, heard at the Midland District Assizes in September 1826, as described by the *Kingston Chronicle* (15 September 1826).

4 For fuller discussion, see Constance Backhouse, *Petticoats and Prejudice: Women and Law in Nineteenth-Century Canada* (Toronto: Women's Press, 1991) at 167-81.

5 Shelley Gavigan, "Petit Treason in Eighteenth-Century England: Women's Inequality before the Law" (1989) 3:2 CWJL 335.

6 Katherine MJ McKenna, "Women's Agency in Upper Canada: Prescott's Board of Police Record, 1834-1850" (2003) 36:72 Social History/Histoire sociale 347 at 362.

7 Lorna McLean, "'Deserving' Wives and 'Drunken' Husbands: Wife Beating, Marital Conduct, and the Law in Ontario 1850-1910" (2002) 35:69 Social History/Histoire sociale 50 at 63.

8 *Statutes of the Province of Ontario*, 1872, 35 Vict, c 16, as cited in McLean, *ibid* at 79.

9 *Statutes of the Province of Ontario*, 1897, 51 Vict, c 23, as cited in McLean, *ibid* at 80.

10 *Custody of Infants*, 1855, 18 Vict, c 126, cited in Lori Chambers, *Married Women and Property Law in Victorian Ontario* (Toronto: Osgoode Society for Canadian Legal History, 1997) at 48.

11 See the Ontario cases discussed by McLean, *supra* note 7 at 65-77.

12 See McLean, *supra* note 7; Annalee E Lepp, *Dismembering the Family: Marital Breakdown, Domestic Conflict and Family Violence in Ontario 1830-1920* (Doctoral Thesis, Department of History, Queen's University, 2000) [unpublished]; Kathryn

Harvey, "'To Love, Honour and Obey': Wife-Battering in Working-Class Montreal, 1869-1879" (1990) 19:2 Urban History Review/Revue d'histoire urbaine 128; Kathryn Harvey, "Amazons and Victims: Resisting Wife-Abuse in Working-Class Montreal, 1869-1879" (1991) 2:1 J Can Hist Assn 131.

13 See Pleck, *supra* note 2 at 3-4.
14 For a description of the legal and policy changes pursued in Canada in the 1980s, see Elizabeth Sheehy, "Legal Responses to Violence against Women in Canada" (1999) 19:1 & 2 Can Woman Stud 62 at 64-65.
15 Lee Lakeman's book *Obsession, with Intent* (Montreal: Black Rose Books, 2005) analyzes the multiple failures of the criminal justice system response to wife battering in Canada. See also Diane Crocker, "Regulating Intimacy: Judicial Discourse in Cases of Wife Assault (1970-2000)" (2005) 11:2 Violence against Women 197. Another study of 100 cases observed during a seven-month period in 2006 in Toronto reported a less vigorous criminal justice response in terms of the seriousness of charges laid and the sentences levied than that observed three years earlier. Women's Court Watch Project, *Court Watch IV 2006, Annual Report: Findings and Recommendations* (Toronto: Woman Abuse Council of Toronto, 2006).
16 See *R v Koyina*, [1989] NWTJ No 94 (SC) (evidence of deceased's prior violence against his common law partner Mary Rose Koyina inadmissible in her murder trial); see also the decision of the Nova Scotia Court of Appeal in *R v Whynot (Stafford)*, discussed *infra* at note 37.
17 She was also known as Jane Whynot, her married name from her first husband, and Jane Stafford, the name that she used while living with Stafford. After her trial, she reverted to her maiden name Hurshman.
18 Judith Lewis Herman, *Trauma and Recovery: The Aftermath of Violence – from Domestic Abuse to Political Terror* (New York: Basic Books, 1992).
19 *Ibid* at 33.
20 *Ibid* at 34.
21 *Ibid* at 86.
22 *Ibid* at 75.
23 Brian Vallée, *Life with Billy* (New York: Simon & Schuster, 1986).
24 The Fifth Estate, *Life with Billy* (CBC, 1984). In the interview, she dissociates on several occasions as she describes Billy's acts of cruelty against her and her children. As Vallée, *ibid* at 6, recounts, "her eyes widened to unnatural proportions."
25 *Ibid.*
26 Brian Vallée, *Life and Death with Billy* (Toronto: Random House, 1998) at 93.
27 *Ibid* at 95-97.
28 *Ibid* at 116.
29 *Ibid* at 126.
30 *Ibid* at 167.
31 Vallée, *Life with Billy, supra* note 23 at 206-7.
32 Vallée, *Life and Death with Billy, supra* note 26 at 165.
33 *Ibid* at 171.
34 *Ibid* at 233.
35 February 1983 issue of *Atlantic Insight*, quoted *ibid* at 174.

36 *Ibid* at 177.
37 *R v Whynot (Stafford)* (1983), 61 NSR (2d) 33 (CA).
38 Vallée, *Life and Death with Billy, supra* note 26 at 186.
39 Vallée, *Life with Billy, supra* note 23 at 241.
40 *Ibid* at 187.
41 *Ibid* at 217.
42 *Ibid.*
43 Brian Vallée, *Life after Billy: Jane's Story: The Aftermath of Abuse* (Toronto: McClelland-Bantam, 1993). Vallée reviews the evidence and concludes that Hurshman committed suicide. Others remain unconvinced; see Deborah Jones, "A Violent End to a Life of Abuse," *The Globe and Mail* (2 March 1992) A5.
44 *Lavallee, supra* note 1 at 876, 883, and 889, casts doubt on the decision of the Nova Scotia Court of Appeal in Hurshman's case (*Whynot (Stafford), supra* note 37).
45 Elizabeth Sheehy, "Battered Woman Syndrome: Developments in Canadian Law after *R v Lavallee*" in Julie Stubbs, ed, *Women, Male Violence and the Law* (Sydney: Institute of Criminology, 1994) 174 [Sheehy, "Battered Woman Syndrome"]; Elizabeth Sheehy, *What Would a Women's Law of Self-Defence Look Like?* (Ottawa: Status of Women Canada, 1995) [Sheehy, *Women's Law of Self-Defence*].
46 *Ibid.*
47 Felicity Hawthorn, "Interviews with Four Battered Women at the Prison for Women Who Are Serving Life Sentences for Murder" (27 April 1992) [unpublished] (on file with the author).
48 Three she recommended for unconditional pardon; three she recommended for sentence remission because they were disqualified from self-defence for using "excessive force" but should have had mitigated sentences on the basis of provocation; and one she recommended for reconsideration of the conviction. Judge Lynn Ratushny, *Self-Defence Review: First Interim Report: Women in Custody* (Submitted to the Minister of Justice of Canada and to the Solicitor General of Canada 6 February 1997); Judge Lynn Ratushny, *Self-Defence Review: Second Interim Report: Women Not in Custody* (Submitted to the Minister of Justice of Canada and to the Solicitor General of Canada 9 June 1997).
49 Government of Canada, "Ministers Respond to Self-Defence Review," News Release (26 September 1997). The government granted conditional, not unconditional, pardons to two of the women who had already completed their sentences and been released; it remitted the sentences of two of the women who had already been released on parole; and the fifth was referred to the courts to determine whether she had "fresh evidence" that would warrant relief. The result was negative. *Reference Re Gruenke*, [1998] MJ No 549 (CA).
50 Judge Lynn Ratushny, *Self-Defence Review: Final Report* (Submitted to the Minister of Justice of Canada and to the Solicitor General of Canada 11 July 1997) at 46; Stephen Bindman, "Bureaucrats 'Scorned' Judge's Probe," *The Ottawa Citizen* (25 July 1997) A1.
51 Elizabeth Sheehy, "Review of the Self-Defence Review" (2000) 12:1 CJWL 197.
52 Sheehy, "Battered Woman Syndrome," and Sheehy, *Women's Law of Self-Defence, supra* note 45; Martha Shaffer, "The Battered Woman Syndrome Revisited: Some Complicating Thoughts Five Years after *R. v. Lavallee*" (1997) 47:1 UT LJ 1.

53 Rebecca Bradfield, *The Treatment of Women Who Kill Their Violent Male Partners within the Australian Criminal Justice System* (DDP thesis, Faculty of Law, University of Tasmania, 2002) [unpublished] at 344.

54 Holly Maguigan, "Battered Women and Self-Defense: Myths and Misconceptions in Current Reform Proposals" (1991) 140:2 U Pa L Rev 379 at 383.

55 I used the keyword of "murder" or "manslaughter" combined with "her boyfriend," "her spouse," "her husband," or "her common law" to search QuickLaw (QL), BestCase, Canadian Newsstand, Canadian Research Index, CPIC, Factiva, Infomart, and ProQuest.

56 Margo Wilson & Martin Daly, "Spousal Homicide" (1994) 14:8 Juristat 1 at 7, reporting on statistics for 1991-92. A more recent study reports that 28 percent of women who killed male partners experienced abuse and that 36 percent of male victims had a history of violence. However, the study's sources were limited to coroner's reports for Quebec 1991-2010; furthermore, the authors were unable to reach a conclusion about whether women who killed had experienced domestic violence in 40.5 percent of the files and whether the male victim had committed prior acts of violence in 36 percent of the files. Dominique Bourget & Pierre Gagné, "Women Who Kill Their Mates" (2012) 30:5 Behav Sci Law 598 at 604, 606.

57 Macguigan, *supra* note 54 at 385, note 12.

58 Elizabeth Sheehy, Julie Stubbs, & Julia Tolmie, "Battered Women Charged with Homicide in Australia, Canada and New Zealand: How Do They Fare?" (2012) 45:3 Aust & NZ J Criminol 383 at 391.

59 The Appendix on page 320 of this book shows twenty-six of them; I also secured the *Lavallee* transcript; the remaining transcripts I ultimately judged to be outside my study parameters.

60 Sentencing decisions for murder are rarely reported because the life sentence is mandatory. The only remaining discretion for the judge is the period of ineligibility before the woman can apply for parole; these decisions might be reported.

61 This figure has been arrived at using Statistics Canada's annual report, *Homicide in Canada*. For the years 1990-94, on average women committed twenty-two homicides of male partners each year; as of 1996, the numbers began to decline; by 2004 and 2005, twelve women each year killed their male partners.

62 See also Ann Jones, *Next Time She'll Be Dead: Battering and How to Stop It* (Boston: Beacon Press, 2000) at 88: "[B]attering ... *is a process of deliberate intimidation intended to coerce the victim to do the will of the victimizer*" [italics in original].

63 Michelle Madden Dempsey, "What Counts as Domestic Violence? A Conceptual Analysis" (2006) 12:2 Wm & Mary J Women & L 301 at 330-31.

64 Murray A Straus, "State-to-State Differences in Social Inequality and Social Bonds in Relation to Assaults on Wives" (1994) 25:1 J Com Fam Stud 7; Douglas A Brownridge & Shiva S Hall, *Explaining Violence against Women in Canada* (Lanham, MD: Lexington Books, 2001) at 230 ("marital violence" linked to patriarchal societies and relationships); Margareta Hyden, *Woman Battering as Marital Act* (Oslo: Scandinavian University Press, 1994) at v (woman battering linked to hierarchical social order). See also Vickie Jensen, *Why Women Kill: Homicide and Gender Equality* (Boulder, CO: Lynne Rienner Publishers, 2001) (women's resort to spousal homicide linked to women's inequality).

65 Jones, *supra* note 61 at 96.

66 "Women have served all these centuries as looking glasses possessing the magic and delicious power of reflecting the figure of a man at twice its natural size." Virginia Woolf, *A Room of One's Own* (New York: Harcourt Brace, 1929) at 35.

67 Melanie Randall, "Domestic Violence and the Construction of the 'Ideal Victim': Assaulted Women's 'Image Problems' in Law" (2004) 23:1 St Louis U Pub L Rev 107 at 112.

68 Lisa A Goodman & Deborah Epstein, *Listening to Battered Women: A Survivor-Centered Approach to Advocacy, Mental Health, and Justice* (Washington, DC: American Psychological Association, 2008) at 8-10. For a rich discussion of the difference between "a hit" and "battering," see Sue Osthoff, "But, Gertrude, I Beg to Differ, a Hit Is Not a Hit Is Not a Hit" (2002) 8:12 Violence against Women 1521.

69 Goodman & Epstein, *ibid* at 9.

70 Randall, *supra* note 67 at 145.

71 *R v Bennett*, [1993] OJ No 1011 (Ct Just) at para 28.

72 *Ibid* at paras 66-68 per Judge Lynn Ratushny. See also the concurring opinion by Justices Claire L'Heureux-Dubé and Beverley McLachlin in *R v Malott*, [1998] 1 SCR 123 at 142.

73 Martha R Mahoney, "Legal Images of Battered Women: Redefining the Issue of Separation" (1991) 90:1 Mich L Rev 1 at 8.

74 Elizabeth Dermody Leonard, *Convicted Survivors: The Imprisonment of Battered Women Who Kill* (Albany: State University of New York Press, 2002) at 79-82; Donald Alexander Downs, *More than Victims: Battered Women, the Syndrome Society and the Law* (Chicago: University of Chicago Press, 1996) at 104.

75 Patrizia Romito, *A Deafening Silence: Hidden Violence against Women and Children* (Bristol: Policy Press, 2008).

76 *Self-Defence Review: Final Report*, *supra* note 50 at 40.

77 *Court Record Access Policy* (Vancouver: Supreme Court of British Columbia, 28 February 2011) at 15.

78 See, for example, Lucie E White, "Subordination, Rhetorical Survival Skills, and Sunday Shoes: Notes on the Hearing of Mrs G" (1990) 38:1 Buff L Rev 1, which describes the constraints in one particular litigation context that shape women's testimony and the partiality of any "truth" distilled from the resulting judgment.

79 Lenore Walker, *The Battered Woman Syndrome*, 3d ed (New York: Springer Publishing, 2009).

80 James Ptacek, *Battered Women in the Courtroom: The Power of Judicial Responses* (Boston: Northeastern University Press, 1999) at 9, relying on the work of historian Linda Gordon, *supra* note 2.

81 Emma Cunliffe, "Untold Stories or Miraculous Mirrors? The Possibilities of a Text-Based Understanding of Socio-Legal Transcript Research," http://ssrn.com/abstract =2227069 [unpublished].

82 Austin Sarat, "Rhetoric and Remembrance: Trials, Transcription, and the Politics of Critical Reading" (1999) 23:4 Legal Stud Forum 355.

83 Sherene H Razack, "Gendered Racial Violence and Spacialized Justice: The Murder of Pamela George" in Sherene H Razack, ed, *Race, Space and the Law: Unmapping a White Settler Society* (Toronto: Between the Lines, 2002) 121.

84 Anne McGillivray & Brenda Comaskey, *Black Eyes All of the Time: Intimate Violence, Aboriginal Women, and the Justice System* (Toronto: University of Toronto Press, 1999).

85 Howard Sapers, *Annual Report of the Correctional Investigator, 2006-2007* (Ottawa: Minister of Public Works and Government Services of Canada, 2007) at 20.

86 *R v Gladue*, [1999] 1 SCR 688.

87 Evan Stark, *Coercive Control: How Men Entrap Women in Personal Life* (New York: Oxford University Press, 2007).

88 *Ibid* at 5.

89 Law Society of Upper Canada, *Rules of Professional Conduct* (Adopted by Convocation 22 June 2000; Amendments Current to 25 November 2010) at 54-55: Rule 4.01 Duty as Prosecutor, Commentary: "When engaged as a prosecutor, the lawyer's prime duty is not to seek to convict but to see that justice is done through a fair trial on the merits. The prosecutor exercises a public function involving much discretion and power and must act fairly and dispassionately."

90 Evan Stark & Anne Flitcraft, *Women at Risk: Domestic Violence and Women's Health* (Thousand Oaks, CA: Sage Publications, 1996).

91 *Citizen's Arrest and Self-Defence Act*, SC 2012, c 9.

92 For full text see *Criminal Code* (RSC, 1985, c C-46), http://laws-lois.justice.gc.ca/eng/acts/C-46/.

93 Kent Roach, "A Preliminary Assessment of the New Self-Defence and Defence of Property Provisions" (2012) 16:3 CCLR 247 at 249.

94 Elizabeth M Schneider, *Battered Women and Feminist Lawmaking* (New Haven: Yale University Press, 2000) at 34.

95 *Ibid* at 36.

Chapter 1: Angelique Lyn Lavallee

1 Statement of Angelique Lyn Lavallee reprinted in *R v Lavallee* (1988), 52 Man R (2d) 274 (CA) App I [*Lavallee* (CA)].

2 "Murder Charge Raises Concern about Violent Women," *The Winnipeg Free Press* (2 September 1986) 3.

3 *Ibid.*

4 *Ibid.*

5 Kim Pate, "Young Women and Violent Offences: Myths and Realities" (1999) 19:1 & 2 Can Woman Stud 39. For critical evaluation of a 34 percent increase in women being jailed for serious crimes in the period 1991-2011, see "Surge in Crime Rates for Women 'Misleading,'" *CBC Online* (25 July 2012), http://www.cbc.ca/. See also Candace Kruttschnitt & Rosemary Gartner, "Female Violent Offenders: Moral Panics or More Serious Offenders?" (2008) 41:1 Aust & NZ J Criminol 9.

6 *Lavallee* (CA), *supra* note 1 at 277.

7 Testimony of Robert Ezako, *R v Lavallee*, Transcript of Proceedings at Trial, Court File No 412/87, Manitoba Court of Queen's Bench, Winnipeg, Volume 2, 17 September 1987 at 562-76 [*Lavallee* (Trial)].

8 Miller's role in the wrongful conviction of another of Brodsky's clients, James Driskell, was criticized by The Honourable Patrick J LeSage, QC, Commissioner,

Report of the Inquiry into Certain Aspects of the Trial and Conviction of James Driskell (Winnipeg, 2007) at 102ff.

9 *Lavallee* (Trial), *supra* note 7 Volume 1, 14 September 1987 at 18.
10 *Criminal Code,* s 651(2).
11 *Lavallee* (Trial), *supra* note 7 Volume 1, 14 September 1987 at 80.
12 *Ibid* at 82-83.
13 *Ibid* at 90.
14 *Ibid* at 103.
15 *Ibid* at 104.
16 *Ibid* at 105.
17 *Ibid.*
18 *Ibid* at 109.
19 He was later promoted to the Manitoba Court of Appeal and became its Chief Justice in 1990 and the Deputy Lieutenant Governor of Manitoba. By 2008, he was the chair of the Canadian Judicial Council's Judicial Conduct Committee.
20 *Ibid* at 110.
21 Keri Sweetman, "Male MPs' Guffaws at Wife Beating Query Enrage Female MPs," *The Ottawa Citizen* (13 May 1982) 4; see also Andrea Levan, "Violence against Women" in Janine Brodie, ed, *Women and Canadian Public Policy* (Toronto: Harcourt Brace, 1996) 319 at 328.
22 Canada, House of Commons, Standing Committee on Health, Welfare and Social Affairs, *Report on Violence in the Family: Wife Battering* (May 1982).
23 The first shelters were opened in Toronto and Vancouver in this year; by 1980, there were sixty-three shelters in Canada; by 1987, there were 264 shelters. Nancy Janovicek, *No Place to Go: Local Histories of the Battered Women's Shelter Movement* (Vancouver: UBC Press, 2007) at 5.
24 See the first such report, by Linda McLeod, *Wife Battering in Canada: The Vicious Cycle* (Ottawa: Canadian Advisory Council on the Status of Women, 1980); see also Debra J Lewis, *A Brief on Wife Battering with Proposals for Federal Action* (Ottawa: Canadian Advisory Council on the Status of Women, 1982).
25 For a broader discussion situating the *Lavallee* trial in the context of the feminist movement in Canada, see Jennie L Abell, *Bringing It All Back Home: Feminist Struggle, Feminist Theory and Feminist Engagement with the Law: The Case of Wife Battering* (LLM Thesis, Osgoode Hall Law School, York University, 1991) [unpublished].
26 For example, Ontario Crown attorneys received a memorandum from Attorney General R Roy McMurtry on the matter on 20 August 1982; Manitoba's pro-charging policy was introduced in 1983 (Jane Ursel & Christine Hagyard, "Winnipeg's Family Violence Court" in Jane Ursel, Leslie M Tutty, & Janice Lemaistre, eds, *What's Law Got to Do with It? The Law, Specialized Court and Domestic Violence in Canada* (Toronto: Cormorant Books, 2008) 95 at 96); and British Columbia's Wife Assault Policy was adopted in 1986 by the Ministry of the Attorney General (British Columbia, *Violence against Women in Relationships Policy* (Victoria: Ministry of Public Safety and Solicitor General, Ministry of Attorney General, and Ministry of Children and Family Development, 2010) at 3).

27 Janovicek, *supra* note 23 at 7.
28 Ursel & Hagyard, *supra* note 26 at 96.
29 *R v Koyina*, [1989] NWT J No 94 (SC).
30 *R v Whynot (Stafford)* (1983), 61 NSR (2d) 33 (CA).
31 Elizabeth M Schneider, *Battered Women and Feminist Lawmaking* (New Haven: Yale University Press, 2000) at 30-31.
32 *State v Wanrow* (1977), 559 P2d 548 (Wash S Ct).
33 *State v Kelly* (1984), A2d 364 (NJ S Ct).
34 Elizabeth Sheehy, *Personal Autonomy and the Criminal Law: Emerging Issues for Women* (Ottawa: Canadian Advisory Council on the Status of Women, 1987) at 36-40.
35 Lisa Priest, *Women Who Killed* (Toronto: McClelland and Stewart, 1992) at 32-33.
36 Bruce Owen, "No Jail for Abused Wife," *The Winnipeg Sun* (24 September 1986) 3, and Canadian Press, "Battered-Wife Defence Accepted in Minaki Case," *The Winnipeg Free Press* (2 May 1986) 12 (Mae Flavell, another Aboriginal woman represented by Greg Brodsky, pled guilty to manslaughter and received a three-year suspended sentence); *R v Chivers*, [1987] NWTJ No 118 (SC) (Judith Chivers was convicted of manslaughter by her jury, but her sentence was mitigated on the basis of evidence of Battered Woman Syndrome); Shirley Fors also pled guilty and relied on Battered Woman Syndrome evidence to mitigate her sentence before Chief Justice Evans in the Ontario Superior Court on 5 May 1987. Monique Poulin, *Le loi à la légitime défense en situation de violence conjugale: Un régime de tutelle pour les femmes* (Mémoire LLM, Université de Laval, 2000) [unpublished] at note 72.
37 *Lavallee* (Trial), *supra* note 7 Volume 1, 15 September 1987 at 130.
38 *Ibid* at 135.
39 *Ibid* at 154.
40 *Ibid* at 174.
41 *Ibid* at 177.
42 *Ibid* at 181.
43 *Ibid* at 187.
44 *Ibid* at 190.
45 *Ibid* at 193, 199.
46 *Ibid* at 206.
47 *Ibid* at 232.
48 *Ibid* at 257.
49 *Ibid* at 263.
50 *Ibid* at 274.
51 *Ibid* at 315-16.
52 *Ibid* at 341.
53 *Ibid* at 349.
54 *Ibid* at 363.
55 *Ibid* at 362.
56 *Ibid* at 365-66.
57 *Ibid* at 366.

58 *Ibid* at 369.
59 *Ibid* at 370.
60 *Ibid* at 372.
61 *Lavallee* (Trial), *supra* note 7 Volume 1, 16 September 1987 at 386.
62 *Ibid.*
63 *Ibid* at 413.
64 *Ibid* at 416.
65 *Ibid* at 419.
66 *Ibid* at 420.
67 *Ibid* at 421.
68 *Ibid* at 423.
69 *Ibid* at 424.
70 *Ibid* at 439.
71 *Ibid* at 443.
72 *Ibid.*
73 *Ibid* at 445.
74 *Ibid* at 454.
75 *Ibid* at 456-57.
76 *Ibid* at 459.
77 *Ibid* at 460.
78 *Ibid* at 468.
79 *Ibid* at 470.
80 *Ibid* at 480.
81 *Ibid* at 481.
82 *Ibid* at 486.
83 *Ibid* at 491.
84 *Ibid* at 506.
85 *Ibid* at 511.
86 *Ibid* at 513.
87 *Ibid* at 523.
88 *Lavallee* (Trial), *supra* note 7 Volume 2, 17 September 1987 at 527.
89 *Ibid* at 528.
90 *Ibid* at 529.
91 *Ibid* at 535.
92 *Ibid* at 553.
93 *Ibid.*
94 *Ibid* at 556.
95 *Ibid* at 560.
96 *Ibid* at 562.
97 *Ibid* at 563.
98 *Ibid* at 577.
99 *Ibid* at 578.
100 *Ibid* at 572.
101 *Ibid* at 568.

102 *Ibid* at 580.
103 *Ibid.*
104 *Ibid.*
105 *Ibid* at 581-82.
106 *Ibid* at 582.
107 *Ibid* at 583.
108 *Ibid* at 588.
109 *Ibid* at 590.
110 *Ibid* at 597.
111 *Ibid* at 591.
112 *Ibid* at 599.
113 *Ibid* at 600.
114 *Ibid* at 601.
115 *Ibid* at 603.
116 *Ibid* at 601.
117 *Ibid* at 608.
118 *Ibid* at 609.
119 *Ibid* at 610.
120 *Ibid* at 636.
121 *Ibid* at 657.
122 *Ibid* at 665.
123 *Ibid* at 669.
124 *Ibid* at 673.
125 *Ibid* at 678.
126 *Ibid* at 680.
127 *Ibid* at 687.
128 *Ibid* at 705.
129 *Ibid* at 706.
130 *Ibid* at 721.
131 *Ibid* at 727.
132 *Ibid* at 728.
133 *Ibid* at 729.
134 *Lavallee* (CA), *supra* note 1 at Appendix 1.
135 *Lavallee* (Trial), *supra* note 7 Volume 2, 17 September 1987 at 759.
136 *Ibid* at 777.
137 *Ibid* at 792.
138 *Ibid* at 793.
139 *Ibid* at 795.
140 *Ibid* at 795-96.
141 *Ibid* at 796.
142 *Ibid* at 805.
143 *Ibid* at 807.
144 *Ibid* at 809.
145 *Ibid* at 811.
146 *Ibid* at 813.

147 *Ibid.*
148 *Ibid* at 814.
149 *Ibid* at 831.
150 *Ibid* at 838.
151 *Ibid* at 844.
152 *Ibid* at 845.
153 *Ibid* at 852.
154 *Kelliher v Smith,* [1931] SCR 672 at 684.
155 *Lavallee* (Trial), *supra* note 7 Volume 2, 17 September 1987 at 854.
156 *Ibid* at 861.
157 *Ibid.*
158 *Ibid* at 878-79.
159 *Ibid* at 880.
160 *Ibid* at 886.
161 *Ibid* at 882, 888.
162 *Ibid* at 889.
163 *Ibid* at 877-78.
164 *Ibid* at 917.
165 *Ibid* at 914.
166 *Ibid* at 902.
167 *Ibid* at 907.
168 *Ibid* at 908.
169 *Ibid* at 910.
170 *Ibid* at 911.
171 *Ibid.*
172 *Ibid* at 919.
173 *Ibid* at 922.
174 *Ibid* at 923.
175 *Ibid* at 927.
176 *Ibid* at 928.
177 *Ibid* at 935-96.
178 *Ibid* at 944.
179 *Criminal Code,* s 651(1).
180 *Lavallee* (Trial), *supra* note 7 Volume 2, 17 September 1987 at 947.
181 *Ibid* at 951.
182 *Ibid* at 952.
183 *Ibid* at 953.
184 *Ibid.*
185 *Ibid* at 996.
186 *Ibid* at 956.
187 *Ibid* at 955.
188 *Ibid* at 954.
189 *Ibid* at 956.
190 *Ibid* at 967.
191 *Ibid* at 958.

192 *Ibid* at 959.
193 *Ibid* at 962.
194 *Ibid* at 965.
195 *Ibid.*
196 *Ibid* at 976.
197 *Ibid* at 999.
198 *Ibid* at 973.
199 *Ibid* at 982.
200 *Ibid* at 983.
201 *Ibid* at 987.
202 *Ibid* at 970.
203 *Ibid.*
204 *Ibid* at 1023.
205 *Ibid* at 1038.
206 *Ibid* at 1039.
207 *Ibid* at 1045.
208 *Ibid* at 1064.
209 *Ibid* at 1049.
210 *Ibid* at 1068.
211 *Ibid.*
212 *Ibid* at 1074.
213 *Ibid* at 1076.
214 *Ibid* at 1130.
215 *Ibid* at 1131.
216 *Ibid* at 1164.
217 *Ibid* at 1173.
218 *Ibid* at 1183.
219 *Ibid* at 1197.
220 *Ibid* at 1199.
221 *Criminal Code*, s 649.
222 Andrew Duffy, "Verdict Hailed as Jury Acquits Battered Wife in Fatal Shooting," *The Winnipeg Free Press* (23 September 1987) 3.
223 Canadian Press, "Battered Woman Mourning Man She Was Forced to Kill," *The [Toronto] Star* (27 September 1987) B8.
224 Canadian Press, "Battered Wife Can't Believe She Was Acquitted of Murdering Husband," *The Ottawa Citizen* (29 September 1987) D18.
225 Duffy, *supra* note 222.
226 Janet McFarland, "Women's Groups Welcome Acquittal as Needed Precedent in Abuse Cases," *The Winnipeg Free Press* (24 September 1987) 8.
227 Duffy, *supra* note 222.
228 *Criminal Code*, s 691(2).
229 *Lavallee* (CA), *supra* note 1 at 284.
230 Stephen Bindman, "Battered Woman Syndrome Key to Case before High Court," *The Ottawa Citizen* (4 November 1989) A2.
231 *Ibid.*

232 *Ibid.*

233 This lecture was developed in 1985 to honour Barbara Betcherman, distinguished lawyer, author, and feminist advocate who co-founded the Toronto Rape Crisis Centre.

234 Bertha Wilson, "Will Women Judges Really Make a Difference?" (1990) 28:3 Osgoode Hall LJ 507.

235 *Ibid* at 515.

236 Brian Bucknall, "Justice Wilson Held Audience Spellbound," Letter to the Editor, *The [Toronto] Star* (24 February 1990) D3, cited in Rosemary Cairns Way & T Brettel Dawson, "Taking a Stand on Equality: Bertha Wilson and the Evolution of Judicial Education in Canada" in Kim Brooks, ed, *Justice Bertha Wilson: One Woman's Difference* (Vancouver: UBC Press, 2009) 278 at 279, note 11. [*One Woman's Difference*].

237 David Vienneau, "Council Rejects Complaint about Top Court Judge," *The [Toronto] Star* (29 March 1990) A15.

238 Ellen Anderson, *Judging Bertha Wilson: Law as Large as Life* (Toronto: University of Toronto Press, 2001) at 219.

239 Robert J Sharpe & Kent Roach, *Brian Dickson: A Judge's Journey* (Toronto: University of Toronto Press, 2003) at 405-6, cited in Constance Backhouse, "Justice Bertha Wilson and the Politics of Feminism" in Jamie Cameron, ed, *Reflections on the Legacy of Bertha Wilson* (Toronto: LexisNexis, 2008) 33 at 46.

240 Anderson, *supra* note 238 at 221.

241 *R v Lavallee*, [1990] 1 SCR 852 [*Lavallee* (SCC)].

242 *The Windsor Star* (3 May 1990) A1.

243 *The [Toronto] Star* (3 May 1990) A1.

244 *The [Montreal] Gazette* (3 May 1990) A1.

245 *[The] Edmonton Journal* (3 May 1990) A1.

246 *The Ottawa Citizen* (3 May 1990) A1.

247 The decision was used as a benchmark by feminist lawyers and researchers in Australia, the United Kingdom, New Zealand, and South Africa. Elizabeth Sheehy, Julie Stubbs, & Julia Tolmie, "Defending Battered Women on Trial: The Battered Woman Syndrome and Its Limitations" (1992) 16:6: Crim L J 369; Katherine O'Donovan, "Law's Knowledge: The Judge, the Expert, the Battered Woman, and Her Syndrome" (1993) 20:4 J L & Soc 427; Nan Seuffert, "Battered Women and Self-Defence" (1997) 17:3 NZU L Rev 292; Lorraine Wohlhuter, "Excuse Them though They Know Not What They Do: The Distinction between Justification and Excuse in the Context of Battered Women Who Kill" (1996) 9:2 SACJ 151.

248 *Lavallee* (SCC), *supra* note 241 at 883.

249 *Ibid* at 874.

250 *Ibid* at 871.

251 *Ibid* at 888.

252 Bill Taylor, "Women's Groups Laud 'Enlightened' Decision by the Court," *The [Toronto] Star* (4 May 1990) A23.

253 "The Lavallee Case," Editorial, *The [Toronto] Star* (4 May 1990) A26.

254 "Court's Ruling Breaks New Ground: Due Weight Given to 'Battered Wife' Syndrome," Editorial, *The [Montreal] Gazette* (5 May 1990) B2; "Myth Takes Battering," Editorial, *The Calgary Herald* (5 May 1990) A4; "Message against Brutality," Editorial,

[The] Edmonton Journal (5 May 1990) A8; "Battered Wife Ruling: More Evidence of Sensitivity," Editorial, *The Ottawa Citizen* (7 May 1990) A8.

255 Trevor Lautens, [no title], *The Vancouver Sun* (10 May 1990) A17; Robert Galbraith, "Landmark or Loose Ends?," *The Kingston Whig-Standard* (15 June 1990) 1.

256 "Women's Groups Hail Battered Wife's Murder Acquittal by Jury," *The Ottawa Citizen* (24 September 1987) A12; "Battered Woman Mourning Man She Was Forced to Kill," *The [Toronto] Star* (27 September 1987) B8; Barb Livingston, "Battered-Wife Defence Could Make Canadian Legal History," *The Calgary Herald* (21 April 1990) J1; Stephen Bindman, "Battered Wife Acquittal Upheld," *The Windsor Star* (3 May 1990) A1.

257 Maggie MacDonald, with Allan Gould, *The Violent Years of Maggie MacDonald* (Toronto: McClelland-Bantam, 1987) at 143.

258 See also the cases discussed *supra* at notes 35-36.

259 See, for example, "multiple, serialized battering," discussed in Chapter 5, and "Coercive Control," discussed in Chapter 6.

260 *R v Lavallee*, Factum of the (Accused) Respondent, filed 6 May 1989, File No 412/87.

261 This is a legal brief offered to the court by a person or group not a party to the litigation, as "a friend of the court," to provide additional information or analysis for the court's consideration.

262 Part 1 of the *Constitution Act, 1982*, being Schedule B to the *Canada Act 1982* (UK), 1982, c 11.

263 Jacqueline R Castel submitted an article for publication just prior to the Supreme Court decision in *Lavallee* arguing that self-defence, and particularly the common law "imminence" requirement, had to be reread in light of the *Charter* right to equality. Jacqueline R Castel, "Discerning Justice for Battered Women Who Kill" (1990) 48:2 UT Fac L Rev 229.

264 Daniel J Brodsky, "Educating Juries: The Battered Woman Defence in Canada" (1987) 25:3 Alta L Rev 461.

265 For example, she relied on Phyllis Crocker, "The Meaning of Equality for Battered Women Who Kill" (1985) 8 Harv Women's LJ 121.

266 Elizabeth Sheehy, "Equality and the Supreme Court: Never the Twain Shall Meet" (2010) 50 SCLR (2d) 329 at 338. Justice Wilson took a similar approach to her analysis of abortion rights in *R v Morgentaler*, [1988] 1 SCR 30, as discussed *ibid* Sheehy at 337.

267 Isabel Grant & Debra Parkes, "Contextualizing Criminal Defences: Exploring the Contribution of Justice Wilson" in Kim Brooks, ed, *Justice Bertha Wilson: One Woman's Difference* (Vancouver: UBC Press, 2009) at 153, 159. For some of the many feminist legal analyses of *Lavallee*, see Donna Martinson *et al*, "A Forum on *Lavallee v. R*.: Women and Self-Defence" (1991) 25:1 UBC L Rev 23; O'Donovan, *supra* note 247; and Christine Boyle, "Battered Wife Syndrome and Self-Defence: *Lavallee v R*" (1990) 9:1 Can J Fam L 171.

268 See Lenore Walker, *The Battered Woman* (New York: Harper and Row, 1979) [*The Battered Woman*]; Lenore Walker, *Terrifying Love: Why Battered Women Kill and How Society Responds* (New York: Harper Collins, 1989); Lenore Walker, *The Battered Woman Syndrome*, 2d ed (New York: Springer Publishing, 1999); and

Lenore Walker, *The Battered Woman Syndrome*, 3d ed (New York: Springer Publishing, 2009) [*The Battered Woman Syndrome*].

269 Walker, *The Battered Woman, ibid* at 95-96, cited in *Lavallee* (SCC), *supra* note 241 at 879.

270 *Lavallee* (SCC), *supra* note 241 at 890.

271 *Ibid* at 888-89.

272 See, for example, Tammy Lyn Papin, acquitted by a Kingston, Ontario, jury in November 1990. Murray Hogben, "Pleading Battered-Wife Syndrome Doctor Says Court Defence Could Extend to Men," *The Kingston Whig-Standard* (2 January 1991) 1. Indeed, defence lawyers had already begun following in Brodsky's footsteps immediately after Lavallee's acquittal at trial and calling Dr Shane as their expert. *R v Mary Rose Koyina*, CR00529, Transcript of Proceedings in the Supreme Court of the Northwest Territories, 20-28 September 1989.

273 See cases discussed in Elizabeth Sheehy, "Battered Woman Syndrome: Developments in Canadian Law after *R v Lavallee*" in Julie Stubbs, ed, *Women, Male Violence and the Law* (Sydney: Institute of Criminology, 1994) 174; Martha Shaffer, "The Battered Woman Syndrome Revisited: Some Complicating Thoughts Five Years after *R. v. Lavallee*" (1997) 47:1 UT LJ 1 [Shaffer, "Syndrome Revisited]; and Judge Lynn Ratushny, *Self-Defence Review: Final Report* (Submitted to the Minister of Justice of Canada and the Solicitor General of Canada, 11 July 1997).

274 *R v McConnell*, [1996] 1 SCR 1075, reversing (1995), 32 Alta LR (3d) 1 (CA).

275 *R v Eagles*, [1991] YJ No 147 (Terr Ct) (uttering a threat to cause death or grievous bodily harm).

276 *R v Lalonde* (1995), 22 OR (3d) 275 (Ct Just) (welfare fraud), discussed by Sheila Noonan, "Lalonde: Evaluating the Relevance of BWS Evidence" (1995), 37 CR (4th) 110.

277 *R v C(TL)*, 2004 ABPC 79 (forgery and fraud); *R v Ryan*, 2011 NSCA 30 (counselling murder), rev'd 2013 SCC 3. See also Martha Shaffer, "Coerced into Crime: Battered Women and the Defence of Duress" (1999) 4 CCLR 271; and Isabel Grant, "Exigent Circumstances: The Relevance of Repeated Abuse to the Defence of Duress" (1997) 2 CCLR 331.

278 David M Paciocco, *Getting Away with Murder: The Canadian Criminal Justice System* (Toronto: Irwin Law, 1999) at 306-7. The author's position on whether Lavallee was properly acquitted is less clear. *Ibid* at 306, 310.

279 *Ibid* at 306.

280 See Sheehy, Stubbs, & Tolmie, *supra* note 247; Isabel Grant, "The Syndromization of Women's Experiences" (1991) 25:1 UBC L Rev 23; and Martha Shaffer, "*R. v. Lavallee*: A Review Essay" (1990) 22:3 Ottawa L Rev 607.

281 Greg Brodsky, interviewed on *As It Happens*, CBC Radio, 3 May 1990, as quoted in Abell, *supra* note 25 at 282.

282 Julie Stubbs & Julia Tolmie, "Gender, Race and the Battered Woman Syndrome: An Australian Case Study" (1995) 8:1 CJWL 122.

283 Shaffer, "Syndrome Revisited," *supra* note 273; Rebecca Bradfield, "Women Who Kill: Lack of Intent and Diminished Responsibility as the Other 'Defences' to Spousal Homicide" (2001-2) 13:2 Current Issues Crim Just 143.

284 Anne Scully, "Expert Distractions: Women Who Kill, Their Syndromes and Disorders" in Mary Childs & Louise Ellison, eds, *Feminist Perspectives on Evidence* (London: Cavendish Publishing, 2000) 191.

285 See, for example, *R v Inwood* (1989), 32 OAC 287, a sentencing decision in which the court held that, because the complainant had separated from the accused after being assaulted a first time by the accused, she was not a true "battered woman," thus relieving the accused of an aggravated sentence because he had not engaged in "wife battering."

286 National Institute of Justice, *The Validity and Use of Evidence Concerning Battering and Its Effects in Criminal Trials: Report Responding to Section 40507 of the Violence against Women Act* (Washington, DC: US Department of Justice, Office of Justice Programs, & National Institute of Justice, 1996) at vii.

287 Aileen McColgan, "In Defence of Battered Women Who Kill" (1993) 13:4 Oxford J Leg Stud 508 at 525.

288 Sheila Noonan, "Battered Woman Syndrome: Shifting the Parameters of Criminal Law Defences (Or (Re)Inscribing the Familiar?)" in Anne Bottomley, ed, *Feminist Perspectives on Foundational Subjects of Law* (London: Cavendish Press, 1996) 191.

289 Stubbs & Tolmie, *supra* note 282.

290 Julie Stubbs & Julia Tolmie, "Defending Battered Women on Charges of Homicide: The Structural and Systemic versus the Personal and Particular" in Wendy Chan, Dorothy E Chunn, & Robert Menzies, eds, *Women, Madness and the Law: A Feminist Reader* (London: Glasshouse Press, 2005) 191; Elizabeth Comack, "Do We Need to Syndromize Women's Experiences? The Limitations of the 'Battered Woman Syndrome'" in Kevin D Bonnycastle & George S Rigakos, eds, *Unsettling Truths: Battered Women, Policy, Politics and Contemporary Research* (Vancouver: Collective Press, 1998) 105; Ruthy Lazar, "Reconceptualizing Victimization and Agency in the Discourse of Battered Women Who Kill" (2008) 45 Stud L Politics & Soc 3.

291 She acknowledges that this study is not random and that it needs replication with a larger sample size. Walker, *The Battered Woman Syndrome, supra* note 268 at 64.

292 *Ibid.*

293 *Ibid* at 42.

294 *Ibid* at 45.

295 *Ibid* at 42.

296 *Diagnostic and Statistical Manual of Mental Disorders,* 4th ed (Washington, DC: American Psychiatric Association, 2000). The 5th edition, released in May 2013, also does not list Battered Woman Syndrome.

297 Walker, *The Battered Woman Syndrome, supra* note 268 at 69.

298 *Ibid* at 73.

299 *Ibid* at 14.

300 *Ibid* at 133.

301 *Ibid* at 139.

302 *Ibid* at 55-56.

303 Schneider, *supra* note 31 at 123.

304 *Ibid* at 126.

305 Melanie Randall, "Domestic Violence and the Construction of 'Ideal Victims': Assaulted Women's 'Image Problems' in Law" (2004) 23:1 St Louis U Pub L Rev 107 at 135-36.
306 *Ibid* at 119.
307 Evan Stark, *Coercive Control: How Men Entrap Women in Personal Life* (New York: Oxford University Press, 2007).
308 National Institute of Justice, *supra* note 286 at ix.
309 Rebecca Bradfield, "Understanding the Battered Woman Who Kills Her Violent Partner: The Admissibility of Expert Evidence on Domestic Violence in Australia" (2002) 9:2 Psychiatry, Psychology & L 177; Patricia Kazan, "Reasonableness, Gender Difference, and Self-Defence Law" (1997) 24:3 Man LJ 549.
310 *Lavallee* (SCC), *supra* note 241 at 870-71.

Chapter 2: Bonnie Mooney

1 *Bonnie Mooney, Michelle Mooney, and Kristy Mooney v Attorney General of British Columbia, Attorney General of Canada, and Constable C Andrichuk,* Transcript of Proceedings at Trial, Docket No C975107, Supreme Court of British Columbia, Prince George, Volume 1, 19 February 2001 at 126, 135, 154, and Volume 2, 21 February 2001 at 195 [*Mooney* (Trial)].
2 Testimony of Bonnie Mooney, *ibid* Volume 1, 20 February 2001 at 170.
3 See Ontario, *Report on the Police Complaints System in Ontario* (Toronto: Ministry of the Attorney General, 2005).
4 *Mooney* (Trial), *supra* note 1 Volume 1, 19 February 2001 at 99.
5 *Ibid* 20 February 2001 at 182.
6 The exceptions are the alibi defence, per *R v Cleghorn*, [1995] 3 SCR 175, and experts' reports, per *Criminal Code*, s 657.3(3).
7 Ministry of the Attorney General of British Columbia, *Policy on the Criminal Justice Response to Violence against Women* [*Violence against Women in Relationships Policy*] (1993).
8 *Mooney* (Trial), *supra* note 1 Volume 2, 21 February 2001 at 194.
9 *Ibid* at 201, 210.
10 *Ibid* Volume 1, 19 February 2001 at 21, Volume 2, 21 February 2001 at 195, 214, 288.
11 *R v Lavallee*, [1990] 1 SCR 852 at 886. For an example of traumatic bonding, see the case of Hedda Nussbaum in Sam Ehrlich, *Lisa, Hedda and Joel: The Steinberg Murder Case* (New York: St Martin's Press, 1989).
12 *Mooney* (Trial), *supra* note 1 Volume 2, 21 February 2001 at 211.
13 Angela Browne, *When Battered Women Kill* (New York: Free Press, 1987) at 129.
14 Quoted in Donald Alexander Downs, *More than Victims: Battered Women, the Syndrome Society and the Law* (Chicago: University of Chicago Press, 1996) at 6. See also Browne, *ibid* at 125, who reports that battered women's "affective, cognitive and behavioural responses are likely to become distorted by their intense focus on survival."
15 Ann Jones, *Next Time, She'll Be Dead: Battering and How to Stop It* (Boston: Beacon Press, 2000) at 131.

16 *Ibid* at 132-33: "Clifton Straw's violence and terrorism disappeared in a puff of rhet-
    oric, utterly overlooked ... Viewers did not have to question the failure of the police
    and courts to protect this woman; they could think instead that Karen Straw might
    simply have walked away."
17 Lyndal Bee, Lian Khaw, & Jennifer L Hardesty, "Leaving an Abusive Partner:
    Exploring Boundary Ambiguity Using the Stages of Change Model" (2009) 1:1 J Fam
    Theory & Rev 38.
18 *Lavallee, supra* note 11 at para 55.
19 See Linda Neilson, "Partner Abuse, Children and Statutory Change: Cautionary
    Comments on Women's Access to Justice" (2000) 18 Windsor YB Access Just 115
    at 134. Women are entitled to child and possibly spousal support, but pursuit of
    support from an abuser can be dangerously provocative and can trigger a demand
    for custody. For women's accounts, see Silke Meyer, "Why Women Stay: A Theoretical
    Examination of Rational Choice and Moral Reasoning in the Context of Intimate
    Partner Violence" (2012) 45:2 Aust & NZ J Criminol 179 at 188-89.
20 *Mooney* (Trial), *supra* note 1 Volume 1, 20 February 2001 at 108.
21 Statistics Canada, *Average Earnings by Sex and Work Pattern* (CANSIM, table 202-
    0102) (2009).
22 Women are paid less for substantially the same work as men; segregated in "pink-
    collar ghettos" where "women's work" in the service sector is devalued; and are less
    likely to be unionized, enjoy full-time work with benefits, or experience job security.
    See Monica Townson, *Women's Poverty and the Recession* (Ottawa: Canadian Centre
    for Policy Alternatives, 2009) at 17-25.
23 See Mary Jane Mossman & Morag Maclean, "Family Law and Social Assistance
    Programs: Rethinking Equality" in Patricia Marie Evans & Gerda R Wekerle, eds,
    Women and the Canadian Welfare State: Challenges and Change (Toronto: Uni-
    versity of Toronto Press, 1997) 117 at 118.
24 Townson, *supra* note 22 at 11. As of 2007, 23.6 percent of women heading sin-
    gle-parent families had incomes below the "low income cut off." Statistics Canada no
    longer uses a "poverty line" but calculates low income as a function of the percentage
    of a family's income dedicated to the bare essentials of shelter, clothing, and food.
25 Aboriginal women have twice the unemployment rate and low income of non-
    Aboriginal women. See Statistics Canada, *Women in Canada: A Gender-Based
    Statistical Analysis*, 5th ed (Ottawa: Ministry of Industry, 2006) at 201-2. "Visible
    minority" women have almost double the unemployment rate and low income rate
    of other women (at 251, 256). Women with disabilities experience similar levels of
    unemployment and low income – approximately twice that of non-disabled women
    (at 297, 299).
26 A legal vacuum exists with respect to matrimonial property rights of Aboriginal
    women on reserve lands: the *Indian Act* laws do not deal with division of property
    issues, and provincial family laws do not apply on reserve lands. The result is that
    Aboriginal women might not be able to secure exclusive possession of their homes
    and, if they leave abusers, can lose their homes and their rights on reserve in turn.
    Native Women's Association of Canada, *Reclaiming Our Way of Being: Matrimonial
    Real Property Solutions Position Paper* (Ottawa: Native Women's Association of

Canada, 2007) at 5. See also Ontario Native Women's Association, *Breaking Free: A Proposal for Change: Aboriginal Family Violence* (Thunder Bay: Ontario Native Women's Association, 1989) at 20-22.

27 Disturbingly, the decision to return to an abusive relationship is often the "best" decision for a woman in a context of "horrendously constrained options." Janet Mosher *et al, Walking on Eggshells: Abused Women's Experiences of Ontario's Welfare System* (Final Report of Research Findings from the Women and Abuse Welfare Research Project, 5 April 2004) at 7. See also Jody Raphael, *Saving Bernice: Battered Women, Welfare, and Poverty* (Boston: Northeastern University Press, 2000).

28 For example, seventeen of thirty-five area administrators interviewed knew of clients who were returned to abusers because they simply could not support their families adequately on welfare. *Ibid* at 8.

29 Ontario welfare recipients are required to make "reasonable efforts" to pursue child or spousal support, which can be waived temporarily (from three to twelve months) if the applicant provides evidence of domestic violence or a restraining order. Ontario Works Directives, *5.5: Family Support* (July 2010) online http://www.mcss. gov.on.ca at 2.

30 Mosher *et al, supra* note 27 at 9.

31 *Ibid* at 55, 56.

32 Mooney suffered a workplace injury and then received worker's compensation benefits for approximately one year.

33 Jill Insley, "Abuser Used Money to Keep Partner in His Power," *The [London] Guardian* (7 December 2008) online http://www.guardian.co.uk/, reports a study by the Women's Aid and Refuge, which found that "89 per cent of respondents report economic abuse as part of their experience of domestic violence."

34 Nina Tarr, *Employment and Economic Security for Victims of Domestic Abuse*, Illinois Public Law and Legal Theory Research Papers Series No 07-01 (18 January 2007) at 12. See also Lisa D Brush, *Poverty, Battered Women and Work in U.S. Public Policy* (New York: Oxford University Press, 2011), particularly Chapter 3, "What Happens When Abusers Follow Women to Work?"

35 A 1998 report by the US General Accounting Office found that between 35 percent and 56 percent of battered women are harassed at work by their batterers; between 55 percent and 85 percent are absent due to battering, including court hearings; and between 24 percent and 52 percent actually lose their jobs for this reason. *Domestic Violence: Prevalence and Implications for Employment among Welfare Recipients* at 7-9, 18-19, as discussed in Tarr, *ibid* at 6.

36 Rosemary Gartner, Myrna Dawson, & Maria Crawford, "Woman Killing: Intimate Femicide in Ontario 1974-1994" in Katherine MJ McKenna & June Larkin, eds, *Violence against Women: New Canadian Perspectives* (Toronto: Inanna Publications, 2002) 123 at 133, describe male unemployment as a risk factor for intimate femicide.

37 *Mooney* (Trial), *supra* note 1 Volume 1, 20 February 2001 at 111.

38 *Family Relations Act*, RSBC 1996, c 128 s 124.

39 These are not necessarily easy orders to obtain. For example, Pamela Behrendt failed to secure such an order from an Ottawa judge and was murdered by her husband when he attacked her with a chainsaw in the summer of 1990. Alana Kainz, "Abused,

Unprotected, Dead: Rally Mourns Victims of Violent Spouses," *The Ottawa Citizen* (26 April 1991) A1.

40 *Mooney* (Trial), *supra* note 1 Volume 2, 21 February 2001 at 265.

41 *Ibid* at 231.

42 *Ibid* at 252.

43 Neilson, *supra* note 19 at 141.

44 Evan Stark, "Re-Presenting Women Battering: From Battered Woman Syndrome to Coercive Control" (1994-95) 58:4 Alb L Rev 973 at 976. See also Meyer, *supra* note 19 at 186-87.

45 Neilson, *supra* note 19 at 135. She discusses women whose children were removed by court order and two others who gave their children to the state because they feared for their safety when fathers were emerging from prison.

46 Carole Curtis, "Representing the Assaulted Woman in Family Law Cases: A Practical Approach" (Toronto: Carole Curtis Barristers and Solicitors, 1999) at paras 37-40.

47 Neilson, *supra* note 19 at 131, 144. Mediators tend to favour joint custody, regardless of abuse. Cynthia Chewters, "Violence against Women and Children: Some Legal Issues" (2000) 20:1 Can J Fam L 99 at 126.

48 Neilson, *supra* note 19 at 125, discusses women's failure to disclose abuse due to self-blame and humiliation and, in consequence, to accede to joint custody.

49 Martha Shaffer, "Joint Custody since *Kaplanis* and *Ladisa*: A Review of Recent Ontario Case Law" (2007) 26:3 Can Fam LQ 315 at 324.

50 *Ibid* at 334.

51 Neilson, *supra* note 19 at 126-27, 137-38, provides illustrations of judicial minimization of men's acts of violence and judicial failure to "see" the patterns and the on-going effects of batterers' violence and control.

52 Although the statistics vary from province to province, in British Columbia lawyers can advise that in a litigation battle joint custody is ordered in 58 percent of cases and sole custody in 42 percent, with women more likely than men (55 percent vs 37 percent vs 8 percent third parties) to end up with the children. Susan Boyd, "Joint Custody and Guardianship in the British Columbia Courts: Not a Cautious Approach" (2010) 29:3 Can Fam LQ 223 at 230, 243. In Ontario, a recent study suggests that joint custody is ordered somewhat less frequently, in 34 percent of the cases studied. Shaffer, *supra* note 49 at 324.

53 See the cases discussed by Neilson, *supra* note 19 at 149-50, and by Shaffer, *supra* note 49 at 332-39.

54 Boyd reports from her study of litigated cases that in approximately one-third of the cases in which joint custody was ordered there was evidence of communication difficulties, parental conflict, non-cooperation, or abuse. *Supra* note 52 at 234. Neilson, *supra* note 19 at 144, reports from a New Brunswick study that "joint, split or full custody was awarded to or obtained by abusers in 23 (16%) of the court-file cases." See also Kimberly Abshoff & Stephanie Lanthier, *Family Action Court Team (FACT) Court Watch Project 2008 Background Paper* (Toronto: Woman Abuse Council of Toronto, 2008). In fact, it can be disadvantageous for a mother to raise concerns about a man's violence if she cannot prove her claim. Kirk Makin, "Warring Couples Misuse Courts, Judge Says," *The Globe and Mail* (9 April 2008) A6.

55 Many studies conclude that witnessing their fathers assault their mothers is detrimental to children, impairing the development of social competence and the ability to develop empathy, and causing depression, worry and frustration, and stress-related disorders. Hearing the assault, seeing the resulting injuries, or becoming aware of their mother's fear and distress have similar impacts on children. See the studies cited in Chewters, *supra* note 47 at 131-36. Further, ten percent of child witnesses are harmed or threatened during the assaults on their mothers. Statistics Canada, *Family Violence in Canada: A Statistical Profile* (Ottawa: Canadian Centre for Justice Statistics, 2001) at 20.

56 See, for example, *V (P) v B (D)*, 2007 BCSC 237 at para 22, discussed by Boyd, *supra* note 52 at 235. The judge awarded joint custody in spite of the ex-husband's violence against his former partner and the judge's acknowledgment that the ex-husband at times made "physical contact with [his daughter]." See also the Ontario cases discussed by Shaffer, *supra* note 49, such as *Brooks v Brooks*, [2006] OJ No 1514 (Sup Ct Just), in which the father had, during the marriage, threatened the mother with a knife and punched holes in the wall and then, post-separation, had been charged with threatening to kill her and was suicidal. He nonetheless succeeded in securing joint custody (discussed at 347-48). Courts can discount mothers' reports of abuse when ordering joint custody but simultaneously place a restraining order on the man or note in disapproval his anger management problem. Shaffer, *supra* note 49 at 324, 342.

57 Neilson, *supra* note 19 at 120, note 21, cites studies that predict that from 20 percent to 50 percent of wife abusers subsequently harm the children. See also Chewters, *supra* note 47 at 128-29, who cites studies that predict that from 30 percent to 75 percent of battering men also harm their children.

58 Boyd, *supra* note 52 at 245, notes that in 37 percent of the cases in which a parent obtained sole custody, the parent was still ordered to share guardianship with the former partner. See, in particular, *Kortlever v Kortlever*, 2007 BCSC 487, discussed at 246, in which charges were pending and a restraining order had been in place against the father for a year and in which both mother and daughter were afraid of the father, yet joint guardianship was imposed.

59 Fiona Kelly, "Enforcing a Parent/Child Relationship at All Cost? Supervised Access Orders in the Canadian Courts" (2012) 49:2 Osgoode Hall LJ 277. Julia Tolmie, Vivienne Elizabeth, & Nicola Gavey, "Raising Questions about the Importance of Father Contact within Current Family Law Practices" (2009) 4 NZ L Rev 659 at 675-79, discuss the experiences of twenty-one women negotiating court-ordered access who reported child neglect and abuse by fathers who refused to administer children's medications, sent them home with feces and urine caked on their clothing, deprived them of warm blankets at night, lost them in malls, and locked them in cars while they shopped. See also Shaffer, *supra* note 49 at 334-39, who reports cases in which access fathers refused to follow medical advice regarding a child's diet, failed to use a special detergent for clothes washing when a child had skin allergies, repudiated school authorities who attempted to provide educational assistance to a special needs child, and took children with them in pizza delivery vans for four-six-hour work shifts.

60 Neilson, *supra* note 19 at 139-40, reports New Brunswick cases in which this was the case.

61 See Marisa L Beeble, Deborah Bybee, & Cris M Sullivan, "Abusive Men's Use of Children to Control Their Partners and Ex-Partners" (2007) 12:1 European Psychologist 54, who report at 56 that 88 percent of the 156 self-identified battered women surveyed reported that their partners used the children to control them by, among other things, getting the children to report on their mothers' activities, trying to turn the children against their mothers, using the contact as an opportunity to harass the mothers, asking the children to persuade their mothers to take them back, and using the children to frighten the mothers. See also Vivienne Elizabeth, Nicola Gavey, & Julia Tolmie, "The Gendered Dynamics of Power in Disputes over the Post-Separation Care of Children" (2012) 18:4 Violence against Women 459; Vivienne Elizabeth, Nicola Gavey, & Julia Tolmie, " ... He's Just Swapped His Fists for the System: The Governance of Gender through Custody Law" (2012) 26:2 Gender & Society 239; and Julia Tolmie, Vivienne Elizabeth, & Nicola Gavey, "Is 50-50 Shared Care a Desirable Norm Following Family Separation? Raising Questions about Current Family Law Practices in New Zealand" (2010) 24:1 NZU L Rev 136.

62 Lisa Priest, "'Revenge Killings' of Children Increasing, Report Says," *The Globe and Mail* (4 May 2005) A10, citing the Ontario Domestic Violence Death Review's findings. For a recent example of a wife abuser murdering his child while on an unsupervised access visit, see Romina Maurino, "Inquest into Jared Osidacz's Death Will Ignore Issue of Domestic Violence: NDP," *The Winnipeg Free Press* (26 February 2009) online http://www.winnipegfreepress.com/. See also Paul Harris, "Violent Fathers Gain Access to Children," *The [London] Observer* (15 December 2002) 4, reporting that in 300 recent UK family court cases 61 percent of fathers had allegations of violence made against them, yet 94 percent of fathers studied achieved access through the courts. He reported that in the previous eight years in Britain, at least nineteen children were killed by access fathers. Furthermore, some judges show little regard for the dangers to children, mothers, and staff posed by access fathers in supervised settings, even when social science evidence about the numbers of attacks and murders that occur on site during supervised access visits is before them. See e.g., *HH v HC*, 2002 ABQB 426 at para 57.

63 Susan Boyd, "Relocation, Indeterminacy, and Burden of Proof: Lessons from Canada" (2011) 23:2 Child & Fam LQ 155, reports that women succeed in only about 50 percent of these applications at trial and that another 45 percent of appeals succeed. The test is the best interests of the child, but judges scrutinize the reasons behind the proposed move, the mother's good faith and behaviour, and whether the mother has facilitated access for the father.

64 Eiah El Fateh, "A Presumption for the Best?" (2009) 25:1 Can J Fam L 73 at 96.

65 *Ibid* at 97.

66 *Mooney* (Trial), *supra* note 1 Volume 2 at 191.

67 *Ibid* at 177.

68 *Ibid* at 340.

69 *Ibid* Volume 1 at 71.

70 *Ibid* at 124.

71 *Ibid* at 123.

72 *Ibid* at 67-68.

73 *Ibid* at 68.

74 *Ibid* at 119.

75 *Ibid* at 120.

76 Martha Mahoney, "Legal Issues of Battered Women: Redefining the Issue of Separation" (1991) 90:1 Mich L Rev 1.

77 Douglas Brownridge *et al*, "The Elevated Risk for Non-Lethal Post-Separation Violence in Canada: A Comparison of Separated, Married and Divorced Women" (2008) 23:1 J Interpersonal Violence 117 at 127.

78 Margo Wilson & Martin Daly, "Spousal Homicide Risk and Estrangement" (1993) 8:1 Violence and Victims 3 at 4, 7; Office of the Chief Coroner, *Seventh Annual Report of Domestic Violence Death Review* (Ontario: Office of the Chief Coroner, 2009) at 20 [*Seventh Annual Report*]. See also Scott Roberts, "Domestic-Abuse Victims Face Extreme Risk of Being Killed," *The Globe and Mail* (2 June 2006) A8, reporting a study by Leslie Tutty of 368 women in ten shelters across the country. Of these women, 77 percent were at extreme or severe risk of murder by their ex-partners based on danger assessment measures.

79 Jacqueline Campbell *et al*, "Risk Factors for Femicide in Abusive Relationships: Results from a Multisite Case Control Study" (2003) 93:7 Am J Public Health 1089 at 1090.

80 Maria Crawford, Rosemary Gartner, & Women We Honour Action Committee, *Woman Killing: Intimate Femicide in Ontario, 1974-1990* (Toronto: Women We Honour Action Committee, 1992); Maria Crawford, Rosemary Gartner, Myrna Dawson, & Women We Honour Action Committee, *Woman Killing: Intimate Femicide in Ontario 1991-1994* (Toronto: Women We Honour Action Committee, 1997).

81 Ninety-eight percent of women were killed by men in Ontario from 1974 to 1994, while 83 percent of men died at the hands of other men. Crawford, Gartner, & Dawson, *supra* note 36 at 137.

82 Statistics Canada, *Family Violence in Canada: A Statistical Profile* (Ottawa: Industry Canada, 2009) at 6 [*Family Violence in Canada (2009)*].

83 Mia Dauvergne & Geoffrey Li, "Homicide in Canada" (2005) 26:6 Juristat 7.

84 Margo Wilson & Martin Daly, "Spousal Homicide" (1994) 18:8 Juristat 7; Campbell *et al*, *supra* note 79 at 1089, where it is reported that "[t]he majority (67%-80%) of intimate partner homicides involve physical abuse of the female by the male before the murder, no matter what partner is killed."

85 Daniel G Saunders, "Are Physical Assaults by Wives and Girlfriends a Major Social Problem?" (2002) 8:12 Violence against Women 1424 at 1432.

86 Gartner, Dawson, & Crawford, *supra* note 36 at 126.

87 Nancy Glass *et al*, "Non-Fatal Strangulation Is an Important Risk Factor for Homicide of Women" (2008) 35:3 J Emergency Medicine 329; Kim Smith, "Strangulation Cases Now Easier to Prosecute," *Arizona Daily Star* (2 January 2011) online http://www.azstarnet.com: "If a woman's boyfriend or husband has ever tried to strangle her, she is 10 times more likely to die from abuse than victims who haven't suffered strangulation," referring to US Department of Justice risk statistics.

88 See Kathryn Laughon *et al*, "Revision of the Abuse Assessment Screen to Address Non-Lethal Strangulation" (2008) 37:4 J Obstetric, Gynecologic and Neonatal Nursing 502.

89 Marisol Bello, "Choking Seen as Prelude to Murder," *USA Today* (24 June 2010) online http://www.usatoday.com/. However, these reforms depend on committed and informed policing and prosecution for their effectiveness. Elizabeth Zavala, "Without Provisions for Training, Enforcing Texas Strangulation Law Proves Complicated," *The [Fort Worth] Star-Telegram* (31 July 2010) online http://www.family justicecenter.com/; Julie Besonen, "A New Crime, but Convictions Are Elusive," *The New York Times* (16 February 2013) online http://www.nytimes.com/ (the first nineteen charges for felony strangulation have all resulted in acquittals due to inadequate collection of evidence).

90 The Domestic Violence Death Review Committee was formed in response to recommendations from coroners' inquests into the murders of Arlene May and Gillian Hadley by their respective partners. It continues the work of the Women We Honour Action Committee in tracking and analyzing intimate homicide in Ontario and in making recommendations based on its findings to prevent such deaths in future. See *Seventh Annual Report, supra* note 78. British Columbia, Manitoba, and New Brunswick have followed suit. *Findings and Recommendations of the Domestic Violence Death Review Panel,* Report to the Chief Coroner of British Columbia (May 2010); Manitoba, "Domestic Violence Death Review Committee Established," News Release (16 June 2010); Communications New Brunswick, "Domestic Violence Death Review Committee Established," News Release (12 February 2010).

91 *Seventh Annual Report, supra* note 78 at 20. Seventy-eight percent of victims experienced the first two risk factors, and 63 percent experienced the third.

92 *Mooney* (Trial), *supra* note 1 Volume 1, 20 February 2001 at 135.

93 Crawford, Gartner, & Dawson, *supra* note 36 at 135; see also *Seventh Annual Report, supra* note 78 at 11.

94 *Seventh Annual Report, supra* note 78 at 20.

95 In the period 1974-94, Crawford, Gartner, & Dawson, *supra* note 36 at 135, found that the "705 cases of intimate femicide resulted in the deaths of 977 persons." The majority of these deaths were offender suicides, but seventy-four other persons were also murdered, mostly children.

96 *Mooney* (Trial), *supra* note 1 Volume 2, 21 February 2001 at 195.

97 Leigh Goodmark, "Going Underground: The Ethics of Advising a Battered Woman Fleeing an Abusive Relationship" (2007) 75:4 UMKC L Rev 999 at 1004, quotes KJ Wilson, *When Domestic Violence Begins at Home: A Comprehensive Guide to Understanding and Ending Domestic Abuse* (Alameda, CA: Hunter House Publishers, 1997) at 89, for the point that "all of the women she knew who successfully concealed themselves went underground without children."

98 *Criminal Code,* s 283; *R v Adams* (1993), 12 OR (3d) 248 (CA); *R v CAV,* [2005] OJ No 1359 (Sup Ct Just); Rebecca Jaremko Bromwich, "Flight: Woman Abuse and the Hague Convention," in Ellen Faulkner & Gayle MacDonald, eds, *Victim No More: Women's Resistance to Law, Culture and Power* (Halifax: Fernwood, 2009) 31.

99 Will Braun, "Abused Mother Seeks Redress after Secret ID Revealed," *The Globe and Mail* (15 August 2011) A3.

100 Goodmark, *supra* note 97.

101 *Mooney* (Trial), *supra* note 1 Volume 2, 21 February 2001 at 212.

102 *Ibid.*

103 Nancy Janovicek, *No Place to Go: Local Histories of the Battered Women's Shelter Movement* (Vancouver: UBC Press, 2007) at 5.

104 Saunders, *supra* note 85 at 1440.

105 There are no guarantees. See Ingrid Peritz, "Quebec Woman Shot to Death at Shelter for Battered Women," *The Globe and Mail* (11 June 1999) A2, which also discusses an earlier attack at a women's shelter in Kenora in 1988, when Elizabeth Mannella was murdered by her husband.

106 Janovicek, *supra* note 103 at 5.

107 Andrea Taylor-Butts, "Canada's Shelters for Abused Women 2005/2006" (2007) 27:4 Juristat 1 at 3 (stays of from one to twenty-one days or from one to eleven weeks).

108 *Ibid* (stays of from three to twelve months).

109 Ontario Association of Interval and Transition Houses [OAITH], *Response to the Long-Term Affordable Housing Strategy Consultation* (Toronto: OAITH, 2009) at 8-9. Its survey of fifty-seven shelters and their clients found a pressing need for subsidized housing units, increased shelter allowances so that women and children do not forgo food for shelter, and increased availability of rent supplements. See also Pamela Pomic & Natasha Jategaeonkar, *Surviving Not Thriving: The Systemic Barriers to Housing for Women Leaving Violent Relationships* (Vancouver: British Columbia Non-Profit Housing Association, 2010).

110 Cassandra Drudi, "Thousands Turned Away from Ottawa Women's Shelters," *The Ottawa Citizen* (7 October 2008) A1. The Ottawa Coalition to End Violence against Women estimates that for every woman served at an Ottawa shelter another six are turned away; see *Hidden from Sight: A Look at Prevalence of Violence against Women in Ottawa* (May 2009) at 3.

111 British Columbia Society of Transition Houses, *24 Hour Census Report: A One-Day Look at Transitional Housing and Children Who Witness Abuse Programs in BC and the Yukon* (2009).

112 For example, Lethbridge turned away 1,186 women in 2005 who were seeking shelter from male violence. Jason Markusoff, "Mayors Call for $20 Million to Help Homeless," *[The] Edmonton Journal* (22 August 2006) A1.

113 For a description of the difficulties that this solution poses, see Interval House of Ottawa, Winter 2008 Newsletter [unpublished] online http://intervalhouseottawa.org/.

114 See, for example, Domestic Violence Death Review Committee, *Annual Report to the Chief Coroner: 2004,* Case No 8 at 18.

115 *Family Violence in Canada (2009), supra* note 82 at 10.

116 Shelters that serve rural, village, and reserve communities make up only 4 percent of shelters in Canada. *Ibid* at 14.

117 *Ibid* at 14: 67 percent of rural and 53 percent of urban shelters.

118 Taylor-Butts, *supra* note 107 at 6: while 28 percent of shelters serve women on reserves, only 5 percent or 30 of 553 shelters were actually located on reserves.
119 For an account of the first shelter run by and for Aboriginal women in Ontario, its philosophy, and its programming, see Janovicek, *supra* note 103 at Chapter 1 (Beendigen shelter, Thunder Bay).
120 *Ibid* at 15.
121 *Ibid* (75 percent wheelchair accessible entrance; 66 percent accessible bedrooms/bathrooms; 22 percent specially equipped telephones; 17 percent sign language interpretation, *etc*). There are very few shelters that have the capacity to serve women with intellectual disabilities. See Springtide Resources, Breaking New Ground project online http://www.springtideresources.org/.
122 Ontario Association of Interval and Transition Houses, "Locked In, Left Out: Impacts of the Budget Cuts on Abused Women and Their Children" in McKenna & Larkin, *supra* note 36 at 413; Marina Morrow, Olena Hankivsky, & Colleen Varcoe, "Women and Violence: The Effects of Dismantling the Welfare State" (2004) 24:3 Critical Social Policy 358.
123 Mandy Bonisteel & Linda Green, *Implications of the Shrinking Space for Feminist Anti-Violence Advocacy* (paper presented at the 2005 Canadian Social Welfare Policy Conference, Forging Social Futures, Fredericton), online http://www.crvawc.ca/.
124 *Mooney* (Trial), *supra* note 1 Volume 2, 22 February 2001 at 306.
125 Celia Wells, "Domestic Violence and Self-Defence" (1990) 140 New LJ 127 at 127, has argued that battered women who fail to contact police "can hardly be blamed for absorbing the social message that this is really a private matter."
126 Statistics Canada, *Family Violence in Canada: A Statistical Profile* (Ottawa: Ministry of Industry, 2011) at 6 [*Family Violence in Canada (2011)*] (22 percent of those self-reporting spousal abuse said that it came to the attention of police).
127 *Ibid* at 12.
128 Marta Burczycka & Adam Cotter, *Shelters for Abused Women in Canada, 2010* (Ottawa: Statistics Canada, 2011) at 15.
129 Stephanie Lanthier, *Documenting Women's Experiences with the Toronto Police Services in Domestic Violence Situations* (Toronto: Woman Abuse Council of Toronto, 2008) at 12.
130 However, one study found that, in many cases in which women called the incident too trivial to report (29 percent), the assault was actually very serious or life threatening (18 percent). Kim Davies, Carolyn Rebecca Block, & Jacquelyn Campbell, "Seeking Help from the Police: Battered Women's Experiences and Decisions" (2007) 20:1 Crim Just Stud 15 at 31.
131 See George Rigakos, "The Politics of Protection: Battered Women, Protection Orders, and Police Subculture" in Kevin D Bonnycastle & George S Rigakos, eds, *Unsettling Truths: Battered Women, Policy, Politics, and Contemporary Research in Canada* (Vancouver: Collective Press, 1998) 82 [*Unsettling Truths*]. Rigakos reports at 87-88 on misogynist beliefs expressed by Delta, British Columbia, police officers surveyed (47 percent of the "beat cops"), who described women reporting protection order breaches by their partners in derogatory terms ("douchebags," "chippy")

and motivated by desires to manipulate custody outcomes or to shift the blame for fights that they started. Lanthier, *supra* note 129 at 15-16.

132 See, for example, *R v BB* (2012), 320 Nfld & PEI R 310 (Nfld & Lab Prov Ct).

133 In a prosecution involving a man who had brutalized his female partner over a four-year period, in which she left and returned to him several times, the woman testified that she returned because she was "'damaged goods' and doubted whether anyone would want her with the state of·her leg – which was shattered when the man allegedly smashed it with a baseball bat." Paula McCooey, "'He Told Me He Loved Me,'" *The Ottawa Citizen* (15 March 2007) C3. She testified that she was too ashamed and afraid to report his violence to the police. Paula McCooey, "Abuse Victim Expected Educated Man to 'Grow Up,'" *The Ottawa Citizen* (14 March 2007) D1: "I thought maybe the police would take him away for a night ... But then he would come back and kill me."

134 Karen Flynn & Charmaine Crawford, "Committing 'Race Treason': Battered Women and Mandatory Arrest in Toronto's Caribbean Community" in *Unsettling Truths*, *supra* note 131 at 93.

135 Dianne Martin & Janet Mosher, "Unkept Promises: Experiences of Immigrant Women with the Neocriminalization of Wife Abuse" (1995) 8:1 CJWL 3 at 26.

136 See Joanne C Minaker & Laureen Snider, "Husband Abuse: Equality with a Vengeance?" (2006) 48:5 Can J Criminol and Crim Just 753. They argue that the newly discovered problem of "husband abuse" has been generated by backlash against feminist victories by men's rights groups and that men's claims that women are as violent as men gain plausibility through equality discourses – hence "equality with a vengeance." See also Molly Dragiewicz, *Equality with a Vengeance: Men's Rights Groups, Battered Women, and Antifeminist Backlash* (Boston: Northeastern University Press, 2011), for an account of the men's rights campaign in the United States that has targeted emergency services for battered women as discriminatory against men.

137 Lanthier, *supra* note 129 at 13, reports on a survey of sixty-three women that found that, when they called police, in 54 percent of cases the man was arrested, and in 11 percent of cases the woman was arrested. Shoshana Pollack, Melanie Battaglia, & Anke Allspach, *Women Charged with Domestic Violence in Ontario: The Unintended Consequences of Mandatory Charge Policies* (Toronto: Woman Abuse Council of Toronto, 2005), interviewed nineteen women who had been charged and four Crown attorneys. Six women had been charged at the same time as the batterer, and thirteen had been the only person charged when they had called the police for help. Seventeen of nineteen women had a history of abuse from the same man; ten of the male partners had criminal records, nine for wife battering; eleven of the women had visible injuries, yet none of this contextualized the woman's behaviour in the eyes of either the police or Crown attorneys. See also Linda Patricia Wood, *Caught in the Net of Zero Tolerance: The Effect of the Criminal Justice Response to Partner Violence* (Master's Thesis, Department of Sociology, University of Manitoba, 2001) [unpublished], and Susan L Miller, "The Paradox of Women Arrested for Domestic Violence" (2001) 7:12 Violence against Women 1339, for further discussion of the US experience in this regard. For a case involving assault charges laid against a woman

arrested for pulling her partner's trouser waist, causing him to fall and experience no physical injury but "an emotional one," see *R v Penner* (2003), [2004] 5 WWR 691 (NWT Terr Ct).

138 *Family Violence in Canada (2011), supra* note 126 at 9, 10, 13, 14, 33. See also Marianne Hester, *Who Does What to Whom? Gender and Domestic Violence Perpetrators* (Bristol: University of Bristol in association with the Northern Rock Foundation, 2009).

139 Pollack, Battaglia, & Allspach, *supra* note 137 at 5: ten of nineteen women arrested and charged were "women of colour," two were Aboriginal, and five spoke English as a second language; at 8-9, the authors provide examples of women's "assaultive" behaviours. See also Valli Rajah, Victoria Frye, & Mary Haviland, "'Aren't I a Victim?' Notes on Identity Challenges Relating to Police Action in a Mandatory Arrest Jurisdiction" (2006) 12:10 Violence against Women 897 at 902, 903, 906, 907; and Carolyn M West, "'Sorry, We Have to Take You In': Battered Black Women Arrested for Intimate Partner Violence" in Kathy A McCloskey & Marilyn H Sitaker, eds, *Backs against the Wall: Battered Women's Resistance Strategies* (New York: Routledge, 2009) 87.

140 Pollack, Battaglia, & Allspach, *supra* note 137 at 5: they report that four of the women lost custody of their children during the criminal process.

141 *Ibid* at 22-23.

142 Statistics Canada, *Family Violence in Canada: A Statistical Profile* (Ottawa: Industry Canada, 2006) at 6. See also Joseph Gillis *et al*, "Systemic Obstacles to Battered Women's Participation in the Judicial System" (2006) 12:12 Violence against Women 1150 at 1160, which reports on a Toronto study of twenty battered women, all of whom stated that they would never again use the legal system.

143 *Family Violence in Canada (2011), supra* note 126 at 11; *Family Violence in Canada (2009), supra* note 78 at 25.

144 *Family Violence in Canada (2009), ibid* at 27.

145 Elizabeth Comack & Gillian Balfour, *The Power to Criminalize: Violence, Inequality and the Law* (Halifax: Fernwood Publishing, 2004) at 167, quote from a woman who explains why she did not call the police when her husband assaulted her children: "Because I did not want to stay home and for him to come and the cops are [at our] home and if nothing would have been done then who knows what he would have done to the kids or me." Amy L Busch, *Finding Their Voices: Listening to Battered Women Who've Killed* (Commack, NY: Kroshka Books, 1999) at 61, provides an account of police who refused to react and threatened to take the woman to the station: "And now they leave and I'm standing in the driveway, and there's Brian and I think, Oh God, he's going to kill me now. I mean, I just called the cops on him, the ultimate sin. And he dragged me in the house and beat me twice as hard. Teaches you not to call the police, you know what I mean? I mean, if you can take a beating that bad and live through it, then you should count your blessings, because if you call the police, then you're probably going to be dead."

146 *Mooney* (Trial), *supra* note 1 Volume 2, 22 February 2001 at 351.

147 He stabbed another man unprovoked and was sentenced to seven years of imprisonment. The victim's mother predicted that "[t]hey will let him out, and he will continue abusing and doing harm to others. It was in 1996 that the nightmare happened for

real." Louise Kennedy, *Sex with All the Wrong Men* (Victoria: Trafford Publishing, 2003) at 207.

148 *Mooney* (Trial), *supra* note 1 Volume 2, 22 February 2001 at 307.

149 Gael B Strack, George E McClane, & Dean Hawley, "A Review of 300 Attempted Strangulation Cases Part I: Criminal Legal Issues" (2001) 21:3 J Emergency Medicine 303 at 308. At 305, they report: "The other symptoms varied including ... vomiting blood, pain to ear, headaches, loss of consciousness, ... hyperventilation, defecation, uncontrollable shaking, pupils not the same size, trouble walking, trouble moving neck, and loss of memory." Other studies report that symptoms include "vision changes, dysphagia [difficulty swallowing], neck pain, and psychiatric problems that include depression and Post Traumatic Stress Disorder (PTSD)." Lee Wilbur *et al*, "Survey Results of Women Who Have Been Strangled while in an Abusive Relationship" (2001) 21:3 J Emergency Medicine 297 at 301.

150 *Mooney* (Trial), *supra* note 1 Volume 2, 22 February 2001 at 302.

151 *Ibid* Volume 1, 20 February 2001 at 126.

152 *Ibid* at 215.

153 *Ibid* Volume 2, 22 February 2001 at 303 [emphasis in the original].

154 *Ibid* at 338.

155 *Ibid* at 305.

156 *Ibid* at 309, 333.

157 Curle testified that the police never assigned guards to hospital patients, with the exception of those who are prisoners. *Ibid* at 326. Neither the police nor hospital practices changed in this regard in the ensuing years. On 20 May 2003, prison guard Bryan Heron walked into his wife's hospital room at the Mission Memorial Hospital in Mission, British Columbia, and shot dead both Sherry Heron and her mother, Anna Adams, only a week after Sherry had gone to the RCMP with his threats of violence. She had told Constable Mike Pfeifer that her husband had threatened to kill her if she left him, that he was being served with a restraining order, that she feared his reaction, that he possessed many guns, and that she had been hospitalized after she tried to call for help from her home and Heron tore the telephone from the wall and began strangling her. See Lee Lakeman, *Obsession, with Intent* (Montreal: Black Rose Books, 2005) at xiv. Just like Andrichuk, Pfeifer took Sherry's complaint but decided that no further investigation was required. Steve Mertl, "Training about Spousal Abuse Urged," *The [Toronto] Star* (2 October 2004) D21.

158 *Mooney* (Trial), *supra* note 1 Volume 1, 20 February 2001 at 131, Volume 2, 21 February 2001 at 244.

159 *Ibid* Volume 2 at 244.

160 *Ibid.*

161 *Ibid* Volume 1, 20 February 2001 at 131.

162 *Ibid* at 135.

163 *Ibid.*

164 *Ibid* Volume 2, 21 Feburary 2001 at 250.

165 *Ibid* Volume 1, 20 February 2001 at 137.

166 *Ibid* Volume 2, 21 February 2001 at 247. Mooney's cross-examination suggests that Neal contacted officer Roberge. *Ibid* at 275.

167 *Ibid* Volume 1, 20 February 2001 at 145.

168 *Ibid.*

169 *Ibid* at 146.

170 See Don Lajoie, "Arsonist Gets House Arrest: Fire Starter Doused Wife with Gas during Dispute," *The Windsor Star* (26 June 2008) A3 (Shawn Prosser pled guilty to aggravated assault and mischief for throwing gas on his wife, threatening to ignite her, then burning down the family home while his wife and three children were inside); Paula McCooey, "'Brutal' Attacks on Wife Put Man in Prison with Four-Year Sentence," *The Ottawa Citizen* (28 June 2007) C6 (accused convicted of assault, aggravated assault, and criminal harassment for having hung his partner by the leg over their eighteenth-floor balcony, attacking her with a baseball bat when she tried to flee, and breaking her leg); and Ross Henderson, "Inflicting 'Ultimate Terror' Draws Two Years," *[The] Edmonton Journal* (14 February 1998) B1 (Ronald Muscat convicted of assault with a weapon and jailed for two years for holding his former girlfriend captive, holding a handgun to her head, and threatening to kill her). See also Myrna Dawson, "Intimacy and Violence: Exploring the Role of Victim-Defendant Relationship in Criminal Law" (2006) 96:4 J Crim L & Criminol 1417. On the other hand, sentencing patterns for men who kill their intimate partners have shifted over the past two decades such that men are more likely to be convicted of murder than manslaughter and to receive longer jail terms. Isabel Grant, "Intimate Femicide: A Study of Sentencing Trends for Men Who Kill Their Intimate Partners" (2009-10) 47:3 Alta L Rev 779 at 793, 799; Myrna Dawson, "Re-Thinking the Boundaries of Intimacy at the End of the Century: The Role of Victim-Defendant Relationship in Criminal Justice Decision-Making over Time" (2004) 38:1 L & Soc Rev 105.

171 *Report of the Criminal Section Working Group on Strangulation* (Uniform Law Conference of Canada, 2006) at 2-7.

172 Wilbur *et al, supra* note 149 at 301.

173 *Mooney* (Trial), *supra* note 1 Volume 1, 20 February 2001 at 147.

174 Some Crown offices have implemented "no drop" policies to curb batterers' efforts to pressure women into recanting. However, sending women to jail for refusing to testify presents serious problems. See Anne McGillivray, "Battered Women: Definition, Models and Prosecutorial Policy" (1987) 6:1 Can J Fam L 15 at 37-43.

175 *Mooney* (Trial), *supra* note 1 Volume 1, 20 February 2001 at 147.

176 *Ibid* Volume 3, 26 February 2001 at 582.

177 *Ibid* at 568.

178 *Ibid* Volume 1, 19 February 2001 at 23.

179 *Ibid,* 20 February 2001 at 151.

180 *Ibid* Volume 3, 26 February 2001 at 580.

181 Edna Erez & Joanne Belknap, "In Their Own Words: Battered Women's Assessment of the Criminal Processing System's Responses" (1998) 13:3 Violence & Victims 251 at 260-61.

182 Melanie Randall, "Domestic Violence and the Construction of 'Ideal Victims': Assaulted Women's 'Image Problems' in Law" (2004) 23:1 St Louis U Pub L Rev 107 at 145.

183 Mooney (Trial), *supra* note 1 Volume 3, 26 February 2001 at 581.

184 Dean Beeby, "Study: Assault Suspects on Bail Likely to Be Violent," *The [Halifax] Chronicle Herald* (6 November 2011) online http://thechronicleherald.ca/, citing Adamira Tijerino & Charlotte Fraser, "Exploring Differences between Those Who Violate Bail and Those Who Successfully Complete Bail among a Sample of Accused Persons at a Domestic Violence Court" (26 November 2010, obtained through Access to Information) [unpublished].

185 *Mooney* (Trial), *supra* note 1 Volume 3, 26 February 2001 at 574.

186 *Ibid* at 572.

187 *Ibid* Volume 2, 21 February 2001 at 223.

188 *Ibid* at 261.

189 *Ibid* at 255.

190 *Ibid* at 261.

191 *Ibid* Volume 3, 26 February 2001 at 578.

192 See "Mountie Convicted of Wife Assault to Head Domestic Violence Unit," *The Ottawa Citizen* (10 March 2000) A6, which recounts RCMP officer Rex Brasnett's conviction for assault causing bodily harm to his wife, who was rendered unconscious by his attack. Queen's Bench Justice Ross McBain called the woman's injuries "relatively minor" and sentenced Brasnett to one day in jail, a fine of $2,000, and a weapons prohibition. Brasnett was elevated to head the Serious Crimes Unit that handles domestic violence in Edmonton ten years later.

193 These passages from Kruska's sentencing hearing are quoted in Mooney's case on appeal: *Mooney v British Columbia (Attorney General)*, 2004 BCCA 402 [*Mooney* (CA)] at para 24, per Donald, J, dissenting.

194 *Mooney* (Trial), *supra* note 1 Volume 2, 21 February 2001 at 262.

195 *Ibid.*

196 *Ibid* at 193.

197 *Ibid* Volume 1, 20 February 2001 at 153.

198 *Ibid* Volume 2, 21 February 2001 at 269.

199 *Ibid.*

200 *Ibid* at 270.

201 *Ibid* Volume 1, 20 Feburary 2001 at 164.

202 *Ibid* at 163.

203 *Ibid* 19 February 2001 at 33.

204 *Ibid* at 40.

205 *Ibid* at 35.

206 *Ibid* Volume 2, 21 February 2001 at 271.

207 *Ibid* Volume 1, 20 February 2001 at 167.

208 *Ibid* Volume 2, 21 February 2001 at 271.

209 *Ibid* Volume 1, 20 February 2001 at 170.

210 *Supra* note 7.

211 *R v Schwartz*, [1998] BC J No 511 (Prov Ct); *R v K (M)* (1992), 12 LW 1219-022 (Man CA).

212 Martin & Mosher, *supra* note 135 at 23.

213 Rigakos, *supra* note 131 at 85-86, discussing police officers' self-reported failure to arrest even when there was a valid protective order reported by a female complainant that was violated by her male partner or former partner.

214 Rigakos, *ibid* at 85: 53 percent of officers in his study recommended a peace bond in the past year; 62 percent instead recommended that women seek a civil restraining order.

215 Violations of s 810 orders are *Criminal Code* offences, whereas breaches of restraining orders are provincial offences.

216 Rigakos, *supra* note 131 at 85: officers had arrested in 35 percent of peace bond breaches and 21 percent of restraining order breaches.

217 *Mooney* (Trial), *supra* note 1 Volume 2, 21 February 2001 at 274.

218 *Ibid* Volume 1, 20 February 2001 at 171.

219 *Ibid* Volume 2, 21 February 2001 at 276.

220 *Ibid* Volume 1, 20 February 2001 at 177.

221 *Ibid* at 174.

222 *Ibid.*

223 *Ibid.*

224 *Ibid* at 174-75.

225 *Ibid* at 161.

226 *Ibid* at 183.

227 *Ibid* at 185.

228 *Ibid* Volume 3, 23 February 2001 at 421. For a more recent example of police failing to "see" the threat and the danger posed by an estranged male partner's behaviour, see Michelle Lalone, "No Threats Alleged by Woman: Officers," *The [Montreal] Gazette* (1 December 2012) A8 (murder of Maria Altagracia Dorval by her violent ex-partner, who was under court orders to stay away from her, five weeks after she asked for police intervention. The officers did not write up a report or perform a data bank search; instead, they advised Edens Kenol to take legal steps to gain access to his children and not to harass Dorval).

229 *Mooney* (Trial), *supra* note 1 Volume 3, 23 February 2001 at 422.

230 *Ibid* Volume 2, 22 February 2001 at 387.

231 *Ibid* at 373.

232 *Ibid* at 374.

233 *Ibid* at 378.

234 *Ibid* at 375.

235 *Ibid* at 381, 383.

236 *Ibid* Volume 3, 23 February 2001 at 442.

237 *Ibid* at 461.

238 *Ibid* at 415.

239 *Ibid* at 453.

240 *Ibid* at 416.

241 *Ibid* at 447.

242 Rigakos, *supra* note 131 at 88.

243 *Ibid* at 91. He notes several studies that put the rate of recantation/non-cooperation by battered women at between 8.8 percent and 15.8 percent. Yet, he says at 90,

"[t]hese images [of battered women as reluctant witnesses] overshadow the hundreds of cases, throughout their collective careers, resulting in guilty pleas, or successful prosecutions."

244 *Mooney* (Trial), *supra* note 1 Volume 3, 23 February 2001 at 408.

245 *Ibid* at 454.

246 *Ibid* at 455.

247 *Ibid.*

248 Statistics Canada, *Measuring Violence against Women: Statistical Trends 2006* (Ottawa: StatsCan, 2006) at 20 *[Measuring Violence against Women]*. See also Saunders, *supra* note 85, for a thorough review of the problems in studies that claim parity, including the ways in which questions are framed and the exclusion of sexual violence, stalking, and controlling behaviour by ex-partners.

249 Yet the police have, armed with the misleading claim that "women are just as violent as men," used "mandatory" arrest policies to arrest women who have called them to report wife assault if their abusive partners claim that "she hit me first" or "look, officer, at this scratch she gave me." See the text accompanying notes 135ff.

250 *Mooney* (Trial), *supra* note 1 Volume 3, 23 February 2001 at 466.

251 *Mooney v Attorney General of British Columbia,* 2001 BCSC 419 *[Mooney* (SC)] at para 52.

252 *Ibid* at para 53.

253 *Ibid* at paras 53-55.

254 *Ibid* at para 63.

255 *Ibid.*

256 *Ibid.*

257 *Ibid* at para 65.

258 *Ibid* at paras 31-32.

259 *Mooney* (CA), *supra* note 193 at para 176.

260 She was appointed to the British Columbia Supreme Court in 2009.

261 *Mooney* (CA), *supra* note 193 at para 120.

262 *Ibid.*

263 *Ibid* at para 112.

264 *Ibid* at para 142.

265 *Ibid* at para 194. For analysis of the court's treatment of the causation issue, see Elizabeth Sheehy, "Causation, Common Sense, and the Common Law: Replacing Unexamined Assumptions with What We Know about Male Violence against Women, or, from *Jane Doe* to *Bonnie Mooney*" (2006) 17:1 CJWL 97.

266 *Mooney* (CA), *ibid* at para 25.

267 *Ibid* at para 81. See also Jamal MacRae, *Relationship Violence and Diversion: A Literature Review on Pro-Charge Policies and Crown Diversion* (Vancouver: British Columbia Institute against Family Violence, 2003) at 7-9.

268 *Mooney* (CA), *ibid* at para 12.

269 *Ibid.*

270 *Ibid* at para 75.

271 *Ibid* at para 94.

272 *Ibid* at para 98.

273 *Ibid* at para 97.

274 *Ibid.*

275 Leave to appeal refused, [2004] SCCA No 428.

276 Jennifer Koshan, "State Responsibility for Protection against Domestic Violence: The Inter-American Commission on Human Rights Report in Lenahan (Gonzales) and Its Application in Canada" (2012) 30:1 Windsor YB Access Just 39. Such decisions are not enforceable in Canada but can exert moral and political suasion.

277 Shelley Page, "Sherri Lee Guy Abandoned When Her Life Was at Risk," *The Ottawa Citizen* (5 May 1995) C1.

278 Katherine Harding, "Children of Slain Alberta Woman Receive Apology from RCMP Officer," *The Globe and Mail* (30 July 2005) A6.

279 Ingrid Peritz & Les Perreaux, "Survivors of Mountie's Rampage Relive Ordeal in Courtroom," *The Globe and Mail* (17 September 2009) A14.

280 Gwendolyn Richards, "RCMP Failed to Protect Woman and Son: Judge," *The National Post* (7 October 2005) A8.

281 Canadian Press, "Woman Suing Police," *The Globe and Mail* (5 September 1995) A4.

282 Statement of Claim No 38857, filed on 6 June 2006, Supreme Court of British Columbia, Vernon Registry, *Audrey Gayle Hull v The Queen in the Right of Canada, the Minister of Public Safety and Solicitor General of British Columbia, the Attorney General for British Columbia, and John Doe.*

283 Hayley Mick, "Threats, Violence and a Family Divided," *The Globe and Mail* (19 December 2006) A3: Wyann Ruso's husband pled guilty to attempted murder after attacking Wyann with an axe and a knife. Her suit against Toronto police for failing to pick him up before the attack was settled out of court.

284 For examples, see Aysan Sev'er, *Fleeing the House of Horrors: Women Who Have Left Abusive Partners* (Toronto: University of Toronto Press, 2002) at 155, and Lakeman, *supra* note 157 at 187.

285 The judicial response to charges against batterers also affects deterrence. One study of seventy-four women found that, when charges against the male partners were stayed, 54 percent of the women were reassaulted; when acquittals were entered, 100 percent of the women were reassaulted. D Plecas, T Segger, & L Marsland, *Reticence and Re-Assault among Victims of Domestic Violence* (Victoria: Ministry of the Attorney General for British Columbia, 2000).

286 See Angela M Moe, "Silenced Voices and Structured Survival: Battered Women's Help-Seeking" (2007) 13:7 Violence against Women 676 at 694: "In instances in which one or several help-seeking mechanisms came through for them, the women's stories illustrated positive outcomes."

287 Jones, *supra* note 15 at 133.

288 See Julia Tolmie, "Police Negligence in Domestic Violence Cases and the Canadian Case of *Mooney:* What Should Have Happened, and Could It Happen in New Zealand?" (2006) 2 NZ L Rev 243.

Chapter 3: Kimberley Kondejewski

1 Testimony of Dr Fred Shane in *R v Kimberley Ann Kondejewski,* Transcript of Proceedings at Trial, Docket No 97.02.46 CR, Manitoba Queen's Bench, Brandon, Volume 5, 20 May 1998 at 17 [*Kondejewski* (Trial)].

2 Kathleen Martens, "Police Study Charges as Suspect Recovers," *The Brandon Sun* (18 May 1997) 1.

3 Scott Gibbons, "Man Shot Dead in Brandon Home," *The Brandon Sun* (17 May 1997) 1.

4 *Ibid.*

5 During the trial, it emerged that the police found over 100 weapons in the home. Scott Gibbon, "Mother's Note to Children: Forgive Me," *The Brandon Sun* (14 May 1998) 1 at 5.

6 *Ibid.*

7 *Ibid.*

8 Scott Gibbons, "Charged with Murder," *The Brandon Sun* (21 May 1997) 1.

9 Canadian Judicial Council, *Model Jury Instructions*, Offence 231.2 – First Degree Murder Planned and Deliberate (s 231(2)), online http://www.cjcccm.gc.ca.

10 *R v Hay*, 2009 ONCA 398.

11 Myrna Dawson, *Criminal Justice Outcomes in Intimate and Non-Intimate Partner Homicide Cases* (Ottawa: Department of Justice, Research and Statistics Division, 2004) at 11. Her study is based on homicide cases in Toronto for the periods 1974-96 and 1997-2002.

12 Kim was released from custody pending trial. "Alleged Killer Released on Bail," *The Brandon Sun* (11 June 1997) 1.

13 Scott Gibbons, "A Litany of Horror," *The Brandon Sun* (13 May 1998) 1 at 2.

14 *Kondejewski* (Trial), *supra* note 1 Volume 1, 12 May 1998 at 12. Either the transcript omitted his opening or Wolson never did deliver an opening address.

15 *Criminal Code*, s 486.1(1).

16 *Kondejewski* (Trial), *supra* note 1 Volume 1 at 33.

17 *Ibid* at 37.

18 *Ibid* at 42-43.

19 This insight is attributable to Professor Emma Cunliffe of the University of British Columbia Faculty of Law.

20 Emma Cunliffe, "Untold Stories or Miraculous Mirrors? The Possibilities of a Text-Based Understanding of Socio-Legal Transcript Research" online http://ssrn.com/.

21 Austin Sarat, "Rhetoric and Remembrance: Trials, Transcription, and the Politics of Critical Reading" (1999) 23:4 Legal Stud Forum 355 at 359.

22 *Kondejewski* (Trial), *supra* note 1 Volume 1 at 47.

23 *Ibid.*

24 Cunliffe, *supra* note 20 at 3.

25 *Kondejewski* (Trial), *supra* note 1 Volume 1 at 74.

26 *Ibid.*

27 Alison Cunningham & Linda Baker, *Little Eyes, Little Ears: How Violence against a Mother Shapes Children as They Grow* (Ottawa: Centre for Children and Families in the Justice System, 2007) at 15.

28 *Ibid* at 8-10, 13-14.

29 *Kondejewski* (Trial), *supra* note 1 Volume 1 at 49.

30 *Ibid* at 50-52.

31 *Ibid* at 53-54.

32 *Ibid* at 50.

33 *Ibid* at 49.

34 *Ibid* at 54.
35 *Ibid* at 56.
36 *Ibid* at 58.
37 *Ibid* at 55.
38 *Ibid* at 75.
39 *Ibid* at 76.
40 *Ibid* at 80.
41 For example, see Julie Stubbs & Julia Tolmie, "Battered Woman Syndrome in Australia: A Challenge to Gender Bias in the Law?" in Julie Stubbs, ed, *Women, Male Violence and the Law* (Sydney: Institute of Criminology, 1994) 192 at 211, where they discuss how an accused woman was portrayed by the expert and her lawyer in simplified and stereotyped terms as "dependent, passive and inadequate."
42 *Kondejewski* (Trial), *supra* note 1 Volume 1 at 81, 83.
43 *Ibid* at 82.
44 *Kondejewski* (Trial), *supra* note 1 Volume 2, 13 May 1998 at 18.
45 *Ibid* at 23-24.
46 *Ibid* at 31.
47 *Ibid* at 38. Constable Bruce Vehrelst testified later to the same effect, adding that he observed firearms improperly and unsafely stored in the bedroom. *Ibid* at 60.
48 *Ibid* at 55.
49 *Ibid* at 91ff: "six hundred and one 22 LR Win Wildcat cartridges"; "two hundred cartridges, 22 LR Federal High Power"; "sixty cartridge 7.62 mm ball clip and bandolier"; "a hundred and one shot shell primers"; "a hundred and eleven primers, large rifle"; "seven strap outer pack for 66 mm rocket"; "seventy-seven hundred primer shotgun, Federal 209A"; "eight thousand primer shotgun, Winchester HW 209's"; "twelve hundred primers, large rifle, 1,045 primers, small rifle"; "thirty kilograms of small arms brass"; "twelve pounds of shotgun powder, 1 MR 700X"; "dummy cartridges, 141 dummy cartridges, 7.62 mm linked"; "four cases of 7.62 mm C1 21 ball cartridges, 1,680 rounds"; "four thousand three hundred and eighty-two rounds of 5.56 mm C 77 ball cartridges"; "smoke grenades"; "rockets"; "rifles, shot guns, high powered rifles, assault guns."
50 *Ibid* at 92.
51 *Ibid* at 95.
52 *Ibid* at 95.
53 *Ibid* at 101.
54 *Kondejewski* (Trial), *supra* note 1 Volume 3, 14 May 1998 at 6.
55 *Ibid.*
56 *Ibid* at 11.
57 *Ibid* at 13-14.
58 *Ibid* at 18.
59 *Ibid* at 14.
60 *Ibid* at 17.
61 *Ibid* at 16.
62 *Ibid* at 18.
63 *Ibid* at 19.

64 *Ibid* at 21.
65 *R v Arcuri*, 2001 SCC 54: if the Crown presents some direct evidence on each element of the offence, then the accused must be committed to trial, regardless of any exculpatory evidence; if the Crown relies instead on circumstantial evidence, then the test is whether a properly instructed jury could reasonably infer guilt if they believed the evidence advanced, in light of the whole of the evidence, including exculpatory evidence.
66 *Kondejewski* (Trial), *supra* note 1 Volume 3, 14 May 1998 at 31.
67 *Ibid* at 33.
68 *Ibid* at 48.
69 *Ibid* at 44.
70 *Ibid* at 40.
71 *Ibid* at 44-45.
72 *Ibid* at 42, 46.
73 *Ibid* at 47.
74 *Ibid* at 50.
75 *Ibid* at 52.
76 *Ibid* at 56.
77 *Ibid* at 63-64.
78 *Ibid* at 69.
79 *Ibid* at 72.
80 *Ibid* at 73, 74.
81 *Ibid* at 75.
82 *Ibid*.
83 *Ibid* at 76.
84 *Ibid*.
85 *Ibid* at 77.
86 *Ibid*.
87 *Ibid* at 78.
88 *Ibid* at 83.
89 *Ibid* at 83-84.
90 *Ibid* at 85.
91 *Ibid* at 84.
92 *Ibid* at 88.
93 *Ibid* at 89-90.
94 *Ibid* at 91.
95 *Ibid* at 86.
96 *Ibid* at 91.
97 Canadian Press, "Wife Charged in Shooting Death Recounts Years of Abuse, Court Hears" (19 May 1998) newswire.
98 *Kondejewski* (Trial), *supra* note 1 Volume 4, 19 May 1998 at 4.
99 *Ibid* at 7.
100 Angela Browne, *When Battered Women Kill* (New York: Free Press, 1987) at 99. See also Vickie Jensen, *Why Women Kill: Homicide and Gender Equality* (Boulder, CO: Lynne Rienner Publishers, 2001) at 49: "High adherence to acceptance of traditional

gender roles ha[s] been found in batterers ... [V]iolence as a way of enacting mascu-
linity becomes most likely when dominance is threatened."

101 *Kondejewski* (Trial), *supra* note 1 Volume 4 at 5.
102 *Ibid* at 34.
103 *Ibid* at 5.
104 *Ibid* at 8.
105 *Ibid* at 10.
106 *Ibid* at 9.
107 *Ibid* at 11.
108 *Ibid* at 16.
109 *Ibid* at 11.
110 *Ibid* at 12.
111 *Ibid* at 13.
112 *Ibid.*
113 *Ibid.*
114 *Ibid* at 17.
115 *Ibid* at 18-19.
116 *Ibid* at 31.
117 *Ibid* at 19.
118 *Ibid* at 31.
119 *Ibid* at 86.
120 *Ibid* at 26.
121 Discussed in the Introduction, *supra* at note 18.
122 *Kondejewski* (Trial), *supra* note 1 Volume 4 at 37.
123 *Ibid* at 38.
124 *Ibid* at 39.
125 *Ibid* at 23.
126 *Ibid* at 40.
127 *Ibid* at 42.
128 *Ibid* at 47.
129 *Ibid* at 49.
130 *Ibid* at 53.
131 *Ibid* at 61.
132 *Ibid* at 66.
133 Browne, *supra* note 100 at 129, 130, reports that changes in severity, nature, or
     frequency of attack indicated to women that death was imminent. "Or an act would
     suddenly be beyond the range of what the women were willing to assimilate.
     Frequently, this involved the physical abuse of a child or the discovery that the man
     had forced sexual activity on a teenage daughter." She further explains: "Their final
     hope had been removed. They did not believe they could escape the abusive situa-
     tion and survive, and now they could no longer survive within it either."
134 *Kondejewski* (Trial), *supra* note 1 Volume 4 at 69 [transcriber's emphasis].
135 Scott Gibbons, "A Nightmare Life," *The Brandon Sun* (20 May 1998) 1.
136 *Kondejewski* (Trial), *supra* note 1 Volume 4 at 79.
137 *Ibid* at 95.

138 *Ibid.*
139 *Ibid.*
140 *Ibid* at 100.
141 See, for example, Gladys Heavenfire's trial, discussed *infra,* Chapter 4.
142 Elizabeth M Schneider, *Battered Women and Feminist Lawmaking* (New Haven: Yale University Press, 2000) at 136-37. Furthermore, mock juror studies indicate that when Battered Woman Syndrome evidence is presented jurors are more likely to see insanity as a plausible defence than if social context evidence is presented to frame the woman's act. Regina A Schuller, "Expert Evidence and Its Impact on Jurors' Decision in Homicide Trials Involving Battered Women" (2003) 10 Duke J Gender L & Pol'y 225 at 244.
143 Schneider, *ibid* at 136.
144 Restoring control to the woman is paramount. Judith Lewis Herman, *Trauma and Recovery: The Aftermath of Violence – from Domestic Abuse to Political Terror* (New York: Basic Books, 1992) at 134-35. See also Evan Stark, *Coercive Control: How Men Entrap Women in Personal Life* (Oxford: Oxford University Press, 2007) at 166: "Their defense lies not in the frailty of their character, personality, sex, class, or culture, not even in the proximate harms they faced from abusive partners. Their defense stems from the irreducible core of autonomy, liberty, and justice on which a free society rests."
145 Stubbs & Tolmie, *supra* note 41 at 212-13.
146 Stark, *supra* note 144 at 389.
147 *Kondejewski* (Trial), *supra* note 1 Volume 5, 20 May 1998 at 8.
148 *Ibid* at 9, 13 (twice), 14 (twice), 18, 19, 22, 30.
149 *Ibid* at 23.
150 *Ibid* at 27.
151 *Ibid* at 28.
152 *Ibid* at 16, 25, 28, 29.
153 *Ibid* at 29.
154 *Ibid* at 27.
155 *Ibid* at 31.
156 *Ibid* at 18.
157 He said *ibid* at 17 that she was "a profound victim of the Battered Woman Syndrome."
158 *Ibid* at 16.
159 *Ibid.*
160 *Ibid* at 54.
161 *Ibid* at 52.
162 *Ibid* at 50.
163 *Ibid.*
164 *Kondejewski* (Trial), *supra* note 1 Volume 6, 21 May 1998 at 1.
165 Canadian Press, "Battered Wife Had to Kill Husband, Lawyer Says," *The [Saskatoon] Star Phoenix* (22 May 1998) A17.
166 *Kondejewski* (Trial), *supra* note 1 Volume 6 at 11 (twice); see also at 2 (twice), 6, 12, 21 (twice), and 22 (three times).
167 *Ibid* at 9.

168 *Ibid* at 10.
169 *Ibid* at 3.
170 *Ibid* at 5.
171 *Ibid* at 7.
172 *Ibid* at 8.
173 *Ibid* at 18.
174 *Ibid* at 24.
175 *Ibid* at 25.
176 *Ibid* at 29.
177 *Ibid* at 30.
178 David Paciocco, "Applying the Law of Self-Defence," paper presented to judges of the Ontario Court of Justice, Kingston Regional Seminar, 10-12 October 2007 [unpublished] at 68.
179 *Kondejewski* (Trial), *supra* note 1 Volume 7, 22 May 1998 at 11.
180 *Ibid* at 19.
181 *R v Cadwallader,* [1966] 1 CCC 380 (Sask CA).
182 *Ibid* at 23.
183 Scott Gibbons, "Kondejewski Not Guilty," *The Brandon Sun* (23 May 1998) 1.
184 *Ibid.*
185 Paul Tim, "Woman Not Guilty of Murdering Husband," *The [Halifax] Daily News* (23 May 1998) 8.
186 Gibbons, "Kondejewski Not Guilty," *supra* note 183.
187 *Ibid.*
188 *Ibid.*
189 *Criminal Code,* ss 745(a), 745(c), 745.2, 745.4.
190 Dawson, *supra* note 11 at 13.
191 Cynthia K Gillespie, *Justifiable Homicide: Battered Women, Self-Defense, and the Law* (Columbus: Ohio State University Press, 1989) at 15.
192 *State v Yaklich,* 833 P2d 758 (Ct App Col 1991) (self-defence rejected where contract homicide would "undermine ancient notions of self-defense"), cited in Kerry McVey, "Battered Women and Contract Killings: Reconciling Fear with Agency" (student paper in satisfaction of LLB degree, University of Ottawa, 2009) [unpublished], on file with the author.
193 Her Honour Judge Lynn Ratushny, *Self-Defence Review: Final Report* (Submitted to the Minister of Justice and the Solicitor General of Canada, 11 July 1997) at 194.
194 See the discussion in the Introduction, *supra* at note 42. See, for example, *R v Perka,* [1984] 2 SCR 232.
195 *R v Ryan,* 2011 NSCA 11 at para 71. The decision of the Court of Appeal affirming the availability of duress as a defence in these circumstances was reversed on further appeal to the Supreme Court of Canada. The Court provided no clear indication of whether self-defence would be available on such facts, but stayed the prosecution of Nicole Ryan instead of returning her for a new trial. *R v Ryan,* 2013 SCC 3. The new self-defence law has abandoned the language of justification. See *infra,* Conclusion.
196 This approach was suggested by Justice Ratushny for one woman in the *Self-Defence Review* and by two sentencing decisions in South Africa: *Self-Defence Review, supra*

note 193 at 126-27; *State v Engelbrecht* (2005), 2 SACR 163 (SCA); and *State v Ferreira* (2004), 2 SACR 454 (SCA).

197 Lenore Walker, *The Battered Woman Syndrome*, 3d ed (New York: Springer Publishing, 2009) at 108.

198 Evan Stark reports that 20 percent of US states have admitted expert testimony on battering and its effects in cases in which battered women have hired third parties to kill their abusers. Evan Stark, "Preparing Expert Testimony in Domestic Violence Cases" in Albert R Roberts, ed, *Handbook of Domestic Violence Intervention Strategies* (Oxford: Oxford University Press, 2002) 216 at 221.

199 Justice Kathleen Satchwell would have afforded self-defence to Ms Engelbrecht at trial, but she was in the minority; the two assessors ruled that Ms Engelbrecht failed to act reasonably, in spite of her seven attempts to flee her husband and the refusal of the police to assist her. *State v Engelbrecht* (2005), 2 SACR 41 (SCA). For a discussion of the decision, see Hallie Ludsin & Lisa Vetten, *Spiral of Entrapment: Abused Women in Conflict with the Law* (Johannesburg: Jacana Media, 2005) at Chapter 4, "Defences for Women Protecting Their Lives."

200 Walker, *supra* note 197 at 108.

201 *Ibid* at 55-56.

202 Gillespie, *supra* note 191 at 51-52, discusses US and UK studies that support this point. One Philadelphia study reported that one-quarter of women killed by male partners were killed by their hands, fists, and feet.

203 Dawson, *supra* note 11 at 48.

204 Susan Edwards, "Ascribing Intention: The Neglected Role of Modus Operandi – Implications for Gender" (1999-2000) 4:3 Contemporary Issues in Law 235; Isabel Grant, "Rethinking the Sentencing Regime for Murder" (2001) 39:3 Osgoode Hall LJ 655 at 678; see also the cases discussed in *PEI Murdered Women 1989-2009* (Charlottetown: Prince Edward Island Advisory Council on the Status of Women, 2010) at 2, 4.

205 See, for example, *R v Klassen* (1997), 95 BCAC 136 (YCA), and *PEI Murdered Women, ibid* at 6, 7. In fact, men's use of bodily force to kill can be construed in law as a mitigating factor. Susan SM Edwards, "Abolishing Provocation and Reframing Self-Defence: The Law Commission's Options for Reform" [2004] Crim LR 181 at 190-91.

206 Marilyn MacCrimmon, "Trial by Ordeal" (1996) 1 CCLR 31 at 39, used this analogy to medieval trial practices as a way of capturing the experience of complainants in sexual assault trials whose therapy records and other private communications are disclosed to the accused and the court in order to "check her records."

207 Manitoba Justice, *Prosecutions: Role of the Manitoba Prosecution Service: The Decision to Prosecute* online http://www.gov.mb.ca/.

208 See *The Federal Prosecution Service Deskbook*, Part V, Section 15 The Decision to Prosecute 15.3.2 (Department of Justice Canada) online http://www.ppsc-sppc.gc.ca/; and Ontario Ministry of the Attorney General, Criminal Law Division, *Practice Memorandum: Charge Screening* (1 October 2002) point 9: "No public interest, no matter how compelling, can warrant the prosecution of an individual if there is no reasonable prospect of conviction."

209 *Self-Defence Review, supra* note 193 at 171.

210 Jack MacAndrew reported in "Charlottetown," *The Globe and Mail* (20 March 2001) A7, that the Crown prosecutor accepted a guilty plea to manslaughter and recommended a ten-year sentence for Frederick Sheppard's homicide of his wife to spare their seven-year-old son from testifying against his father.

211 *Criminal Code*, s 486.4; Jane Doe, "What's in a Name?" in Ian Kerr, ed, *Privacy, Identity and Anonymity in a Network Society: Lessons from the Identity Trail* (New York: Oxford University Press, 2009) 265.

212 E Margareta Hyden, *Woman Battering as Marital Act* (Oslo: Scandinavian University Press, 1994) at 109, reports that half the men in her study used *"their fists because they did not want to hear any more words"* [italics in the original]. She comments at 110: "As a well-tried means for enforcing the subordination of others, the use of violence offered these men the best option for achieving what they wanted ... [T]hey beat their wives into silence."

213 Elaine Scarry, *The Body in Pain: The Making and Unmaking of the World* (New York: Oxford University Press, 1985).

214 Elaine J Lawless, *Women Escaping Violence* (Columbia, MO: Missouri University Press, 2001) at 105.

215 *Ibid* at 152.

216 Patrizia Romito, *A Deafening Silence: Hidden Violence against Women and Children* (Bristol: Policy Press, 2008), describes these strategies as euphemizing, dehumanizing, psychologizing, naturalizing, legitimizing, and denying, among others.

217 She relied on the work of Felicity Hawthorn, "Interviews with Four Battered Women at the Prison for Women Who Are Serving Life Sentences for Murder" (27 April 1992) [unpublished], and Sheila Noonan, "Strategies of Survival: Moving beyond the Battered Woman Syndrome" in Claudia Currie & Ellen Adelberg, eds, *Too Few to Count* (Vancouver: Press Gang, 1993) 247.

218 Stephen Bindman, "Inmates' Freedom Hinges on Review," *The Ottawa Citizen* (14 July 1995) A3.

219 Judge Stuart Leggatt was asked in 1980 by the Minister of Justice to assess whether eighty-seven persons held indefinitely as "habitual offenders" under predecessor legislation should be released in light of the changed criteria in the 1977 legislation that permitted indefinite detention only for "dangerous offenders." The Honourable Judge Stuart Leggatt, *Report of the Inquiry into Habitual Criminals in Canada* (Ottawa: Government of Canada, 1984).

220 See Elizabeth Sheehy, "Review of the Self-Defence Review" (2000) 12:1 CJWL 197 and discussion *supra,* Introduction at note 49.

221 "This situation causes me serious concern. It means that women may be pleading guilty to manslaughter when they are legally innocent because they acted in self defence." *Self-Defence Review, supra* note 193 at 163. See also Martha Shaffer, "The Battered Woman Syndrome Revisited: Some Complicating Thoughts Five Years after *R. v. Lavallee*" (1997) 47:1 UTLJ 1, who found that, of sixteen cases post-*Lavallee*, nine of the women pled guilty to manslaughter, relinquishing strong claims to have acted in self-defence; Elizabeth Sheehy, "Developments in Canadian Law after *R v*

Lavallee" in Stubbs, *supra* note 41 at 174; and Sylvie Frigon, *L'homicide conjugal au feminine* (Montréal: Éditions du Remue-Ménage, 2003).

222 Constitutional challenges to mandatory minimum sentences for homicide offences have thus far been rejected by the Supreme Court, even though two justices have suggested that their impacts might be unfair for battered women. *R v Morrisey,* 2000 SCC 39 (per McLachlin and Arbour JJ). For an exploration of the distorting effects of the mandatory life sentence on battered women's trials, see Elizabeth Sheehy, "Battered Women and the Mandatory Minimum Sentence" (2001) 39:2 Osgoode Hall LJ 529.

223 *Self-Defence Review, supra* note 193 at 160-61.

224 *R v Pintar* (1996), 30 OR (3d) 483 at 483 (CA).

225 *Self-Defence Review, supra* note 193 at 161-62.

226 Karyn M Plumm & Cheryl A Terrance, "Battered Women Who Kill: The Impact of Expert Testimony and Empathy Induction in the Courtroom" (2009) 15:2 Violence against Women 186 at 201.

227 See Chapter 2, *supra* at note 132.

228 Women who fight back against violent male partners are more likely than men who assault female partners to experience depression, fear, and anxiety, to feel guilty about and assume responsibility for their actions, and to recount in detail their acts of violence. Leigh Goodmark, "When Is a Battered Woman Not a Battered Woman? When She Fights Back" (2008) 20:1 Yale J L & Feminism 75 at notes 105-8, 111.

229 Schneider, *supra* note 142 at 144-46; Sue Osthoff, Preface, in J Parrish, *Trend Analysis: Expert Testimony on Battering and Its Effects in Criminal Cases* (Philadelphia: National Clearinghouse for the Defense of Battered Women, 1994) at v.

230 See *Report of the Attorney General's Advisory Committee on Charge Screening, Disclosure and Resolution Discussions* (Honourable G Arthur Martin, Chair) (Toronto: Queen's Printer, 1993) at 293, 295, discussed in the *Self-Defence Review, supra* note 193 at 178-79.

231 Joan Brockman, "An Offer You Can't Refuse: Pleading Guilty When Innocent" (2010) 56:1 Crim LQ 116 at 119-22.

232 *Self-Defence Review, supra* note 193 at 179.

233 Kim Pate, Executive Director, Canadian Association of Elizabeth Fry Societies.

Chapter 4: Gladys Heavenfire and Doreen Sorenson

1 Emma LaRocque, "The Colonization of a Native Woman Scholar" in Christine Miller & Patricia Chuchryk, eds, *Women of the First Nations: Power, Wisdom, and Strength* (Winnipeg: University of Manitoba Press, 1996) 11 at 11.

2 Mario Toneguzzi, "Woman Charged in Shepard Shooting," *The Calgary Herald* (28 August 1990) B2.

3 In fact, domestic violence is more prevalent in rural Canada. Melissa Northcott, "Domestic Violence in Rural Canada" (2011) 4 Domestic Violence Research Digest, Chapter 2.

4 Sherene H Razack, "Gendered Racial Violence and Spacialized Justice: The Murder of Pamela George" ["Pamela George"] in Sherene H Razack, ed, *Race, Space and the*

Law: Unmapping a White Settler Society (Toronto: Between the Lines, 2002) 121 at 129 [*Race, Space and the Law*].

5 Kim Lunman, "Pastor, Prosecutor Strives to Be Fair," *The Calgary Herald* (15 November 1992) A3.

6 *Ibid.*

7 Don Thomas, "Native Justice Task Force to Meet Drumheller Inmates," *[The] Edmonton Journal* (3 May 1990) A7.

8 Canada, Canadian Centre for Justice Statistics, *Family Violence in Canada: A Statistical Profile*, Catalogue No 85-224-XPE (Ottawa: Statistics Canada, 2001) at 2. Note that Aboriginal men committed spousal homicide at a rate eighteen times greater than non-Aboriginal men.

9 Sheila Noonan, "Battered Woman's Syndrome: Shifting the Parameters of Criminal Law Defences (Or (Re)Inscribing the Familiar?)" in Anne Bottomley, ed, *Feminist Perspectives on Foundational Subjects of Law* (London: Cavendish Press, 1996) 191 at 207.

10 *R v Gladue*, [1999] 1 SCR 688, discussed in Chapter 5, *infra*.

11 Constance Backhouse, *Colour-Coded: A Legal History of Racism in Canada, 1900-1950* (Toronto: Osgoode Society for Legal History, 1999) at 12-14; Yasmin Jiwani, "The Criminalization of Race/the Racialization of Crime: There Are No 'Race Shield Laws'" in Wendy Chan & Kiran Mirchandani, eds, *Crimes of Colour: Racialization and the Criminal Justice System in Canada* (Toronto: University of Toronto Press, 2001) 67; David M Tanovich, "The Charter of Whiteness: Twenty-Five Years of Maintaining Racial Injustice in the Canadian Criminal Justice System" (2008) 40 SCLR (2d) 655. See also Gloria Galloway & Tavia Grant, "Canadians Increasingly Reporting Aboriginal Identity," *The Globe and Mail* (1 July 2013), online http://www.the globeandmail.com.

12 Sharon McIvor & Teressa Nahanee, "Aboriginal Women: Invisible Victims of Violence" in Kevin D Bonnycastle & George S Rigakos, eds, *Unsettling Truths: Battered Women, Policy, Politics, and Contemporary Research in Canada* (Vancouver: Collective Press, 1998) 63 at 65.

13 *R v Heavenfire*, No 9101-0133-CO, Alta QB, Calgary, Volume 5, 24 June 1991 at 640, per CM Jones, Crown Attorney [*Heavenfire* (Trial)].

14 Kim Heinrich, "The Battle over Bail: Recent Court Decisions Spark a New Round of Debate over the Ability of Accused Killers to Remain Free Pending Trial," *The Calgary Herald* (25 August 1995) B6.

15 Monica Zurowski, "Bar Scrap Preceded Slaying, Trial Told," *The Calgary Herald* (19 June 1991) B2.

16 She is now a justice of the Alberta Court of Appeal.

17 *Heavenfire* (Trial), *supra* note 13 Volume 1, 7 June 1991 at 3.

18 *Ibid* at 14.

19 *R v Williams*, [1998] 1 SCR 1128 at 1158.

20 *Heavenfire* (Trial), *supra* note 13 Volume 2, 18 June 1991 at 124.

21 *Ibid* at 250.

22 *Ibid* Volume 3, 19 June 1991 at 284.

23 *Ibid* at 306.

24 *Ibid* at 284.

25 *Ibid* at 318. The content of these other four police records was never revealed.
26 Patricia Monture, "Lessons in Decolonization: Aboriginal Overrepresentation in Canadian Criminal Justice" in David Long & Olive Patricia Dickason, eds, *Visions of the Heart: Canadian Aboriginal Issues*, 2d ed (Toronto: Harcourt, 2000) 361 at 371.
27 Anne McGillivray & Brenda Comaskey, *Black Eyes All of the Time: Intimate Violence, Aboriginal Women, and the Justice System* (Toronto: University of Toronto Press, 1999) at 29.
28 Jo-Anne Fiske, "Colonization and the Decline of Women's Status: The Tsimshian Case" (1991) 17:3 Feminist Stud 509 at 513.
29 *Stolen Sisters: A Human Rights Response to Discrimination and Violence against Indigenous Women in Canada* (Ottawa: Amnesty International Canada, 2004) at 13.
30 McGillivray & Comaskey, *supra* note 27 at 34.
31 Janice Acoose argues that these stereotypes live on in Canadian literature. See her *Iskwekwak – Kah' Ki Yaw Ni Wahkomaxanak: Neither Indian Princesses Nor Sq**w Drudges* (MA Thesis, Department of English, University of Saskatchewan, 1992) [unpublished]. I use ** for this term on the advice of Professor Darlene Johnston.
32 Emma LaRocque, "Written Presentation to Aboriginal Justice Inquiry Hearings" (5 February 1990) in *Report of the Aboriginal Justice Inquiry of Manitoba* (Winnipeg: Queen's Printer, 1991) at 479: "The portrayal of the sq**w is one of the most degraded, most despised and most dehumanized anywhere in the world. The 'sq**w' is the female counterpart to the Indian male 'savage' and as such she has no human face; she is lustful, immoral, unfeeling and dirty. Such grotesque dehumanization has rendered all Native women and girls vulnerable to gross physical, psychological and sexual violence ... I believe that there is a direct relationship between these horrible racist/sexist stereotypes and violence against Native women and girls."
33 McGillivray & Comaskey, *supra* note 27 at 33. In fact, colonization was deeply implicated in the prostitution of Aboriginal women. Jackie Lynne, "Colonialism and the Sexual Exploitation of Canada's First Nations Women," paper presented at the American Psychological Association 106th Annual Convention, San Francisco, 17 August 1998, online http://www.prostitutionresearch.com/; Melissa Farley & Jacqueline Lynne, "Prostitution in Vancouver: Pimping Women and the Colonization of First Nations" in Rebecca Whisnant & Christine Stark, eds, *Not for Sale: Feminists Resisting Prostitution and Pornography* (London: Spinifex Press, 2005) 106.
34 Associate Chief Judge Murray Sinclair, "A Presentation to the Western Workshop of the Western Judicial Education Centre" (14 May 1990), reproduced in Jennie Abell, Elizabeth Sheehy, & Natasha Bakht, eds, *Criminal Law and Procedure: Cases, Context, Critique*, 5th ed (Concord, ON: Captus Press, 2012) 86 at 90.
35 *Heavenfire* (Trial), *supra* note 13 Volume 3, 19 June 1991 at 339. See also Lynne Sears Williams, "Failure to Pursue Indications of Spousal Abuse Could Lead to Tragedy, Physicians Warned" (1995) 152:9 Can Med Ass J 1488 at 1489.
36 *Heavenfire* (Trial), *supra* note 13 Volume 3, 19 June 1991 at 343.
37 *Ibid* at 344.
38 *Ibid* at 326.
39 *Ibid* at 380.
40 *Ibid.*

41 *Ibid* at 310.
42 *Ibid* at 382.
43 *Ibid* at 389.
44 *Ibid* at 395.
45 Repeated in the transcript in the defence counsel's address to the jury. *Ibid* Volume 5, 24 June 1991 at 625.
46 *Ibid* Volume 4, 20 June 1991 at 432.
47 *Ibid.*
48 *Ibid* at 441.
49 *Ibid* at 447-48.
50 *Ibid* at 449.
51 *Ibid* at 452.
52 *Ibid* at 453.
53 *Ibid* at 457-58.
54 *Ibid* at 459.
55 *Ibid* at 462.
56 *Ibid* at 475.
57 *Ibid* at 482.
58 *Ibid* at 488.
59 *Ibid* at 489.
60 *Ibid* at 491.
61 *Ibid* at 499.
62 *Ibid* at 500.
63 *Ibid* at 501.
64 *Ibid* at 516.
65 *Ibid* at 512, 515.
66 L Kevin Hamberger & Clare E Guse, "Men's and Women's Use of Intimate Partner Violence in Clinical Samples" (2002) 8:11 Violence against Women 1301 at 1319.
67 *Heavenfire* (Trial), *supra* note 13 Volume 4, 20 June 1991 at 515.
68 *Ibid* at 514.
69 *Ibid* at 537.
70 *Ibid* at 547.
71 *Ibid* at 549.
72 *Ibid* at 553.
73 *Ibid* at 557.
74 *Ibid* at 558.
75 *Ibid* at 561.
76 *Ibid* at 562-63.
77 *Ibid* at 564.
78 *Ibid* at 566.
79 *Ibid* at 567.
80 *Ibid* at 568.
81 *Ibid* at 573.
82 *Ibid* at 584.
83 *Ibid* Volume 5, 24 June 1991 at 626.

84　*Ibid* at 640.
85　*Ibid* at 638.
86　*Ibid* at 655.
87　*Ibid* at 668.
88　*Ibid* at 687.
89　*Ibid* at 695.
90　However, Mary Rose Koyina was earlier acquitted in 1989, after Lavallee's trial acquittal. See Chapter 1 at note 272. Heavenfire seems to have been the first Alberta woman to be acquitted on this basis. Williams, *supra* note 35 at 1488.
91　Canadian Press, "Battered Woman Acquitted of Killing," *The [Montreal] Gazette* (25 June 1991) A8 ["Battered Woman Acquitted"].
92　Williams, *supra* note 35 at 1488.
93　Monica Zurowski, "Woman Found Not Guilty of Murdering Husband," *The Calgary Herald* (25 June 1991) A7 ["Woman Found Not Guilty"].
94　"Battered Woman Acquitted," *supra* note 91.
95　"Woman Found Not Guilty," *supra* note 93.
96　Monica Zurowski, "Weapon of Death Was a Gift," *The Calgary Herald* (25 June 1991) A1.
97　Razack, "Pamela George," *supra* note 4 at 154-55, discusses how racelessness or colour blindness was deployed as a legal strategy in the murder trials of two white men who beat Pamela George to death.
98　*Ibid* at 142.
99　*Ibid* at 128. Razack describes the "making of the white, masculine self as dominant through practices of violence directed at a colonized woman."
100　Mary Eberts, *In Harm's Way: The Legal Construction of Aboriginal Women as Prey* (Toronto: Native Women's Association of Canada, 2005) at 22.
101　Statistics Canada, *Measuring Violence against Women: Statistical Trends* (Ottawa: Canadian Centre for Justice Statistics, 2006) at 67.
102　Ontario Native Women's Association, *Breaking Free: A Proposal for Change to Aboriginal Family Violence* (Thunder Bay: Ontario Native Women's Association, 1989).
103　Aboriginal women are more likely to be injured than non-Aboriginal women (59 percent vs 41 percent) and to have feared for their lives (52 percent vs 31 percent). Shannon Brennan, "Violent Victimization of Aboriginal Women in the Canadian Provinces, 2009" in Statistics Canada, *Juristat*, Catalogue No 85-002-X (Ottawa: Minister of Industry, 2011) at 10.
104　McGillivray & Comaskey, *supra* note 27.
105　*Ibid* at 5-6.
106　Kristen Gilchrist, "'Newsworthy' Victims? Exploring Differences in Canadian Local Press Coverage of Missing/Murdered Aboriginal and White Women" (2010) 10:4 Feminist Media Stud 373.
107　Warren Goulding, *Just Another Indian: A Serial Killer and Canada's Indifference* (Calgary: Fifth House, 2001), especially Chapter 17, "Did Anyone Notice?" For a comparison of how Crawford's victims were treated in the media as opposed to those of Paul Bernardo, see Denise McConney, "Differences for Our Daughters: Racialized Sexism in Art, Mass Media, and the Law" (1999) 19:1 & 2 Can Woman

Stud 210. See also Jasmin Yiwani & Mary-Lynn Young, "Missing and Murdered
Women: Reproducing Marginality in News Discourse" (2006) 31:4 CJ Communication 895.

108 *Stolen Sisters, supra* note 29.
109 David Hugill, *Missing Women, Missing News* (Halifax: Fernwood Press, 2010) at 46.
110 Brennan, *supra* note 103 at 10 (69 percent of Aboriginal women said that they did
     not report compared with 76 percent of non-Aboriginal women).
111 McGillivray & Comaskey, *supra* note 27 at 95-96.
112 *Ibid* at 96-97.
113 *Ibid* at 100.
114 *Ibid* at 82.
115 *Ibid* at 93.
116 *Ibid* at 92. See also Kelly A MacDonald, "Justice Systems' Response: Violence against
     Aboriginal Girls" (Submitted to The Honourable Wally Oppal, Attorney General of
     British Columbia, September 2005), and the accounts documented in Human Rights
     Watch, *Those Who Take Us Away: Abusive Policing and Failures in Protection of
     Indigenous Women and Girls in Northern British Columbia, Canada* (2013), online
     http://www.hrw.org/reports/.
117 McGillivray & Comaskey, *supra* note 27 at 100.
118 See, for example, *R v Scarff,* [1994] YJ No 6 (Terr Ct), in which the severely beaten
     woman was acquitted of assault charges for stabbing her batterer, based on ample
     evidence that he was the aggressor and she the defender. Her wrongful arrest set off
     a chain of events and multiple charges against her. She was acquitted of mischief for
     later retracting her initial report of his assault based on his threats of retaliation. She
     was also acquitted of assault on a police officer because the arresting officer had en-
     gaged in an illegal strip search in her bathroom. She yelled and rushed at the officer;
     he threw her to the ground and kicked her. Scarff was acquitted of mischief for dam-
     aging the jail light fixture, on which she took out her frustration when the officer at
     the station removed the mattress in her cell for no reason. She was, however, con-
     victed of threatening him when, en route to jail, she uttered threats because she was
     afraid that she would lose custody of her children.
119 McGillivray & Comaskey, *supra* note 27 at 106.
120 Tracey Lindberg, Priscilla Campeau, & Maria Campbell, "Indigenous Women and
     Sexual Assault in Canada" in Elizabeth Sheehy, ed, *Sexual Assault in Canada: Law,
     Legal Practice and Women's Activism* (Ottawa: University of Ottawa Press, 2012) 87;
     Those Who Take Us Away, supra note 116 at 33-34, 50-56, 59-65.
121 See the studies reviewed in Leigh Goodmark, "When Is a Battered Woman Not a
     Battered Woman? When She Fights Back" (2008) 20:1 Yale J L & Feminism 75 at 129.
122 *Ibid* at 96, 102.
123 Canadian Association of Elizabeth Fry Societies & Native Women's Association of
     Canada, "Women and the Canadian Legal System: Examining Situations of Hyper-
     Responsibility" in Patricia A Monture & Patricia D McGuire, eds, *First Voices: An
     Aboriginal Women's Reader* (Toronto: Inanna Publications, 2009) 382 at 386 [CAEFS
     & NWAC].

124 Elisabeth C Wells, "'But Most of All, They Fought Together': Judicial Attributions for Sentences in Convicting Battered Women Who Kill" (2012) 36:3 Psych of Women Q 350 at 357.

125 *Ibid* at 358. See also the sentencing judge's portrayal of Constance St-Hilaire in Quebec in 1996, discussed in Barbara Hamilton & Elizabeth Sheehy, "Thrice Punished: Battered Women, Criminal Law and Disinheritance" (2004) 8 Southern Cross U L Rev 96 at 116-19.

126 Beth E Richie, *Compelled to Crime: The Gender Entrapment of Battered Black Women* (New York: Routledge, 1996) at 119.

127 *US v Whitetail,* 956 F 2d 857 (8th Cir 1992), discussed in Susan Edwards, *Sex and Gender in the Legal Process* (London: Blackstone Press, 1996) at 252.

128 See the judicial overreaction to a racial profiling argument by counsel in *R v Brown* (1993), 64 OR (3d) 161 (CA), and police reaction – through a suit in defamation – to a suggestion by defence lawyers that two white girls would not have been strip searched by the police as were their African Canadian clients in *Campbell v Jones,* 2002 NSCA 128.

129 See *R v RDS,* [1997] 3 SCR 484, in which Judge Corinne Sparks's comments in acquitting an African Canadian teen were challenged as displaying judicial bias against (white) police, and Sherene Razack's comment on the case in *"RDS v Her Majesty the Queen*: A Case about Home" in Gayle MacDonald, Rachel L Osborne, & Charles C Smith, eds, *Feminism, Law, Inclusion: Intersectionality in Action* (Toronto: Sumach Press, 2005) 200.

130 See Sheila Dawn Gil, "The Unspeakability of Racism: Mapping Law's Complicity in Manitoba's Racialized Spaces" in Razack, *Race, Space and the Law, supra* note 4 at 157, describing the ejection of MP Oscar Lathin, a Cree man, from the Manitoba legislature for using the word "racist," which was declared "unparliamentary language."

131 *Fatality Inquiry into the Deaths of Connie and Ty Jacobs,* 13 April 1999 at 3427.

132 *Ibid* 23 November 1999 at 8278-79.

133 Williams, *supra* note 35 at 1489.

134 *Ibid.*

135 *Ibid* at 1491.

136 *R v Doreen L Sorenson,* Transcript of the Proceedings, Saskatchewan Queen's Bench, Saskatoon, QBJ No 4 of AD 2005, Volume 2, 28 March 2006 at 330, Testimony of Tansu Oktay [*Sorenson* (Trial)].

137 *Ibid* Volume 1, 27 March 2006 at 148 (Testimony of Daniel Cunningham).

138 *Ibid* at 144.

139 *Ibid* at 136.

140 *Sorenson* (Trial), *supra* note 136 Volume 3, 3 April 2006 at 696.

141 *Williams, supra* note 19.

142 Justice Rothery stated in *Sorenson* (Trial), *supra* note 136 at 6, that "counsel have not advised me that there are any issues there, so I'm only anticipating a type of challenge called a peremptory challenge."

143 Thomas Claridge, "Half of Would-Be Jurors Stumble in Test of Impartiality," *The Globe and Mail* (1 October 1994) A3.

144 Challenges for "cause" are decided by two other persons pulled from the pool of potential jurors. *Criminal Code* s 640(2.1), (2.2), (3). Failing exclusion on this basis, both lawyers in a murder trial have twelve peremptory challenges, which they can use to exclude potential jurors without explaining or justifying their decision. *Criminal Code* s 634(2).

145 Betty Adam, "Woman Goes on Trial in Husband's Stabbing," *The [Saskatoon] Star Phoenix* (28 March 2006) A7.

146 Testimony of Sergeant James Gerard Engel under cross-examination. *Sorenson* (Trial), *supra* note 136 Volume 1, 27 March 2006 at 111-21.

147 *Ibid* Volume 3, 3 April 2006 at 693.

148 *Ibid* Volume 2, 29 March 2006 at 376.

149 *Ibid* 28 March 2006 at 264-65, 270.

150 *Ibid* at 277.

151 *Ibid* at 276.

152 *Ibid* at 304.

153 *Ibid* at 318.

154 *Ibid* at 325, 326.

155 *Ibid* at 320.

156 *Ibid* at 330.

157 *Ibid* Volume 3, 29 March 2006 at 493.

158 *Ibid* 30 March 2006 at 573.

159 *Ibid* at 613.

160 *Ibid* Volume 4, 3 April 2006 at 756.

161 *Ibid* at 770: "A black eye, broken ribs, he kicked her and kicked her"; at 771, "my dad hit her in the forehead with a hammer and she had this black goose egg."

162 *Ibid* at 774.

163 *Ibid* at 775.

164 *Ibid* at 779.

165 *Ibid* at 784.

166 *Ibid* at 787.

167 *Ibid* 4 April 2006 at 817-18.

168 *Ibid* at 823.

169 *Ibid* at 920.

170 *Ibid* at 828.

171 *Ibid* at 834.

172 *Ibid* at 836.

173 *Ibid* at 833.

174 *Ibid* at 836.

175 *Ibid* at 838.

176 *Ibid* at 842.

177 *Ibid* at 860.

178 *Ibid* at 925.

179 *Ibid* at 873.

180 *Ibid* at 854.

181 *Ibid* at 857.

182 *Ibid* at 926.
183 *Ibid* at 925.
184 *Ibid* at 875.
185 *Ibid* at 930.
186 *Ibid* at 905-6.
187 *Ibid* at 907.
188 *Ibid* at 917.
189 *Ibid* at 932.
190 *Ibid* Volume 5, 5 April 2006 at 1044-46.
191 *Ibid* at 1120.
192 As discussed in Chapter 1, Dr Walker defines a battered woman as a woman who has been through the cycle of violence at least twice.
193 *Sorenson* (Trial), *supra* note 136 Volume 5, 5 April 2006 at 1134.
194 *Ibid* at 1141.
195 *Ibid* at 1143.
196 *Ibid.*
197 *Ibid* at 1147.
198 *Ibid* 10 April 2006 at 1200.
199 *Ibid* at 1210.
200 *Ibid* at 1227.
201 *Ibid.*
202 *Ibid* at 1250.
203 *Ibid* at 1260.
204 *Ibid* at 1252-53.
205 Janai Gopal, "Woman Receives Three Years in Prison for Stabbing Death," *The [Saskatoon] Star Phoenix* (18 May 2006) A3.
206 *Ibid.*
207 CAEFS & NWAC, *supra* note 123 at 386.
208 Many Aboriginal people in Saskatoon were aware of this police practice long before it was officially recognized as a criminal matter. *Two Worlds Colliding* [DVD] (Ottawa: National Film Board of Canada, 2004).
209 Susanne Reber & Robert Renaud, *Starlight Tour: The Last Lonely Night of Neil Stonechild* (Toronto: Random House, 2005).
210 Shamita Das Dasgupta, "Just like Men? A Critical View of Violence by Women" in Melanie F Shepard & Ellen L Pence, eds, *Coordinating Community Responses to Domestic Violence: Lessons from Duluth and Beyond* (Thousand Oaks, CA: Sage Publications, 1999) 202 at 211.
211 *Sorenson* (Trial), *supra* note 136 Volume 2, 28 March 2006 at 324.
212 Razack, *supra* note 4 at 144.
213 *Ibid* at 147.
214 McConney, *supra* note 107 at 212.
215 Razack, *supra* note 4 at 156.
216 *Ibid* at 153.
217 *Ibid.*
218 *Ibid* at 146.

Chapter 5: Donelda Kay, Denise Robin Rain, and Jamie Gladue

1 *R v Gladue* (1997), 98 BCAC 120 at 128 [*Gladue* (CA)].
2 *R v Gladue*, [1999] 1 SCR 688 at 696 [*Gladue* (SCC)].
3 Section 718.2 (e) of the *Criminal Code*, SC 1995, c 22.
4 The Supreme Court reasoned that for such serious offences the punishment sought by both Aboriginal and non-Aboriginal communities would implicate imprisonment. *Gladue* (SCC), *supra* note 2 at 739. See also Jean Lash, "Case Comment: *R. v. Gladue*" (2000) 20:3 Can Woman Stud 85.
5 *Gladue* (CA), *supra* note 1 at 138.
6 *Ibid* at 128.
7 To withdraw her guilty plea, she would have required proof of incompetent legal advice. *Ibid*.
8 *R v Kay*, Transcript of Proceedings at Trial, QBC No 8 of 1994, Queen's Bench of Saskatchewan, Regina, Volume 1, 6 June 1994 at 213 [*Kay* (Trial)].
9 *Ibid* at 27.
10 *R v Lifchus*, [1997] 3 SCR 320 at 334.
11 *Ibid* at 335.
12 *Kay* (Trial), *supra* note 8 at 119.
13 *Ibid* at 43.
14 *Ibid* at 89, 125.
15 *Ibid* at 88.
16 Fran Sugar & Lana Fox, "Nistum Peyako Séht'wawin Iskwewak: Breaking Chains" (1989-90) 3:2 CJWL 465 at 473: "self-mutilations that are not suicide attempts, but the relief of tension and anger, physical pain self-inflicted as escape from what lies within."
17 *Kay* (Trial), *supra* note 8 at 83.
18 She was stripped, placed in oversized men's coveralls, and left barefoot.
19 *Ibid*.
20 *Ibid* at 84.
21 *R v Stillman*, [1997] 1 SCR 607: the police have no authority to simply pull hair samples from persons whom they arrest. Kay's right to be secure against search and seizure pursuant to *Charter* s 8 was arguably violated by this conduct.
22 *Kay* (Trial), *supra* note 8 Volume 1, 7 June 1994 at 138.
23 *Ibid* at 156.
24 *Ibid* at 191.
25 *Ibid*.
26 *Ibid* at 207, 212.
27 *Ibid* at 204, 234, 235, 243.
28 *Ibid* Volume 2 at 254, 255.
29 *Ibid* at 256-58.
30 *Ibid* Volume 1 at 213, Volume 2 at 252.
31 *Ibid* Volume 2 at 268-69.
32 *Ibid* at 275.
33 *Ibid* at 277.
34 *Ibid* at 284.

35 *Ibid* at 287.
36 *Ibid* at 324.
37 *Ibid* at 320-21.
38 *Ibid* at 333.
39 *Ibid* 8 June 1994 at 351.
40 *Ibid* at 366.
41 *Ibid* at 376.
42 *Ibid* at 369.
43 *Ibid* at 412.
44 *Ibid* Volume 3, 9 June 1994 at 576.
45 *Ibid* at 578.
46 *Ibid* at 581.
47 *Ibid* at 584.
48 *Ibid* at 587-88.
49 *Ibid* at 592.
50 *Ibid* at 596.
51 See e.g., Dene Moore, "Hundreds Join RCMP Harassment Case," *The Globe and Mail* (31 July 2012) A5.
52 *Kay* (Trial), *supra* note 8 Volume 3, 9 June 1994 at 598-600.
53 *Ibid* at 606-10.
54 *Ibid* at 610-11.
55 *Ibid.*
56 *Ibid* at 615.
57 *Ibid* at 616.
58 *Ibid* at 615.
59 *Ibid* at 617-18.
60 Canadian Criminal Justice Association, *Aboriginal Peoples and the Criminal Justice System* (Ottawa: Special Issue of the Bulletin, 2000) at Part 4, online http://www.ccja-acjp.ca/ [CCJA].
61 Stephanie Fryer-Smith, *Aboriginal Benchbook for Western Australia Courts* (Melbourne: Australasian Institute of Judicial Administration, 2002) at Chapter 5, "Language and Communication," at 5-8.
62 Furthermore, he warned, the expert cannot testify as to the "voracity" [sic] of Donelda Kay. *Kay* (Trial), *supra* note 8 Volume 3, 13 June 1994 at 627.
63 *Ibid* at 634.
64 *Ibid* at 635-36.
65 *Ibid* at 650.
66 *Ibid* at 651.
67 *Ibid* at 684.
68 *Ibid* at 687.
69 *Ibid* at 689.
70 *Ibid* at 690.
71 *Ibid* at 696.
72 *Ibid* at 700.
73 *Ibid* at 706.

74 *Ibid* at 707.
75 *Ibid* at 713.
76 *Ibid* at 714.
77 *Ibid* at 717.
78 Lorraine Greaves *et al*, "Substance Use among Women in Shelters for Abused Women and Children" (2006) 97:5 Can J Pub Health 388 at 392, discuss the search for long-term housing, employment, or welfare, criminal and family law issues, as well as chronic physical, mental health, and relational issues as major stressors for battered women who use substances.
79 *Kay* (Trial), *supra* note 8 Volume 3, 13 June 1994 at 718.
80 Sharon McIvor & Teressa Nahanee, "Aboriginal Women: Invisible Victims of Violence" in Kevin D Bonnycastle & George S Rigakos, eds, *Unsettling Truths: Battered Women, Policy, Politics, and Contemporary Research in Canada* (Vancouver: Collective Press, 1998) 63 at 65.
81 *Kay* (Trial), *supra* note 8 Volume 3, 13 June 1994 at 726.
82 *Ibid* Volume 4 at 737.
83 *Ibid* at 738.
84 *Ibid* at 743.
85 *Ibid* at 725, 761.
86 *Ibid* 14 June 1994 at 774.
87 *Ibid* at 790.
88 *Ibid* at 789.
89 *Ibid* at 814.
90 *Ibid* at 819.
91 *Ibid* at 820.
92 *Ibid* at 850.
93 *Ibid* at 853-54.
94 *Ibid* at 855.
95 *Ibid* at 856.
96 *Ibid* at 859.
97 *Ibid* at 860.
98 *Ibid* at 864.
99 *Ibid* at 886.
100 *Ibid* at 867.
101 *Ibid* at 894.
102 *Ibid* at 869.
103 *Ibid* at 879.
104 *Ibid* at 871.
105 *Ibid* at 872.
106 *Ibid* at 881.
107 *Ibid* at 887. See also Beth E Richie, *Compelled to Crime: The Gender Entrapment of Battered Black Women* (New York: Routledge, 1996) at 90, 92, where she discusses the experience of African American battered women of "detachment from their bodies, self-neglect, and shame that 'deepened' social isolation and alienation."

Battering results in "a *particularly* painful loss of identity, confidence, and self-esteem" [italics in original].

108 *Kay* (Trial), *supra* note 8 Volume 3, 14 June 1994 at 888.
109 *Ibid* at 889. She objected that Dr Neilson should not be permitted to testify to the ultimate issue of self-defence, which is for the jury to decide.
110 *Ibid.*
111 *Ibid* at 894.
112 *Ibid* at 895.
113 *Ibid* at 906.
114 *Ibid* at 907-8.
115 *Ibid* at 902.
116 *Ibid.*
117 *Ibid* at 908.
118 *Ibid* at 914.
119 *Ibid* at 915.
120 *Ibid* Volume 5, 16 June 1994 at 926.
121 *Ibid* at 941.
122 *Ibid* at 938.
123 *Ibid* at 949.
124 *Ibid* at 950.
125 *Ibid* at 947.
126 *Ibid* at 952-53.
127 *Ibid* at 957.
128 *Ibid* at 963.
129 *Ibid* at 965.
130 *Ibid* at 971.
131 *Ibid* at 972.
132 *Ibid.*
133 *Ibid* at 975.
134 *Ibid* at 978.
135 When a jury is struggling to reach a unanimous verdict, judges are required to carefully urge the jurors to attempt to find common ground, without influencing the verdict or in any way suggesting that the minority bend to the majority opinion. *R v G (RM)*, [1996] 3 SCR 362.
136 *Kay* (Trial), *supra* note 8 (Jury Deliberations) Volume 5, 18 June 1994 at 1037.
137 *Ibid* at 1039.
138 The Supreme Court subsequently adopted this interpretation of s 34(2). *R v McIntosh*, [1995] 1 SCR 686.
139 Barb Pacholik, "Kay Cleared of Murder," *The [Regina] Leader-Post* (20 June 1994) A1.
140 *Kay* (Trial), *supra* note 8 (Jury Deliberations) Volume 5 at 1073.
141 Pacholik, *supra* note 139.
142 *Kay* (Trial), *supra* note 8 Volume 5 at 1074.
143 *Ibid* at 1075.

144 Pacholik, *supra* note 139.

145 Aspects of Worme's opening and closing replicate those of Brodsky's almost to a word.

146 Susanne Reber & Robert Renaud, *Starlight Tour: The Last Lonely Night of Neil Stonechild* (Toronto: Random House, 2005) Prologue at 10.

147 He also served the Federation of Saskatchewan Indian Nations, the Association of Métis and Non-Status Indians, and the World Assembly of First Nations.

148 Kay (Trial), *supra* note 8 Volume 3, 13 June 1994 at 719 (per Della Kay).

149 Anne McGillivray & Brenda Comaskey, *Black Eyes All of the Time: Intimate Violence, Aboriginal Women, and the Justice System* (Toronto: University of Toronto Press, 1999) at 9.

150 *Ibid.*

151 *Ibid* at 11.

152 *Kay* (Trial), *supra* note 8 Volume 2 at 283.

153 *Ibid* Volume 1 at 87.

154 McIvor & Nahanee, *supra* note 80 at 63.

155 David Hugill, *Missing Women, Missing News: Covering Crisis in Vancouver's Downtown Eastside* (Halifax: Fernwood Publishing, 2010), argues that the media focus on a serial killer and police negligence effectively concealed the role of government policy – the contraction of social welfare, for example, and the dispossession of Aboriginal women of their homes and communities – in throwing women into poverty, homelessness, and prostitution. See also Beverley Jacobs, "Gender Discrimination under the Indian Act: Bill C-31 and First Nations Women" in Gayle McDonald, Rachel L Osborne, & Charles C Smith, eds, *Feminism, Law, Inclusion: Intersectionality in Action* (Toronto: Sumach Press, 2005) 175.

156 *R v Denise Robin Rain*, Transcript of Proceedings at Trial, No 99012429801, Alberta Queen's Bench, Edmonton, 27 March 2000 at 4 [*Rain* (Trial)].

157 Murder is tried by a jury unless the Crown and accused both agree otherwise. *Criminal Code*, s 536(2).

158 *Rain* (Trial), *supra* note 156 at 4.

159 *Ibid* at 97.

160 *Ibid* at 27.

161 *Ibid* at 37.

162 *Ibid* at 48.

163 *Ibid* at 53.

164 *Ibid* at 67.

165 *Ibid* at 69.

166 *Ibid* at 70.

167 *Ibid* at 73.

168 *Ibid* at 74.

169 *Ibid* at 77, 80.

170 *Ibid* at 86.

171 *Ibid* at 87.

172 *Ibid* at 89.

173 *Ibid* at 90.

174 *Ibid* at 91.
175 *Ibid* at 92.
176 *Ibid* at 107.
177 *Ibid* at 108.
178 Loraine Bacchus, Gill Mezey, & Susan Bewley, "A Qualitative Exploration of the Nature of Domestic Violence in Pregnancy" (2006) 12:6 Violence against Women 588.
179 *Rain* (Trial), *supra* note 156 at 114.
180 *Ibid* at 120.
181 *Ibid* at 123.
182 *Ibid* at 127.
183 *Ibid* at 128.
184 *Ibid* at 143.
185 *Ibid* at 145.
186 Mary Becker, "The Passions of Battered Women: Cognitive Links between Passion, Empathy and Power" (2001) 8:1 Wm & Mary J Women & L 1 at 17.
187 *Ibid* at 11, 16.
188 Michouche Kandel, "Women Who Kill Their Batterers Are Getting Battered in Court" *Ms* (July-August 1993) 88 at 89, quoting Valoree Day.
189 Becker, *supra* note 186 at 15.
190 *Rain* (Trial), *supra* note 156 at 200.
191 *Ibid* at 161.
192 *Ibid* at 168.
193 *Ibid* at 167.
194 *Ibid* at 177.
195 *Ibid* at 179.
196 *Ibid.*
197 *Ibid* at 180.
198 *Ibid* at 183.
199 *Ibid.*
200 *Ibid* at 192.
201 *Ibid* at 204.
202 *Ibid.*
203 *Ibid* at 206.
204 *Ibid* at 210.
205 *Ibid* at 215.
206 *Ibid* at 217.
207 *Ibid* at 298-99.
208 *Ibid* at 301-2.
209 *Ibid* at 302.
210 *Ibid.*
211 *Ibid.*
212 *Ibid.*
213 *Ibid* at 317.
214 *Ibid* at 330.

215 See, for example, *R v Eyapaise* (1993), 20 CR (4th) 246 (Alta CA), in which the accused was disentitled from self-defence when she stabbed a man whom she did not know who thrice sexually assaulted her. The presiding judge believed that she could have telephoned the police or her husband, left in a taxi, or called for aid from her cousin.

216 A report by Indian and Northern Affairs, *Aboriginal Women and Family Violence*, Final Report (DSS File No A0107-053090/001/CY) (2006), describes how women's access to support and services is compromised by distance, lack of transportation, poor relationships with the police, and lack of privacy in accessing resources, among other problems. See also Native Women's Association of Canada [NWAC], *Aboriginal Women: Police Charging Policies and Domestic Violence* (Ottawa: NWAC, 1994), which discusses the wide variation in charging practices by police in Aboriginal communities across the country.

217 Department of Justice Canada, Federal-Provincial-Territorial Meeting of Ministers Responsible for Justice, *Report on Sentencing for Manslaughter in Cases Involving Intimate Relationships* (Calgary, 4-6 November 2002), reports that women offenders were likely to receive sentences of two years less a day, including suspended sentences, conditional sentences (served in the community), and probation.

218 See Appendix, page 320 of this book.

219 For the specific factors that ought to be addressed in the sentencing of Aboriginal women after *Gladue*, see Angela Cameron, "R v Gladue: Sentencing and the Gendered Impacts of Colonialism" in John D Whyte, ed, *Moving toward Justice: Legal Traditions and Aboriginal Justice* (Saskatoon: Purich Publishing, 2008) 160.

220 Toni Williams, "Intersectionality Analysis in the Sentencing of Aboriginal Women in Canada: What Difference Does It Make?" in Emily Grabham *et al*, eds, *Intersectionality and Beyond: Law, Power and the Politics of Location* (Oxon: GlassHouse Books, 2009) 79 at 88. The overall incarceration rate dropped by almost 20 percent from 1996 to 2003. Non-Aboriginal women's incarceration at the federal level increased by 14 percent from 1996 to 2006, and Aboriginal women were one in five federal female prisoners in 1996 but as of 2006 constituted one in three. See also Cameron, *ibid* at 175-80 (harsh sentences imposed on two Aboriginal women that failed to fulfill the *Gladue* requirements), and Gillian Balfour, "Falling between the Cracks of Retributive and Restorative Justice: The Victimization and Punishment of Aboriginal Women" (2008) 3:2 Feminist Criminol 101.

221 Williams, *ibid* at 95.

222 Sugar & Fox, *supra* note 16.

223 Patricia A Monture-Angus, "Lessons in Decolonization: Aboriginal Overrepresentation in Canadian Criminal Justice" in David Long & Olive Patricia Dickason, eds, *Visions of the Heart: Canadian Aboriginal Issues*, 2d ed (Toronto: Harcourt, 2000) 361 at 379.

224 Sugar & Fox, *supra* note 16 at 476.

225 She had missed several menstrual periods; only after the homicide did her doctor rule out pregnancy. Her cessation of menstruation was attributed to extreme stress.

226 *R v Gladue*, Proceedings at Preliminary Inquiry, Day 1, No 34897 & 34897C (21 May 1996), Provincial Court, Nanaimo at 40 [*Gladue* (Preliminary Inquiry)].

227 *R v Gladue,* Proceedings at Sentence, Day 1, No 34897 (12 February 1997), Supreme Court of British Columbia, Nanaimo at 7 [*Gladue* (Sentencing)].

228 JC Campbell, C Oliver, & L Bullock, "Why Battering during Pregnancy?" (1993) 4:3 AWHONNS Clin Issues Perinat Women's Health Nurs 343 (women battered during pregnancy more frequently and severely battered).

229 *Gladue* (Preliminary Inquiry), *supra* note 226 at 34.

230 *Ibid* at 47.

231 *Ibid* at 58.

232 *Gladue* (Sentencing), *supra* note 227 at 14.

233 *Gladue* (Preliminary Inquiry), *supra* note 226 at 24.

234 *Ibid* at 37.

235 *Ibid* at 75-76.

236 *Ibid* at 67.

237 *Report of the Royal Commission on Aboriginal Peoples: Gathering Strength,* Volume 3 (Ottawa: Supply and Services Canada, 1996) at 167.

238 CCJA, *supra* note 60. This report relies on *Report of the Royal Commission on Aboriginal Peoples, ibid* at 167, 171.

239 Pauline De Jong, *Legal Service Provision in Northern Canada: Summary of Research in the Northwest Territories, Nunavut, and the Yukon* (Ottawa: Government of Canada, 2004) at 4.2.

240 Aboriginal & Torres Strait Islander Social Justice Commissioner, *Social Justice Report 2003* (Sydney: Human Rights and Equal Opportunity Commission, 2003) at 184.

241 Julie Stubbs & Julia Tolmie, "Battered Women Charged with Homicide: Advancing the Interests of Indigenous Women" (2008) 41:1 Aust & NZ J Criminol 138 at 148-49.

242 Affidavit of Theresa Hamilton, Solicitor, reproduced in *R v Kina,* Qld CA No 221, 1993.

243 "The doctor who saw Robyn Kina in the cells directly after the fatality, and who observed her to have sustained considerable bruising, was not interviewed by the solicitors until after the first, unsuccessful appeal in November 1988. The social worker who provided a report to the trial solicitors about his increasingly open discussions with Kina was told by Kina that her solicitors wished he would cease to interfere and he was not called or proofed for possible testimony. The Aboriginal Health Services worker who sent a letter to these solicitors about the exposure of Robyn Kina to brutalising domestic violence at the hands of the deceased was not called to discuss those observations – at all." Sarah Ford & Kate Auty, "One Indigenous Woman and What 'Her' Jury Did Not Hear" in Kate Auty & Sandy Toussaint, eds, *A Jury of Whose Peers? The Cultural Politics of Juries in Australia* (Crawley: University of Western Australia Press, 2004) 84 at 91.

244 Canadian Association of Elizabeth Fry Societies & Native Women's Association of Canada, "Women and the Canadian Legal System: Examining Situations of Hyper-Responsibility" in Patricia A Monture & Patricia D McGuire, eds, *First Voices: An Aboriginal Women's Reader* (Toronto: Inanna Publications, 2009) 382.

245 *Ibid* at 385.

246 Sugar & Fox, *supra* note 16 at 476. See also Rudy Wiebe & Yvonne Johnson, *Stolen Life: The Journey of a Cree Woman* (Toronto: Alfred A Knopf Canada, 1998).

247 Diana Eades, *Aboriginal English in the Courts: A Handbook* (Brisbane: Queensland Government, Department of Justice, 2000); Adam Alter, *Aborigines and Courtroom Communication: Problems and Solutions*, Working Paper 2004/2 (Canberra: Australian Human Rights Centre, 1994).

248 Alter, *ibid* at 4, 5.

249 Eades, *supra* note 247, describes questioning strategies, gratuitous concurrence, quantifiable specification, negative questions, pronunciation, grammar, and non-verbal contact as problem areas. Alter, *supra* note 247, discusses the different cognitive universes inhabited by those who speak different languages, different communication norms, and the underuse of interpreters as additional problems. See also *Submissions of the Aboriginal and Torres Strait Islanders Social Justice Commissioner on Common Problems Facing Aboriginal Witnesses* in *Giblet et al v Queensland and Uniting Church of Australia*, No QUD300/2005 (Fed Ct Aust, Queensland Registry).

250 McGillivray & Comaskey, *supra* note 149 at 65.

251 *Ibid* at 66.

252 Elisabeth C Wells, "'But Most of All, They Fought Together': Judicial Attributions for Sentences in Convicting Battered Women Who Kill" (2012) 36:3 Psych of Women Q 350 at 356.

253 Alicia H Clark & David W Foy, "Trauma Exposure and Alcohol Use in Battered Women" (2000) 6:1 Violence against Women 37 at 38.

254 Sara E Gutierres & Christina Van Puymbroeck, "Childhood and Adult Violence in the Lives of Women Who Misuse Substances" (2006) 11:5 and Violent Behaviour 497 at 503.

255 Canadian Panel on Violence Against Women, *Changing the Landscape: Ending · Violence – Achieving Equality*, Final Report (Ottawa: Minister of Supply and Services Canada, 1993) at 180 [*Changing the Landscape*], quotes drug and alcohol treatment centres as reporting that "the vast majority of addicts have suffered from violence as children and adults." These centres have long waiting lists, and local communities have few resources to provide support for those who return after completing programs.

256 Gutierres & Van Puymbroeck, *supra* note 254 at 501. See also *Changing the Landscape, ibid* at 180. The report quotes the Anishinabeck of Ontario for the proposition that "alcohol and drug abuse does not cause violence but that the two are often present together because they have the same root causes: low self-esteem, racism by the general population, social and economic conditions and the loss of Aboriginal social structures which were respectful of women, children and elders."

257 Michael Jackson, "Locking Up Natives in Canada" (1989) 23:2 UBC L Rev 215 at 218, argues that "the stereotypical view of native people" reflects "an equation of being drunk, being an Indian and in prison." This view, he argues, has "power in the popular imagination and ... [shapes] decisions of the police, prosecutors, judges and prison officials." Quoted in Sheila Noonan, "Battered Woman Syndrome: Shifting the Parameters of Criminal Defences (Or (Re)Inscribing the Familiar?)" in Anne

Bottomley, ed, *Feminist Perspectives on the Foundational Subjects of Law* (London: Routledge, 1996) 191 at 213, footnote 107.

258 Anthony Doob, Michelle Grossman, & Raymond Auger, "Aboriginal Homicides in Ontario" (1994) 36:1 CJ Criminol 29 at 47; see also Amber Richelle Dean, *Locking Them Up to Keep Them "Safe": Criminalized Girls in British Columbia* (Vancouver: Justice for Girls, 2005) at 24-25 (prosecutors more likely to overstate or claim a substance abuse problem for First Nations girls).

259 Debra Redhead died in a police cell when her injuries from her partner's violence went untreated because the police thought that she was inebriated even though her mother described her injuries as profound and obvious. Canadian Press, "Autopsy Finds Pregnant Native Died in Cell of Head Injuries," *The Ottawa Citizen* (27 July 1994) A5. Minnie Sutherland died in Hull, Quebec, after the police labelled her an intoxicated "sq**w" and left her on a snow bank rather than calling an ambulance. In fact, she had been hit by a car and suffered fatal head injuries. John Nihmey, *Fireworks and Folly: How We Killed Minnie Sutherland* (Toronto: Hushion House, 1999). See also Scott Edmonds, "Métis Allege Police Racism," *The [Toronto] Star* (27 April 2001) A7, reporting on the police failure to respond to five 9-1-1 calls made by two Métis women who were ignored by the police based on their belief that one of the women let her former boyfriend, against whom she had a restraining order, into the home and that they were all drinking together.

260 *R v Daviault*, [1994] 3 SCR 63.

261 Elizabeth Sheehy, *The Intoxication Defence in Canada: Why Women Should Care* (Ottawa: Canadian Advisory Council on the Status of Women, 1995); Corinne McKay, *Reform of the Law of Intoxication: A First Nations Women's Analysis* (Whitehorse: Yukon Women's Directorate, 1994); Elizabeth Sheehy, *A Brief on Bill C-72* (Ottawa: National Association of Women and the Law, 1995). The courts have found that s 33.1 violates *Charter* ss 7 and 11(d) but have divided on whether it can be upheld pursuant to s 1. Compare *R v Brenton*, [1999] NWTJ No 113 (SC) with *R v SN*, 2012 NUCJ 02, in which the court upheld the law, in part because the rate at which Aboriginal women experience intoxicated male violence is "stunning" (at para 48).

262 Noonan, *supra* note 257 at 212.

263 *Ibid* at 213-14, discussing *R v Raymond*, [1993] NWT J No 86 (Terr Ct). See also Cameron, *supra* note 219 at 172, who reviews three cases in which Aboriginal women's "drug and/or alcohol addictions were given little mitigating weight."

264 Monture-Angus, *supra* note 223 at 378: "Alcohol was introduced into Aboriginal nations by European traders who learned they could accumulate great profits when they relied on alcohol as a trade commodity."

265 Caroline L Tait, "Simpering Outrage during an 'Epidemic' of Fetal Alcohol Syndrome" in Monture & McGuire, *supra* note 244, 312 at 316. Tait critiques the discourse around "Fetal Alcohol Syndrome," as contrasted with "the larger discourse of 'intergenerational trauma,' that has been adopted by Indigenous peoples to explain the negative health and social impacts of colonization." Fetal Alcohol Syndrome discourse recasts "intergenerational trauma" "not as collective suffering that at an individual level manifests itself as psychological and emotional distress, but one

grounded in biology, and specifically a cognitive deficit that exists beyond the bounds of Indigenous healing."

266 For example, Jean Toner, "Resistance and Recovery: Three Women's Testimonies" in Ellen Faulkner & Gayle MacDonald, eds, *Victim No More: Women's Resistance to Law, Culture and Power* (Halifax: Fernwood Publishing, 2009) 163, explores substance abuse and recovery strategies as resistance to "status oppression," including the loneliness and isolation caused by racism, among Indigenous women in the United States.

267 Aboriginal women's incarceration rate exploded by 151 percent between 1997 and 2007, making them 32 percent of federally incarcerated women even though they are 3 percent of Canadian women. Howard Sapers, *Annual Report of the Correctional Investigator, 2006-2007* (Ottawa: Minister of Public Works and Government Services of Canada, 2007) at 20. Over the past decade, the number of Aboriginal women in federal custody increased by 86.4 percent, while the number of Aboriginal men increased by 25.7 percent. *Annual Report of the Office of the Correctional Investigator 2010-2011* (Ottawa: Minister of Public Works and Government Services of Canada, 2011) at 50.

268 Aboriginal women accounted for 45 percent of maximum security women in 2007. *Ibid.* See also Paul Verbrugge & Kelley Blanchette, "The Validity of the Custody Rating Scale for the Initial Classification of Aboriginal Women" (2002) 14:3 Forum on Corrections Research online http://www.csc-scc.gc.ca/.

269 Statistics Canada, *Measuring Violence against Women: Statistical Trends* (Ottawa: Canadian Centre for Justice Statistics, 2006) at 68 (speculating that Aboriginal women's higher reporting rate is in keeping with the more severe levels of violence and injuries that they experience).

270 See media statements by men jurors after Paul Bernardo's trial in which they claimed that Karla Homolka was not a "battered woman" in spite of front-page news photos showing her bruised and swollen face when she contacted the police. Kirk Makin, "Homolka Just as Guilty as Bernardo, Juror Says," *The Globe and Mail* (16 September 1995) A5. Women jurors responded; see Estanislao Oziewicz, "Homolka Was Battered Woman, Jurors Say," *The Globe and Mail* (21 September 1995) A8. See also Anne McGillivray, "'A Moral Vacuity in Her which Is Difficult if Not Impossible to Explain': Law, Psychiatry and the Remaking of Karla Homolka" (1998) 5:2 & 3 Int J Legal Prof 255.

Chapter 6: Lilian Getkate

1 Pat McCann, opening address to the jury, *R v Lilian Getkate*, Transcript of Proceedings at Trial, Court File # 95-20433, Ontario Court of Justice (General Division), Ottawa, Volume 1, 15 September 1998 at 29 [*Getkate* (Trial)].

2 Peter Hum, "Accused Describes Years of Abuse," *The Ottawa Citizen* (25 September 1998) B1.

3 *R v Getkate*, [1996] OJ No 5297 (Ct Just Prov Div) at paras 28, 29 (statements ruled "voluntary" and therefore admissible for the purposes of the preliminary inquiry) [*Getkate No 2*].

4 *Ibid* at para 34.

5 Although there are no comparable Canadian studies, British researchers have concluded that "women are much more likely to answer police questions." Tom Bucke & David Brown, *In Police Custody: Police Powers and Suspects' Rights under the Revised PACE Codes of Practice* (London: Home Office, 1997) at 36, and David Dixon, *Law in Policing: Legal Regulation and Police Practices* (Oxford: Clarendon Press, 1997) at 264, as described in Law Reform Commission, New South Wales, *Report 95: The Right to Silence* (2000) at para 2.119. This report states that women "are also less likely to request legal advice than males and are more likely to make admissions than men." *Ibid* at note 207, citing Bucke & Brown at 20, 33.

6 Cynthia Gillespie, *Justifiable Homicide: Battered Women, Self-Defense, and the Law* (Columbus: Ohio State University Press, 1989) at 15: "There is seldom any question about who did the killing: in the typical case, it is the woman herself who calls the police and freely acknowledges that she wielded the knife or pulled the trigger." She writes that the police then proceed to build a murder case, carefully choosing language that supports a theory of premeditated murder, attributing motives to the accused women, and sometimes starkly revealing police vindictiveness. *Ibid* at 18.

7 See *R v Coté*, 2011 SCC 46; *R v Way*, 2010 NBQB 154; and Brian Vallée, *The War on Women* (Toronto: Key Porter Books, 2007) at 186-87 (Alan Ferrier, on behalf of Jane Hurshman, unsuccessfully argued for the exclusion of her statements to the police: "The course of the evening was in fact designed to tire and frustrate a woman who was obviously very placid and quiet; who was under the influence of drugs [Valium]; and it was a design on their part to create an atmosphere of sympathy – to give her the impression that they understood her ... She was almost constantly with one police officer or another for a period of nine hours."

8 *R v Getkate*, [1998] OJ No 4198 (Ont Ct Just Gen Div) at paras 2, 3 [*Getkate No 3*]. Even when she asserted that she wanted to contact counsel, the officer purported to respect her request by verbally acknowledging it but continued to interrogate her, eventually securing her confession.

9 James Ptacek, *Battered Women in the Courtroom: The Power of Judicial Responses* (Boston: Northeastern University Press, 1999).

10 *Ibid* at Chapter 8, "Disorder in the Courts: Battering and Judicial Responses" at 174. Ptacek uses Figure 8.2 on this page to redraft the Duluth Power and Control Wheel using examples from the court process under the same headings in order to make vivid the parallels. See also examples provided in TK Logan & Jody Raphael, "Book Review: Evan Stark, *Coercive Control: How Men Entrap Women in Personal Life*" (2007) 13:8 Violence against Women 885 at 889 (woman required by judge to show how she was beaten with a hanger on her hands and knees).

11 Justice Jean Bienvenue made several inappropriate comments while presiding over Tracy Théberge's murder trial in Trois-Rivières in December 1995. He was removed from the bench. See *Report to the Canadian Judicial Counsel by the Inquiry Committee Appointed under Subsection 63(1) of the Judges Act to Conduct a Public Inquiry into the Conduct of Mr Justice Jean Bienvenue of the Superior Court of Quebec in R v T Théberge* (June 1996). A new trial was ordered for Théberge.

12 Province of Ontario Ministry of the Attorney General, *Crown Policy Manual: Spouse/Partner Offences* (21 March 2005). Prosecutorial policies, as well as other

innovations such as "domestic violence courts," are discussed by the essayists in Jane Ursel, Leslie M Tutty, & Janice leMaistre, eds, *What's Law Got to Do with It? The Law, Specialized Courts and Domestic Violence in Canada* (Toronto: Cormorant Books, 2008).

13 Angela Browne, *When Battered Women Kill* (New York: Free Press, 1987) at 128-29.

14 Cheryl Hanna, "The Paradox of Progress: Translating Evan Stark's Coercive Control into Legal Doctrines for Abused Women" (2009) 15:12 Violence against Women 1458 at 1476.

15 Dianne Noel, quoting statements made by Lilian Getkate while in detention. Examination in Chief, *Getkate* (Trial), *supra* note 1 Volume 5, 23 September 1998 at 509.

16 *R v Getkate*, [1995] OJ No 4291 (Ct Just Gen Div) [*Getkate No 1*].

17 *Getkate No 3*, *supra* note 8 at para 9.

18 *Ibid* at paras 9, 21.

19 *R v Taylor* (1992), 77 CCC (3d) 551 (Ont CA), called it a "limited cognitive capacity test."

20 If successful, this defence results in a verdict of "not criminally responsible." The person is then assessed at a disposition hearing to determine whether she or he can be released either unconditionally or on supervision or must be detained. *Criminal Code*, ss 672.11, 672.34, 672.45.

21 *Getkate No 1*, *supra* note 16 at para 28.

22 *Getkate No 3*, *supra* note 8 at para 18.

23 *Ibid* at para 21. Justice Chadwick decided that there was a reasonable basis for counsel's decision, namely securing his client's pre-trial release, even though it had long-term implications for her trial. He further found that there was no evidence that this decision fundamentally altered the trial strategy. *Ibid* at paras 21, 22.

24 Evan Stark & Anne Flitcraft, *Women at Risk: Domestic Violence and Women's Health* (Thousand Oaks, CA: Sage Publications, 1996) at 45, citing Frances Cobbe, "Wife Torture in England" (April 1878) 32 Contemporary Rev 55.

25 *Getkate* (Trial), *supra* note 1 Volume 1 at 21, 22.

26 *Ibid* at 27.

27 *Ibid* at 28.

28 *Ibid* at 29.

29 *Ibid* at 48.

30 *Ibid* at 47.

31 *Ibid* at 73.

32 *Ibid* at 75.

33 *Getkate* (Trial), *supra* note 1 Volume 2, 16 September 1998 at 163.

34 *Ibid* at 204.

35 *Ibid* at 218.

36 *Ibid* at 265.

37 *Ibid* at 263.

38 *Ibid* at 270.

39 *Ibid* at 273.

40 *Ibid* at 274.
41 *Getkate* (Trial), *supra* note 1 Volume 4, 22 September 1998 at 341.
42 *Ibid* at 309.
43 *Ibid* at 313, 315-16, and 328.
44 *Ibid* at 316.
45 *Ibid.*
46 *Ibid* at 314.
47 *Ibid* at 315.
48 *Ibid* at 316.
49 *Ibid* at 314.
50 *Ibid* at 316.
51 *Ibid* at 318.
52 Browne, *supra* note 13 at 101. See also Lori Haskell & Melanie Randall, "Politics of Women's Safety: Sexual Violence, Women's Fear and the Public/Private Split" (1999) 26:3 & 4 RFR 113 at 141-42 (40 percent of battered women interviewed felt unable to refuse unwanted sexual contact by the abusers).
53 *Ibid.* See also Beth E Richie, *Compelled to Crime: The Gender Entrapment of Battered Black Women* (New York: Routledge, 1996) at 89, and Maryse Rinfret *et al*, "A Survey on Violence against Female Partners in Québec, Canada" (2004) 10:7 Violence against Women 709 at 716 ("35% of sexually violent behaviours occurred six times or more during the preceding year").
54 Holly Johnson, "Limits of a Criminal Justice Response: Trends in Police and Court Processing of Sexual Assault" in Elizabeth Sheehy, ed, *Sexual Assault in Canada: Law, Legal Practice and Women's Activism* (Ottawa: University of Ottawa Press, 2012) 613.
55 Jennifer Koshan, "The Legal Treatment of Marital Rape and Women's Equality: An Analysis of the Canadian Experience" (September 2010) online http://www.theequalityeffect.org at 17.
56 *Getkate* (Trial), *supra* note 1 Volume 4 at 324.
57 *Ibid* at 324-25.
58 *Ibid* at 327.
59 *Ibid.*
60 *Ibid* at 322.
61 *Ibid.*
62 *Ibid* at 332-33.
63 *Ibid* at 346.
64 *Ibid* at 347.
65 *Ibid* at 351-53. See also Sara E Gutierres & Christina Van Puymbroeck, "Childhood and Adult Violence in the Lives of Women Who Abuse Substances" (2006) 11:5 Aggression and Violent Behaviour 497 at 504. "[M]erely asking if one has 'ever been raped?' is insufficient because so many marital rape survivors do not identify the sexual violence as rape. Women should be asked whether their partners 'have forced them to do things sexually they were uncomfortable with,' 'pressured them to have intercourse,' 'had intercourse with them while they were asleep,' 'forced them to have sex against their will,' and so forth." Raquel Kennedy Bergen, *Marital Rape:*

New Research and Directions (National Online Resource Center on Violence against Women, Applied Research Forum, February 2006) online vawnet.org/Assoc_Files_VAWnet/AR_MaritalRapeRevised.pdf at 8.

66 *Getkate* (Trial), *supra* note 1 Volume 4 at 373-74.

67 *Ibid* at 375.

68 *Ibid* at 380.

69 Evan Stark, "Preparing for Expert Testimony in Domestic Violence Cases" in Albert R Roberts, ed, *Handbook of Domestic Violence Intervention Strategies* (Oxford: Oxford University Press, 2002) 216 at 252 [Stark, "Preparing for Expert Testimony"].

70 Mary Becker, "The Passions of Battered Women: Cognitive Links between Passion, Empathy and Power" (2001) 8:1 Wm & Mary J of Women & L 1 at 50-51.

71 Re-examination is limited to exploring matters raised on cross-examination.

72 *Getkate* (Trial), *supra* note 1 Volume 4 at 385.

73 *Ibid* at 397.

74 *Ibid* at 402.

75 *Ibid* at 394.

76 *Ibid* at 403.

77 *Ibid* at 400.

78 *Ibid* at 401.

79 *Ibid* at 403-4.

80 *Ibid* at 410.

81 *Ibid* at 406.

82 *Ibid* at 408.

83 *Ibid* at 418.

84 *Ibid* at 422.

85 *Ibid* at 431.

86 *Ibid* at 453.

87 *Ibid* at 450.

88 *Ibid* at 454.

89 *Ibid* at 464-65.

90 *Ibid* at 461.

91 *Ibid* at 463.

92 *Getkate* (Trial), *supra* note 1 Volume 6, 24 September 1998 at 699.

93 *Getkate* (Trial), *supra* note 1 Volume 5, 23 September 1998 at 492.

94 *Ibid* at 493.

95 *Ibid* at 509.

96 *Ibid* at 509-10.

97 *Ibid* at 504.

98 *Ibid* at 505.

99 *Ibid* at 513-14.

100 *Ibid* at 514-15. Lilian testified: "[H]e had me phone him when I got there and when we were on the phone he would tell me what he is doing, where he is at with what he is doing, and where he was going, and that kind of stuff, what time I was going to be home, and that sort of thing, and I had already told him before I left how long I thought I would be." *Getkate* (Trial), *supra* note 1 Volume 6 at 684.

101 *Getkate* (Trial), *supra* note 1 Volume 5 at 515.
102 *Ibid* at 519.
103 *Ibid* at 520.
104 *Ibid* at 524.
105 *Ibid* at 516.
106 *Ibid* at 524.
107 *Ibid* at 525. Lilian testified that Maury made it increasingly difficult for her to get from the house with the children and into the car for church. He would stop them at the door, criticizing their dress, and complaining about the four dollars in church collections that they would spend (at 688-90).
108 *Ibid* at 526.
109 *Getkate* (Trial), *supra* note 1 Volume 1 at 52.
110 *R v Getkate*, [1998] OJ No 4199 (Ct Just Gen Div) at paras 12, 13 [*Getkate No 4*].
111 Hum, *supra* note 2.
112 *Getkate* (Trial), *supra* note 1 Volume 6 at 569-70.
113 *Ibid* at 575.
114 *Ibid* at 576-77.
115 *Ibid* at 578-79.
116 *Ibid* at 581.
117 *Ibid* at 583.
118 *Ibid* at 589.
119 *Ibid* at 585-86.
120 *Ibid* at 597.
121 *Ibid* at 607.
122 *Ibid* at 608.
123 Hum, *supra* note 2.
124 *Getkate* (Trial), *supra* note 1 Volume 6 at 610.
125 *Ibid* at 611.
126 *Ibid* at 629.
127 *Ibid* at 630.
128 *Ibid* at 634.
129 Robbin S Ogle & Susan Jacobs, *Self-Defense and Battered Women Who Kill: A New Framework* (Westport, CT: Praeger, 2002) at 80.
130 *Getkate* (Trial), *supra* note 1 Volume 6 at 643.
131 *Ibid* at 694.
132 *Ibid* at 642.
133 *Ibid* at 648.
134 *Ibid* at 656.
135 *Ibid* at 657.
136 *Ibid* at 651.
137 *Ibid* at 652.
138 *Ibid* at 666.
139 *Getkate* (Trial), *supra* note 1 Volume 5 at 529.
140 *Getkate* (Trial), *supra* note 1 Volume 6 at 692.
141 *Ibid* at 679.

142 *Ibid* at 695.
143 *Ibid* at 698.
144 *Ibid* at 708.
145 *Ibid* at 710.
146 *Ibid.*
147 *Ibid* at 711.
148 *Ibid* at 714.
149 *Ibid* at 718-19.
150 *Ibid* at 723.
151 *Getkate* (Trial), *supra* note 1 Volume 7, 25 September 1998 at 727.
152 *Ibid* at 728.
153 *Ibid* at 741.
154 *Ibid* at 759.
155 *Ibid* at 760.
156 *Ibid* at 760-61.
157 *Ibid* at 761.
158 *Ibid* at 762.
159 *Ibid* at 763.
160 *Ibid* at 745-46.
161 *Ibid* at 746.
162 *Ibid* at 801.
163 *Ibid* at 827.
164 *Ibid* at 764-65.
165 *Ibid* at 765.
166 *Ibid* at 767-68.
167 *Ibid* at 863.
168 *Ibid.*
169 *Ibid* at 884.
170 *Ibid* at 885-86.
171 Koshan, *supra* note 55 at 21.
172 *Getkate* (Trial), *supra* note 1 Volume 7, 25 September 1998 at 906-8.
173 *Ibid* at 911.
174 *Ibid.*
175 *Ibid* at 926.
176 *Ibid* at 919.
177 Donald Alexander Downs, *More than Victims: Battered Women, the Syndrome Society and the Law* (Chicago: University of Chicago Press, 1996) at 62 [italics in original].
178 *Ibid*, quoting Anthony Giddens, *Modernity and Self-Identity: Self and Society in the Late Modern Age* (Stanford, CA: Stanford University Press, 1991) at 53. For example, Downs at 63 discusses a battered woman who "lacked a sense of a continuum of time to such an extent that the defense team had to work hard to instil one in order for her testimony of abuse to have credibility. Mueller [her lawyer] explicitly linked this lack to Ronda's general inability (at that period of her life) to show emotion and a sense of injustice about the abuse she had suffered."
179 *Getkate* (Trial), *supra* note 1 Volume 7 at 927.

180 *Ibid.*
181 *Ibid* at 783.
182 *Ibid* at 784.
183 *Ibid* at 784.
184 *Ibid* at 786.
185 *Ibid* at 811 (two times).
186 *Ibid* at 794.
187 *Ibid* at 791.
188 Gillespie, *supra* note 6 at 77, noting post-separation femicides and increased risks associated with attempts to utilize other social resources.
189 Alyce D LaViolette & Ola W Barnett, *It Could Happen to Anyone: Why Battered Women Stay,* 2d ed (Thousand Oaks, CA: Sage Publications, 2000) at 58-61 (discussing the scandal of the Los Angeles Police Department's protection of its own officers from wife assault prosecution); Diane Wetendorf, *When the Batterer Is a Law Enforcement Officer: A Guide for Advocates* (Battered Women's Justice Project, 2004) online http://www.vaw.umn.edu/. She reports at 4 that women in the "police family" "repeatedly showed me how police abusers' institutional power makes safety planning very complicated. Remedies such as safe houses, shelters, address confidentiality, or identity change are undermined by a police officer's knowledge of investigative techniques and his access to all types of personal information through private and government data base searches. Victims had all been warned: 'There is nowhere you can hide that I won't be able to find you.'" See also Gina Gallo, "Airing Law Enforcement's Dirty Laundry" (2004) 31:6 Law Enforcement Technology 132, who discusses the paucity of research but notes cases in which the police failed to file domestic violence reports against fellow officers.
190 *Getkate* (Trial), *supra* note 1 Volume 7 at 806.
191 *Ibid* at 809.
192 *Ibid* at 811.
193 *Ibid* at 832.
194 *Ibid* at 837.
195 *Ibid* at 828.
196 *Ibid* at 827-28.
197 *Ibid* at 840.
198 *Ibid* at 841.
199 *Ibid* at 851.
200 *Ibid* at 845.
201 *Ibid* at 874-75.
202 *Ibid* at 876.
203 *Ibid* at 878.
204 *Ibid* at 855.
205 Ogle & Jacobs, *supra* note 129 at 47, note "the contribution of failed attempts to utilize outside assistance to escalating danger in these relationships." At 76, they state that "[e]fforts to utilize inadequate resources in the past are likely to have resulted in increased violence, control regained by the batterer, and a lesson for the victim on the batterer's power and her isolation."

206 *Ibid* at 77 [italics in original].

207 *Getkate* (Trial), *supra* note 1 Volume 7at 855.

208 *Ibid* at 857.

209 *Ibid* at 856, 860.

210 *Ibid* at 868.

211 *Ibid* at 871.

212 *Ibid* at 931-32.

213 *Ibid* at 938, 944-46.

214 Dr Glancy, quoting Lilian Getkate, *Getkate* (Trial), *supra* note 1 Volume 8, 28 September 1998 at 1009.

215 *Ibid* at 954.

216 *Ibid* at 977-78.

217 *Ibid* at 980.

218 *Ibid* at 964.

219 *Ibid* at 990.

220 *Ibid* at 985.

221 *Ibid* at 968.

222 *Ibid* at 971.

223 *Ibid* at 981.

224 *Ibid* at 975.

225 *Ibid* at 986-87.

226 *Ibid* at 994-95.

227 *Ibid* at 1030-31.

228 *Ibid* at 1000.

229 *Ibid* at 1003.

230 *Ibid* at 1006.

231 *Ibid* at 1022.

232 American Psychiatric Association, *Diagnostic and Statistical Manual of Mental Disorders,* 4th ed (Washington, DC: American Psychiatric Association, 2000). The 5th edition was released in May 2013, but has not changed in this regard.

233 *Ibid* at 1021.

234 This slippage among PTSD, Complex PTSD, and Battered Woman Syndrome illustrates how the broad and often "absolute" discourse of "the syndrome" can take over even when it is disavowed by the expert. For discussion, see Melissa Hamilton, *Expert Testimony on Domestic Violence: A Discourse Analysis* (El Paso: LFB Scholarly Publishing, 2009) at 76-77.

235 *Getkate* (Trial), *supra* note 1 Volume 8 at 1026.

236 *Ibid* at 1027-28.

237 *Ibid* at 1032.

238 *Ibid* at 1035.

239 *Ibid* at 1049, 1071.

240 *Ibid* at 1063.

241 Statistics Canada, *Measuring Violence against Women: Statistical Trends 2006* (Ottawa: StatCan, 2006) at 14; Peter Jaffe *et al, Children of Battered Women* (Newbury Park, CA: Sage Publications, 1990).

242 *Getkate* (Trial), *supra* note 1 Volume 8, 28 September 1998 at 1065.
243 *Ibid* at 1066.
244 *Ibid* at 1086. He was presumably referring to *R v Malott*, [1998] 1 SCR 123, released earlier that year, in February 1998, per L'Heureux-Dubé and McLachlin, JJ, concurring.
245 *Getkate* (Trial), *supra* note 1 Volume 8 at 1098.
246 *Ibid* at 1100.
247 *Ibid* at 1092-93.
248 *Ibid* at 1094.
249 *Ibid* at 1096.
250 *Ibid* at 1102.
251 *Ibid* at 1103.
252 *Ibid* at 1040.
253 *Ibid* at 1111-12.
254 *Getkate* (Trial), *supra* note 1 Volume 9, 29 September 1998 at 1133.
255 *Ibid* at 1161.
256 *Ibid* at 1143.
257 *Ibid* at 1199.
258 *Ibid* at 1148.
259 *Ibid* at 1161.
260 *Ibid* at 1159.
261 *Ibid* at 1196.
262 *Ibid* at 1178.
263 *Getkate* (Trial), *supra* note 1 Volume 10, 30 September 1998 at 1231, 1239, 1249.
264 *Ibid* at 1233.
265 *Ibid* at 1226.
266 *Ibid* at 1251.
267 *Ibid* at 1252.
268 *Ibid* at 1253.
269 *Ibid* at 1267. This is a paraphrase of Sir Matthew Hale's debunked claim that "[r]ape is an accusation easily to be made and hard to be proved and harder to be defended by the party accused though never so innocent." Sir Matthew Hale, *The History of the Pleas of the Crown*, George Wilson, ed (London: Little-Britain, 1800) at 634.
270 *Getkate* (Trial), *supra* note 1 Volume 10 at 1268.
271 *Ibid* at 1290.
272 *Getkate* (Trial), *supra* note 1 Volume 11, 1 October 1998 at 1310.
273 *Ibid* at 1318.
274 *Ibid* at 1325.
275 *Ibid* at 1350.
276 *Getkate* (Trial), *supra* note 1 Volume 12, 4 October 1998 at 1364.
277 *Ibid* at 1366.
278 Patrick FD McCann, "Getkate's Sentence Was Just," Letter to the Editor, *The Ottawa Citizen* (16 November 1998) B5.
279 *Ibid*.
280 Rebecca Bradfield, "Women Who Kill: Lack of Intent and Diminished Responsibility as the 'Other' Defences to Spousal Homicide" (2001-2) 13:2 Current Issues Crim Just 132.

281 Micheline Vaillancourt was not acquitted by her jury but by the appeal court when it overturned her murder conviction. *R v Vaillancourt,* [1999] JQ No 571 (CA).

282 Regina Schuller, "Expert Evidence and Its Impact on Jurors' Decisions in Homicide Trials Involving Battered Women" (2003) 10 Duke J Gender L & Pol'y 225 at 243.

283 *R v Krieger,* 2006 SCC 47.

284 *R v MacDonald,* 2008 ONCA 572.

285 In fact, they can be prosecuted under the *Criminal Code,* s 649, for revealing their deliberations.

286 *R v Morgentaler,* [1988] 1 SCR 30; for criticism, see Edward M Goldberg, "The 'Bad Law' Argument in *Morgentaler v The Queen*" (1989-90) 3:2 CJWL 584.

287 According to Robert E Korrach & Michael J Davidson, "Jury Nullification: A Call for Justice" (1993) 139 Military L Rev 131 at 139, discussed in Elisabeth Ayyildiz, "When Battered Woman's Syndrome Does Not Go Far Enough: The Battered Woman as Vigilante" (1995-96) 4:1 Am U J Gender & L 141 at 164, Maryland and Indiana permit jurors to be told about their power to nullify. In June 2012, New Hampshire also adopted a nullification law that provides: "In all criminal proceedings the court shall permit the defense to inform the jury of its right to judge the facts and the application of the law in relation to the facts in controversy." US, HB 146, *Relative to the right of a jury to judge the application of the law to the facts in controversy,* Reg Sess, NH, 2012.

288 See *infra* at notes 315-17.

289 Evan Stark, "Re-Presenting Woman Battering: From Battered Woman Syndrome to Coercive Control" (1995) 58:4 Albany L Rev 973 at 1000 [Stark, "Re-Presenting Woman Battering"].

290 "[B]atterers learn effective coercive control tactics by trial and error, revising them to see which work best in the given situation with a given partner." Logan & Raphael, *supra* note 10 at 887.

291 Stark, "Re-Presenting Woman Battering," *supra* note 289 at 1009.

292 See *Thigpen v State,* 546 SE 2d 60 (Ga Ct App 2001), discussed by Hanna, *supra* note 14 at 1472.

293 Evan Stark, *Coercive Control: How Men Entrap Women in Personal Life* (New York: Oxford University Press, 2007) [Stark, *Coercive Control*].

294 *Ibid* at 5.

295 *Ibid* at 278.

296 See *R v Craig,* 2011 ONCA 142. Dr Evan Stark testified on behalf of Teresa Craig in her first-degree murder trial for stabbing her husband while he slept. She denied violence or sexual assault by her husband but testified that she was very afraid of him. She was convicted of manslaughter.

297 Stark, *Coercive Control, supra* note 293 at 276-77.

298 Lisa A Goodman & Deborah Epstein, *Listening to Battered Women: A Survivor-Centered Approach to Advocacy, Mental Health, and Justice* (Washington, DC: American Psychological Association, 2008) at 17-18, citing JC Campbell, P Sharps, & NE Glass, "Risk Assessment for Intimate Partner Violence" in GF Pinard & L Pagani, eds, *Clinical Assessment of Dangerousness: Empirical Contributions* (New York: Cambridge University Press, 2000) 136.

299 Ogle & Jacobs, *supra* note 129 at 81-85. See also Martha R Mahoney, "Legal Images of Battered Women: Redefining the Issue of Separation" (1991) 90:1 Mich L Rev 1.

300 Ogle & Jacobs, *supra* note 129 at 82-83.

301 Stark, "Preparing for Expert Testimony," *supra* note 69 at 230.

302 Stark, *Coercive Control, supra* note 293 at 5.

303 Stark, "Re-Presenting Woman Battering," *supra* note 289 at 1017-19.

304 Emma Williamson, "Living in the World of the Domestic Violence Perpetrator: Negotiating the Unreality of Coercive Control" (2010) 16:12 Violence against Women 1412 at 1415: "The impact of living within an unreality of someone else's making is that you become paralyzed. This woman cannot do anything because whatever she does is wrong."

305 Stark, "Re-Presenting Woman Battering," *supra* note 289 at 1003-4, describes the trial of Donna B: "During the trial ... [the log book that she was forced to keep] became emblematic of how her every movement had been scrutinized, entered and regulated, thereby reproducing the sense of suffocation she must have experienced during the last beating."

306 Goodman & Epstein, *supra* note 298 at 9.

307 Stark, "Re-Presenting Woman Battering," *supra* note 289 at 1009-10.

308 *Ibid* at 1003. See also William R Downs, Barb Rindels, & Christine Atkinson, "Women's Use of Physical and Nonphysical Self-Defense Strategies during Incidents of Partner Violence" (2007) 13:1 Violence against Women 28; Dana-Ain Davis, "Non-Violent Survival Strategies in the Face of Intimate Partner Violence and Economic Discrimination" in Kathy A McCloskey & Marilyn H Sitaker, eds, *Backs against the Wall: Battered Women's Resistance Strategies* (New York: Routledge, 2009) 113; and Melanie Randall, *Agency and (In)Subordination: Victimization, Resistance and Sexual Violence in Women's Lives* (PhD dissertation, Political Science, York University, 1996) [unpublished].

309 Stark, "Re-Presenting Woman Battering," *supra* note 289 at 1023.

310 Peter Hum, "Getkate Convicted on Lesser Charge," *The Ottawa Citizen* (5 October 1998) B1 at B2.

311 *Ibid.*

312 *Ibid.*

313 Peter Hum, "'This Abuse Thing Is a Crock,'" *The Ottawa Citizen* (5 October 1998) B1.

314 *R v Getkate*, [1998] OJ No 6329 (Ct Just Gen Div) at para 12 [*Getkate No 5*].

315 *Getkate* (Trial), *supra* note 1 Volume 13, 10 November 1998 at 1368.

316 *Ibid* at 1370.

317 Peter Hum, "Getkate Won't Go to Jail: Lenient Sentence for Killing Spouse Angers Crown, Victim's Family," *The Ottawa Citizen* (11 November 1998) C1. [Hum, "Getkate Won't Go to Jail"].

318 *Criminal Code*, s 236(a).

319 Hum, "Getkate Won't Go to Jail," *supra* note 317.

320 "Appeal Rejected in Manslaughter Case," *The [Vancouver] Province* (10 December 1998) A12.

321 Sharon Lamb & Susan Keon, "Blaming the Perpetrator: Language that Distorts Reality in Newspaper Articles on Men Battering Women" (1995) 19:2 Psych of Women Q 209.

322 Letter from the Status of Women Council of the Northwest Territories to Justice Minister Allan Rock, 2 November 1994 (on impact of a Supreme Court ruling on "extreme intoxication").

323 Geraldine Finn, "Taking Gender into Account in the Theatre of Terror: Violence, Media, and the Maintenance of Male Dominance" (1989-90) 3:2 CJWL 375; see also the evidence of Micheline Vaillancourt in her murder trial. *Vaillancourt, supra* note 281 at paras 10, 11. She testified that as she contemplated asking her husband for a divorce, she read to him a news item about a man who strangled his wife when she had proposed divorce, in order to gauge his reaction.

324 Compare Jessica A Wozniak & Kathy A McCloskey, "Fact or Fiction? Gender Issues Related to Newspaper Reports of Intimate Partner Homicide" (2010) 16:8 Violence against Women 934, and Jordan Fairbairn, *I Loved Her... I Killed Her: The Construction of Intimate Partner Homicide in Canadian Print Media* (MA Thesis, Department of Sociology and Anthropology, University of Guelph, 2008) [unpublished].

325 Peter Hum, "Getkate Hit Daughter 'as Hard as He Could,' Court Hears," *The Ottawa Citizen* (24 September 1998) D3; Peter Hum, "Accused Describes Years of Abuse," *The Ottawa Citizen* (25 September 1998) B1; Peter Hum, "Getkate Fits Bill for Abused Wife, Psychiatrist Says," *The Ottawa Citizen* (30 September 1998) C3.

326 Dave Rogers, "Doubt Cast on Getkate's Defence: Psychiatrist Doesn't Believe Claim of Battered-Wife Syndrome," *The Ottawa Citizen* (23 September 1998) C3; Peter Hum, "Slain Man Described as Calm, Gentle," *The Ottawa Citizen* (17 September 1998) D1; Peter Hum, "Getkate Had Trouble 'Sticking to a Story,' Lawyer Argues," *The Ottawa Citizen* (26 September 1998) C2; Peter Hum, "'Desperate for a Way Out of Her Marriage,'" *The Ottawa Citizen* (1 October 1998) B1; Hum, "'This Abuse Thing Is a Crock,'" *supra* note 313. For a sophisticated analysis of media reporting on a mother's homicide trial, see Emma Cunliffe, *Murder, Medicine and Motherhood* (Oxford: Hart Publishing, 2011) at Chapter 8, "Media Monster."

327 Leonard Stern, "Wife Charged in Psychologist's Slaying," *The Ottawa Citizen* (9 December 1995) A1; Brenda Branswell, "Psychologist Shot Twice, Autopsy Reveals," *The Ottawa Citizen* (10 December 1995) A1; "Police, Friends Seek Motive for Killing of Psychologist," *The Ottawa Citizen* (11 December 1995) B2; "Wife of RCMP Psychologist to Stand Trial for His Murder," *The Ottawa Citizen* (2 November 1996) C5.

328 "An Insult to Our Sense of Justice," Editorial, *The Ottawa Citizen* (12 November 1998) B4.

329 *Ibid.*

330 "Battering Justice," Editorial, *The National Post* (27 November 1998) A19.

331 *Ibid.*

332 *Ibid.*

333 Ron Corbett, "'I'm Getting On with My Life': Lilian Getkate, the Woman Who Shot Her Husband Dead and Didn't Go to Jail for It, Says She's Shocked, and a Little Angry over the Media's Handling of Her Case," *The Ottawa Citizen* (26 November 1998) C1. [Corbett, "'I'm Getting on with My Life'"].

334 Ron Corbett, "Appeal Rejected, Book Closes on Getkate Case," *The Ottawa Citizen* (10 December 1998) C3.

335 Peter Hum, "Killer's 'Stay-at-Home' Jail Term Pushes Crown to Request Appeal," *The Ottawa Citizen* (13 November 1998) B3.

336 Peter Hum, "Husband-Killer Spared Prison: 'Appalling Message': No Independent Evidence of Abuse, Crown Points Out," *The National Post* (11 November 1998) A6; "No Appeal of Sentence in Husband Killing," *The National Post* (10 December 1998) A9.

337 "Killer Mom Home Free: Tearful Mother: 'I Just Want to Go Home with My Kids,'" *The [Vancouver] Province* (12 November 1998) A1.

338 "Killers Deserve Time behind Bars," Editorial, *The Ottawa Citizen* (9 February 1999) C4.

339 Robert W Sterling, "Judge Ignored His Duty in Sentencing Getkate," Letter to the Editor, *The Ottawa Citizen* (14 November 1998) B6 (arguing that the judge defeated the will of the legislator and usurped legislative power by refusing to apply the new *Criminal Code* amendments requiring a mandatory four-year sentence to Getkate, even though they did not take effect until three weeks after her criminal act – something that the judge is prohibited from doing not only by the *Criminal Code* but also by the *Constitution*); Michael Kroitor, "Murder Should Be Totally Unacceptable," Letter to the Editor, *The Ottawa Citizen* (20 November 1998) B5 (stating that he was "very frightened" by the sentence and that "millions upon millions of dollars ... go into funding battered women's shelters, policing as well as mandates for doctors and health-care workers to report abuse when it is suspected"); Tom Chapman, "Gender Bias Evident When Women Only Get 'Slap on the Wrist,'" Letter to the Editor, *The [Vancouver] Province* (25 November 1998) A41 (lamenting that "our media reports and public perception ha[ve] been ... grossly influenced by women's rights and violence against women").

340 *CFRA-AM and CHO-TV re The Lowell Green Show*, CBSC Decisions 98/99-0157, 0158, and 0177, decided 17 June 1999 (Canadian Broadcast Standards Council, Ontario Regional Council).

341 McCann, *supra* note 278.

342 *Ibid*, referring to *R v Ferguson*, [1997] OJ No 2488 (Sup Ct).

343 *Ibid*.

344 Suzanne Vezina, "If Women Must Kill to Protect Selves, So Be It," Letter to the Editor, *The Ottawa Citizen* (16 November 1998) B5.

345 Donna Johnson, "Why Prosecute Women for Self-Defence?," Letter to the Editor, *The Ottawa Citizen* (15 October 1998) B4.

346 *Ibid*.

347 Ron Corbett, "Getkate: 'I Was Packed to Go to Jail,'" *The Ottawa Citizen* (26 November 1998) A1.

348 Corbett, "'I'm Getting On with My Life,'" *supra* note 333.

349 Julianne Parfett, "Beyond Battered Woman Syndrome Evidence: An Alternative Approach to the Use of Abuse Evidence in Spousal Homicide Cases" (2001) 12 Windsor Rev Legal & Soc Issues 55 at 62.

350 For provocation, she seems to be suggesting the attenuation of the "suddenness" requirement: "The defence of provocation needs to be reformulated in order to take

into account that, in an unequal relationship, it may not be possible for the weaker party to react to the provoking action immediately." *Ibid* at 93.

351 *Ibid* at 67.

Chapter 7: Margaret Ann Malott and Rita Graveline

1 *R v Margaret Ann Malott*, Transcript of Proceedings at Trial, Court File No C-13886, Ontario Court (General Division), Windsor, Volume 4, 24 September 1992 at 191 [*Malott* (Trial)].

2 *Ibid* Volume 10, 6 October 1992 at 138-39.

3 *R v Graveline*, Cause No 550-01-002547-992 (Cours Supérieure, Chambre Criminelle, Hull) 20 février 2001 at 77 [*Graveline* (Trial)], per Marc Desjardins.

4 *Ibid* at 166, per Luc Bastien.

5 Pascal Monpetit, "Wife Distraught after Shooting," *The Ottawa Citizen* (22 February 2001) C8.

6 Rita was described as a "doting grandmother." See "Grandmother Arrested," *The National Post* (12 August 1999) online http://www.nationalpost.com/.

7 *Malott* (Trial), *supra* note 1 Volume 3, 23 September 1992 at 108. Testimony of Mary Featherstone, mother of Paul Malott.

8 Although severance of charges is within a judge's discretion pursuant to *Criminal Code*, s 591(3)(a), and can be ordered when the person will be prejudiced by being tried on both charges in the same trial, severance is very difficult to secure because of the competing interest in avoiding the cost of two trials. Here, because both charges arose out of the same transaction (*Criminal Code*, ss 589, 591(1), and 789(1)(b)), Margaret was denied severance.

9 *Malott* (Trial), *supra* note 1 Volume 1, 21 September 1992 at 103-13.

10 *Ibid* at 116.

11 *Ibid* at 124.

12 *Ibid* at 128-32.

13 *Malott* (Trial), *supra* note 1 Volume 2, 22 September 1992 at 161-62.

14 *Ibid* at 157.

15 *Ibid* at 176.

16 *Ibid* at 209-10.

17 *Ibid* at 211.

18 *Ibid* at 215.

19 *Ibid* at 216.

20 *Ibid* at 227.

21 *Ibid* at 222.

22 *Ibid* at 226.

23 *Ibid* at 231.

24 *Malott* (Trial), *supra* note 1 Volume 3, 23 September 1992 at 108.

25 *Ibid* at 114-15.

26 *Ibid* at 120.

27 *Ibid* at 125, 121.

28 *Ibid* at 141.

29 *Ibid* at 122.

30 *Ibid* at 125.
31 *Ibid* at 130.
32 *Ibid* at 143.
33 *Ibid* at 159.
34 Roseann Danese, "Woman Describes Being Shot, Knifed by Boyfriend's Wife," *The Windsor Star* (24 September 1992) A3.
35 Nick Pron, "Man Killed, Lover Injured in Trailer Park Shooting," *The [Toronto] Star* (25 March 1991) A2.
36 *Malott* (Trial), *supra* note 1 Volume 3, 22 September 1992 at 174.
37 *Ibid* at 191.
38 *Ibid* at 192.
39 *Ibid* at 180.
40 *Ibid* at 182.
41 *Ibid* at 198.
42 *Ibid* at 201.
43 *Ibid* at 224.
44 *Ibid* at 240.
45 *Ibid* at 260, 246.
46 *Ibid* at 169.
47 "Helmuth Buxbaum, Convicted of 1980s Murder, Dies in Jail," *CBC News* (2 November 2007) online http://www.cbc.ca/.
48 *Malott* (Trial), *supra* note 1 Volume 3, 22 September 1992 at 182.
49 *Ibid* at 183.
50 *Ibid* at 184.
51 *Ibid* at 188.
52 *Ibid* at 190.
53 Charles Patrick Ewing, *Battered Women Who Kill: Psychological Self-Defense as Legal Justification* (Lexington, MA: Lexington Books, 1987) at 62.
54 *Ibid.*
55 *Malott* (Trial), *supra* note 1 Volume 3 at 203.
56 *Ibid* at 232.
57 *Ibid* at 231.
58 *Ibid* at 235.
59 *Ibid* at 237.
60 *Malott* (Trial), *supra* note 1 Volume 5, 25 September 1992 at 103.
61 *Ibid* at 105.
62 *Ibid* at 109.
63 *Ibid* at 128.
64 *Ibid* at 122.
65 Evan Stark, "Re-Presenting Woman Battering: From Battered Woman Syndrome to Coercive Control" (1995) 58:4 Alb L Rev 973 at 1003, describes a battered woman being weighed by her husband each week. See also the Kondejewski and Getkate trials, Chapters 3 and 6 respectively.
66 *Malott* (Trial), *supra* note 1 Volume 5 at 141.
67 *Ibid* at 148.

68 *Ibid* at 154.
69 *Ibid* at 162.
70 *Ibid* at 165.
71 *Controlled Drugs and Substances Act*, SC 1996, c 19, s 4(2).
72 *Malott* (Trial), *supra* note 1 Volume 5 at 177.
73 *Ibid* at 178.
74 *Ibid* at 178-79.
75 *Ibid* at 179.
76 *Ibid* at 184.
77 *Ibid* at 189.
78 *Malott* (Trial), *supra* note 1 Volume 6, 26 September 1992 at 104.
79 *Ibid* at 110.
80 *Ibid* at 115.
81 *Ibid* at 141.
82 *Ibid.*
83 *Ibid* at 143.
84 *Ibid* at 142.
85 *Ibid* at 144.
86 *Ibid* at 145.
87 *Ibid* at 148.
88 *Ibid* at 159.
89 *Ibid* at 161.
90 *Ibid* at 160.
91 *Malott* (Trial), *supra* note 1 Volume 7, 1 October 1992 at 120.
92 *Ibid* at 189.
93 *Ibid* at 193.
94 *Ibid* at 196.
95 *Ibid.*
96 *Malott* (Trial), *supra* note 1 Volume 6 at 230.
97 *Ibid* at 229.
98 *Ibid* at 232.
99 *Ibid.*
100 *Ibid* at 230.
101 *Ibid* at 246.
102 *Ibid* at 257.
103 *Ibid* at 262.
104 *Malott* (Trial), *supra* note 1 Volume 7 at 147.
105 *Ibid* at 175.
106 *Ibid* at 234.
107 *Ibid* at 245.
108 *Ibid* at 232-33.
109 Raquel Kennedy Bergen, "Marital Rape" (March 1999), National Electronic Network on Violence against Women, Applied Research Forum, online http://www.hawaii. edu/.
110 *Malott* (Trial), *supra* note 1 Volume 7 at 138.

111 *Malott* (Trial), *supra* note 1 Volume 6 at 258.
112 *Malott* (Trial), *supra* note 1 Volume 7 at 164.
113 *Ibid* at 159.
114 *Ibid* at 256.
115 *Ibid* at 106.
116 *Ibid* at 106-7.
117 *Ibid* at 133.
118 *Ibid* at 109.
119 *Ibid* at 110.
120 *Malott* (Trial), *supra* note 1 Volume 6 at 265; *Malott* (Trial), *supra* note 1 Volume 7 at 112.
121 *Malott* (Trial), *supra* note 1 Volume 7 at 130.
122 *Ibid* at 116.
123 *Ibid* at 267.
124 *Ibid* at 126-27.
125 *Ibid* at 113.
126 *Ibid* at 264.
127 *Ibid* at 242.
128 *Ibid* at 151.
129 *Ibid* at 163.
130 *Ibid* at 150.
131 *Ibid* at 149.
132 *Ibid* at 166.
133 Lenore Walker refers to the forms of psychological torture advanced by Amnesty International, *infra* note 137, and reports that "[m]ost battered women experience most or all of them." Lenore Walker, *The Battered Woman Syndrome*, 3d ed (New York: Springer Publishing, 2009) at 393.
134 This definition comes from the Preamble of the *Declaration of Tokyo*, adopted by the World Medical Association in 1975 during its 29th General Assembly. For a thorough analysis of domestic violence as torture, see Shannon Selden, "The Practice of Domestic Violence" (2001) 12:1 UCLA Women's LJ 1. She argues that domestic captivity gives the torturer constant access to the victim. His use of violence "has the twofold effect of torture: the infliction of injury reduces the victim to physical pain and the verbal acts accompanying the injury make the woman appear to be the source of her [own] suffering." *Ibid* at 41.
135 John Locke, *Two Treatises of Government*, Peter Laslett, rev ed (Cambridge: Cambridge University Press, 1960) at 320, quoted in Ewing, *supra* note 53 at 83.
136 Frances Cobbe, "Wife Torture in England" (April 1878) 32 Contemporary Rev 55 at 72 [italics in original].
137 "Biderman's Chart of Coercion" in Amnesty International, *Report on Torture*, 2d ed (London: Duckworth and Amnesty International, 1975) at 53.
138 "Psychological and Physical Torture Have Similar Mental Effects" (6 March 2007) *ScienceDaily* online http://www.sciencedaily.com/.
139 "Psychiatric Impact of Torture Could Be Amplified by Head Injury" (8 November 2009) *ScienceDaily* online http://www.sciencedaily.com/.

140 *Criminal Code,* s 228.
141 *Malott* (Trial), *supra* note 1 Volume 7 at 140.
142 *Ibid* at 150.
143 *Ibid* at 182.
144 *Ibid* at 247.
145 *Ibid* at 248.
146 *Ibid* at 252.
147 *Ibid* at 135.
148 *Ibid* at 132.
149 *Ibid* at 147.
150 *Ibid* at 198.
151 *Ibid* at 204-5.
152 *Ibid* at 215.
153 *Ibid* at 218.
154 *Ibid* at 219.
155 *Ibid* at 220.
156 *Ibid* at 225.
157 *Ibid* at 228.
158 *Malott* (Trial), *supra* note 1 Volume 8, 2 October 1992 at 103.
159 *Ibid* at 111.
160 *Ibid.*
161 *Ibid* at 112.
162 *Ibid* at 150-51.
163 *Ibid* at 132.
164 *Ibid* at 134.
165 *Ibid* at 142.
166 *Ibid* at 154.
167 *Ibid* at 143.
168 *Ibid.*
169 *Ibid* at 164.
170 GB Strack *et al,* "A Review of 300 Strangulation Cases, Part I: Criminal Legal Issues"
     (2001) 21:3 J Emergency Medicine 303 at 309, as cited in Mindy B Mechanic *et al,*
     "Risk Factors for Physical Injury among Help-Seeking Battered Women: An Ex-
     ploration of Multiple Abuse Dimensions" (2008) 14:10 Violence against Women
     1148 at 1160.
171 GE McClane *et al,* "A Review of 300 Strangulation Cases, Part II: Clinical Evaluation
     of the Surviving Victim" (2001) 2:31 J Emergency Medicine 311 at 315, as cited in
     Mechanic *et al, ibid* at 1160.
172 *Malott* (Trial), *supra* note 1 Volume 8 at 174.
173 *Ibid* at 175.
174 *Ibid* at 198.
175 *Ibid.*
176 *Ibid* at 200.
177 *Ibid* at 201.

178 *Ibid* at 203.
179 *Ibid* at 221.
180 *Ibid* at 246-47.
181 *Ibid* at 242.
182 *Ibid* at 232.
183 *Ibid* at 234.
184 *Ibid* at 240.
185 *Ibid* at 249.
186 *Ibid* at 224-25.
187 Evan Stark & Anne Flitcraft, *Women at Risk: Domestic Violence and Women's Health* (Thousand Oaks, CA: Sage Publications, 1996) at 10: "Whereas physicians saw 1 of 35 of their patients as battered, a more accurate approximation is 1 in 4; whereas they traced 1 presenting injury in 20 to partner assault, the actual figure approached 1 in 3 (30%)."
188 Twenty-four percent of battered women versus nine percent of non-battered women are prescribed drugs. *Ibid* at 13.
189 According to Stark and Flitcraft's study of 520 women who presented at the emergency room of a major urban hospital in a one-month period, "battered women had a relative risk of attempting suicide that was 8 times as great as normal, a risk of drug abuse that was 6 times greater, a rate of alcohol abuse that was 15 times as great, and a rate of hospitalization in the state mental health facility that was 14 times as great." *Ibid* at 12.
190 "[P]ersons with MTBI are highly vulnerable to the potentially adverse effects of medications." National Institutes of Health, "Rehabilitation of Persons with Traumatic Brain Injury" (1999) 282:10 J Am Med Ass 974 at 980, as cited in Hélène Jackson *et al,* "Traumatic Brain Injury: A Hidden Consequence for Battered Women" (2002) 33:1 Professional Psychology: Research & Practice 39 at 44. See also Stark & Flitcraft, *supra* note 187 at 20.
191 Stark & Flitcraft, *supra* note 187 at 21. Furthermore, 15 percent of battered women versus 4 percent of non-battered women are given psychiatric referrals. *Ibid* at 13.
192 *Ibid.*
193 One woman reports: "I used it to cope with the violence and would then put up with more violence. Using only served to numb me – that was the only benefit." Quoted in Nancy Poole *et al,* "Substance Abuse by Women Using Domestic Violence Shelters" (2008) 43:8 & 9 Substance Use & Misuse 1129 at 1139.
194 According to Stark and Flitcraft, "the general consequence is to isolate abused women from resources and to reduce their capacity to understand, adequately respond to, or resolve their crisis by leaving the violent home or struggling through to autonomy against the hurt inflicted by a malevolent other." *Supra* note 187 at 21.
195 *Ibid* at 22.
196 *Malott* (Trial), *supra* note 1 Volume 8 at 242.
197 *Ibid* at 257.
198 *Ibid* at 258.
199 *Ibid* at 259-60.

200 *Ibid* at 265.

201 *Ibid* at 269.

202 *Ibid* at 271.

203 Roseann Danese, "Killing of Abuser: Was It Self-Defence?," *The Windsor Star* (6 October 1992) A3. I use a news article here because the transcript inexplicably omitted the closing addresses of both counsel.

204 *Ibid.*

205 *Ibid.*

206 *Ibid.*

207 *Ibid.*

208 *Ibid.*

209 *Ibid.*

210 *Malott* (Trial), *supra* note 1 Volume 10, 6 October 1992 at 122.

211 *Ibid.*

212 *R v McCraw*, [1991] 3 SCR 72, interpreting s 264.1(1)(a) of the *Criminal Code.*

213 Harrison also objected to the charge, arguing that the judge had not sufficiently reviewed the evidence undercutting Margaret's credibility.

214 Roseann Danese, "Appeal Pondered as Battered Wife Jailed for Murder," *The Windsor Star* (9 October 1992) A1. [Danese, "Appeal Pondered"].

215 *Malott* (Trial), *supra* note 1 Volume 10, 8 October 1992 at 237-38.

216 Danese, "Appeal Pondered," *supra* note 214.

217 *Ibid.*

218 Grace Macaluso, "Battered Wife Syndrome: The Justice System Is Being Forced to Look at the Phenomenon as a Legal Defence for Abused Women," *The Windsor Star* (15 October 1992) C1.

219 *Ibid.*

220 Danese, "Appeal Pondered," *supra* note 214.

221 Macaluso, *supra* note 218.

222 *Ibid.*

223 See *R v Robinson*, [1996] 1 SCR 683, in which the Supreme Court held that s 7 of the *Charter* requires a focus on actual intent rather than incapacity. If the medical evidence has centred on incapacity, then a "two step" charge will be appropriate, whereby the jury is first instructed on incapacity and then directed to consider the accused's actual intent. Since Margaret was still in the judicial system through her appeal, she was entitled to the benefit of this constitutional ruling. See *R v Sarson*, [1996] 2 SCR 223.

224 *R v Malott* (1996), 30 OR (3d) 609 (CA) at 640 [*Malott* (CA)].

225 Kiranjit Ahluwalia & Rahila Gupta, *Provoked: The Story of Kiranjit Ahluwalia* (Noida: HarperCollins India, 2007).

226 *R v Ahluwalia*, [1992] 4 All ER 889 at 894-96. The Court cautioned, however, that "the longer the delay and the stronger the evidence of deliberation on the part of the defendant, the more likely it will be that the prosecution will negative provocation." "Cumulative provocation" for battered women was accepted in *R v Humphries*, [1995] 4 All ER 1008 (CA); in *R v Thornton (No 2)*, [1996] 2 All ER 1023, the Court held that Battered Woman Syndrome can inform the "ordinary person" test for provocation.

227 *Malott* (CA), *supra* note 224 at 629.

228 *Ibid* at 630.

229 See, for example, Katherine O'Donovan, "Defences for Battered Women Who Kill" (1991) 18:2 JL & Soc 219 at 223.

230 Wayne Gorman, "Provocation: The Jealous Husband Defence" (1999) 42:4 Crim LQ 478; Victoria Nourse, "The New Normativity: The Abuse Excuse and the Resurgence of Judgment in the Criminal Law" (1998) 50:4 Stan L Rev 1435 at 1451: "[T]he reasonableness of such arguments [that a reasonable person would lose self-control when his wife cheats] is assumed."

231 Victoria Nourse, "Passion's Progress: Modern Law Reform and the Provocation Defense" (1997) 106:5 Yale LJ 1331 at 1345, in which she reports that 65 percent of men's provocation defences were raised in the context of women's decision to end the relationship.

232 Isabel Grant, "Intimate Femicide: A Study of Sentencing Trends for Men Who Kill Their Intimate Partners" (2009-10) 47:3 U Alta LR 779 at 809, in which she reports that provocation was raised in 15 percent of the reported decisions from 1990 to 2008 and succeeded in 19 percent of those cases. This undercounts provocation defences because the Crown might accept provocation as a basis for a plea bargain. *Ibid* at 810. In contrast, Andrée Coté's earlier study of Quebec cases found that at least one-third of men charged invoked provocation, often at the plea bargaining stage. Andrée Coté, *La rage au coeur: Rapport de recherche sur le traitement judiciaire de l'homicide conjugal au Quebec* (Baie-Comeau: Regroupement des Femmes de la Côte-Nord, 1991).

233 See the cases discussed by Grant, *ibid* at 811-12.

234 See *R v Gladue*, [1997] BCJ No 2333 (CA), and *R v Drake*, [1995] OJ No 4375 (Ct Just).

235 See *R v Getkate*, [1998] OJ No 6329 (Gen Div), and *R v Ferguson*, [1997] OJ No 2488 (Gen Div).

236 "Provocation" (10 January 2001), *The Fifth Estate*, CBC Television, Toronto, CBC Archives.

237 *R v Stone*, [1999] 2 SCR 290 at 303.

238 *R v Thibert*, [1996] 1 SCR 37 at 59.

239 *Ibid* at 59-60.

240 Kathleen Engman, "4 Years in Love-Triangle Slaying," *[The] Edmonton Journal* (2 November 1996) B3; "Crimes of Passion: Episode 102 – Norman Thibert" (Summerhill Television, 2007).

241 *R v Tran*, 2010 SCC 58 at para 34.

242 *Ibid.*

243 *Ibid* at para 29 [emphasis in original].

244 See Andrée Còté, Diana Majury, & Elizabeth Sheehy, *Stop Excusing Violence against Women! NAWL's Position Paper on the Defence of Provocation* (Ottawa: National Association of Women and the Law, 2000); two Australian states, Tasmania and Victoria, the United Kingdom, and New Zealand have abolished provocation as a defence. However, the United Kingdom introduced a new defence of "sudden loss of control" (resulting in manslaughter rather than murder), which has been interpreted

in a manner suggestive of the former defence of provocation. Oliver Quick & Celia Wells, "Partial Reform of Defences: Developments in England and Wales" (2012) 45:3 Aust & NZ J Criminol 337. Victoria introduced a new mitigated offence (also resulting in manslaughter rather than murder) that accommodates provocation-like facts and has served male accused. Jenny Morgan, "Homicide Law Reform and Gender: Configuring Violence" (2012) 45:3 Aust & NZ J Criminol 351; Kate Fitz-Simmons & Sharon Pickering, "Homicide Law Reform in Victoria, Australia" (2011) 52:1 Br J Criminol 159.

245 *Malott* (CA), *supra* note 224 at 620-21.
246 *Ibid* at 624.
247 *Ibid* at 638.
248 *Ibid* at 640.
249 *R v Malott*, [1998] 1 SCR 123 at 138-39 [*Malott* (SCC)].
250 *Ibid* at para 43.
251 *Graveline* (Trial), *supra* note 3 23 février 2001 at 50. Testimony of Kelly Graveline, Rita's daughter.
252 Don Campbell, "Woman Charged in Husband's Slaying: Domestic Violence Darkened Marriage of Luskville Couple," *The Ottawa Citizen* (12 August 1999) D1.
253 Juror number seven was excused for a death in her family on 23 February 2001, leaving ten women and one man. *Graveline* (Trial), *supra* note 3 at 121.
254 Mendo said: "The judge will instruct you on the Defence that we're planning to use and you must already be aware of it since my colleague has asked you several questions when you were chosen as jurors, asked you if you were knowledgeable in the matter of battered wife syndrome, it's a legitimate Defence." *Ibid* 19 février 2001 at 22. This statement suggests that the trial judge gave the prosecutor leeway to ask additional questions of the potential jurors, but the legal basis for this cannot be discerned from the record.
255 *Ibid* at 23.
256 *Ibid* at 30.
257 *Ibid* at 35.
258 *Ibid* at 46.
259 *Ibid* at 65.
260 *Ibid* at 60.
261 *Ibid* at 64.
262 *Ibid* at 70.
263 *Ibid* at 68.
264 *Ibid* 20 février 2001 at 43.
265 *Ibid* at 52.
266 *Ibid* at 56.
267 *Ibid* 21 février 2001 at 87.
268 *Ibid* at 131, 109, 112.
269 *Ibid* at 151.
270 She testified that he said "we're going to end it tonight and I got so scared and I thought, ah, better marry him." *Ibid* 27 février 2001 at 21.
271 *Ibid* 22 février 2001 at 34.

272 *Ibid* at 123.

273 *Ibid* at 43.

274 *Ibid* at 51.

275 *Ibid* at 21.

276 *Ibid* at 63.

277 *Ibid* at 64-65.

278 *Ibid* at 84.

279 *Ibid* at 75.

280 *Ibid* at 92.

281 *Ibid* at 186.

282 *Ibid* at 220.

283 Judith Lewis Herman, *Trauma and Recovery: The Aftermath of Violence – from Domestic Abuse to Political Terror* (New York: Basic Books, 1992) at 87.

284 *Graveline* (Trial), *supra* note 3 22 février 2001 at 196.

285 *Ibid* at 202.

286 *Ibid* at 210.

287 *Ibid* at 135.

288 *Ibid* at 108.

289 *Ibid* 23 février 2001 at 116.

290 *Ibid* at 119-20.

291 *Ibid* at 127.

292 Mechanic *et al*, *supra* note 170 at 1163.

293 *Graveline* (Trial), *supra* note 3 23 février 2001 at 163.

294 *Ibid* at 164, citing John Gunn & Pamela J Taylor, *Forensic Psychiatry: Clinical, Legal, and Ethical Issues* (Oxford: Butterworth-Heinemann, 1993).

295 *Ibid*, citing Benjamin J Sadock & Virginia A Sadock, *Kaplan and Sadock's Synopsis of Psychiatry: Behavioral Sciences/Clinical Psychiatry,* 10th ed (Philadelphia: Lippincott, 2007) 665.

296 *Ibid* at 170-71.

297 *Ibid* at 187.

298 *Ibid* 26 février 2001 at 9.

299 *Ibid* at 12.

300 *Ibid* at 16.

301 *Ibid.*

302 *Ibid* at 26-27.

303 *Ibid* at 29.

304 *Ibid* at 40.

305 *Ibid* at 42.

306 *Ibid* at 44.

307 *Ibid* at 43.

308 *Ibid* at 58-59.

309 *Ibid* at 60.

310 *Ibid* at 91.

311 *Ibid* at 96.

312 *Ibid* at 104.

313 *Ibid* at 98.
314 *Ibid* at 104.
315 *Ibid* at 106.
316 *Ibid* at 127.
317 *Ibid* at 108.
318 *Ibid* at 121-22.
319 *Ibid* at 123.
320 *Ibid* at 129.
321 *Ibid* at 142.
322 *Ibid* at 168.
323 Pascal Monpetit, "Wife Was Fed Up with Being 'Treated like a Dog': Woman Confessed to Killing Husband 'Believed I Loved Him,'" *The Ottawa Citizen* (28 February 2001) F1.
324 *Ibid.*
325 *Graveline* (Trial), *supra* note 3 27 février 2001 at 29.
326 *Ibid* at 31.
327 *Ibid* at 32.
328 *Ibid.*
329 *Ibid* at 95.
330 *Ibid* at 36.
331 *Ibid.*
332 *Ibid* at 64.
333 *Ibid* at 37.
334 *Ibid* at 54.
335 *Ibid* at 49-50.
336 *Ibid* at 52.
337 *Ibid* at 60.
338 *Ibid* at 75.
339 *Ibid.*
340 *Ibid* at 76.
341 *Ibid* at 112.
342 *Ibid* at 114.
343 *Ibid* at 117.
344 *Ibid* at 120.
345 *Ibid* at 122.
346 *Ibid* at 136.
347 *Ibid* at 138.
348 *Ibid* 28 février 2001 at 21.
349 *Criminal Code*, s 265.
350 Nancy Berns, *Framing the Victim: Domestic Violence, Media, and Social Problems* (New Brunswick, NJ: Transaction Publishers, 2004) at 46-52.
351 Wendy S Deaton & Michael Hertica, *Growing Free: A Manual for Survivors of Domestic Violence* (Binghampton, NY: Haworth Maltreatment and Trauma Press, 2001) at 9.

352 Fern Martin, *A Narrow Doorway: Women's Stories of Escape from Abuse* (Burnstown, ON: General Store Publishing, 1996) at 16, 67.

353 Sara E Gutierres & Christina Van Puymbroeck, "Childhood and Adult Violence in the Lives of Women Who Misuse Alcohol" (2006) 11:5 Aggression and Violent Behaviour 497 at 504: "Many victims of violence ... do not identify their experiences as 'abuse' per se ... Inquiring about specific events is more likely to elicit an accurate endorsement of experiences with violence."

354 *Graveline* (Trial), *supra* note 3 27 février 2001 at 139.

355 *Ibid* 28 février 2001 at 12.

356 Pascal Monpetit, "'I Don't Want to Remember,' Wife Says," *The Ottawa Citizen* (1 March 2001) F6.

357 *Graveline* (Trial), *supra* note 3 28 février 2001 at 19.

358 *Ibid* at 50.

359 *Ibid* at 59.

360 *Ibid* at 67-68.

361 Crown prosecutors are not normally allowed to "split the case" in this way as it can be highly prejudicial to the defence: *R v Biddle*, [1995] 1 SCR 761.

362 *Graveline* (Trial), *supra* note 3 28 février 2001 at 127.

363 *Ibid* at 123.

364 *Ibid* at 103-4.

365 *Ibid* at 180-81.

366 *Ibid* at 152.

367 *Ibid* at 179.

368 *Ibid* at 188.

369 Her call was not recorded due to a malfunction of the computer system. *Ibid* 20 février 2001 at 77, per Marc Desjardins, 9-1-1 operator.

370 *Ibid* 1 mars 2001 (Audition/Addresses to the Jury by Counsel) at 8.

371 *Ibid* at 9.

372 *Ibid* at 32.

373 *Ibid* at 12.

374 *Ibid* at 28.

375 *Ibid* at 16-17.

376 *Ibid* at 17.

377 *Ibid* at 19.

378 *Ibid* at 24.

379 *Ibid* at 26.

380 *Ibid* at 28.

381 *Ibid* at 30.

382 *Ibid* at 37.

383 *Ibid* at 39.

384 *Ibid* at 54.

385 *Ibid* at 74-75.

386 *Ibid* at 76-77.

387 *Ibid* at 79.

388 *Ibid* 1 mars 2001 (Hors Jury/Voir Dire) at 3.

389 *Ibid* 1 mars 2001 (Audition/Address to the Jury by the Court) at 40.

390 *Ibid* at 36.

391 *Ibid* at 49.

392 *Ibid.*

393 *Ibid* at 52.

394 *Ibid* at 56.

395 *Ibid* at 55.

396 *Ibid* at 77.

397 *Ibid* 1 mars 2001 (Hors Jury/Voir Dire) at 10-11.

398 Douglas Quan, "Woman Who Shot Sleeping Husband Goes Free: Abused Wife Suffering from 'Amnesia' When She Killed Her Husband; 'Now I Can Do Things with My Family Again,'" *The Ottawa Citizen* (4 March 2001) A1.

399 Nathalie Trepanier, "Abused Spouse Freed: Shot Husband in 'Automaton' State," *[The] Toronto Sun* (4 March 2001) online http://www.fact.on.ca/.

400 *Ibid.*

401 Canadian Press, "Jury Acquits Woman of Killing Husband," *The [Halifax] Daily News* (4 March 2001) 9.

402 *Ibid.*

403 Quan, *supra* note 398.

404 *Ibid.*

405 "A Disturbing Court Acquittal," Editorial, *The Ottawa Citizen* (7 March 2001) D4.

406 *Ibid.*

407 Margaret Wente, "How to Get Away with Murder (for Women Only)," *The Globe and Mail* (10 March 2001) A15.

408 "Woman Acquitted in Killing of Abusive Husband," *[The] Edmonton Journal* (4 March 2001) B11.

409 *Ibid.*

410 *Supra* note 237.

411 *R v Falconer* (1990), 171 CLR 30 (HC Australia), is the only case that I have found in which a battered woman argued that she was dissociated, based on a psychological blow, when she killed her batterer. The High Court ordered a new trial so that she could advance her defence. See also Stella Tarrant, "A New Defence in Spouse Murder?" (1992) 17:2 Alternative LJ 67.

412 Maggie MacDonald, discussed in Chapter 1 at note 257, was acquitted on this basis, as was Linda Lutchmin Haslam. *R v Haslam* (1990), 56 CCC (3d) 491 (BCCA) (aggravated assault).

413 In a later decision, the Court clarified that the accused need only make out an "air of reality" to get the defence to the trier of fact and that ordinarily "the logically probative opinion of a qualified expert" will suffice: *R v Fontaine*, 2004 SCC 7 at para 89.

414 The mental disorder defence, if successful, results in a verdict of "not criminally responsible." In turn, the person will be subject to a disposition hearing in which either the court or the Review Board will make an order about the accused person's need for further detention and treatment taking into consideration his or her mental

condition and rights and liberties as well as the need to protect the public from dangerous persons. *Criminal Code,* s 672.45.

415 *Stone, supra* note 237 at 260.
416 *Ibid* at 394-95.
417 Automatism requires proof on a balance of probabilities.
418 *R v Graveline,* 2005 QCCA 574 at para 80.
419 *Ibid* at para 76.
420 *Ibid* at para 48.
421 *Ibid* at para 96.
422 *R v Graveline,* 2006 SCC 16 at para 10.
423 *Ibid* at para 18.
424 See the case of Dorothy Joudrie, found not criminally responsible for the attempted murder of her husband on the basis of mental disorder automatism. Audrey Andrews, *Be Good, Sweet Maid: The Trials of Dorothy Joudrie* (Waterloo: Wilfrid Laurier University Press, 1999).
425 See, for example, Rebecca Bradfield, "Women Who Kill: Lack of Intent and Diminished Responsibility as the Other 'Defences' to Spousal Homicide" (2001-2) 13:2 Current Issues Crim Just 143 at 157. However, Bradfield's critique is levied against cases in which women were convicted of manslaughter based on no intent defences, not in which they were acquitted outright, as was Rita.
426 See, for example, "Head Injuries in Football," *The New York Times* (10 December 2012) online http://topics.nytimes.com/, and Cathy Gulli, "Concussion: The Untold Story," *Maclean's* (19 May 2011) online http://www.macleans.ca/.
427 Tracey Covassin, C Buz Swanik, & Michael L Sachs, "Sex Differences and the Incidence of Concussions among Collegiate Athletes" (2003) 38:3 J Athletic Training 238, and Anahad O'Connor, "Concussions May Be More Severe in Girls and Young Athletes," *The New York Times* (10 May 2012) online http://well.blogs.nytimes.com/.
428 Kathleen Monahan & K Dan O'Leary, "Head Injury and Battered Women: An Initial Inquiry" (1999) 24:4 Health & Social Work 269 at 270. See also Albert R Roberts & Jung H Kim, "Exploring the Effects of Head Injuries among Battered Women: A Qualitative Study of Chronic and Severe Woman Battering" (2005) 32:1 J Social Service Research 33 at 34: "[T]here is a shortage of research on the consequences of head, face and neck injuries sustained by battered women."
429 One study found that 92 percent of battered women sampled had been hit in the head during battering incidents. See Jackson *et al, supra* note 190 at 39. Another reports that the heads, necks, and faces of between 40 percent and 70 percent of battered women are targeted by abusive men. See DN Kyriacou *et al,* "Risk Factors for Injury to Women from Domestic Violence" (1999) 341:25 New England J Medicine 1892 at 1898.
430 Jackson *et al, supra* note 190 at 39.
431 *Ibid* at 40.
432 Deborah Kotz, "Evidence of Brain Damage from Head Injuries Mounts," *The Boston Globe* (3 December 2012) online http://www.bostonglobe.com/.
433 Jackson *et al, supra* note 190 at 41.

434 *Ibid.* Ninety-one percent of fifty-three battered women had been hit in the head in the past year, with a mode frequency of between two and five times; 88 percent had been hit in the past five years, also between two and five times; and 25 percent had been hit in the head more than twenty times in the past five years, 8 percent in the past year.

435 Roberts & Kim, *supra* note 428 at 45; Mechanic *et al, supra* note 170 at 1160.

436 DA Slagle, "Psychiatric Disorders Following Closed Head Injury: An Overview of Biopsychosocial Factors in Their Etiology and Management" (1990) 20:1 Int J of Psychiatry in Medicine 1 at 35.

437 Roberts & Kim, *supra* note 428 at 37.

438 A study of 362 battered women found that 45 percent had experienced loss of consciousness, 72 percent from strangulation and 46 percent from blows to the head. Mechanic *et al, supra* note 170 at 1160.

439 Monahan & O'Leary, *supra* note 428 at 272, referring to mild to severe head injury.

440 Roberts & Kim, *supra* note 428 at 42.

441 Monahan & O'Leary, *supra* note 428 at 272.

442 *Ibid* at 275. See also Jackson *et al, supra* note 190 at 43: "Thus, despite intervention, women who have sustained MTBI may be even less able to extricate themselves from abusive relationships."

443 Monahan & O'Leary, *supra* note 428 at 275, citing K Sperling *et al,* "Emotionally Charged: Why Do Head Injuries Make People Seem Out of Control?" (1990) 1 Headlines 2 at 3.

444 National Institutes of Health, *supra* note 190 at 983, cited in Jackson *et al, supra* note 190 at 40. See also Associated Press, "Doctor Describes Chris Benoit Brain Injury" (5 September 2007) online http://boards.library.trutv.com/. This piece describes the possibility that an intimate femicide committed by a professional wrestler can be partially attributed to his brain injuries.

445 See *supra* note 190.

446 Jackson *et al, supra* note 190 at 40, citing D Gronwall, "Cumulative and Persisting Effects of Concussion on Attention and Cognition" in HS Levin *et al,* eds, *Mild Head Injury* (New York: Oxford University Press, 1989) at 161.

447 Evan Stark, "Preparing for Expert Testimony in Domestic Violence Cases" in Albert R Roberts, ed, *Handbook of Domestic Violence Intervention Strategies* (Oxford: Oxford University Press, 2002) 216 at 252.

448 Victoria Seddon was acquitted of manslaughter on the basis of self-defence even though she too was in a dissociated state and could not testify about her fear. *R v Seddon,* Ruling of the Honourable Mr Justice Shabbits, 19 January 1993, Supreme Court of British Columbia, No 26656S.

449 Tarrant, *supra* note 411 at 70, explains: "Whose interests would be served if automatic or 'unwilled' actions on the one hand and acts of defence or protection on the other were not mutually exclusive?"

450 Walker, *supra* note 133 at 135. See also Mary Becker, "The Passions of Battered Women: Cognitive Links between Passion, Empathy, and Power" (2001) 8:1 Wm & Mary J Women & L 1 at 50: "Sometimes they snap or dissociate at the time of killing and cannot remember it happening at all."

Conclusion

1 Rita Graveline seems to have been acquitted on the basis of automatism. *R v Graveline*, 2006 SCC 16 at para 18. Micheline Veilleux was acquitted because the Crown could not prove that her act caused the death. "Micheline Veilleux est acquitée du meurtre de son ex-conjoint," *Nouvelles Télé-Radio* (11 novembre 2003) online http://www.infomart.ca. However, Micheline Vaillancourt was acquitted on appeal on the basis of self-defence. *R v Vaillancourt*, [1999] JQ No 571 (CA).

2 *Criminal Code*, s 675(1), governs appeals by persons convicted of indictable offences.

3 *R v Palmer*, [1980] 1 SCR 759.

4 Jean Millar won a new trial but was convicted of manslaughter at her second trial. Canadian Press, "Woman Jailed for 4 Years for Killing Abusive Husband," *The [Montreal] Gazette* (10 December 1992) B5. Darlene Alice Young was granted re-trials twice but plead guilty to second-degree murder before her third trial took place. Castanet Staff, "Falkland Woman Confesses to Murder" (5 November 2009) online http://www.castanet.net. Elaine Trombley was acquitted at her retrial. Donald McArthur, "Windsor Woman Found Not Guilty of Manslaughter: Wife Said She Feared for Her Life When She Stabbed Husband," *The National Post* (21 March 2000) A8. Vaillancourt was acquitted on appeal. *Supra* note 1.

5 Debra Parkes & Emma Cunliffe, "Wrongful Conviction: Asking the 'Woman Question'" [unpublished], on file with the author.

6 Elizabeth Rapaport, "Staying Alive: Executive Clemency, Equal Protection, and the Politics of Gender in Women's Capital Cases" (2001) 4:2 Buff Crim L Rev 967 at 1005.

7 Gaile Owens in Tennessee refused to take the stand in order to protect her children from hearing about her abuse. The state governor commuted her death penalty after she spent twenty-five years on death row. Travis Loller, "Gaile Owens, Former Death Row Inmate, Freed from Tennessee Prison," *The Huffington Post* (10 July 2011) online http://www.huffingtonpost.com.

8 *Criminal Code*, s 236(a).

9 *Criminal Code*, s 742.1; this exclusion has been continued under Bill C-10, the *Safe Streets and Communities Act*, SC 2012, c 1, s 34.

10 Patricia Gagné, *Battered Women's Justice: The Movement for Clemency and the Politics of Self-Defence* (New York: Twayne Publishers, 1998) at 180.

11 The experience of one woman jailed in the United States for killing her abuser is described as follows: "Despite all of the emotional, physical, and sexual abuse this woman had endured, she found the strip search required of all inmates to be demoralizing and degrading. Somehow, even after the efforts of her husband to take away all her self-worth and sense of humanity, some shred of dignity remained. The prison managed to find it." *Ibid* at 178.

12 For example, Justice Oliphant said, when refusing to jail Emily Brown and instead giving her a suspended sentence, "So far as I'm concerned, Ms. Brown served that period of incarceration during the years leading up to the death of Wesley Chaske when she became virtually a prisoner in her home and was subjected to brutal violence at the hands of Mr. Chaske." Nilu Balsara, "Killed Abusive Husband, Manitoba

Woman Freed: Judge Ruled Justice Would Not be Served by Jail Sentence," *The Globe and Mail* (12 August 1991) A5. Mary Ann Keeper's sentencing judge, Justice Patrick Ferg, made a similar comment after her twelve-day sentencing hearing: "She's already been put through hell. She need not go through more hell as far as I'm concerned." "Killer 'Went through Hell,'" *The [Vancouver] Province* (4 June 1993) A31.

13 Angela Cameron, "R v Gladue: Sentencing and the Gendered Impacts of Colonialism" in John D Whyte, ed, *Moving toward Justice: Legal Traditions and Aboriginal Justice* (Saskatoon: Purich Publishing, 2008) 160 at 180.

14 Canadian Association of Elizabeth Fry Societies, "Submission of CAEFS to the Canadian Human Rights Commission for the Special Report on the Discrimination on the Basis of Sex, Race and Disability Faced by Federally Sentenced Women" (10 May 2003) online http://www.elizabethfry.ca at 21.

15 Gagné, *supra* note 10 at 170-71.

16 *Ibid* at 194.

17 Correctional Association of New York, "Domestic Violence Survivors in Prison Fact Sheet," *Women in Prison Project,* March 2002 online http://www.prisonpolicy.org/. Veronica Lewin, "Alternative Sentences Sought for Domestic Violence Victims," *Legislativegazette.com* (13 June 2011) at 3, quoting the memo in support of New York Bill A.7874-a/S.5436, the *Domestic Violence Survivors Justice Act:* "[O]f the 38 women convicted of murder and released between 1985 and 2003, not a single one returned to prison for a new crime within a 36-month period of release – a zero percent recidivism rate." See also Linda L Ammons, "Symposium: Why Do You Do the Things You Do? Clemency for Battered Incarcerated Women: A Decade's Review" (2003) 11:2 Am U J Gender Soc Pol'y & L 533 at 564-65, reviewing Ohio recidivism data for battered women who received clemency.

18 Her Honour Judge Lynn Ratushny, *Self-Defence Review: Final Report* (Ottawa: Department of Justice and Solicitor General of Canada, 1997) at 163 [*Self-Defence Review*].

19 *Ibid* at 180.

20 *Ibid* at 164, where Judge Ratushny describes these cases as possible "miscarriages of justice."

21 *R v Kay,* Transcript of Proceedings at Trial, QBC No 8 of 1994, Queen's Bench of Saskatchewan, Regina, Volume 4, 14 June 1994 at 914.

22 Only Margaret Malott (Chapter 7); Micheline Vaillancourt, *supra* note 1; and Darlene Young were convicted by their respective juries of second-degree murder (Young was twice convicted by juries, then before her third murder trial pled guilty to second-degree murder). *Supra* note 1.

23 She did not extend her recommendation to first-degree murder because she questioned whether "planning and deliberation" ought to rule out leniency. *Self-Defence Review, supra* note 18 at 194.

24 *Ibid* at 195.

25 The United Kingdom, three states of Australia, New Zealand, US federal law, and five US states (California, Florida, Kentucky, Minnesota, and New York). *Ibid* at 183-92. Elisabeth Ayyildiz discusses Washington as well in "When Battered Woman's

Syndrome Does Not Go Far Enough: The Battered Woman as Vigilante" (1995-96) 4:1 Am U J Gender & L 141 at 161.

26 Only California's and New York's sentencing regimes are as or more severe than Canada's. *Self-Defence Review, supra* note 18 at 192.

27 Stephen Bindman, "Call for Leniency Gets Wide Support," *The Ottawa Citizen* (25 July 1997) A3, quoting Steve Sullivan, then Executive Director of the Canadian Resource Centre for Victims of Crime.

28 See *R v Morrisey*, 2000 SCC 39 at para 83, where Justice Louise Arbour, joined by Chief Justice Beverley McLachlin, suggested that the mandatory prison sentence for criminal negligence causing death using a firearm might be unconstitutional on the basis of "gross disproportionality" when an abused woman has killed her partner with a gun.

29 Ryan Elias Newby, "Evil Women and Innocent Victims: The Effect of Gender on California Sentences for Domestic Homicide" (2011) 22:1 Hastings Women's LJ 113 at 125, 140.

30 See *R v Ferguson*, [1997] OJ No 2488 (Sup Ct Just) at para 23. See also the jury's efforts in the case of Dixie Shanahan, sentenced by an Iowa judge to fifty years of imprisonment for killing her husband as he lay in bed, to have her sentence reduced by appealing to the governor. Staci Hupp, "Chances of Being Pardoned Slim for Shanahan," *The Des Moines Register* (29 May 2004) 1A, discussed in Leigh Goodmark, "The Punishment of Dixie Shanahan: Is There Justice for Battered Women Who Kill?" (2006) 55:2 Kansas L Rev 269 at 270.

31 *An Act to Amend the Criminal Code (Exception to Mandatory Minimum Sentences for Manslaughter and Criminal Negligence Causing Death).* This is a Senate bill that she hopes to introduce in the fall of 2013 (on file with the author).

32 *R v Kay, R v Rain,* both discussed in Chapter 6; see also *R v Massetoe*, [1993] BCJ No 585 (Prov Ct).

33 Camellia Britt, Rachael Fisher, Valerie Kahpeasewat, Patricia Kay, and Cherie Wasicuna.

34 Most provincial legal aid schemes use the probability of jail to determine eligibility for funded counsel. The constitutional test for the right to funded counsel is whether the charges are serious (implicating a probability of incarceration if convicted or loss of custody of one's children to the state) or complex. As for complexity, if defending a refusal to provide a breath sample is not "complex" (one of the more technical areas of criminal practice), according to the Alberta Court of Appeal in *R v Rain*, 1998 ABCA 315, then neither is domestic assault.

35 Aboriginal Justice Inquiry of Manitoba, *Report of the Aboriginal Justice Inquiry of Manitoba, Volume 1: The Justice System and Aboriginal People* (Winnipeg: Queen's Printer, 1991) at 366-67.

36 Shoshanna Pollack, Vivien Green, & Anke Allspach, *Women Charged with Domestic Violence in Toronto: The Unintended Consequences of Mandatory Charge Policies* (Toronto: Woman Abuse Council of Toronto, 2005) at 17-19.

37 Mary Becker, "The Passions of Battered Women: Cognitive Links between Passion, Empathy, and Power" (2001) 8:1 Wm & Mary J Women & L 1 at 55, 60-61.

38 *Ibid* at 56.
39 *Ibid.*
40 *Ibid.*
41 *Ibid* at 66.
42 *R v Malott*, [1998] 1 SCR 123 at 144.
43 Mike Blanchfield, "Lawyer Punished for Running Letterman-Style Contest," *The Ottawa Citizen* (8 January 1993) B2.
44 See also Fiona E Raitt, "Gender Bias in the Hearsay Rule" in Mary Childs & Louise Ellison, eds, *Feminist Perspectives on Evidence* (London: Cavendish Publishing, 2000) 59.
45 *Citizen's Arrest and Self-Defence Act,* SC 2012, c 9.
46 Kent Roach, "A Preliminary Assessment of the New Self-Defence and Defence of Property Provisions" (2012) 16:3 CCLR 247 at 249.
47 VF Nourse, "Self-Defense and Subjectivity" (2001) 68:4 U Chi L Rev 1235 at 1284.
48 For example, a guilty plea to manslaughter was entered by Greg Brodsky on behalf of Nancy Cowley in part because she did not face life-threatening or serious injury but "another beating." *R v Cowley,* [1995] OJ No 592 at para 5 (Ct Just Gen Div).
49 *R v Pétel,* [1994] 1 SCR 3; *R v McConnell,* [1996] 1 SCR 1075.
50 Michael J Glennon, "The Fog of Law: Self-Defense, Inherence, and Incoherence in Article 51 of the United Nations Charter" (2002) 25:2 Harv J L & Pub Policy 539 at 552-53, cited in Shana Wallace, "Beyond Imminence: Evolving International Law and Battered Women's Right to Self-Defense" (2004) 71:4 U Chi L Rev 1749 at 1776. See also Jane Campbell Moriarty, "'While Dangers Gather': The Bush Preemption Doctrine, Battered Women, Imminence, and Anticipatory Self-Defense" (2005) University of Akron School of Law, Public Law and Legal Theory Working Paper Series No 05-14.
51 Moriarty, *ibid* at 26.
52 Wallace, *supra* note 50 at 1777.
53 Elizabeth Sheehy, *What Would a Women's Law of Self-Defence Look Like?* (Ottawa: Status of Women Canada, 1995) at 23.
54 Elizabeth Sheehy, Julie Stubbs, & Julia Tolmie, "Defences to Homicide for Battered Women: A Comparative Analysis of Laws in Australia, Canada and New Zealand" (2012) 34:3 Sydney L Rev 467 at 474-79, discussing the laws of Victoria and Queensland.
55 Victoria, Department of Justice, *Review of Defensive Homicide* (Discussion Paper, 2010) at 33-38.
56 Kate Fitz-Gibbon & Sharon Pickering, "Homicide Law Reform in Victoria, Australia" (2012) 52:1 Br J Criminol 159; Kellie Toole, "Self-Defence and the Reasonable Woman: Equality before the Law" (2012) 36:1 Melb U L Rev 250.
57 Sheehy, Stubbs, & Tolmie, *supra* note 54 at 480-81.
58 *R v Faid,* [1983] 1 SCR 265.
59 *R v Cadwallader* (1966), 1 CCC 380 (Sask QB); *R v Bogue* (1976), 13 OR (2d) 272 (CA).
60 *Self-Defence Review, supra* note 18 at 142.

61 Danielle R Dubin, "A Woman's Cry for Help: Why the United States Should Apply Germany's Model of Self-Defense for the Battered Woman" (1995) 2:1 ILSA J Int'l & Comparative L 235 at 259.

62 Sheehy, Stubbs, & Tolmie, *supra* note 54 at 478.

63 See Jennifer Koshan, "The Legal Treatment of Marital Rape and Women's Equality: An Analysis of the Canadian Experience" (September 2010) online http://www.theequalityeffect.org; Melanie Randall, "Sexual Assault in Spousal Relationships, 'Continuous Consent,' and the Law: Honest but Mistaken Judicial Beliefs" (2008) 32:1 Man LJ 144; and Ruth Lazar, "Negotiating Sex: The Legal Construct of Consent in Cases of Wife Rape in Ontario, Canada" (2010) 22:2 CJWL 392.

64 *R v Paice*, 2005 SCC 22 per Fish J at para 41.

65 *Criminal Code*, s 2.

66 *R v McCraw*, [1992] 3 SCR 72.

67 Several judges have held that the use of a weapon by a woman resisting sexual assault amounts to excessive force, disqualifying her from self-defence. See *R v Eyapaise*, [1993] AJ No 1080 (QB) (defence denied); *R v Cochrane*, [1969] 2 NBR (2d) 665 (Co Ct) (defence denied), as discussed in Shira Bernholtz & Jill Pomerantz-Redinger, "A Legal Defence of Self-Defence: Future Guidelines to Fighting Back" (1985) 6:2 Can Woman Stud 63 at 64; *R v Jiang*, (2010) 2011 ABQB 182 (defence denied); and *R v SFC*, 2001 BCCA 17 (self-defence rejected by jury, either on the basis that the accused did not face "grievous bodily harm" or because she used "excessive force"); but see *R v Kalleo*, 2008 NLTD 157 (accused acquitted). See also *R v Doyle*, [1992] NBJ No 24 (QB) (accused abandoned self-defence and pled guilty to manslaughter in spite of evidence corroborating attemped rape), and *R v SFC*, 2001 BCCA 17 (self-defence rejected by jury, likely on the basis of the use of "excessive force").

68 See also Annalise Acorn, "Response to *What Would a Women's Law of Self Defence Look Like? By Elizabeth Sheehy for Status of Women Canada, 1995*" (1995) [unpublished] at 7, on file with the author.

69 *Osland v The Queen* (1998), 159 ALR 170 per Kirby J, as discussed in Gail Hubble, "Self-Defence and Domestic Violence: A Reply to Bradfield" (1999) 6:1 Psychiatry, Psychology & L 51 at 54.

70 In *R v Ryan*, 2011 NSCA 11 at para 71, Chief Justice MacDonald said that, had Nicole Ryan's efforts to hire a hit man to kill her violent ex-husband been successful, she would have been denied access to self-defence: "After all, her conduct is not the type that we would expect to justify, let alone the type that we would 'praise' or 'assist.'" At the Supreme Court, this issue was left unaddressed. *R v Ryan*, 2013 SCC 3 at para 31.

71 Paris De Soto, "Feminists Negotiate the Judicial Branch: Battered Women's Syndrome" in Cynthia R Daniels, ed, *Feminists Negotiate the State: The Politics of Domestic Violence* (New York: University Press of America, 1997) 53 at 64, refers to critics of Charles Ewing's proposal as well as a mock juror study that found a success rate for "psychological self-defence" of 44 percent.

72 Evan Stark, *Coercive Control: How Men Entrap Women in Personal Life* (New York: Oxford University Press, 2007) at 365.

73 See Sheehy, Stubbs, & Tolmie, *supra* note 54 at 476, discussing New South Wales, Victoria, South Australia, the Northern Territory, and Tasmania. No case law has interpreted these laws to date.

74 Counsel for Valentina Potselouva also secured her acquittal without expert testimony, though he was denied the opportunity to present this evidence by Justice Humphrey. *R v Valentina Potselouva*, Court File No P930/95, Ontario Superior Court of Justice, Toronto, 4, 5, 6, 7, and 11 March 1996.

75 *R v Graveline*, Cours Supérieure, Hull, 19 février 2001 at 22.

76 *R v Ferguson*, Submissions, Challenge for Cause Application, Volume C, Court File No 93-080132, Superior Court of Justice, Ottawa, 10 January 1997.

77 Martha R Mahoney, "Legal Images of Battered Women: Redefining the Issue of Separation" (1991) 90:1 Mich L Rev 1 at 14, suggests, in light of the data, that "at least four of the fifteen or more actors in an average criminal action – jurors, judges, and attorneys – probably will have experienced or committed at least one domestic assault." For a summary of questions that might be posed to potential jurors in a trial involving a battered woman, see Sara Lee Johann & Frank Osanka, *Representing ... Battered Women Who Kill* (Springfield, IL: Charles C Thomas, 1989) at Chapter 9, "Voir Dire," 321-25.

78 Kevin Rollason, "Battered Woman Spared Jail Term," *The Winnipeg Free Press* (3 June 1993) B1.

79 *R v Seddon*, Ruling of the Honourable Mr Justice Shabbits, 19 January 1993, Supreme Court of British Columbia, No 26656S.

80 See *R v Sinclair*, 2011 SCC 40.

81 See, for example, Erica Meltzer, "Expert in 'Battered Woman Syndrome' Questioned at Midyette Hearing," *Colorado Daily* (14 November 2011) online http://www. dailycamera.com/. Molly Midyette's appeal counsel argued that Molly had received ineffective assistance of counsel at trial because "she was so emotionally abused and so psychologically manipulated ... that she was incompetent to assist in her own defense." She lost her appeal on 22 November 2011.

82 This accusation was levied against Lilian Getkate.

83 Albert R Roberts & Jung H Kim, "Exploring the Effects of Head Injuries among Battered Women: A Qualitative Study of Chronic and Severe Woman Battering" (2005) 32:1 J Soc Service Research 33 at 45; Hélène Jackson *et al*, "Traumatic Brain Injury: A Hidden Consequence for Battered Women" (2002) 33:1 Professional Psychology 39 at 39.

84 Jackson *et al*, *ibid* at 44.

85 See also the acquittal of Victoria Seddon, *supra* note 79.

86 Regina A Schuller, "Expert Evidence and Its Impact on Jurors' Decisions in Homicide Trials Involving Battered Women" (2003) 10 Duke J Gender L & Pol'y 225 at 242.

87 Richard Morris, in a more recent case outside my study's parameters, was the first criminal lawyer to call and qualify an expert to testify about Coercive Control, over the vigorous resistance of Crown counsel. See *R v Craig*, 2011 ONCA 142.

88 Regina A Schuller & Gwen Jenkins, "Expert Evidence Pertaining to Battered Women: Limitations and Reconceptualizations" in Mark Costanzo, Daniel Krauss, & Kathy

Pezdek, eds, *Expert Psychological Testimony for the Courts* (Mahwah, NJ: Lawrence Erlbaum Associates Publishers, 2007) 203.

89 Schuller, *supra* note 86 at 244.

90 Both of these forms of racist abuse were practised by the husbands of Theresa Kneiss (Diana Coulter, "Court Hears of Abusive Marriage: Defendant Recalls Violence," *[The] Edmonton Journal* (29 May 1992) B3) and Teresa Craig, *supra* note 87.

91 See Erica Lawson & Amanda Hotrum, "Equity for Communities: Integrating Counsel and Critical Race Theory" in Gayle MacDonald, Rachel L Osborne, & Charles C Smith, eds, *Feminism, Law, Inclusion: Intersectionality in Action* (Toronto: Sumach Press, 2005) 41 at 47.

92 Use of the term "fighting" has already been noted; in another file, the accused woman described the deceased as "bothering her" when she was trying to sleep. Her lawyer was able to explain to the sentencing judge that this innocuous word is used to convey sexual assault. *R v Marie Valerie Kahypeasewat,* Provincial Court of Saskatchewan, Huculak, J, Regina, Sentence, Volume 2, 26 June and 24 August 2006 at 151 per Ms LeClair-Harding.

93 Gena Rachel Hatcher, "The Gendered Nature of the Battered Woman Syndrome: Why Gender Neutrality Does Not Mean Equality" (2003-4) 59:1 NYU Ann Survey Am L 21 at 41. See also Sheehy, *supra* note 53 at 18.

94 Hatcher, *ibid* at 47.

95 See, for example, Lee Lakeman, *99 Federal Steps: Toward an End to Violence against Women* (Toronto: National Action Committee on the Status of Women, 1993).

96 "Largest Global Study on Violence against Women Finds Feminist Movements Hold Key to Change," *The San Fransico Chronicle* (28 September 2012) online http://www.sfgate.com/, referring to Mala Htun & S Laurel Weldon, "The Civic Origins of Progressive Policy Change: Combatting Violence against Women in Global Perspective, 1975-2005" (2012) 106:3 Am Pol Sci Rev 548.

97 Rosemary Gartner, Myrna Dawson, & Maria Crawford, "Woman Killing: Intimate Femicide in Ontario 1974-1994" in Katherine MJ McKenna & June Larkin, eds, *Violence against Women: New Canadian Perspectives* (Toronto: Inanna Publications, 2002) 123 at 128.

98 In 2011, seventy-six women were the victim of intimate partner homicide, compared to thirteen men: Samuel Perreault, *Homicide in Canada, 2011,* Juristat, Statstics Canada Cat no 85-002-X (Ottawa: Ministry of Industry, 2012) at 11.

99 Frances Power Cobbe, "Wife Torture in England" (April 1878) 32 Contemporary Rev 55 at 84 [italics in original].

100 Deborah Tuerkheimer, "Recognizing and Remedying the Harm of Battering: A Call to Criminalize Domestic Battering" (2004) 94:4 J Crim L & Criminol 959; Deborah Tuerkheimer, "Renewing the Call to Criminalize Domestic Violence: An Assessment Three Years Later" (2007) 75:3 Geo Wash L Rev 613; Alafair Burke, "Domestic Violence as a Crime of Pattern and Intent: An Alternative Reconceptualization" (2007) 75:3 Geo Wash L Rev 552.

101 Stark, *supra* note 72 at 383.

102 *Ibid* at 382.

103 Loi no 2010-768 du 9 julliet 2010 relative aux violences faites specifiquement aux femmes, aux violences au sein des couples et aux incidences de ces dernieres sur les enfants, JO, 9 July 2010 online http://www.legifrance.gouv.fr.

104 Susan Sachs Paris, "France's Spousal Mental Cruelty Law Hits Obstacles," *The Globe and Mail* (26 November 2011) A16.

105 Cheryl Hanna, "The Paradox of Progress: Translating Evan Stark's Coercive Control into Legal Doctrines for Abused Women" (2009) 15:12 Violence against Women 1458.

106 Walter S DeKeseredy & Molly Dragiewicz, *Shifting Public Policy Direction: Gender-Focused versus Bi-Directional Intimate Partner Violence, Report Prepared for Stakeholder Relations and Policy Development Division, Ontario Women's Directorate* (Toronto: Queen's Printer for Ontario, 2009). For a feminist conceptualization of the prosecutorial function, see Michelle Madden Dempsey, *Prosecuting Domestic Violence: A Philosophical Analysis* (Oxford: Oxford University Press, 2009).

107 Roma Luciw, "Risk Assessment Could Have Saved Slain Woman: Advocacy Groups," *The Globe and Mail* (23 June 2000) A3 (re murder of Gillian Hadley); Debra Black, "Trying to Predict Spousal Assaults," *The [Toronto] Star* (4 December 2004) L10 (re Domestic Violence Evaluation [DOVE]); Angela Eke *et al*, "Intimate Partner Homicide: Risk Assessment and Prospects for Prediction" (2011) 26:3 J Fam Violence 211 (re Ontario Domestic Assault Risk Assessment [ODARA]). The risk assessment tools have not been validated for assessing the specific risk of lethal or near-lethal assaults. Bing Guo & Christa Harstall, *Spousal Violence against Women: Preventing Recurrence* (Edmonton: Institute of Health Economics, 2008) at 20-21 (reviewing risk assessment tools). However, the ODARA is able to predict the risk of more severe assaults; see Eke *et al, ibid*. Some of these tools are used by the police, prosecutors, and judges. See, for example, *R v Lalumiere,* 2010 ONSCJ 3810, and *R v JKB*, [2009] OJ No 4441 (Sup Ct Just).

108 The RCMP incorporated a Primary Aggressor Policy in its *Violence in Relationships Policy* after the Vernon Ghakal murders in 1996. Linda Light, *Police-Reported Spousal Violence Incidents in BC in which Both Partners Are Suspects/Accused: An Exploratory Study* (Victoria: British Columbia Ministry of Public Safety and Solicitor General, 2009) at 11.

109 See Janet K Stoever, "Transforming Domestic Violence Representation" (2013) 101:3 Ky LJ 483, for a discussion of how the new model for understanding the process by which battered women disentangle from violent relationships, the Stages of Change model, should shape responses by lawyers.

110 "Family Violence Is Manifestation of Male Power in Society: Wilson," *The Lawyer's Weekly* (7 June 1991) 15.

111 Evan Stark & Anne Flitcraft, *Women at Risk: Domestic Violence and Women's Health* (Thousand Oaks, CA: Sage Publications, 1996) at 41.

112 See, for example, Carrie L Yodanis, "Gender Inequality, Violence against Women, and Fear: A Cross-National Test of the Feminist Theory of Violence against Women" (2004) 19:6 J Interpersonal Violence 655 at 670: in countries where the status of women is low, the rates of sexual violence against women tend to be higher:

"[A] structure of gender inequality is associated with a culture of violence against women."

113 See Lakeman, *supra* note 95 at 3.

114 Elizabeth Dermody Leonard, "Convicted Survivors: Overview of Original Research," Hearings of the State of California Joint Legislative Committee on Prison Construction and Operations, California Institute for Women (12 October 2000) online http://www.freebatteredwomen.org/.

115 Gail Barnes, "Private Violence, Gendered Justice" (1999) 24:2 Alternative LJ 67 at 70, compares the legal and media treatment of Said Morgan, a detective senior constable who killed his brother-in-law, who was suspected of sexually abusing his daughters and a family friend, and Heather Osland, who, with her son, killed her violent husband: "Morgan was portrayed within legal and public discourse as a hero, an exemplary male whose actions were rational and whose acts could legitimately be conceptualised as self-defence. Yet, Heather Osland's involvement in a lethal assault on a brutal husband and father from whom there was no escape was seen as totally unreasonable and unjustified." See also Anthony Reinhart & Anna Mehler Paperny, "Shopkeeper Taught His Lesson in Acquittal," *The Globe and Mail* (30 October 2010) A7.

116 Ayyildiz, *supra* note 25 at 149.

Select Bibliography

Books

Browne, Angela. *When Battered Women Kill* (New York: Free Press, 1987).

Busch, Amy L. *Finding Their Voices: Listening to Battered Women Who've Killed* (Commack, NY: Kroshka Books, 1999).

Downs, Donald Alexander. *More than Victims: Battered Women, the Syndrome Society and the Law* (Chicago: University of Chicago Press, 1996).

Ewing, Charles Patrick. *Battered Women Who Kill: Psychological Self-Defense as Legal Justification* (Lexington, MA: Lexington Books, 1987).

Frigon, Sylvie. *L'homicide conjugal au feminine* (Montréal: Éditions du Remue-Ménage, 2003).

Gagné, Patricia. *Battered Women's Justice: The Movement for Clemency and the Politics of Self-Defense* (New York: Twayne Publishers, 1998).

Gillespie, Cynthia K. *Justifiable Homicide: Battered Women, Self-Defense, and the Law* (Columbus: Ohio State University Press, 1989).

Hamilton, Melissa. *Expert Testimony on Domestic Violence: A Discourse Analysis* (El Paso: LFB Scholarly Publishing, 2009).

Herman, Judith Lewis. *Trauma and Recovery: The Aftermath of Violence – from Domestic Abuse to Political Terror* (New York: Basic Books, 1992).

Jensen, Vickie. *Why Women Kill: Homicide and Gender Equality* (Boulder, CO: Lynne Rienner Publishers, 2001).

Johann, Sara Lee, and Frank Osanka. *Representing ... Battered Women Who Kill* (Springfield, IL: Charles C Thomas, 1989).

Jones, Ann. *Next Time She'll Be Dead: Battering and How to Stop It* (Boston: Beacon Press, 2000).

Lakeman, Lee. *Obsession, with Intent* (Montreal: Black Rose Books, 2005).

LaViolette, Alyce D, and Ola W Barnett. *It Could Happen to Anyone: Why Battered Women Stay,* 2d ed (Thousand Oaks, CA: Sage Publications, 2000).

Lawless, Elaine J. *Women Escaping Violence* (Columbia: Missouri University Press, 2001).

Leonard, Elizabeth Dermody. *Convicted Survivors: The Imprisonment of Battered Women Who Kill* (Albany: State University of New York Press, 2002).

Ludsin, Hallie, and Lisa Vetten. *Spiral of Entrapment: Abused Women in Conflict with the Law* (Johannesburg: Jacana Media, 2005).

McGillivray, Anne, and Brenda Comaskey. *Black Eyes All of the Time: Intimate Violence, Aboriginal Women, and the Justice System* (Toronto: University of Toronto Press, 1999).

Ogle, Robbin S, and Susan Jacobs. *Self-Defense and Battered Women Who Kill: A New Framework* (Westport, CT: Praeger, 2002).

Pleck, Elizabeth. *Domestic Tyranny: The Making of American Social Policy against Family Violence from Colonial Times to the Present* (New York: Oxford University Press, 1987).

Ptacek, James. *Battered Women in the Courtroom: The Power of Judicial Responses* (Boston: Northeastern University Press, 1999).

Richie, Beth E. *Compelled to Crime: The Gender Entrapment of Battered Black Women* (New York: Routledge, 1996).

Schneider, Elizabeth M. *Battered Women and Feminist Lawmaking* (New Haven: Yale University Press, 2000).

Sev'er, Aysan. *Fleeing the House of Horrors: Women Who Have Left Abusive Partners* (Toronto: University of Toronto Press, 2002).

Stark, Evan. *Coercive Control: How Men Entrap Women in Personal Life* (New York: Oxford University Press, 2007).

Stark, Evan, and Anne Flitcraft. *Women at Risk: Domestic Violence and Women's Health* (Thousand Oaks, CA: Sage Publications, 1996).

Vallée, Brian. *Life with Billy* (New York: Simon and Schuster, 1986).

Walker, Lenore. *The Battered Woman Syndrome,* 3d ed (New York: Springer Publishing, 2009).

Articles and Chapters

Ammons, Linda L. "Symposium: Why Do You Do the Things You Do? Clemency for Battered Incarcerated Women: A Decade's Review" (2003) 11:2 Am U J Gender Soc Pol'y & L 533.

Ayyildiz, Elisabeth. "When Battered Woman's Syndrome Does Not Go Far Enough: The Battered Woman as Vigilante" (1995-96) 4:1 Am U J Gender & L 141.

Balfour, Gillian. "Falling between the Cracks of Retributive and Restorative Justice: The Victimization and Punishment of Aboriginal Women" (2008) 3:2 Feminist Criminol 101.

Barnes, Gail. "Private Violence, Gendered Justice" (1999) 24:2 Alternative LJ 67.

Becker, Mary. "The Passions of Battered Women: Cognitive Links between Passion, Empathy and Power" (2001) 8:1 Wm & Mary J Women & L 1.

Boyle, Christine. "Battered Wife Syndrome and Self-Defence: *Lavallee v R*" (1990) 9:1 Can J Fam L 171.

Bradfield, Rebecca. "Understanding the Battered Woman Who Kills Her Violent Partner: The Admissibility of Expert Evidence on Domestic Violence in Australia" (2002) 9:2 Psychiatry, Psychology & L 177.

—. "Women Who Kill: Lack of Intent and Diminished Responsibility as the Other 'Defences' to Spousal Homicide" (2001-2) 13:2 Current Issues in Crim Just 143.

Cameron, Angela. "R v Gladue: Sentencing and the Gendered Impacts of Colonialism" in John D Whyte, ed, *Moving toward Justice: Legal Traditions and Aboriginal Justice* (Saskatoon: Purich Publishing, 2008) 160.

Canadian Association of Elizabeth Fry Societies and Native Women's Association of Canada. "Women and the Canadian Legal System: Examining Situations of Hyper-Responsibility" in Patricia A Monture and Patricia D McGuire, eds, *First Voices: An Aboriginal Women's Reader* (Toronto: Inanna Publications, 2009) 382.

Castel, Jacqueline R. "Discerning Justice for Battered Women Who Kill" (1990) 48:2 UT Fac L Rev 229.

Cobbe, Frances. "Wife Torture in England" (April 1878) 32 Contemporary Rev 55.

Comack, Elizabeth. "Do We Need to Syndromize Women's Experiences? The Limitations of the 'Battered Woman Syndrome'" in Kevin D Bonnycastle and George S Rigakos, eds, *Unsettling Truths: Battered Women, Policy, Politics and Contemporary Research* (Vancouver: Collective Press, 1998) 105.

Crocker, Phyllis. "The Meaning of Equality for Battered Women Who Kill" (1985) 8 Harv Women's LJ 121.

De Soto, Paris. "Feminists Negotiate the Judicial Branch: Battered Women's Syndrome" in Cynthia R Daniels, ed, *Feminists Negotiate the State: The Politics of Domestic Violence* (New York: University Press of America, 1997) 53.

Dubin, Danielle R. "A Woman's Cry for Help: Why the United States Should Apply Germany's Model of Self-Defense for the Battered Woman" (1995) 2:1 ILSA J Int'l & Comparative L 235.

Edwards, Susan. "Ascribing Intention: The Neglected Role of Modus Operandi: Implications for Gender" (1999-2000) 4:3 Contemporary Issues in Law 235.

Ford, Sarah, and Kate Auty. "One Indigenous Woman and What 'Her' Jury Did Not Hear" in Kate Auty and Sandy Toussaint, eds, *A Jury of Whose Peers? The Cultural Politics of Juries in Australia* (Crawley: University of Western Australia Press, 2004) 84.

Gartner, Rosemary, Myrna Dawson, and Maria Crawford. "Woman Killing: Intimate Femicide in Ontario 1974-1994" in Katherine MJ McKenna and June Larkin, eds, *Violence against Women: New Canadian Perspectives* (Toronto: Inanna Publications, 2002) 123.

Goodmark, Leigh. "Going Underground: The Ethics of Advising a Battered Woman Fleeing an Abusive Relationship" (2007) 75:4 UMKC L Rev 999.

—. "The Punishment of Dixie Shanahan: Is There Justice for Battered Women Who Kill?" (2006) 55:2 Kansas L Rev 269.

—. "When Is a Battered Woman Not a Battered Woman? When She Fights Back" (2008) 20:1 Yale J L & Feminism 75.

Grant, Isabel. "Exigent Circumstances: The Relevance of Repeated Abuse to the Defence of Duress" (1997) 2 CCLR 331.

–. "The Syndromization of Women's Experiences" (1991) 25:1 UBC L Rev 23.

Grant, Isabel, and Debra Parkes. "Contextualizing Criminal Defences: Exploring the Contribution of Justice Wilson" in Kim Brooks, ed, *Justice Bertha Wilson: One Woman's Difference* (Vancouver: UBC Press, 2009) 153.

Hamilton, Barbara, and Elizabeth Sheehy. "Thrice Punished: Battered Women, Criminal Law and Disinheritance" (2004) 8 Southern Cross U L Rev 96.

Hatcher, Gena Rachel. "The Gendered Nature of the Battered Woman Syndrome: Why Gender Neutrality Does Not Mean Equality" (2003-4) 59:1 NYU Ann Survey Am L 21.

Kazan, Patricia. "Reasonableness, Gender Difference, and Self-Defence Law" (1997) 24:3 Man LJ 549.

Koshan, Jennifer. "State Responsibility for Protection against Domestic Violence: The Inter-American Commission on Human Rights Report in Lenahan (Gonzales) and Its Application in Canada" (2012) 30:1 Windsor YB Access Just 39.

Lash, Jean. "Case Comment: *R. v. Gladue*" (2000) 20:3 Can Woman Stud 85.

Lazar, Ruthy. "Reconceptualizing Victimization and Agency in the Discourse of Battered Women Who Kill" (2008) 45 Stud L Politics & Soc 3.

Maguigan, Holly. "Battered Women and Self-Defense: Myths and Misconceptions in Current Reform Proposals" (1991) 140:2 U Pa L Rev 379.

Mahoney, Martha R. "Legal Images of Battered Women: Redefining the Issue of Separation" (1991) 90:1 Mich L Rev 1.

Martinson, Donna, *et al.* "A Forum on *Lavallee v. R.*: Women and Self-Defence" (1991) 25:1 UBC L Rev 23.

McColgan, Aileen. "In Defence of Battered Women Who Kill" (1993) 13:4 Oxford J Leg Stud 508.

McIvor, Sharon, and Teressa Nahanee. "Aboriginal Women: Invisible Victims of Violence" in Kevin D Bonnycastle and George S Rigakos, eds, *Unsettling Truths: Battered Women, Policy, Politics, and Contemporary Research in Canada* (Vancouver: Collective Press, 1998) 63.

Moriarty, Jane Campbell. "'While Dangers Gather': The Bush Preemption Doctrine, Battered Women, Imminence, and Anticipatory Self-Defense" (2005) U Akron School of Law, Public Law & Legal Theory Working Paper Series No 05-14.

Noonan, Sheila. "Battered Woman Syndrome: Shifting the Parameters of Criminal Law Defences or (Re)Inscribing the Familiar?" in Anne Bottomley, ed, *Feminist Perspectives on Foundational Subjects of Law* (London: Cavendish Press, 1996) 191.

–. "Strategies of Survival: Moving beyond the Battered Woman Syndrome" in Claudia Currie and Ellen Adelberg, eds, *Too Few to Count* (Vancouver: Press Gang, 1993) 247.

Nourse, Victoria. "The New Normativity: The Abuse Excuse and the Resurgence of Judgment in the Criminal Law" (1998) 50:4 Stan L Rev 1435.

O'Donovan, Katherine. "Law's Knowledge: The Judge, the Expert, the Battered Woman, and Her Syndrome" (1993) 20:4 J L & Soc 427.

Plumm, Karyn M, and Cheryl A Terrance. "Battered Women Who Kill: The Impact of Expert Testimony and Empathy Induction in the Courtroom" (2009) 15:2 Violence against Women 186.

Randall, Melanie. "Domestic Violence and the Construction of the 'Ideal Victim': Assaulted Women's 'Image Problems' in Law" (2004) 23:1 St Louis U Pub L Rev 107.

Rapaport, Elizabeth. "Staying Alive: Executive Clemency, Equal Protection, and the Politics of Gender in Women's Capital Cases" (2001) 4:2 Buff Crim L Rev 967.

Razack, Sherene H. "Gendered Racial Violence and Spacialized Justice: The Murder of Pamela George" in Sherene H Razack, ed, *Race, Space and the Law: Unmapping a White Settler Society* (Toronto: Between the Lines, 2002) 121.

Schuller, Regina A. "Expert Evidence and Its Impact on Jurors' Decision in Homicide Trials Involving Battered Women" (2003) 10 Duke J Gender L & Pol'y 225.

Schuller, Regina A, and Gwen Jenkins. "Expert Evidence Pertaining to Battered Women: Limitations and Reconceptualizations" in Mark Costanzo, Daniel Krauss, and Kathy Pezdek, eds, *Expert Psychological Testimony for the Courts* (Mahwah, NJ: Lawrence Erlbaum Associates Publishers, 2007) 203.

Scully, Anne. "Expert Distractions: Women Who Kill, Their Syndromes and Disorders" in Mary Childs and Louise Ellison, eds, *Feminist Perspectives on Evidence* (London: Cavendish Publishing, 2000) 191.

Seuffert, Nan. "Battered Women and Self-Defence" (1997) 17:3 NZU L Rev 292.

Shaffer, Martha. "The Battered Woman Syndrome Revisited: Some Complicating Thoughts Five Years after *R. v. Lavallee*" (1997) 47:1 UT LJ 1.

–. "Coerced into Crime: Battered Women and the Defence of Duress" (1999) 4 CCLR 271.

–. "*R. v. Lavallee:* A Review Essay" (1990) 22:3 Ottawa L Rev 607.

Sheehy, Elizabeth. "Battered Woman Syndrome: Developments in Canadian Law after *R v Lavallee*" in Julie Stubbs, ed, *Women, Male Violence and the Law* (Sydney: Institute of Criminology, 1994) 174.

–. "Battered Women and the Mandatory Minimum Sentence" (2001) 39:2 Osgoode Hall LJ 529.

–. "Causation, Common Sense, and the Common Law: Replacing Unexamined Assumptions with What We Know about Male Violence against Women, or, from *Jane Doe* to *Bonnie Mooney*" (2006) 17:1 CJWL 97.

–. "Legal Responses to Violence against Women in Canada" (1999) 19: 1 & 2 Can Woman Stud 62.

–. "Review of the Self-Defence Review" (2000) 12:1 CJWL 197.

Sheehy, Elizabeth, Julie Stubbs, and Julia Tolmie. "Battered Women Charged with Homicide in Australia, Canada and New Zealand: How Do They Fare?" (2012) 45:3 Aust & NZ J Criminol 383.

–. "Defences to Homicide for Battered Women: A Comparative Analysis of Laws in Australia, Canada and New Zealand" (2012) 34:3 Sydney L Rev 467.

–. "Defending Battered Women on Trial: The Battered Woman Syndrome and Its Limitations" (1992) 16:6 Crim L J 369.

Stark, Evan. "Preparing Expert Testimony in Domestic Violence Cases" in Albert R Roberts, ed, *Handbook of Domestic Violence Intervention Strategies* (Oxford: Oxford University Press, 2002) 216.

–. "Re-Presenting Women Battering: From Battered Woman Syndrome to Coercive Control" (1994-95) 58:4 Alb L Rev 973.

Stubbs, Julie, and Julia Tolmie. "Battered Woman Syndrome in Australia: A Challenge to Gender Bias in the Law?" in Julie Stubbs, ed, *Women, Male Violence and the Law* (Sydney: Institute of Criminology, 1994) 192.

–. "Battered Women Charged with Homicide: Advancing the Interests of Indigenous Women" (2008) 41:1 Aust & NZ J Criminol 138.

–. "Defending Battered Women on Charges of Homicide: The Structural and Systemic versus the Personal and Particular" in Wendy Chan, Dorothy E Chunn, and Robert Menzies, eds, *Women, Madness and the Law: A Feminist Reader* (London: Glass House Press, 2005) 191.

–. "Gender, Race and the Battered Woman Syndrome: An Australian Case Study" (1995) 8:1 CJWL 122.

Tarrant, Stella. "A New Defence in Spouse Murder?" (1992) 17:2 Alternative LJ 67.

Toole, Kellie. "Self-Defence and the Reasonable Woman: Equality before the Law" (2012) 36:1 Melb U L Rev 250.

Wallace, Shana. "Beyond Imminence: Evolving International Law and Battered Women's Right to Self-Defense" (2004) 71:4 U Chi L Rev 1749.

Wells, Elisabeth C. "'But Most of All, They Fought Together': Judicial Attributions for Sentences in Convicting Battered Women Who Kill" (2012) 36:3 Psych of Women Q 350.

Williams, Toni. "Intersectionality Analysis in the Sentencing of Aboriginal Women in Canada: What Difference Does It Make?" in Emily Grabham *et al*, eds, *Intersectionality and Beyond: Law, Power and the Politics of Location* (Oxon: Glass House Books, 2009) 79.

Wohlhuter, Lorraine. "Excuse Them though They Know Not What They Do: The Distinction between Justification and Excuse in the Context of Battered Women Who Kill" (1996) 9:2 SACJ 151.

Index

81-82; appeal judge's comments, 85; contradictory testimony at *Mooney* trial, 80-81; criminal record search on Kruska, 81; decision of trial judge in *Mooney,* 83-84; excuses for not probing Mooney's statement, 82-83; superiors' finding of incompetent investigation, 81; *Violence against Women in Relationships Policy* not followed, 78. *See also Mooney* lawsuit (trial)

appeals: basis for, 46, 274, 297; grounds to dismiss, 292; ineffective assistance of counsel, 124, 162; "fresh evidence" rule, 162, 297; limits of, 297; miscarriages of justice, 194, 297; requirement for judges to consider Aboriginal background when sentencing, 127, 146, 161. *See also* criminal justice system, changes recommended

Armitage, Frank, 202-3

Atleo, Georgette, 190, 191

Austin, Allan, 273

Australia: barriers to fair trials for Aboriginal Australians, 193-95; defence of "excessive self-defence," 306; "defensive homicide" offence, 305-6; gratuitous concurrence by Aboriginal Australians, 168-69; self-defence available to prevent or terminate unlawful deprivation of liberty, 309; wrongful conviction of Robyn Kina, 194, 395n243

automatism and dissociation: as survival strategy, 17, 232, 278; batterers target women's heads, faces, and necks, 293; blows to head and dissociated states, 50, 289; burden of proof, 282; criteria for, 290-91; Getkate's state at time of homicide, 226, 232, 237; Graveline's state at time of homicide, 17, 245, 277-78, 282-83, 285; incompatibility of automatism and self-defence, 287,

292; internally caused and externally caused, 292; judge's charge to jury re dissociation in *Getkate* case, 232; judge's charge to jury re automatism in *Graveline* case, 287-88; Malott's state at time of homicide, 245, 293; mental disorder automatism, 287, 290; mischaracterized as alcohol abuse for Aboriginal women, 196; non-mental disorder automatism (externally caused), 289-91; psychological blow, 196, 289, 291, 293, 295, 310, 311, 424n411; role of traumatic brain injuries and post-concussive syndrome, 293-95; symptom of BWS, Complex PTSD, and PTSD, 54, 232, 292-93. *See also Getkate, R v* (trial); *Graveline, R v* (trial); *Graveline, R v* (Supreme Court of Canada); *Malott, R v* (trial); mild traumatic brain injuries; strangulation

Ayyildiz, Elisabeth, 319

Bail: Aboriginal peoples, 193; for battered women (Heavenfire, 128, 150), (Getkate, 202-3), (Graveline, 280-81), (Kondejewski, 371n12); for batterers, 75, 105 (Kruska, 193); benefits of, 128, 310; recidivism by batterers on bail release, 367n184; risk assessment needed for abusive men, 317

Bailey, Donald, 247

Balis, Donna, 235

Baptiste, Eldon, 145

Barbara Betcherman Memorial Lecture, 46-47

Barnes, Peter, 303

Battered Woman Syndrome (BWS): Complex PTSD as alternative theory, 56, 312-13; criteria for, factors in, and description of syndrome, 54-55, 137, 168, 174, 224-26; "cycle of violence," 51, 173, 175; dissociation, 17, 232, 278, 292-93; duration of relationship and, 175; expert evidence in *Getkate*

Steven Bittle
Still Dying for a Living: Corporate Criminal Liability after the Westray Mine Disaster (2012)

Jacqueline D. Krikorian
International Trade Law and Domestic Policy: Canada, the United States, and the WTO (2012)

Michael Boudreau
City of Order: Crime and Society in Halifax, 1918-35 (2012)

David R. Boyd
The Environmental Rights Revolution: A Global Study of Constitutions, Human Rights, and the Environment (2012)

Lesley Erickson
Westward Bound: Sex, Violence, the Law, and the Making of a Settler Society (2011)

Elaine Craig
Troubling Sex: Towards a Legal Theory of Sexual Integrity (2011)

Laura DeVries
Conflict in Caledonia: Aboriginal Land Rights and the Rule of Law (2011)

Jocelyn Downie and Jennifer J. Llewellyn (eds.)
Being Relational: Reflections on Relational Theory and Health Law (2011)

Grace Li Xiu Woo
Ghost Dancing with Colonialism: Decolonization and Indigenous Rights at the Supreme Court of Canada (2011)

Fiona Kelly
Transforming Law's Family: The Legal Recognition of Planned Lesbian Motherhood (2011)

Colleen Bell
The Freedom of Security: Governing Canada in the Age of Counter-Terrorism (2011)

Andrew S. Thompson
In Defence of Principles: NGOs and Human Rights in Canada (2010)

Aaron Doyle and Dawn Moore (eds.)
Critical Criminology in Canada: New Voices, New Directions (2010)

Joanna R. Quinn
The Politics of Acknowledgement: Truth Commissions in Uganda and Haiti (2010)

Patrick James
Constitutional Politics in Canada after the Charter: Liberalism, Communitarianism, and Systemism (2010)

Louis A. Knafla and Haijo Westra (eds.)
Aboriginal Title and Indigenous Peoples: Canada, Australia, and New Zealand (2010)

Janet Mosher and Joan Brockman (eds.)
Constructing Crime: Contemporary Processes of Criminalization (2010)

Stephen Clarkson and Stepan Wood
A Perilous Imbalance: The Globalization of Canadian Law and Governance (2009)

Amanda Glasbeek
Feminized Justice: The Toronto Women's Court, 1913-34 (2009)

Kim Brooks (ed.)
Justice Bertha Wilson: One Woman's Difference (2009)

Wayne V. McIntosh and Cynthia L. Cates
Multi-Party Litigation: The Strategic Context (2009)

Renisa Mawani
Colonial Proximities: Crossracial Encounters and Juridical Truths in British Columbia, 1871-1921 (2009)

James B. Kelly and Christopher P. Manfredi (eds.)
Contested Constitutionalism: Reflections on the Canadian Charter of Rights and Freedoms (2009)

Catherine Bell and Robert K. Paterson (eds.)
Protection of First Nations Cultural Heritage: Laws, Policy, and Reform (2008)

Hamar Foster, Benjamin L. Berger, and A.R. Buck (eds.)
The Grand Experiment: Law and Legal Culture in British Settler Societies (2008)

Richard J. Moon (ed.)
Law and Religious Pluralism in Canada (2008)

Catherine Bell and Val Napoleon (eds.)
First Nations Cultural Heritage and Law: Case Studies, Voices, and Perspectives (2008)

Douglas C. Harris
Landing Native Fisheries: Indian Reserves and Fishing Rights in British Columbia, 1849-1925 (2008)

Peggy J. Blair
Lament for a First Nation: The Williams Treaties of Southern Ontario (2008)

Lori G. Beaman
Defining Harm: Religious Freedom and the Limits of the Law (2007)

Stephen Tierney (ed.)
Multiculturalism and the Canadian Constitution (2007)

Julie Macfarlane
The New Lawyer: How Settlement Is Transforming the Practice of Law (2007)

Kimberley White
Negotiating Responsibility: Law, Murder, and States of Mind (2007)

Dawn Moore
Criminal Artefacts: Governing Drugs and Users (2007)

Hamar Foster, Heather Raven, and Jeremy Webber (eds.)
Let Right Be Done: Aboriginal Title, the Calder *Case, and the Future of Indigenous Rights* (2007)

Dorothy E. Chunn, Susan B. Boyd, and Hester Lessard (eds.)
Reaction and Resistance: Feminism, Law, and Social Change (2007)

Margot Young, Susan B. Boyd, Gwen Brodsky, and Shelagh Day (eds.)
Poverty: Rights, Social Citizenship, and Legal Activism (2007)

Rosanna L. Langer
Defining Rights and Wrongs: Bureaucracy, Human Rights, and Public Accountability (2007)

C.L. Ostberg and Matthew E. Wetstein
Attitudinal Decision Making in the Supreme Court of Canada (2007)

Chris Clarkson
Domestic Reforms: Political Visions and Family Regulation in British Columbia, 1862-1940 (2007)

Jean McKenzie Leiper
Bar Codes: Women in the Legal Profession (2006)

Gerald Baier
Courts and Federalism: Judicial Doctrine in the United States, Australia, and Canada (2006)

Avigail Eisenberg (ed.)
Diversity and Equality: The Changing Framework of Freedom in Canada (2006)

Randy K. Lippert
Sanctuary, Sovereignty, Sacrifice: Canadian Sanctuary Incidents, Power, and Law (2005)

James B. Kelly
Governing with the Charter: Legislative and Judicial Activism and Framers' Intent (2005)

Dianne Pothier and Richard Devlin (eds.)
Critical Disability Theory: Essays in Philosophy, Politics, Policy, and Law (2005)

Susan G. Drummond
Mapping Marriage Law in Spanish Gitano Communities (2005)

Louis A. Knafla and Jonathan Swainger (eds.)
Laws and Societies in the Canadian Prairie West, 1670-1940 (2005)

Ikechi Mgbeoji
Global Biopiracy: Patents, Plants, and Indigenous Knowledge (2005)

Florian Sauvageau, David Schneiderman, and David Taras, with Ruth Klinkhammer and Pierre Trudel
The Last Word: Media Coverage of the Supreme Court of Canada (2005)

Gerald Kernerman
Multicultural Nationalism: Civilizing Difference, Constituting Community (2005)

Pamela A. Jordan
Defending Rights in Russia: Lawyers, the State, and Legal Reform in the Post-Soviet Era (2005)

Anna Pratt
Securing Borders: Detention and Deportation in Canada (2005)

Kirsten Johnson Kramar
Unwilling Mothers, Unwanted Babies: Infanticide in Canada (2005)

W.A. Bogart
Good Government? Good Citizens? Courts, Politics, and Markets in a Changing Canada (2005)

Catherine Dauvergne
Humanitarianism, Identity, and Nation: Migration Laws in Canada and Australia (2005)

Michael Lee Ross
First Nations Sacred Sites in Canada's Courts (2005)

Andrew Woolford
Between Justice and Certainty: Treaty Making in British Columbia (2005)

John McLaren, Andrew Buck, and Nancy Wright (eds.)
Despotic Dominion: Property Rights in British Settler Societies (2004)

Georges Campeau
From UI to EI: Waging War on the Welfare State (2004)

Alvin J. Esau
The Courts and the Colonies: The Litigation of Hutterite Church Disputes (2004)

Christopher N. Kendall
Gay Male Pornography: An Issue of Sex Discrimination (2004)

Roy B. Flemming
Tournament of Appeals: Granting Judicial Review in Canada (2004)

Constance Backhouse and Nancy L. Backhouse
The Heiress vs the Establishment: Mrs. Campbell's Campaign for Legal Justice (2004)

Christopher P. Manfredi
Feminist Activism in the Supreme Court: Legal Mobilization and the Women's Legal Education and Action Fund (2004)

Annalise Acorn
Compulsory Compassion: A Critique of Restorative Justice (2004)

Jonathan Swainger and Constance Backhouse (eds.)
People and Place: Historical Influences on Legal Culture (2003)

Jim Phillips and Rosemary Gartner
Murdering Holiness: The Trials of Franz Creffield and George Mitchell (2003)

David R. Boyd
Unnatural Law: Rethinking Canadian Environmental Law and Policy (2003)

Ikechi Mgbeoji
Collective Insecurity: The Liberian Crisis, Unilateralism, and Global Order (2003)

Rebecca Johnson
Taxing Choices: The Intersection of Class, Gender, Parenthood, and the Law (2002)

John McLaren, Robert Menzies, and Dorothy E. Chunn (eds.)
Regulating Lives: Historical Essays on the State, Society, the Individual, and the Law (2002)

Joan Brockman
Gender in the Legal Profession: Fitting or Breaking the Mould (2001)

Printed and bound in Canada by Friesens

Set in Segoe and Warnock by Artegraphica Design Co. Ltd.

Copy editor: Dallas Harrison

Indexer: Patricia Buchanan